THE POWER
OF DELIGHT

THE POWER
OF DELIGHT

A Lifetime in Literature:
Essays 1962 – 2002

JOHN BAYLEY

Selected by Leo Carey

W. W. Norton & Company
NEW YORK • LONDON

Manufacturing by RR Donnelley, Harrisonburg, VA
Book design by Brooke Koven
Title page photograph by Jonathan Brade / Photonica
Production manager: Anna Oler

Library of Congress Cataloging-in-Publication Data
Bayley, John, 1925–
The power of delight : a lifetime in literature : essays, 1962–2002 /
John Bayley; selected by Leo Carey.—1st ed.
p. cm.
Includes index.
ISBN 0-393-05840-9 (hardcover)
1. Literature, Modern—history and criticism. 2. Literature,
Modern—Book reviews. I. Carey, Leo. II. Title.
PN710.B345 2005
809'.03—dc22   2005002273

W. W. Norton & Company, Inc., 500 Fifth Avenue, New York, N.Y. 10110
www.wwnorton.com

W. W. Norton & Company Ltd., Castle House, 75/76 Wells Street, London W1T 3QT

1 2 3 4 5 6 7 8 9 0

Audi

What seas what shores what grey rocks and what islands . . .
—T. S. ELIOT, from "Marina"

Contents

III: *Mother Russia*

IV: *American Poetry*

V: *Out of Eastern Europe*

VI: *Aspects of Novels*

VII: *Correspondences*

VIII: *How It Strikes a Contemporary*

Introduction

T HE ASPIRANT OF literary criticism (perhaps one should use the word in its old continental military sense of the cadet serving and hoping, often vainly, for promotion) has one advantage over the budding poet or promising young novelist. He is not on his own, with his own self-sought measure of originalities. He has not been told by Ezra Pound to "make it new"; he need not attempt to astonish a Jean Cocteau. An editor has told the aspiring critic what to write about, in how many words, and by when. This can stabilize him, even cheer him up, as he attempts the frightening task of getting words on paper for his first review. He begins to practice his craft in the welcome knowledge of supervision, and with an experienced and more or less well-disposed arbiter just behind him.

But as the young critic grows not only in confidence but in knowledge of his trade's techniques—in knowledge, too, of the scale and scope of the texts he writes about—he will want to put forward a personality of his own, and to show where he stands in relation to colleagues and rivals. This process may be either instinctive or deliberate. Some friends may have told him, "Whatever you do, don't start writing like X, or with the insufferable self-regard of Y. Be natural," as if anyone in the world of criticism, or indeed perhaps of art itself, has ever succeeded in being that.

It is good advice all the same, however impossible of fulfillment, and it leads to the important related question of what *line*, in a general way, should the beginning critic propose to take. Is he to lay about him in all directions, become numbered with well-known *féroces*, or will he choose to be one of the soft men, who are in practice seldom so kindly and so well disposed as they seem, even if they are not Chaucer's "smiler with the knife under the cloak," or the critic of Pope's *Acquaintance*, who would "just hint at fault and hesitate dislike."

In general, as the critic matures, he discovers that he can change his mind, but not his basic attitudes. Those are more instinctive. The great nineteenth-century Russian critic, Vissarian Belinsky, known to writers of the day as "Furious Vissarian," was steadfast in his belief that the function of writing was to reform ideas, institutions, and the people; but, as Edmund Wilson, a great admirer, pointed out, his taste for, and his sense of, good writing—Pushkin's most notably—was unerring, and as finely tuned as that of any aesthetic critic, who proclaimed and believed in Art for Art's sake. By the same token, a staunch believer in the political correctness of today may nonetheless relish authors to whom the whole idea of such correctness is or would be a joke, and who believes that it can be the conscious function of much good art—as with the writings of Philip Larkin or Evelyn Waugh, for instance—to be as politically incorrect as possible.

Many of the best critics can be what one of them, the distinguished American Matthew Prince, described as "dramatists of literary ideas." And certainly ideologies can never be avoided by the critic. Even when he takes no interest in them, or thinks he does not, he cannot avoid referring to them in relation to the authors he deprecates, or admires, or even loves. Perhaps the best as well as the most comforting advice for the aspirant was given by Dr. Johnson, the least likely person to want to lay down any kind of critical system. "It is a good service one reading man does another when he tells him his own manner of being pleased." All of us have different ways of being pleased by books—*quot homines, tot sententiae*, as the Romans used to say—and a reader's life would be very boring if he found himself in agreement with all other readers. Iris Murdoch, once a junior member of the Communist Party, used to amuse one later on in her life by repeating the old rhetorical query that she and her fellow members had once applied to all things, great or small: "What's the Party Line on this one, comrade?" That attitude is about as far as can be from Dr. Johnson's view of the matter. It gave us a good laugh, whether we were discussing *Dr. Zhivago* or wondering whether to buy a more expensive brand of coffee. Must first find out and follow the Party Line.

Wandering through these reviews of fifty years, which have been admirably selected and collected by *New Yorker* editor Leo Carey, I found the most interesting thing for me is the question of whether the piece would make me want to read again the book or author I had once reviewed. Very often I found I did want to; and I began to wonder whether that wasn't, perhaps, the most valuable service a critic could render: not only inspiring a member of the reading public to read the book, but to persuade some of them who had read it to read it again. Sterne's *Tristram Shandy*, for instance, is not a book which in my experience many people much enjoy the first time. They may feel they *ought* to be enjoying it, because it is generally acknowledged to be a comic masterpiece, and yet they often find themselves irritated or baffled. But if they can bring themselves to read the book again, on some later occasion, they may well feel the genuine and spontaneous delight in wit, pathos, deft and ingenious bawdy, that somehow passed them by the first time. A friend's wife has read *War and Peace* twice with the keenest pleasure, not missing a line, and proposes to read it a third time as soon as the occasion offers. I felt inspired by this to have another go myself, although after once writing on *War and Peace* I had felt I should never be up to tackling it again as a book for pleasure. But when I tried, I found I was reading it in a more relaxed way, and the pleasure was unconscious and in a way less demanding. The greater power of book delight is in its spontaneity, whether we are discovering pleasure or rediscovering it.

There is no point in continuing to talk about my own views and outlooks and methods when these things will of necessity reveal themselves to anyone who is prepared to read some of the pieces that follow. The proof of the pudding is in the eating. As the novelist Anthony Powell observes in the pages of that great epic seen from the standpoint of a writer's life, *A Dance to the Music of Time*, "a writer writes what he is." And this is as true of a critic as of a novelist or poet.

Every reviewer knows that of the work he produces over a span of fifty years or more very little will deserve to see the light of day again, and of that little he is in luck if some of it actually does get reprinted. Leo Carey has an excellent nose for the kind of thing that might be hoped to deserve exhumation, and I should like to thank him again for the charitable but judicious eye he has brought to making this selection. I must also thank Bob Weil at W. W. Norton for thinking up the project in the first place and believing that the results might justify it; also for his admirable work on the book as a general editor.

In 1955, when I started teaching English literature at Oxford University, it was normal for a college Tutor to teach the whole syllabus, from Chaucer and earlier, to the nineteenth and twentieth centuries. Of course he or she did not know it all equally well—gutsy, from the Tutor's point of view at least, but there were some advantages to this method. We got to know the students better, and if we and the students got along well together we shared our knowledge and impressions to equal advantage, over a continuous period. At the same time as I started teaching I also started reviewing, and I found the two activities went well together: teaching literature and writing about it seemed and seem complementary activities.

The pair of them inspired as well sudden flurries of enthusiasm for this or that author, not necessarily one that I was teaching or happened to be writing about. I recall being bowled over by Robert Lowell's poetry, particularly *The Life Studies*, but that seemed as it were a private matter, and it was not until some time later that I wanted to write about him, or teach him, and eventually met the poet himself. But I thought then, and still think, that Lowell's poetry is some of the very best produced anywhere in the century. He and Philip Larkin admired each other's poetry, and they were both excellent judges.

After I had been teaching and reviewing English literature for some time, I suddenly developed a strong urge to learn enough Russian to read Pushkin. I had read Tolstoy and Dostoevsky, Turgenev and Chekhov with immense and varied pleasure, and without any great sense that I was missing something important by not being able to read them in the original. But Pushkin was another matter. I felt encouraged by Edmund Wilson's pioneer essay, in which he suggests that Pushkin, of all poets, needs his own words, and quite simple words they always are to make his own extraordinary impact. I found I was delighting in those words even when I barely knew what they meant. It was not like a learning process, but more a sudden thrill of discovery. Later on I wrote a book about him, *Pushkin: A Comparative Commentary*, in which I tried to show what the poet was like by relating him to other European and American writers—not necessarily of the same period—in order to bring out both his uniqueness and his own kind of magical accessibility. The power of sheer pleasure in reading and remembering Pushkin's verse is as great as anything one is likely to experience in a lifetime with words. Moreover, the pleasure of reading in translation the great Russian novelists, Russian poets too, is in some mysterious way greatly enhanced by the feeling of Pushkin's presence in the work of his successors, and the knowledge that they had all felt and known that presence so keenly.

One of the pleasures of reviewing comes when the reviewer is asked to take on some author with whom he is most familiar or one whom he has largely forgotten. He learns again, and the lesson he learns, so to speak, may turn out quite a different one. I had fixed ideas in my head from earlier readings of Dickens, Trollope, and Orwell, among many others. Reviewing those authors not only drastically revised those ideas but also made me conscious of a different kind of pleasure in rereading them. The same goes for Hardy and Kipling, two writers to whose novels, poems, and stories I had been deeply attached since childhood, without quite knowing why. Again, the pleasure of reading about them and reviewing them caused me to ponder more deeply why I had loved them and why I still did, although perhaps in different ways and from a different perspective.

Occasionally I have felt that I might have missed or ignored a writer completely if I had not been asked for a review. The pleasure of meeting and enjoying the wonderful work of the Polish-Jewish writer Bruno Schulz, and the haunting poems in German of Paul Celan, is something for which I shall always be deeply grateful. Doing a review brought us together. To have missed Celan in particular would have been to forfeit not only delight in the wonderful strangeness of his verse but also some of the deepest and most painful experiences that any writer of our age has described in art.

—John Bayley
Oxford, May 2004

PART I

English Literature

1

The Genius of Shandy Hall

Laurence Sterne (1713–1768)

Laurence Sterne: The Later Years
by Arthur H. Cash

THE ONLY PEOPLE whom Laurence Sterne did not get on with were other writers. Not that his universal good nature was in the least competitive, but he had an involuntary knack of suborning their confidence in themselves and spoiling their image. Even Dr. Johnson withdrew when the author of *The Sermons of Mr. Yorick* held forth at one of Joshua Reynolds's parties, nominally because of his impropriety, but actually, one suspects, because the Johnsonian style was insensibly rebuked by Sterne's genius. This is one of the many glimpses that Arthur Cash provides in the second volume of his superlative life.*

It is at once very easy and very difficult to imagine the scene. Touchy literary men who expect to dominate a gathering are found in every age, and will not forgive any rival who shows them at a disadvantage. But if Johnson's memory is to be trusted, Sterne's conduct on this occasion would certainly now seem to us rather odd. He had just received permission from Lord and Lady Spencer to dedicate to them "The Story of Le Fever," that sentimental little masterpiece in *Tristram Shandy* in which Uncle Toby and Corporal Trim take into their care a dying French officer and his son. A manuscript preserved at Spencer House endorsed in

*The first volume was *Laurence Sterne: The Early and Middle Years*.

Lord Spencer's hand "The Story of Le Fever, sent to me by Sterne before it was published." Sterne had just come from the Spencers' to Reynolds's house, and there he pulled the dedication out of his pocket, and, as Johnson says, "sponte suâ, for nobody desired him," began to read it out loud to the assembled company. Johnson sourly observed that it was "not English," whereupon Sterne pulled from his other pocket "a drawing too indecently gross to have delighted even in a brothel." This "attempt at merriment" from a clergyman of the Church of England was too much for Johnson, who left in disgust; and Reynolds took good care afterward not to invite Sterne if Johnson was to be present. One suspects that the merry cleric was deliberately teasing the good doctor.

Yet the episode is more significant than it appears. Sterne was an archetype of the eighteenth century, Johnson was not. Although his father had been only a half-pay ensign in a marching regiment, Sterne had connections with the aristocracy—his great-grandfather had been Archbishop of York—and it was the most natural thing in the world for him to exercise his wits in high life, and expect from lords and ladies benefits, financial and otherwise, in return for the entertainment. Jealous of his independence, Johnson distrusted the aristocracy, upheld the dignity of authors, was a pillar of the new middle-class morals and proprieties. He belonged to the world of Samuel Richardson, even to the later world of Jane Austen, rather than to the happily spontaneous and unregenerate old eighteenth century championed by Sterne.

Every detailed page of Cash's excellent biography makes the point more clear. When he observed that *Tristram Shandy* "did not last" Johnson was expressing a half-truth. What did not last was the age that produced *Tristram Shandy*. It is probably still true that those who see no point in Sterne belong, as it were, to the perennially new generation of serious-minded persons, from Dr. Johnson to Dr. F. R. Leavis, who turn their backs on the frivolity and irresponsibility of a past age. Sterne's devotees, on the other hand, are natural denizens of the eighteenth century and its witty, ribald, self-confident ways. One of Sterne's most devoted admirers was old Lord Bathurst, who had been the friend and patron of all the great Augustan writers. Sterne afterward recalled Bathurst's kindness when he first met him in 1760:

This nobleman is an old friend of mine—You know he was always the protector of men of wit and genius; and has had those of the last century, Addison, Steele, Pope, Swift, Prior, etc. etc. always at his table.— The manner in which his notice began of me, was as singular as it was polite.—He came up to me, one day, as I was at the Princess of Wales's court. "I want to know you, Mr. Sterne; but it is fit you should know, also, who it is that wishes this pleasure. You have heard," continued he, "of an old Lord Bathurst, of whom your Popes, and Swifts, have sung and spoken so much: I have lived my life with geniuses of that cast; but have survived them; and, despairing ever to find their equals, it is some years since I have closed my accounts, and shut up my books, with thoughts of never opening them again: but you have kindled a desire in me of opening them once more before I die; which I now do; so go home and dine with me."

Running on as he does, Sterne nonetheless involuntarily makes it clear, in such a passage, of the extent to which *Tristram Shandy*, and the world he created in it, was less of an innovation than a survival.

Writers like Tobias Smollett felt the same, and Sterne returned the compliment, though good-naturedly, caricaturing "Smelfungus" in *A Sentimental Journey*. Sterne's friendship with the Bluestocking group, led by Elizabeth Montagu, a distant cousin of his wife's, also suffered from a misunderstanding based upon apparent novelty and the manners of a past age. Studious, learned, animated, a great reader—she would make her reputation with her *Essay on the Writings and Genius of Shakespeare*—Elizabeth Montagu was friendly and well-disposed to Sterne, who cultivated her favors as much as he could. He embarked on a flirtation with her friend and fellow Bluestocking, Elizabeth Vesey, a lively Anglo-Irish woman known as "the Sylph" because, in the words of a friend, she belonged to "a race of air rather than of earth," but who was married to a decidedly earthy character with the interesting first name of Agmondesham, who detested his wife's assemblies and spent his time gambling and whoring.

But both ladies ceased to appreciate Sterne, as Cash explains. Like Bishop Warburton, that upright and learned figure who had first taken up Sterne with enthusiastic kindness but dropped him hastily on realizing how much harm Parson Yorick might do to the new image of the Church, the ladies shared the new, unspoken, perhaps only half-understood assumption that authors had the duty to spread the gospel of middle-class virtue, the good news that honesty, duty, and chastity were not only possible, but immediately rewarding. The new millennium would be one of sentimental fiction. And here they made their mistake about Sterne. Moved by the sweetness in his story, they did not fully recognize that he was a subversive who delighted in being naughty and believed that people were most lovable when their imperfections showed. They would eventually withdraw from him.

For Sterne the new sentimentality was in many ways the old Georgian licentiousness writ large, though with more warmth and lightness, more elegance and spontaneity. But the Bluestockings saw the danger and were quick to sheer off. There was nothing feminist about *Tristram Shandy*, which was much closer to *Tom Jones* than to the new novel of sentiment with which Sterne was to become, almost accidentally, identified. Eminently fashion conscious, Sterne was prepared to identify with the new rage for feeling just as, during his time in France, he reveled in the company of the free-thinking *Encyclopédistes*, especially d'Holbach and Diderot, who, as Cash dryly remarks, "made free use of the existing social structure to lead a comfortable life while carrying out their subversive activity." Diderot was under the protection of the crown as a member of the French Academy, and he was shortly to write, in imitation of *Tristram Shandy*, his novel *Jacques le fataliste*. Both books would be a decisive influence in the future of the European novel and the fashion for fiction without a story, beginning and ending in anecdotal wit and conversation. Shandy Hall and its denizens, their humors and obsessions, generate a novel without the need for any extraneous narrative.

On Cash's cover and frontispiece is a delightful picture, showing Sterne in his most congenial milieu, an uproarious eighteenth-century wine and oyster party. It is a caricature group by John Hamilton Mortimer, an accomplished artist in the genre, with Sterne carousing at the artists' club in the company of John Ireland, the watchmaker and biographer of Hogarth, and Dr. Arne, the musician and composer, whose sister Susannah wrote "Rule Britannia." (Sheridan memorably described

Arne's eyes as "two oysters on an oval plate of stewed beetroot.") Sterne, a lanky six-footer in a fashionable apple-green coat, has opened his shirt front to disclose a heart-shaped locket containing the picture of his "sentimental" ladylove, Mrs. Eliza Draper. His expressive face is split in an enchanting grin, and the picture has more animation and gives more sense of Parson Yorick, in his habit as he lived, than even the famous study by Reynolds in the National Portrait Gallery, which Cash reproduced in his first volume. He acknowledges that the attributions in this picture group, including that of Sterne himself, remain conjectural, but they certainly carry conviction.

Painted in the late 1760s, the picture gives a vivid impression of that boisterous high point in the fortunes of England, which, with the accession of George III and the subsequent loss of the American colonies, were never to be quite the same again. Seventeen fifty-nine had been the *annus mirabilis* of the Seven Years' War against France; Canada and India had been conquered and America protected; audiences at every play and public entertainment used to burst into "Rule Britannia" at the drop of a hat. All this is somehow immanent in the picture group of Sterne and his cronies, just as it was in the gaiety and fizzing high spirits of *Tristram Shandy* itself.

It was also a civilized and a truly international age, before the French Revolution and the nationalist Napoleonic Era. Though England had been at war with France for years, English visitors could come and go freely in France and on the Continent, with only the mild inconvenience of having to obtain a passport, as related in the early part of *A Sentimental Journey*. The first volume of Cash's biography describes Sterne's time as a student, his struggle for Church preferment, and his unlucky marriage. *The Later Years* opens with Sterne's breakthrough into fame and success as an author, and his preferment, through the good offices of Lord Fauconberg, to the living of Cox-wold near York, with a parsonage—still surviving, now a museum—which Sterne delighted in, and which his friends were to dub "Shandy Hall."

Sterne had the right temperament for success and happiness, although it was certainly true, as he wrote to his most valued patron, Lord Rockingham, that "every word" of the first hilarious volumes of his novel had been written in affliction; & under a constant uneasiness of mind. Cervantes wrote his humorous Satyr in a prison — & Scarron his, in pain & Anguish — such Philosophers as will account for every thing, may explain this for me.

Sterne's life itself provides an explanation, as Cash says. "Trapped in an unhappy marriage and a disintegrating body, he sought laughter as an anodyne to pain, wherever he could find it." Given his temperament Sterne's marriage could not have been all that unhappy, although there is plenty of testimony to the exasperating and lowering qualities of his wife Elizabeth, as of his daughter Lydia, who evidently took after her mother. Yet Sterne in his own way was fond of both of them, doting on Lydia's pleasure in the "poney" he gave her, and arranging the details of travel and ménage with care and affection when they traveled in France and finally settled in Toulouse.

Sterne was equally affectionate and loyal toward his mistress, Catherine Fourmantel, a singer of Huguenot extraction whom he met in the Assembly Rooms at York. During his period of fame and celebrity in London she came to join him there. Sterne was not like Leigh Hunt, caricatured in Dickens's portrait of Harold Skimpole, a careless butterfly sort of man, abounding in fine feelings, who loved his fellow men and let them pick up the pieces. "Sentiment" in Sterne's time had not, as it were, gone that far. His good nature had no irresponsibility about it, and he ministered and gave himself to wife, daughter, mistress, friends, and lovers with genuine tenderness and concern; sitting, for instance, at the bedside in France of the dying George Oswald, a casual acquaintance who had no sort of claim upon him, looking after him in his last days, and arranging his affairs after his death. From obscure correspondence and chance references, for Sterne's life is by no means well documented, Cash has ferreted out a number of such cases, and their accumulated effect adds a significant dimension to the picture we have of Sterne the man.

Tuberculosis had of course dogged him since he had been an undergraduate at Cambridge, where he had once woken up to find he had "filled the bedclothes with blood." Like D. H. Lawrence he survived not so much by willpower as by sheer vividness of being, saving himself by incessant laughter and entertainment as Lawrence did by letter writing and travel. In neither case could it last, but while the candle burned at both ends and in the middle it burned brightly. There is also in Sterne something of Pushkin's verbal and temperamental exuberance. The Russian author delighted in him (though he read him in French) and, in his brilliant little play *The Stone Guest*, produced a Don Juan figure with a marked resemblance both to himself and to Sterne—a brightly and innocently genial lover who keeps the affection of all his conquests and meets his fate in a new access of tenderness. Puritanical critics used to disapprove of Sterne's "nasty philandering," as they did of the constant sexual innuendoes in his writing: smut, like promiscuity, can be, and generally is, both disagreeable and boring. But there are shining exceptions and Sterne is emphatically one of them, witness the famous joke that begins *Tristram Shandy*, when Tristram is being inefficiently begotten by his father, to whom his mother observes, "Pray, my dear, did you remember to wind the clock?"

He said so himself; and that may be one of the reasons his detractors disliked him. Cash tells the story of how he once asked a Yorkshire lady if she had read *Tristram Shandy*.

"I have not, Mr. Sterne," was the answer, "and, to be plain with you, I am informed it is not proper for female perusal."—"My dear good lady," replied the author, "do not be gulled by such stories; the book is like your young heir there, (pointing to a child of three years old, who was rolling on the carpet in his white tunics) he shews at times a good deal that is usually concealed, but it is all in perfect innocence!"

That would not win over Sterne's more fastidious detractors, and indeed there is only a hair's breadth of difference, in Sterne's prose, between a true innocence and a false one. We must get used to the tone, and as with certain other writers—Virginia Woolf is one—listen to a voice rather than attending to written sentences.

Johnson may have had this in his mind when he said of Sterne's writing that "nothing odd will do for long," unconscious of the ironic fact that his own speaking tone would be immortalized in Boswell's recollections. Sterne wrote as if he were talking; Johnson talked as he wrote. Sterne's method was to draw humorous attention to the *provisional* nature of human experience, Tristram's nonexperiences, as he finds he is living 365 times faster than he is writing—"I shall never overtake myself"—making it impossible for what literature knows as his "life" ever to get going. As Jean-Jacques Mayoux pointed out in "Variations on the Time-sense in Tristram Shandy," an essay in his book *Winged Skull*, both Tristram and his Uncle Toby exist in order to continue existing: the misadventures that befall Tristram, from his conception onward, being paralleled by Uncle Toby's quest for health and recovery from his wound. I think Sterne might well have had Pope's famous line in mind when he invokes the absence of anything but trifles "to help me through this long disease, my life." Sterne intuited better than any writer the essential egoism of existence. When the sad news arrives at Shandy Hall that Tristram's brother Bobby is dead, the "foolish fat scullion" speaks for us all when she says: "So am not I."

Sterne's own death was an easy one, for his disintegrated lungs brought on the usually euphoric condition of oxygen starvation. Shortly before his death, a fellow parson from Yorkshire called at his London lodgings and passed two girls who were going down the stairs laughing. Sterne told him that if he had come a bit earlier he would have found as many as thirteen at the party. Nor had jest yet finished with Yorick, for his grave was broken into and the corpse stolen by medical students, who spirited it away to Cambridge for dissection. The students had probably never heard of Sterne, but at Cambridge his features were recognized by a professor, who had the body conveyed discreetly back to the London cemetery.

Cash has unearthed many new facts not only about this Shandean episode but about the future careers of Sterne's lady friend, Eliza Draper, who returned to her husband in India, and those of his wife and daughter. They went back to France, "making enemies till the last," and were soon wrangling over the proceeds of Yorick's "sermons," which reveal Sterne's basic theological orthodoxy rather than his wit. "The quietest man in the world," as Sterne described himself in a letter, was spared "the ingratitude and unquiet spirit of a restless unreasonable Wife whom neither gentleness nor generosity can conquer." Lydia married a Frenchman, Jean-Baptiste Medalle, four years younger than herself, whose father was principally intent on getting all Sterne's literary capital for her dowry. She also had a go at forging her father's letters for sale. Tuberculosis must have become well entrenched in the family, for Sterne's two poor little grandsons were both dead in a few years, as was their grandmother, while Lydia herself only lived to the age of thirty-two. Her husband long survived her, and although he remarried, always proudly identified himself as the "son-in-law of Sterne, the author of the famous Sentimental Journey."

The New York Review of Books, 1987

2

Double Life

Jane Austen (1775–1817)

─────────

The Life of Jane Austen
by John Halperin

A Goodly Heritage: A History of Jane Austen's Family
by George Holbert Tucker

IN ONE OF Barbara Pym's novels a young man has occasion to find himself marveling "at the sharpness of even the nicest women." The sharpest are also the nicest. Even the nicest are sharp. The comment is loaded with cunning and we can take it either way. Jane Austen would have endorsed it instantly, and with amusement. She would have been amused, too, by the way her critics tend to divide into those who emphasize how sharp she was, and those who loyally proclaim how nice she was. No doubt she was both, and in the highest degree, in her art as in her life, "biting of tongue but tender of heart," as Virginia Woolf put it.

Critics are not required to marry the author they criticize, but many of Jane Austen's now write as if they had either proposed and been rejected, or had thought better of it. After the sickly adulation of "dear Jane" in the nineteenth century, a domestic charmer and helpmate comparable to the author of *Cranford*, came what Professor Halperin engagingly refers to as "the bitchmonster" of our own time. The letters between her and her elder sister, which had once seemed so cosy and delightful, gave E. M. Forster the horrors and made him think of the cackling of a pair of harpies. Harold Nicolson and H. W. Garrod attacked her dreadful sexlessness and her deprecation of masculinity. D. W. Harding proclaimed her the mistress of a virulent literary mode—"regulated hatred." The honeymoon was definitely over.

Halperin's publishers claim on the dust jacket that his biography "revises forever our understanding of the woman and the novels she wrote." In a curious way the claim is not unjustified. Halperin's great merit as a biographer is that he is the most unlikely spouse imaginable for Jane Austen. He resembles the lover of Vinnie, the heroine of Alison Lurie's *Foreign Affairs*, whom she comes to love because he is in every way so unlike herself. Halperin teases his Jane as he admires her, and by being so completely from another world does indeed make us see her in a different way. He takes her right out of the incestuous love or hate embrace in which Janeites and anti-Janeites have concealed her so long. That is quite an achievement.

I like his style too, which is a bit like that of Miss Bates, full of details and exclamations and quotes from the letters. Cassandra has been suffering at Godmersham from Mrs. Stent, who was in fact probably the original of Miss Bates. "Poor Mrs. Stent!" wrote Jane in reply. "It has been her lot to be always in the way; but we must be merciful, for perhaps in time we may come to be Mrs. Stents ourselves, unequal to anything and unwelcome to everybody." Halperin comments that this was "a jolly thought: she was nearing thirty." A jolly thought indeed, and it conveys the actual predicament of the two sisters. Whether we love Jane Austen, or fear and dislike her, it is difficult to imagine ourselves back into the actual insecurity of her existence. We can no longer see her as leading a life in which she didn't know what was to become of her, and was in constant fear of ending up dependent, despised, and in the way. And it is this predicament which Halperin's brash manner vividly restores to us, on its daily basis.

Eternity has changed her into herself, as Mallarmé would say, but Halperin ruthlessly puts her back among the contingencies, the fears and hopes of uncharted existence. How did she get on with her mother, for instance? It is obvious to Halperin that she got on badly, and once he shows us this we see that it must have been so, though the point has not been made by any biographer with such cogency before. A daughter living at home (elder sister Cassandra was frequently away, staying with the

Godmersham branch of the family and helping at her sister-in-law's many confinements) and daily exposed to the whims of a lively, tiresome, hypochondriac mother, who was to survive her by many years—how could it have been otherwise? Of course there was affection; and the mother's fussy hypochondria was probably cunningly transposed and immortalized in the sympathetic figure of Emma's father. Mrs. Austen was one of those genial, sociable creatures who always put themselves first; Jane was dutiful, sweet-natured, and sharp: her "cheerful disposition" must have had a lot to put up with, as anyone else's would have done. Particularly at Bath, which Mrs. Austen seems to have enjoyed as much as her daughters disliked it, and where social life was both exigent and screamingly dull.

Jane loved her clever, amiable father, and when he died suddenly in Bath wrote to her brother Frank that the corpse "preserves the sweet, benevolent smile which always distinguished him." This tenderness is very exact, as Halperin says, though it is no doubt what all nice kind girls feel about nice kind fathers. His death in 1805 (one of her brothers at sea narrowly missed taking part in the battle of Trafalgar the same year) was a low-water mark in their fortunes, though as Jane's letters twice rather sharply indicate her mother took it very well. Four years earlier, when the family had been on holiday, probably at Sidmouth, a young clergyman staying with his physician brother had appeared to fall in love with Jane, and she to return his feelings. The holiday ended without a proposal however, though tradition tells that the two families made plans to meet again. Some time later the doctor wrote that his brother had died. Had Jane written to him in the meantime? We don't know. Had he taken fright and gone to ground? Halperin is inclined to believe that something of the kind may have happened, and that posterity has romanticized and tidied up the enigmatic episode.

The next year occurred what he calls "yet another bizarre incident in the history of Jane Austen's 'love' life," a description that does indeed enable us to see it more accurately as well as more vividly. Cassandra and Jane were staying at Manydown, the home of old friends, the affluent Bigg Wither family. It was near Steventon, where Jane's father had been parson. Jane, nearly twenty-seven, was proposed to by Harris Bigg Wither, just twenty-one and preparing to enter the Church. Another parson, but a much better catch financially—he could have given Jane a good establishment and a handsome house. She accepted the young fellow, but after what must have been a night of appalling strain and indecision, changed her mind in the morning. Did elder sister Cassandra, herself still unmarried, and like Jane to remain so, influence the decision? The girls had always been close and were to become closer, till Jane died in Cassandra's arms. Young Bigg Wither, says Halperin, was "a recluse who stammered and had a mean temper"—she was not in love with him and was never likely to be. The embarrassment was smoothed over as much as possible. But it must have been a brutal situation, and unhelped in fact by Jane knowing in theory how to deal with it. Had she not coolly and brilliantly done so when she was writing *Pride and Prejudice* nearly five years before? (Halperin is of the school that believes that novel was her first—the one offered by her father to a publisher who declined it sight unseen, preferring to bring out the ever popular Mrs. Radcliffe.)

Halperin's treatment draws attention to the sharp difference between life and art: in life the artist gets just as bothered and upset as the rest of us, and just as ready to discard his theoretically superior knowledge, values, and principles. Jane knew she knew one married for "intelligent love"; in their various ways all her heroines do. Like her mother she was unmaternal, but her mother had brought up a large, cheerful, happy family (except for one deaf, retarded little boy, who was boarded out at a cottage and not spoken of again), and she might well have done the same. The "second trilogy"—*Mansfield Park, Emma, Persuasion*—would certainly not have got written if she had. Her own niece, with literary ambitions and encouragement from her aunt, finally burned her own unpublished novel manuscripts after years of marriage. So much of the buried tension in the later novels—and on publication Jane thought of them all as her children—comes from the knowledge and pondering of two kinds of life, between which she both did and did not make a choice. A contemporary version of the same kind of choices and deprivations, trench humor and tears, can be read in Barbara Pym's superb diaries. Let us be thankful, all the same, that Jane Austen did not keep one.

Halperin's admirable sense of the minutiae of the Austen ménage, the alarms and tranquilities, the things to drink and to eat ("You know how interesting the purchase of a sponge-cake is to me"), and the grim amusement over things that can nonetheless be enjoyed ("We are to have a tiny party here tonight. I hate tiny parties—they force one into constant exertion") lead him also to some unexpected and penetrating critical judgments. He points out the marked contrast between Jane Austen and many other creative artists, those for whom "adversity is a catalyst, the grain of sand in the oyster . . . in her, adversity blanketed energy and aspiration; she wrote only when she was relatively content and secure." The importance of the point is open to misunderstanding. Of course she was not like Dostoevsky, composing with maximum speed and vigor when most overwhelmed with financial and domestic problems. During her "dark" period at Bath and later at Southampton, before they were able to settle into the house at Chawton, Jane Austen composed nothing but *The Watsons*, the beginnings of a novel which she soon gave up and never afterward resumed work on.

Why was that? Emma Watson, with "a lively Eye, a sweet smile, and an open countenance" seems a promisingly spontaneous character, and the other persons and situation might have shaped up well too. But what has gone wrong is something to do with the tone, which Jane must have recognized and looked back on with dislike. Into *The Watsons* she was putting directly all the fears and frustrations she was feeling at the time: the family's comparative poverty; her fear of increasing poverty, and the cold or careless patronage that went with it; the "dreadful mortifications of unequal Society," the insolence of young men who disregard intelligent young women, the knowledge that "it is very bad to grow old & be poor & laughed at." Short as it is, the fragment of *The Watsons* is full of resentment and bitterness, feelings given their head because they were being felt in full measure at the time of writing.

This is not the case with the "first trilogy"—*Pride and Prejudice, Sense and Sensibility*, and *Northanger Abbey*—and Halperin is surely wrong to suggest that the latter in particular is full of "bitter irony." He claims that it is the work of "a caustic, disappointed woman," and that "in Catherine's early failures with men, we may perceive the novelist's." Maybe so, but Jane Austen has taken great care, as it seems she could not do when she came to start on *The Watsons*, to metamorphose such experience into a delicious and Mozartian humor. Halperin for once completely misunderstands the tone of the passage he quotes in support of his argument: "She had reached the age of seventeen, without having seen one amiable youth who could call forth her sensibility; without having inspired one real passion, and without having excited even any admiration but what was very moderate and very transient." "What heartbreaking disappointment lies behind those words," Halperin says, but they afford the clearest possible case of the author having her fun, indulging in the kind of deadpan humor she enjoyed. Real disappointment is a world away from this sort of virtuosity.

Since *Jane Eyre* we have regarded the explosion of strong feelings in a novel, particularly perhaps a woman's novel, to be a sign of authenticity and power. But "Such is my fate, O Reader" would have seemed to Jane Austen a formula for bad workmanship as well as bad taste. Emma Woodhouse may sit musing on "the difference of woman's destiny," but these things must be obliquely approached; far better to have a heroine like her, "handsome, clever, and rich," or a gracious country estate, like Mansfield Park, a heroine and a setting where sharpness can be exercised and sadness revealed with tranquility and elegance.

Jane Austen's instinct was right for herself, and perhaps right, in a more profound sense, for the novel. The light is the best foil for the dark: boredom, misery, and despair are revealed the more sharply and effectively through a surface of serenity, comedy, and good humor. Doing it the other way around is far more difficult, as many powerful and sincere novelists have found to their cost; indeed a true double picture cannot be achieved by such direct means at all, and it is significant that the novelists of our time who have really managed to learn from Jane Austen (itself a rare feat) are those with the surest instinct for this lesson. Ivy Compton-Burnett, Elizabeth Bowen, Elizabeth Taylor, Barbara Pym, all learned it in their different ways.

This double focus is the real clue to Jane Austen, to her life as to her art; and it is her art that makes a clear case of what must be, after all, a fairly universal situation. When an aunt gives the wrong advice, or a tiresome old woman is thoughtlessly snubbed, we apprehend with piercing clarity the dual nature of things, the heaven and hell in which we simultaneously live. The crack in the teacup opens, as Auden writes, a lane to the land of the dead. Jane Austen would have laughed at this view of her novels, or found it tasteless and incomprehensible, which is why the modern criticism of her novels often seems unreal in relation to their actual world. Princeton professor Walton Litz rightly says that her dilemma is "an epitome of the dilemma faced by the free spirit in a limited world," but that does not indicate what her art is doing in practical terms, which is to make the savagery and monotony of ordinary life delightful to read about. It is deeply misleading to say there is a "real" Jane Austen, quite unlike the delightful Jane who, as Henry James dryly observed, was so much to everyone's advantage.

Halperin's achievement is to imply nothing of the sort, while at the same time suggesting with considerable vividness what it must actually have felt to live like Jane Austen, and even to die like her at forty-one of adrenal tuberculosis, a disease now easily controlled by cortisone. His biography is admirably complemented by George Holbert Tucker's history of the Austen family, a labor of love more traditionally accomplished and clearly set out so that the reader can follow the fortunes of each relation in turn. It contains a long and detailed account of what must have been the most dramatic event among the Austen relatives—the arrest and trial of Jane's rich and formidable aunt, Mrs. Leigh Perrot, on a charge of shoplifting in Bath. Clearly she had been blackmailed by an unscrupulous shopkeeper—she was found not guilty—but had the verdict gone against her she would have been transported to Botany Bay, and the youthful Jane, who had volunteered to stay with her in prison—an offer gratefully declined—would have had a convict among her relations.

It is unlikely she would have used the incident for "copy." Though she loved jaunts and visits she had no impulse to widen the scope of her experience or to bring new aspects of society into her art. She excused herself from attending a grand party at her sister-in-law's to meet Madame de Staël, and that may have been not only from shyness but from an instinct to avoid anything resembling competition. Had she lived another twenty-eight years, like her elder sister, the pair would no doubt have grown contentedly old together in Chawton. How many more novels would have been written? Would there have been a falling-off in her powers? No way to tell, but there is a certain fitness about the fact that her life and work had the same sort of pattern, the same tragic completeness, as those of her romantic contemporaries, Keats, Shelley, and Byron, about whom, insofar as she knew of them, she registered little beyond amusement.

The New York Review of Books, 1985

3

Best and Worst

Charles Dickens (1812–1870)

———

Dickens: A Biography
by Fred Kaplan

S o VARIOUS IS Charles Dickens, so contradictory and disconcerting, that it is natural for anyone writing about him to seek a clue to his complex genius, something for ourselves and the critic to hold on to. G. K. Chesterton, in what is still one of the best introductions to the Dickens world, stressed the immense joviality—the bacon in the rafter and the wine in the wood—a Pickwick feast of snowballs and plum puddings. Humphry House, more sober and social-minded, wrote a book with the title of *The Dickens World*, which has lasted well, and which stresses Dickens's extraordinarily multiform relation, as personality and author, with virtually every reform and aspiration of the time, with the problems of Victorian London and the woes of industrialized England.

The more recent tendency is to emphasize Dickens's subjective side, to plunge him back into the maelstrom of oddity in which he reveled, the Freudian nightmare of purity and corruption, fascination and horror. In a very penetrating little book, *The Violent Effigy: A Study of Dickens' Imagination*, John Carey dwelt on Dickens's obsession with dolls and waxworks, with young girls as sugar models and the elderly as limp puppets or gesticulating masks. Who but Dickens, he asked, could make us laugh at the idea of dead babies while almost simultaneously reaching for our handkerchiefs when one of his little dears—Jo the sweeper or Paul Dombey—is about to expire? Oscar Wilde in a sense summed the matter up when he remarked that one needed a heart of stone not to laugh at the death of Little Nell.

Admirably comprehensive, balanced, and informative, and showing an encyclopedic knowledge of minor Victorian writers and journalists and hostesses long forgotten, Fred Kaplan's book goes a long way to redress the balance and give us a Dickens who demands all-around attention rather than present a single elemental clue to the source of genius. But even Professor Kaplan cannot resist dwelling on one leitmotif, and it is a decidedly spooky one. When in early 1857 Dickens produced *The Frozen Deep* with Wilkie Collins, himself taking the leading role, part of the melodrama's huge success was due to public interest in Sir John Franklin's ill-fated expedition to the Arctic ice in quest of the Northwest Passage. Not only were the explorers never seen again but it was rumored they had been forced to practice cannibalism.

Dickens was fascinated and went into the evidence in his magazine *Household Words*, giving a sensible verdict of "not proven" but remaining absorbed by the idea itself. It certainly connects with much that fueled his creative imagination, and not only in *The Frozen Deep*, which had been inspired by the Franklin tragedy. Not only is eating itself of huge importance in the Dickens world, where "there was never such a mutton chop," such a barrel of oysters, such a steak and onions, but in a broad sense all his characters are engaged in eating each other, or being eaten. Sexuality itself is seen as a process of ingestion, and so sometimes is murder. The terrifyingly vital little Daniel Quilp, in *The Old Curiosity Shop*, is ready to eat his wife anew every day, and of course regards Little Nell herself as a particularly desirable morsel. In his last unfinished novel, Dickens's young Edwin Drood might well have disappeared because the mysterious villain John Jasper, who lives in two worlds, has had him consumed in some abominable Eastern rite. Jasper certainly wishes to devour, in a more socially acceptable sense, the heroine, Rosa Bud. "I could eat you" is the unspoken wish of Dickens's liveliest characters. Even a Dickensian cat has to be removed from a room where a corpse is laid out in case . . . we know what, though Dickens of course does not tell us.

Indeed Professor Kaplan is right to recognize that Dickens nowhere else mentions cannibalism specifically. He does not have to; and I feel that Kaplan might have made even more of this insight if he had wanted, for he does not refer it specifically to the energies and spirit of the novels. His purposes are not critical, although his detailed commentary suggests on the way, as in this instance, more illuminating ideas than occur in most critical studies of Dickens's work. Understanding of the Dickens phenomenon is probably best served, in any case, not by theories about him but by facts—all the swarming lot of them. There is something unreal now about the pronouncements on the novels by those two formidable critical lawgivers of Cambridge, England, Dr. and Mrs. Leavis, who spent years decreeing what could be "saved" in the novels and what could not. Leavis himself originally gave out the bizarre instruction that *Hard Times*, with its satiric parable on utilitarianism, was the only novel of Dickens that deserved serious study by grown-up people. Attitudes have changed a good deal since then, and Dickens's reputation as an artist, once even more in the doldrums than those of his fellow Victorians, has continued to rise to almost Shakespearean heights.

Naturally enough Kaplan has no new or sensational material about Dickens's secret life, or his affair in middle age with the actress Ellen Ternan, but he shows a matter-of-fact interest and sympathy, that of a modern man well accustomed to such matters, which is itself a good corrective to those previous biographers who were more eager to speculate, praise, or condemn. The surprising thing is that Dickens did not have many more affairs: his energy and frenetic sexual imagination might seem to have required them. But Dickens lived in an age when there was no shame, as it were, in keeping sex in the head rather than laying upon it the duty—and especially where such a celebrity was concerned—of ceremonially frequent physical expression. Very likely he was not highly sexed or promiscuous by nature, although he may have had adventures that we know nothing of.

Certainly his great friend Wilkie Collins did: he was a gentle, self-effacing man who kept two mistresses and families on a regular basis, as well as other unspecified commitments. But Collins never married, whereas something in Dickens required to be plunged into the bosom of blameless domesticity as if into a hot bath or a feather bed, from which he would periodically rush out in revulsion against family life in all its aspects. "It was the best of times. It was the worst of times." The famous beginning of A *Tale of Two Cities* sums up much of Dickens's own mental and physical existence, which, like that of his last and most haunting hero-villain figure, John Jasper, alternated between light and dark, grim secrecy and ebullient openness. He could be astonishingly cruel to his family, particularly to his wife, Catherine, for whose cloying affectionate simplicity he came to feel a cold detestation. It was easy to revere the memory of her sister Mary, the sweet sixteen-year-old who had died in his arms not long after his marriage; or to be chums with Catherine's other and more vivaciously practical sister, Georgina, who virtually ran the household for many years.

"A misplaced and mismarried man," Dickens wrote about himself in his notebook. Rightly I think, Kaplan refers the prison of his marriage, as he came to conceive it, to his early relations with his mother, that fecklessly endearing and much enduring woman who had danced on the night he was born, and who had shown no sympathy with and little awareness of the nightmare life he suffered when he was put to work at the age of fourteen in the notorious blacking factory. Kaplan does not overdo the Freudian angle, but Dickens is certainly a treasure-house for Freudian interpretation—almost too obviously. Part of Dickens's universal appeal must come not so much from the extraordinary characters he dreamed up as from his essentially "comic strip" private imagination: the world of giants, demons, ogres, and beautiful princesses that had such a rapturous fascination for him in shows and pantomimes when he was young and for which he found counterparts in Victorian life. In a sense his inner world never changed. In 1858, at the age of forty-six, he was telling his friend Macready of dreams in which he acted the part of the fantasy hero, striving to recapture from her enemies "the Princess whom I adore . . . nothing would suit me half so well . . . as climbing after her sword in hand, and either winning her or being killed."

As Kaplan dryly remarks, "that the princess was Ellen Ternan mattered less than that he needed a princess." Dickens had no desire for a contented old age, and he felt that to die rescuing her would make him happy. He needed happiness, or rather the sheerness of joy, in order to be able to write, and his naive definition of happiness to himself was the absence of his mother-wife and the promise of his princess-mistress. Human, all too human, as Nietzsche might have said, and certainly all too familiar. That the Dickens who indulged in these fantasies was also the Dickens whose brilliantly intuitive intelligence and perceptive humor could analyze the consciousness of David Copperfield, or of Pip in *Great Expectations,* is much more remarkable, is indeed the miracle involved in his genius. He could be remorselessly intelligent, as well as sympathetic, about his characters—their needs, their destiny, their conditioning—but he disdained to extend the same insight to his own problems, or the same kind of sympathy. Had he done so he might have lost his creative spirit, lapsed into the introversion of the Coleridgean sage. He had to keep going, and the only way to do that was to invent and write, and to act out in recitals and dramatic shows the parts once adored in juvenile fancy.

Of course it was tough on others. What must poor Kate have thought when he rose from the marital couch at 2:00 A.M. and walked all the way from Tavistock Square in Bloomsbury to their place on Gads Hill in Kent—"over 30 miles through the dead night. I had been very much put-out; and I thought, 'After all, it would be better to be up and doing something, than lying here.' So I got up and did that." He also worked on a Christmas number for *Household Words,* which he planned with great care and entitled "The Perils of Certain English Prisoners." These perils took place in China and India, both dangerous places for the English invaders in the mid-nineteenth century, and at the center of the story was a dramatized version of himself as Saint George, rescuing a fair-haired maiden, Lady Maryon, whose hand the hero cannot aspire to since she is well above his social station. He is happy to serve her for no reward.

Both in his life and in his novels Thomas Hardy also indulged in romantic aspirations about aristocratic girls. It must have been a common Victorian fantasy, and in *Tess of the D'Urbervilles* Hardy has things ingeniously both ways by making his heroine a peasant girl of aristocratic origins and demeanor. Dickens did the same with a real-life Ellen Ternan, putting her on a pedestal as a princess while at the same time aiding her career as a struggling chorus girl (her stage parts were hardly more exalted than that) and setting her up in a secret little establishment of her own. His circle of intimate friends clearly knew all about it but remained silent and loyal. His elder sons came to know, too. It was, after all, a familiar middle-class situation of the time, though in the case of such a celebrity as Dickens it had to be kept a close secret.

Kaplan wisely makes no pretense of succeeding where so many others have failed in penetrating the mysteries of "the great Detective," but it seems possible that the couple had a child whose paternity remained unknown, perhaps even to himself. It seems more likely than the now discredited story that Hardy had one too. Dickens and Ellen traveled about a good deal—he once thought of taking her to America—and on a return from Paris, in 1864, accompanied by her mother, both were involved in what became known as the great Staplehurst Railway Disaster, with ten passengers killed. Suddenly transported from fantasies of peril and rescue into the real thing, Dickens behaved with great courage and resource, carrying brandy to the wounded and dying and calling the distracted guards to order by saying sharply: "Do you know me?" "We know you very well, Mr. Dickens," they meekly replied. Ellen herself was hurt, though not seriously, and Dickens's own health was so shaken that he never really recovered in the six years that remained to him.

His rhetorical order to the railwaymen, a question very definitely expecting the answer "Yes," shows the extent to which he had become not only a public figure, but one whose authority he himself felt to be unquestionable. A year or so after the railway incident a deputation of London's Jewish citizens waited on him to complain about the famous portrait of Fagin, the Jewish crook who runs the thieves' kitchen for young criminals in Oliver Twist. Dickens promised like royalty to put the matter right, and inserted the good Jew Riah into Our Mutual Friend, which he was working on at the time. Riah is not only virtuous and beneficent but the reluctant instrument of an odious and dishonest young Gentile and financial yuppie, "Fascination" Fledgeby.

As a character, however, Riah is hardly a success, and one feels that what he is, and is intended to be, might well be a source of greater irritation to Jewish readers than is the memorably nightmarish early portrait of Fagin. Fagin, like Shylock, is a victim, despite his villainy, and the account of him in prison before his execution is one of the most powerful things in the novels. But, as Chesterton remarked, it pleased Dickens "to be taken for a judge in Israel," and to compensate graciously for what might seem an injustice. What no one seems to have noticed is that the name Fagin was taken from that of the uncouth but kindly boy who befriended Dickens in the blacking factory: a remarkable instance of the ruthless way in which he exorcised his most painful memories by transferring them to his picture of the juvenile gang in *Oliver Twist*.

He was not such a lawgiver at the time of his American visit in 1842, but it seems likely that he irritated a good many Americans by airing his views, just as he did when he came to portray the young country in *Martin Chuzzlewit*. James Fields, the Boston publisher, found him "the Emperor of Cheerfulness on a cruise of pleasure," and, as Kaplan says, "though he came as a private traveler, he could not resist stepping onto the public platform that his American hosts assumed was his natural place." Painful misunderstanding was bound to occur, for there was no room in America for the secret, reticent, and private side of Dickens, nor did he make himself popular by saying what he thought about slavery and the need for international copyright. Dickens could be both fearless and tactless, but there was something admirable about his determination to speak out, as when he scornfully rejected the stories that most slaves were in fact well treated, just as he had belabored back in England the economists who had advocated humane child employment in factories, or properly organized prostitution.

Like every great entertainer he sacrificed his health to his public without a thought. His friend and biographer Forster besought him not to go on with the recitals that were killing him, and which toward the end of his life he came much to prefer to writing new novels. The novels for him achieved their true reality—"so real are my fictions to myself"—on the boards, and he needed the ecstatic crowds. He was delighted when rows of girls were dragged out from his Sikes and Nancy performance in dead faints. He also needed the money, but of the two the applause was more vital to him. The secret side that had originally produced the London horrors, the grim fears so marked even in the apprentice *Sketches by Boz*, and in the interior fantasy of Quilp or Mrs. Gamp, could be driven further into the darkness by more and more spectacular public success.

Kaplan is particularly good—it is one of the strengths of his biography—on the shape and perspective of Dickens's career, his relation with his younger siblings, all of whom he outlived, and with his own children and their developing private lives. To be fully understood as a writer he needs to be put in this sort of family frame. But it is as a writer that he remains most vivid to us here, unforgettable, describing himself as

> prowling about the rooms, sitting down, getting up, stirring the fire, looking out of window, tearing my hair, sitting down to write, writing nothing, writing something and tearing it up, going out, coming in, a Monster to my family, a dread phenomenon to myself.

His most remarkable summing up of his own sense of himself was "a wild beast in a caravan, describing himself in his keeper's absence." Fortunately the keeper was absent pretty frequently. Like so much else in his frenetic existence, being a literary genius was for Dickens both the best of fates, and the worst of them.

The New York Review of Books, 1989

4

Living with Trollope

Anthony Trollope (1815–1882)

The Chronicler of Barsetshire: A Life of Anthony Trollope
by R. H. Super

Trollope: Living with Character
by Stephen Wall

*He Knew She Was Right: The Independent Woman in the Novels
of Anthony Trollope*
by Jane Nardin

THERE IS AN amusing scene in Anthony Powell's *roman-fleuve*, *A Dance to the Music of Time*, in which a brigadier demands of a very junior officer what he thinks of Anthony Trollope. It is wartime, 1940, and the novelist has suddenly become popular again. The junior officer is the narrator: in fact the author himself. After a difficult moment wondering whether truth or respectfulness would be more in order he replies that he has never found Trollope "particularly easy to read." An explosion follows, and he is required to produce the name of a novelist whom he does like. "Well, Sir, there's Balzac." Another explosion.

Bus drivers and brigadiers were in fact reading Trollope during the war, as they were reading *War and Peace*. The atmosphere of crisis and boredom in the Battle of Britain made a red-letter day for the classic novelists, offering the comfort and relaxation of a complete and credible alternative world. That was what counted, and made the classics during that time more acceptable than romances or junk novels. There was also no doubt a general feeling, encouraged by skillful BBC propaganda, that the crusade against Hitler required, during its moments of relief, a correspondingly elevated class of reading matter. Whatever the reason there is no doubt that Trollope's reputation and sales rose greatly during those years, and his reputation has remained high ever since. Academia is now prepared to take him as seriously as it takes Dickens, though the Trollope industry is not yet on the same scale.

But does the Balzac addict find Trollope as easy to read, or as profitable? At a big dinner Trollope once made a speech toasting Balzac. "I am told that he was the man who invented that style of fiction in which I have attempted to work. I assure any young men around me who may be desirous of following the same steps that they cannot possibly find any style easier." Hmm. R. H. Super quotes that in his elegant and scholarly biography, and goes on to wonder whether it may be referred to Trollope's amusement, a year or so earlier, when he overheard two clerics at the Athenaeum Club depreciating Mrs. Proudie, the bishop's wife in the Barsetshire series. According to his *Autobiography* Trollope revealed himself on that occasion, telling the clergymen that he would go home and kill off Mrs. Proudie. Which he did.

It would be agreeable to imagine Henry James, the attentive eavesdropper of Max Beerbohm's cartoon, hearing some fellow clubmen criticizing the Princess Casamassima (who had, after all, appeared in two of his novels) and vowing to go home and do her in straightaway. Agreeable but, alas, impossible. James's sense of the novelist's calling was too high, too august: he could never have compromised it by so brutally vulgar an attitude as that which Trollope took pleasure in revealing to the public who read his *Autobiography*. James, who revered Balzac, expressed a fearful admiration for Trollope, like a visitor to the zoo admiring the carnivore's appetite. He was amazed by the majestic insensitivity of Trollope's work habits. Why, he even wrote in his cabin at sea, and James admitted that the man who could close his eyes to the discomforts of "a pitching Cunarder," and open them on the loves and sorrows of Lily Dale, had a faculty that could take to itself wings. James's wonder hints, nonetheless, that this remarkable process passes beneath the reader's gaze like the conveyor belt of a soap opera.

The *Autobiography* made Trollope his own worst enemy in advancing his literary reputation, yet its no-nonsense attitude impressed other writers and even spurred them to emulation. Henry Adams wrote that after seeing how Trollope "can destroy the last vestige of heroism in his own life, I object to allowing mine to be murdered by anyone except myself." Henry James thought it "one of the most curious and amazing books in all literature for its density, blockishness, and general thickness and soddenness," but he too began in consequence to think seriously of writing about himself. Trollope had an unsettling but secretly inspiring effect upon those who practiced High Art. Yeats adored him, but furtively, his official love being Balzac. It may indeed have been Trollope's example that prompted the division of the novel by the critics, about the time he died, into highbrow and lowbrow, a distinction that would have meant nothing to Dickens, or to his readers. And yet Trollope soon ceased to be a popular taste. What made him "not particularly easy to read"?

James may supply the answer when he spoke of his "great, the inestimable merit" being "a complete appreciation of the usual, . . . a delicate perception of the actual." These are not qualities that make a popular novelist. Ordinary novel readers expect more fantasy, and what James calls "a strong grasp of the possible," rather than of the usual. Balzac's grasp of society's workings strongly applied to his readers because of its fertile spawning of monsters, male and female, and the vivid detail in which he created their customs and habitat. Many readers wish to feel that their novelist is himself an extraordinary man, and the extraordinariness of Trollope was not the kind that readers require. It is the kind that makes ordinary people seem infinitely surprising when you get to know their little ways. But there is no drama about it, none of the sibylline authority of George Eliot, or the tremendous invention of Dostoevsky. Interestingly it was not the reading public but other writers who showed themselves most aware of Trollope's true singularity. James's tribute speaks for itself; George Eliot both admired and envied him; and Tolstoy—even more surprisingly—once exclaimed that "Trollope kills me, kills me with his mastery"—an ambiguous compliment perhaps, but a very positive one.

Trollope specializes in our "little ways." He sees that they are the most important thing about most of us. But they are also the hardest thing to make continuously interesting and absorbing to the reader. Trollope had the knack, however he got it, of converting our little ways into a tale, a story of ourselves that has both the truths of monotony and the compulsions of an increasing momentum. His most obvious triumphs in this genre are the Reverend Crawley, the clergyman in *The Last Chronicle of Barset* who is accused of stealing a check; or Louis Trevelyan, the obsessed and jealous husband of *He Knew He Was Right*. The latter has more than "little ways," it is true, yet his trouble is essentially a small habit grown to infernal proportions.

In a perspicacious study from a feminist angle Jane Nardin comes near to suggesting, perhaps without quite meaning to, that Trollope became a kind of protofeminist as an author because it suited his method better. Social determinism bears harder on women than on men, and "little ways" develop as a means both of circumventing and coming to terms with it. Hardy, of all nineteenth-century novelists the most inclined to make drama out of determinism, has Elizabeth Jane in *The Mayor of Casterbridge* find that the only way to be happy in this world is to cultivate minute forms of contingent gratification, the kind that offer themselves daily to the humble heart who accepts a subordinate position. One of his characters makes this discovery but the rest of them, and his novels too, don't act on it. Homely Hardy is surprisingly inept at conveying the actual homeliness of existence on a daily basis, although he can suggest it indirectly in moving and imaginative touches.

But Trollope can do it continuously and brilliantly. Perhaps it went with that unfailing daily session at his desk, from five to seven-thirty each morning. If women have the drudgery of habit forced upon them, he elected it as a personal literary method and made it the basis of a lifetime's success. Perhaps because he understood the art of the possible so well he saw the best scope for it in his female characters. Nardin's *He Knew She Was Right* suggests that "in a society where power is largely reserved for the male, men may wilfully seek tragedy" (the reference is to Louis Trevelyan) "but are far less likely than women to have it thrust upon them." That puts the matter very well. Trollope is always at his best with characters who have things thrust upon them.

Jane Nardin has also written an excellent study of Barbara Pym's novels; and in a memorable image Barbara Pym compared a woman's usual experience of life to having a large white rabbit thrust into one's arms.

Halfway between Lewis Carroll and Samuel Beckett, the picture is certainly a potent one for half of human experience. It is comic too, and comedy is never far away from Trollope's exact sobrieties, beneath which lurk in demure seclusion the small comforts and incongruities of life chronicled in the world of Barbara Pym. The bishop in bed with his wife in the Barsetshire series is a surprising Victorian emblem, but one as significant for Trollope as the rabbit to Pym. Neither the bishop nor his lady quite knows how he and she got there. For the bishop bed stands both for comfort and for exasperation: for his wife it is the center for scheming and for the enjoyment of power; but also, we intuit, for the reassurance and support which this masterful woman unreflectingly takes from her supine spouse.

Stephen Wall's study is subtitled "Living with Character," and this seems to me to go to the heart of the matter. Trollope is always in bed with his characters, metaphorically speaking; he seems not to have invented them but to have found himself in their company. Wall's is the most unpretentious but also the most original study I have read on Trollope's novels, and does more to explain their true appeal than does anything previously written on the novelist. Living with his characters in what Trollope called "the full reality of established intimacy," a quaint but highly suggestive phrase, Trollope knows them as a wife was once said to know her husband, or a valet his master. He knows them from the inside out, from the weak, uncertain interior to the armored persona that has grown up for public use.

John Grey, in *Can You Forgive Her?*, is a characteristic figure here, and Wall produces a telling example from the Palliser novels. Trollope understands Plantagenet Palliser as a political animal but also as a vulnerable creature, with little ways that are an endearing aspect of his vulnerability. He and his wife, Glencora, are talking one day about Rosina de Courcy, a decayed old aristocrat come down in the world. Plantagenet is sententious about her. "Perhaps there is nothing so sad in the world as the female scions of a noble but impoverished stock." That is the kind of pontification we might expect of a politician off duty, and Palliser is not only a politician but prime minister. But Trollope is not just "placing" the tone and personality of one of his specimens: that would not go with the way he lives with them. Certainly the remark is sententious, fully meriting

Glencora's sharp retort—"Nothing so dull certainly." But Trollope then goes on to show how a politician's armor of sententiousness can overlay genuine human feeling and touching personal need. "People are not dull to me, if they are real," replies Palliser.

What he means by "real" here goes both to the inside of his own nature and the inside of Trollope's process. "Reality" of being in these novels is something both internal and involuntary, something the human actor cannot will for himself, or cultivate. Role-playing in Trollope subtly and invisibly contrasts with the way we actually are, the little ways which make us real. Women in particular disclose them. Right at the beginning of *The Eustace Diamonds* we are introduced to Lady Linlithgow, the heroine's aunt.

> Lady Linlithgow was worldly, stingy, ill-tempered, selfish, and mean. She would cheat a butcher out of a mutton-chop, or a cook out of a month's wages, if she could do so with some slant of legal wind in her favour. She would tell any number of lies to carry a point in what she believed to be social success. It was said of her that she cheated at cards. In backbiting no venomous old woman between Bond Street and Park Lane could beat her—or, more wonderful still, no venomous old man at the clubs. But nevertheless she recognised certain duties, and performed them, though she hated them. She went to church, not merely that people might see her there—as to which in truth she cared nothing—but because she thought it was right.

In Trollopian reality Lady Linlithgow rivals her niece Lizzie Greystock, the heroine of the novel, and the contrast between them is a telling one. It is also typical of Trollope, as it is not of Dickens, that the major character should be just as "real," in his peculiar sense, as the minor one. But he establishes the nature of reality in a manner very different from that of Dickens, as becomes clear if we go back to the odd relation between Palliser and Lady Rosina. Accustomed to the behavior and pretenses of politicians, Palliser is soothed by the genuineness of the old woman, but Trollope manages to make it clear that this is only because she is a genuine aristocrat. Palliser could not—unlike Wordsworth's characters, or Kipling's—have found anything elevating or soothing in the society of common folk; but he enjoys conversing with Lady Rosina about cork soles.

> "I always have thick boots—I am very particular about that—and cork soles."
> "Cork soles are admirable."
> "I think I owe my life to cork soles," said Lady Rosina enthusiastically. "There is a man named Sprout in Silverbridge who makes them. Did your Grace ever try him for boots?"
> "I don't think I ever did," said the Prime Minister.
> "Then you had better. He is very good and very cheap too."

Whatever they think he means by "real," philosophers like A. J. Ayer, the distinguished author of *Language, Truth, and Logic,* read Trollope with passion and precision, in a way they would never read Dickens. Connoisseurs of legal and political theory relish him too. Shirley Letwin's lively study, *The Gentleman in Trollope,* suggests that Trollope's ladies—notably Madame Max in *Phineas Finn*—fit supremely well into his category of gentlemen. Feminist as she is Jane Nardin allows that. She is brilliant on Lily Dale, the popular heroine of *The Small House at Allington,* about whom Trollope shocked the readers of his *Autobiography* by calling her a "female prig." And like all good Trollope critics, such as James Kincaid and A. O. J. Cockshut, she is more concerned with questions of human nature than with literary theory.

Once or twice she cannot resist a modish pronouncement, as when she claims that *The Claverings* "offers a commentary on the kind of comedy it pretends to be," but her normally shrewd and penetrating discussion of Trollope's characters shows that she must have found analyzing him in formalist or structuralist terms a singularly barren exercise. He is still unfashionable with the higher criticism, which explores metaphysical light and darkness in Dickens or Joyce or Melville, but which has a horror—almost a *pudeur*—about discussing the actual quirks of human beings. The great merit of Stephen Wall's book is that it is as uncomplicated as Trollope's own approach to fiction, and as illuminating. The way in which people are judged and talked about by their fellow men and women is far more important in relation to Trollope's world than the ways in which novels are written.

The "established intimacy" in which Trollope lived with his characters is less commonplace than the idea of it, promulgated by Trollope himself, might suggest. Many novelists talk of "getting to know" their characters, and popular romances try to persuade their readers that their heroes and heroines act, as it were, freely and spontaneously. The element of popular romance in Trollope associates with a lonely childhood in which he compulsively told himself stories; and also with the fact that his vivacious but usually absent mother had herself become a prolific novelist, and on occasion a best-seller. Frances Trollope is seldom read today, but the formulas of romance were in the blood, and there are times, both with Trollope and his mother, when they are all too obviously on the page as well. Trollope's father was ineffectual, but perhaps taking up his mother's gift was for the neglected son a way of regaining, and monopolizing, her affection?

The lonely child's stories ended happily; and with that can go a sentimentalization of women's feeling about themselves, as in the touching but also distinctly soppy *Miss Mackenzie*. Such winking made Anthony Powell's young narrator claim rather desperately to the incensed brigadier that Trollope had no true sense of woman at all. If that were the case it would indeed make him "not particularly easy to read" for the fastidious; but in fact his women, like his men, divide very positively into those he can live with, and those with whom he does not try or bother to do so. The striking thing about Trollope's familiarity with his characters is the way it can alternate the cynical ease of popular romance with sudden shrewd insights and piercing sympathies.

The lonely child telling himself stories grew into a hard and masterful tycoon who quickly learned how to exploit their market value, and became as well a resourceful and hardworking post office executive, who had much to do with that institution's early success. In his capacities for multiple employment, hard work, and hard play, Trollope was the yuppie *beau ideal*. Writing before dawn, riding to hounds four times a week, incessant traveling to check on offices and employees, running magazines and organizing literary society, finding the wholly suitable wife, and raising the good family—this paradigm of complete living would conceal, were Trollope the protagonist of a modern novel, some desperate inner vacuum, longings corrosive and unfulfilled.

But there is no evidence that it did anything of the sort. There are no dramas or disclosures in Trollope's life, and yet Professor Super's biography manages to give it as much fascination as that of Dickens or Tolstoy, if not more so. Super's mastery of the period, its details and its dailiness, makes his chronicle the perfect accompaniment to one of Trollope's own novels, and he is as comprehensive about plots and sales as he is about dinners and travels and the vast circle of friends.

Not everyone liked Trollope; many found him repellent. His voice was loud and harsh and his manner could be overbearing and aggressive. He made up to the great and the useful, and was not always nice to servants. But of course he could be charming, and he had a special *tendresse* for vivacious and vigorous women, particularly American women. In 1860 he met an American girl, Kate Field, with whom, as Jane Nardin puts it, "he was to carry on a Platonic love affair for the rest of his life." He was frank about this in his *Autobiography*, remarking that he could "always strike a spark by thinking of her," and in a letter to a friend he admitted that the relationship sometimes "teased" his wife. But his wife, Rose, was a sensible woman, although at parties and receptions she could seem to onlookers a little absurd, sometimes coquettishly wearing a rose in her prematurely white hair. Kate Field was in any case too busy acting, writing, lecturing, and advocating women's rights to want to set her cap at Trollope. She was a kind of muse to him all the same: his portraits of women who possess and can use power owe her a great deal.

In the speech honoring Balzac and advocating the "style of fiction" in which he had himself attempted to work, Trollope went on to say that "the carrying on of a character from one book to another is very pleasant to the author; but I am not sure that all readers will participate in that pleasure." Trollope need not have worried (if indeed he did), as Wall's study most effectively demonstrates. Not only recurring characters, as with Balzac or Barbara Pym, but recurrent situations directed and explored in different ways, are Trollope's greatest strength as a novelist. He loves to see how the same people will respond to a different challenge, and new characters to a familiar one. It is a familiarity that seldom palls, and that for his admirers is easy to appreciate. If he finished a novel during his early morning stint he immediately began another, as if he were his own Scheherazade. It was well for him that he died of a stroke when he did, aged sixty-seven, for life without a novel going would have been death to him. Such a compulsion is itself awe-inspiring. Henry James, who in his own way shared it, may be allowed the last word. As a twenty-two-year-old reviewer of *Miss Mackenzie* when it appeared in 1864, he observed magisterially: "We have long entertained for Mr. Trollope a partiality of which we have yet been somewhat ashamed." Trollope has survived that embarrassment. No one need feel ashamed of reading him today.

The New York Review of Books, 1989

5

Eminent Victorian

George Eliot (1819–1880)

George Eliot: The Last Victorian
by Kathryn Hughes

THAT FAMOUS OPENING of L. P. Hartley's novel *The Go-Between* — "The past is a foreign country: they do things differently there" — has become a cliché of the present time. But some things in the past are more different than others. The philosopher Isaiah Berlin used to say that some things change and some things don't, and that it is important for the historian of ideas to sense by instinct which is which. Take the case of George Eliot—Mary Ann Evans as she then was—an ardent and naive young woman in 1845. Like all young women she had a special girlfriend, Sara Hennell, and, Hughes writes, "there was no room in Mary Ann's life for another significant emotional attachment." Still, her halfsister Fanny Houghton thought she had found a nice boy for Mary Ann, a good-looking young picture restorer, himself prepared to take a keen interest in this plain but intelligent and articulate young woman. All went well: the sound of wedding bells almost audible. But quite abruptly Mary Ann decided no: she couldn't love or respect him enough to marry him. And the decision gave her a series of psychosomatic headaches.

And so Mary Ann Evans, child of worthy yeoman farm contractors in the English Midlands, was saved from becoming Mrs. Somebody or other, to become in time George Eliot. But the point is how familiar that particular situation and its outcome still seems to us today, give or take a few minor changes in social and sexual expectation. Mary Ann Evans was an ordinary woman who had not yet become George Eliot the Victorian, separated from us in a culture that really does seem different from our own, in outlook, in ideas, and in behavior. Jane Austen feels far closer. George Eliot, always wary of her great predecessor and sometimes down-right rude about her, feared above all her lack of reverence. For if there is one thing that makes the high-minded Victorians appear marooned in an age and a country that is irrevocably, terminally foreign, it is the way so many of them clung to a rigid uncompromising reverence in the midst of an equally uncompromising disbelief. The believer can laugh at what he believes: the disbeliever has no choice but to be wholly serious about the ethical commandments that have taken its place.

That at least became true of George Eliot, and more fatally true the more her successive books and her growing legend were greeted by her Victorian contemporaries with reverence, even with awe. She was the first novelist whose work was accepted as on the same level of the intel-lect as the works of the other great Victorian thinkers. Henry James, who seems as much our contemporary today as any figure from the past does, remarked that the notion and purpose of the novel became perverted if it was placed in a museum: its function as art was to record and to pass on. George Eliot's works of fiction became monumental in her own lifetime. And the girl who giggled with her friend Sara Hennell and both wanted and did not want the love of her erstwhile suitor—the girl who might belong in any age—was in time to become the majestic sibyl seated in the corner of her salon, to whom her lover and partner George Henry Lewes would lead up grave admirers one by one for a strictly rationed dose of sibylline discourse.

No wonder George Eliot fell from favor after her death, a death which, as her biographer Kathryn Hughes rightly suggests, can stand sym-bolically for the closing of the high Victorian age. "Within ten years of her death no one was reading George Eliot. . . . The intellectual elite, the opinion formers, had already moved on." Virginia Woolf might state that *Middlemarch* was "the first English novel for adults," but the praise was two-edged: Woolf's new kind of novel was proclaiming and practicing a philosophy of subjectiveness and helplessness wholly alien to the magis-terial certainties of George Eliot. The revival in George Eliot's fortunes which occurred during and after the Second World War was due not only to an increased interest in Victorian fiction generally but to the specific efforts of critics like F. R. Leavis, who in his study *The Great Tradition* rehabilitated her and placed her firmly, as he thought, at the front of the greatest practitioners of the novelist's art.

Does that judgment still stand today? Only up to a point. *Middlemarch* is still required reading in university English courses, although among the merely bookish it has been partially displaced by the cult of Trollope, more particularly his equally comprehensive social novels like *The Way We Live Now*. Trollope is less bossy in his judgments, more pragmatic, more ready to accept in his easygoing way the complexity of human weakness and social interrelation, less foreign, in fact, from our own contemporary viewpoint. Remaining addicts of George Eliot (Henry James in his time was after all one of them) can enjoy with reservations the full gamut of her work, *Daniel Deronda* and even *Romola* included; her companion guardian Lewes said of her first effort, *Scenes of Clerical Life*, "I think your pathos is better than your fun," but both now seem more than a trifle *voulu* and heavy-handed. We feel more at home with that sort of thing in Dickens.

Kathryn Hughes has, naturally enough, nothing new to say about the life story, and is too honest to pretend she has, but she writes shrewdly and well, neither patronizing her subject nor unduly attempting to champion her. She is good on the human weakness and vanity which underlay George Eliot's proclaimed convictions and certainties, and points out how very little sympathy she would have had with feminist positions today, whether moderate or extreme. Rather sensibly she preferred, whenever she could, to avail herself of the best of both worlds: "warmth and femininity" when these qualities came in question, and intellectual rigor and masculine superiority when they did not. She found no trouble in separating the two sides of herself—not becoming a "whole woman."

She said she would have liked to have children, but as the mistress of a married man she deferred to society's conventions and refrained. This was fortunate not only for her reputation, which became ever more august and respectable, but because in any case she did not really care for children: she cordially disliked Lewes's tiresome boys, offspring of his wife, Alice, who had early gone off with Leigh Hunt's son into a truly bohemian world. Characteristically she did her best to love the Lewes children when they appeared; but if she had become permanently entangled with Herbert Spencer or the raffish George Bray, with both of whom she may have had an affair, she might well have found herself in a subordinate position which would have stifled her writing. Imprisoned with a normal husband and a brood of her own she would have been even worse off. She was lucky enough to be and to do what suited her best, while the confidence in being right about everything which underlies all her work, fiction and philosophy alike, stems from that primal good fortune. She knew she was right because everything had turned out right for her. She did just what she wanted; and her partnership with Lewes gave her the greatest possible encouragement to do it.

It is this factor that may have produced the curious uncertainty in her remarkable heroines which Kathryn Hughes has perceptively noted. They have all their creator's fine qualities—nobility, idealism, the moral imperatives of virtue and high thinking—but since they cannot be George Eliot, and achieve what she achieved, what else can they manage to do? There is nothing for them apparently commensurate with the interest with which George Eliot has succeeded in charging their situations in the eyes of the reader. Dorothea Brooke marries and settles down with an ordinary working MP; Romola devotes all her learning and her powers of study to looking after the poor; Gwendolen Harleth, politely rejected by that improbable pioneer of Zionism, Daniel Deronda, dwindles into the vague role of do-gooder. Only meek little Milly, the uncomplaining put-upon wife of the Reverend Amos Barton in *Scenes of Clerical Life*, seems to find her proper role and to earn her author's unreserved praise in fulfilling it. She dies in her husband's arms, and he is helpless and inconsolable in consequence. It is Milly who seems the most suitable candidate for "the Choir Invisible," singing of goodness rather than of godliness, to which George Eliot, most high-minded of atheists, announced that she aspired to belong.

"O May I Join the Choir Invisible"—the devotional rhapsody she composed for herself and other *bien pensants*—is George Eliot in her most Victorian and to us today her least congenial mood. High-minded as it may be, it also did her no good in the eyes of the godly, and of the clerical establishment. It was discovered after her death that she had been so far from immune to the satisfactions of a posthumous celebrity that she had expressed a wish in her will to be buried in Westminster Abbey. Normally there would have been no bother about so illustrious a writer being commemorated with Shakespeare and the others in Poets' Corner. But Dean Stanley of Westminster Abbey, though he had been a personal friend of hers and Lewes's, took it upon himself sharply to intervene. She had ignored the sanctity of marriage; still worse she disbelieved the truths of Christianity. It must not be. And it was not. George Eliot was interred along with Karl Marx in Highgate Cemetery.

Her young husband of a few months, John Cross, the banker, was deeply shocked by the Dean's decision. But poor John Cross!—he had the heavy weight of her reputation to support, sustain, and, if it were possible, augment still further. Marriage to the great lady, who loved him all the more fervently since, unlike Lewes, he was a real husband, had already proved something of a strain. On their honeymoon in Venice he jumped from their hotel balcony into the Grand Canal. It seems to have been a nervous breakdown, albeit one which never subsequently recurred. But malicious gossip was not slow to suggest that he had leaped out to escape the amorous importunity of a wife not only many years older but "magnificently, awe-inspiringly ugly," as the young Henry James had wonderingly described her.

Sadly, and after only a few months of great happiness, George Eliot was to die of a kidney ailment, aged sixty-one. Her health had never been good; she suffered from a formidable array of psychosomatic ailments— racking headaches attacked her whenever she wrote—but she was tough too and always a great traveler. Her death came as a shock to the new husband who had looked after her so devotedly, just as the death of her beloved partner Lewes had come as a bewildering shock to her. If any woman ever needed a man it was George Eliot, and she was lucky to have acquired two good men who made it their life's work to look after her, although Lewes remained mercurial and frivolous to the end, and it may well be, unfaithful on occasion.

Someone asked Henry James what Cross must have felt when his wife died. After prolonged rumination James replied: "Surprise? Regret? Remorse? Relief." And Cross never married again. Once was enough for him, and the burden of being Chief Worshipper at the great lady's shrine was to prove as onerous as were the spousal duties Cross had originally taken on. There was the Life to write, a massive three-volume Victorian affair, epitomizing the pieties and concealments which Lytton Strachey was to deride and excoriate when he himself came to write *Eminent Victorians*. As Kathryn Hughes well puts it, the Eliot of Cross's biography is "the Sibyl, the Sage, the earnest talking head who urges the world to try harder." Prime Minister Gladstone, another great Victorian not remarkable for iconoclasm or salacious curiosity, was nonetheless heard to murmur as he read it, "It is not a Life at all. It is a reticence in three volumes."

The fate of lawgivers and sibyls, in literature if not in life, is to have no lasting influence. George Eliot's precepts can be said to have perished with her. She had tried to turn the novel into too blunt an instrument not only of culture and duty but of what Matthew Arnold called "sweetness and light." She should have heeded what her contemporary Emily Dickinson (of whom of course she had never heard) was to do, and "tell all the truth but tell it slant." Henry James, the novelist who did indeed learn from her but who was also her most searching and clear-eyed critic, did just that. But as Kathryn Hughes implies in her admirably sensible and workmanlike biography, George Eliot can reveal much to us today precisely because she and her mindset and her philosophy of life seem so far off, so irrevocably in a past which has become and will no doubt remain totally a matter of history. Shakespeare may be "our contemporary," to say nothing of Pushkin or Proust or the metaphysical poets, but George Eliot is emphatically not. It is true that many young women even today do not feel that Dorothea Brooke or Gwendolen Harleth are remote from them and read about them with passion. But Eliot herself remains forever the Great Victorian, as well as the last. She lives in a distant and now unrecoverable country of her own.

The New York Review of Books, 1999

6

The Two Hardys

Thomas Hardy (1840–1928)

Thomas Hardy: A Biography
by Michael Millgate

The Short Stories of Thomas Hardy
by Kristin Brady

The Collected Letters of Thomas Hardy: Volume 3, 1902–1908
edited by Richard Little Purdy and Michael Millgate

THOMAS HARDY AT one time seemed the very spirit of subversion and pessimism, the author whose last novel, *Jude the Obscure*, was burned by a bishop—in despair "presumably," as Hardy observed, "at not being able to burn me." As late as 1905, when he went to receive an honorary degree at Aberdeen University, he was forcibly attacked in the Scottish press. To his friend Sir George Douglas he wrote that Swinburne had shown him a cutting which stated: "Swinburne planted, & Hardy watered, & Satan giveth the increase." A year later he wrote to Millicent Fawcett, the women's suffrage leader, stating his principles in terms that still sound an echo today.

I think the tendency of the woman's vote will be to break up the present pernicious conventions in respect of manners, customs, religion, illegitimacy, the stereotyped household (that it must be the unit of society), the father of a woman's child (that it is anybody's business but the woman's own . . .), sport (that so-called educated men should be encouraged to harass & kill for pleasure feeble creatures by mean stratagems), slaughter-houses . . . & other matters which I got into hot water for touching on many years ago.

Hardy's first novel, *The Poor Man and the Lady*, was turned down for being, in a jejune way, too radical; forty years later his views seem almost those of a *bien pensant*, and his personality had begun to produce in literary circles a general respect and reverence, almost veneration. His friend the wartime poet Siegfried Sassoon praised his calm and saintly personality; the novelist Charles Morgan wrote of the hidden fires that seemed to glow beneath his gentle homely exterior. Even Virginia Woolf was impressed by her meeting with him. That view held until about the early Seventies, Hardy's stock having continued to rise steadily in the meantime, when prolonged and elaborate biographical investigation at last began to bear fruit.

It has long been accepted that Hardy was somewhat close, self-protective: that he had written his own biography under the name of his second wife, giving a mildly romantic version of his origins and early life, and a respectably innocuous one of his domestic and social career as an increasingly famous man of letters. That was all very well, a deception in the interest of privacy and modesty that was positively endearing, and how charmingly innocent of the old man to suppose his simple stratagem could stand up to modern methods of investigation. It was blown at once, of course, but oddly enough that only increased a general sense of Hardy's quaint kind of unworldly integrity.

Not for long, however. When Robert Gittings's masterly two-volume biography appeared it presented a very different image of Hardy, and was at once accepted as definitive by critics who prefer to think the great not only have feet of clay but are constructed of that substance throughout.* The picture seemed all the more accurate because Gittings, a scholarly biographer who had taken immense pains, eschewed the wilder speculations about a dark and possibly incestuous secret in Hardy's life, and dis-

---

Young Thomas Hardy; Thomas Hardy's Later Years.

missed the story that his cousin Tryphena Sparks may have secretly borne him a male child.

Such sins as these might be tolerated, even admired. The Hardy who emerges from Gittings's narrative would not have been man enough for them. He is a mean man, of frigid purposes and slow reptile determinations, snobbish, selfish, uncompassionate and unfeeling, calculating in high society, obsequious to great ladies, nasty to servants, heartless to his wives. Gittings's Hardy was also a voyeur who preferred a girl glimpsed on top of a motorbus to a real one living beside him at his Dorchester villa; even a sadist whose most memorable encounter was with a lady poisoner at a public hanging that he attended in his early teens. Very handsome and shapely she looked, all in black silk, turning slowly around and around in the rain. Hardy was particularly impressed by the way in which the cloth hood over her face grew wet, and the features showed through. The episode throws a rather different light on the epigraph from Shakespeare with which Hardy prefaced *Tess*: "Poor wounded name! my bosom, as a bed / Shall lodge thee." Gittings also seemed to take *au pied de la lettre* the cruel remark which a no doubt much-tried Emma aimed at her husband on the occasion of the notorious Crippen trial in 1910. From Hardy's appearance, she is alleged to have said, he might well be taken for the murderer.

To Gittings it did not seem to occur that Hardy might, so to speak, have enjoyed the joke. Might he not have taken a sardonic pleasure not only in the morbidity with which he was regularly taxed by earnest critics and public spokesmen but also in the knowledge that he was himself a man of very ordinary tastes, tastes of a kind that in respectable society people keep strictly to themselves. His poems were the outlet of his feelings, and indeed of his self-knowledge. The man who in his actions and in the impression he left on others comes to dominate the Gittings biography as the true Hardy could never have written those touching lines at the end of "After a Journey," one of the poems that poured out of him after Emma's sudden death in 1912, in which Hardy imagined himself returning to the wild Cornish coast where he had first met her.

> Trust me, I mind not, though Life lours,
> The bringing me here; nay, bring me here again!
> I am just the same as when
> Our days were a joy, and our paths through flowers.

"Just the same"—not worse, not better, the habitual self as when Emma used to "muse and eye me" in the days of courtship at Beeny Cliff. Hardy's passionate pronouncement has the marvelous honesty of art, the assertion of the self as its own kind of self-knowledge, as in Shakespeare's sonnet.

> No, I am that I am, and they that level
> At my offences reckon up their own.

In both cases the art that so triumphantly blows away secretiveness could only have been produced by a secretive man.

And that paradox is particularly marked in Hardy's case. Gittings quoted Edward Clodd's comment, probably based on something said to him by the second Mrs. Hardy, that Hardy was "a great writer but not a great man." But that is not so much deadly as affectionate: one does not want one's friends to be "great men," and Clodd, a banker by trade, had clearly become very attached to Hardy, attached in the same quasi-maternal way that the second Mrs. Hardy herself was. They teased each other, Clodd sending Hardy a cutting from a local paper about a Thomas Hardy who had just been sent to trial for stunning one of his relatives with a bust of Gladstone. The touchy, vain, and morbidly sensitive author manifested in the Gittings biography would hardly have put up with this sort of thing from the hearty and rather philistine Clodd, any more than he could have written the lines at the end of "After a Journey" about the neglected wife whom her often almost equally neglected successor used dryly to refer to as "the late espoused saint."

Apart from its scholarship and its lively narrative style, Gittings's biography was salutary in that it compelled Hardy lovers to confront (if they had not already privately done so) the contrast between the calculating egotist of Max Gate and the wistfully, vulnerably, and totally sincere poet and novelist. Sincerity, as Aldous Huxley observed, is mainly a matter of talent, but temperament comes into it too. Hardy the poet just does not know how to be bogus: his forthcomingness always rings true. To illustrate this it would not be unfair to quote in apposition to "After a Journey" the last stanza of Richard Aldington's poem "After Two Years," praised by Herbert Read (whose very phrase is an unwitting kiss of death) as "one of the most perfect lyrics in the English language."

> She is as gold
> Lovely and far more cold.
>   Do thou pray with me,
> For if I win grace
> To kiss twice her face
>   God has done well to me.

Aldington may well have been a nicer man than Hardy, a more passionate lover, a more devoted husband, but all one can say of such a poem is that one does not believe a word of it. The gambits and devices of intimacy ("Do thou pray"), of modesty and understatement ("God has done well") would not deceive a child. The poem appears false throughout, and its technical accomplishment merely compounds the falsity. It strikes one as not even intended to be believed in, while every line of Hardy's poetry compels belief, not excluding that line—"I never cared for life, life cared for me"—to which W. H. Auden took such violent exception on just these grounds. "*Never* cared for life?—Well, *really*, Mr. Hardy!" But yes, Hardy the poet never did care for life in this sense, however much he may have cared for moments of living, moments that have been "great things, great things to me." The general life has to be put up with, by making "limited opportunities endurable." However apparently disingenuous, Hardy's art can never lie in the teeth of its own technique.

It is nonetheless true that Hardy was in some sense a split personality, a divided man, and that this takes the form to which we have been accustomed by modern studies and analyses of the Victorian mind and personality. Gittings was doing to Hardy, though with a much greater authority of research, what Lytton Strachey had done many years before to the eminent Victorians, Matthew Arnold and Cardinal Manning and General Gordon. The division there was that those men of power and charisma were something else inside, or so it was claimed, something which sub-verted and contradicted the Victorian ideal of the great man. That would not do in Hardy's case, for he had never made the implicit claims of Arnold or Tennyson, or set up a corresponding façade to theirs. But Git-tings was able to suggest that Hardy was not even in reality "up to" the measure of his own negativism and pessimism and the great scenes of tragedy and disillusionment he had created in the novels.

In fact, the true division was perhaps a very simple one, with nothing Victorian about it. Like D. H. Lawrence, Hardy was exceptionally close to parents of markedly different temperament. Lawrence possessed all his mother's fierce repressive puritanism, as well as his father's zest for living. Hardy's father had a passive, contemplative nature, his mother a canny initiative and an iron will. Their eldest son inherited both tendencies, in all the measure of a genius. And as Lawrence's stories reveal more directly than his novels the two biological sides of his nature, Hardy's too have the same tendency. They encapsulate in miniature, and in an elemental way not found in his poems or novels, both the bleak, close determination of his being, and its tender, vulnerable passivity. The characters in the best of the stories tend, significantly, to represent one side or the other, misfor-tune resulting from collision between the two.

Thus in "The Son's Veto" it is the mother who is tender, open, and lov-ingly docile while her clerical son is a mean-minded tyrant who refuses to let her find happiness in marriage to a tradesman, since a connection with him would lower his own social status. These transposed contrasts reveal Hardy's understanding of the lurking hardness in family situations, in indi-viduals' capacity for concealment, and the pathos of the needs they con-ceal: Ned Hipcroft in "The Fiddler of the Reels," though manly in behavior and appearance, is not really interested in sex and acquiesces in his wife's relation with the fiddler; but is passionately—even pitilessly—concerned to keep and to father the fiddler's child Carry. In "On the West-ern Circuit," one of Hardy's best stories, the childless and neglected wife "falls in love" with the young barrister who has seduced her servant, on whose behalf she has written to him engaging love letters; but she secretly and almost unconsciously wishes to keep the servant girl for herself in a quasi-lesbian relation, and to mother her expected child. To add a spe-cially Hardyan twist the barrister is in love with the letters, not with the woman who wrote them or the girl he has seduced. Most writers of good short stories, like Maupassant and Somerset Maugham, exhibit in them in a virtuoso way both the authors' toughness and their worldly-wise understanding. Hardy conceals his under the guise of a homely tale.

Nonetheless the stories reveal with remarkable accuracy the two sides of Hardy's nature, so closely bound up not only with his parents but with social class. The close exclusive kinship of his mother's family, the Hands, and the Hardys, was a function of the Dorset peasant class from which they sprang, despite all Hardy's later attempts to represent his father as a professional builder and his family as the offshoot of an ancient stock which had come down in the world. It is surprising that these tales have not been more quarried by biographers, or inquirers into the Hardy enigma who might employ a Freudian approach, for they would reveal much of personal significance. Kristin Brady has written a workmanlike study of the stories and she has some good insights, particularly about *A Group of Noble Dames*, but neither she nor Hardy's latest and most authoritative biographer of all, Michael Millgate, draws attention to the starkness and simplicity with which the two sides of Hardy's nature come together in the tales.

In one of his poems, "The Convergence of the Twain," the liner *Titanic* and the iceberg that sank her are imagined as growing up together, though far distant from each other, until the moment of their fatal match and marriage. It is a homely but sinister conceit of the kind in which Hardy was fond of indulging. Other poems suggest that he saw the convergence of himself and Emma, from their two remote rural backgrounds, in the same light; and it may well be that he was also aware of a personal image of the cold, dominant will in him coming into its unique relation in his life and art with his warm, receptive, and wondering side.

There is no doubt that Michael Millgate has in his own way projected a more convincing "convergence" than any previous biographer, and has produced what will surely be the definitive life. It is easy to read, continuously interesting, and crammed with facts—some curious and new— mild, peaceable, and understanding in tone. Whatever Hardy himself might have thought of those who dug on his grave, he would no doubt be fair-minded enough to view it, and the picture of himself which it gives, with a grudging lack of resentment.

Millgate effectively pulls together the mean and stark little Thomas with the great writer Hardy. One of the ways he does this is quietly to emphasize Hardy's remarkable sense of duty and fidelity, his unswerving loyalty to two incompatibles: his own close-knit family and the two wives who represented his own elected separation from it. His implacable and indomitable mother Jemima would have liked to decree that her four children would live celibate, in two pairs. She actually made this known to them: her younger son Henry, who followed his father in the building trade, and her two daughters, who became schoolteachers, in fact never married and lived more or less in each others' pockets all their lives.

The death of Hardy senior in 1892 offers a good illustration of the kind of thing that went on. His tranquilly reflective good nature had acted as a sort of buffer; wife and mother were now in direct confrontation, and Jemima expected her son to be in constant attendance. A first-class argument broke out, with Hardy's sisters being virtually forbidden the entry at Max Gate—of course the mother had never come there—and this prohibition continued until Emma's death. Hardy stoically retained his relation with both sides and saw nothing incongruous in burying his first wife beside her old enemy and rival. They were all of the one family, and whatever had happened in life there was to be no division between them in death.

Millgate is very good at slipping through the walls of family silence, without actually summoning them to fall down as his predecessor Gittings had done. If Hardy's stories reveal in many cases a transmutation into art of the two sides of his nature, his novels use his sense of his own life in a different way. Millgate remarks of *The Return of the Native* that in it Hardy seems to try out another version of what might have gone wrong for him. A return to his native heath and a disastrous marriage leave Clym as the archetypal defeated and impotent intellectual, eventually reduced to a purely passive state and tolerated by society as a sort of quietistic and broken-down lay preacher.

There may be an element of wish fulfillment here, as in the background of so many great novels, for the real Hardy was constantly aggrieved and resentful at the attitude of publishers and public toward events and attitudes in his fiction. Emma particularly detested *The Hand of Ethelberta*, in which Hardy tries himself out as the daughter of a London butler who has succeeded in society as a kind of actress and poet-improvisatore and frequently finds herself at dinner tables where she is waited on by her own father. Like all really good plotting imaginations Hardy's was decidedly epicene: before the final, rather mechanical chapters he informs Ethelberta with a good deal of original and erotic life of his own; and in *Tess* the process is carried almost to its logical conclusion, Hardy being both the deer and the hunter, the persecuted girl and her pursuers.

The correspondence, which Millgate is editing in a meticulously produced series of seven volumes in collaboration with that other doyen of Hardy studies, Richard Purdy, tends in the third volume to bear out the general temperateness of his approach to the skeletons in the Hardy cupboard. Between 1902 and 1908 Emma's relations with her husband have usually been taken to be at their lowest ebb. She had detested *Jude the Obscure*; even more perhaps she had detested *The Well-Beloved*, whose pages bore ample evidence of Hardy's views on the impossibility of marriage and the hopeless pursuit of romance. She complained of Hardy to visitors, sometimes asserting that she was a writer too, almost in the same class as her husband: she had sacrificed her life to him and he had never given her thanks or encouragement. She wrote bitterly about this in her diary, which her husband read after her death. She retreated to two upper attics in Max Gate and led a hermitlike existence. It was even rumored that she was certifiable, and Hardy wrote a poem with the epigraph: "I saw the form and shadow of madness seeking a home."

But this gloomy picture was not the whole truth or even in a sense the half of it. That old affections and intimacies continued unabated, and that they were by no means wholly perfunctory is shown by Hardy's letters to her during this period. They take for granted a life in common, passing on tidbits of news, giving a blow-by-blow account of visitors to Max Gate, if Emma was away, and of social life in London if she had remained in the country. Hardy remained a pertinacious attender of grand social occasions, but his letters show him doing this, as often as not, to give pleasure to relatives or dependents like his niece by marriage Lillian Gifford. He reports to Emma:

I ate no dinner yesterday, & although I had to undergo the fatigue of taking Lilian to the Academy Crush, I felt no worse. It was such a novelty & a delight to her that I was so glad I took the trouble; she never saw anything at all like it before, poor child, & though I felt past it all, I enjoyed it in an indirect way through her eyes.

The important thing about that letter is that it is as true in feeling as is "After a Journey," the poem about revisiting the dead Emma. Hardy's observations are always in their way as "true" as those of the characters in Shakespeare, and his life has all the richly intermingled aspects of muted comedy and tragedy that one finds in the plays. Hence perhaps the kind of interest we take in it. Hardy, like an aging Othello, is reporting to a Desdemona who had once lovingly urged him "to feed on nourishing dishes" and to keep warm. In the same spirit he had been, while his family was alive, in the position of a Hamlet obliged by deep and atavistic loyalties to keep in with his father's ghost as well as with his mother and his uncle Claudius.

A sharing of the commonplace and the pleasure of others is an elementary connubial satisfaction the Hardys never seem to have forgone, even in these years. More unexpectedly they shared their literary experiences.

I have been reading H. James's "Wings of the Dove"—the first of his that I have looked into for years & years. I read it with a fair amount of care—as much as one would wish to expend on any novel, certainly, seeing what there is to read besides novels—& so did Em; but we have been arguing ever since about what happened to the people, & find we have wholly conflicting opinions thereon. At the same time James is almost the only living novelist I can read, & taken in small doses I like him exceedingly, being as he is a real man of letters.

Much emerges from that, besides Hardy's views on the novel and on "the man of letters." He thought the latter a superior concept to the novelist *tout court*, and no doubt preferred to count himself as one. On Henry James he conferred the same dignity, for Hardy would not have agreed with or even understood James's sense of the novelist's high calling.

That letter is to Florence Henniker, daughter of that earlier "man of letters," Monckton Milnes, and wife of a distinguished but philistine British officer. Hardy had met her in Dublin in 1893 and been smitten at once, though she seems to have kindly but firmly demarcated the lines and progress of their relationship, possibly to his secret relief. The letters to her during this period have a slightly resigned philosophical air, as if he were gently reproaching her for her prudence while at the same time tacitly endorsing it. To "Em" Hardy made no secret of this relation.

There are four short letters to Florence Dugdale, the quiet little secretary with literary aspirations whom Hardy was to marry in 1914, two years after the death of his first wife. At this stage he encouraged her attempts to write but gave up doing so after they got married. He wrote after their first meeting: "I do not think you stayed at all too long, & hope you will come again some other time."

The strength of Millgate's biography lies not so much in its scholarship, which the reader can take for granted, as in its balance and its natural sympathy with the subject. Almost everything that is likely to be known about Hardy is now known, but Millgate has made nonetheless one important discovery which will be of considerable interest to devotees. Hardy met Eliza Nicholls, whose father was a coast guard at Kimmeridge in Dorset, sometime in 1862 when he was working as an architect's assistant, and they seem to have been more or less formally engaged from 1863 to 1867. (They kept it quiet, but Millgate has turned up more or less conclusive evidence.) A serious and deeply religious young woman, Eliza seems to have been of considerable support to the youthful Hardy, but her seriousness and her religion may eventually have caused them to drift apart. Though probably more deeply attached to him than he to her, she was no doubt shocked by his growing agnosticism and the freethinking intellectuals whose tuition he sought, like his great friend and mentor Horace Moule, who was to commit suicide in 1873.

Eliza would no doubt have been no more successful as a wife for Hardy than her sister Jane Nicholls (with whom he seems to have flirted), or Tryphena Sparks, or Louisa Harding ("To Louisa in the Lane"), all of whose pretty features look out from the excellent photographs in Millgate's volume. Hardy was no Don Juan, and it is unlikely he had intimate relations with any of them, though Millgate rather surprisingly speculates that Emma may eventually have "caught" her evasive suitor by pretending to be pregnant, the same device that Arabella uses in *Jude*. Sexually Emma was probably more like Sue Bridehead than Arabella, though this in itself need not have seriously thrown the relationship off balance: Hardy was clearly more attracted to girls glimpsed twirling a sunshade than to girls in bed. Any that came there could not forever have nestled in his imagination and been commemorated in his poems. Yet that "I am just the same as when . . ." is never insincere, even on the occasion he told Edmund Gosse that the young Helen Paterson, his "best illustrator" who had done the pictures for *Far from the Madding Crowd*, was the woman he should have married "but for a stupid blunder of God Almighty." Wisely, no doubt, she married the fifty-year-old poet William Allingham in the same year in which Hardy began to take an interest in her.

> Had we mused a little space
> At that critical date in the May-
> time,
> One life had been ours, one place,
> Perhaps, till our long cold clay-
> time.

Perhaps. But one enduring fascination of Hardy's Life to its readers, as to readers of the novels themselves, lies in the way his imagination fuses the literal and the humdrum with the might-have-been, with what his great admirer the poet Philip Larkin called

> the long perspectives
> Open at each instant of our lives.
> They link us to our losses.

Life is never really suited to our imaginations of it, as Hardy continually found, and is continuously reminding us.

The New York Review of Books, 1982

7

The King's Trumpeter

Rudyard Kipling (1865–1936)

The Long Recessional: The Imperial Life of Rudyard Kipling
by David Gilmour

BEFORE RUDYARD KIPLING, the art of polemics in poetry had
scarcely been practiced in England since the days of Dryden and
Pope. Apart from his other achievements in verse and prose,
Kipling revived this art, and he transformed it as well. Dryden and Pope
were professionals, superb artists in social and political satire who did not
bother to believe passionately what they were saying, or to loathe with
equal passion what their opponents stood for. Kipling, equally skillful as
a writer in action, did both these things. He never laughed or mocked his
opponents as Dryden had done—"showing his teeth with a smile," as
Mark Van Doren put it in his study of Dryden. He hated them, and his
hatred was in deadly earnest, often—if he genuinely felt the Empire, or
his idea of it, was threatened—to the point of shrillness and hysteria.

Take the famous case of the Marconi Scandal of 1912, which nearly
brought down the British government of the time. David Gilmour,
always equable and fair-minded about his excitable subject's often exag-
gerated reactions to such matters, tells this revealing story of the imperial
twilight in a particularly masterful way. Godfrey Isaacs, the managing
director of the Marconi Company in Britain, negotiated a contract for
wireless stations around the Empire, which would be highly useful in
peace and invaluable in war. Kipling, convinced that war—"Armaged-
don," as he put it—would come, and come soon, was, as usual, passionately

concerned with the protection and welfare of the British Empire. Others, and in high government circles, were more concerned to make money out of the transaction. Three of the Liberal ministers in particular were involved in the furtive bout of insider trading which followed the announcement of the Marconi deal, one of whom was the brother of Godfrey Isaacs, the attorney-general Rufus Isaacs, not long after to be appointed Lord Chief Justice. ("Thou barely 'scaped from judgment, / Take oath to judge the land," as Kipling was to write.)

A great fuss was soon being made, and the offenders were lucky to get away with it, although Kipling bitterly blamed members of the Conservative opposition for not doing more in a case where shady dealings on the government side had been so clearly shown, particularly in the cases of Lloyd George, the chief whip Alexander Murray, and Rufus Isaacs. *The Times*, still "The Thunderer" in those days, devoted no fewer than six leaders to the case, while Hilaire Belloc and Cecil Chesterton (brother of G. K.) were not above tapping the old resources of anti-Semitism—the Isaacs brothers came from an assimilated and distinguished Jewish family.

Kipling's response was, as it had so often been before, to write a poem, and "Gehazi" is one of the most brilliant and mordant pieces he ever produced. English poetic satire had always drawn naturally on the Bible, the Old Testament in particular, for example and precedents; indeed the Church of England's mythology is virtually based on the model of England as ancient Israel. Dryden presented Charles II and his court in the guise of David and the Jewish Kingdom. Himself from god-fearing Yorkshire stock, Kipling knew his Bible backward, and the story of Gehazi and Elisha might have been made for his hand.

After Elisha has cured the Syrian captain Naaman of his leprosy, and refused all reward, his servant Gehazi runs after Naaman and says his master has changed his mind and will accept a gift of money after all. Elisha questions Gehazi on his return, and finding out the truth, curses him and his seed with leprosy forever.

The marvelous passage from the Bible that begins with Elisha's question "Whence comest thou, Gehazi?" is made good use of by Kipling in the opening stanza of this superbly vitriolic poem:

"Whence comest thou, Gehazi,
So reverend to behold,
In scarlet and in ermines
And chain of England's gold?"
"From following after Naaman
To tell him all is well,
Whereby my zeal hath made me
A Judge in Israel."

Gehazi "went forth a leper as white as snow," and at the end of his poem Kipling imagines the same figurative fate for the Lord Chief Justice, whom he would no doubt have wished to see as an outcast, disgraced in the eyes of decent society. The poem has of course been labeled anti-Semitic, a charge that Gilmour rebuts in this case, and rightly, although Kipling puts a venom into his lines, based as they are on an old Hebrew story familiar to generations of devout English churchgoers, which would have fitted less well for the other delinquents in the case (a Welshman and a Scot as it happened). The thrust of the poem is in its satire on corruption in high places, and as Gilmour observes, "its characters were evoked not because they were Jewish," but because, as the case of Elisha and Gehazi, they could be used as a moral precept to illustrate the good and the bad.

Kipling was typical of his time and class in having Jewish friends but being, as it were, cheerfully anti-Semitic in an unreflecting way. But, as Dickens had done, he portrays both good and bad Jews in his tales and fictions, as if to show that he has no hard feelings, and some of his characters, like the old Jewish moneylender in *Puck of Pook's Hill*, who inadvertently help to lay the foundations of imperial justice, are vividly and memorably evoked. So is young Glass, in a late story celebrating the Scout Movement, who is no good at doing whatever Scouts are supposed to do, but who can at least cook for them and cook brilliantly. So although "Gehazi" is one of Kipling's most trenchant and dynamically savage poems, and Gilmour is surely right to single it out to illustrate these violent tendencies in its author, he is also right when he says that the poem "has often been condemned as evil and anti-Semitic. It is neither."

Coincidentally, although Gilmour does not mention it, Kipling wrote another poem a good deal later which also makes use of the story of Naaman and Elisha, and which also cannot fairly be called anti-Semitic. Kipling loathed the exploitation of the early film industry—which with his usual interest in technological advances he hoped might be useful for the spread of education at home and throughout the Empire—by the film moguls of Hollywood who were indeed mostly of Jewish origin:

And here is mock of faith and truth, for children to behold;
And every door of ancient dirt reopened to the old;
With every word that taints the speech, and show that weakens
thought;
And Israel watcheth over each and—doth not watch for naught.

"Naaman's Song"

In view of this, Naaman decides to give Jordan a wide berth and wash in the waters of Damascus, "whose strength is from on high / And if they cannot cure my woes, a leper will I die." The poem has little of the rhetorical fire and intensity of "Gehazi," but both show not only Kipling's agility and strength as a polemicist in verse but his determination to use them on behalf of his own particular and often idiosyncratic vision of England and Empire.

"Gehazi" and "Naaman's Song" were not the only poems in which Kipling made a natural and instinctive use of Bible stories, and the more dramatic they were, the better. Gilmour is right to single out for its powerful economy an early verse written in India which makes pungent use of the tale of Bathsheba and Uriah the Hittite. Desiring the beautiful Bathsheba, King David ordered her husband Uriah to be placed in the forefront of the battle, where he is duly killed. In imperial India, hints Kipling, the same thing was happening all the time. The poem tersely relates how Jack Barrett was dispatched to an unhealthy station in Baluchistan by a senior civil servant with a partiality for his pretty wife. Jack Barrett goes, of course—as a servant of Empire he can do no other—leaving his wife in the salubrious hill station of Simla on "three fourths his monthly screw," and of course attended by her senior admirer. Jack

Barrett "died at Quetta ere his next month's pay he drew." For the poet, as in the Bible, there will nonetheless come, one day, a day of judgment:

> When Quetta graveyards give again
> Their victims to the air
> I shouldn't like to be the man
> Who sent Jack Barrett there.

By way of postscript I remember once being assured by an old Anglo-Indian hand, who was amused by the poem, that the climate of Quetta is actually a particularly good one—healthy, even bracing. But it was a place and a word that served Kipling's turn, and the journalist in him always knew how to make the best use of a graphic idea. His knowledge of India was indeed considerable as well as varied, but it was always the kind of knowledge that can be used for immediate literary effect, rather than the kind which goes deep and sees all sides of a question. As in the case of many of the "Departmental Ditties" which made Kipling's reputation in Anglo-India, the real facts about Jack Barrett were indeed known, if only to a few, and the story had a basis in stark reality, as had many of the tales and episodes which Kipling put into his even more successful prose collection of the time, *Plain Tales from the Hills*.

Because he felt more at home with them, and because they supplied most of the best recruits for the native army of the Raj, Kipling preferred Muslims to Hindus. Although a heroic Babu plays his part in *Kim* in the spy service of the Raj, and the immortal Gunga Din, the regimental water carrier of *Barrack Room Ballads*, is from his name clearly a Hindu, Kipling disliked and distrusted both the Brahmins and the educated Babu class of Bengal. A part of the long recessional in Kipling's eyes was the way in which Indians were taking over, and were being trained by the English of the civil service to take over, the running of the Raj. In common with almost all the other English in India, Kipling was outraged when the viceroy, Lord Ripon, approved a bill which for the first time made provision for English plaintiffs or wrongdoers to be tried in a court presided over by an Indian judge or magistrate.

This was in 1883, not much more than thirty years after the great Indian uprising, and the English were peculiarly sensitive to the possibility that their women might be tried by an Indian judge, supporting their prejudices by the argument that Indians treated their own women very badly, often keeping them in the virtual imprisonment of purdah. By 1923, when E. M. Forster wrote *A Passage to India*, the issue was virtually a dead letter, and the brilliantly dramatic trial scene in the novel, which shows that an Indian can successfully preside as a judge, had become distinctly anachronistic.

Kipling, Gilmour tells us, scornfully referred to Lord Ripon as a "circular and bewildered recluse of religious tendencies." On the whole he took a poor view of viceroys and civil service high-ups, preferring, as he claimed to do in almost all circumstances, the humble man on the spot who actually does the work, or the woman on the spot, like his character Mrs. Hauksbee in *Plain Tales from the Hills*, who knows how things are done, and knows how to arrange them. The book of stories was by then becoming highly successful in England as well as in Anglo-India, and Oscar Wilde referred to it admiringly as giving him the feeling that he was sitting "under a palm-tree reading life by superb flashes of vulgarity."

When Kipling returned to England after his long spell as a working journalist he might have behaved like any other promising and ambitious young writer. He might have mingled with his fellows, sought a metropolitan reputation in the daringly fashionable magazines like *The Yellow Book*, hobnobbed with Oscar Wilde and Frank Harris and a whole gang of up-and-coming London writers. His reputation for literary brilliance and originality was already so great that the best magazines clamored for his articles; the editor of the *St. James's Gazette* wondered in print if he might become yet greater than Dickens. All seemed set, Gilmour writes, for what Kipling himself now called "that queer experience known as a literary career."

What he might have written in that case is anybody's guess, but it is an odd fact that he never found his métier and his subject in the sense that Dickens had done, and that his friend Henry James was doing. His one young man's novel, *The Light That Failed*, was itself a failure; it is significant that the best bits in it, about the campaign against the Mahdi in the Sudan, show a hankering for the life of a war correspondent, and the dread of failure as an artist through choosing the wrong things to write about. From then on Kipling abandoned the idea of form and the *chef d'oeuvre*, and—in verse, stories, articles, a general mix of literary enterprises—found his material wherever he needed it, wherever he happened to be, and wherever his natural restlessness took him. By mingling not with writers but with men who had jobs—jobs of any and every kind—he became what C. S. Lewis, although he detested Kipling's outlook and personality, rightly and admiringly called "the poet of work." Some of his best tales take up this theme in the early collection of stories he called "The Day's Work."

C. S. Lewis also wrote an essay called "The Inner Ring," expressing abhorrence of an atmosphere of secretive authority in what are nowadays called the corridors of power, and implying that Kipling's passion for all things imperial arose from his lust as an outsider to be accepted, and to belong, in those circles where power really lay. Gilmour does not refer to this essay, but his subtle and gradual unfolding of Kipling's developing attitudes shows effectively how unfair is the charge that Lewis brought. *The Long Recessional* is in this context a perfect title, for Kipling was indeed haunted all his adult life by a sense of the hollowness of power, and the fragility and brevity of all imperial dreams:

> Cities and Thrones and Powers,
> Stand in Time's eye,
> Almost as long as flowers,
> Which daily die.

The famous "Recessional," writes Gilmour, was published in *The Times* in 1897, "on the same page as a message from Queen Victoria expressing her gratitude for the spontaneous outburst of loyalty and affection that had greeted her sixty years on the throne." The two effusions were jointly awarded a leading article in which the newspaper commended the note of "moral responsibility" ringing out "as clearly in the simple grandeur of the Queen's message as in Mr. Kipling's soul-stirring verses." The combination of royalty and poetry with political and national uplift and fervor was unique at the time, and produced a reaction—"the deepest response of our race," Kipling wrote—which, for better or worse, had never been seen before and never since. No wonder that when the rhetoric of Mussolini and Hitler came along in the Twenties and Thirties of the twentieth century, the *bien pensants* thought they had once recognized in the imperial Kipling the same signs of Fascist tendencies.

But to do Kipling justice the tone was as different as the message. The fervor of "Recessional," while not exactly defeatist, strikes a note of solemn warning. Its eloquence really amounts in the end to saying, "As a people and as an Empire we are trying to do too much, and it can't last."

> Far-called, our navies melt away;
> On dune and headland sinks the fire:
> Lo, all of our pomp of yesterday
> Is one with Nineveh and Tyre!

Underneath the rhetoric is the note of a somber insurance policy—better watch out, and take precautions while you can. But more moving than the message is the high quality of the medium. Kipling the strident or semi-facetious versifier can abruptly become the poet who can produce the unexpected magic of lines like "On dune and headland sinks the fire."

Kipling certainly saw America as the emergent and deserving power to whose keeping Britain would hand on the imperial torch. Americans were usually not pleased about this, although Teddy Roosevelt was the exception. He became a friend of Kipling's and was deeply admired by him. Nonetheless Roosevelt showed judgment in remarking that Kipling's poem "The White Man's Burden" was "rather poor poetry." It came out in America in *McClure's Magazine*, as Gilmour tersely notes, "on the day the Filipino revolt broke out, and a day before the American Senate voted as Kipling had urged them" to

> Take up the white man's burden—
> The savage wars of peace . . .

Roosevelt may have been right about the sentiments and the shrill tone of the poem, and yet it is hard to fault technically: it contains some of the poet's most effective and enduring epigrams, and as we know to our cost "the savage wars of peace" are still very much with us today. The characteristically dry and droll American comic awareness was soon very busy with Kipling's effusion, however, and, as Gilmour tells us, "newspapers from the *Buffalo Express* to the *Iowa State Register* competed to publish parodies with titles such as 'The Black Man's Burden,' 'The White Woman's Burden,' and even 'The Old Maid's Burden.' One assiduous collector of Kiplingiana pasted over eighty such parodies into his scrapbook."

Nonetheless the United States did become involved in Cuba and in the Philippines, although Kipling himself could hardly take the credit for those first reluctant steps in what some saw as imperial business. Kipling's own enthusiasm for America, boundless at first, had been diminished, if only temporarily, by the argument he had had with his brother-in-law, Beatty Balestier, when the Kipling family had been living in Brattleboro, Vermont. More serious, though again only in the short run, was the crisis of 1895, when Britain and the United States appeared to be on the brink of war over the Venezuelan boundary dispute, of which Gilmour gives a sardonic account.

Gold had been discovered in the disputed area on the border of British Guiana; and the British prime minister, Lord Salisbury, had remarked rather tactlessly that the Monroe Doctrine was all very well, but that Guiana had belonged to the British crown before Venezuela (and by implication the United States) had been born or thought of. American Anglophobia rose to a frenzy, and the secretary of state, Richard Olney, instructed his ambassador to tell the British government that the United States "was practically sovereign on this continent," which, as Gilmour points out, must have been news to Canadians, Mexicans, and South Americans generally.

The storm in the teacup soon abated, of course, helped by a tumble on the New York stock market when British investments looked as if they were being withdrawn, but Kipling's naive idea in his new book of poems, *The Five Nations*, of an Anglo-American condominium over half the world had left its author's enthusiasms somewhat diminished. He had scarcely improved matters by his playful suggestion that the new anthem or marching song of this super-country "should combine 'The British Grenadiers,' 'Marching Through Georgia,' and other songs to create 'the greatest song of all, The Saga of the Anglo-Saxon all round the earth.' " Tact, as Gilmour observes, was never his strong point, and for so intelligent a man he remained as innocently unaware as a child about the feelings and prejudices of other people and other nations. Anyone who thought that the marching song of Sherman's army would inspire universal enthusiasm in the States must have been naive indeed, or very ill-informed.

Undoubtedly Kipling became a wiser man as time went by, and the First World War, in which he lost his only son, shattered any of his latter-day hopes of imperial expansion and peace among nations. His last stories—"The Kipling Whom Nobody Read," as Edmund Wilson called them—are intricate and often mysterious, but technically of great interest, and worthy at their best of Henry James. Many of his poems of the Twenties and Thirties are somber warnings of another and even more horrific war to come. His later work shows an interest in the unseen world and in God, who, as Gilmour says, "had played a minor and intermittent role in his life," but whom he knew "did not abandon His people at the end of their days."

He had suffered dangerously and painfully for years from a peptic ulcer and was rushed to the hospital in 1936, with his last book, a terse, brilliant, and reticent memoir he called *Something of Myself*, still unfinished. King George V, with whose stiff, philistine personality Kipling had always felt at home, died two days after him, bringing the long recessional of Empire almost to its end. "The King has gone," so it was said at the time, "and taken his trumpeter with him." Gilmour's considerable achievement is to show just how and why Kipling and his writings were so important and influential in their own time. Today he is most read not for this imperial message but because everything he wrote, from the Indian stories to *Shalky & Co.*, is unputdownable.

In her book of family history, *Bowen's Court*, Elizabeth Bowen records an occasion during the early "troubles" when her house was occupied by the IRA. She was astonished to find several fervent young nationalists sitting in her library, spellbound by the stories of Kipling, who detested everything they stood for. But, as Auden wrote in his elegy on Yeats, time is not interested in the convictions of personalities but will pardon "Kipling and his views" because it "worships language and forgives / Everyone by whom it lives." In that sense Kipling's words are still very much alive.

The New York Review of Books, 2002

8

Life in the Head

John Cowper Powys (1872–1963)

Wolf Solent
by John Cowper Powys, with an introduction by
    Robertson Davies

Weymouth Sands
by John Cowper Powys, with an introduction by James Purdy

JOHN COWPER POWYS was born in 1872 in Derbyshire, England, and died in 1963 in the small Welsh village of Blaenau Ffestiniog. He grew to maturity as slowly as a tree, and his long life included more than twenty-five years spent lecturing in the United States before he published anything of significance. Powys inherited the charisma of his father, a Church of England parson, and he could discourse with eloquence on almost any subject—Homer, Shakespeare, Blake, the Bible, ancient romance, and modern materialism. He had been at Cambridge University, and in English literature and the classics he was prodigiously well read.

In America he preferred nonacademic audiences, but in the early days of imagism, and before their emigration to Europe, Ezra Pound, HD, and their friends came under his spell and followed him around the lecture circuit, sitting at his feet in the intervals in cafés and hotel bedrooms. There was nothing vain or sinister in this appeal. Powys was never ambitious to establish a dominant literary persona. Modest, chivalrous, the least power hungry of men, he was quite out of place in the ambitious bohemian world of the prewar literati, but he was also quite unself-conscious, accepting and being accepted by them. His early marriage in England had broken down, but he supported his wife and child all their lives, and because he was a Catholic never divorced her. Latterly he lived with a young admirer, Phyllis Playter, with whom he remained for many years, and who was with him when he died.

His powers as a preacher certainly left their mark on Powys's writings, but an equivocal one. Every literate person has to know about Faulkner or Kafka or Lawrence, but it is permissible in literary academic circles to be barely aware of Powys. His name crops up as a crackpot mystagogue, the kind associated with druid festivals and Stonehenge societies. His admirers, on the other hand, have the wrong sort of fervor, comparing him freely to Tolstoy, Dostoevsky, Cervantes. Such comparisons may in fact be quite justified but they are not reassuring. He has never become a universal property like other great writers; his legend and reputation belong to a cult. All cults are tiresome, but this one paradoxically shows something very attractive about Powys—his ineradicable amateurishness, his lack of self-dedicated ambition. Less attractive geniuses—Frost, Yeats, Thomas Mann—do not need a little church of devout acolytes to cherish them. Nobel Prize seekers have a better sense of timing. Powys did not bother. What he wrote is all over the place. He never artfully planned and brought forth the pattern or sequence of masterpieces that would have established him definitively.

His remarkable siblings, to whom he was very close, were better at this than he was. Theodore, who wrote as T. F. Powys, had a great critical success with *Mr. Weston's Good Wine*, which appeared in 1927, two years before *Wolf Solent*. In 1939, the year of his death from tuberculosis, there appeared Llewelyn Powys's idyll of dreamy pastoral wish fulfillment called *Love and Death*, which is still moving and readable. But their elder brother, whose numerous novels and didactic potboilers (with titles like *The Meaning of Culture* and *The Pleasures of Literature*) stretched right back before the First World War, and forward well beyond the second, never desired or achieved such definitive literary moments. His best-known novel, *The Glastonbury Romance*, has great things in it, but is so huge and unwieldy that it obscures his two much more effective masterpieces, chronologically on either side of it, *Wolf*

Solent and *Weymouth Sands*. The ivy of Powys's occasional writings covers and obscures such masterpieces with its leisurely profusion. Welshness abounds in his later work, and his grand old age produced such misty marvels as *Porius* and *Owen Glendower*, much admired by some, and full of superb Arthurian scene and vision, but as unproportioned as are most historical fantasies.

Nor is Powys really at his best in his autobiography, composed in the Thirties in his cottage in upstate New York. A wonderfully mercurial presence in his novels, the Powys personality face to face is no less genial, but forfeits its strange powers of creation and romance, becomes garrulous and quirky, exhibits the stigmata of the confiding obsessive. It is characteristic of Powys to seem to have no idea that this might be so: there is no division in him between artist and man. The character Wolf Solent derives from Powys himself—the clumsy young schoolmaster with his beaky nose and angular frame, inseparable from his hat and walking stick, loquacious, unself-conscious, enthusiastic—and *Weymouth Sands* contains three or four partial self-portraits. But his remarkable vitality as a novelist transforms these familiar self-images, and with great humor, into the swirling vortex of the tale, into its vigorous play of multiple consciousnesses.

The Powys cult has done him a disservice in obscuring the true gift so evident in these two novels—that of a highly idiosyncratic but essentially *domestic* novelist, as domestic as Jane Austen, a genius like her at creating a cast of characters as part of a comedy, and in a comic setting. Like her, too, he is at his best in the home or family, in a small historic town whose traditions and way of life mingle with the fantasies and illusions of its inhabitants. In the interrelation of these fantasies flourish not only comedy and pathos but *joie de vivre* and a kind of deep holy satisfaction in the intricacies of being and in the small, ever-present details of nature—leaves, wheel-ruts, bright beetles, small dry twigs. His earliest novel, *Wood and Stone* (1915), set like the later ones in Hardy's Wessex, which Powys knew intimately from his childhood and schooldays, makes apprentice use of Hardy's plotting in dire coincidence and fatality, but is basically and irrepressibly cheerful. It is also dedicated to Hardy, who had not long since been censured by conservative critics for writing *Jude the Obscure*. Powys's Wessex is a different world, though it has a subtle kinship with Hardy's, just as the fabulous world of sex in a Powys novel seems both unconscious of D. H. Lawrence and yet in affinity with him.

While Powys is just as brilliant an explorer of our erotic being as Lawrence, he is also happily tolerant, relaxed, diffusive, spacious. The erotic world he offers is too enchanting to be viewed with intensity. Powys's heroes are never self-protective, and in personality as in diction he is fundamentally easygoing. He seems not to mind something sounding clumsy and banal, old-fashioned, even secondhand. Smart academic critics avoid him because it is so hard to show succinctly why he is good. It is no use pointing to key passages, in the way that a critic can demonstrate the mastery of Lawrence, Joseph Conrad, or George Eliot, and assign them their place in a "Great Tradition." As his stories go on, Powys's fascinations are accumulative, their movement peristaltic. His themes, if analyzed, appear lacking in original insight. In his second novel, *Ducdame*, the autobiographical elements are particularly strong, and prefigure a situation enriched and varied in the later novels—that of a young man whose emotional life is divided among several women— wife, mother, mistress. Young Wolf Solent is torn between his wife Gerda, a marvelously realized, down-to-earth creation, and an ethereal "soulmate," Christie, who is in every way Gerda's antithesis.

Stated thus the plot of *Wolf Solent* sounds sufficiently banal, verging on soap opera, but the reader is won over by the immense lyrical and humorous energy with which Powys gets into these characters. Living in the rustic setting they do they maintain convincingly egalitarian relations, although the question of class is always present. Wolf is a gentleman whose dotty, life-loving father—an active presence in the book—has died in the poorhouse, and he supports his vain, active, sardonic mother. Another disturbing presence in Wolf's life is that of Miss Gault, his old headmaster's daughter, whose face, hideously disfigured by a huge birthmark, looks "like an ancient theatre full of dusky gladiators." All these people are driven by the passions and illusions of love, but they are not presented as eccentrics and we soon cease to regard them as such.

Trivialities loom as satisfyingly large as in a novel by Jane Austen or Barbara Pym. We share Wolf's anguish when both his mother and his mother-in-law threaten to come to tea the same day. After a tiff with his wife he is comforted by looking into the "strangely-coloured eyes" of his friend

Darnley, and has "that peculiar sensation of relief which men are wont to feel when they encounter each other after the confusion of sex-conflicts."

> Wolf heard nothing of what he was saying, so occupied was he with a sudden question, gaping like a crack in a hot stubble-field in the very floor of his mind, that had just then obtruded itself. Was he really in love, in the proper sense of the word, with his sweet bedfellow?

That gives an idea of Powys's curiously resonant use of cliché, and the images of landscape that mingle with and represent consciousness.

> His feeling was like a brimming stream between reedy banks, where a wooden moss-covered dam prevents any spring-flood, but where the water, making its way round the edge of the obstacle, bends the long submerged grasses before it, as it sweeps forward.

The Coleridgean delicacy and zest are accompanied in the novel by images and suggestions of mystery and fatality that show why a writer like James Purdy so much admires Powys. *Wolf Solent* possesses a full intimacy in description and humor which Powys never quite approached again. Squire Urquhart, a memorable character at once sinister and commonplace, who is compiling a scandalous history of Dorset, says "my book must grow like a living thing, till it frightens us by its reality." The death of Mr. Malahide, father of the Christie whom Wolf illusorily supposes to be his soulmate, is one of the great comic scenes in English literature, both perturbing and, in an odd sense, profoundly reassuring. Although not to Wolf. When he attempts to offer philosophical comfort to Christie, who may have pushed her father downstairs, she rejects him with a scream of rage and misery which seems to disclose a region of feeling into which neither he nor his author can penetrate. "You great, stupid, talking fool! What do *you* know of me or my father? What do *you* know of my real life?" This cry from the girl whom Wolf for most of the book has regarded as his "one true love" shows us a great deal about Powys's unique attitude toward the characters he creates.

Originally published in England as *Jobber Skald*, because the corporation of Weymouth objected to the use of their town's name in its title, *Weymouth Sands* has a greater breadth of cast than *Wolf Solent* and a more dramatic concentration of scene—the harbor town and the island of Portland (Hardy's "Isle of Slingers"), which the young Powys had known well, and which he continually returns to in his early fiction. The plot turns on emotions of hatred and sadism—the projected revenge of Jobber Skald, a formidable jack-of-all-trades, against a powerful brewer who has wronged him—but, as in the other big novels, the fantasies and incongruities of love and daily living take a more important place than does the apocalyptic theme that has caused Powys's admirers to compare him with Faulkner and Dostoevsky.

Indeed in his most natural and absorbing vein Powys noticeably avoids "big scenes," preferring to refer to them as imminent and to assume their importance after they have gone by. This increases our sense of many and diverse consciousnesses leading their own lives, regardless of the author's speculations and enthusiasms. Unlike Hardy and Lawrence, unlike Tolstoy, with whom George Steiner has compared him, Powys does not assume a complete understanding of his characters—he hardly seems to take responsibility for them at all. He does not own them psychologically, or pursue their fates in order to turn them into models of fictiveness. It is their fantastic but homely contact with life, always fresh and droll, that really takes hold of us, making its own tacit and good-natured commentary on the more mystical inventions of the story. An exuberance unlike any other in fiction keeps breaking in—"that basic human necessity for some degree of cheerfulness in one's lair," as Powys calls it—which is the most striking and engaging feature of his novels.

At the end of the novel, Wolf Solent feels he is "a 'vegetable animal' wrapped in a mental cloud." He lives, like other Powys characters, by "mythology," by "life-illusion." There is nothing mystic about this; it is just a fact of life, as of the eroticism which for Powys fills most life-consciousness. He knows the truth that Lawrence always angrily and absurdly denied, that sex is "in the head," part of our general dream of consciousness. For Lawrence "sex in the head" was the great deception; for Powys it is the great and obvious reality. "The best love was not lust; nor was it passion. Still less was it any *ideal*. It was pure Romance."

Nothing could be more of a cliché than that exclamation in *Wey-*

mouth Sands, and yet the sexual encounters and relations in these novels—Gerda's with Wolf, Perdita's with Jobber Skald, Mary's with John and Nell's with Sam in *A Glastonbury Romance*—give it a new kind of force and fascination. "Romance," which can be more shamelessly, explicitly, and polymorphously erotic than Lawrentian sex, is the excitement which attaches our selfhood to the details of the world about us—erotic details especially—while at the same time keeping us separate in our own peculiar forms of self-satisfaction. This "life-illusion," as Powys calls it, unites the odd and the conventional, the simple and the sophisticated. Wolf Solent reflects that the rival who has perhaps cuckolded him, the lecherous little grocer Bob Weevil, who thinks that "girls' legs are the most beautiful things in the world," has the same good fortune in his daydreaming consciousness that he himself enjoys. "We both have the sort of intense life-illusion which protects human beings from the futility of the commonplace."

One of Lawrence's truest perceptions was that a great novelist made the novel form "incapable of the absolute." This is especially true of Powys. There are no ultimate revelations in his world, or solutions for his characters; naturally enough, since for Powys personal illusions are the saving conditions in which we live. Although *Wolf Solent* has the form of a *Bildungsroman*, its hero learns nothing and is not subject to that stock fictive evolution common to both Lawrence's Paul Morel and Joyce's Stephen Dedalus, as well as, incidentally, to the heroines of Jane Austen. In their urban or rural setting Powys's lovers are as timeless in their erotic fixations as Queen Phaedra or Helen of Troy. And his narrative proffers all sorts of metaphysical suggestions only to circumvent them, as trees and plants grow around artificial obstructions; sudden vital "discoveries," often emphasized by italics, are soon absorbed back into the leisurely ganglion. Even as it absorbs and compels us, the novel seems to be inviting us not to take it seriously.

This has disconcerted the critics who evaluate the novel as a serious art form. They can do little with Powys—his substance is too elemental—and his devotees usually resort to their fervently inflationary comparisons. The *Saturday Review of Literature* decided that he was "by turns an Emily Brontë; a subtle introspective Proust; a nature-enthralled Wordsworth; . . . a Dostoevsky shaking with the mystic fever; even, at rare moments, a

Shakespeare." The critic of *The New York Times* was nearer the mark in calling *Weymouth Sands* "a novel which takes people as it finds them." Professor Robertson Davies has produced a similarly temperate and perceptive appreciation in the introduction to his edition of *Wolf Solent*. Few great novelists have the unusual gift of taking their characters as they find them, and the best we can do is to return Powys the compliment, hoping at the same time that these two splendid novels will never be taught in the English literature departments as part of what Mary McCarthy, in one of her satirical novels, called "the Proust-Joyce-Mann course." The best tribute is the short poem Stevie Smith wrote for Powys in his old age.

> This old man is very wise.
> He knows the truth, he tells no lies.
> He is as deep as a British pool.
> And Monsieur Poop may think him a fool.

The New York Review of Books, 1982

9

Nothing Nasty in the Woodshed

P. G. Wodehouse (1881–1975)

———————

Yours, Plum: The Letters of P. G. Wodehouse
edited by Frances Donaldson

WITTGENSTEIN HAD A phrase about the "great heart of Beethoven," the rider to which was that it would make no sense to talk about the "great heart" of Shakespeare. So much the worse for Beethoven, might be the sentiment of a non-philosopher who did not share Wittgenstein's passion for music. But his point has its ramifications. Like Tolstoy, whose didactic tales he revered as the best that mere literature could do, Wittgenstein was distinctly a non-Shakespearean. He distrusted and feared literature's rich dishonesty, its endless begging of the question. Writers disappeared into their own dreams and vanities: their great hearts were not on display.

Did Wittgenstein read P. G. Wodehouse? Probably not, but had he done so he might have got on with him very well, as he did with the conventions of early cinema. With such things you knew where you were, and a philosopher likes that: Gilbert Ryle, so it is said, thought Schopenhauer and Wodehouse the most sensible authors he knew, and the two who wrote the best. When not studying the one he was relaxing with the other. As well as writing a hundred-odd sensible books, Wodehouse also wrote some highly sensible letters, like this one to his stepdaughter Leonora, known as Snorky, who had consulted him about names for her forthcoming baby.

I'm glad you're feeling better. Jolly sensible taking that three weeks in bed. Nothing like it. Stephanie. Oke with me, though Mummie says it reminds her of the Rector of Stiffkey. I once knew a girl named Stephanie Bell. I like the name.

A touch of the great heart about that one? No pretenses, suspicious forthcomingness, concealed reservations. Snorky certainly knew where she was with Plum, and he loved her fondly without any further complexity of feeling. His responses always seem to have been both immediate and final, like the effects in his own books. In 1956 he reminded Richard Usborne, author of *Clubland Heroes*, of the source of a quotation.

Smiling, the boy fell dead. Mr Usborne, *really*! I thought everyone knew Robert Browning's poem 'An Incident in the French Camp'. Young lieutenant comes to Napoleon with the news that they have taken Ratisbon. Napoleon quite pleased. He notices that the young man isn't looking quite himself.

> 'You're wounded!' 'Nay,' the soldier's pride
> Touched to the quick, he said:
> 'I'm killed, Sire!' and his chief beside
> Smiling the boy fell dead.

There is no suggestion of a score off Usborne: the "I thought everyone knew" has nothing snide about it, no secret pleasure in being one up. The moment is like one out of his books, and that means like one of the books themselves. The repetition of "quite" is exemplary; and as recalled and presented by Wodehouse, the episode is as if Bertie Wooster has at last found a way of doing something spiffing for Jeeves. He isn't feeling quite himself but never mind: we can't let Aunt Dahlia down; the plot must thicken: the show must go on.

Malice and snobbery seem to have fallen off Wodehouse unregarded, playing absolutely no part in his life, just as they are absent in the novels. He knew nothing of their source, or how they operated. William Connor, the *Daily Mirror*'s Cassandra, notoriously attacked him in the war for broadcasting "on behalf of the Germans" when he was interned after the

French debacle: a particularly malicious lie, because Wodehouse was obviously sending no more than reassuring messages to American friends and public. Always eager to disapprove, and to spurn a fallen idol, the public welcomed the story, and Wodehouse was, as he put it, in the dog house for years. But he replied by writing his usual sort of letters to Connor, who seems to have been gratified to have his author, as it were, after eating him. He had originally sneered at Wodehouse's Christian names, Pelham and Grenville, and Wodehouse wrote to him as "Dear Walp," suggesting that his initials stood for "Walpurgis Diarmid, or something of that sort." The suggestion of establishment grandeur in his given names, which only a malicious snob would impute, is lost by Wodehouse, and turned into a mutually jokey fantasy from the world of Catsmeat Potter-Pirbright and Gussie Fink-Nottle.

Intellectuals, and journalists looking for worms in the apple, find it hard to forgive Wodehouse for being so apparently sunny and straightforward. Surely there must be some dark secret somewhere? Reviews of his letters have contained such phrases as "something withheld"—"wears too fixed a smile"—"self-suppression everywhere." These seem to be symptoms of reviewer's terror, a well-known complaint like athlete's foot, which hamstrings the reviewer's normal responses through the fear that he must have missed some quite obvious point all his colleagues will have picked up. It must be said that Wodehouse's books might be much more interesting if there were things lurking in the background—instead of the pulse beating its happy rhythm on and on, unconscious of history and society and change and all the rest of it. Or rather not unconscious. The letters do wonder at times "whether they will think my sort of story out of date nowadays . . . but I don't believe people care a damn, so long as the story is funny." He may be "archaic," assuming a state of affairs as out of date as *Three Men in a Boat*: but "I believe that people will jump at something that takes them away from modern conditions." "I read a book about Dickens the other day which pointed out that D was still writing gaily about stagecoaches etc, long after railways had come in. I don't believe it matters and I intend to go on hewing to the butler line, let the chips fall where they may."

Ah, but the difference is that the Wodehouse world lives because it never existed. Like the young French lieutenant, Bertie falls dead as he smiles: it is his métier: no one believes in Blandings Castle any more than in heaven and the saints, which is why the idea of them is so restful. Like the saints, Wodehouse was single-minded: to ask what he thought of it all would be like asking St. Francis if he was really so attached to brother mouse and sister sparrow. The act of devotion is what counts.

> My war history has been a simple one. I have just sat in my chair and written all the time. When the Germans occupied Le Touquet I was in the middle of a Jeeves novel, *Joy in the Morning*. I continued plugging away at this for exactly two months, when they took us all off in a van to internment. After a few weeks spent in prisons, barracks etc we were dumped down at the lunatic asylum at Tost in Upper Silesia, where it was possible to resume writing and I started a new novel called *Money in the Bank* . . . I had to write in pencil in a room full of men playing darts and ping-pong, which made it a slow job. After my release my wife joined me, bringing me what I had done of *Joy in the Morning*. I finished this . . .

The hermit's point was being a hermit, not lamenting what was going on in the world. Suffering is indeed permanent, obscure, and dark, and if Wodehouse had been conscious of it, could he have gone on doing his thing? That might be the difference between him and the saint. In *The Borough* Crabbe has a parson of whom he writes that

> Never a man has left this world of sin
> Quite so unchanged as when he entered in.

That may be bitter, but there is a surly admiration in it too.

For it is rare not to pretend to feel what you don't, and not to seem chastened by experience into the role of *bien pensant*. To Usborne Wodehouse mentions his childhood, much of it spent with aunts while parents were in Hong Kong, and in rectories where the rector's wife dumped him on the housekeeper or butler while she confabulated with the Lady Bountiful at the Great Hall. There was some basis to Jeeves country, and Wodehouse himself was like Jane Austen and many other people in having some grand though distant connections at one end and ordinary humble ones at the other. None of that seems to have interested him, or perhaps like sex and other matters it never entered his head. He was the reverse of clubbable, and indeed resigned from the Garrick. He hated company—the face of Bertie's Uncle Tom "wore the strained haggard look it wears when he hears that guests are expected for the weekend." That is from a letter to Denis Mackail, while his wife was sprucing up their house at Remsenburg, Long Island, and building a bar. "She really loves solitude as much as you and I do, but she has occasional yearnings to be the Society hostess and go in for all that 'Act Two, The Terrace at Meadowsweet Manor' stuff." Women are funny, of course, but dogs seem to keep them happy. Wodehouse's own sex life is an open book, as suggested in another letter to Mackail:

there always seems such a lot to do. Work in the morning, at twelve watch a television serial in which I am absorbed, lunch, take the dog to the post office which covers two to three, brood on work till five, bath, cocktails, dinner, read and play two-handed bridge, and the day is over. The same routine day after day and somehow it never gets monotonous.

St. Benedict might have said the same of his rule.

He read everything, and not to take himself "away from modern conditions." Plotting wasn't his natural flair, and J. P. Marquand's novels gave him the occasional idea for one. He was somewhat in awe of his friend Denis Mackail, brother of Angela Thirkell and like her a best-seller. Their names remind one that the status of what used to be called 'escapist' literature has subtly changed. No doubt there is still plenty of one sort of the old style, as indicated by the success of Mills and Boon: but the reading public hardly recognizes the fact that sex and brutality and fearless realism are now pretentiously exploited to achieve the same ends. We still jump at something that takes us away from the conditions of our lives, but prefer to think it is Life we are getting, things as they really are. There is also a certain resemblance between Wodehouse and a modern master like Samuel Beckett. Both are, verbally speaking, performing fleas, but with Beckett you have the illusion that you are, as Plum might have put it, getting the goods on life. Jeeves and Wooster never pretended to give you that. There is no "human interest" in either writer, but his admirers would shy away from Beckett being described as "a master of English prose," the accolade freely given to Wodehouse. The vocabulary of appreciation changes our mode of response from age to age.

Raymond Chandler went as a schoolboy to Dulwich the year Wodehouse left, and there is a reference to him in the letters as a writer to be admired and read more of. C. S. Forester was at the same school and Wodehouse would have known about him too, for he zealously kept up with all the school's sporting activities and its old boys. Not too fanciful to discern a resemblance, in terms of mastery of English prose, between all three writers; but the other two combine their skills with daydreams — being a private eye or captaining a ship of the line — in a way that discloses interior personality, the secrecy of a human case. Nothing like that happened with Plum.

Frances Donaldson has done a superb job of editing and writing an informative and perceptive introduction. She arranges the letters under the heading of subject and recipient, which gives a much better and clearer impression than the usual chronological hodge-podge, and it is a method that might be commended to all compilers of literary correspondence. One section, headed "Spiritualism," is very brief, containing two letters of a couple of lines each to William Townend, a friend of longstanding. One says: "I want to talk to you about Spiritualism. I think it's the goods." The other, two years later, in 1927:

> That was rather queer about the planchette and Kate Overy. Do you remember she and her brother both committed suicide. I knew her fairly well. Have you had any more results?

Planchettes were quite the thing around 1927 — see A Dance to the Music of Time — and so was communication from the great beyond. Wodehouse received several letters dictated by Townend to a medium after his death. The message was that "life continues here in the most delightful way," and communication ran from 1967 to 1970, a few years before Wodehouse died. "To what extent Plum believed all these things is not known to anyone." So the editor remarks, adding that books on Spiritualism, including Townend's favorite, *The Wisdom of the Gods* by H. Dennis Bradley, were found in his study after Wodehouse's death. Bertie would have made a joke of it, but Jeeves would have understood.

London Review of Books, 1990

10

Like Ink and Milk

D. H. Lawrence (1885–1930)

———————

Sons and Lovers: The Unexpurgated Text
by D. H. Lawrence, edited by Helen Baron and Carl Baron

D. H. Lawrence: The Early Years, 1885—1912
by John Worthen

Sons and Lovers
by Michael Black

T HE NOVEL IS a natural vehicle for superiorities. In an age which took competition for granted the novelist possessed a means of distancing himself, morally, socially and sexually, from his contemporaries; and many of them seized the opportunity, D. H. Lawrence no less than Jane Austen. That establishing and disengaging of the self became in the nineteen century more and more a part of the classic writer's instinct, and merges with the novel's own unique form of self-therapy. Dickens explores himself through it and Lawrence cures his sickness: Hardy assuages his Biblical "astonishment and fear" at the horror of life: Jane Austen overcomes helplessness, malice, and contempt.

Fiction had also taken over the sermon. From George Eliot to the present day, bossing the reader about with your own view of things—no longer with the sermon's universal assumptions—has been the simplest mode of being superior. But of course the form has its own deep ways of compensating for all this. It overflows, given half the chance, with its own involuntary generosity. Rereading *Sons and Lovers* is to be filled afresh—more even than at a first reading—with the truth of F. R. Leavis's old dictum that here is "where life flows," as well as with that of Lawrence himself: trust the tale and not the teller. It is not the tale which absorbs one here, however, so much as the closeness and richness of experience that comes fizzing out of words and pages. Lawrence's message, and even his insight into this classic Oedipal situation, have become as a tale that is told; but the genius of people, place, and language is more vivid and compelling than ever, the very top of that abundance and generousness the great classic novel had and ought to have. It exhales a prodigious, at times comically portentous concentration upon the self, but none of that superiority which has become at once second nature, style, and integument to the combative and cosmopolitan literary milieu of Lawrence's novels.

Suspected as a spy in Metz, the highly sensitive German frontier fortress in which Frieda's father held a humdrum position as garrison adjutant and engineer, Lawrence sat down to pass the time, while his intended engaged in distracted conclave with her family by writing some pieces round the incident for the *Westminster Gazette.* "How a Spy Is Arrested" was set up in type but never printed: the *Westminster's* editor, Stephen Spender's uncle, was mildly pro-German in 1912, and he also turned down a piece called "In Fortified Germany." But the third and fourth articles made it—Lawrence's debut as a travel writer—and they already exhibit their author's hedgehog defences against other people's superiorities. A German officer in a flowing cloak of bluey-grey—"like ink and milk" (a wonderfully characteristic phrase)—looks at him "coldly and inquisitively. I look at him with a 'Go to the devil' sort of look and pass on." Much more important to Lawrence than German-occupied Alsace were his own reasons for being there, which overflowed into the piece he was writing. England, he implies, would also give in to the conqueror. "Nowadays it is easier not to live than to live . . . to suffer than to insist." The English instinct is "to forgo life . . . I know a certain woman wants to love me. I know I want to love her." Was he to renounce her, in typically English way, because "there are plenty of well-shaped women in England and Germany who would love me enough in a licentious fashion"? One wonders what an editor not privy to Lawrence's situation as he was writing made of all this.

As John Worthen justly observes, "it is hard to imagine Lawrence writing like this before meeting Frieda or hearing Frieda talk." It is also hard to imagine any biographer telling the tale with more dispassionate sympathy and insight than Worthen does: his biography of Lawrence's early years is a masterpiece of its kind, and by far the most illuminating study of Lawrence we now possess. We are apt to take the elopement for granted as a bold bid for life and freedom culminating in the idyll on Lake Garda. As Worthen shows in detail, it was anything but that. For all Frieda's "splendour" and emancipated sexual code, it was not principles that counted here but power, just as it would be when the nation's went to war two years later. Lawrence as England won this power struggle, refusing to forgo: showing indeed an utter ruthlessness worthy of the German General Staff, or later Hitler himself. Worthen comments with his usual insight that "in the hectic Muddle and confusion of those days Lawrence had one single advantage: he was the only person who knew exactly when he wanted." Lawrence was Machiavel, not derelict: it was a far cry from the abandoned and self-abandoned Paul Morel at the end of *Sons and Lovers*; and yet *Sons and Lovers* in its present form would never have existed if it had not been for Frieda, her new perspective upon writing—Lawrence worked on it as he awaited the outcome of the power struggle—and the circumstances of their flight.

Michael Black's admirable little book in the Landmarks in World Literature series, analyzing in close and illuminating detail the plan and growth of *Sons and Lovers*, and emphasizing Frieda's sense of the novel's "form," makes the proper companion piece to Worthen. Aldous Huxley called Frieda the stupidest woman he had ever met, and no doubt she was, in his sense: but at this stage of their relationship her intuition had an uncanny understanding of what Lawrence himself hardly knew he was doing, or trying to do. It was she who recognized what she called "the amazing brutality" of *Sons and Lovers*, the Sophoclean brutality of a "relation brought into the open, unmentionable in that epoch of Brushwood Boys and Peter Pans. Jessie Chambers wrote her own version of events in a novel she called *The Rathe Primrose* (Milton's "rathe primrose that forsaken dies") which Frieda found touching and "lovable," while even Lawrence said "it wasn't bad." This "faded photograph," as Frieda also called it, which was never published and which Jessie later destroyed, made Frieda intuit even more forcibly the "amazing brutality" of Lawrence's own novel, then still at the fetal stage.

Worthen's blow-by-blow account shows Lawrence using his single-minded determination to betray what he knew to be the wishes and expectations of the woman he loved. Her ideas of their relationship counted for nothing against his will. Both Henry James and Choderlos de Laclos would have deeply admired the skill with which Lawrence exploited his apparent powerlessness in the face of three amoral but powerful and realistic women—Frau von Richthofen and her two daughters—scheming to give him his "affair" and then get rid of him. Their counsels were not divided as to ends, only to means: but while they argued the best way to deal with him, Lawrence preempted their schemes by writing to Frieda's husband, Professor Weekley, back home in Nottingham, telling him he had carried off Frieda, and was to marry her.

After that, there was nothing much the three ladies could do. The initiative, seized by Lawrence, passed to Weekley, who took full advantage of it. Lawrence had deliberately put all the cards in his hands. Oddly enough, both he and Frieda had perfectly good reasons for being in Germany—she to see her sisters and parents, he to visit his uncle and cousin at Waldbrol. Theirs was no romantic elopement: Frieda assumed, as did her relatives, that a discreet "holiday" would take place, followed by the return to Nottingham and the parental happiness which she not only expected but wanted. She had had affairs with the Austrian psychiatrist Otto Gross, and back home with a well-off lace manufacturer, her son's godfather; and these had ended amicably, without her husband suspecting anything. She had learnt from Gross, who wrote to her in terms which strangely prefigure what Lawrence would write to and about her, to obey every sexual impulse that came her way while at the same time bestowing on her chief lover the absolute sense of *Sicherheit* that was in her special gift. Lawrence, too, already knew about and wanted this, and was prepared to do anything to get it.

It could and perhaps should be, of course, the gift of a mother to her children. Lawrence needed to take it from the Weekley children and have it himself. He made Frieda reveal to Weekley her past as well as her present infidelity, thus ensuring that he could and would cut her children totally off from her by the terms of a divorce. It is interesting to speculate how a present-day Lawrence would solve this question: Lawrence himself could share Frieda with her casual lovers, but not, or at least not till long after, with her children. What he must have was a "counter-mother," who he need not worship or adore or "Love," as he had done his own mother, but who would give him the same absolute security while dwelling with him in a state of total war, instead of the saccharine peace of his own home circle.

The remarkable thing was that Frieda obeyed him, in that way if in no other, as if assigning the stronger maternal claim to him rather than to her own children, whatever the cost to her other feelings. Guilt takes odd forms, and the pathetic letters from a close woman friend at home imploring her not to leave little Monty and Barbie and Elsie ("Monty *must* have a mother to protect him . . . don't you remember the night Monty was born?") may have helped to harden her heart, however much she really did love and need her own children. As Worthen remarks, the battery of letters from Weekley and his family and friends, as well as from her own family, may have driven her to Lawrence. She needed him "to overcome her guilt at having made such a dreadful mess of her husband's life—and of her children's lives." She had no humor exactly, but both she and Lawrence had a great instinct for the high comic-grotesque, in their own and others' lives—a sense both Dostoevskian and Germanic. It must have made them roar when her husband's sister Maude compared her to the *Titanic* (which had just gone down), not seeing the mischief she did any more than the iceberg. At the same time, using him as a "dose of morphia" in the midst of all this high drama, she was going to bed with her old friend Udo von Henning. With perceptive venom Lawrence reckoned that she made him "more babyfied." She would not do that to Lawrence: nor would he plead his case, or comfort her, or let her blackmail him with love-possessiveness. He knew now what he wanted from a mother, and it was the exact opposite of what he had got from his own mother in the past.

Nonetheless he had his own kind of guilt—a writer's guilt. It begins to emerge even in *The Rainbow* as a kind of pomposity, a determination of superiority which glosses over what he had actually done and what he actually needed. From then on, he would browbeat the rest of the world into seeing him as the only one in step, and make a mystique of the elemental needs of his own individuality. He was indeed exceptional, and so was Frieda: *Anna Karenina*, which Frieda read compulsively during their early days together, gives an exhaustively accurate forecast of what would happen to most people who chose their sort of situation. And the first and most spontaneous writing that Lawrence came out with at the time—the wonderful travelogue of his and Friedas journey down to Garda in *Mr. Noon*—shows a Lawrence without superiorities, the comical and merry youth who used to amuse his friends with spontaneous self-mockery and self-parody. *Mr. Noon* could have been the best thing he ever wrote: but he dropped it after four hundred pages. It was too shameless, too disarmingly personal in its sense of the real relation between Gilbert Noon and Johanna, the "livanted" couple who were Frieda and Lawrence. Their adventures are a comedy of vivid and sometimes ignobly gruesome misfortune, their sex life is scrappy and unsatisfactory: but they can only enjoy life together, and Lawrence's quick infallible prose shows us how and why. They are the exact opposite of Mellors and Lady Chatterley.

Nothing could be less portentous than *Mr. Noon*. And Worthen is surely right in taking *Mr. Noon* as the index of Lawrence's true feelings and responses at the time, and in telling the reader his grounds for doing so. By the time of *The Rainbow and Women in Love*, the journey abroad together, vivid and memorable though it is, has become a sort of mystic pilgrimage, and the relation of Birkin and Ursula, is similarly hagiographical. Symbol and meaning have become like the Alps. Such a change of approach may have been necessary if Lawrence was to have the authority he required, and reach the mass audience he wanted: but it involved a very real sacrifice—that of his young authentic being. Imagine Lady Chatterly telling Mellors in a fit of pique that she had made love to a friend of his, and being "forgiven," much to her fury, as Mr. Noon feels it proper to do when his Johanna makes such a malicious confession? Both Gilbert Noon and Johanna have the true and moving absurdity of life in that situation: Mellors and Lady Chatterly have the unintentional absurdity of idealized constructs. Gilbert Noon's discomfiture when Johanna's rage and irritation at him is only increased by his "understanding" of her feminine being is one of the funniest things in Lawrence's writing, and the truest to the sense of self and life which his relation with Frieda at first gave him. The spirit and—more important—the persona of Gilbert Noon is often found in the stories, particularly in "The Captain's Doll," but it disappears from the novels.

Cambridge has published the unexpurgated text of *Sons and Lovers* in their edition of Lawrence. Helen and Carl Baron have also produced a less annotated version of the same complete text, before Edward Garnett's editing of it, "in a form and at a price intended for anyone who appreciates great literature." Garnett's editing used to be praised for giving the novel proportion, and bringing out its meaning. The Barons, probably rightly, maintain that it weakened Lawrence's scope and purpose. Garnett cut 2,050 lines, about 10 percent, from the manuscript; and although their restoration does not make the novel feel any weightier or read very differently, it does shift the perspective a little.

Scenes were trimmed which show Paul's mother with neighbors and tradesmen—scenes which brought out more fully her subtle social isolation. The family as a whole was more fully represented: Garnett had thought the main character should stand out by himself against a generalized social background. The elder brother William's charm and amorous activity, and his mother's reaction to them, were more fully documented. As the Barons point out, the title itself implies multiple treatment within a family; it is not just a generalization. A previous editor, Keith Sagar, found the facetious detail about the elder Morel brother "insufferable": and yet it shows among other things Lawrence's awareness of different approaches to growing up and falling in love among the males of a family. William is as vivid a character as any in the book, his death one of its most moving moments: it can only help to have more of him.

The same might apply, though with less force, to the deleted passages about the contemporary role of women, and about current debates on science and sociology—passages reminiscent of H. G. Wells, whose presence was to reveal itself even more strongly in the first part of *Mr. Noon*. Some of these passages looked forward to Lawrence's later dogma about the sexes. Paul observes to his mother that he doesn't think he "could be a woman better than a woman is one herself," and she says: "We could do better than men."

"Perhaps you could, mother," he said.

"Well—!" she replied, with her little amused sniff, "anything that is natural is pleased to be itself. And when a woman wants very badly to be a man, you may back your life she's not much good as a woman."

"I hate it when a woman wants to be a man," he said.

"It shows her pride as a woman is pretty low," she answered. He always came to his mother, making her the touchstone.

No comment on the relevance of the passage seems necessary, but it may have mildly irritated Garnett's emancipated views on the sex question. Other sexual matters he may not have minded himself, but simply had a professional eye for what could offend susceptibilities at the time. Clara Dawes's breasts came in for a good deal of excision, and some of the dialogue with her was also cut out. Garnett preferred the novel to concentrate on the treatment of Miriam. One extraordinary Lawrentian touch which he got rid of describes Paul's behavior when he stays the night at Clara's mother's house, and has faint hopes that Clara may later contrive to come to his room, despite the dragon's watchfulness. Some of her possessions are in the little room he has been given. Garnett's text reads: "He sat up and looked at the room in the darkness, his feet doubled under him, perfectly motionless, listening." After "darkness" the full text has:

Then he realised that there were a pair of her stockings on the chair. He got up stealthily, and put them on himself. Then he sat still and knew he would have to have her. After that he sat erect on the bed, his feet doubled under him.

The Barons seem a bit at a loss as to how to pigeonhole the incident sexually, hesitating between transvestism and latent homosexuality. But it seems quite normal, though probably only Lawrence at the time could have said so. If you want the girl you want her stockings, and if you put the stockings on you want her still more. Whatever he felt about it himself Garnett must have at once seen it wouldn't do—not for the reading public of the time.

The printers also re-punctuated Lawrence's manuscript, applying their own house style in about five thousand cases. Not much of this mattered, but sometimes it did. Meaning can depend upon it. Lawrence wrote that "Miriam saw what Paul was seeking: a sort of baptism of fire in passion, it seemed to her. She realised that he would never be satisfied till he had it. Perhaps it was essential to him—as to some men to sow wild oats." The printer changed that to "Perhaps it was essential to him, as to some men, to sow wild oats." That makes quite a difference.

London Review of Books, 1992

11

Baby Face

William Gerhardie (1895–1977)

William Gerhardie: A Biography
by Dido Davies

Memoirs of a Polyglot
by William Gerhardie

Futility
by William Gerhardie

God's Fifth Column: A Biography of the Age, 1890–1940
by William Gerhardie, edited by Michael Holroyd and
    Robert Skidelsky

WHO SAID OF WHOM: "I have talent but he has genius"? Evelyn
Waugh had been reading *Futility*, which first came out in 1922,
but his favorite William Gerhardie novel was to be *Jazz and
Jasper*. This almost forgotten work appeared in 1927, two years earlier than
Vile Bodies. Its author wanted to call it *Doom*, a title not adopted until the
1974 edition. In 1947 it made a brief appearance as *My Sinful Earth*, and
the 1928 American edition was called *Eve's Apples*, the American publisher having decided, no doubt wisely, that the word "jazz" had been
"worn threadbare" in crossing the Atlantic.

This mirage of various titles, all perfectly suitable, seems proper for a
writer more famous in his day for being a genius than for any specific

work of art. Even his own name had variations: the family name was Gerhardi, to which he sometimes but not always preferred to add an "e," and which he pronounced soft, as in George. Its distant origins, not unlike those of the Beerbohms, were sober Protestant German, with a talent for sticking to business. On a commercial foray in the cosmopolitan capitalist world of the 1850s the author's grandfather married a Flemish girl, came back to England, and then tried Russia, where the cotton business was booming. Industrious colonies from Yorkshire and Lancashire where settling in beside the Neva and Moskva rivers, and Gerhardi's mother was named Clara Wadsworth. His father prospered and owned a large mansion and warehouse in St. Petersburg. A solid family, despite their later forced exiles and polyglot adventures, and William's brother Victor, who was to settle down in business in Finland, sounds rather boringly British. William, too, was English in his own way, which may have been one of the things about him that Evelyn Waugh admired.

He borrowed from him too. In her highly fascinating and erudite biography, Dido Davies notes some of the echoes of *Jazz and Jasper* in *Vile Bodies*. Gerhardie's Lord Ottercove, based on the ubiquitous literary model of Beaverbrook, shouts "Faster! Faster!" like Agatha Runcible. Beaverbrook seems to have genuinely and deeply admired Gerhardie and made a kind of mascot of him, dragging him off to nightclubs and grooming him in every possible way for publicity. Waugh was never so much petted and encouraged by the news tycoon: he had the good sense to keep his distance, and the kind of secret dedicated independence Gerhardie lacked. Gerhardie's lack of balance and center was part linguistic, part social: Russian came easier to him than English, in the use of which he never seems to have obtained an instinctive confidence. All things Russian were madly fashionable in the early Twenties, and Gerhardie found himself lionized and invited everywhere, but on a basis of mild but permanent misunderstanding. Bernard Shaw, he noticed, had a red nose and he wondered whether the famous abstinence was really as severe as claimed. Shaw said to him: "If you're English you're a genius, but if you're Russian . . . well then . . . of course . . ." "I am English," cut in Gerhardie.

That was partly the trouble: he was, but he made his reputation as an exotic. Unlike Ronald Firbank, who had his own niche as a homosexual and a rare stylistic innovator, Gerhardie could not in the end claim to be anything specially, not even an eccentric. Although he had a close and lifelong relationship with his mother Clara, his own tastes were promiscuous and heterosexual: a great deal of falling in love, and even more brief affairs with shopgirls and waitresses, to whom he was kind but also rather mean, as he never had any money to speak of, in spite of his run of success in the Ottercove world of society and journalism. While Waugh settled into a self-created world of Catholicism as a mock-aristocratic patriarch, Gerhardie remained an indeterminate sort of adventurer to the end, dying in 1977 at the age of 82 in his little flat near the BBC, for whom he had worked in the war years. For a long time he had been toiling in obscurity on what he hoped would be his masterpiece, a mixture of history and memoir, biography and literary criticism, a successor to *God's Fifth Column*. It was discovered after his death, in a folder querulously inscribed "Do not crush."

Certainly he remained uncrushable. Like most butterflies, he was far too tough to be broken on the wheel. But his work is very well worth reviving, and not just for its local chronicle interest. It had something which deeply impressed his contemporaries and made the older hands feel "not only out of date but dead and buried." Something in the way the early novels were done made them look like the literary future, not just to Evelyn Waugh but to Rebecca West and Arnold Bennett—the young and the old alike—H. G. Wells, Elizabeth Bowen, Olivia Manning, Anthony Powell. In his time Gerhardie was at least as potent a literary influence in England as Hemingway, and more prevasive, more part of the new metropolitan air that English authors breathed: they absorbed him as Dostoevsky and the Russian writers had breathed the air of Gogol and come out from under his overcoat, and if that seems an excessive claim, read the pages of *Futility* and *The Polyglots* and taste a sort of comprehensive ur-flavor of the inter-war novel, the Graham Greene to Henry Green.

And yet his words and sentences, unlike theirs, are never quite in place, never quite add up to a novelist's "world," the sort that has a good chance of standing outside time. But Gerhardie had an absolutely natural sense of the new incongruity principle, the thing that flickers like immortal sheet lightning in *The Waste Land*, published in the same year as *Futility*—those nightingales and dirty ears. This is not, as has some-times been supposed in the case of Gerhardie, a vulgarization of Chekhov, to whom he was of course devoted, and whose three sisters he borrows, transmogrifies, and gently lampoons in *Futility*. Gerhardie's mode of unseriousness has a cutting edge, a new dimension of experience kept immanent—a tremendous potential of threat and promise—behind the disheveled economy of the manner. True, he can become sentimen-tal (so can Graham Greene), and also vulnerable to his own stereotype. A tender scene in *The Polyglots* is suffused with a sudden disgusting smell of burning fish-bones from somewhere behind the arbor where it takes place. An old device, but one that is used by Gerhardie, as later by Nabokov, to enhance the experience of both kinds of perception, rather than to diminish them. *Futility* has a gusto at variance with its title and overt tendency. Nabokov does the same sort of thing in *Lolita*, where the comically magic night of love with the nymphet is rendered more piquant, more alluring in consciousness, from the fact that the hero finds himself not very well in the morning, and decidedly constipated. Though he had no Russian blood, Gerhardie certainly had the Nabokovian gift of enjoying life's rich tapestry, as it were, no matter in what form it unfolded.

Another thing that has ensured Gerhardie's comparative nonsurvival as a writer seems to be his lack of a decided and involuntary personality. It goes, in some way, with the polyglot background, even with the large numbers of possible titles for his novels; and with the difficulty he had in acquiring by intuitive means the authority of background which a novelist needs for his creations. He lacked much sense of others. Tall and baby-faced, he was attractive to many women and pursued them obsessively, but he had a dandy's coldness and was too fastidious to be physically in love. He never married, though he once pursued a razor-blade heiress with what seems to have been a fair amount of determination. He and Beaverbrook obviously had much in common, and he seems to have possessed the art of simultaneously teasing and flattering the great man. But Ethel Mannin, a powerful figure in the literary and social world of the time, did not take to him at all, declining to be seduced, and addressing him scornfully, at least in her memoirs, as "You, with your pale baby face, and stone-cold blue eyes, you're a sadist." Antipathy was mutual, Gerhardie referring to her as the meanest woman he ever met.

Coldness as an aid to stylishness was admired by writers of Waugh's and Anthony Powell's generation, and to be fair to Gerhardie, his attitudes never strike one as repulsive, or even unsympathetic. Also, like the father of the three sisters in *Futility*, he was at the same time a detached and a devoted family man.

In that respect, he resembled Chekhov, and Chekhov's masterpiece "The Lady with the Dog" is in a sense in the background of the novel he hoped would be his own masterpiece. *Of Mortal Love* was published in 1936, the story of a casual love affair that turns into the real thing. Katherine Mansfield, who had deeply admired *Futility*, had urged him many years back to attempt "one of those stories of a simple heart," and both her advice and his eager acceptance of it show that both possessed the strong streak of sentimentality coveted by their essentially worldly temperaments. Gerhardie probably did not know enough about that sort of love to write about it very well. But the opposite kind of thing he can do beautifully, and with the kind of light touch—Desmond MacCarthy much admired in his writing "the ever-shifting and changing *sense of being alive*"—which impressed readers reacting from the heavy-handedness of John Galsworthy, and not enamored of D. H. Lawrence's use of a new sort of heavy-handedness. In *Futility*, the Russian extended family with one of whose daughters the narrator is in love, has ended up at last in Vladivostok, itself in the final convulsion of civil war.

> It had been snowing in the night, prematurely for the season; now the snow was thawing and the ground was muddy. The sun was yellow, honey-coloured, and her sidelong look seemed warmer in the sunshine.
>
> "Will you marry me?" I said.
>
> "No." She shook her head. "I am tired of you."
>
> "I know that," I replied, and walked silently beside her.
>
> "If I were really tired of you I wouldn't tell you."
>
> "Then why do you tell me?" I took it up, hungering for something positive, however small.
>
> "I don't always say what I think," was the answer.
>
> We walked on.
>
> "We are leaving in any case," she said.

It is deceptively simple, but oddly effective in conveying the fact that consciousness is not really an affair of feeling, emotion, action, but of something more intangible, though no less active. The Russian "manner" is only there in order to bring out a more genuinely novel way of seeing and doing the thing, which we shall recognize a decade or so later in Anthony Powell's *Venusberg* Hugh Walpole, who had himself jumped on the bandwagon during the war by bringing out two novels with Russian settings, spoke of Gerhardie with envy and admiration to Virginia Woolf, who seems herself to have implied an admission that he managed the new consciousness without drawing attention to it in the way she needed to do.

At the same time, he did not sell. After *Futility*, which was in any case by no means a commercial success, he rarely managed to earn the publisher's advance. Yet his reputation never really declined. Robert Donat was keen to do *The Polyglots* as a film, but eventually decided that "only Hollywood or Alexander Korda could do justice to the story." Basil Dean, who had filmed *The Constant Nymph*, was enthusiastic as well, but that too came to nothing.

Dr. Davies never claims too much for Gerhardie's achievement and reputation; her scholarship has produced an absorbing account in detail of the London literary life of the time. Vera Boys, the original of Dinah in *Of Mortal Love*, was said by Beaverbrook when Gerhardie introduced them to be "the most beautiful woman in London," but to her irritation she heard him say the same thing to another young woman the next evening. Gerhardie was named as co-respondent in her divorce case and was cautious with married women thereafter, for his Yorkshire-German antecedents, as well as an affectionate regard for the feelings of his mother and sisters, made him reluctant to play the overt bohemian. But how different the events of life from all the ways there are of making novels about them! While Gerhardie was working as a liaison officer in Vladivostok, and unconsciously gathering material for *Futility*, he recorded in his diary; "Played tennis in the afternoon; then had a woman; then a bath, and afterwards witnessed a revolution." That might seem to be what it all boiled down to in the end.

12

The Last Puritan

George Orwell (1903–1950)

Orwell: Wintry Conscience of a Generation
Jeffrey Meyers

IN ANTHONY POWELL's *Memoirs*, which contain a great many shrewd and perceptive observations about writers of the memoirist's time, there is a little anecdote which, trivial as Powell admits it to be, sheds a great deal of light on George Orwell's complex character. On one occasion, when Orwell was visiting him, Powell left the room to fetch a book, leaving Orwell alone with his young son. Returning he found Orwell assiduously examining the pictures on the wall. Inside the baby's cot was an enormous jackknife. Orwell looked embarrassed and said he had given it to the child to play with.

The incident illustrated his shyness, "part genuine, part assumed," and his odd taste for sentimental vignettes:

> Why, in the first place, should he want to burden himself, in London, with a knife that looked like an adjunct of a fur-trapper's equipment? Echoes perhaps of Dangerous Dan McGrew? Why take such pains to avoid being found playing with a child? . . . Why leave the knife behind as evidence? It was much too big to be forgotten.
>
> I think the answer to these questions is that the whole incident was arranged to create a genre picture in the Victorian manner of a kind which, even though he might smile at the sentimentality, made a huge appeal to Orwell's imagination, and way of looking at things. He

was, so to speak, playing the part of a strong rough man, touched by the sight of a baby, but unwilling to confess, even to himself, this inner weakness. At the same time, he had to be discovered for the incident to achieve graphic significance.

Like many others who are masochists—not sexually but in their need for some sort of punishment—Orwell wanted simultaneously to act a part and to be caught out in acting it. His personal and political nature was both romantic and masochistic, and the twin impulses are to be found in combination throughout his work, no doubt contributing in no small measure to their notoriety and to a popularity which could have never been achieved by any amount of political and social theorizing.

Like T. E. Lawrence in *The Seven Pillars of Wisdom*, Orwell unconsciously strove both to be a man of action and destiny and to reveal what a fraud he was in that role; in consequence Orwell's admirers were as much mesmerized as Lawrence's were, though in subtler, more interesting, and more various ways. All Orwell's novels and personal records, from *Keep the Aspidistra Flying* and *Down and Out in Paris and London* to *Animal Farm* and *Nineteen Eighty-Four*, embody the same kind of human contradiction: clarity and concealment, the stark and the sentimental, side by side but never recognizing each other's existence.

Winston in *Nineteen Eighty-Four*, the closest that Orwell came in his work to a dramatized self-portrait, is fascinated by O'Brien, the Thought Police chief who behaves toward him with alternate cruelty and geniality, expounding very Orwellian views on the inevitability of the tyrant state while behaving in accordance with the best *Boys' Own Paper* tradition of the gloating villain. Winston himself, significantly, is not a political being at all: his pattern of life lies between a swooningly abject submission to the categorical imperative of O'Brien's brutality, even though his conscious intelligence revolts from everything O'Brien stands for, and a nostalgic delight in the old-fashioned pleasures and customs of the "proles" who still survive in this odious new society, and whom he sees as the sole hope and force for good in an otherwise Stalinized world. The most memorable scenes in the novel are the delight a Victorian "snowstorm" paperweight gives to Winston and his girlfriend, and its destruction by the

Thought Police, who torture the pair and let them go when they are no longer capable of feeling their former love for each other, with no emotion or desire left, except for Victory Gin.

The character of O'Brien, incidentally, was partly derived from Orwell's ambivalent feeling for Georges Kopp, a Belgian-raised Communist and adventurer whom Orwell encountered while serving with a separatist revolutionary party in Catalonia during the Spanish Civil War. A heroic figure, Kopp served the cause devotedly throughout that war and the world war which followed, although he lost his Communist faith and died in obscurity not long afterward. There was clearly much about him that repelled as well as attracted Orwell; and Jeffrey Meyers, in his new biography, is surely right in suggesting the presence of the figure of Kopp in Orwell's creative work. Kopp's life and his importance to Orwell are just one of the many details that Meyers has discovered or investigated: his book is probably richer in Orwelliana than any of its predecessors; and it is the first study of Orwell to make full use of Peter Davison's superb twenty-volume edition of Orwell's complete works. Meyers presents a story full of new angles and anecdotes, and rich with quotation from a diversity of sources culled from an unusually active and talented literary epoch.

A romantic epoch above all. Without emphasizing the parallels too plainly, Meyers demonstrates the similarities between political and literary romanticism at the opening of the nineteenth century, when, as Wordsworth put it in *The Prelude*, "Bliss was it in that dawn to be alive," and the warring but passionate idealisms of the Twenties and Thirties of our own century in Europe. Whatever the kind and degree of his disillusionment, Orwell never shook off the power and the appeal of these romanticisms: he would have found it impossible to live and work without the commitment they offered, any more than a medieval thinker could have shaken off the power of belief and its warring factions within doctrinal Christianity.

Malcolm Muggeridge, who liked Orwell though he was amused by his attempts to adapt a proletarian manner and style of clothing, was himself notorious in his own time for his continued fascination with the apparatus and ideology of communism, in all its different manifestations and changes. He no longer believed in communism, perhaps never had believed in it, but he could not live without it, as a kind of aesthetic refuge. Orwell had the same kind of involvement with his time, though emphatically not an aesthetic one: his contradictory and complex emotional temperament declared itself in brilliant but also bizarre ways. Like a religious saint he needed to suffer, even though the suffering may have been deliberately invited or self-induced. He suffered in the cause of decent folk everywhere, whatever kind of ideology tyrannized them. And he distrusted all forms of political correctness.

He certainly wanted his readers to become aware of his need for self-punishment, for he had an obscure Saint Teresa–like sense of humor. The early reviewers grasped at once that the man who wrote *Down and Out in Paris and London* had suffered a great many vivid and picturesque hardships but had no real occasion to have suffered them. He had never been an authentic vagrant, a genuine tramp, any more than T. E. Lawrence had been or could have been a real Arab guerrilla. Both men needed self-exposure; and the second romantic epoch, if for convenience we may call it that, contained a necessary element of acting and make-believe. Acting the part was even necessary in the dangerous world of Nazi uniforms and rallies, or of Communist "comrades" and Party lines. Orwell came to see both the danger and the fascination of this, perhaps because it mirrored his own novelist's appetite for display and response, the genre picture and the significant scene. But he could not stand back from the scene as Muggeridge did, and survey it with absorption but also with detachment.

Meyers does not quote Anthony Powell's anecdote of Orwell and the baby, a scene contrived, as Powell suggests, because it made such an appeal to Orwell's imagination and to his "way of looking at things." But Meyers emphasizes in detail and to great effect the many other oddities of Orwell's domestic behavior. Because his real name was Eric Blair and his Scottish ancestors moderately aristocratic, he coined for himself the name of George Orwell, George being uncompromisingly bourgeois and British, Orwell the name of a small river in East Anglia, a part of the Home Counties with which Blair/Orwell had no regional connection at all. Again he can be compared with T. E. Lawrence, whose family was Irish, but who in a highly self-conscious bid to escape from the fabulous personality he had acquired in the war called himself first Ross and then Shaw, two uncompromisingly English names. Blair/Orwell was in fact a connoisseur of class distinctions, referring to his family as "lower upper-middle class," a category worthy of Henry James himself and charmingly at variance with the sturdy proletarian persona Orwell admired and adopted.

But perversity and unexpectedness are the most endearing aspects of his personality both as man and writer. The book he most admired, and the one that most influenced the way he wrote, was Swift's *Gulliver's Travels*, but his favorite books were boys' adventure stories and stirring yarns like Rider Haggard's *King Solomon's Mines*. His occasional essays, which are among the best things he wrote, refer often and nostalgically to such topics, and he invented the useful concept of "good bad books," such as the ones he habitually enjoyed reading, and "good bad poetry," which included Macaulay's *Lays of Ancient Rome* and Tennyson's "The Charge of the Light Brigade" with other rousing patriotic verses. His tastes were also puritan: he detested anything *louche* or even mildly pornographic, and wrote an essay denouncing James Hadley Chase's thriller *No Orchids for Miss Blandish*, a work which by modern standards of thriller-writing seems innocence itself.

Anthony Powell told me an engaging story to illustrate this strong streak of puritanism in Orwell, with whom Powell had been at school and who remained a close friend. In keeping with his affection for old-fashioned lower-class customs, Orwell loved vulgar seaside postcards, which Powell used to send him, on one occasion dispatching one of a mildly risqué sort. A sultry shop assistant is asked by a meek little bespectacled customer, "Do you keep stationery?" to which she replies, "Sometimes I do and sometimes I give a little wiggle." To Powell's consternation Orwell's response was glacial: like Queen Victoria he was most definitely not amused.

They shared a taste for military uniforms however—Orwell as a young man served in the Burma police—and Powell, an officer during the war, was in uniform when he met Orwell in the Café Royal. He was surprised to be asked in tones of "considerable tenseness," "Do your trousers strap under the foot?" Reassured, Powell said they did, and Orwell observed solemnly, "Those straps under the foot give you a feeling like nothing else in life." Meyers mentions this story, and comments too on the curious way in which Orwell mingled in his personal life romantic affection for modest proletarian comforts—the sausage and crumpets, the coal fire and the cat on the hearth rug—with an insistence on more middle-class standards of domestic elegance. His first wife, Eileen, was amused when they were living on no money in a workman's cottage to be told she must serve the jam in a dish and not in the jar; Orwell cherished and polished his few bits of family silver and displayed them on the sideboard.

Orwell's father, a severe but ineffectual man who had been a colonial administrator in India, had urged his son to try for the Burma police. Orwell made no objection. He had disliked his time as a schoolboy at Eton, where he had not been popular with the masters and had not made an impressive record: he was keen to get away from England. In Burma, like his colleagues, he had native mistresses and was reasonably competent at a highly demanding and responsible police job. He also acquired useful experience for his later writing, notably the essays about shooting an elephant and seeing a man hanged and the less original novel *Burmese Days*, which borrows from E. M. Forster's *A Passage to India*. But during his time in Burma, although he clung to the idea that he might one day become a writer, he seems to have had no literary skills at all and none of a born writer's instinctive groping toward a style and a manner of his own.

Meyers is excellent and detailed on the provenance of Orwell's early work and on the overwhelming impression it gives of ordinariness, of the *via dolorosa* trodden by every young failed untalented writer. Ruth Pitter, a poet of the period now lost sight of but at her best remarkably good, is one of the many witnesses, critics, reviewers, and casual friends whom Meyers has talked to, or whose comments at the time he has tracked down. Ruth Pitter helped Orwell find a room in the squalid and broken-down part of London where she was living, but she was skeptical about his future as a writer:

> Ruth gave practical support, but shared his [Orwell's] parents' view of his literary ambitions. Mocking his lack of imagination, his earnest if amateurish efforts, she emphasized the egoistic aspects of being a writer. Though she was a poet herself, she dismissed him out of hand: "he was a wrong-headed young man who had thrown away a good

career, and was vain enough to think he could be an author. . . . We lent him an old oil-stove and he wrote a story about two young girls who lent an old man an oil-stove. . . . One story that never saw the light of day began 'Inside the park, the crocuses were out.' Oh dear, I'm afraid we did laugh."

Yet this was the man whom V. S. Pritchett was to describe as "the wintry conscience of a generation." As well as being himself a self-punishing romantic, Orwell offers another contrast: the writer who did not seem a talented or remarkable young man who goes on to become a saint, sage, and seer almost by accident.

Or rather by a series of accidents. As a child and young man Orwell had always had a bad chest and lungs and was in a condition later to be described by a doctor as pre-tubercular. He needed to take care of himself, but given his temperament, care was the last thing he was prepared to take; nor were his "lower upper-middle class" parents the sort to make a fuss over him. One can hardly blame them since their difficult son treated them with impatience and scarcely concealed boredom. Bad food and endless "tramping" in bad weather in his quest not only for what Meyers aptly calls "the joy of destitution" but for literary material out of which to construct his writing made it certain that the lung condition would steadily worsen.

So it did, but as in the case of D. H. Lawrence, not to mention so many geniuses of the first romantic period, tuberculosis and the arts can go hand in hand and can turn out to be the most productive of bedfellows. Art, and its fulfillment, care nothing about the artist's own life, which is usually forfeited in the process. Lawrence and Orwell at least survived a good deal longer than did most of their nineteenth-century predecessors.

Then came the Spanish war. Orwell was probably too self-willed and too egotistic ever to be a convinced Communist, but here was the perfect moment for both having a hard time and finding something real and urgent to write about. His experience at the front, where he was wounded, and still more in Barcelona, soon banished from his heart and mind all considerations except disillusion and intense anger. He had joined the Anarchists' faction in the Republican cause: its members were his comrades in the common struggle, and yet they were soon being hunted down like rats by the Stalinists on their own side and shot whenever found. Orwell and Georges Kopp themselves barely escaped. Back in London Orwell wrote his first remarkable book, indeed for many good judges his best book, *Homage to Catalonia*, which he had great difficulty getting published in the climate of a London intelligentsia secretly or openly in sympathy with Stalinism and the Party line.

For Orwell loyalty and decency were overwhelmingly what counted, and here they had been outraged by those Communists who were still the official heroes of the Spanish war. Orwell characteristically remained unmoved by the fact that if the war was going to be won, the Stalinists were crucial to winning it: they alone possessed the iron discipline which later made it possible for Russia to win the war against Hitler. What counted for Orwell was that his fellow fighters against Franco were being killed by Communists and that this fact had become obscured in the conventional left-liberal accounts of the war.

Orwell had the same sort of trouble getting *Animal Farm* published. The left-wing firm of Gollancz would not look at it, alleging that while the war was on it was our duty to support our Soviet ally, presumably as much in its politics as its military endeavors. The conservative T. S. Eliot at Faber and Faber was equally cautious but more insinuating. His letter of rejection to Orwell was all Jesuitical courtesy, pointing out with some justification, in view of what was to come in *Nineteen Eighty-Four*, that the overall effect is simply one of negation:

> After all, your pigs are far more intellectual than the other animals, and therefore the best qualified to run the farm—in fact, there couldn't have been an Animal Farm at all without them: so that what was needed (someone might argue) was not more communism but more public spirited pigs.

Meyers is quick to point out the speciousness of this argument:

> Eliot willfully ignored the crucial passage—inspired perhaps by Orwell's first exhilarating visit to revolutionary Barcelona—in which he wrote that after [the farm animals] drove out Farmer Jones and

before the pigs took over, "the work of the farm went like clockwork. The animals were happy as they had never conceived it possible to be."

Nonetheless Eliot's argument remains a cogent one. In Orwell's two last and by far his most popular books—runaway successes that have been translated into many languages—the overall effect, politically speaking, is purely negative, amounting to a good deal less even than Voltaire's calm advice at the end of *Candide*: "*Il faut cultiver notre jardin.*" For Orwell there is "hope" only in the "proles," just as there was hope in the sturdy decency and limited intellect of Boxer the cart-horse, whom the pigs send to the slaughterhouse when he can no longer work.

Allegories are notorious simplifiers, and Orwell liked to see political matters in simple black-and-white terms. There is something prophetic all the same about the negativism of *Animal Farm* and of *Nineteen Eighty-Four*: they look forward to the climate of today, and to our contemporary indifference to ideology, as well as history. Despite the timidity of the publishers, the two books were in fact perfectly timed to catch the rising alarm at the methods of Soviet communism and its international threat, as well as a more general distrust of the secretive and authoritarian regimes that had inevitably grown up under wartime procedures in both England and America. Propaganda was not just a Nazi or a Communist instrument of government, and Orwell's satire on it—crude but frightening and easy to understand—passed at once into current speech and attitude. Some animals were indeed more equal than others, as every citizen was able to perceive, and Meyers ingeniously quotes the opinion of Eve in Milton's *Paradise Lost*, which he may well be right in suggesting was in Orwell's mind: Eve's ambition is to be "more equal" and sometimes "superior."

What seems most moving and most memorable today in Orwell's famous books is also what is most innocent and indeed naive: the character and fate of Boxer the cart-horse, and the simple pleasures of love and private possessions (the Victorian paperweight again) which still survive in the nightmare world of *Nineteen Eighty-Four*. And yet crafty old Eliot was no doubt right in suggesting that the good, simple, decent animals, with their naive ideals, could not have run a farm successfully. Orwell may have felt sure they could have, but for him, as for most idealists, human nature was how he preferred to see it rather than what the centuries had shown it to be.

He was a good man and a gallant fighter notwithstanding, although his personal life was dogged, as might all too clearly have been expected, by the kind of bad luck that masochists sometimes attract. Orwell longed for children, but he was probably sterile as a result of tuberculosis, while Eileen had troubles which may in any case have prevented conception and led to the tumor from which she died. They adopted a little boy, on whom Orwell lavished loving but clumsy attention. After his wife died he went to live with the child on the island of Jura, one of the most remote and inhospitable of the Hebrides, with a vile climate—a home about as unsuitable as could be imagined for a tubercular writer who had to keep in touch with London's journals and literary scene. It was a paradise for self-punishment, but even Orwell was forced to make it a little more inhabitable after the phenomenal success of *Animal Farm* and *Nineteen Eighty-Four*.

In his last months Orwell married Sonia Brownell, an attractive woman who had been an editorial assistant on Cyril Connolly's magazine *Horizon*, and she did much to cheer him up at the end. Not that he had ever been short on ladies to cherish and support him. Meyers is particularly good on a sex life more colorful and varied than had been previously supposed in so overtly puritanical a man. But Meyers also quotes some bitterly misogynistic diaries written shortly before Orwell's death accusing some women of being congenitally dirty and slovenly as well as sexually insatiable. To the end there was much of Swift in him.

Would he have written more and more remarkable books had he survived? He was so ill when finishing *Nineteen Eighty-Four* that he could barely complete it, joking indomitably that no writer died until he had said all that he wanted to say. As "the wintry conscience of a generation" his work had been well done, and as his biographer rightly claims, its qualities, shining "like pebbles in a clear stream," remain "universally appealing." His death at the age of forty-seven was a sad loss to letters, as it was to writers and public men of conscience and integrity. Anthony Powell told me the funeral was the most heartbreaking he had ever attended.

The New York Review of Books, 2001

13

Mr. Toad

Evelyn Waugh (1903–1966)

Evelyn Waugh
by Selina Hastings

WHEN *Put Out More Flags* was published in March 1942, Alan Pryce Jones reviewed it in the *New Statesman*, praising the writer's "dead-accurate" social sense and his vituperative use of "the unpopular weapons of economy and proportion," and yet concluding that the book and its author were "fundamentally without humor." A surprising charge: but, on reflection, surprisingly accurate. Waugh, in his black style, had no more humor than P. G. Wodehouse in his rosy style. Waugh deeply admired Wodehouse, and read and re-read him all his working life.

But humor in fiction is about an interest in real people, and Waugh had no such interest. Neither, probably, had Wodehouse. Both knew what they could do, and did it to perfection. "I shall have to go on hoeing the old butler row," remarked Wodehouse in a letter, with his usual sunny equability. Waugh, as his last stories reveal, could not do without his Ambrose Silks and Agatha Runcibles and Peter Pastmasters. But one must not press the analogy too far. Waugh did become interested in himself as a literary model—very much so—and *The Ordeal of Gilbert Pinfold* is a masterpiece of self-portraiture, one of the very best in English fiction. Even so it might never have been created had it not been for the remarkable things that happened to its author and his consciousness, as a result of a cocktail of alcohol and assorted drugs, and of the true events which are graphically examined in its story.

Up to middle age, Waugh had all the adventurer's disdain for self-scrutiny, and his vision of the Catholic faith and of high society—the world, the flesh, and the devil—came to have an inflexible and objective conviction about it. He thought he saw what was, and what should be; and his fascination with the idea of high society was closely connected with a contempt for the way it actually was. The Church of Rome was the model of rational and historical perfection, and an aristocracy, or at least an upper class, worthy of the name should live up to it. His satires batten on the discrepancy, but he has no real interest in the individuals who actually have to make up such a society, even at the highest level.

It is here that his achievement as a novelist is so different from that of his contemporary Anthony Powell. Both were influenced by cinema, but while the early Waugh film is run at manic speed the Powell is reduced to slow motion. Powell's narrator spends a lot of time "reflecting" on the people he meets, their differences and their resemblances. He is fascinated by them, and his fascination is communicated to the reader. Waugh, for example, in the persona of Guy Crouchback in the *Men at Arms* series, is only seduced by a vision of what should be: wife, Church, family, class—all in their proper places. Such idealism is hardly appropriate for a novelist, no matter how he may feed on the negative consequences of its failure.

Yet people evidently entered Waugh's emotional life from time to time (at least up to the time of his second marriage) about whom his novels could not, and could never have had, anything to say. In the bleak period after his divorce, before he knew from the officials of his Church whether he would ever be allowed to remarry, he seems to have forced himself to fall in love with, or at least to pursue, any congenial girl who came his way. Such sins were perfectly acceptable to a Church with all the apparatus of penance and atonement. But Waugh's heart was not in it, and he seems also to have lacked sexual confidence and drive. The result was a certain amount of harm done to other people, the sort of people for whose individuality he could have had no feeling or interest. What must he have thought, for instance, of this letter that he received from one of his brief lovers of the period? There is no way in which it or its sender could have been used in a novel: it has nothing to do with stage figures like Brenda and Tony Last.

> It is too difficult not to write to you now, Evelyn, because things have not been going well—because it's nearly March 13th which was the day you jokingly suggested we might meet—each year till I am 70. And so I suppose that day will be for me a kind of lovely agony for ever and ever . . . I think of you all the time when I am making love, until the word and Evelyn are almost synonymous! And in the darkness each night & the greyness of each morning when I wake I remember you face—& your voice and your body and everything about you so earnestly and intensely that you become almost tangibly beside me. And after that I can forget you for the day (except when I am alone) . . . It is only for the next few years. After I am forty I won't want to see you . . . Then even the impossible possibility of having your child will be gone.

The letter was from Joyce Gill, whom Evelyn had known as Joyce Fagan when he was an undergraduate. Selina Hastings quotes it in her biography without any particular comment, but something in her style and approach shows how much she is aware of its import.

For this is a biography of such exceptional perception and sympathy that it quite revived my own interest in Waugh, which overkill in the industry had definitely led to flag. Martin Stannard's two big volumes were thoughtfully written and well researched, but they set out from a contemporary standpoint to portray Waugh as a monster and a grotesque, redeemed in part by a staunch belief and conviction of sin. That is no doubt true enough; but like all biographical puttings of people in their place, it avoided the homelier and more contradictory texture of the Waugh being. That love letter, for instance, what did he feel about it, what unexpectedly endearing aspects of himself had inspired this cry of loving desolation? It was a far cry from the bright young people, and from the world of Waugh's own aborted first marriage, about which Selina Hastings is a great deal more intelligently though unemphatically understanding than any previous commentator. How would Waugh actually deal with a person who might write a letter like that? How indeed had he

already dealt with her? She could only be wholly excluded from his literary and creative imagination, the imagination that had transformed, in its
wounded and brilliant malignancy, his own young wife and her lover into
the Brenda Last and John Beaver of A *Handful of Dust*.

It had been essential for Waugh to transmute what had gone on and
what had not gone on during that brief marriage into what John Cowper
Powys would call his "Life Illusion": the sense of things, that is, by which
we all need to exist in our separate ways. In Waugh's case such a "life illusion" was unusually pugnacious and positive. Very fully, yet in what
comes to seem almost in passing, Selina Hastings shows us the young
couple—He-Evelyn and She-Evelyn—setting up house in Canonbury,
among the bright little pieces of furniture Waugh had made, and pasted
over with colored cuttings and old postage stamps. An idyllic scene and
almost a Pooterish one, not so distant from the menage which his parents
had once set off with together in the North End Road. Snobbishness does
not seem to have been at all the problem, although She-Evelyn came
from a much grander background than he did. For A *Handful of Dust*
Waugh turned himself into the last of a line of doomed country gentry,
cursed with a fickle Guinevere, but the diminutive, bright-eyed, squirrel-
like couple their friends saw seemed perfectly suited to each other, and to
their bijou North London residence.

And yet the worm was already in the bud. On their honeymoon She-
Evelyn at once fell ill, and with such alarming symptoms that doctors and
nurses had to be got, at great expense since they were by then in Port
Said. Evelyn tried sitting at his wife's bedside like a model young husband
and reading her P. G. Wodehouse, but for relief he soon rushed away to
stay with old friends in Athens. It turned out that she loathed having
Wodehouse read to her in any case, though she did not say so; and she
was also convinced he was really hating her for being ill. In reality, he
does not seem to have had much idea of her at all, and when they got
home again he was soon off to the old pub near Oxford where he was
accustomed to write. He set about *Vile Bodies*. Left alone in London,
She-Evelyn went to as many parties as she could—she adored parties and
Waugh did not—and she met and went out with John Heygate, an amiable and talented young man about town who, like Waugh, worked on
the newspapers. She also went to bed with him, and then confessed to her

husband. Heygate was having a leisurely motoring holiday in Germany with Anthony Powell, to whom the husband dispatched an Aeschylean telegram. "Instruct Heygate return immediately Waugh."

The fateful episode is worth dwelling on at some length, not only because it became so central to Waugh's subsequent life and outlook but because his biographer has so admirably contrived to fill in the cracks in what is now an almost legendary story with the ordinary humdrum matter of daily existence. Waugh's real life, like everybody else's, was of course full of the ordinariness which biography and legend have ignored, without necessarily seeking to avoid. There are people and events, like the woman of the love letter, which have not part in the story others told about him, and the "illusion" on which he based his own personality. All such matters come crowding in here, although the book is not over-long by modern standards of biography, and its spare and elegant presentation is commendably uncluttered by the kind of tales with which devotees of Waugh and his circle are already too familiar. The picture of him that emerges is thus in the subtlest and best sense an unusual one.

Not only could Waugh never have digested in his art the kind of real people with whom he necessarily came in daily contact, but he could never admit the crushing banality of ordinary life and its motivations. "What shall I do?" She-Evelyn asked her flat-mate Nancy Mitford when things began to come out.

> To Nancy, the problem was not serious: it was the sort of mischance at a party which could happen to anyone. "Tell Evelyn it wasn't your fault," she said, "and that you love him." "But I don't love him," She-Evelyn replied, going on to confess that she had never loved her husband, had married only to get away from home.

This was not the sort of humdrum situation to which even Nina and Adam in *Vile Bodies* could afford to be subject; nor would a Waugh persona sit smoking his pipe and reading Wodehouse to his wife, when she longed to be showered with anxiety and endearments. Oddly enough, too, Waugh seems to have been as cool about sex as it can be inferred that Wodehouse also was. Art, in both their cases, has to sustain itself at a remarkably artificial level above existence, although Waugh's great skill consists in part of appearing to demonstrate starkly to his reader that this is not so.

His friend Henry Green, quite a different sort of performer as a novelist, got a cold reception when he made the same point in a letter about *A Handful of Dust*. Yet he was the first to see that Waugh's brand of realism in fact depends on a rather cozy kind of fantasy, verging on self-parody in *Scoop*, where William Boot of Boot Magna Hall, and his column "Lush Places" in the *Daily Beast*, bear an odd resemblance to the goings on in another of Waugh's lifelong favorites, *The Wind in the Willows*. Waugh's Catholic and hierarchic nostalgia for the Great Good Place blends with deceptive ease into a more conventional Edwardian nostalgia; while Boot Magna, as Selina Hastings points out, is Waugh's idealized version of a place he actually detested: his in-laws', the Herberts' house at Pixton. It becomes in the book "the ultimate haven, where there is no pressure to do anything, and one day, one year, is exactly like the last . . . William's mother and his three uncles sat round the table. They had finished eating, and were sitting there, as they often sat for an hour or so, doing nothing at all. Priscilla alone was occupied, killing wasps in the honey on her plate." Killing wasps "with a teaspoon" is not only one of the few incongruously blood-thirsty activities indulged in by Wodehouse's heroes and heroines, but has an odd status in the Waugh family archive. In his unfinished memoir, *A Little Learning*, Waugh blandly records that his paternal grandfather killed a wasp that was buzzing round his wife by pressing it against her forehead with the knob of his cane.

Selina Hastings brings out very well this deceptive Waugh formula for achieving widespread popularity. He knew how to combine sentiment of a very English sort with the new cynicism, a bracing heartlessness appropriate to the modern age. But when the formula failed, as with the character of Julia in *Brideshead*, we are virtually in the world of Ouida and the Sheiks. The enormous middle-brow success of *Brideshead* was ironical, for Waugh's grand friends all thought it rubbish. Waugh told Ronnie Knox that Katherine Asquith "had detested the book to the end and beyond, and said the characters did not exist either in real life or faery," adding sadly that he had after all "grown up in Metroland, and didn't know any other world except at secondhand or at a great distance." Perhaps the real trouble was that he had never shown any true curiosity about the nature of that world, or examined its denizens with absorbed and conscientious relish, as Ted Jeavons does in the *Dance to the Music of Time* series of Anthony Powell.

Waugh's second wife, with whom he lived in great harmony, was the perfect example of an aristocrat who gently declined to play the game that Waugh expected of the class as a whole. He expected polished silver and white tablecloths, and "Laura, shouldn't there be two salt cellars when there are more than four people?" — but, as his biographer observes, she preferred to live her own way, "anxious only to keep the peace and her husband in a good mood," though "if necessary she could be scathing. 'When Evelyn is in one of his bad moods,' she said with feeling to a surprised Ann Rothermere, 'we send him to a witch in Somerset who spits at him.'"

His army career probably did as much as anything to show Waugh the difference between his view of things and what really went on in life: he was certainly brave, and he assumed he was being a good soldier even when he involuntarily escaped all the slog of the war by making himself so intolerable that no officer would trust or employ him. The upshot genuinely saddened him. The Don Quixote or Mr. Toad that lurks in all of us was with him ever rampant; and the dyer's hand could never have been subdued to the service it worked in. But it made him sadder and wiser, and disillusion with himself and his role in the army is the most telling aspect of *Brideshead*, as it is the origin of the masterpiece he produced in *The Ordeal of Gilbert Pinfold*.

This excellent biography not only humanizes him, by playing down his more outrageous aspects, but by understanding the true nature of the world he aspired to live in, it shows how so idiosyncratically good a writer actually needs, in his own way, to get things wrong. Not that he always did. About some things, such as the world of newspaper journalism, he was dead right, and is proved more right every day. Who can forget the fairy-tale William Boot's wholly down-to-earth associates, Corker, Shumble, Whelper, and Pigge, "who had loitered together of old on many a doorstep, and forced an entry into many a stricken home"?

London Review of Books, 1994

14

God's Greene

Graham Greene (1904–1991)

The Captain and the Enemy
by Graham Greene

Graham Greene
by Neil McEwan

A Reader's Guide to Graham Greene
by Paul O'Prey

THE GENRE OF thrillers and detective stories has strong appeal to deconstructural critics, to whose gimlet eyes its repetitive rituals and devices are wide open. But its more common readers generally make a more downright Johnsonian distinction between those they enjoy and the ones they don't go for. It is the simple distinction between what is convincing and what is not, what seems "real" and what seems false or made-up. No use the literary lads telling us that it's *all* made-up, that the whole thing is composed not of life but of "literariness." We know what we like, and cling sturdily to the old distinction.

Thus, for me, Raymond Chandler is real, so is even Ian Fleming, so above all is Sherlock Holmes. Unreal and therefore not good are Agatha Christie, Len Deighton, Father Brown, Dorothy Sayers, and too many others. It would take far too long for me to try to rationalize the crude distinction, nor could it be done satisfactorily, but two requirements emerge: one, that the work must have some inner intensity, the need and thus the belief of the writer behind it; and, that the "side effects," the ones that really matter, should not only have a personal appeal but must exhibit the author's natural enjoyment, relish, individuality, and curiosity. Ian Fleming's tense inward phobia contrasts with this pleasure and his capacity for sharing it, so that traveling, drinking, meeting people in his books all become vividly pleasurable to the reader.

Graham Greene has the inner intensity all right, but not, for me, the convincing side effects. All essentially thrillers, his books create their own world, as Conan Doyle's do, but here the rituals and repetitions are not merely formulaic—a trait common to the genre—but have a deliberate and unremitting monotony about them, like that of the old dentist's drill. It is as if Greene had hit on the idea of making the properties of the genre itself its penance and its *via dolorosa*, as if he were telling us that the things we enjoy in thrillers are themselves an earnest of what is most boring, most detestable, and most damned about life. An ingenious device, certainly, for it uses the artifice of the genre against itself, standing the tricks or pleasure and suspense on their heads and making them seem like the monotonous capers of the damned. That, Greene seems to indicate with a sour smile, is how to bring real life into the wholly made-up world of art.

The method has its drawbacks. You cannot parody Conrad, or even, convincingly, Ian Fleming, because the great artist constantly surprises and delights and absorbs us in something new, and even the more modest one has his comparable moments. But a good parody of Graham Greene not only sounds like him but *is* like him, and would go on being so until the end of a whole book. (Greene once won a *New Statesman* competition for a parody of his style by sending one himself, anonymously.) He himself is well aware of the fatal flaw in his technique, and all his books can be seen as obsessional efforts to break out of it—into comedy, the picaresque, the apparently insouciant. All come to grief on the same miscalculation, which is also, no doubt, the bedrock of Greene's own nature. By bringing his own vision of reality into his novels as a literary device he has committed the thriller writer's ultimate sin: he has used the properties that should give the impression of the real—no more and no less—as if they revealed a pre-existing truth. The contemporary cinema does much the same thing. It uses all the devices, but—a long way now from its innocent and unpretentious beginnings—insists on being taken "seriously" as a precondition of using them.

Greene's remarkable fecundity, and popularity, testify nonetheless to the success of his method. A thriller mixed with spirituality—always the same, always reassuring and reliable—has shown itself over the years to be a formula that cannot fail to appeal. The gloom and despondency that Greene achieves have proved a more satisfying draw than happy endings. In one sense Greene has invented a prose equivalent of the Sad Ballad and the Shropshire Lad, and with a strong flavor of the cinema. Who can forget that moment at the end of the movie *The Third Man* when at the funeral of the villanous Harry Lime, played by Orson Welles, whom she had loved, the actress Alida Valli walks without a glance straight past the hopeful hero Joseph Cotton, and away down an artful perspective of a somber road? A film critic in the Thirties, ultimately on the short-lived but influential periodical *Night and Day*, Greene had a passion for Erich Von Stroheim, about whom he wrote as "climbing a ladder in skin-tight Prussian breeches towards an innocent bed." The words are recalled in Anthony Powell's *Memoirs*, where he also tells the tale of the libel action against Greene and the magazine *Night and Day* on behalf of Shirley Temple, an action whose award against the magazine finally undid its shaky finances and caused it to close down.

Greene had—characteristically—committed the unforgivable sin of suggesting that Shirley was not quite as sexually innocent as she looked. His books have always had their own variation on the "broken blossoms" theme: that of the young girl, like Rose in *Brighton Rock* and Helen in *The Heart of the Matter*, who is innocent indeed, but also desperately avid for love and sex. Avid, in fact, for damnation. As Paul O'Prey reports in his helpful little book, the master of having it both ways was deeply impressed when he was writing *Brighton Rock* in the early Thirties by the essay on Baudelaire that T. S. Eliot had just published. It contained the following sentence:

So far as we are human, what we do must be either evil or good; so far as we do evil or good we are human; and it is better, in a paradoxical way, to do evil than to do nothing; at least we exist.

There is a Greene model broken blossom in his novel *The Captain and the Enemy*: Liza, a waif who loves the mysterious confidence man, the Captain, but is made pregnant by the young narrator's father, who compels her to have an abortion. By way of compensation the Captain virtually kidnaps the narrator from his boarding school and presents him to Liza. He then slips away. Neither is particularly gratified by this arrangement, but it lasts until Liza dies of cancer, and the narrator prepares to join the Captain in his strange, romantic, and nefarious doing, now going on in Panama. The feeling between Liza and the Captain is genuinely touching, as such relationships usually are in Greene; and the Captain himself is a variation on a reliable model: the dashing liar with a secret sorrow and a heart of gold. Greene may even unconsciously have had in mind Alan Breck in Stevenson's *Kidnapped*, about whom Henry James admiringly wrote that his creator "both sees through him and admires him." Seeing through and admiring are as one to Greene, for whom the Captain is a useful adjunct to the kind of modern thriller, like his own fairly recent one, *The Human Factor*, in which the spy is working for both sides, or possibly for neither, and in which motive and outcome remain corrupted but enigmatic.

Greene's admirers would no doubt retort that unlike other thriller writers he manages to inject into such works a genuine sense of right and wrong, of both human decency and a terrible expression of human indifference and callousness. That may well be so, but right and wrong have always had a rather incongruous and ineffective relation in Greene's novels to Good and Evil. The latter has always put the alcohol in the drink, as Greene admits in *Brighton Rock*, where the decent but insipid Ida, with her sense of what's right, is eclipsed by the doomed Rose and unspeakable Pinkie, whose taste has been "extinguished by stronger foods—Good and Evil." It is part of Greene's strategy in his postwar novels—in fact since *The Quiet American*—to cut down on the Catholic membership and ritual (even the Third Man was one, as we learn from a single sentence), and the Captain and young narrator have no evident religious affiliations. Even so, the Captain while shaving "turns solemnly away from the mirror, lifting his razor much as a priest lifts the host." Built up as a shady and equivocal figure, illustrating Greene's favorite lines from "Bishop Blougram's Apology" about our interest being "on the dan-

gerous edge of things," the Captain has all the literary and spiritual privileges enjoyed by the damned (who of course never are damned) in
Greene's world.

This is something of a handicap in creating suspense, because as soon
as we meet the Captain we know he is "one of those," a sinner, a nonbor-
ing man, ultimately a protégé of the Holy Ghost. So it comes as no surprise when he finally takes off in a crazy little plane to try to blow up
Somoza (today it would be to go after the Contras). For sheer unreality
masquerading as "realism" it would be difficult to beat the closing
sequences, which have a strong flavor of Humphrey Bogart and Ingrid
Bergman in *Casablanca*, with Greene's remorseless pessimism merely
the calculated obverse of the optimism required by the film. Even the
narrator, a singularly irritating young man, gets his comeuppance, when
he has "written" the story (he hopes to be a writer) in a trick ending which
the film version, should there be one, will no doubt enjoy doing its own
way. Only the Captain is capable of love and of inspiring love, the accolade bestowed on all Greene's sinners, from Scobie in *The Heart of the
Matter* to the Third Man. One even suspects a certain irony in Greene's
epigraph from the works of George A. Birmingham, which makes a great
showing on the title page. "Will you be sure to know the good side from
the bad, the Captain from the enemy?" Of course we will, because this is
Greeneland.

However sophisticated his story there is indeed something basically
childlike about Greene's good guys and bad guys, the former being
mostly Communists and some Catholics; sinners and criminals and traitors; blacks and underdogs. The latter tend to include all establishment
figures, the rich, the innocent, and Americans. One suspects that some of
his most enthusiastic readers come from the bad class and enjoy slum-
ming. No good asking, either, how "serious" all this is, for Greene protects himself with an invulnerable cover of frivolity, which suggests,
reasonably enough, that out of frivolity come all the really important matters in life. He is frivolous, but for me he is never genuinely funny; humor
requires a simple enjoyment of life which is of course not in Greene's
nature. He manipulates black fun as carefully as he does his scenarios,
which like the films they resemble are set up with all appropriate artifice.
As much as in a good film or a play, say, by Racine, the frame is too care-

fully determined, too founded in traditional belief, to allow for what Hannah Arendt called the banality of evil. Impossible to imagine Greene making a story out of those Catholic priests who set up an escape line for the mass murderers of the SS who had incinerated Europe's Jews. Even Greene could hardly get out of that one, or convert such men into the good guys of his mythology. He prefers a villain who has been endangering the lives of children by watering down the penicillin. That is selected drama.

Excellent and useful compilations as O'Prey's and McEwan's books both are—Neil McEwan is particularly good on recent developments in Greeneland—neither introduction to his work asks the simple but fundamental question: is it false or true? In his summing-up McEwan writes:

> The innocents who ought to know better, the successful and the complacent, the uninvolved comedians of his books, may be believers— Pyle [*The Quiet American*] dies for democracy and Rycker [*A Burnt-Out Case*] thinks himself a good Catholic—but because they are blind to the real world, which appalls and dizzies the Characters who see it honestly, their allegiances are worthless.

That is good, and plausible, but the real problem remains unsolved. The real ambiguity is never in the story but in the author himself. Belief here, or what Coleridge called "the willing suspension of disbelief," is total: we either believe in him or we don't. It is possible to believe, say, in Sherlock Holmes as a creation but not in Greene as a creator. Ultimately his world stands or falls by whether or not we believe a word he says. Greene has, perhaps by accident, got himself into the position of God.

It is an interesting literary irony, and one that would not in the least concern us in the case of Kipling or Conrad, who live in, and present us with, a relative world. It may reveal that Greene is too naive to be claimed as a great writer. If he is not, as it were, God, the power and glory are in the end no more than literary devices: not themselves deceptions, but whose tale in the end is only of himself.

A story from his own autobiography, *A Sort of Life*, may serve as a final illustration. As a student at Oxford he suffered from fits of boredom and depression, and took to going for solitary walks carrying a small revolver.

In some quiet spot he would spin the cylinder, loaded in one of the six chambers, put the muzzle to his temple, and fire, with one chance in six of being killed. This is known as Russian roulette, and as a reviewer was quick to point out it involves an ingenious deception. A single bullet in a revolver whose cylinder can be spun freely will always—well, nearly always—be carried by its weight to the bottom of the cylinder when it comes to rest, and thus will not be fired when the trigger is next pulled. Did Greene know that he was giving God not a one in six chance of ending the affair, but more like a one in six thousand? The point caught the imagination of the readers of the periodical in which the review appeared, and a brisk correspondence ensued, in which the Master himself, however, took no part, remaining enigmatic. The terms of the treaty, or the tricks of the trade, were not divulged.

The New York Review of Books, 1989

PART II

The English Poets

15

Family Man

William Wordsworth (1770–1850)

The Love Letters of William and Mary Wordsworth
edited by Beth Darlington, published by Cornell University Press

My Dearest Love: Letters of William and Mary Wordsworth
edited in facsimile by Beth Darlington, foreword by Jonathan
    Wordsworth, published by The Trustees of Dove Cottage and
    printed by the Scolar Press

WILLIAM WORDSWORTH'S POEMS are like one's parents' clothes—always out of fashion. John Donne is always our contemporary, even more so is Stendhal, who was in fact Wordsworth's contemporary. How does one name these feelings, or rather how can one rationalize them? Why have Donne and Stendhal in their writings a modern mind and Wordsworth an irremediably dated one? He is as egotistic as they, as intent on impressing his own consciousness on paper. But perhaps, as Keats intuited, it is because Wordsworth in his poetry appears as the "Egotistical Sublime." That, where posterity is concerned, is a fatal combination. Most artists redeem their natural solipsism as artists by continual suggestions in their art of personal chaos, drama, disaster, accident-proneness, what Auden calls "human unsuccess." They are not in the least sublime, they are "human, all too human"; and we respond to that. We admire the artist's talent for self-destruction.

But no poet could be less accident-prone than Wordsworth. If he fell he always fell on his feet. He is carried away by the Revolution; he meets a charming French girl; he gets her pregnant. Ten years later—the war having conveniently come between them—he is engaged to a charming English girl. He meets his former flame and illegitimate daughter. He explains; he regrets. They quite see the point. Annette must have been an admirable, generous woman. These qualities are probably what attracted William to her in the first place; his own virtues had the knack of bringing out the virtues in others. Women loved him, but, more remarkably, they loved him unpossessively. When he married his childhood sweetheart Mary Hutchinson, his sister Dorothy lovingly accepted the situation with no evident strain, and became a sister to his wife and a second mother to his children.

"The family of love" their friends called them. Do we detect in that fond phrase a faint note of exasperation? Too close an exposure to the domestic sublime seems to have alienated Coleridge, who when he stayed with his old friends became withdrawn and lapsed into old habits of nipping at the brandy and the laudanum. His feelings were further exacerbated by his own love for Sara Hutchinson, Mary's sister, but she, like the other women, had no eyes for anyone but William. William took their attentions sublimely for granted, but, as these new letters reveal, he was deeply and privately in love with his wife and loved her more with every month that passed. He had made the perfect choice.

> A creature not too bright or good
> For human nature's daily food. . . .
> A perfect woman, nobly planned,
> To warn, to comfort, and command.

We don't talk about it like that anymore, and most writers never have; nor, in the midst of connubial bliss, would they be murmurously walking up and down composing *The Excursion* and revising *The Prelude* ("Yet another / Of these remembrances . . .") until summoned in for a mid-morning snack of "two fresh scones baked by the cook."

> God and the cook are very good,
> Says William, relishing his food

jingled Dorothy fondly. Ladies later on took a different view. "God, what a *Pa*-man!" Katherine Mansfield noted in her journal, after reading some Wordsworth memoirs. Coleridge, in all his troubles, seems to have thought so too, and this is probably at the back of his remarks on the subject to Henry Crabb Robinson in 1811. "Wordsworth is by nature incapable of being in Love, tho' no man more tenderly attached; hence he ridicules the existence of any other passion, than a compound of Lust with Esteem & Friendship, & confined to one Object, first by accidents of Association, and permanently, by the force of Habit & a sense of Duty."

This is a judgment with two interesting implications. Coleridge suggests that Wordsworth knew nothing of the wildness of the emotion, in life or in poetry, nothing of deep romantic chasms and women wailing for their demon lovers. But, more damagingly, that he had all the complacent connubial satisfactions of Monsieur Prudhomme, the phrases "confined to one Object" and "a sense of Duty" implying that something furtive on the side would not necessarily have come amiss if it could be arranged. Coleridge, in fact, while appearing to present his old friend as *honnête homme* and warmly honorable family man, in fact, and perhaps by intention, suggests how morally and emotionally commonplace he is.

This presentation is in a sense much more subtly depreciatory than Shelley's jibe in *Peter Bell the Third* about Wordsworth as a "solemn and unsexual man" who "touched the hem of Nature's shift / Felt faint and scarcely dared uplift / The closest, all-concealing garment." An ascetic in spiritual love with nature is, or was at that time, a more impressive poetic persona than Coleridge's philistine who scoffs at passion and sees himself and his fellows habituated to a mere mechanical uxoriousness. Shelley's Peter Bell Wordsworth is a rum cove, a bit ludicrous, but hauntingly absorbed, single-mindedly intent on the places in which he finds poetry, the stones on the highway to which he gives a moral life.

It may be that Shelley's lampoon is more just and more understanding than Coleridge's utterances of friendship, though Coleridge at this time was writing in sorrowful envy and resentment. And yet perhaps Wordsworth *was* in essence a very ordinary man, an ordinary man speaking to men, and perhaps Keats's exasperated phrase recognizes that in him mere human egotism did aspire, and not always without incongruity, to the quality and style of the sublime. From the beginning, and not just by 1810–1812, the dates of the most recently discovered letters published by both Cornell University Press and the Trustees of Dove Cottage, the sublime was in the style rather than in the man himself. Indeed this must be the nub of our feeling that Wordsworth does belong so completely to the past, and more specifically to the poetic past as represented by the eighteenth century.

It was natural in that period for the man and his style to be two separate things, representing two recognized aspects of social behavior. Wordsworth changed both, but equally in his curious way kept them separate. We look in vain in his work for the true ease, the rambling and inconsequential but always growing and vivifying speech of Coleridge as poet and man combined. In his simplest poems Wordsworth has put on his singing robes, however unusual their design. Coleridge is not only more like us because of his habits of thought, but more like a modern poet because they are also his natural utterance and expression.

There is something both Augustan and wholly Wordsworthian about what Wordsworth wrote to his wife, his "dearest Mary," as he looked forward to rejoining her in June 1812, after his absence from her in London. "That very evening, viz Tuesday, I had been reading at Lamb's the Tintern abbey, and repeated a 100 times to myself the passage 'O Sylvan Wye thou Wanderer through the woods,' thinking of past times, & Dorothy, dear Dorothy, and you my Darling." Who but Wordsworth would have talked about his own poem as "*the* Tintern abbey" in this way—that definite article is unmistakably characteristic—and what other poet than he would linger with such unabashed fondness on a poem he had written many years previously? Many poets, as one can tell from the way they recite their poems, abandon them after they have done with them and put them out of mind. Not so Wordsworth, and the relish with which he recalls the poem is like a family man fondly remembering a Christmas past, an anniversary, or shared family treat. Even his poems were sacred lares and penates for him, to be mused over again and again in the bosom of his family.

What a Pa-man indeed, and one who combined all the paternal virtues and affections idealized in the eighteenth century with poetry's new-style egotism (which we still so abundantly accept and possess), making them—incredibly—into one and the same thing. Wordsworth is both the modern poet creating and inhabiting his own unique and personal world of art, and the sublimely domestic family man. The two are not separated; and it is this that disconcerts and often repels the modern sensibility. We ought to respect and admire it—why don't we?

The answer must lie deep in our tradition of dissociation of poetry from the family. "Get out as early as you can / And don't have any kids yourself." Philip Larkin jests in his own way, but that way is on the level: he has remarked that deprivation is to him what daffodils were to Wordsworth, and daffodils stand for the whole of Wordsworth's natural-domestic style.

Of course the clever men at Yale and elsewhere, as well as the devoted work of the poet's direct descendant, the scholar Jonathan Wordsworth, have—if one may try to use the word without any hint of patronage—rehabilitated the poet humanly as well as intellectually. They have put him back in fashion, in a visionary company which includes all the best people, as one of ourselves today. But this has been done by deconstructing the style, tracing the way tropes work, and analyzing such out-of-the-way and fascinating pieces as the "Essays upon Epitaphs": it has not been done by restoring to us any intimacy with Wordsworth the man-poet and poet-man.

So will the discovery of these letters do the trick? It depends really what we want to see done; whether we feel that a red-blooded Wordsworth of not only warm domestic affections but of ardent sexual longings, a Wordsworth who passionately missed his wife in bed when he was away from her, is such a surprising and welcome figure to discover after the event. The publicity used in connection with the finding of the letters that revealed "Wordsworth in love" seems to me rather to miss the point here, and probably with intention. To think the more of a poet because he is revealed to have been sexually in love with his wife—this has surely all the vulgarity of the modern age about it.

The real interest of the letters is quite different. They show us neither a highly sexed man nor an egotistically sublime poet, but a comically familial human being, pouring out to his wife on paper what he was doing and whom he was meeting, what was the state of his digestion, his bowels, and his chronic piles (his "old enemy" as he called them); whether she should advise his leaving off wine altogether, and how the heavy breakfasts at grand houses made him feel uncomfortable all day. These domesticities are blended, often in a single and continuous sentence, with shrewd social and political comment, and even shrewder comments on the appearance and developments in their friends and relations. But—and this is the point—all such things are mixed up, too, with ecstatic avowals and happinesses of intimacy, which come caroling out of him all the more compellingly for the accents in which they are uttered.

> My sweet love how I long to see thee; think of me, wish for me, pray for me, pronounce my name when thou art alone, and upon thy pillow; and dream of me happily and sweetly.

It would not be quite true to say that any happy husband might write as artlessly as that, and in such heartfelt tones, for an artist has a way of conveying art's own sincerities even in his most informal moments. But this is certainly Wordsworth at the furthest remove from the egotistical sublime, at the closest to all uxorious and happy husbands. What is more, in declaring his feelings his tone confirms hers, for even if we had no letters of Mary's to match these we could be sure she felt about him the same way; and sure, too, that she would know he took as close and devoted an interest in all her views and ways, feelings and doings, as she in his. William required, nay, clamored, for as much and as detailed information about her poor sore mouth as he himself was furnishing about his poor sore behind.

This is the blessed small change of any truly happy relation. Whether it makes the discovery of these letters an important literary event is another matter. One thing that becomes plain is that William, like other young men, was prepared to sow wild oats abroad but certainly not at home. He *had* been very much attracted to Mary, once his childhood friend, and when she stayed for six months with him and Dorothy at Racedown in 1797 he fell deeply in love with her. An early letter almost uncannily anticipates a Hardy poem in its lyrically tender evocation of what *might* have happened.

> . . . unable to part from each other we might have come in sight of those hills which skirt the road for so many miles [the Malverns], and

thus continuing our journey (for we should have moved on at small expense) I fancied that we should have seen so deep into each others hearts, and been so fondly locked in each others arms that we should have braved the worst and parted no more. Under that tree I thought as I passed along we might have rested, of that stream might have drunk, in that thicket we might have hidden ourselves from the sun and from the eyes of the passenger.

Typically, and most endearingly, the passage mingles amiable thoughts of a nice cuddle under the bushes with an image of Adam and Eve in *Paradise Lost*. But it was not to be. Their financial situation made the idea of immediate marriage and a family not to be "braved" by a prudent young couple. William recalls it without regret, indeed as a natural augmentation of the love he now bears her ("O Mary I love you with a passion of love which grows till I tremble to think of its strength") and also with a desire for her to be with him now to share whatever he sees ("not having you at my side my pleasure is so imperfect that after a short look I had rather not see the objects at all").

William really did have cause to believe in a power that changes, as *The Excursion* informs us, "all accidents, converting them to good." Nothing mystical involved, he had found it empirically. Shortly after this correspondence closes, his little daughter Catharine and little son Thomas both died. Such child mortality was common, though Mary was heartbroken and William too. But the sorrows did not change, one feels, his profound inner conviction that mortal chances were on his side in some secret sense, that as a poet he was the equivalent of one of those favored generals of Napoleon who were considered "lucky."

This is the cause of his prolonged and in reality permanent estrangement from Coleridge. Coleridge was not lucky. The blind goddess had never been known to do him a good turn, even arranging (if his own report is to be trusted) that a person from Porlock should cut short the effusion of one of his greatest poems. Oddly enough the effective cause of these love letters between William and his wife was William's absence in 1812, staying in Grosvenor Square with his patrons Sir George and Lady Beaumont; his chief purpose was to effect a complete reconciliation with his old friend.

In this he was only partially successful. The trouble had started when Coleridge had been staying with the Wordsworths at Allan Bank, not too propitiously; and a rich friend, Basil Montagu, had suggested making a home for him in London, keeping him as tame poet and talker. Wordsworth very prudently warned Montagu of the possible drawback of Coleridge's habit and was going to counsel Coleridge against the scheme too, but found no opportunity. In consequence Montagu told Coleridge what Wordsworth had said, and it wounded Coleridge deeply. The formal reconciliation in London was at last made, but there was no getting over the real cause. Besides the old friends were now in some sense rivals; both in their various ways had made the fashion that was now sweeping polite society in England: for scenery and for cultured conversation. The wars had cut off the traditional Continental sources of these commodities. William was clearly gratified to find he was quite a lion in London circles, but Coleridge had set out to exploit the situation more methodically.

> Coleridge is to commence a course of six Lectures; One guinea the course upon the Drama. This is a most odious way of picking up money, and scattering about his own & his friend's thoughts. Lady B[eaumont] has taken 30 tickets, which she will have to force upon her friends and where she cannot succeed must abide by the Loss.

Alas, "his own and his friend's thoughts" tells us all. The two friends who had once held every inspiration in common were now assiduously cultivating their own sensibilities, their own plots of the new ground. And Coleridge, thought Wordsworth writing to Mary, was not only using his old friend's ideas but was doing his best to horn in on Wordsworth's particular patrons, the Beaumonts, and even slandering him to them. No, certainly that much-publicized reconciliation was in name only.

Nonetheless Wordsworth enjoyed London, enjoyed being taken seriously, being made much of in society. Eighteen hundred and twelve was the year of England's greatness as the forge and center of war planning and production; the titanic struggle with Napoleon was at its height, the unnecessary American sideshow just coming on. No need for Wordsworth to mention these matters, or what he thought of them; but he attended the debate in the House at which that silly radical Sir Francis Burdett, who thought that civil liberties were more important than beating Boney, was ably answered by the prime minister, Spencer Perceval. Two days later Perceval was dead, shot down in the lobby of the House by a crazy Liverpool merchant who had lost goods and money in the war at sea. The poet's sentiments on the subject were very much to the point.

. . . the Country is in a most awful state. The Monster is to be executed on Monday Morning. I hope to procure, by means of the Poet Bowles a stand upon the Top of Westminster Abbey whence I may see the Execution without risk or danger.

Meanwhile Mary was pouring out her own news and doings. "What would I not give to wander with thee in the opposite meadow that looks so green & so beautiful—the trees by the pool & the one in the court are ready to burst into leaf, but there is not a *green* leaf to be seen, except upon the goose berry trees, & here & there upon a shy hawthorn that has been in compleat shelter." The nature poet watches executions in London and his wife the budding of the hawthorn at Grasmere—well, no doubt that is what life is all about.

It remains, and perhaps rather ungraciously late in the day, to praise without stint the editorial work that has been done on these letters. Beth Darlington's utility edition from Cornell University Press is a model of how to carry out such a task: there is a first-rate introduction, and just the right amount of information interspersed between the sections of letters at the right moments. The nature of the letters is such—their extraordinary density and charm of domestic detail—that the grand Trustees edition's meticulous facsimiles, in which each printed page exactly mirrors the manuscripts opposite, gives an astonishing feel of their true and scribbled actuality. For the layman at least comparatively few facsimile manuscripts are worth reading in this way, but here we have one: the difference is between the tap water of plain print, and the writhing mass of preserved animalculae—each onrush and error of actual composition—brought under one's eye as if in a powerful microscope, the very seconds and sentience of the past still wriggling about on paper. However daunting the price, the magificent Trustees edition is worth having for this experience alone.

Most sumptuously bound and produced editions by private presses today merely reproduce some well-known classic—*Lycidas, The Song of Songs*, or whatever. This edition really justifies itself by its wholly novel and fascinating material; and for that reason alone its value is bound to appreciate.

Though it has done a superb job, the Scolar Press is in fact only the printer. Publishing and editorial design have been carried out by the Trustees of Dove Cottage and the Wordsworth Museum at Grasmere. All proceeds from sales go to the Wordsworth Heritage Appeal, to rehouse and re-equip the library at Grasmere, which contains more than 90 percent of Wordsworthian manuscripts, and which must be the only institution of its kind where a great poet's writings can actually be read and examined on the site where they were composed. The excellence of this cause would justify the price even if it were excessive, which considering the material and the production it is certainly not. The whole enterprise must be among the truly worthwhile publishing ventures of recent years.

And from where did the letters suddenly appear? There are still mysterious vanishings and reappearances of such historic material in England, unregarded hoards of Aspern papers which have escaped from any family keeping and responsibility. A large collection of such Wordsworthiana was auctioned at Sotheby's as "the Property of a Gentleman." To the firm their client's name was sacrosanct, and to this day the Wordsworth family has not been able to find out exactly what took place. But it seems that a Carlisle stamp dealer had a garden shed full of papers which he had bought for their value as "franks," the printed signs on correspondence that preceded the attachable stamp of 1840. Even family solicitors have periodically to clear out their cellars, and thus the mass of papers set out on their anonymous journey, like the wares of a peddler in one of Wordsworth's own poems.

Besides this correspondence the sale included the hitherto unknown manuscript of Coleridge's "Dejection, An Ode," the great love poem which he wrote to Sara Hutchinson, and which her sister Mary transcribed and kept among her papers. Neither Coleridge, nor Mary, nor William—most certainly not William—would have wished the world to see these letters, which had been placed in sequence by the couple as a keepsake for the one who survived the other. Henry James would have had a fit, too, and Miss Bordereau, the heroine of *The Aspern Papers*, would certainly have denounced those responsible for these editions as "publishing scoundrels." But other times, other manners. It is impossible not to feel more warmly toward Wordsworth after reading these letters, even though they bring his personality no further in line with contemporary fashion. A great poet becomes his admirers, as Auden wrote in his poem on the death of Yeats. Wordsworth has vanished so utterly that it is idle even to ask how much he would have resented our intrusion. As we read them, the letters, and the facsimiles especially, give back almost uncannily what Auden called "his last afternoon as himself."

The New York Review of Books, 1982

16

Unmisgiving

John Keats (1795–1821)

———————

John Keats
by John Barnard

Keats as a Reader of Shakespeare
by R. S. White

THE ARTIST Benjamin Haydon said of John Keats, probably with affectionate disapproval, that "one day he was full of an epic poem!—another, epic poems were splendid impositions on the world, & never for two days did he know his own intentions." Haydon's canvases have something in common with Keats's more ambitious poems in that they lack the basic confidence of genre; they are trying to do something new according to an old recipe. It was a romantic dilemma, and the fact that anything could be tried out made what might be termed a natural originality difficult to obtain. The many "modernisms" of the twentieth century found it much easier. In terms of style and genre, Wordsworth and Coleridge continued to rely on the eighteenth century tradition of ballad and didactic poem, while Byron had successfully romanticized the more robust traditions of Dryden and Pope. Keats would read himself into style through a much more unstable and challenging model—Shakespeare.

The process is fairly familiar, but R. S. White, the author of two excellent books on Shakespearean romance and tragedy, has examined it in detail and come up with a host of fresh examples and insights. His book makes a good complement to John Barnard's more general but also innovative study in the Cambridge introductions to "British and Irish Authors," a high-quality series which includes Patrick Parrinder on James Joyce and John Batchelor on H. G. Wells. Barnard gets a great deal into his short book, presenting a rather different Keats from that of the many other Keats scholars and biographers. Keats's vividness has been present to his admirers in many forms. In *Abinger Harvest* E. M. Forster had the idea of doing a kind of anonymous life of a young man in Regency London, quoting Keats's letters and describing his hopes and fears and his family and financial troubles, but not mentioning him by name. It brought the actual Keats, before the legend began, very close. Barnard's treatment has something of the same literalizing effect.

Indeed, he sees the word "literal" as having a quite special importance in relation to Keats.

> The ultimate literalness of Keats's mind is that of the common reader. The directness and uncomforting honesty of the questions he proposes allow neither the poet nor his reader to slip past them. As a post-Romantic the modern reader inhabits the situation defined by the claims and disclaimers of Keats's poetry.

This is true. Keats's existence, and his sense of it, is a very contemporary one: it is post-romantic and post-Nietzschean. Shelley seems old-fashioned beside him, a man still living in a settled world of religion and ideology. Yet at the same time Keats's art, and his true sense of it, is extraordinarily "conservative," as that of the common reader usually is. His most natural feeling for art is as an escape route from human ills, an escape into romance, into women's magazines, into poetry, where all disagreeables evaporate. In the ferment of creation they are all muddled together. Hence Keats's strenuous and touchingly impressive attempts to distinguish chambers of maiden thought in vales of soul-making, to write grave allegories about art and the human condition, to write finally and bitterly that he had no faith whatever in poetry—"I only wonder that people read so much of it." The reference must be to the fact that there was money in poetry if you wrote the right sort—like Sir Walter Scott's—because people, chiefly women, did indeed read so much of it. The young Keats read Mary Tighe's verses with pleasure, and the Misses Porter, of romance fame, admired his "Endymion." Barnard is right to emphasize just how important the market for poetry was, which was why Taylor and Hessey, the young firm which took over Keats's *Poems* of 1817 from Charles Ollier, were prepared to treat him so generously. They did the same for Clare. In the event, neither poet made it commercially: in Keats's case, because success had to be on his own terms, and these went against the grain of his natural genius.

He did not want to write the sort of "unmisgiving" poetry (Leigh Hunt's remarkable adjective) which came, with help from Shakespeare, like the leaves to the tree. If Keats had possessed the native cynicism of Leigh Hunt himself, or—a rather different kind—of Robert Bloomfield, the rustic poet who in 1804 had been paid nearly four thousand pounds for his two little volumes, he would have ruined his gift but he might have made big money. As it was, his best things are so good because they were not the things he wanted to do. The leaves the tree put out neither satisfied his ambition nor made for commercial success. But Leigh Hunt shrewdly opined that "The Eve of St. Agnes" was the best poem he wrote, and modern criticism is just beginning uneasily to wonder if he may not have been right. Scott had made his fortune out of poetry even before he began writing novels, and a Keats cast in Leigh Hunt's mold might eventually have followed him, making a trinity with Mrs. Radcliffe.

For it was "Mother Radcliffe" whom Keats had in mind when he borrowed the Romeo and Juliet motif and turned it into Gothic romance for the poem he always referred to as "St. Agnes Eve." The formula worked beautifully, and goodness knows how many Victorian young ladies identified with Madeline, even though Mrs. Carlyle was sourly to remark that the poem read as if a seamstress had eaten something too rich for supper and then gone to sleep on her back. And of course Keats turned against the poem, as he habitually did when he had done something marvelous: either that or ignored it, as he did with the "Ode to Autumn." As Barnard points out, he detested the thought of writing for a female public, and in two successive prefaces he had done his utmost to put both public and reviewers against him by proclaiming that this was youthful, rubbishy stuff which he hoped to get over soon.

Keats turned against the poem because it was mawkish and might seem to appeal to women. Oddly enough, some rather similar ideas were going through Byron's head when he gave up writing romances and turned to *Don Juan*, that—in intention—derisively masculine poem. But the change that Keats wished on "St. Agnes Eve" spoilt its old effect without producing a convincing new one, as his friends and publisher pointed out. He wanted the seduction to be no romance, but explicit and cynical, and went on about how he would have been ashamed to leave a young lady in the virgin state he found her; and instead of the magic of those ages long ago in which his lovers fled away into the storm, he announced that in the concluding lines of the poem he wished to "leave on the reader a sense of pettish disgust."

> Angela went off
> Twitch'd by the palsy: and with face deform
> The Beadsman stiffen'd—'twixt a sigh and laugh
> Ta'en sudden from his beads by one weak little cough.

That is bad in every way, but chiefly in its pretension to be tough, realistic, and lifelike. It misses out on everything, yet it is full of Keats's touchingly expressed wish to write poetry that "cannot be laughed at in any way."

He was in an impossible position, which might well have led him, had he kept his health, to have given up writing poetry altogether. Self-criticism never really helped him, and he could not see how the incongruous factors in "St. Agnes Eve" nonetheless worked together to make it the kind of masterpiece adored by the Victorians. Porphyro, "brushing the cobwebs with his lofty plume" in true "Mother Radcliffe" style (yet who but Keats would have *seen* a helmet plume as brushing the cobwebs?), is a figure of complex human and poetic origins, a voyeur and would-be seducer who is also a rapt adoring lover longing to make Madeline his bride. Troilus, Iachimo, and Romeo are present in him, but he is also very much his Keatsian self, like one of the "carved angels, ever eager-eyed." There is a strong contrast, very typical of Keats's poetry, between the raptness of this "unmisgiving" mixture and Keats's own touchy self-consciousness about how he wanted a public—and a masculine public—to respond to it, the men who, represented by Byron, were prepared to think "Hyperion" very fine. R. S. White points out that Keats paid very special attention to Touchstone's words in *As You Like It* about an audience's failure to understand what a poet would be at. "When a man's verses cannot be understood, nor a man's good wit seconded with the forward child Understanding, it strikes a man more dead than a great reckoning in a little room." Keats was less interested in Shakespeare's reference to Marlowe's sudden slaying in the Deptford tavern than in Touchstone's plea for understanding, a "greeting of the spirit," in which the poet's audience engages in a collaborative reading of his meanings. And he went so far as to quote the whole passage in an attack on Dr. Johnson's notes at the end of the play.

The whole dilemma is more significant than perhaps even Keats realized. He hated the idea of an audience, mostly of ladies, who would swoon at the romantic beauties in his story, as they had done over the "Last Minstrel," and Parisina, and the Giaour, and so he tried hard to appeal to manly sophistication and knowingness. His friend Woodhouse saw the point, but took a defeatist line in Keats's eyes: "As the poem was orig. written, we innocent ones (ladies & myself) might very well have supposed that Porphyro, when acquainted with Madeline's love for him . . . set himself at once to persuade her to go off with him . . . to be married. But, as it is now altered, as soon as M has confessed her love, P instead winds by degrees his arms round her, presses breast to breast, and acts all the part of a bona fide husband, while she fancies she is only playing the part of a Wife in a dream . . . and tho' all is left to inference, and tho' profanely speaking, the interest on the reader's imagination is greatly heightened, yet I do apprehend it will render the poem unfit for ladies, & indeed scarcely to be mentioned to them among the 'things that are.'" The real point, perhaps is that both Keats and Woodhouse are underestimating the taste, sense, and understanding of the "ladies." Jane Austen and her readers would have seen what the poem would be at, in either version; and would realize how much it was dealing with "things that are," as Shakespeare dealt with them, just because of "the interest on the reader's imagination." Keats is as usual his own worst enemy, his genius profoundly at odds with his intentions. When those intentions are really in control, as in the two "Hyperion" poems, and he is producing something gravely and nobly masculine, the poetry, in spite of superb lines and phrases, goes two-dimensional and dead. But it would tax a Roland Barthes to do justice to the inner life of "St. Agnes Eve," as of the Odes, and all their supremely felicitous incongruity. And it is essentially Shakespearean. Here again Keats misunderstood himself. He imagined he could only be Shakespearean by "writing a few fine plays." But into the verbal texture of "St. Agnes Eve" and the Odes he got more of the Shakespearean spirit than any other poet had done then, or has done since. This is not to say that the poems are not things of their own kind, highly romantic poems, which in the case of "St. Agnes Eve" make an important contribution to Victorian romanticism. That romanticism could be defined as a genre which, knowingly or unknowingly, exploited with great elaboration the rich difference between "things that are" and things that the day-dreaming and self-sustaining imagination created and cherished. In the "Morte D'Arthur," "The Lady of Shalott" and other such poems, Tennyson was to show that he well understood where the distinction lay. He and other Victorians worked with feeling, and finally with complacency, the poetic ore that Keats had both unmisgivingly and unintentionally turned up. And the human and artistic problems involved, the literal questions that absorbed and distracted Keats, they took for granted with the kind of graceful obeisance to suffering humanity that Tennyson makes in "The Palace of Art."

Keats could not understand how much "things that are" had got into "St. Agnes Eve," into its vision and feel for life. He was bogged down among the unmentionables, details and queries which are certainly absurd, but whose very absurdity is part of the livingness of a poem. Jack Stillinger, who in spite of his scrupulous editing takes the rather insensitive view that the poem is showing Madeline up as a silly girl whose seduction is her own fault, concludes that whether it "is a good poem depends in large part on the reader's willingness to find in it a consistency and unity that may not in fact be there." Of course the critic can always find them, but in the sense in which he uses the terms in relation to Keats they are not worth having. The poem sustains its own incongruities, artistic and psychological. Of course Madeline is a silly girl, but she is also good, loving, warm-hearted. Porphyro, the voyeur who takes advantage of her, is also a good, and honorable young man. Keats has boxed himself comically in, where the emphasis of his own alteration is concerned, by insisting that his hero make love, like an incubus, to a sleeping girl, and without waking her up: an undeniably difficult feat, even if the girl were not, as Madeline is, a virgin. A nice point, as *Punch's* Handelsmann might say, but one that any Victorian poem based on the kind of distinction and incongruity I have indicated would invisibly accommodate. The Victorian public accepted without question the sex in Christina Rossetti's "Goblin Market" and her brother William Michael was one of Keats's most enthusiastic critics. Did not Tennyson return a robust reply when his friend Edward FitzGerald objected that his Lady of the Lake could hardly have forged Excalibur *sitting down*? ("Nine years she wrought it, sitting in the deeps / Upon the hidden bases of the hills.")

Barnard has a sensible grasp of the complex issues which contribute to the rich success of "St. Agnes Eve"—Keats's own turbulent and dissatisfied attitude being one of them. Clearly he wrote much of the poem—much of all his poetry—in the mood of Porphyro himself, gazing with entranced devotion on Madeline's "empty dress." But the poem itself also contains his disillusion with that mood, quite apart from his willful insistence on changing the poem's end. All his greatest poetic effects are founded on this kind of instability, deep inside their verbal texture. The word "rich," naturally a favorite with Keats, is itself both casual and devout. The line in the Nightingale Ode—"Now more than ever seems it rich to die"—sounds the tone both of the romantic sorrowful daydreamer and of a negligently vulgar young man laughing with his friends about how it would be rich to run down to Putney with their girlfriends and a dozen of claret. Keats does not aim for such an effect, but it is present nonetheless in all its verbal immediacy, as it is in the second stanza of the "Ode to Melancholy."

> Or if thy mistress some rich anger shows,
> Emprison her soft hand, and let her rave,
> And feed deep, deep upon her peerless eyes.

As Barnard points out, the mistress is both girlfriend and goddess, the personified being of the next stanza who

dwells with Beauty, beauty that must die
And Joy whose hand is ever at his lips
Bidding Adieu.

"The lines invite the charge of callous, even sadistic, indifference to the mistress's feelings," says Barnard. In defence it has been argued that this is an example of Keatsian intensity."

The girl is both mistress and goddess, but while

> this ambiguity helps some of the way, it does not altogether answer the objection and raises another. Ought a lover to allow his mistress to rave, while he feeds on her eyes? Is it in character for the goddess Melancholy to "rave" at her devotee? The human and fictive levels do not satisfactorily support one another.

Here we are back at the Keatsian "literals," and the trouble they cause, even though that trouble is very much a part of the experience of real concentration on the poetry. Barnard's close criticism of the Odes is as revealing as R. S. White's detailed exposition of Shakespeare parallels. Yet Barnard cannot resist adding a note of moral and aesthetic disapprobation, as so many Keatsian scholars—notably Garrod—have done. Should a lover seduce a sleeping girl, or encourage his mistress to rave by imprisoning her hand? In the "Ode to Melancholy" Keats did his best to strike a worldly note, and a suitably masculine world-weary attitude, with which "to upset the drawling of the bluestocking literary world." He even wrote, and canceled, a knowingly grotesque first stanza, which Harold Bloom maintained gave the Ode its proper tone. But there is no proper tone here, any more than there is in the other Odes—only the "human and fictive," interchanging in their typically and unmisgivingly Keatsian manner: real girls and marble girls, goddesses and mistresses, nightingales actual and mythological, always and naturally mixed up. The ladies wouldn't have minded. The last irony for poor Keats is that it is the gentlemen whom he was trying to impress, and to get on his side, who have been most apt to do so.

17

The All-Star Victorian

Alfred, Lord Tennyson (1809–1892)

Tennyson: The Unquiet Heart
by Robert Bernard Martin

The Tennyson Album: A Biography in Original Photographs
by Andrew Wheatcroft

WHEN TENNYSON was a young man the French poet Gérard de Nerval used to walk about with a lobster on a lead, observing that "it doesn't bark and it knows the secrets of the sea." Such behavior, or variations on it, is wholly familiar and comprehensible where poets are concerned, in any post-romantic age. Eccentricity seeks familiarity, and in obtaining it yields up any claim to be inveterately peculiar. Charles Baudelaire and Dylan Thomas would have understood each other very well, and both of them are on easy terms with the modern spirit in poetry, easy terms with John Berryman, with Frank O'Hara, with Robert Lowell, with Ezra Pound and T. S. Eliot. Eliot was, figuratively speaking, leading his lobster about when he wrote his notes on *The Waste Land*.

This relation of the sacred monster with his client, both sophisticated and collusive, is quite unlike any relation that we have with the great Victorian poets. Not that the effect of their poetry was necessarily so different. Both kinds could equally depend on incantation, mystery, suggestiveness. But Cyril Connolly was right in remarking that the sonnets of Nerval have the modern spirit in them. Their mysteriousness addresses us intimately, their incantation seeks out the response of a fellow-feeling and intelligence, the family understanding of Baudelaire's "*mon semblable, mon frère.*" Such effects in the poetry of Victorians like Tennyson are, by contrast, entirely popular and democratic, as wide open as their own movement and rhythm. They make no hidden arcane appeal.

The presence of such an appeal in modern poetry shows the diminishment of its audience, even in an age of mass culture and education. Poetry is now the captive maiden of the English departments, neither expecting nor receiving a wider readership. More important from the biographer's point of view, it shows how little worthwhile it would be to do and redo the life of a modern poet. Because of the nature of their appeal to us there is nothing in the least unimaginable in the lives and sensibilities of Eliot or Lowell or Berryman, and the same goes for Nerval or Baudelaire. But Tennyson presents the biographer with a perennial challenge. What was the secret of his appeal? What actually went on behind the hair and beard and glowing eyes, under the black hat? The past is not necessarily a foreign country, and they do not always do things differently there, but the popular charisma of the great Victorians has a quality about it which is unlike anything today. How can it be recaptured and made comprehensible to us?

On the whole it can't, which is the source of the abiding fascination, but there are clues and parallels. Take Gérard de Nerval's lobster again, which we might meet up with now at any happening, any experimental play or poetry reading. Compare it, and the motives of its master, with a recorded event in the life of Tennyson. In 1859 the Duke of Argyll was staying with him in the Isle of Wight. Tennyson took the nobleman for a long walk, in the course of which he complained incessantly about the unscrupulous copying of his unpublished poems. Then, as a mark of respect and favor, he led his guest into the middle of a large stubble field, in which no unauthorized copyists could possibly be lurking, and recited to him in conspiratorial tones a new poem, "Boädicea."

Now where today in the world of poetry have we anything—anything at all—like that? Of course we haven't, but the same kind of ingredients could come together in quite a different context. Tennyson was a pop star, one of the most successful and famous ever. It is all there—his own curious classlessness and the wide appeal to persons of all classes; the relations with the *beau monde*, with royalty and riches; the spontaneities, the simplicities, the suspicions; the generosities; the secluded estates and publicized progresses, the words on every lip, the public appearance known to all. In Tennyson a great poet became a great impresario, a magic performer, a legend. For perhaps the only time in its history, real poetry was as potent and as widespread as pop music, and the man who made it as much of a star.

No wonder the reaction against it all was so intense. "Modern" poetry retreated into cult and fashion, secreted itself among connoisseurs and those in the know. It rejected Tennysonian popularity just as decisively as Bloomsbury sneered at Tennysonian manners and morals. Virginia Woolf's feeble little charade, "Freshwater," has a lot of what it feels to be superior fun with the absurdities of Tennysonian domesticity, the tears and recitals, the fervors and the reticences. Julia Margaret Cameron hovered adoringly about the bard with her photographic apparatus, taking those portraits which for depth and fidelity of expression have never been surpassed. Tennyson's vanity was as open as everything else about him, and he was fascinated by her pictures, particularly the one which he called "the dirty old monk"; he wanted her to give him lessons in the techniques of photography.

But the style of living that seemed so hopelessly old-fashioned and comic to Bloomsbury now seems open, dignified, rather splendid. It is Bloomsbury itself which now appears grotesquely old-fashioned, affected, alienated; at least insofar as it claimed to stand for a return to honesty and clear-sighted intelligence after the era of Victorian evasiveness and hypocrisy. The fact is that Victorian art, as embodied and represented in Tennyson's production and performances, was enjoyed by all and accessible to all. Together with Dickens he represented the peak of the Victorian populist achievement, an achievement which high art has not risen to since, nor seems likely to again. We have to leave those kinds of achievement now to other sorts of idols—the actor and film director, the football player, pop singer, and sportsman.

The "rehabilitation" of Tennyson has been in many ways as misleading as the post-Victorian slighting of him. Harold Nicolson in his book on Tennyson* took the view that there *was* a good Tennyson, the neurotic

Tennyson: Aspects of His Life, Character, and Poetry.

young writer of black moods and haunted cadences, straying about the dreary wastes of the Lincolnshire seashore, the Tennyson of "Mariana" and "The Dying Swan" and "A spirit haunts the year's last hours."

> The air is damp, and hush'd and close,
> As a sick man's room when he taketh repose
>   An hour before death;
> My very heart faints and my whole soul grieves
> At the moist rich smell of the rotting leaves,
>   And the breath
>   Of the fading edges of box beneath,
> And the year's last rose.

Success and recognition destroyed this darkly melodious poet, who then produces for the rest of his life official verses of little merit and conventionally popular sentiment. This reduced Tennyson to a minor Rimbaud, a blighted poet of the fin de siècle type, acceptable to an age which rejected the Victorian achievement.

Nicolson, it is true, later recanted. Professor Martin quotes a letter to his wife, Victoria Sackville-West, in which he said that Tennyson "truly was a poet, darling, and I wish I had realized that more deeply when I wrote that slight book about him." But there persisted the idea of Tennyson as a true and strange small poet struggling to get out of a big and bloated official reputation. He had to be defended, championed, stuck up for. The excellent life by his grandson, Charles, is defensive in tone,* so is J. H. Buckley's valuable *Tennyson, The Growth of a Poet.* Christopher Ricks's fine edition of the poems marked a real step forward in Tennyson appreciation, but his critical and biographical study is in subtle ways more misleading than earlier depreciations of the poet.[†] Perceptions about the detailed virtues of the verse are punched out as precisely as on a computer, and as mechanically, the suggestion created that a finely tuned machine for producing poetical effects is being brilliantly decoded.

But Tennyson was not Herbert or Donne. His poetry, however full of

*Alfred Tennyson.
[†] *Tennyson.*

"good things," is essentially and continuously naive, moving us altogether if it moves at all. Ricks's is the last refinement of the intellectualized Tennyson which with the best intentions has been reconstructed out of the old blank Victorian image, to make him at home with modernism, able to rub shoulders with Eliot and Yeats. What makes Professor Martin's to my mind the best biography that has appeared so far is the way in which he has been able to rid it of all such special pleading. He feels comfortable with Tennyson: he accepts him for what he feels him to be. Neither apologies nor rebuttals nor original claims are made. The result is a Tennyson whose success story, both financial and psychological, comes alive in simple human terms.

For simplicity is very much the clue, the kind of simplicity which is opposed to "seriousness." Matthew Arnold, most thoughtful of Tennyson's early detractors, thought his poetry provincial, lacking in the idea of "high seriousness" which Arnold had invented as the criterion of great European poetry. The idea is of course a phantom of Arnold's own wishes for and about his own creative powers, but it has had a prolonged and damaging effect: "serious" is still a cliché word which any novelist asked about his intentions, or any critic on the radio, finds it necessary to come out with to indicate that what he is writing, or what he is praising, seems to him good.

Wordsworth, Arnold's chief inspiration, is certainly a serious poet in his sense of the word; Tennyson is not. The young Tennyson, surrounded by his friends, was not unlike the idol of a rock group, picking out his music amid the hubbub, smoking pot (the strongest shag tobacco in Tennyson's case), and delighting the others with recitals which had something of the quality of an improvisation. As Martin shows, Tennyson was a far more social person than the image of the solitary neurotic would suggest. He needed company, camaraderie of the kind that his friends Hallam and Spedding had a gift for, as he needed work, and uncritical admiration for his touch and his performance.

This is the atmosphere of *The Princess*, a kind of elaborate and aborted early musical, the theme of which Gilbert was later to turn into comic opera. Young men shouting and smoking and rolling sonorous vowels is the setting for the *Morte d'Arthur*, a setting significantly different from what it became when Tennyson blew up the whole thing many years later into the *Idylls of the King*, though even there an element of the shared and wondrous *joke* is never far away, as in the lines which Gladstone was so enchanted by, describing a guardsman at Arthur's court surprised by news when eating a sandwich.

> He spoke: the brawny spearman let his cheek
> Bulge with the unswallowed piece, and turning stared;

It was probably in the same spirit that Tennyson solicited his friend Edward FitzGerald's enthusiasm for his lines about the Lady of the Lake, and how she made the sword Excalibur.

> Nine years she wrought it, sitting in the deeps
> Upon the hidden bases of the hills.

Every effective Tennysonian "hit" is on the basis of extravaganza. Who but Tennyson could take a line from Shakespeare and blow it up into the extraordinary tone-poem of "Mariana," a mixture of topographical realism and pure mood, so potent in its effect on the most unlikely auditors that Queen Victoria could say with touching pathos to her Poet Laureate many years later, after the Prince Consort's death: "I am your Mariana now."

Indeed what is remarkable about Tennyson's later popularity at court and among social and political grandees is the atmosphere of his early friendships and the style of life that made him the shy, uncouth, simple hero of an intellectual and apostolic band. He had the gift of putting his foot in it in such a way that everyone was pleased. In his first meeting with the Queen after Albert's death all he could think of to say in desperation was what a good king Albert would have been. "I lost my head—big fool that I was." But of course as was usual with Tennyson, who had the kind of luck that Napoleon would have envied, it was just the right thing to say: it had always been a sore point with the Queen that her subjects underrated her adored husband, and that the politicians would allow him no power. She was melted wholly, and invited the whole family to Osborne, where Tennyson's wife Emily was overcome by the euphoria of the occasion.

She gave me her hand & I found myself on my knees kissing it but I
don't exactly know how I got there. . . . Ally talked very eloquently
with the Queen & we all laughed & talked. . . . We talked of everything in heaven & earth almost—Jowett, Huxley, the stars, the Millennium. I never felt it so easy to talk with any stranger before.

Both Tennysons found the royal touch surprisingly easy to come by.

A short while before Tennyson had been in the Pyrenees with friends,
walking along the valley of Cauteretz which he had visited with Arthur
Hallam in 1830, when they were young men together. The result was
what he believed to be the finest lyric he ever wrote.

> Brook that runnest madly, brook that flashest white
> deepening thy voice with the deepening of the night
> All along the valley where thy mad waters go
> I walked with Arthur Hallam two & thirty years ago.
>
> All along the valley thou ravest down thy bed
> Thy living voice to me is as the voice of the dead
> All along the valley by rock & cave & tree
> The voice of the dead is a living voice to me.

That first version holds in its most concentrated form the self-absorbed
melody of Tennyson. There is in the fourth line, as so often in Tennyson's
verse, a kind of immanent comicality which is immensely effective and
touching, the sonorous movement of the line taking in its stride the
pedestrian syllables of the name, the real thing that had once been a real
person. In fact, as Tennyson knew quite well, though he later claimed to
have forgotten it ("A brute of a critic has discovered that it was thirty-one
years and not thirty-two") he had altered the timing in the interests of
euphony, and in revising the poem he changed the name to "one I
loved." But the haunting second line was unchanged, and the "popular"
motif that sings itself in a recurrent rhythm was further accentuated.

The whole thing is a remarkable instance of Tennyson's powers of
ingesting more deliberate kinds of poetry and giving them his own trademark melody. The landscape is brought to life by means of three other
poems—one of Hallam's called "The Soul's Eye," an echo of Meredith's

Love in a Valley, and a direct reference to Wordsworth's "A Slumber did my spirit Seal." The dead girl in Wordsworth's lines is "rolled round in earth's diurnal course / With rocks and stones and trees." The sense of Hallam's presence is more manic, more theatrical, and appealing more to a mass audience. The mechanical noise of the water tearing along itself becomes dead, but it brings in the very impersonality of its energy a sense of the vanished individual life. In the revised version Tennyson weakened this effect by changing "where thy mad waters go" into "where thy waters flow."

Martin is the first biographer to have been able to make extensive use of the Tennyson correspondence. He combines encyclopedic Tennyson scholarship with a great deal of intuitive common sense, a dry sympathy and intimacy with his subject, a leisurely and domestic awareness of the poet. He certainly gets in more *about* Tennyson than any previous biographer, and his book makes a foil to Christopher Ricks's brilliantly incisive—too incisive—shorter study. To be comprehensible Tennyson needs space and calm, the calm that his own poetry made out of deprivations and resentments, boredom and unhappiness. We recognize the quality of the pop star, almost the sleepwalker's capacity for success and survival, but the relation between unhappiness and fame is one that present sensibilities can make little of. Neurosis, with us, produces—if it produces at all—the kinds of creativity that lead to violence and self-destruction, our twin snobberies, the forms of authenticity most admired in the imagination of the writer, and in its preoccupations and inventions. We escape from coddled, uneasy boredom into willed and gratuitous horrors: the Victorians preferred to be taken out of themselves to nicer places.

Their fashions were for gracious pasts, Arthurian dignities of living; their literature did not admire the degradation by drugs and alcohol which was overwhelmingly present to their daily view. Tennyson was not proud of the madness of one of his brothers, the opium addiction of another (Charles, also a poet, and a good one), and of his own steady boozing—his tipple was cheap port, drunk in the fumes of strong shag tobacco. When famous he once poured a glass of hot water into the decanter of peerless '34 vintage at some grand dinner. He was embarrassed by the general embarrassment and muttered, feebly defiant, that Horace used to water his Falernian.

There seems no doubt that public reaction, whether favorable or unfavorable, constantly took Tennyson by surprise. All his best poems have a quality of absurdity in their self-absorption that is sublime; Tennyson seems to have been genuinely taken aback by their success, as much as by the kind of criticism they attracted. His attachment to *Maud*—rightly—was so total, and his disappointment at its reception so obsessive, that he insisted on giving two-hour readings of it to all his friends—Jane Carlyle, though she adored him, was bored to tears—and he was still doing it years later. "That was rather a debauch wasn't it?" the poet Clough remarked to his wife after one such reading; and an unwary guest at Farringford, who had told the two young Tennysons how much he enjoyed their father's poetry, was trapped upstairs while changing his wet clothes, and compelled to listen, shiveringly, to the whole performance. But perhaps the most signal instance of Tennyson's unawareness of other people's responses was much earlier, when he included "O Darling Room" in his *Poems* of 1833, a selection including some of the best he ever wrote.

> O darling room, my heart's delight,
> Dear room, the apple of my sight,
> With thy two couches soft and white,
> There is no room so exquisite,
> No little room so warm and bright,
> Wherein to read, wherein to write.

That gave the reviewers a field day. It was clear from the rest of the poem, with its reference to the German tour Tennyson had lately been on with Hallam, that this was not a dramatic effusion supposed to have been written by a girl—even then it would have seemed pretty artless—but a poem about the poet's own room at Somersby Rectory. Croker in the *Quarterly* rubbed his hands. "In such a dear *little* room a narrow-minded scribbler would have been content with *one* sofa, and that one he would probably have covered with black mohair, or red cloth, or a good striped chintz; how infinitely more characteristic is white dimity!—'tis as it were a type of the purity of the poet's mind." Prurience, in its robust Victorian way, could produce hints of a certain complexity. Why did the poet need two couches? In view of his exquisite tone—what Bulwer Lytton called the "eunuch strain"—perhaps the other was not intended for a lady? In fact the explanation was very simple. The rectory was cramped; Tennyson and a brother, now absent, had shared the room: sometimes a guest, like Hallam himself, doubled up for the night.

Tennyson could only have produced such stuff because he had no idea of how it might be taken. This enormous, shaggy, thick-wristed man, the epitome of slovenly and tobacco-drenched masculinity, had a feminine side that came out in his poetry so naturally that he was unconscious of the fact. This is the key to the whole tone of *In Memoriam*. It embarrassed the Victorians—though not Queen Victoria, she had too much sense and feminine perception—by its feminine abandonment to the spirit of the dear departed. One reviewer, when it was still anonymous, thought it must have come from the full heart of a widow, an uncommonly talented one.

> A spectral doubt which makes me cold
> That I shall be thy mate no more . . .

The reviewer could hardly be blamed.

> Stoop soul and touch me: wed me: hear
> The wish too strong for words to name.

That manuscript version became, as Ricks remarks, even more disconcerting in the published version. "Descend, and touch, and enter: hear . . ." But the clue was supplied by Tennyson himself, who as usual woke up too late to the implications of what he had written. About the line "Oh, wast thou with me, dearest, then . . ." he remarked: "If anybody thinks I ever called him 'dearest' in his life they are much mistaken, for I never even called him 'dear.' " Exactly. It is because Hallam is dead that the poem can adopt a tone never imagined or contemplated in his lifetime; and in so doing has achieved that extraordinary universality of tenderness which has moved, and indeed comforted, so many readers ever since.

Hallam had an unsuspected cerebral deformity which hemorrhaged when he was sight-seeing with his father in Vienna, and he died instantly. Perfectly possible that he might have survived and dragged out a vegetable existence indefinitely, in which case not only would the poem, or anything like it, never have been written, but Tennyson himself would probably have managed to put him out of mind, as he had done in the case of his own mad brother, confined up in Edinburgh. Hallam, who comes across in his letters and in the many memoirs as an enchantingly attractive character, had literally saved Tennyson, by his discerning admiration, his gaiety, the warmth of his affection. He was engaged to Tennyson's sister; in saving her brother he had saved, adopted, virtually wedded, the whole family. But his work was done; the legend remained. Had he lived on, even in perfect health, there could only have been a diminution in the relationship, as occurred with Tennyson's many other and lesser friendships. As so often happened in Tennyson's strangely fortunate career, the death itself was a kind of last blessing, a benefaction.

Tennyson is the great master of what may in general be a romantic invention, and is certainly something developed and exploited by the Victorians—the art of letting the incongruous die in the embrace of the elaborate. The most deeply soothing and comforting thing about *In Memoriam* is the strangeness of its honesty, clinging both to the total nothingness of death and the dead, and the wonderful constructions that living human sensibility can make out of that fact. It is like making a fortune or a factory as a response to the departure of God and the totality of death; and the Victorians, who were frequently doing things of that sort, must have felt that Tennyson and his poem were very much on their side, one of them. Nor were they wrong. A long poem of Tennyson is like an industrial enterprise, undertaken in the face of spiritual darkness and religious collapse. The death of Hallam was like the death of God, but it could be overcome; a poem could be written about it; language survived, like other forms of human enterprise.

> But, for the unquiet heart and brain,
>   A use in measured language lies;
>   The sad mechanic exercise
> Like dull narcotics, numbing pain.

That is a sound, an admirable, a proper response to the fact that

> He is not here; but far away
> The noise of life begins again,
> And ghastly thro' the drizzling rain
> On the bald street breaks the blank day.

But Tennyson's model, insofar as he had one, was not Victorian at all. It was Shakespeare's *Sonnets*, deeply admired, and having the same air of occasional poems, lucidly reasoned and hauntingly metaphored, on a theme of friendship. In both cases the idea of that friendship was transformed in the writing.

T. S. Eliot observed that the faith of *In Memoriam* was a poor thing, but the doubt in it was a very intense experience. Martin queries this, suggesting that both are dramatized in an equally effective way. I feel he is right, and I would also feel that what really matters is the creation of a living poetry in the place of both. The poetry seems lucidly argued, rangingly reflective, but the important thing is its hypnotic authority as poetic statement, a statement that satisfies in itself and by its own being. The Victorians clearly underwent the force of this satisfaction: it was the source of Tennyson's power alike over the philistine great and the ignorant poor. Lord Dufferin, who often came in his yacht to Farringford, and treated the poet with the most admiring deference, once told Tennyson that his poetry had suddenly shown him what poetry was all about—he had never been able to see the point of it before.

Noblemen can flatter as successfully as lesser mortals or more, but this is the kind of praise that rings true, and points to the source of the popularity. It was Lord Dufferin, incidentally, who when Viceroy of India won Kipling's admiration for saying that "there can be no room for good intentions in one's work." There are certainly none in Tennyson's best work—perhaps the intention is in any case irrelevant to the genesis of good poetry—and when he did have them the poetry suffers, not only in such obvious cases as the *Idylls of the King*, but where the scale is much smaller:

> Flower in the crannied wall,
> I pluck you out of the crannies,
> I hold you here, root and all, in my hand,

Little flower—but *if* I could understand
What you are, root and all, and all in all,
I should know what God and man is.

That is surely as tiresome a little poem as "O Darling Room," but Tennyson's absorption has now grown portentous, however little deliberately so. He has no talent at all for the Why and the Wherefore of things, the questions that Browning and Hardy could ask in their poetry in their own way. Martin perceptively says that Tennyson has to imagine himself into physical reality "so that it melts into metaphor": he cannot just wonder and record. In spite of the stately accuracy of detail in his verse—things like "as black as ash buds in the front of March"—he was emphatically not a man like Hardy, who "used to notice such things": and of course, like Yeats, he was extremely short-sighted.

Reality melts into metaphor in a way that will surely remind us—once we have accepted how bizarre the process can be—of a more modern poetry, and specifically of the poetry of Wallace Stevens. Hugh Kenner remarked, with the same note of exasperation often found in comments by the more intellectual critics among Tennyson's contemporaries, that for forty years Stevens's poetry "revolves about nothing more profound than bafflement with a speechless externality which poets can no longer pretend to animate." "Nothing more profound" used to be the note of complaint where Tennyson's poetry is concerned; but the point would be that both Tennyson and Stevens *are*, in their different ways, animating externality: it is precisely what such poets in an age of materialism learn to do. In Stevens's case the process is both self-conscious and in a muffled way deliberately funny: but his poems, especially the long ones, have something of the *Idylls of the King* about them. Those stately narratives should not be read as narratives about people and events at all but as prolonged and luxurious metaphor into which Tennyson has melted the externality of the tale. The incongruity between metaphor and tale is comical and should be seen as such; comedy represents a kind of triumph, as in Wallace Stevens, over externality, showing how the poet still can, and does, animate it in his own way.

But the American poet who most closely resembled Tennyson and revealed the continued vitality in his style of metaphor is Edwin Arlington Robinson. There is a George Crabbe side to Robinson but there is a Tennysonian side too, shown most obviously in the success in the early Twenties of his long narrative poem *Tristram*. Robinson of course didn't *believe* in "knights in iron clothing," but he was still able to write about them, and for the same sort of reasons that Tennyson could. Both poets had the temperament that thrives on anachronism, and both gave it their own sort of new look. They knew they could do nothing but write poetry, and that composition—the "sad mechanic exercise," like embroidering or doing the dishes—was what kept them going, was as Tennyson put it, the thing

> that handles daily life
> That keeps us all in order more or less.

They wrote poetry as they drank, in large but controlled amounts that saved them from excess. And this form of composition has its own fascination for the public, who take to it largely because they feel that if they themselves wrote poetry then this is the kind they might be able to write. (Dufferin's compliment suggests the same sort of reaction.)

It is a totally nonprogressive kind of poetry, just as it has nothing apparently original about it but suggests the timeless solidity of a purely verbal craft. That again makes for the deep reassurance in its popularity, and for its continual impulse to self-parody, turning movement into metaphor majestic and circular.

> And like a downward smoke, the slender stream
> Along the cliff to fall and pause and fall did seem.

Henry James, no mean judge of such matters, saw Tennyson's style as poised and stationary—"the phrase always seems to me to pause and slowly pivot upon itself." Even when movement takes place it is a movement that melts into its own confidence and sureness of movement, rather than into an advance of sense; and this process has a secret hilarity about it, the kind that must lurk in all eloquence that transforms the speechless externality of things. Undoubtedly the finest parody of Tennyson ever written is Robinson's famous sonnet, "The Sheaves," a poem which miniaturizes the whole process in fourteen lines which are as beautiful as they are subliminally funny. The field of wheat "waited there, the body and the mind";

> And with a mighty meaning of a kind
> That tells the more the more it is not told.

"Like a tale of little meaning though the words are strong," as Tennyson put it in "The Lotos Eaters." Nothing of course can be said of the wheat, except that it is there, and the poem knows this quite well, but it turns the tables on its own profundity by slipping into metaphor, giving the scene an incongruous and unexpected animation. As the season (and the sonnet) draws on

> A thousand golden sheaves were lying there,
> Shining and still, but not for long to stay—
> As if a thousand girls with golden hair
> Might rise from where they slept and go away.

The scene, imagined literally, is pure James Thurber, like his lady who leaps into the cartoon declaiming: "I come from haunts of coot and hern." Robinson's metaphor usurps the blankness of nature just as effectively as Tennyson's, and with an exuberance which adds his own trademark to the original.

Martin is particularly good on Tennyson's later life, and his relations with wife and children, matters which most biographers have tended to pass over rather perfunctorily. In spite of the virtual madness of his own father, and his lifelong resentment against the parvenu uncle at Bayons Manor whose side of the family had successfully engrossed its wealth and status, Tennyson had on the whole a happy childhood; and he was an adoring father to his own two sons, not at all the heavy Victorian paterfamilias, and treated them as equals. The elder, Hallam, returned that adoration for the rest of his life, remaining fixated on his father's memory after his death. He, more than anyone else, helped to create the Tennyson legend. The second son, Lionel, was very different and caused his parents considerable anxiety. Where the psychological strain of being the great man's son caused the elder to bury his being wholly in the legend, the younger was determined to get away, if he could.

But to escape that sort of encumbrance is not easy. Sent to Eton, Lionel developed a bad stammer, became a dandy and a womanizer. Several muffled scandals preceded and followed his marriage to a beauty, Eleanor Locker, daughter of an old friend of his parents. Determined to make his own way and become financially independent, he entered the India office where he was a success, and then he died of typhoid on the way home after a routine tour of the Indian provinces. The same Lord Dufferin who admired his father's poetry so much had been very kind to him; and his father, utterly stricken by Lionel's death, wrote to the Viceroy a most moving poem, which revived the *In Memoriam* stanza, and inevitably recalled the ship which had brought home "the dark freight" of Hallam's body.

> But ere he left your fatal shore,
>   And lay on that funereal boat,
>   Dying, 'Unspeakable' he wrote
> 'Their kindness,' and he wrote no more;
>
> And sacred is the latest word;
>   And now the Was, the Might-have-been,
>   And those lone rites I have not seen,
> And one drear sound I have not heard,
>
> Are dreams that scarce will let me be,
>   Not there to bid my boy farewell
>   When That within the coffin fell,
> Fell—and flashed into the Red Sea,
>
> Beneath a hard Arabian moon
>   And alien stars. To question, why
>   The sons before the father die,
> Not mine! and I may meet him soon.

Tennyson could do anything with that stanza. The encapsulation within it of his son's own gratefully polite, inevitably banal words, is deeply and directly touching.

In his later years Tennyson attempted, as Henry James was to do, a success upon the stage (it was about this time that the young James met him at a dinner party and had borne in upon him "the full, the monstrous demonstration that Tennyson was not Tennysonian"). The immensely long *Queen Mary* was a financial disaster, and Henry Irving, who found himself saddled with Tennyson's ambitions as a playwright, confided to a friend as he struggled with the next play, *Becket*, "he is a great poet but he cannot write plays; what a pity he tries—they are the greatest rubbish." Tennyson did try, however, and there is something engagingly indomitable about the old wizard plugging on—for money very largely—in hopes of scoring a West End hit. Immediately after *Becket* he was off on another, *The Falcon*, about a proud and impoverished count who serves up his falcon as the only food left in the house.

One wonders whether he felt anything symbolic in the old story, the falcon being the poetry he now hardly wrote. In keeping with Victorian ideas of staging, a real bird was put on, which terrified the actors until it killed itself accidentally and had to be replaced with a stuffed understudy. Then came *The Cup* (ancient history), *The Foresters* (on Robin Hood), and finally *The Promise of May*, a melodrama in prose about seduction and remorse in rural Lincolnshire. Its total flop induced the poet to abandon the stage at last, bitterly disappointed. Biographers have tended to ignore the whole episode, but Martin shows how significant it was in terms of Tennyson's sense of his popularity, and what it could do.

Old, toothless, and rather bald, he had become the prisoner of his own image—that "defiling and disfiguring shape," as Yeats called the persona of an aged poet—but his strong-willed wife remorselessly maintained the Tennysonian image, and living up to it did not improve his temper. Tennyson's friends were never quite sure whether or not it had been a good thing that he married Emily Sellwood. Certainly she looked after him as only a Victorian wife could do. But it may be that insensibly she came to exercise a kind of censorship over his poetry, and her habit of applying to their friends for subjects for her husband to write on, although it suited his methods of composition, certainly resulted in a good many inferior poems. The publication of *In Memoriam* and his appointment as Poet Laureate meant that Tennyson became a rich man within a year of his marriage, though he had not been exactly poor before. He still grumbled however. He told his envious friend Henry Taylor that he was making about two thousand pounds annually, "but, alas, Longfellow receives three thousand, and there is no doubt that Martin Tupper makes five."

His old friend FitzGerald was sure that the marriage was a mistake. "She is a graceful lady, but I think that she and other aesthetic and hysterical ladies have hurt AT, who, *quoad Artist,* wd have done better to have remained single in Lincolnshire, or married a jolly woman who would have laughed and cried without any reason why." A subtle diagnosis of the loss of the old Tennysonian spontaneity which he and Carlyle had so much valued. But Fitz's affection for Tennyson was, or had been, certainly homosexual, though Tennyson was quite unaware of that, and his feeling of estrangement both from the poet himself and his work made him increasingly bitter. Edward Lear took quite a different view. The gentle creature adored Mrs. Tennyson and said of the marriage: "I believe no other woman in all this world could live with him for a month." But Lear abominated Julia Cameron, whose arrival at Freshwater to be near Tennyson, to a house she called "Dimbola" from her Indian past, spelled the end of the peace and quiet he had previously enjoyed with the Tennyson family.

Julia Cameron is inevitably the heroine and presiding genius of the superb pictorial biography which Andrew Wheatcroft has put together, and to which John Betjeman, most Tennysonian of contemporary poets and most adept at bringing out the latent ebullience of his rhythms, contributes an introduction. The text is perceptive, and excellent on the relation of the poet with various friends, fellow poets, illustrators, tutors, and the two children of amazing beauty who appear like slightly disheveled angels against the background of Farringford House. Wheatcroft has assembled a fine collection of Victorian notables and nonentities, contemporaries of the poet, filling his margins with out-of-the-way information about them, and his book is certainly the best record of its kind. Not all the other photographers are outshone by Julia Cameron: Oscar Rejlander, a Swede who achieved a great reputation in England as a pioneer of high art photography—a forerunner of Cecil Beaton—and I. Mayall both run her close. Rejlander's picture of the family in the garden is uncanny in the way it brings together the vanishment and unknowability of the Victorians with the ordinary, faintly complacent simplicity with which an author's family might be snapped for the Sunday papers in their garden today.

The New York Review of Books, 1980

18

An Art of Self-Discovery
Edward Thomas (1878–1917)

Collected Poems
by Edward Thomas

*A Language Not to Be Betrayed: Selected Prose of
    Edward Thomas*
selected and with an introduction by Edna Longley

Edward Thomas: A Portrait
by R. George Thomas

EDWARD THOMAS belongs to an odd class of poet—the disappointed, dispossessed ones, who unexpectedly realize their hidden gifts as a result of some external pressure. If A. E. Housman had not fallen in love with a fellow undergraduate called Moses Jackson he would almost certainly never have written the poems that make up *A Shropshire Lad*; and had he not heard of Jackson's death many years later, the further series called *Last Poems* would not have poured from his pen. Thomas's case is not so dramatic as that, but it is recognizably the same.

His true personality and voice were not the ones he supposed he had, even wanted to have. He was born in fairly humble circumstances, the son of a schoolmaster who became a well-known socialist and polemicist. The pair were not at all mutually congenial. Young Thomas was no Jude the Obscure, but he yearned naturally for the kind of new life—the life of cottage culture and emancipated relationships—that seemed to offer itself around 1900 to the idealistic young. A classier version of the same ethos was already being practiced in Bloomsbury. Thomas managed to get to Oxford where he did not do well academically. While still almost a schoolboy he had met Helen Noble, the daughter of family friends, and she began to exercise in his life the kind of influence that Miriam did for young Paul in *Sons and Lovers*. In the course of an idyllic hike through the Oxfordshire countryside a child was conceived. That was all fine, and in accordance with the middle-class sexual mores of the new century, but Thomas Hardy, raised in an epoch of more worldly pessimism, would have smiled grimly at the prospects it implied.

The trouble—ironically enough—was the opposite of that in *Jude the Obscure*. Helen was the perfect partner for the sort of man Thomas supposed he was, and that she initially supposed he was. In any case she possessed the wonderfully equable temperament that comes serenely through any amount of estrangement on the part of a difficult spouse. As her autobiographical recollections, *As It Was* and *World Without End*, make clear, she never faltered either in love or in confidence. Neither did Thomas seem all that difficult: less so, probably, than most young men of his type. They were poor, but he had shown that he could earn their living by journalism and reviewing, comparatively a quite highly paid profession in those days. They seemed set for a tranquil life of domestic order and cottage industry.

Of course it did not work out that way. Thomas worked hard; wrote an immense amount—criticism, essays, hundreds of pieces on the beauty of the English countryside, the subject so fashionable at the time. He earned a respectable amount. They had two nice children. But all this was dust and ashes where the unknown poet in him was concerned. He suffered increasingly from fits of black depression. A grainy photograph reproduced in R. George Thomas's admirably detailed biography, and duplicated on the cover, shows his handsome half-profile and fine eyes set in a concentration of misery so deep as to be almost frightening, as it must have frightened whoever held the camera. Who was it? The picture seems posed, the sitter not entirely indifferent to the portrait he made, and yet sunk beyond any ordinary comfortable sort of conceit; though one notices he always turned the same right profile to the camera in all the photos reproduced. The one of him in despair makes a striking contrast with a photograph of the young Robert Frost, just after he had arrived in England.

With A Boy's Will and North of Boston already behind him Frost looks entirely pleased with himself, his poetry, his status, and his future. He was the opposite kind of poet, who had found himself early and completely. It used to be debated whether he received more from Thomas than he gave, in poetic imponderables. Thomas's biographer, who has also done a superlative edition of his poems, makes it clear, I think, and with all the unassuming authority of his scholarship, that the debt was wholly on Thomas's side. It was no Wordsworth-and-Coleridge relationship. Thomas found he could unburden himself entirely to Frost, whose sympathy and intuition were amazing (he later offered to take Thomas's son Merfyn, with whom his father had been unable to get on, back to America with him). Apart from this service to morale, Frost showed Thomas what he could do with his feeling for locality, a feeling which up till then had only found a fairly commonplace Georgian utterance in essays, descriptive sketches, a biography of Richard Jefferies. But "A Nature Note" could become something else, something which a trick of eye or of style could turn into a new sort of poetry. Thomas, already a thorough professional and craftsman, was well aware of this, as a letter to Frost shows.

> Sometimes brief unstrained impressions of things lately seen, like a drover with six newly shorn sheep in a line across a cool woody road on a market morning and me looking back to envy him and him looking back at me for some reason which I can't speculate on. Is this North of Bostonism?

It was, in a sense; but Thomas was to use it much more diffidently and intimately, to discover the inscape of a self previously unexpressed — on the verge of, but prevented from, inventing itself in art — rather than to bring an already confident self to the shaping of new perceptions. Thomas was to write some poems, like "Up in the Wind," which are almost imitations of Frost stories, but one cannot imagine him striking that exquisitely comfortable Frost note of self-assurance which is so memorable in swinging the birches, or stopping by woods on a snowy evening, or seeing a crow shake snow off a branch, or having a lover's quarrel with the world. Thomas is more like Housman in discovering an idiom of reticence to reveal himself completely.

It is the reticence that gives interest to what is revealed: that, and the reader's awareness that it could only have been done in this new-found poetry, poetry which "began to run," in R. George Thomas's felicitous phrase, specifically for this purpose. Thomas had always been a direct and sensitive critic of his contemporaries' poetry, on which he had written innumerable newspaper reviews, but there is a new note of eagerness and excitement in what he wrote in July 1914 about the English edition of *North of Boston*. He calls it "one of the most revolutionary books of modern times," and after praising especially "The Wood Pile" and "The Death of the Hired Man" ends with the deceptively simple comment that this "is poetry because it is better than prose," a phrase which exactly describes what he wanted from the poetry that he himself was on the verge of writing.

Frost is the greater poet, as Thomas himself would have been the first to recognize. Had he survived the war, instead of being killed by a shell at Arras in 1917, Thomas would have written more no doubt, but would not have increased his reputation, might even have diminished it. Frost had inspired him, by making the critic in him see what the poet might do. But the best of his poems are quite unlike Frost's, and there are not many of them: indeed to revisit his collected poems is to be aware of a sense of disappointment that they are so few. Those that depend too much on "A Nature Note," and Frost's own rhythms, have not worn well. The war itself was the more potent factor in bringing the true Thomas into being. It sharpened and distanced the material he used, and gave him, as it gave so many others, a new and decisive role to play in life. The photograph of him as a gunner officer, about to leave for France, shows a new and mature man who has found himself, and revisits only in his poetry the days when he contemplated suicide, despaired of his future, strove to escape the bonds of his family.

A soldierly personality embodied the Housman side of Thomas. It is instructive to learn, too, that while he was an undergraduate and his wife was expecting their first child, he fell in love with a handsome fellow student. "And all this," his notebook records, "about a boy—with abundant black hair, pale, clear face, piercing and frank grey eyes, red lips and a boyish voice! Some people made indecent suggestions to explain my liking, suggestions which I trust he will never hear."

The reader of Thomas's poetry was never to hear it either, except very obscurely, in the depth of his most individual poetic effect, his sense of obscure guilt, and of a yearning for distance, silence, and oblivion. This haunting quality, an elusive sense of personality fulfilled in its own disappearance, is Thomas's special trademark. We hear it in poems like "It rains" and "Tall Nettles" (nettles are another Housman motif) and in "Lights Out":

> The tall forest towers:
> Its cloudy foliage lowers
> Ahead, shelf above shelf:
> Its silence I hear and obey
> That I may lose my way
> And myself.

"Old Man" is one of the few poems in which the Frost manner and meter are used with complete individuality by Thomas, a strange poem about "The hoar-green feathery herb, almost a tree," known as Old Man or Lad's love. The poet sniffs its elusive scent and can think of nothing it reminds him of.

> No garden appears, no path, no hoar-green bush
> Of Lad's-love, or Old Man, no child beside,
> Neither father nor mother, nor any playmate;
> Only an avenue, dark, nameless, without end.

The same poetry of longings and extinctions, a theme that was as traditional to Shelley or to Hardy as it would be to Philip Larkin, makes an incongruous appearance even in the famous "Adlestrop."

> Yes, I remember Adlestrop—
> The name, because one afternoon
> Of heat the express-train drew up there
> Unwontedly. It was late June.

The steam hissed. Someone cleared his throat.
No one left and no one came
On the bare platform. What I saw
Was Adlestrop—only the name

And willows, willow-herb, and grass,
And meadowsweet, and haycocks dry,
No whit less still and lonely fair
Than the high cloudlets in the sky.

And for that minute a blackbird sang
Close by, and round him, mistier,
Farther and farther, all the birds
Of Oxfordshire and Gloucestershire.

All too famous anthology piece as it is, it illustrates better than any other poem the way in which Thomas used and transformed, to his own obscure purpose, the comfortable archness of the Georgians, their often self-congratulatory rural reveries, and the meditative phonetic skills of Robert Frost, who in a letter to a friend had written: "I give you a new definition of a sentence. . . . It is a sound in itself." The sentences of the poem illustrate this, from "the sound in itself" of the first word. The third stanza with its pseudoarchaism ("No whit less still") might have been written by any Georgian poet among Thomas's friends, but it serves perfectly to set off the mysterious ending, the birdsong receding, as it were, into Thomas's own being, and "farther and farther" into the dark perspective in which so many of his best poems end, the unknown counties of his mind. It is a very secret poem, masquerading as a very simple and open one, a combination somehow typical of Thomas's brief and new-found personality as a poet.

But of course it is also a very sober and exact poem. Thomas, like Hardy, was a man "who used to notice such things"—in this case the phenomenon of a bird singing in a sudden man-made silence, and the effect of receding part song as each bird strikes up to vie with others closer or farther off. He used to notice things, too, in his capacity as reviewer. The mostly short pieces in A Language Not to Be Betrayed (the phrase is

Thomas's own) show what a good critic he was, though they have dated as his poetry has not. To earn his living Thomas deliberately subdued his hand to the idiom of the age, and wrote as other reviewers did. Edna Longley has arranged the extracts well, and has made a telling connection by putting a review of the imagists' anthology, containing poems by Pound, Joyce, HD, Richard Aldington, and Ford Madox Ford, next to the pieces on Frost.

The result shows that there were two distinct new techniques, around 1914, for writing poetry that was "better than prose"—a phrase that Pound himself might have used—and that the imagist way preferred, as Thomas put it, to avoid "the commonplaces of verse" by sounding like a translation. "Mr. Pound, again, has seldom done better than here under the restraint imposed by Chinese originals or models." Thomas had found a different way of avoiding the commonplace: by becoming in his poetry the sort of man he really was.

The New York Review of Books, 1986

19

Fun While It Lasted

Rupert Brooke (1887–1915)

The Neo-pagans: Rupert Brooke and the Ordeal of Youth
by Paul Delany

THE BRITISH PUBLIC SCHOOL, which as everyone knows is really a private school, grew out of the grammar schools, those admirable and ancient places where an excellent formal education was given to promising children of the locality, rich and poor alike. They were charitable institutions, endowed by local merchants and gentry. The young Shakespeare attended grammar school at Stratford, of which his father, who afterward went bankrupt, had been a minor benefactor. But in the nineteenth century, amid all the strains of a new industrial society, the status and function of these schools underwent a radical change. They became upwardly mobile, in the direst sense, extracting comparatively large fees from pupils no longer local and deserving, and at the same time they strove to give themselves a new and artificial image, patriotic, clean-limbed, and high-minded.

The personality and legend of Rupert Brooke can only be properly understood in this public school setting. His father was a housemaster at Rugby, the most successful of the new model schools and the one most determinedly in competition with the much older and more impersonal foundations of Winchester and Eton. The great headmaster Thomas Arnold, father of Matthew Arnold, had imprinted the place with his own dedicated and inspiring personality. It was the scene of that Victorian classic *Tom Brown's Schooldays*. It produced more administrators and servants of empire, men of integrity and serious ideals, than anywhere else. It fostered a new idea of the gentleman, and the obligations of class.

In his third novel, *The Longest Journey*, published in 1907, E. M. Forster gave a brilliantly terse and venomous account of the metamorphosis of an old local grammar school into one of the pretentious new places, and showed how at the time he was writing even the dynamism had gone, replaced by a cult of games and "colours" and aimless snobbishness. Forster knew: he had been at Tonbridge School, from which he had escaped to the haven of Cambridge. Kipling knew too, but he belonged to a previous generation, and in *Stalky & Co.* he tried to inject a new style of pseudo-iconoclasm into the business, and celebrate a vigorous breed of imperial officers who despised "the flanneled fools," but who in their tight-lipped way were just as devoted to ideals of service and family. In the case of both writers, too, there was a powerful mother figure in the background, suggesting a region that revolt could never quite overcome, or irreverence make its own. Forster's Mrs. Moore and Mrs. Wilcox, and Kipling's mother in *The Brushwood Boy*, have a lot in common.

Rupert Brooke had a mother too, one of those angelic strong-willed matrons whose children "adore" them, and often die of it. None of her three sons reached thirty. Not her fault directly, but they had the death wish, like Peter Pan, and knew that dying was a much bigger adventure than growing up. The Great War gave them their chance, although only one was killed in action. Parker Brooke, their father, was a weak man held up by the system and by a wife who—it was said—sent him out at night to collect horse droppings off the roads for her rose garden. An honorable activity, one would have thought, if he had been allowed to do it openly, and in the day.

Rupert's second name, Chawner, was in honor of one of his mother's ancestors, a fanatical Roundhead. Rupert was the second son and she wanted a girl; but he was delicate and became her favorite anyway. Ironically he was named after Prince Rupert, the Roundheads' stoutest adversary. In the splendid photography of mother and younger sons discovered by Dr. Delany she looks like a cavalry commander herself, poised for a charge she could never lead. Rupert inherited her eager profile.

He also inherited his father's weakness. As Delany brilliantly shows, he suffered from all his friends assuming he had an unbeatable hand—

brains, poetic talent, ravishing looks, admiration enough to make him "a future Prime Minister"—while inside he was all timidity, cold self-hatred, and self-distrust. Not an uncommon modern dilemma, perhaps, and perhaps one that has always been with us, but that has now been more precisely diagnosed by the modern consciousness. Rupert could hardly have been invented by a novelist, as Scott Fitzgerald invented Gatsby, out of himself and his own keen sense of the age. He was not interesting enough for that, although to friends and contemporaries he seemed so achieved a character that there could be no latency in him for a novelist to sense and to exploit. Delany is going over familiar ground, but he does it so well and with so much detached humor and understanding that he makes the situation of Brooke and his circle smaller, more sympathetic, more natural, less of a fable to be revered once and now derided. He makes them seem, in Auden's phrase, "silly like us." If none of them look very nice in retrospect, that is something we can hardly afford to feel superior about: time is not likely to deal with us any better, if it bothers to do so at all.

The term "Neo-pagans" was coined by Virginia Woolf. Standing with one foot in Bloomsbury, with its more sophisticated and metropolitan atmosphere, she gave a quizzical glance at the young men and women, many from Cambridge like her brother and his friends, who preferred a more bracing and open-air existence. She was even prepared to join them on occasion. Under Brooke's tutelage she bathed naked at Byron's pool by Grantchester, where Brooke enjoyed showing off his party trick to the company: jumping into the river and emerging with an instant erection. But there was nothing priapic in these caperings; they were curiously asexual, hearty, good clean fun. The Neo-pagans, as Virginia Woolf probably saw, were really just public school types by other means, exploring their own variation of the tribal rites. Like most revolutionaries they settled for a more high-souled and censorious version of the old regime.

At any rate Bloomsbury was prevailed on to attend a Neo-pagan camp at Dartmoor in the summer of 1911—"Bloomsbury under canvas," as Brooke called it. Virginia roughed it nobly, if quizzically. Maynard Keynes was there, putting up an unexpectedly good show at rising with the dawn and sleeping on the ground. Lytton Strachey, who had come with an eye to the young men, wisely preferred the comfort of a neighboring guest house, and after a single night's ordeal in the open his brother James joined him there, his caution provoking an extempore couplet by Rupert:

> In the late evening he was out of place
> And utterly irrelevant at dawn.

Also present, and in charge of most of the cooking arrangements, were the famous Olivier sisters, whose nephew still to be, Laurence, would one day become the most celebrated actor of his time. Children of a handsome colonial governor, the sisters were noted for their beauty, and in their parents' absence had lived together rather like the Lost Boys in *Peter Pan*. They were perfect female Neo-pagans, and not lost girls in any sexual sense, for though they did their best to attract the new eligible youth they remained determinedly chaste. Rupert at various times was in love with the two youngest, Bryn and Noel. They liked adding his scalp to their belts, but had no more intention of settling down yet than he had. In time Noel, whose deep eyes were her great attraction, would become a doctor and marry a nonentity in the same profession. James Strachey, who became a psychiatrist, loved her hopelessly for many years. As a middle-aged mother she suddenly returned his love and they had a long and passionate affair. She had certainly loved Rupert, but her instinct was to keep away from him, and he had become heavily involved with Ka Cox, another of the Neo-pagan circle. Virginia Woolf found Ka motherly but was also sexually attracted to her and called her "Bruin."

Did it all amount to no more than Hilaire Belloc's sardonic view of the in-groups of his day, who "Talk of their affairs / In loud and strident voices"? Yes and no. That reptilian old idealist and aristocrat Bertrand Russell was never taken in by the Neo-pagans:

> I went to Grantchester . . . to tea with Jacques Raverat who is to marry Gwen Darwin. He has immense charm, but like all people who have superficial and obvious charm, I think he is weak and has no firm purpose. He is staying with Rupert Brooke whom I dislike. . . . Young people now-a-days are odd— . . . great familiarity, rendered easy by a complete freedom from passion on the side of the men.

Russell, who was just getting rid of his wife Alys the better to pursue his affair with Lady Ottoline Morrell, was inclined to despise the Neo-pagans' lack of sex drive. Although their mild and malicious polymor-phousness suited Virginia Woolf, it was a strain on the young men, who found themselves in the false position of carrying on public school mores in other situations. Those schools at least had never tried to idealize ado-lescent sex and make it part of the bracing and enlightened regime of mixed camps and nude bathing, sandals and uplift. Most of the young Neo-pagan men, and many of the girls, were to have more or less serious breakdowns based on the unnaturalness of their lives and feelings. Scien-tology and such movements have had the same effect, less picturesquely, in our own time.

But the men who were in a sense behind Neo-paganism—Badley, the founder of Bedales School, Reddie of Abbots-Holme, Edward Carpenter with his Millthorpe community, which influenced a generation of homo-sexuals like E. M. Forster—were not in it for money or power. They were genuinely innocent and good, though no doubt with a large slice of Eng-lish middle-class hypocrisy transferred to a new sort of social area. Many of the Neo-pagans were from Bedales and spread the gospel when they teamed up with old Rugbians like Rupert, and even the more worldly Bloomsbury fringe. The Oliviers were connected with the Fabian move-ment, their father a friend of Bernard Shaw; Rupert and his associates strove to bring the Cambridge ideal of "good states of mind" to the lower classes; even Virginia Woolf gave lectures at working-class colleges in London. Feminism, socialism, pacifism were officially taken for granted.

Then why did the whole thing ring so false in what they said and in what they wrote—particularly in what Rupert wrote? Even their atheism sounds kitschy and bogus, perhaps because it was merely an inversion of and a reaction against the sickly pieties of public school religion, and playing the game. Could anyone, even at the time, not have been embar-rassed by some of Brooke's rhapsodies? "We'll be children seventy-seven years instead of seven," he vowed in what is virtually a Neo-pagan mani-festo to Jacques Raverat:

We'll *live* Romance, not *talk* of it. We'll show the grey unbelieving age, we'll teach the whole damn World, that there's a better Heaven than the . . . harmonium-buzzing Eternity of the Christians, . . . a Heaven of Laughter and Bodies and Flowers and Love and People and Sun and Wind, in the only place we know or care for, ON EARTH.

The styles may differ, but all flower children say much the same things; the exciting words of the Sixties sound like rubbish today. Yet the idiom of Rupert and his circle, and the personality behind it, still have a special power to set our teeth on edge. Perhaps that is why we keep going back to it, and remolding it in a new image of disillusion.

Delany quotes some of Rupert's poetry but has little to say about its quality. And yet to reappraise it, at least in part, might seem a worthwhile project, if he and his circle are again to be studied seriously. Henry James, who fell for Rupert at first sight—his physical charm appealed equally to young women and to homosexuals—inquired anxiously whether he was any good as a poet, and was relieved to get a negative response from Rupert's close friends, who were not as easily impressed as outsiders. The Master felt that those looks, and poetic genius as well, would have been altogether too much.

Lacking originality or an inspiring model—the days of Pound and Eliot were still to come—Rupert tried to write like a Georgian poet and a country lover. But by temperament he was too waspish and irreverent for the form: there was a discrepancy between his nature and the way he tried to write which I. A. Richards probably spotted when he remarked that Brooke's poetry had no "inside" to it. He seems indeed, as Delany rereads him, to have been oddly lacking in personality. He and his close friend Jacques Raverat, who was half-French and who later became an artist, were would-be poets together "talking from breakfast to midnight of poetry, art, sex, suicide, the ridiculous superstitions about God and religion, the absurd prejudices of patriotism and decency, the grotesque encumbrances called parents." But they were a long way from Rimbaud; this childish irreverence was not *"le dérèglement de tous les Sens,"* but the high spirits of those who are never going to grow up. Raverat died young of multiple sclerosis, and Brooke of an infected mosquito bite before he reached wartime Gallipoli.

It is this quality of being "slightly insincere to myself," as Brooke complacently phrased it in a letter to Geoffrey Keynes, which helps to make the language of most of his poems so shoddy and embarrassing. Memorable too in a sense. People who don't read real poetry can always remember the bits about "is there honey still for tea?" and the breeze at Grantchester "sobbing through the little trees." His best talent was satirical, his best poem the remarkable "Fish," for once a performance both lighthearted and genuinely heartfelt, for Rupert had an uninhibited sexual passion for water as he did for neither man nor woman. Sex, the true poetic drive, comes into this poem with real fervor. The only flicker of life in the famous wartime sonnets is his private identification of the coming struggle with bathing nude—"swimmers into cleanness leaping." But whether daring or coy, most of his verse smells of the school magazine; had he survived he would almost certainly have returned to Rugby, and dwindled into an embittered pedagogue like his father.

Frances Cornford, one of the Neo-pagans who survived into old age, possessed a slight, but compared with Rupert's an individual, poetic talent (her anthology poem is on the fat white woman who walks through the field in gloves), and the sight of Rupert laughing and talking with his friends inspired her to write when young her well-known quatrain:

> A young Apollo, golden-haired,
> Stands dreaming on the verge of strife;
> Magnificently unprepared
> For the long littleness of life.

"Long littleness," which made Hardy into a poet, would certainly not have done the same for Rupert. When the golden dream was over life merely became "perfectly foul." Gwen Darwin, who married Jacques Raverat, summed up a general feeling when she wrote, "I don't believe there is anything compensating in age and experience. We are at our very best and most livingest now—from now on the edge will go off our longings and the fierceness from our feelings and we shall no more swim in the Cam. . . . I don't believe in getting old—I hate it, I hate it." So did they all, and the breakdown Rupert suffered three years before the war seems as much due to the terror of age as to the sexual puritanism that (as with D. H. Lawrence) was his mother's legacy. Having coldly broken his virginity with a boyfriend, he experienced nothing but depression from going to bed with Ka Cox and Cathleen Nesbitt, however much he might desire them theoretically. He was not specially homosexual but he was incorrigibly narcissistic. The letters Delany quotes make disagreeable reading, as much from their idiom—lots of locutions like "most livingest"—as from their emotions and prejudices. Social conversation was less racially inhibited then than now, but Rupert's venomous superiorities and his anti-Semitism, which he probably acquired from Hilaire Belloc via Jacques Raverat, would make repulsive reading in any age.

Necessary legends care little for such things. Rupert was to remain fixed as the golden boy of the war and the future, the tragic flower of his country's youth. Sir Philip Sidney had meant much the same to the Elizabethans, with more justification, for he was a poet and scholar of international repute, but even so Ben Jonson had not been able to refrain— fifty years on—from belittling his image and claiming he had had an ugly spotty face. No iconoclast could deny Rupert Brooke's facial beauty, but, as he himself knew very well, there was something sufficiently ugly about the rest of him. All "public schools" tend to be horrible at the time, joyous in retrospect, and there is something both repellent and pathetic about the taste of an age which exalts such a school product as its national ideal, whether that ideal comes from Rugby or from Bedales. Let us return to real education and give up the mystique—soppy or bracing—which used to surround such schools. That should be the moral of Delany's valedictory study, though he wisely refrains from pointing any.

Neo-paganism was not just a provincial English phenomenon. In another guise it had appeared in progressive Germany, where all good Neo-pagans went whenever they could. Rupert wrote his poem "Grantchester" while sitting in a café in Berlin; and in Austria both Musil the novelist and Rilke the poet were to write with horrified fascination about the "public school" type of academy they had both attended. The young volunteers on both sides in 1914 had much the same ideals; the cult of the young continued after the war, fostered by Mussolini and that romantic idealist, Adolf Hitler. The English Neo-pagans perhaps showed good sense in letting the movement fade out in the comparative harmlessness of a myth to look back on, although Auden—a great poet—and his friend Isherwood revived their own schoolboy version of it when they were young in the Thirties. But youth must end, somehow or other, in every generation. Gwen Raverat pronounced the Neo-pagans' final epitaph in a letter to Virginia Woolf:

All the others are dead or have quarrelled or gone mad or are making a lot of money in business. It doesn't seem to have been a really successful religion, though it was very good fun while it lasted.

The New York Review of Books, 1987

20

Gallant Pastiche

Cecil Day Lewis (1904–1972)

————————

The Complete Poems
by Cecil Day Lewis, with an introduction by Jill Balcon

THE CHASTE GREEN and purple cover (appropriately enough the colors of the Wimbledon tennis club) has inset on the back a modest-size picture of the poet. He is posed by the photographer like an eighteenth-century author for his portrait—leather-bound books in the background; the right arm, in oxford shirt cuff and well-cut tweed, resting on another volume; the tie and waistcoat prosperously in place; curly hair copious, but well brushed and cut; handsome cheeks creased in a leisurely smile. It is an infections grin really, making the beholder want to smile himself; for it so clearly if stealthily invites him to see the cocky little boy dressed up as the poet who has more than made it; who has become an advertisement for the graciousness of culture, and its mandarin-tycoon.

The poet, like his picture, was endearing; and all the more so today when the image of poets and poetry, and of culture itself, has so drastically and it seems irrevocably changed, not necessarily for the better. Cecil Day Lewis was once thought of as one of the forward-looking poets of the urgent Thirties, a comrade in verse and in politics of Auden, Spender, MacNeice—"the Macspaundays," as they had been scornfully but perhaps enviously christened by the reactionary South African poet Roy Campbell. In the same age group, they seemed peers and equals, their talents committed to the same causes. So in a sense they were, because the spirit of the times required it of them, but in reality they were wholly different from one another; and the era of "the young poets exploding like bombs" and dashing forward "like hussars," as Auden referred to it, was soon to be over. They settled down then to cultivate their separate talents: Auden the true genius; MacNeice the scholarly poet, full of unexpected originalities; Day Lewis the debonair craftsman. He could produce glittering pastiche, from homely Hardy to Frost or Browning or Hopkins, turn out elegant detective novels, sing madrigals, recite verse incomparably well, and chair with charm any metropolitan literary gathering.

None of the "Macspaundays" went mad, or died in a garret or on the battlefields of Spain or of Hitler's war. All were in fact decidedly success-ful in a worldly way. The age in which Day Lewis had imagined himself singing "on a tilting deck," with the sea about to destroy him, turned out in the end unexpectedly benevolent to poetry and to poets. They became privileged academics, jet setters, pickers-up of bursaries and international awards; and the less the citizens read them the more publicity they got from university departments and the cultural journalists. They even started to get a good living from teaching the young to write poetry, an occupation that would have aroused scornful amazement in Dr. Johnson, but would have been thoroughly understood and accepted among the scalds of Viking society or in the lodges of the Trobrianders. Day Lewis was the kind of poet who would have been perfectly at home in such a society, and eminently useful.

For he could write in any sort of style. Since the romantic movement we have been so conditioned to the poet who finds and speaks in his own voice that we forget the larger and more ancient tradition of a poetry that is still practiced by skill alone. Of course Catullus had his own voice, but it came from studying the Hellenic poets of the Greek Anthology, all of whom were writing in the same spirit and with the same conventions. The workshop or campus poets of today would probably do best to stop trying to speak in individual tones, which in practice merge into involun-tary unison: but in spite of T. S. Eliot's efforts to promote a doctrine of impersonality, that choice is not really open to the poets of our self-conscious age and society. Nor does Day Lewis's poetry strike the reader today as attempting unavailingly to find its own voice. On the contrary:

the still lively fascination of his verse seems to depend on the variety of tones he could pick up, change, and discard at will. Pushkin well understood the charms of such a virtuoso performance, presenting in his poem "Egyptian Nights" an improviser who can take up any topic an audience suggests and compose on it instantly, as if possessed by its appropriate and tutelary spirit.

And so the "Complete" Poems (an adjective more effective in its context than "Collected" would be) are uniformly full of a poetry to please and be admired. Day Lewis was well aware of what he could do and how to set about doing it, never staying long in the same place.

> Tenure is not for me
> I want to be able to drop out of my head,
> or off my rock and swim to another,
> ringed with a roundelay of sirens

In 1940 he translated Virgil's *Georgics*—exceedingly well. A few years before he made a spirited compound of elegy and epic, "A Time to Dance," commemorating the death of a teacher colleague, "a brilliant cricketer and amateur actor," as his widow Jill Balcon notes, and also celebrating the flight home after the First World War of two Australian airmen in a battered DH-9. Often anthologized, this remains a brilliantly satisfying performance, drawing its strength from the whole surge of the narrative, like all good verse of the kind, but lively enough to be quoted in part.

> Baghdad renewed a propeller damaged in desert. Arid
> Baluchistan spared them that brought down and spoiled
>   with thirst
> Armies of Alexander. To Karachi they were carried
> On cloud-back: fragile as tinder their plane, but the winds
>   were tender
> Now to their need, and nursed
> Them along till teeming India made room for them to alight.
> Wilting her wings, the sweltering suns had moulted her bright
> Plumage, rotten with rain

The fabric: but they packed her with iron washers and tacked her
Together, good for an hour, and took the air again.

The style is wholly nonpersonal, cunningly constructed, like the airplane
itself, from the flimsy but graceful stuff of tradition, given a more modern
edge by the echoes from Hopkins's "The Wreck of the Deutschland," and
from Auden's use of Old English alliteration. The effect is a dazzling
composite, replete with appropriate emotion and salutation: to courage,
grit, endurance—all the qualities supposed to be inculcated by the English public school values which these poets (they had all been schoolmas-
ters) had outwardly repudiated. The same goes for "The Nabara," an
epical account of a sea fight in the Spanish civil war between Basque
Republican ships and Franco forces. It adopts every metrical and rhetorical strategem that Tennyson had made memorable in "The Charge of
the Light Brigade" and "The Last Fight of the Revenge," and at the time
it was urgent with what seemed the best propaganda for the best sort of
cause. Those "men of the Basque country, the Mar Cantabrico" were
Stakhanovites, heroes of the future, whose deeds should not go unsung.

But the future has already dated. The battle of Madrid was not being
won on the playing fields of Oxford and Cambridge, as Day Lewis's
poems cannot, with hindsight, help giving that impression. Like other
long poems, by Stephen Vincent Benét or Edgar Lee Masters or Vachel
Lindsay, which rely on bringing traditional materials up to date, Day
Lewis's poetry of the period seems to have entered that "World of Lost
Things" visited in the *Orlando Furioso*, which Anthony Powell movingly
brings in to the last section of *A Dance to the Music of Time*. But the fact
remains that the lost things of such a world are often worth resurrecting,
and always worth investigation. They are, and should be, a subject of true
academic study, and in the case of poems their publication by a distinguished academic press is a gain for scholarship as well as for poetry.

It has to be said, however, that the true Lost Things in their peculiar
world never thought they would be lost—their assumption of permanence is a part of their pathos and their attraction. Day Lewis had no such
illusions. His modesty was genuine and profound, giving his verse texture
its winning versatility, its air that "tenure is not for me." Another poetic
charmer, Walter de la Mare, whose long career overlapped with Day

Lewis's, can leave the same impression; but de la Mare was one of those fortunate poets who produced a few undoubted masterpieces among a great many inferior journeyman poems, while nothing that Day Lewis wrote is lacking its own sort of ephemeral though rediscoverable effectiveness. He was well aware of this, and it was a part of his modesty, as Jill Balcon points out in her thoughtful and sensitive introduction. Like Edna St. Vincent Millay, who is also being rediscovered today, he was, as Jill Balcon suggests, a particularly honest kind of hero-worshiper. He wrote revealingly about this himself, observing that he had been "enabled to clarify my thoughts, by such diverse poets as Yeats, Wordsworth, Frost, Virgil, Valéry, Auden and Hardy. They suggested to me ways of saying what I had to say. Any given poem thus influenced is not necessarily secondhand." A reader might find, he adds, "as much difference as similarity between a poem of mine, influenced by him, and one of Hardy's own."

There is a certain pathos but also a subtle self-amusement in that—not for nothing was Day Lewis's provenance an Anglo-Irish one—as well as a sound critical point. It is quite true that there is a difference between a poem of Hardy's or Frost's and a related one by Day Lewis; and the latter's poetry can throw a searching light on the inwardness of the verse it hero-worships. This is especially true in the case of Frost. No one—certainly no critic—has as it were "got" Frost more exactly than Day Lewis did in some of his own poems, most notably of course in their concluding lines. It is a nice point whether the upshot is not to diminish the Frost poem rather than to elevate the Day Lewis; but in any case the contact is so persuasive that a new and fascinating sort of effect is, as R. P. Blackmur would have said, added to the sum of poetic reality.

In 1957, when Frost was on a visit to London, the poets spent an afternoon together at sheepdog trials in Hyde Park and composed an exercise in friendly competition on the event. Like dissimilar twins, the product of what Day Lewis referred to as a "stylised game" in "intuitive wit" compels a particularly droll form of attention on the reader's part. The sheepdog is like the poet, "for a kind of / Controlled woolgathering is my work too."

When Day Lewis held the Charles Eliot Norton chair at Harvard in 1964–1965 he pulled off another Frost, one of his own favorites, in the poem "On Not Saying Everything." As a variation on the woolgathering process, the last line deftly tucks home the point that a poem must be in

one sense self-limiting, finding its clue "from the not saying everything."
An earlier stanza, as sometimes happens too in Frost's own poems, foretells the apt conclusion.

> A poem, settling to its form,
> Finds there's no jailer, but a norm
> Of conduct, and a fitting sphere
> Which stops it wandering everywhere.

A poem by Hardy or Philip Larkin, no less than one by Wallace Stevens
or Emily Dickinson, does indeed wander everywhere, through the mysterious implications of its own exactness. The craftsmanlike precision of
Frost and Day Lewis belongs to an older tradition—Georgian, even
Augustan—when poetic diction was not afraid to have certain worldly tri-
umphalism about it, even though the self-congratulation of their own
speech is hidden beneath unpretentious homeliness.

 The incorrigibly public nature of Frost's diction—always "scoring"
but finally self-limiting—is revealed in Day Lewis's most touchingly
domestic poems, like the well-known "Walking Away," written for his eldest son, Sean, who had just come of an age to go to school on his own,
and to play football. The small "hesitant figure," seen off by dad, "has
something I never quite grasp to convey / About nature's give-and-take."

> I have had worse partings, but none that so
> Gnaws at my mind still. Perhaps it is roughly
> Saying what God alone could perfectly show—
> How selfhood begins with a walking away
> And love is proved in the letting go.

The arresting nature of that seems to come from the invisible collision
between a private and a public utterance, two conventions normally
more distinguishable in the rhetoric of verse than in any other context.
God, like love itself, has in this poem a stylized place as a poetic property:
a property that belongs to the public rather than to the private sphere.
Day Lewis never separated the two—perhaps did not want to—never
quite managing to steer his course, as he ironically remarked of his Geor-

gics translation, between "the twin vulgarities of flashy colloquialism and perfunctory grandiloquence." He was more harsh in his own self-knowledge than was justified, because the division itself did endow him with his own unique sort of poetic personality. Yet the consciousness of it was a deep pain to him, as is shown in the collection's most self-revealing poem, "Almost Human."

> The man you know, assured and kind,
> Wearing fame like an old tweed suit—
> You would not think he has an incurable
> Sickness upon his mind.

The tongue that "for the listening people / Articulates love, enlivens clay" is also disgusted with its own facilities. Yet in the man is something "that must for ever seek,"

> To share the condition it glorifies,
> To shed the skin that keeps it apart,
> To bury its grace in a human bed—
> And it walks on knives, on knives.

The word "grace" located in so deadly a fashion in that last stanza is nonetheless justified in the dimension of the poems. Their historic interest is indeed poignant, for they show us a civilization that began to apologize for its own culture, its own sense of the beautiful. Day Lewis loved Italy and all its artifacts, pictures, and buildings; and his book of poems *An Italian Visit* (1953) significantly combines his love of what he saw—the fountains in the streets, the pictures in the galleries—with a series of graceful poems in the style of poets he loved: a tacit admission that "beauty" in the old sense, however exuberantly enjoyed and celebrated, had become an affair of imitation, of touristic culture.

But the pastiche poems—a Della Robbia in the manner of Hardy, a Donatello by Yeats, a superlative Leonardo Annunciation by Frost—justify and carry the whole scheme of such verse, which with its lengthy borrowing from the metrics of Clough's Victorian "Amours de Voyage" might otherwise lose even the well-disposed reader's attention. A note by

Jill Balcon at the beginning of *An Italian Visit* records that the poem was written in 1948 and 1949, at the end of Day Lewis's long liaison with the novelist Rosamond Lehmann, who asked him not to publish it for several years, a request which he loyally honored.

Personal guilt, and a more complex guilt about the nature of its poetic stance, are never far away in this poetry, and give its easy nature in the end a compelling resonance. A real love of art made Day Lewis always passionately wish to join in.

> And if I miss that radiance where it flies,
> Something is gained in the mere exercise
> Of strenuous submission, the attempt
> To lose and find oneself through others' eyes.

It is these things, and the touch of unexpected obsession about them, which in the end win for the poetry a personality of its own. His grave in Stinsford churchyard in Dorset is close to Hardy's, as he wished it to be; and he died as Poet Laureate, an honor Hardy would probably not have declined had it been offered to him. In the few years left him he loved being Laureate, remarking with his usual charming grin that if he could produce appropriate verse for civic and municipal occasions, "I shall feel I've really achieved something." He wrote the epitaph now carved on his gravestone not long before he died. Characteristically it carries echoes from Hardy, from Housman, and from Walter de la Mare; yet it is different from any of them, a difference expressed not so much in the song he composed and the verse he recited but in the nature of the "pleasing anxious being" behind them.

> *Shall I be gone long?*
> For ever and a day.
> *To whom there belong?*
> Ask the stone to say,
> Ask my song . . .

It is not in the nature of stones, or of songs, to give such information, as the poem and the poet are well aware. Like a parting smile the irony shows how far the poetry had progressed since early days, when with *The Magnetic Mountain* in 1933 Day Lewis had leapt into action beside Auden ("Look west, Wystan, lone flyer, birdman, my bully boy!"), and what his poetry seemed to be up to; the result is a travesty which today sounds both absurd and touching.

> And if our blood alone
> Will melt this iron earth,
> Take it. It is well spent
> Easing a saviour's birth.

Such a verse, whose metaphor is as unreal as its sentiment, really does belong to the world of "Lost Things," of what Auden in "Spain" called "the ephemeral pamphlet and the boring meeting," although it was published in the year Hitler came to power, and in celebration of the poet's belief in the coming victory of communism, the new faith. Auden's poetry drew its own mysterious inner strength from the time: Day Lewis's tried loyally to make itself relevant and expedient to a history that has now discarded it. But poets' developments remain unpredictable. Because he never cared about "tenure" but threw himself into whatever appealed at the time, Day Lewis's poetry traveled in the end further than Auden's, however unexpectedly: Auden, for all his different interests, was stuck with his inescapable persona: his admiring disciple was free to derive a poetic voice from anywhere he chose—from Italy to the English past, other voices and other rooms. For anyone who likes poetry there is real interest here in that complete record.

The New York Review of Books, 1993

21

The Best of Betjeman

John Betjeman (1906–1984)

———————

John Betjeman's Collected Poems
compiled and with an introduction by the Earl of Birkenhead

Church Poems
by John Betjeman

IN ANTHONY'S BURGESS'S NOVEL, *Earthly Powers*, there is a parody of a Betjeman poem.

> Thus kneeling at the altar rail
> We ate the word's white papery wafer.
> Here, so I thought, desire must fail,
> My chastity be never safer.
> But then I saw your tongue protrude
> To catch the wisp of angel's food.

In a brilliant piece of wordplay the angel food cake of the children's tea party becomes the Host: sex, worship, and childhood come together on the tip of the darting tongue that demurely holds it. Essence of Betjeman, it would seem, compressed in a few workman-like lines. But not so. Betjeman himself is never so explicit in his real poetry. It escapes, in fact, from its always apparently so intrusive subject matter.

How this happens is itself a comment on the way a lot of poetry works, and the kind of world it creates and at times departs from. Burgess's parody shows what Betjeman is *not* like, because he singles points and ideas out for treatment in the same way that his own prose makes points, is chatty, ingenious, witty, informative. Burgess, one might say, turns art into non-art, fascinating, energetic, even suspenseful non-art, rather as his novel about Shakespeare sought to turn the art into the man. In this, he is not unlike those actual Elizabethan writers—Hall, Nashe, Greene—who created a whole great literary Elizabethan world of non-art, hardly read today but still well worth reading. In any fertile age there is a great deal of it, and our own is no exception.

But Betjeman's poetry is a particularly clear case of a poetry that does not contain its subject matter. Never "of its time," it has turned itself into a separate space-time continuum in which there is nothing but the poetry. This may seem so grotesque a point to make about the churchy, snobby, peopled, artlessly confiding and revealing world of Betjeman that it requires some clarification. Take the early poem "Death in Leamington"—Betjeman's "Lake Isle of Innisfree," as it has been called. The source of its amazing new reality is not at all easy to find. It is certainly not about death in any sense, though death and the fear of death are frequently emphasized in Betjeman's poetry, offered to us as a theme with a too insistent abandon. It is not even about architecture ("From those yellow Italianate arches / Do you hear the plaster drop?"), or the sense of place, or all three things coming together. Its effectiveness, going with the new and awkward life put into the simple meter, is an entirely new way of seeing things, an abandonment so unlike anything else as to become impersonal, disconnected with the poet.

> She died in the upstairs bedroom
>> By the light of the ev'ning star
> That shone through the plate glass window
>> From over Leamington Spa

The unexpectedness of plate glass in this context goes with the archaizing laboriousness of the dropped trisyllable in "evening." But neither is emphasized in a pantomimic or hammed-up way, as things so often are in less successful Betjeman, and in the Burgess parody. The thing is completely rapt and self-absorbed.

We meet the window again and learn something else about it.

> She bolted the big round window,
> She let the blinds unroll . . .

The nurse's activities, soothingly purposive, ungracefully habitual, dominate the poem, sinking to a conscious hush in the last two lines.

> And tiptoeing gently over the stairs
> Turned down the gas in the hall.

Before, she had moved into the room—"Breast high 'mid the stands and chairs"—another line of deeply penetrative awkwardness, "breast high" suggesting, among other things, the dense growth in some creature's native haunt, which is being explored. And who but Betjeman would have written "over the stairs" instead of "down the stairs"? Sensible laced black shoes are carefully picked up for the quiet negotiation of each riser.

The impact of the poem depends on the unseen but felt working of these actions—inter-relations of actions and things—with the bald vulgar lines of nudging statement or exclamation, obviously arranged to be somehow offensive.

> But the fingers that would have work'd it
> (the crochet)
> Were dead as the spoken word,

and

> But nurse was alone with her own little soul
> And the things were alone with theirs,

and

> Oh! Chintzy, chintzy cheeriness,
> Half dead and half alive!

Even as the poem takes him in, the reader notes and objects to the juvenile getting-above-himself of those comments, but their feebleness as comments does nonetheless mingle with the deep singular art of the poem's tone and movement. In depriving it of seriousness, they confirm its effectiveness as art. If the poem was what the American poetess Aline Kilmer, earnest disciple of Emily Dickinson, meant when she said in a poem that "things have a terrible permanence when people die," it would be banal. The world of the poem is so unusual that the platitude of death has no part in it.

Platitudes are, in fact, used instead as a way of pointing to the poem's originality. And that is the only true function of comment in Betjeman's poetry. A poem in which Betjeman imagines his own death—a much later poem—again acquires its chilling force from the way in which cliché and detail combine without having anything in common.

> Say in what cottage hospital
> Whose pale-green walls resound
> To the tap-tap-tap on the parquet
> Of inflexible nurses' feet
> Shall I myself be lying
> When they range the screens around?

The imitation of poetic language ("Say in what . . .") and of popular trench humor ("When they range the screens . . .") does nothing to detract from the fact that this is a real nightmare place. Death, and the deaths of others, is a platitude, but one's own death is something unique, singular with the same perfect singularity achieved by the poem.

No doubt the modish thing today would be to give Betjeman the same label that has been stuck on Gavin Ewart: "a deeply serious poet." That is the mechanical accolade, the last infirmity of contemporary clichés. Its irrelevance consists in the fact that no good poetry can be other than serious, whereas poetry written to be serious today is seldom good. The word has been deeply tainted by post-Arnoldian use, and should be retired indefinitely. Seriousness in nineteenth-century poetry hangs out self-consciously, as even Keats's does in "Hyperion" and Tennyson's in "Morte d'Arthur" ("Lest one good custom should corrupt the world"). Betjeman's poetry is founded on these nineteenth-century models and on the atmosphere of the Victorian age, and he makes as idiosyncratic a use of its gravity as of its rhythms and meters.

The difficulty, of course, is that he cannot "hang out" from his world: it is too much its own place for that. At times, this very fact can be used against itself, and to accentuate the note of Betjemanic comedy. In "Beside the Seaside," a relaxed and rambling account of Cornish childhood holidays, the central "event," which might have been got up in prose by almost any indifferent short-story writer, is the disillusion of Jennifer, aged twelve or so, when she finds that this summer she is no longer the little favorite on the beach.

> And here it was the tragedy began,
> That life-long tragedy of Jennifer
> Which ate into her soul and made her take
> To secretarial work in later life
> In a department of the Board of Trade.

This parodies, and deliberately crudely, the pregnant psychological episode favored not only by such stories, but by somber or sentimental Victorian narratives as well, where the "blighted life" is a favorite theme. The parody is of course "unserious," and to find its frivolity gratuitous would be to make heavy weather. Nonetheless, the tone *is* irritating just because it does "hang out," presenting a deliberate challenge to the serious. The tone is too much one of interior understanding, of a joke shared with the reader. It is precisely because good poetry is never "serious" that when here it deliberately chooses not to be so it brings up the whole irritating question and rubs it the wrong way.

Jennifer and her family are first presented in the poem with the same rapt attention and delight that looks into the Betjeman world and sees church interiors and Pams and Joan Hunter-Dunns. But meter and manner preclude those bursts of lyric magnificence: Betjeman essays the mock-sententious. He becomes knowing, over-conscious, collusive with the reader; the local and parodic tone invites a mockery of its own world, and of course the people inside it.

A single topic occupies our minds.

'Tis hinted at or boldly blazoned in
Our accents, clothes and ways of eating fish,
and being introduced and taking leave,
'Farewell', 'So long', 'Bunghosky', 'Cherribye'—
That topic all-absorbing, as it was,
Is now and ever shall be, to us—CLASS.

Very true no doubt, or at least very likely. But the lines make a point of being pleased with the effect of their own complacency, and ask us too winningly to share the pleasure. Perhaps it is churlish not to join in, but the summons to togetherness is not the most attractive feature of Betjeman's poetry. The really great poems—"A Subaltern's Love-Song," "Indoor Games near Newbury," "Upper Lambourne," "Spring Morning in North Oxford," "Youth and Age on Beaulieu River," and most of all, "Love in a Valley," are outbursts of erotic pleasure in the people that go with places. The adoration is classless, and the pleasure not only erotic but solipsistic. No togetherness there.

In these poems, Betjeman is a complete original: no other poet had perceived or expressed these things before, although the poetry is not concerned with being itself but is quite happy to be poetical and to borrow indiscriminately from poetic convention. In that, as in much else, Betjeman is like Wordsworth. The genuineness does not depend on a new style but on a new kind of perception, and in both poets there are "two voices." Wordsworth enjoying and Wordsworth expatiating are very different things, and the same is true with Betjeman. He is versatile; he has many tones; but only the passion rings true. His satire, his erudition and descriptive passages, even his enthusiasm and his humor, have something not quite right about them. I suppose this is part of the camp effect, which his fans revel in as much as they revel in everything else about him, but at his best Betjeman is emphatically not a camp poet. He is, though, when in "Beside the Seaside" he strikes the warm-hearted line about the holiday pursuits (this was in the Thirties) of the vulgar Brown family:

with allowances
For this and that and little income tax,
They probably earn seven times as much
As poor old Grosvenor-Smith. But who will grudge
Them this, their wild spontaneous holiday?
The morning paddle, then the mystery tour
By motor-coach inland this afternoon.
For that old mother what a happy time!

This can be taken as either straight or not straight, but either way it is no more satisfactory than the end of "Margate 1940":

And I think, as these fairy-lit sights I recall,
It is these we are fighting for, foremost of all.

The Poet Laureate would have no bother writing in the Soviet Union, because his fervent celebration of the Gleaming Heights of Socialism or kind hearts at the Kolkhoz could be taken according to taste. But banality in "Leamington Spa" and other masterpieces is doing a real job, no hanging out, but integral with the intensity of the perception. Betjeman at his best ("The Best of Betjeman," as we learn from *Summoned by Bells*, was a work the author dreamed up at school in Highgate and submitted to one of the temporary masters, T. S. Eliot, who made no comment) has the totality of childhood, or rather of adolescence, when emotional ecstasies find their consummation in the sight of a packet of Weights pressed in the Surrey sand, in the makes of Rovers and Austins and Lagondas, in rhododendrons ("Lucky the rhododendrons") casually swiped at by the tennis racquet of a girl with an arm "as firm and as hairy as Hendren's." Surprised by these joys, the reader is swept into them as if with Kubla Khan in Xanadu, or in Keats's castle on the Eve of St. Agnes.

Betjeman's joys and sorrows go straight back to the early Romantics. He is not a bit like Hardy and Philip Larkin, who are often associated with him. No comparison could be more misleading. Their idiom is one of deprivation, of that pleasure in things going wrong, or never having been right, which has become so much a part of English culture and consciousness. But Betjeman's gaiety, like his sense of glory, is the most genuine thing about him. Hardy and Philip Larkin cheer us up, and themselves, by the tender scrupulousness with which they couple the unshapely ills of existence with noticings and perceptions that reconcile us to those ills. Deprivation is associated in them with the hiding-places of comfort. Their poems are not out to please or to exhibit pleasure, and they have no social sense at all. Betjeman's poems are not exactly *about* "How to Get On in Society" (the title of the famous one that starts "Phone for the fish-knives, Norman"), but they reflect the personality of someone who is obviously getting on very well indeed.

Laugh the Betjeman way and the best people will laugh with you. D. H. Lawrence had a comparable power, the jester's vitality that attracts the upper crust, and the social "feel" in his verse has odd affinities with Betjeman's: both are obviously—in their works and out of them—the life and soul of a "set." There is of course no more to it than that—Betjeman's preoccupations having nothing of Lawrence in them—but the butterfly moods and the inspired mimicry have a curious relation: Betjeman's world of things is as authentic as Lawrence's beasts, birds, and flowers. There is a sharp distinction in both writers, too, between the solitary and the social personality, and the real poet in each is the solitary one.

In such cases, no doubt, the social comes in the end wholly to preponderate. To be in Betjeman's "set" is to enjoy the things he enjoys, the churches, the architecture, the nostalgically or exuberantly self-mocking Anglican emotions.

> Dear old, bloody old England
> Of telegraph poles and tin . . .

That struck the right note, but anything graver and more satirical is apt to fall flat. Larkin has, rather oddly, referred to Betjeman as a "committed writer," an adjective which might seem as beside the point as "serious" would be. And yet perhaps not. A committed writer is more concerned with what he says than how he says it, and that, oddly enough, is both what impresses about the bulk of Betjeman's work, and what goes wrong. It takes a committed poet to express his convictions and feelings with such forcible flatness. That, after all, is an aspect of Betjeman's Wordsworthian side, and Wordsworth wrote a hundred or so "Ecclesiastical Sonnets" which are pretty unreadable today.

Readable Betjeman always is, though his Anglican ditties and "Poems in the Porch," now reprinted with others as *Church Poems*, do not go very far back in terms of Anglican tradition. There is nothing Elizabethan about them, nothing of the sharpness of Donne or the mysterious sweetness of Herbert. He does not think in his poems, as they did or seem to do; he does not even ruminate, as Philip Larkin so impressively does in his poem "Church Going." But why should he? His faith is in the ongoing power of Church—necessities, restorations, and revampings of prayer book notwithstanding.

> The Church's restoration
>   In eighteen-eighty-three
> Has left for contemplation
>   Not what there used to be.

No, where Betjeman is concerned it has left more, much more. He is identified with a new sort of revival, unserious but certainly committed in its own way, done with all the fervor of the nineteenth-century hymns but sending itself up at the same time. The dual response is important: it is because the hymn is so robustly absurd that we sing it with the delight that we do. A mutual admiration society perhaps, a "set" again, but what else has the social side of religion, in its vitality and in its complex utilities, ever been? Betjeman relishes and reveres every historic and contemporary aspect, from "Undenominational / But still the church of God"—

> Revival ran along the hedge
>   And made my spirit whole
> When steam was on the window panes
>   And glory in my soul—

to the elaborate Art Nouveau of Holy Trinity, Sloane Street:

The tall red house soars upward to the stars,
The doors are chased with sardonyx and gold,
And in the long white room
Thin drapery draws backward to unfold
Cadogan Square between the window-bars
And Whistler's mother knitting in the gloom.

Church poems, like poems of plain works of art with a sub-clerical interest and flavor, could hardly have occurred without Betjeman's preparation of the ground.

In their poems Hardy and Larkin are natural dramatists. They intensify anonymous moods, invent situations; only the settings and the noticings are immediately and personally "true." With Betjeman it is different. Although his imagination is so Victorian, he does entirely without the odd Victorian gift for disingenuousness, for pretense and concealment. Like a certain sort of church he fancies, with carved pilasters and gilt commandment boards, where

pre-Tractarian sermons roll'd
Doctrinal, sound and dry,

his natural voice is that of the late-eighteenth-century poets whose tones converge in the spacious decorum of Wordsworth's *Prelude* and *Excursion*. Betjeman has no persona: he is simply himself. That explains the immense popularity of *Summoned by Bells*, the verse autobiography with real names in it, real parents and reactions to them, all the youthful experiences and impressions complete, up to the age of leaving Oxford without a degree and taking perforce a prep-school job where

Harsh hand-bells harried me from sleep
For thirty pounds a year and keep.

As in all the best autobiographies, from Edmund Gosse to Jocelyn Brooke, the flavor of personal experience is exactly caught.

All silvery on frosty Sunday nights
Were City steeples white against the stars.
And narrowly the chasms wound between
Italianate counting-houses, Roman banks,
To this church and to that. Huge office-doors,
Their granite thresholds worn by weekday feet
(Now far away in slippered ease at Penge),
Stood locked. St Botolph this, St Mary that,
Alone shone out resplendent in the dark.
I used to stand by intersecting lanes
Among the silent offices, and wait,
Choosing which bell to follow: not a peal,
For that meant somewhere active; not St Paul's,
For that was too well-known. I liked things dim—
Some lazy rector living in Bexhill
Who most unwillingly on Sunday came
To take the statutory services,
A single bell would tinkle down a lane:
My echoing steps would track the source of sound . . .

Such things are as authentic as the skating or climbing episodes in the
Prelude, the singularity of the poet's taste being substituted for the shock
of recognition which surprises the reader of Wordsworth. Betjeman's
emotions are both intense and narcissistically self-aware.

'Twas not, I think, a conscious search for God
That brought me to these dim forgotten fanes.
Largely it was a longing for the past,
With a slight sense of something unfulfilled;
And yet another feeling drew me there,
A sense of guilt increasing with the years—
'When I am dead you will be sorry, John'—
Here I could pray my mother would not die.
Thus were my London Sundays incomplete
If unaccompanied by Evening Prayer.
How trivial used to seem the Underground,

How worldly looked the over-lighted west,
How different and smug and wise I felt
When from the east I made my journey home!

It has the same flat accuracy of tone, however effectively crafted, that will later tell us, after the author has been sent down from Oxford for failing in Divinity (of all things!), that

Maurice Bowra's company
Taught me far more than all my tutors did.

The personal Betjeman is compulsive, but the rare impersonal one — the one who has disappeared wholly into ecstasies of subalterns and their girlfriends, and the fir-dry alleys round Camberley bungalows, and the waste water running out into the dark — is even better. That is what I meant by the two voices in his poetry, and how one of them escapes from the humor and the in-jokes, from the idiosyncratic subject matter, escapes beyond parody into a world no longer its own, one for which no reader of poetry could feel the incomprehension or distaste which might legitimately be felt for the personal Betjeman, the in-Betjeman. That world belongs to the ages.

London Review of Books, 1981

22

The Flight of the Disenchanter

W. H. Auden (1907–1973)

Early Auden
by Edward Mendelson

BOTH HUMPHREY CARPENTER in his biography and Edward Mendelson in his very illuminating critical study emphasize the vulnerability of the younger Auden, and perhaps the Auden of any age. A secure childhood, but accompanied by a sense of failure and inadequacy at school and in relation to others; a fear of appearing dull and anxious and uncouth, compensated for by making himself the legendary figure who seems to understand everyone and everything—"Hunt the lion, climb the peak, / No one guesses you are weak"—this dualism is commonplace among the gifted of all ages, particularly the gifted young. Most such persons, though, have a secure place, a secret wholeness of self-satisfaction into which they can withdraw. We can detect it, even enter it to our own corresponding satisfaction, in the poems of Edward Thomas, of Hardy, of Eliot. But not in Auden's. He is not even on terms of intimacy with the "Wound" to which he writes the letter.

The act of working—and Auden became a workaholic as well as a heavy drinker—obscures most effectively the question of who one is. "The soul doubtless is immortal where a soul can be discerned." The poem's immortality, in Auden's case, does not depend on the survival in it of a self. It is interesting that he instinctively sought one, at the time of his juvenilia, in the poems of Hardy and Edward Thomas, twin voices to be imitated. A special favorite was one of Thomas's most characteristic poems, "Lights Out". "I have come to the borders of sleep . . ."

> The tall forest towers;
> Its cloudly foliage lowers
> Ahead, shelf above shelf;
> In silence I hear and obey
> That I may lose my way
> And myself.

The poet's desire to get lost in sleep reveals his actual presence in the poem more subtly and strongly than anything else could do, as it does in Philip Larkin's poem with the repeated line: "Beneath it all, desire of oblivion runs." Those negations disclose an individuality as nothing in Auden does. His sort of equivalent would be to write, as he does in "Oxford," "Here too the knowledge of death / Is a consuming love"—and the tone of that could be paraphrased from a guidebook or a work of psychology.

"All I have is a voice," he wrote, in his early work, and its potency depended on its impersonal authority. Charles Madge's reaction— "There waited for me in the summer morning, / Auden, fiercely, I read, shuddered and knew"—was common among those at the time who understood the nature of new utterance in poetry and were unconsciously awaiting it. That it was not the voice of an individual was, in terms of the Zeitgeist, so much the better: a bleak impersonal severity was in fashion, as was the idea of communal enterprise, in poetry as in society. But Auden never did develop his individuality. The cozy mannerisms of his latter period are no more personal than the youthful tones, but are just as much something in the air, the sound of the leader of a group or fashion, though no longer one that was minatory and exhilarating.

Not infrequently it happens that the tone was not altered at all between the early and the late periods. As soon as the undergraduate of 1926 was introduced by his friend Tom Driberg to *The Waste Land* he took to writing stanzas like

> In Spring we waited. Princes felt
> Through darkness for unwoken queens;
> The itching lover weighed himself
> At stations on august machines

which has not only ceased to be Eliot and become Auden but is the same Auden—although not as accomplished—as the one who around 1950 was to write for Cyril Connolly that most plumy of camp poems, "The Fall of Rome."

> Fantastic grow the evening gowns;
> Agents of the Fisc pursue
> Absconding tax-defaulters through
> The sewers of provincial towns.

The always questionable relation between self and group is characteristic of this poetry, the sign of a duality both accepted and exploited by the poet. Mendelson observes that as he began his career Auden wanted "both absolute isolation and absolute community, one for the mind, the other for the flesh," and "in his poems he had no need for a dramatic mask; he was invisible without one." This may be a way of saying that the poems do not necessarily believe in their own air of complete confidence, of assertiveness over and rapport with the reader. They seem to be in personal charge but disappear into the isolation of art. Barbara Everett comments that "it is the sound of a man who knows that he sounds like this, assents to sounding like this, but is not like this." Then what is he like? Nothing else. The art is all, as it is in Mozart or Shakespeare: it is the art (as Auden put it in "The Age of Anxiety") of "the sane who know they are acting," rather than "the mad who do not." Sanity for this poet is keeping the show on the road.

The poet is what the poetry seems; part of the art of the contraption is to make up an impression—a disconcerting or alluring one—of the man inside it. The uniqueness of Auden's poetry lies in its being the result of an act of will. A similar act of will might have made him a doctor, a geologist, a brilliant teacher. That he turned out to be a brilliant poet does not alter the essential arbitrariness of his decision to become one. And his attitude to his art ("we may write, we *must* live") remained permanently affected by that decision. The paradox is that other poets who have, as it were, found themselves in their poetry, take their dedication to it for granted: their art is for them the most important *human* activity, proclaiming poet as man and man as poet, paired in harmony. Gabriel Josipovici blames Auden for his attitude to art, rightly seeing in it a rejection of the slow, painful exploratory process which results in the organic creation of a Mallarmé, a Joyce, an Eliot, a Wallace Stevens, or a Montale. Auden's act was that of scald or court poet, lead man in a team, the analogy again being with modern activities likes physics or filmmaking. For such an act, art must be highly decorated but untrustworthy, halcyon but bogus, beautifully made to be true to nothing else. Auden is the "half-witted Swedish deckhand" whom Basil Wright and Harry Watt, the directors of *Night Mail*, saw scribbling "the most beautiful verse" for them on an old GPO table and telling them to "just roll it up and throw it away" when its profuseness had to be checked. *Night Mail* is the strongest magic ever brewed by Auden, a magic that completely enchants and dispossesses what it celebrates.

The brilliant creature who looks like a Swedish deckhand is also an image of the Mozart who so affronted the serious Salieri, a legend dramatized with elegant intensity by Pushkin and vulgarized in the play *Amadeus*. Artists dedicated as and for themselves recognize such genius but secretly, almost unconsciously, hate and envy it, for it discredits their labors to bring their own special gifts to fruition. "Negative capability" takes on a special meaning in Auden's case. He comes as close as any poet in the post-romantic age to what Coleridge said of Shakespeare—"a very Proteus of the fire and flood"—naming and inhabiting people and things, entering into being while having no being of his own. In our time this primary activity of the naïve poet is no longer possible. Auden could not get into things and people, but he got instead into the spirits and sense of the age, into its moods and dreams, its fears and neuroses, its fashions and crazes, from Homer Lane to Sheldon, from the yo-yo to the carbon date. He turned into hard magic everything in the consciousness of the time that was questioning and uncertain, muddled and apprehensive, everything that was reaching out, as the poetry itself seemed to be doing, for new devices and solutions, new images of wholeness and salvation.

Poetry eternalizes these things, but also embodies in the process the very weakness it transforms, it "flat ephermeral" nature. Poetry only survives "in the valley of its making." That marvelous poem "Spain," which chastened liberals disapprove of today, gets its power from its accurate conjuration of the illusions of a special moment, its fidelity to that moment's sense of "Today, the struggle," and tomorrow (which never comes in poem or history) the idyllic social utopia. Auden, as he told Isherwood, knew they could only live among lunatics, and the same is true of his poems. Unlike most great poetry they do not beckon to another world but make one out of the absurdities of the present.

Of course, if that had been the poet's intention the magic would not have worked: the young Auden wrestled with real problems as other intellectuals were doing. Mendelson is not only his most perceptive critic but executor, guardian, and scholar-chief of Auden studies, and this study tells us more than any other about the background of his early work and the scaffolding and ideas behind his poetry, particularly of the big stuff, ambitious raids on significance like *The Orators* and *The Ascent of F6*. Mendelson's tone is humorous and humane, and he never tries to impose a paraphrase of an interpretation, but he is up against the problem that all Auden critics face. Since his art was not evolved and explored but magical and ephemeral, Auden's poems lose their point in the focus of commentary, just as they frequently did when he himself revised them at a much later date ("Oxford" lost everything when its syntax was made more plausive). I recall the sensible and humanitarian glosses made by Richard Hoggart in his early study, and my own feeling when I was working on Auden that they were in a frustrating way both true and not true; that one could neither take the poems as magic anecdotes and incantations nor as (what for instance "Just as his dream foretold" or "Our hunting fathers" seemed to be) coherent meditations on social and personal states.

The success of an Auden poem, especially an early one, depends on its simplicity. When he pursues a complex argument as in "Meiosis," which Mendelson analyzes, the poem sustains the complexity by making a special thing of it, like an ingenious pump or gear, but calls in magic, too, as an insurance (the Dantesque last line) and ends up with all its bits and pieces seeming strewn on the page around it. Mendelson picks them up, observing that the poem explores a heterosexual conceit, the progress of the seed into the womb, with all the consciousness this must imply of imperfections passed on and inspissated traumas perpetuated; yet because love is the universal and functional instinct the seed-giver is not depressed by this knowledge. The poem is an impressive, even satisfying contraption, but there is no life in it. In his maturity Auden would have been more genial, more cunning, and more clear, but it is doubtful if he would have been more inspiring. The poem lacks sex and its excitement of the group, the excitement that is so extraordinary and has such controlled success in "Consider":

> Then, ready, start your rumour, soft
> But horrifying in its capacity to disgust
> Which, spreading magnified, shall come to be
> A polar peril, a prodigious alarm,
> Scattering the people, as torn-up paper
> Rags and utensils in a sudden gust,
> Seized with immeasurable neurotic dread.

As the Airman would say: "Much more research needed into the crucial problem—group organization." Mendelson feels that energy like this is "a projection of the Airman's (Auden's) contradictory desire for order and no order at once." But where do we find Auden at all in such a poem? Granted his near-obsession with organization and meaning, and with the importance, which he often stressed, of a subject, the fact remains that the personality and behavior of the Airman exist only as a secret excitement or glee. In "Consider" it seems likely that the rumor "horrifying in its capacity to disgust" is in fact connected with homosexuality, and the secret group knowledge that goes with it. But this again is a case of Auden's talent for disappearing not only into the overwhelming atmosphere of the poem but into the general sense of apprehension and impending disaster ("It is later than you think") which the poem has conjured up.

The ideal Auden poem of this date always moves outward into a public scene imagined in its significant details and observed as if from the air or by radio ("Supplied elsewhere to farmers and their dogs / Sitting in kitchens in the stormy fens"). The torn-up paper is reminiscent of the famous shot in *Things to Come*, where the camera focuses on a ragged scrap of newsprint caught on wire, giving news of ultimate war-horrors. The image of the helmeted airman, with his lordly perspective, is superb but farcical, too, just as his exhortation is also a spell of comfort against the horrors that a demoralized society imagines are awaiting it. Auden's poetry is deeply aware that the group want both to be thrilled by their bard and to joke with him, and that the ideal shaman is both a power and a figure of fun. The Airman is related to the curious persona of "Mother" which Auden adopted socially in his late maturity, when in addition to the role defined in the saying "Your mother knows best" he would present mother as a clown figure, reciting the first line of Spender's poem as "Your old mother thinks continually of them that are truly great." Reading Benedict and Malinowski, the young Auden was no doubt well aware of the function of this kind of thing in group anthropology: the fear of mothers or bears was negated by the shaman taking on their role.

Mendelson quotes a letter written in 1932 in which Auden revealed the source of *The Orators*, probably with a touch of parody of Eliot's notes to *The Waste Land*:

> The genesis of the book was a paper written by an anthropologist friend of mine about ritual epilepsy among the Trobriand Islanders, linking it up with the flying powers of witches, sexual abnormalities etc.

The friend was John Layard, who had shot himself through the head in Berlin two years before, out of jealousy over a boy Auden was also interested in. Amazingly he failed to kill himself and was taken to hospital by Auden, after which he made a full recovery. Despite his depressions and instability he was a remarkable theorist and original thinker, and the papers he wrote for the *Journal of the Royal Anthropological Institute*—"Flying Tricksters, Ghosts, Gods and Epileptics," and "Shamanism: an Analysis Based on the Flying Tricksters of Malekula"—are the specific influences, behind *The Orators*, mixed with the doctrines of D. H. and the personality of T. E. Lawrence, and with the image of a revolutionary hero that came from Lenin and the early romance of Nazism and *Führerprinzip*.

Together with the charade *Paid on Both Sides, The Orators* developed the Auden technique later adopted in the plays he wrote with Isherwood: exotic and mythical matter from the past and present and transposed into the group life of English schools and homes. Such a transposition was standard practice among the modernists—Eliot had used it in *The Waste Land*—but Auden gave it not only the special emphasis of a game among initiates but a corresponding and disarming frivolity (though *Paid on Both Sides* is significantly more serious, and more moving, than *The Orators*). As usual there is a discrepancy, particularly grotesque in the latter case, between the impact of the work of art and what the artist and his critics have said about it. Auden wrote to Naomi Mitchison that "the theme was the failure of the romantic conception of personality"; and expressing dissatisfaction to another correspondent he said the result was "far too obscure and equivocal"—what was intended as a critique of the Fascist outlook "might be interpreted as a favourable exposition." That, indeed, is one reason why *The Orators* comes off as well as it does, for Mendelson emphasizes that however much the early Auden wanted to respond "positively" to the challenge of the time and become the young poet spokesman for enlightenment and left-wing ideals, his art would not oblige. The group was essential to it, the cause was not. And neither was the Message. However much he tinkered with *The Ascent of F6*, the end remained a muddle, though the individual speeches and poems are so effective; and compared with its group liveliness, the satire of *The Dog Beneath the Skin* operates on the most elementary level.

The most significant comment on *The Orators* was made by Auden himself in a preface to a new edition in 1966. He cannot, he says, "think myself back into the frame of mind in which I wrote it. My name on the title page seems a pseudonym for someone else, someone talented but near the border of sanity, who might well in a year or two become a Nazi." Its central theme, he then felt, was hero-worship, but had he ever been a hero-worshipper? Had he in fact, before he went to America and fell in love with Chester Kallman, ever been anybody, except a brilliant and dispossessed talent? The later Auden does not recognize the earlier, just as the writer of the early poems seems wholly different from the anxious and wretched being of his Journal and Diaries. Keats is Keats in letters as in poems, but Auden is not Auden. No wonder his early work and his manifestos to friends are so obsessed with "wholeness"; and it is highly ironical that Madge and other readers ("My states of mind were broken. It was untrue / The easy doctrine which separated things") should have been so struck by the force of the new doctrine. Mendelson comments: "Madge had it backward. Auden implied connections and relations only to announce their absence or failure." It is rather, perhaps, that Auden's early poetry is always having the opposite effect to the one proclaimed, delighting when it threatens, reassuring when it warns, relaxing when it sets out to brace. No wonder Leavis, the apostle of true wholeness, was so disillusioned.

With great acuteness, Mendelson traces the wholeness of the problem to an early essay called "Writing" which Auden did for Naomi Mitchison who was editing a collection called *An Outline for Boys and Girls and Their Parents*. Written in a simple family style, it discusses the connection of words with isolation and self-consciousness. In trying to bridge a gulf and restore wholeness, language in fact connives at the disjunction it tries to overcome. A hunting group learns to talk when it tries to recreate the communal excitement of the hunt (was Auden recalling Tolstoy's theory of art, here?) but words are naturally antagonistic both to user and referent. In reconstituting experience they separate us from it and from the wholeness we seek to attain. Mendelson suggests that Auden's account of language's origin in a sense of absence, its ineffectual efforts to bridge a gap, comes close to structuralist theory "a generation before Derrida and Lacan,") although the poet's schoolroom style in the essay is at the furthest possible remove from the opacity of later theoreticians. Be that as it may, the piece certainly sheds light on the way Auden's diction gets its characteristic effects, and the gap his poems make between subject and response, a gap that becomes virtually an aesthetic weapon. Mendelson's nose for what is relevant in unlikely places—critics, as he says, have written off this essay because of the book it came out in—is typical of the sensitive and detailed scholarship he brings to this period of Auden's life.

One might add that the even more effective weapon with which the poetry both underlines and combats the alienation of language is what might be termed the Saving Personification. Direct appeals fail: it seems merely out of place when at the end of that ambitious poem "The Malverns" Auden invokes the words of Wilfred Owen and Katherine

Mansfield ("Kathy in her journal") to rub the message home; as out of place as when in 1929 ("It was Easter as I walked in the public gardens") he introduces us to an actual dropout on a bench. It is true that "The Malverns" is a superlatively absorbing poem, and also the first poem in which Auden's settled maturity is forecast, with its caressing verbal catalogues and its simplistic ingenuities of appeal. It humanizes the helmeted airman and introduces us for the first time to that totally unintimate intimacy which from now on will be the tone of a poet "assuming to sound like this," as he does in the Byron pastiche in *Letters from Iceland*.

The reader's feeling of intimacy with most poets takes two forms. First, that the poet is revealing to him, quite naturally and by the act of composition, something he could not reveal to anyone else; second, and conversely, that the poet "in touching our hearts by revealing his own," as Hardy puts it, also reveals that he has a self to keep back. The second does not apply to later confessional poetry, like Lowell's and Berryman's, whose convention is a complete avowal to the reader; and neither applies to Auden. His early intimacy of threats and promises is like the disclosures of an older and dazzling schoolboy prodigy to the reader as younger child; and this changes to the reader being accepted as one of a group of comrades and initiates, the poet forthcoming and unbuttoned but retaining his powers of fascination and omniscience. The poems written in Brussels in 1938–1939, "Musée des Beaux Arts," "Gare du Midi," "The Capital," and "Epitaph on a Tyrant"—are good examples of this, and the success of such a style of communication reveals the hollowness, embarrassment even, when the group seems to have disappeared, and the poet of "Lay your sleeping head" and "I sit in one of the dives / On Fifty-Second street" is talking to us on our own. The residue of discomfort and unreality in such poems is produced by a suggestion of contrived aloneness, a person-to-person relation does not come naturally.

It is here that the Saving Personification comes to the rescue. These feats have an air of the unintentional, of inadventure, of something the poet does not bother about and the reader can carry away with him.

> And, gentle, do not care to know,
> Where Poland draws her eastern bow,
>   What violence is done,

> Nor ask what doubtful act allows
> Our freedom in this English house
> Our picnics in the sun.

The simple reference to Poland holds considerable complexity. Poland under Pilsudski is a tyrant appropriately armed. But the bow is also that a violin and musician, the vulnerable instrument of peace, while the pictorial referent in the personification is Rembrandt's Polish Rider, the taut and soldierly masculine figure with the features of a girl; more generically, Poland plays the part in history of both victim and rebel. The beauty of the image seems serenely independent of the pushy insistence of the poet as leader and lecturer. It is the same with the green heraldic glimpses of English landscape that Auden lifted from Anthony Collett's *The Changing Face of England*:

> Calm at this moment the Dutch sea so shallow
> That sunk St Paul's would ever show its golden cross
> And still the deep water that divides us still from Norway.

Perhaps the plunge into what seems a limpid imagination is the effect of true secrecy, not elsewhere found in Auden, the poet concealing his simple debt in Eliot's remembered dictum that "the bad poet imitates, the good poet steals." I think that John Fuller, the doyen in England of Auden minutiae, has also pointed out Auden's extraordinary debt to Collett's handbook, whose barely altered phrases nonetheless suffer a sea change, calming and stabilizing the compositional alembic. All the personifications do that.

> As Fahrenheit in an odd corner of great Celsius' kingdom
> Might mumble of the summers measured once by him.

This might be borrowed, too, but the effect of all Auden's borrowing—whether of phrases, ideas, or doctrines—is to emphasize the immense spread and richness of his achievement, and the retreat, too, by personification into a kind of shyness.

To find those clearings where the shy humiliations
Gambol on sunny afternoons, the waterhole to which
The scarred rogue sorrow comes quietly in the small hours.

The most pellucid and complete of all such things in Auden's poetry is probably the madrigal "O lurcher-loving collier," set to music by Benjamin Britten, which Auden wrote to ornament the last moments of *Coal Face*, a short documentary film about mining.

Everything that the young Auden wrote has a bottom of good sense. His poetry's hospitality toward crazes of every kind, crackpot or otherwise, carries into its art one of the most universal of human tendencies, and corrects it with a faith and a skepticism that, again as with most human beings, are almost identical. "You cannot have poetry unless you have a certain amount of faith in something, but faith is never unalloyed with doubts." A true magic is its own antidote. For Auden as for Nabokov, "art is a game of intricate enchantment and deception," but Auden also wrote that "in so far as poetry, or any of the arts, can be said to have an ulterior purpose, it is, by telling the truth, to disenchant and disintoxicate." It was by his genius for resolving this paradox that Auden became, as Mendelson justly claims, "the most inclusive poet of the twentieth century, its most technically skilled, and its most truthful."

Times Literary Supplement, 1981

23

The Last Romantic

Philip Larkin (1922–1985)

Philip Larkin
by Andrew Motion

WHY IS PHILIP LARKIN so different from other poets of today? The simple question is not easy to answer, although every appreciative critic and lover of poetry has his own solution and his own diagnosis of Larkin's virtues. Long ago the Poet Laureate referred to him as "the John Clare of the building estates," a decidedly quaint though no doubt heartfelt compliment, in line with Eric Homberger's later summing-up of Larkin as "the saddest heart in the post-war super-market," or the more magisterial pronouncement that his poetry is "representative of the modern English condition: a poetry of lowered sights and diminishing expectations." These judgments suggest his glum accuracy about places and emotions—particularly his own—an unillusioned accuracy beautifully, and in a very English way, satisfying both the poet and ourselves with what another critic has called "a central dread of satisfaction." As Larkin has himself wryly remarked: "Deprivation for me is what daffodils were for Wordsworth." What is perfect as a poem is what is imperfect in life.

More recently the Larkin effect has been defined in terms of his own peculiar use of symbolism, the symbolism that Yeats got from the French poets, especially Mallarmé. In her essay "Philip Larkin: after Symbolism" Barbara Everett has pointed out these French echoes; the fact that, for example, "Sympathy in White Major" is a kind of symbolist parody of

Gautier's "Symphonie en blanc majeur," and "Arrivals, Departures" echoes Baudelaire's "Le Port." It is quite true that Larkin's brand of rhetoric, as it suddenly flowers at the end of poems like "Absences" ("Such attics cleared of me! Such absences."), "Next Please," and "High Windows," has the sound of French eloquence, or rather a uniquely effective English adaptation of it. Larkin is also adept at the Baudelairean device of dislocating the pulse and rhythm of lines from the actual things they are speaking of—Baudelaire's decaying corpses or *affreuses juives*, Larkin's trains and hospitals and bed-sitters and death-fears—so that a different and disembodied image is created, something that is nowhere and endless, forever "out of reach," like the landscape of "Here."

A more direct borrowing can be found at the end of "An Arundel Tomb." Of the stone effigies of the earl and countess we are told in the last stanza that "Time has transfigured them into / Untruth." The reference must be to Mallarmé's lines on the tomb of Poe: *"Tel qu'en lui-même enfin L'éternité change."* The reversal is not ironic. Untruth is the home of poetry, the only place of transfiguration. Time, for Mallarmé, takes away what is irrelevant in Poe's life: for Larkin, it removes actuality from the history of the stone figures and their touching hand-in-hand pose (including the detail that the pose itself was added by a Victorian restorer, a fact presumably not known to Larkin, though it would have given him pleasure). Transfiguration is into a kind of poetic absence which includes only the idea of love, not its quotidian betrayals or fulfillments. "What remains of us is love" in the sense that love equates with self-extinction. I think Larkin here gives his own entombed precision to the Symbol, which for the symbolists gave out nothing but its own powers of suggestion. To Larkin it suggests the comfort of disappearance, selflessness, away-ness, and in the universe this is no doubt the true comfort of love.

The Symbol can deepen and reverse the familiarity of a poem, changing its nature like a symphony. For Hardy the nature of a poem on a tomb would be its fidelity in a homely historical way. Larkin in a radio talk said he wanted to write different sorts of poems. "Someone once said that the great thing is not to be different from other people but different from yourself." He wished he could write more often like the last line of "Absences" ("Such attics cleared of me . . .") A highly personal poet, he uses symbolism as a mode of the impersonal, to liberate the poem from its own world.

Barbara Everett in her essay looked at Larkin from a new angle, and in his short book on Larkin in the Methuen Contemporary Writers series Andrew Motion emphasizes even more the symbolist side of Larkin. Although what he has to say is always perceptive it brings out once again, as every critic has done, the seeming capacity of Larkin to escape from his poems, not to be pinned down in them. The critic is not wrong or misguided, and yet Larkin is not there any more. Like the brides in "The Whitsun Weddings" we travel with him on the same train, bound for the same destination, but when our procedures and projects get under way he has already departed elsewhere. Indeed that word, as I shall hope to show, stands for something very important in his poetry.

That absence from the critic, even from the reader, is unusual in the poetry of today, which in general is distinguished by togetherness and communality, a complex and clever intimacy with the reader. Poets understand each other because they write for each other. It is not a new phenomenon; it has happened with all collective poetry, with the metaphysicals and with the poets of the "Tribe of Ben." But Larkin is not like that. He seems to be present in his poetry historically, and as it were histrionically, as a nineteenth-century poet might now seem to us present in his poetry. His seeming intimacy can be startling and yet he is both shameless and reticent, confidential and yet invulnerably refined, wholly unself-conscious and yet inevitably withdrawn, unavailable to us and yet totally forthcoming, absent in presence. His presence is its own style of "elsewhere." The interior of his poetry, like a Vermeer interior, is both wholly accessible and completely mysterious.

As a student Larkin adored Yeats, feeding upon his music and his mystery, though disliking his ideas. After his influence was worked out there still lurked in Larkin's verse that riddling transition from loftiness to intimacy—those "magnanimities of sound" as Yeats called them—which the old wizard could modulate so well. Yeats is eloquent about a great creator like himself being "forced to choose / Perfection of the life or of the work." In Larkin this high destiny undergoes a characteristic shift, though it is equally insistent. Now it is a domestic choice, presented with comic drabness. Yeats compared himself with the soldiers of the civil war, and Larkin ponders the active life of Arnold, the married man.

> To compare his life and mine
> Makes me feel a swine . . .

Comedy with Larkin never dis-elevates decorum, the eloquence of rhythm and tone.

Nor does it affect the role in his poetry of "elsewhere," as it appears in that deceptively simple short poem, "The Importance of Elsewhere." Elsewhere is a fairy place, but it is not insubstantial.

> You can see how it was:
> Look at the picture and the cutlery.
> The music in the piano stool. That vase.

It is also sex. Sex can only be its real self in the other world, in the imagination, in the head. Where have we come across this before? Not in any place as recondite as Symbolist poetry, but in one of the most famous of romantic poems.

> And this is why I sojourn here
>   Alone and palely loitering,
> Though the sedge is withered from the lake,
>   And no birds sing.

For Keats, as for many other nineteenth-century imaginations, sex was a fairy world that vanished in consummation. Larkin in his own way inherits the tradition, inherits, too, its legacy of disillusion. The erotic is elsewhere. "Dry Point," in *The Less Deceived*, is a more explicit and more metaphysical poem than "La Belle Dame Sans Merci," but it makes the same point with the same kind of intensity. When the erotic is trapped in the one-way street of sex, "the wet spark comes, the bright blown walls collapse,"

But what sad scapes we cannot turn from then:
What ashen hills! What salted, shrunken lakes!

"Elsewhere" is an avoidance of what in the poem "Deceptions," a central poem in *The Less Deceived*, is "fulfilment's desolate attic." The two forms contrast in the plot of Larkin's first novel, *Jill*, whose hero, a young undergraduate, has his own private romance of elsewhere, based on the invention of a girl called Jill. Keats found himself losing in company any sense of identity, and John Kemp has the same experience with fellow students and their girlfriends; his real being is invested in Jill, and all the details of her life, details set up in the manner of one of Larkin's own poems. When Kemp first sees and then actually meets the "double" of Jill, a real girl called Gillian, who turns out to be the cousin of his roommate's girl, he begins to go completely to pieces. His personality, already meager, seems to take leave of the reader, and after a symbolic consummation when he embraces Gillian and kisses her, he is thrown into a fountain by her friends, catches a severe chill, and collapses in the college sickbay into delirium and disillusionment.

As gripping in its way as a Larkin poem, the novel tells a tale very similar to Keats's "Lamia." The hero of that poem invents, as it were, a wonderful woman, with whom he becomes so enamored that he insists on marrying her at a public festival, though she warns him of the dire consequences. She changes back into a serpent, and he swoons into death ("in its marriage robe, the heavy body wound"). In both poem and novel the man who creates and contemplates romance is extinguished by its realization or fulfillment. ("To me it was dilution," as the narrating "I" says of propagation, in "Dockery and Son.")

Both Larkin's novels vanished into the past, as is the way of the best fiction that is not followed up, and have only been revived by his solid fame as a poet. A third novel, begun as soon as Larkin had finished the second, was never completed. Surprisingly Andrew Motion considers the first, *Jill*, the more successful. For me its successor, *A Girl in Winter*, is far more subtle in its handling of the same theme, and the girl, Katherine, far more effective than Kemp, both as a character in her own right and as a focus of consciousness. It is "The Eve of St. Agnes" to *Jill*'s "Lamia," though I doubt that the author was conscious of any affinity with either of

Keats's poems. But the plot resemblance is as striking with the one as is the magic atmosphere—the kingdom of cold, the kingdom of warmth—is in the case of the other. In fact the novel was first called *The Kingdom of Winter*, and Larkin changed the title at the publisher's request. (A girl is always a good thing in a title: Kingsley Amis claims to have found *Jill* in a Soho bookstore, next to *High-heeled Yvonne*. That would have delighted Keats.)

Wallace Stevens said that "a poet looks at the world as a man looks at a woman." Stevens and Larkin are romantics of a very different color—in any case what about poets who *are* women?—but as regards both Keats and Larkin the remark is certainly suggestive, almost literal. As the sight of almost any woman may be a fantasy for a man, so their world of looking and language is to them. In revising "The Eve of St. Agnes" Keats was very conscious of the contrast between poetic daydream and the physical reality of a seduction. He wouldn't think much of his hero, he said, if he left the heroine in the virgin state in which he found her. The ribald comment is not a part of the poem, as Keats knew very well, and yet the poem makes its own solution between romantic fantasy and undeceived awareness, a solution that seems to leave the poet out. Larkin it leaves very much in: there is no gap for him between romantic vision, "ever eager-eyed," and boring bleak reality. Disillusion is a working part of the dream. With its own kind of beauty, as the last words of the novel tell us, and "not saddening." As it ends, his couple have no further interest in or desire for each other; nothing to look forward to but sleep. Like icefloes, "in slow orderly procession," their "unsatisfied dreams" move "from darkness further into darkness"; and the girl's watch ticks persistently in the man's ears, counting the time till death.

For Larkin disillusionment intensifies the enchanted comforts of elsewhere and becomes a part of them. So even, at least from the view of art, does social vapidity and commonplace. In a poem from *High Windows*, "Vers de Societé," Larkin converts social chit-chat ("Canted / Over to catch the drivel of some bitch / Who's read nothing but 'Which'") into elsewhere. Would he shun an invitation, preferring the solitude of dreams, as Madeline leaves the baronial party on St. Agnes' Eve? Or would he hasten to accept and attend?

In a pig's arse, friend.
Day comes to an end.
The gas fire breathes, the trees are darkly swayed.

But he goes to the party, for the world of elsewhere is also the acceptance world. Who but Larkin would juxtapose the exotic obscenity and the romantic line in such a way that instead of their making a brisk, glib contrast between real "undeceived" life and deceptive dream, as they would do in the work of most moderns, they come quietly together in their own secret, consolatory meaning? Change of key in Larkin is never for contrast but obscurely rich enhancement, as in the consoling grandeur that rises out of the witty levity of "Next Please."

Only one ship is seeking us, a black-
Sailed unfamiliar, towing at her back
A huge and birdless silence. In her wake
No waters breed or break.

Symbolist technique marries in Larkin with the no-nonsense manner of "the Movement," represented in sex terms by Kingsley Amis's Dai Evans and his earthy perky view of appetites and needs. Romance there is a silly cow with someone's hand up her skirt. In Larkin, so to speak, the hand is there but is part of the inviolable dream of "Sunny Prestatyn."

Come to sunny Prestatyn
Laughed the girl on the poster,
Kneeling up on the sand . . .

Whatever disfigurement is inflicted on her image by the traveling public, culminating when "a great transverse tear / Left only a hand and some blue. / Now *Fight Cancer* is there"—the girl in the poem remains inviolable, a Virgin with ballpoint moustaches offering herself to the odium which does not alter her transcendent nature. "She was too good for this life"; but living, as seen in Larkin's poems, always is.

The critics who have seen the importance there of latter-day symbolist technique would seize on the phrase "some blue"—Mallarméan

Azur—as highly significant. The poems are indeed full of such cunning pointers. In the last stanza of "Next Please" that memorable adjective "birdless" is no doubt carrying two senses; in colloquial and especially northern English bird can mean girl. But in Larkin's, as opposed to more contemporary poetry, such things don't want to be noticed, any more than does the deft adaptation of "Movement" style, or the beautiful rhyme and stanza patterns, often modified from Spenser or Yeats or Donne. Such influences give his poetry no trace of anxiety; it has no obligations to them, disappearing into its own elsewhere, the romantic premise of simultaneous expectancy and disillusion, and Larkin's own proclaimed if unemphasized version of romantic solitude, the corsair's freedom,

> Drafting a world where no such road will run
> From you to me;
> To watch that world come up like a cold sun,
> Rewarding others, is my liberty.

The romantic has no possessions or commitments, and a secret sorrow. In a world of sexual and material acquisitiveness his elsewhere can never be possessed, least of all by the poet himself. Larkin's main difference is in this buildup of absence. It makes him pleasurably unpredictable, each poem unfamiliar. There is no place today where his poetry obviously lives, as there is, say, a Ted Hughes country and a Seamus Heaney land, a place domesticated by poets. Keats said that Hampstead had been "damned" by Leigh Hunt, and the Lakes by Wordsworth. For Larkin elsewhere can only be completely authentic ("a real girl in a real place / In every sense empirically true!") if

> I have never found
> The place where I could say
> *This is my proper ground,*
> *Here I shall stay . . .*

The absolute reality of elsewhere only "underwrites my existence"—the end of "The Importance of Elsewhere" is, as one might expect, both downright and mysterious—if that existence is almost aggressively hum-drum. Of reviewers who once wondered at this existence Larkin said: "I'd like to know how they spend their time . . . do they kill a lot of dragons for instance?"

The tone is a Larkinian updating of the tone of Keats's letters, the refusal to be romantic which—kidding on the level—conceals a con-sciousness wholly devoted to romance. Yes, Larkin in his poems does in a sense kill dragons, just as he writes his own versions of the Nightingale Ode in such poems as "Here," "The Large Cool Store," "Essential Beauty," "Days." In their deft, immaculate way these poems wonder at the quotidian realities they turn into fairylands forlorn, provided the beholder does not possess them but remains an equivalent of the figure parodied by Yeats's idea of Keats. ("I see a schoolboy when I think of him / With face and nose pressed to a sweet-shop window.") Often, as in "Essential Beauty," Larkin parodies them himself, his art finding the ways in which all true romance is intensified by parody. "Our live imperfect eyes / That stare beyond this world . . . seeking the home / All such inhabit" may find in advertisement

> that unfocused she
> No match lit up, nor drag ever brought near

but the silent, poignant joke in the poem is that its art is itself an adver-tisement for elsewhere, feeding our "bad habits of expectancy" that depend on nonfulfillment. "Where can we live but days?"—but that question conjures up a vision as memorable as Keats's "perilous seas"— "the priest and the doctor / In their long coats / Running over the fields."

The most famous of all Larkin's poems presents the "I" as voyeur at Endymion-like rites of initiation and fulfillment. Hardy might well have written about finding himself on a trainful of brides about to start their married lives, and he would have taken his usual grimly compassionate pleasure in imagining their lives-to-be. His musings would certainly have been erotic, but nothing like so erotic as Larkin contrives to be in "The Whitsun Weddings." Everything in that poem is charged with the pecu-liar potency of Larkinian sexual arrest.

and for
Some fifty minutes, that in time would seem
Just long enough to settle hats and say
  I nearly died,
A dozen marriages got under way.

The fascinated concentration is on the fact of change which takes the form of stasis, like the lovers on St. Agnes' Eve.

They glide, like phantoms, into the wide hall;
  Like phantoms, to the iron porch, they glide . . .

The just-married couples "watched the landscape, sitting side by side," for this moment voyeurs themselves, watched by a voyeur. Just the same double tactic is used throughout *A Girl in Winter*, a marvelous and sustained erotic prose poem, in which the girl Katherine, a foreigner without a surname, watches the English in what seems their elsewhere, and is herself watched by the author and his readers. So Madeline attends a vision of her future lover while he is gazing on her from hiding, and the reader of the poem on both. In the focus of this sort of poetry everything can be sexier than sex, for everything is seen as if in the sweet-shop window. Having her first meal in an English train Katherine is fascinated by clear soup joggling in white plates; when she has to take a colleague to the dentist she watches him drop into a glass of water a pink tablet which "sank furiously to the bottom." Through the poet's eyes the wedded couples watch train details of mesmeric significance and exactitude, and are then themselves plunged forward into an unending metaphor of Arthurian power and mystery, "an arrow-shower / Sent out of sight, somewhere becoming rain." The paradox of elsewhere, as glimpsed in this "travelling coincidence," is that the unchanging human progress through sex to birth and death can be seen out of time, in the right words.

And they are not knowing words. Larkin's deepest romanticism is neither knowing nor overtly symbolic, but concentrated solely on its own vision and its own frankness. The double self and the dual vision are fixed counters which give the vision and the personality behind it an unexpected variety, as well as a kind of instant grip. He is the only sophisticated poet today who needs no sophisticated response from the reader; apparently not interested in art, its cozy responses and communal strategies, the poetry knows every sense of the difference between living in the world and looking in on it. Both activities are necessary to each other, but their interchange produces instant fiction in depth inside every poem. He is the only poet since Hardy really to use the novel, and the way he does it, inside an apparently limited poetic field, makes the "confessional" poetry written since the Sixties, as well as the "communal" poetry of today, seem one-dimensional.

The brevity of his poems, as of Hardy's, is an aspect of their robust variety. The personal and the fictional join hands in them, and with the novels, which are also in Larkin's case long poems. Hardy said the poet "touches our hearts by revealing his own," and the simple sentiment fits Larkin as well as himself, all the more so because both in their own way express simple and forceful sentiments with which we may disagree. They share the essential simplicities of romanticism, and neither (in Hardy's case over a very long span) could be said to "grow up" or mature. A kind of arrest becomes poetry in Larkin as it does in Keats, and has the same direct power to move us, partly by seeming ever young, undiminished, fixed in essential concentration. Keats might have stopped being a poet as Larkin, in one sense, stopped being a novelist.

Keats wrote that poetry "simply tells the most heart-easing things." The heart can be eased by unexpected things, as Larkin's poetry knows. It never seems to want to move us, or ease our hearts, but they escape into comfort nonetheless. Today nobody uses the word "escapism," a common term of disapproval in the days when romanticism was being consciously reacted against. Larkin's poetry profoundly understands it, and the popular need for it, its increasing if unfashionable importance in a religionless age. He is a connoisseur of its most paradoxical instincts and of its place in the romantic tradition.

The man who is "not deceived" is also the true escapist. Keats wrote to Reynolds: "Until we are sick we understand not." As an "old-type natural fouled-up guy" Larkin makes a joke of it, but it means much for the stance of his art. Escapists make good novelists, and Larkin observed that he had found "how to make poems readable as novels." Like the tip of an iceberg his poems imply depths of lives and selves, a mass of material not written, or not revealed. In understanding the importance of elsewhere the undeceived also know that it "tolls me back from thee to my sole self," and Larkin's poems are made from this relationship. His kind of romanticism is now out of fashion, and his curious version of "escapism" would be frowned on if it were more widely recognized for what it is. His popularity, like that of many great idiosyncratic artists, rests on various sorts of misconception where the critics are concerned, and on the sound unexamined instincts of a more general public. It is nonetheless remarkable for that, and nonetheless deserved.

PART III

Mother Russia

24

Cutting It Short

Alexander Pushkin (1799–1837)

O F ALL GREAT WRITERS Pushkin left the greatest number of incomplete or fragmentary works. Even when something is finished it still has an air of potential, of development that might have been carried on had not the author felt that his art had done its mysterious job and that it was not for him to press it further. *Don Juan* comes to an end because Byron can not keep up the pressure and think up further adventures to which his imagination can really respond, and so he loses interest. *Evgeny Onegin* does not end in this sense at all. In it Pushkin tells us that when he began what he calls his "free novel" he did not know how it would end. His story breaks off, but his hero and heroine seem to live on. Their destiny is fulfilled in the form of the narrative, but we continue to ask questions about their future. Would Evgeny have continued to pursue Tatiana? Would she (as Nabokov opined) in time have relented? Russian readers, and writers too, have always speculated about them.

Pushkin's most subtle originality, in fact, could be said to anticipate and even to make a principle out of Henry James's comment: "Properly speaking, relations stop nowhere, and the task of the artist is eternally but to draw the circle in which they shall happily appear to do so." James's way of doing this was to squeeze the orange, as it were—to saturate his subject with all its meanings while avoiding everything about it that was not "meaning." Pushkin's solution was plainer, opener, more sybilline and yet more emphatic. He would take matters to the point at which the reader could take over. Above all, he would have no facile, sentimental, or melodramatic endings, no suicides for love or honor, no stock wedding bells, no feasts of sugarplums.

In the romantic heyday, when literature was becoming ever more popular and popular literature was supplying all these things with ebullience and abandon, his task was not easy. Romantic history plays, facile as *Hernani*, fateful as *The Cenci*, were bursting out on all sides. Pushkin seems to have determined, in *Boris Godunov*, to write a history play showing how uncooperative history is with romance, with happy endings or with tragic ones. History just goes grumbling on. Dramatically *Boris Godunov* is a disappointing play: everybody said so—"nothing in this piece is complete," complained Pushkin's old enemy Bulgarin. But as a kind of tableau of historical inquiry it is extraordinarily suggestive. It ends on an anti-climax, an anti-demonstration. The crowd are ordered to shout: "Long live Dimitri Ivanovich" (the pretender who has displaced Boris's son). They do so. End of play. But not quite, because the censor objected, and said it would be more decorous to orthodox Tsarist ears if the crowd were silent. Very well, said the amused author, and he wrote a final stage direction—"*Narod besmolvstvuet*," "the people are silent"—which has become a Russian proverb. As Pushkin must have seen, from the point of view of history, from the point of view of an anti-romantic history tableau, the two endings were the same. No opinion is uttered: there is only the finality of openness.

The theory of openness came to Pushkin from Shakespeare. In his admirable study—his "other Pushkin" is the storyteller, and novelist, not the poet—Paul Debreczeny quotes Pushkin's comments on Shakespeare's characterization. They go hand in hand with inconclusiveness, and show why it is that though Shakespeare had to finish the play, his characters never do. They are not completed by their dramatic role, observes Pushkin. "Shylock is not only miserly but resourceful, vindictive, child-loving, witty." By contrast, Moliere's miser, like his hypocrite, is exhausted by being what he is and doing what he does; he can offer no further interest to us.

Pushkin implies here that if your character is not doing just what the piece requires of him then you cannot "finish" the piece. You break it off at the right moment. And this is what he does in his *Little Tragedies*, which he called "Dramatic Investigations." In "Mozart and Salieri" the composer Salieri is so scandalized by the sheer insouciance of genius, its refusal to take itself seriously and to display the *gravitas* proper to a great musician, that he resolves to poison Mozart. But the wonderful clean lines of the poetry carry a note of hesitancy, of the lack of self-knowledge behind Salieri's bleak and self-righteous convictions. Is he perhaps animated by low envy, the involuntary hatred of the lesser for the great? The piece ends with such questions hanging in the air, and in our minds. In "The Stone Guest" Don Juan meets his fate at the hands of the commander whose wife he has seduced, but with whom, before they die together, he has perhaps fallen deeply and irrevocably in love.

Though he does not comment on the fact, as he comments on what might now be called Pushkin's Law of characterization, Pushkin seems to have connected the open ending with his own conviction that his art—his "rubbish," as he sometimes referred to it—came from outside him, was the visitation of a god who sometimes condescended to enter and inspire this quite ordinary man about town, Pushkin, who normally spent his time gambling with fashionable friends and making up to the girls. Naturally the god withdrew before the work he had fathered reached anything as laborious as birth. This is itself the theme of "Egyptian Nights." A fashionable young man, a secret poet, befriends a poor and rather ridiculous Italian *improvisatore*, another kind of self-portrait of Pushkin. To earn him money, the poet arranges for the improviser to declaim verses on any subject suggested by a fashionable audience. The subject is "Cleopatra and Her Lovers," which occasions titters, but the improviser, after looks of timid apology and uncertainty, abruptly turns pale as the god possesses him and proceeds to declaim line upon line of magnificent verse, some of Pushkin's very best.

The story up to then has been in prose, but when the improviser suddenly breaks off, having sketched a situation without a dénouement, it has reached its end. The god has departed: the points have been made with Pushkin's usual inscrutability. His vivid spontaneous genius combined in a unique way with a detached interest in form and theory, a taste for almost scientific demonstration. He abhors any use by the artist of unexamined cliché, and there was plenty of that around at the time. Sometimes his "fragments" mingle verse and prose, as if in ironic comment on the virtues and limitations of each. The situation in "Egyptian

Nights" is set out in terse and simple prose ("plain water" was his prose ideal) and the superb and deliberate romanticism of the verse "improvisation" contrasts with it, displaying the fact that if the god inspires him, the most banal subject can be turned by the poet into deathless verse.

When Charsky first tested the improviser's powers, he asked him to declaim on the theme of inspiration, and the Italian made a magnificent defense of the poet's freedom to scorn the crowd and choose any subject he wishes, even the most trivial and vulgar ones, "as the great eagle sails past tower and crag to perch on a withered stump." The unspoken irony is not only that the improviser will accept any subject he is given, confident (like Pushkin himself) that his freedom lies in his possession by the inspirative power, but also that he is free to break off whenever he feels like it, when the inner message is delivered, and not to toil on to the end of some fabricated story for the sake of his laborious listeners. The improviser breaks off at the moment when the great queen has offered herself to all takers, the price of a night of her favors being death, and three have accepted—an older soldier, a philosopher, and a youth on whom Cleopatra bestows a quick glance of regret. The couch is spread; the poem ends.

D. M. Thomas, who has made some excellent translations of Pushkin's poems, has also been daring enough to include in his novel *Ararat* (successor to *The White Hotel*) a verse continuation of this story. He has the soldier and the philosopher submit successively to the eunuch's blade as they leave the queen's chamber in the morning. The youth, however, drugs the queen, slays the eunuch and departs in triumph. Thomas may have his own esoteric reasons for arranging this dénouement, but on the face of it nothing could better illustrate Pushkin's implicit contrast between banality of theme and banality of treatment. No situation can be too banal to provoke and intrigue the imagination of the poet, and of his reader: but to pursue it to a conclusion worthy of a swashbuckling serial or the *Arabian Nights* is to ruin the imagination of the thing, rather as an explicit sex scene in a film spoils whatever suggestive appeal a love scene can have.

Thomas's treatment is the more surprising because of his admiration for Pushkin's most inspired dramatic fragment, "Rusalka," the story of a miller's daughter seduced by a prince, who drowns herself and becomes a "cold powerful *rusalka*," seeking revenge. Again the theme appears banal but its suggestiveness is highly penetrating and poetic. It breaks off just at the moment when "revenge," in the conventional sense, might seem about to be consummated. There is all the difference between this kind of effect and those that are sought by Barry Cornwall in his "dramatic fragments," a reading of which in French had given Pushkin his model. Very much in the spirit of the age, Cornwall had sought to wring every ounce of romantic melodrama out of the situations he treated. Pushkin does just the opposite. He arrests the mechanism of the melodrama and the stock situation and probes their inward dimension and their inner psychology. As with *Boris Godunov* his gaze is not on the auditorium—"Rusalka" would spoil in the acting, just as would the *Little Tragedies*—but on the calm calculation of what a "god" of dramatic inspiration has brought him. Nevertheless "Rusalka" is among the most haunting, and the most moving, of Pushkin's works.

In forbearance and precision there are deep affinities between Pushkin's poetry, drama, and prose, though for most readers there is no point in claiming, as Tsvetaeva did in a remarkable essay on *The Captain's Daughter*, that prose and poetry are for him the same medium. That may be true in some higher sense, but the distinction is nonetheless clear and plain, and in his excellent detailed study—probably the first in English—Paul Debreczeny is not concerned with metaphysical questions but with Pushkin's prose as prose, though the two sometimes intermingle as in "Egyptian Nights." His critical volume is complemented by a volume containing for the first time in English all the novels, stories, and fragments, jottings and ideas, together with a detailed and informative textual apparatus and notes.

Everyone who has read Tolstoy's life knows that the germ of *Anna Karenina* was a fragment of Pushkin's that begins, "The guests were arriving at the dacha," and Tolstoy's enthusiastic comment that this was just how a novel should open. Now that they can read the pieces that Pushkin actually wrote they may be surprised to find that Tolstoy's debt to Pushkin in *Anna Karenina* goes far beyond that first sentence. Pushkin's "novel," if that was what it was to be, concerns a headstrong, odd, charming, fascinating girl who moves in the best St. Petersburg society. She is called Volskaia or Zinaida. She married for advantage, is dissatisfied with her life without knowing why, takes a lover, and goes to live in a little house—"in

the corner of a small square" is how the alternative fragment opens—
where he visits her. What clearly intrigued Pushkin as a subject is the
oppression of a free soul in what she feels should be a "free" relationship—a situation perennially relevant for the novelist and never more so
than today. It irks her lover equally.

> He had never meant to tie himself down with such bonds. He hated
> boredom, feared every obligation, and valued his egotistical inde-
> pendence above all else. But it was a *fait accompli*. Zinaida remained
> on his hands. He pretended to be grateful, but in fact he faced the
> pain of his liaison as if performing an official duty, or getting down to
> the tedious task of checking his butler's monthly accounts.

That becomes very much Vronsky's situation, though Tolstoy does not do
it with Pushkin's swift and light touch, nor with the humor. The other
fragment gives an excellent brief instance of Pushkin's Law, where characterization is concerned. "Not suspecting that frivolity could be joined
with strong passions, he foresaw a liaison without any significant consequences." That compresses in one sentence an immense amount of
social and psychological knowledge. Of course Tolstoy widened everything, weighed it, and filled it in, but *Anna Karenina*, especially in its earlier drafts, owes a very great deal to Pushkin's offhand but telling scrutiny
of character and a situation.

Pushkin himself owed a lot to his sources—Constant's *Adolphe*, for
instance. But his prose is a remorseless exposer of other men's clichés,
event those of authors with great talent. Constant's hero and heroine are
not only disingenuous with each other and with themselves: their creator
is disingenuous too—because "love," in the French context, is too hallowed an idea to be treated with Pushkin's sympathetic, casual-seeming
perspicuity. The fact that Adolphe and Ellénore are mutually disenchanted, while remaining mechanically attached, is a truth from which
Constant flinches, writing as he is within a basically reverent convention.
Apart from his genius, Pushkin is in a coincidentally strong position. He
inherits all the French incisiveness and power of analysis, and yet is
emancipated from the blinkers of their cultural and linguistic tradition.
At the same time he can draw, through French, on Shakespeare and the

English novelists and romantics, and be equally impartial in the use he makes of them.

One must not exaggerate his success. He needed money and was prepared to compromise for it. But much of his prose reveals his extraordinary intuition of the fatalities in the history of Russian power. The figure of Peter the Great fascinated him, and his first essay at historical fiction, "The Negro of Peter the Great," was based on the career of his own maternal forebear, Ibrahim Gannibal, a black page presented to Peter, who rose to the rank of general in his army. Interestingly, Pushkin attempted the technique of omniscient and impersonal narrator, one which was normal for the later nineteenth-century novelist but was avoided on the whole by Scott—an instinctively crafty storyteller—as it was even by Dickens. Clearly the kinds of historical inanity—anecdote, local color, "picturesque" speech—which were the stock-in-trade of the genre, soon exasperated Pushkin, and he abandoned the novel. Its clichés, in this context, could not be made use of or transformed into a true or different kind of reality. He found the same difficulty when he attempted a different kind of story, "Dubrovsky," which is set in comparatively recent times and has the promising theme of a small and honorable landowner persecuted and finally dispossessed by a large and aggressive one. It shows Pushkin's growing interest in social unrest, its origin in naked power and in the lack of rights at any level of Russian society. But once again the clichés of romantic fiction steal in, showing themselves to be indispensable and uncontrollable. Dispossessed, the young Dubrovsky becomes a bandit; the big landowner's daughter falls in love with him; there are flights, ambushes, assignations. The kind of stuff that Scott can produce with perfect equanimity, and without compromising his essential virtues, is alien to Pushkin's almost scientific turn of mind as a conscious artist. Once again he abandoned the project.

The only historical novel he actually finished, *The Captain's Daughter*, was written at a later stage, when Pushkin's productivity and popularity as a poet were waning, and when he needed money even more urgently. It is a fine achievement but there is something fatigued about it, which suggests to me that when he died in a duel at the age of 37 he was, if not written out, unlikely to have realized a great future potential. The first person narrator, Grinev, is a young officer of Catherine the

Great's time, who gets involved in Pugachev's revolt, and he does just what the piece requires of him. He derives from Scott's young hero Waverley, who is also involved in a rebellion "sixty years since," and who like his Russian counterpart is carried along passively by the torrent of event. But "sixty years since" is much more grimly significant and prophetic in a Russian context than it would be in a Scots and English one. Scott makes a comfortable English-style compromise with Waverley, allowing him to participate in romanticism and rebellion and to fall in love with a wild Scots lady, and then bringing him safely home to a hereditary estate and marriage with an English rose. The formula is more perfunctory in Pushkin but also more effective in the detail of the text. Grinev's efforts at achievement in the romantic style are pointedly ineffective, and his expectations fade away before the flat economy of the narrative, which resembles the bare steppes where he sees the fortress—a low black palisade and a few wooden buildings which his imagination had pictured as looking like something out of the Scottish Highlands. Ingeniously but without vitality, Pushkin merely borrows the ending from *The Heart of Midlothian*, sending Grinev's financée to intercede for him at St. Petersburg in a gracious interview with Catherine the Great.

That is a nadir by his standards, but there are admirable scenes in *The Captain's Daughter* as in "Dubrovsky"—the rebels' capture of the fort, the meeting with Pugachev in the snowy night, the fire at the manor house in which the lawyers persecuting Dubrovsky are accidentally incinerated. Grinev, too, has interesting affinities with a later style of romantic hero, even though he is fundamentally a copybook figure, like the heroines. Pushkin's real interest is in the figure of Pugachev and in the Pugachevschina, the rebellion associated with him. At the time of *The Captain's Daughter* he had already written an official history of the revolt, commissioned by the Tsar, Nicholas I, who following his act of pardon to Pushkin after the Decembrist revolt had appointed himself as the poet's patron and personal censor. The bland patronage of the tyrant became in time an intolerable burden, but we owe to it some of Pushkin's most perceptive and mature reflections on the nature of power in Russia, which the Tsar was remarkably acute at elucidating and commenting on. In his notes to the Tsar, Pushkin pointed out that all Russian revolts of true significance had followed the same pattern: a mutiny in what was virtually the colonial army—the Cossacks—joined by all the disaffected and ill-treated in Russia's ever-growing empire. The Tsar was particularly exercised by Pushkin's comparison of the Pugachevschina with the mutiny of Stenka Razin a hundred years earlier. Pushkin's history is a model of its kind for detachment, perspicacity, and clarity of style. Its calm recital of the horrors of the revolt, the demoralization of the ruling class, the eventual success of the methods of suppression, led by two effective generals, Mihkelson and the great Suvorov himself, and not least the contradictory character of Pugachev, a real-life instance of Pushkin's Law—all this makes a telling comparison with fictional discourse employed in *The Captain's Daughter*.

As always, though, Pushkin needed a *form*. He had made the fragment into one, though his aborted romances and novels do not count as "fragments"; they are merely drafts which the author could not or did not wish to complete. There are undoubted traces of agoraphobia when he tries the omniscient authorial manner; when, for example, he makes use of a Russian gentleman in "The guests were arriving at the dacha" to make a disquisition on the Russian class system, the decay of the original aristocracy, and the reliance of Tsarism on a new class of apparatchik and time-server. Himself very conscious of belonging to the old nobility, Pushkin knew all about the new order and his remarks are as relevant today as would be those he made to Nicholas about the causes of revolt in Russia. But they are too obviously personal, lacking Pushkin's calmly objective identification with a form, even the form of the fragment.

With hindsight we can say that he saw what the big novel would be like, in its nineteenth-century heyday, but that he could not reconcile that knowledge with the ways in which he could make use of the limitations of existing romantic forms, undercutting and subtly transforming them. In one "Boldino Autumn," those few weeks of the year when he used to give himself up to intensive creation on his small country estate, he produced among many other things the *Tales of Belkin*, a series of stories purporting to be written by the acquaintance of a country squire, and collected by him. Belkin is a figure of inimitable unconscious humor, and the tales are gems of deadpan comedy whose parodic implications it is the joy of Russian scholars to unravel, Dostoevsky pillaged them, both the spirit and material, while reserving his total reverence for the story written three years later, which he called "the height of artistic perfection"—"The Queen of Spades."

Here Pushkin again tries the omniscient mode of narration, but overcomes the agoraphobic effect it had on him by stuffing his tale with every kind of stock romantic and melodramatic situation. These contrast with the understanding, reasonable, slightly amused tone of the narrative. Inconspicuously the narrator enters into the psychology, the small hopes and irritations and ennuis of a young girl who is the paid companion of a tyrannical old countess. He is equally good at showing with sympathy the Countess's own life, the horrors of old age, and how she clings to her place in an *haut monde* which has forgotten her and acknowledges her existence only with the most perfunctory show of good manners. Though she does nothing and says little, the girl Lizaveta is one of his most effective characters, and it is typically Pushkinian that—contrary to what the reader might at first suppose—her heart is not broken nor her hopes ruined. She makes a suitable marriage with a very nice young man, the son of the Countess's former steward, who has a good position in the service. Those unobtrusive concluding details are typical of the method.

The Countess and her attendant are really much more important in the story than are the popular melodramatic elements, chief of which is the hero himself, the Napoleonic Hermann, the young German engineer who makes up to Lizaveta and tries to force from the Countess her family secret of how to win at cards. Hermann is certainly a figure of great potential, borrowed from Balzac and from Stendhal's young heroes of the will, and bequeathed to Dostoevsky, and yet one feels that Pushkin himself had too much sense to be fascinated by him. In a subtle way he is presented as a fundamentally *boring* character. What the story does brilliantly is to reconcile a depth and leisureliness of insight with narrative excitement and suspense—the apparition of the Countess, the fatal sequence of cards—so that each mode of feeling and describing enhances the other. The aspect of the story's success which most pleased Pushkin, characteristically, was that to bring them luck his young gambler friends in St. Petersburg started to bet, as Hermann had done, on the three, seven, and ace.

Pushkin's refusal to be portentous about his materials is as typical as his talent for bringing their rather banal constituents into a memorable whole, though the tale is not, in my opinion, the absolute masterpiece that Dostoevsky claimed. The term is hardly applicable to anything in Pushkin's prose, except perhaps to the parodic skill and finish of the *Tales of Belkin*. What does lurk in "The Queen of Spades" is Pushkin's genius for incompletion. Several suggestions in it remain as strategically placed queries; the past broods over the present without leading into it; the future is claimed by Hermann but never conquered; in the face of superstition the supernatural remains enigmatic.

Pushkin declines to commit himself to melodrama and its emotions, as Dostoevsky would do, just as he had refused to play the conventional game as he had found it in Richardson and Constant. No heroine of his could die like Clarissa, and Debreczeny points out that he wrote "Rubbish" in his copy of *Adolphe* at the point where the hero throws himself on the ground and wishes to be swallowed up. Ellénore's death when deserted must have struck him as equally *voulu*. He was irritated by the higher sentimentality; the ordinary vulgar kind simply amused him, as is shown by his indulgence to two gushing young friends who were upset by the plot of *Evgeny Onegin*. One of them wanted the poet Lensky, killed by Onegin in the fatal duel, to have been only wounded. "Then Olga could have looked after him and they would have grown even fonder of each other." The other would have had Onegin wounded, "so that Tatiana could have looked after him and he would have learnt to value and love her."

The anecdote shows what Pushkin was up against. Where the novel was concerned popularity was all, and Pushkin never succeeded in reconciling the conventions of the novel in his time with the intuitions he must have had of its later use as a vehicle for unrestrained intelligence and observation. He needed forms to work on, undercut, and re-create, and here there was none suitable to hand. His history of Pugachev is not only a model historical study but shows a concentration of style and perspective which few historians at the time had any notion how to achieve. "The Queen of Spades" is a brilliant *tour de force*, which makes stories like Balzac's *Sarrasine* and *La Peau de Chagrin* look shallow, unfeeling, merely smart. But the two fragments of Pushkin's prose that are truly and significantly prophetic are "The guests were arriving at the dacha" and "In the corner of a small square." The heroine glimpsed in those few pages could have been one of the most memorable of nineteenth-century fictional portraits.

Debreczeny's detailed study is useful reading for Russian students and a valuable text for anyone seriously interested in fiction and its techniques. His translations of the prose—almost as difficult a problem in its different way as translating Pushkin's poetry—are always adequate, and in the case of the Pugachev History outstandingly good, though the stories contain some odd things like "tersity" for "terseness," and there is clumsiness in the use of colloquial English. (Grinev's servant Savelich, among the best of Pushkin's characters in *The Captain's Daughter*, would hardly exclaim "Egad!") Walter Arndt supplies an impressively vivacious rendering of the improviser's verses in "Egyptian Nights."

25

Under the Overcoat

Nikolai Gogol (1809–1852)

The Collected Tales of Nikolai Gogol
by Larissa Volokhonsky, translated by Richard Pevear

"**G**OGOL WAS MADE uneasy by his works," notes Richard Pevear in his introduction to his and Larissa Volokhonsky's admirable translation of the collected tales. It is an understatement that would have appealed to Gogol himself. He came to regard his extraordinary gift for writing prose as something sent from the devil, something that only prayer, fasting, and slavish obedience to his father confessor might exorcise and expiate. He fasted so fanatically that he died at forty-three. The story of his last years and months makes harrowing reading, more particularly for readers who are themselves fascinated and seduced by the power of words, and by their capacity in the hands of a great artist to exist marvelously and uncannily on their own, like the nose which, to the consternation of its respectable owner, seems to have escaped, even from the tale of which it is the title, to lead a phantom life of its own in the streets of St. Petersburg.

Andrei Sinyavsky's study *In Gogol's Shadow* analyzes Gogol's gift for language—one could speak of it as the equivalent in Russian prose of Pushkin's primal genius as Russian poet—that shifts "from the object of speech to speech as a process of objectless intent, interesting in itself and exhausted by itself. . . . That is why we perceive Gogol's prose so distinctly as prose, and not as a . . . form of putting thoughts into words. . . . It has its content and even, if you wish, its subject in itself—this prose which steps forth in the free image of speech about facts worth mentioning, speech in a pure sense *about nothing*." No wonder Gogol came to think that such objectless speech must come from the devil—Satan, in fact, finding words for idle mouths to utter. Pushkin hinted that laughter and tears are the same in Gogol—the same because neither has significance beyond the pure play of the words that convey them? And naturally, as the critic Richard Pevear comments, the images that Gogol's prose produces "are too deeply ambiguous to bear any social message."

Nonetheless they must have come from somewhere, and be about something. And indeed they are, and they have: Gogol's laughter itself is neither sane nor mad, but it is totally and magically localized. He was born in the provincial depths of Little Russia, or the Ukraine, in the village of Sorochintsy near the town of Dikanka. His mother, the dominant factor in his emotional life, had a small estate; his father, a more shadowy figure who died young, had been an amateur playwright; Gogol's sole apparent talent at school was as an actor and mimic. Like many an ambitious young provincial, he went to try his luck in the capital; and a setting more different from his home town in the Ukraine could hardly be imagined. As Pevear observes, the road from the depths of Little Russia intersected with the glittering "all-powerful Nevsky Prospect," in Gogol's words, and "his art was born at that crossroads."

Pushkin and Lermontov, we should remember, like Tolstoy after them and Dostoevsky, too, were men of the metropolis; the cosmopolitan world was in their blood, however much a writer like Tolstoy might will himself to identify with the life of the peasants and of primitive holy Russia. Tolstoy's peasants and small folk are creatures of his ideological need: he sees them from above, and is determined that should be how he sees them. Gogol had no idea how to see things: they crowded eerily onto his page, as independent as the nose in his story. Or perhaps rather, as Sinyavsky emphasizes, he preserved, throughout the time of his fame and success in St. Petersburg, a provincial's "naive, external, astonished and envious outlook."

And yet within a remarkably short time Gogol was a success in the capital and an established writer, hailed by Pushkin himself as a phenomenon "so unusual in our present-day literature that I still haven't recovered." Pushkin had been reading *Evenings on a Farm near Dikanka*, the tales from the Ukraine which appeared in two volumes in 1831 and 1832, and make up more than half of Gogol's total output of stories.

Their author was only twenty-two. His first attempt at publication, at his own expense, had been an epic poem so bad that he bought back all the copies and burned them. That was a very provincial gesture, something that Balzac and Flaubert would have understood. All his short life Gogol was apt to do the wrong thing at the wrong time and place. After he became famous as a writer he managed to get himself made professor of history at St. Petersburg University, an episode that ended in predictable disaster and humiliation. Cut off from his homeland, always an outsider in the capital, he rushed off abroad in 1836, at the height of his fame and just after the triumph of his play *The Inspector General*. He spent most of the sixteen years left to him in Switzerland, Paris, and Rome, able to feed only in memory on the Russian localities which had nourished and inspired him. Most of his unfinished masterpiece about Russian provincial life, *Dead Souls*, was composed abroad.

In his brilliant and original little study of Gogol, Nabokov was inclined to belittle the early Ukraine tales and to concentrate on the last and greatest of the stories with a St. Petersburg background, the famous "Overcoat." Pushkin was surely nearer the mark in exclaiming with pleasure and surprise at the extraordinary freshness and originality of the Dikanka series—"Here is real gaiety—honest, unconstrained, without mincing, without primness!"—qualities that the present translators have contrived to reveal to the non-Russian reader at last, and virtually for the first time. They have managed the almost impossible task of finding expressions and equivalents in English for the onward rush of Gogol's prose, at once disheveled and uncannily precise, and packed with inconsequential detail. In his Gogol study Nabokov gave a bravura rendering of the passage in *Dead Souls* describing the luxuriant entanglement of the miser's garden, with a huge broken birch tree slanting whitely upward like a ruined classical column. (Gogol wrote the passage when he was in Rome.) Gogol's precipitate ramblings, which can find time in their rapid flow for all sorts of still-life detail—provided those details are irrelevant enough—are equally well rendered by the present translators, who have succeeded in conveying the early Dikanka stories in all their complicated richness and humor.

The black earth of the Ukraine produces weeds as luxuriant as its crops, and Gogol seems himself to luxuriate in the feel of their opulent density.

> Except for one path beaten down on household necessity, the rest was hidden by thickly spreading cherry trees, elders, burdock that stuck its tall stalks with clingy pink knobs way up. Hops covered the top of this whole motley collection of trees and bushes like a net, forming a roof above them that spread over to the wattle fence and hung down it in twining snakes along with wild field bluebells. Beyond the wattle fence that served as a boundary to the garden, there spread a whole forest of weeds which no one seemed to be interested in, and a scythe would have broken to pieces if it had decided to put its blade to their thick, woody stems.

Gogol's pleasure in a kind of suggestive indelicacy—without mincing or primness, as Pushkin noted—is possibly more a Ukrainian than a Russian trait. That path "beaten down on household necessity" (to the privy presumably) suggests it well; and the translation finds a Dickensian equivalent for the tendency of Gogol's characters to express themselves in reductive convolutions of normal language. Afraid of a beating from the Cossack hetman, the "philosopher" seminarian in "Viy" observes that "everybody knows what a leather whip is: an insufferable thing in large quantities." Gogol's apparently artless prose seems mildly surprised that one seems to be interested in the forest of weeds that flourishes beyond the already weed-crowned and decorated garden, while it is the scythe itself that has to make the "decision" not to risk being broken on the sturdy weed stems.

Gogol's world is full of objects rank and vegetable in their nature, with lives of their own. Together with the way his characters talk, as if the sophistications of Beckett or Pinter were to have become wholly destylized and naïve, Gogol's prose seems ripe to bursting with too many other preoccupations to bother about plot. And yet of course there is a plot, concocted by the author along the lines of Ukrainian folk or fairy tale, but reversing the normal expectations of the genre. The classic Russian simpleton or Holy Fool, who undergoes miraculous trials and torments but gets the girl in the end, is replaced in "Viy" by an ecclesiastical hanger-on, a down-at-heels "philosopher" merely hoping to get by somehow or other, but who in the course of a binge finds himself jumped on by a witch and ridden through a kaleidoscopic Gogol landscape, rendered brilliantly by the translators:

A reverse crescent moon shone in the sky. The timid midnight radiance lay lightly as a transparent blanket and steamed over the earth. Forest, meadows, sky, valleys—all seemed to be sleeping with open eyes. Not a flutter of wind anywhere. There was something damply warm in the night's freshness. The shadows of trees and bushes, like comets, fell in sharp wedges over the sloping plain. Such was the night when the philosopher Khoma Brut galloped with an incomprehensible rider on his back. He felt some languid, unpleasant, and at the same time sweet feeling coming into his heart. He lowered his head and saw that the grass, which was almost under his feet, seemed to be growing deep and distant and that over it was water as transparent as a mountain spring, and the grass seemed to be at the deep bottom of some bright, transparent sea; at least he clearly saw his own reflection in it, together with the old woman sitting on his back. He saw some sun shining there instead of the moon: he heard bluebells tinkle, bending their heads. He saw a water nymph swim from behind the sedge; her back and leg flashed, round, lithe, made all of a shining and quivering. She turned toward him, and her face, with its light, sharp, shining eyes, with its soul-invading song, now approached him, was already at the surface, then, shaking with sparkling laughter, withdrew—and then she turned over on her back, and the sun shone through her nebulous breasts, matte as unglazed porcelain, at the edges of their white, tenderly elastic roundness. Water covered them in tiny bubbles like beads. She trembles all over and laughs in the water . . .

The philosopher in his turn manages to change places and ride the witch until she sinks down utterly exhausted, revealing herself as a beautiful young woman. Later he finds himself summoned by a rich Cossack hetman, whose daughter the young witch turns out to be, and who is now lying at the point of death. Her father commands our hero to say prayers for her soul in an empty church, where she suddenly sits up in her coffin, her green eyes blank and sightless, and attempts to possess him and to steal his soul. He escapes her, and then tries to escape from the Cossacks, but they catch him and force him to continue reading the prayers until he too falls down, dead of terror in the fiend-ridden church.

In "Viy," the richest and most suggestive of the Dikanka stories, Gogol's lyrically evasive eroticism gradually gives way to real nightmare when the assembled witches, cavorting about the church and churchyard, summon the shapeless monster Viy, who kills the unfortunate philosopher with the touch of his iron finger. (The word "Viy," incidentally, is virtually the Russian for "you": a Gogolian indication of the place where nightmares actually come from.) But of course it is Gogol's electrifying power over words that frightens at the same moment as it absorbs and delights us, rather than the comparative banality of his spooky apparatus. The lyrical passages in "Viy," like the brilliantly shining description of the river Dnieper in another of the stories, retain all Gogol's normal air of frenetic detachment. The philosopher's death is itself a contingent incident, as offhand as the rapid demise of poor Akaky in Gogol's last and most famous St. Petersburg story, "The Overcoat." Unlike Dickens's, Gogol's words are never interested in exploiting emotion or in their own luxuriant freedom and sentiment: they are much too absorbed in themselves.

This can make their abrupt impact unexpectedly piercing at moments, when a different sort of writer would be systematically pulling out the stops of tenderness and compassion. In "The Diary of a Madman," one of the St. Petersburg stories, poor Mr. Poprishchin, who is Gogol's most intimate and sympathetic character, finds himself by making the discovery that "there's no place" for him "in the world." In the same spirit, and as if something really terrible had just occurred to him, the meekly contented Akaky of "The Overcoat," happily absorbed in his dull copying job, startles himself and his fellow clerks by asking with sudden intensity why they persecute him, ordering them to leave him alone. He behaves, in fact, totally out of character.

Such moments are quickly over, but they are as telling as Akaky's own outburst; and it is revealing to compare the way Gogol's own words (like Akaky's fellow clerks) themselves treat Akaky with the lingeringly insistent fashion in which Melville writes about his clerk Bartleby. Bartleby is too much of a subject: Akaky, we may feel, is too humble to get much attention from Gogol's language, absorbed as it is with the dreamlike details of St. Petersburg life, its ranks and humiliations, fingernails, watermelon rinds, hemorrhoids, onions, cockroaches, and of course the great overcoat itself, the obsession for which Akaky comes to live and to die. In Gogol's St. Petersburg the homely and contingent shabbiness of living is itself both a dream and a kind of squalid nonreality, lost in the same vast physical space, like the endless square which poor Akaky is attempting to cross when the overcoat robber assaults him.

The overcoat, whose physical reality has been so satisfyingly and so laboriously established—we remember how the tailor Petrovich brought it wrapped in a clean cloth which he then folded and pocketed "for further use"—vanishes into thin air like one of the props of a Ukrainian sorcerer from the fantasy tales. "Realism" is for Gogol just another aspect and source of verbal magic. It is surprising that he has never been claimed, so far as I know, as the father of Magic Realism, perhaps because his writing is in fact far more free-floating and evasive than anything by that genre's more conventional practitioners. As Pevear says, Gogol imitates the cautionary tale which has something to tell us, some admonishment to offer, just as he imitated the full-blown epic style of old Cossack and country legend. In reversing expectation he is doing what Pushkin did in his *Tales of Belkin*, but Pushkin's prose is always calm and sane and open, in contrast to Gogol's slipperiness and excitement. The genuine function of magic in Gogol's tales, and one that came to frighten its owner as if he were indeed a sorcerer's apprentice, is to make the very possibility of message and meaning vanish away like the overcoat.

Because, as Pevear puts it, "he does not know where the act of writing will lead him," Gogol's stories leave nothing that can be passed on. At first his magic words merely seem surprised by this, but in his last years it became a source of torment for him, of real spiritual misery. No wonder the influential social critic Belinsky, and Dostoevsky after him, strove to straighten out Gogol, and to put him on the side of those who were using literature in the fight for political reform, or in Dostoevsky's case, for moral and spiritual regeneration.

In the second part of *Dead Souls*, embarrassingly lifeless as it is, Gogol strove to meet such objections, to make sure that he knew what he wanted to tell his audience before he began to write. Total failure in consequence. Belinsky, a brilliantly perceptive critic as well as a man of dogma, clung to the conviction that Gogol, great writer as he undoubtedly was, must for that reason be—could only be—a champion of the Little Man, and of his struggle against an unjust society. Does not the persecuted Akaky cry out words of protest which have as their echo "I am your brother"? So he does, but the story forgets it at once, just as Akaky himself doubtless did. Gogol's prose bustles him on, and the reader with him.

Poor clerks like Akaky were becoming a feature of Russian writing in what is known as its Golden Age. Pushkin's tale of the stationmaster and his daughter, in *Tales of Belkin*, and of the demented clerk Evgeny in *The Bronze Horseman*, reverse in their own remarkable way the sentimental genre represented by Karamzin's popular tale "Poor Liza." In his own way the young Dostoevsky was concerned to bring back into fashion such direct and earnest sentiment as Karamzin's.

The clerk Makar Devushkin in Dostoevsky's first novel, *Poor Folk*, a tale of St. Petersburg, actually reads Gogol's "Overcoat" in the course of the narrative, and is deeply offended by it—"a nasty little book." He accuses Gogol of dehumanizing Akaky. "It's not even possible there could be such a civil servant," he objects. "I will make a complaint . . . a formal complaint." There is a touch here, it may be, of Dostoevsky's own Gogolian brand of humor, but it remains nonetheless the case that Dostoevsky is trying deliberately to humanize the clerk figure, to give him an inner life, a need to love, and even the wish to be a writer and critic himself. Ironically, in view of such good intentions, it is Makar Devushkin who comes to seem a puppet in his creator's hands, while Akaky is not only moving and highly memorable but independent as well, with that eerie independence Gogol came to mistrust so much, just as he came to fear and distrust his own powers as a writer. It seems likely that Stravinsky remembered Gogol's story in the ballet *Petrushka*, where the showman's puppet, killed off during the performance, returns at the finale into a life of his own, confounding the showman's assurance to the audience that he was only a puppet made of straw and sawdust.

"My Tatiana has gone and got married," wrote Pushkin to a friend as he was composing the last part of *Evgeny Onegin.* "I should never have believed it of her!" In his own lighthearted way Pushkin is expressing the same wonder at the seeming independence of his own creative power that was eventually to cause Gogol such heartfelt anguish. It is this primal power of creation that distinguishes Russia's "Golden Age" of writing, an age of Shakespearean freedom, innocent of social messages or ideological intentions. Those were to come later, with stern critics like Belinsky, who bossed Turgenev around as he would like to have bossed Gogol, and with the great committed and opinionated geniuses of Dostoevsky and Tolstoy. And yet, as Dostoevsky himself is said to have remarked, "We all came out from under Gogol's Overcoat."

The New York Review of Books, 1999

26

The Strengths of His Passivity

Ivan Turgenev (1818–1883)

─────────

First Love and a Fire at Sea
by Ivan Turgenev, translated by Isaiah Berlin

Turgenev's Letters
edited and translated by David Lowe

A GAME MIGHT BE PLAYED about the great Russian authors: With which of them do we feel most at home? Feeling at home with them is important, for it explains their extraordinary popularity with English-speaking readers from the time translations of their work first appeared. The Victorian intellectuals deeply respected Goethe and the German philosophers and admired Balzac and Victor Hugo, but Tolstoy and Turgenev, and later on Dostoyevsky as well, they really took to their hearts. Of course, their enthusiasm was for the charm of the unknown, which suddenly seemed wonderfully accessible and familiar. But that enthusiasm was based on an often remarkable ignorance. In the course of a rhapsodic review of the French translation of *Anna Karenina*, Matthew Arnold broke off to remark patronizingly that "the crown of literature is of course great poetry" and the Russians had not produced a great poet. Presumably he had never heard of Pushkin.

But Arnold certainly knew all about Turgenev, who was taken up in England as much as or more than in cosmopolitan Germany and France; he was invited out shooting on great estates and was given an honorary degree at Oxford. The English (and Henry James) saw him as one of themselves. Not only was he obviously a gentleman, but his art—to borrow the perhaps unintentionally ironic verdict of the literary historian Prince Mirsky—"answered to the demands of everyone." The right admired its sensitivity and aesthetic beauty and the left its liberal tendencies, which they saw as embodying their own radical and revolutionary program. But the danger of pleasing everyone is that in the end you please no one; that happened to Turgenev, even in his own lifetime. More than any other factor, perhaps, it has contributed to the gradual eclipse of his once great reputation.

One feels that Turgenev's novels should have increased in stature by virtue of their wise and civilized impartiality, while those of Tolstoy and Dostoyevsky should appear more and more clearly as having been written by opinionated fanatics. But art does not work that way. Turgenev's humanity now looks like weakness. As his best biographer, Leonard Schapiro, has observed, "Much of Turgenev's life and work can be explained in terms of a longing and admiration for the kind of all-consuming will he himself lacked." Probably he never recovered from the capricious domination of his mother, a rich, embittered, and often sadistic woman, who flogged the serfs on her large estate and sometimes treated her son as if he were one of them. Though he had one or two affairs with servant girls, and produced an illegitimate daughter whom he looked after but who remained a constant source of worry to him, Turgenev never achieved a mature relationship with a woman. All his later life he clung to Pauline Viardot, the masterful Parisian opera singer who, together with her husband, provided him with a ready-made home and family.

There seems to be a connection between weakness of will in an author and the length at which he can most successfully work. Turgenev admired Tolstoy's stories but abominated *War and Peace*. The repetitive patterns in his own novels—indecisive men and pure, strong-hearted women—make them predictable and boring before they end; but weakness comes into its own in the forms Turgenev was best at—the sketch, the story, and the personal letter. "A Sportsman's Sketches," which is supposed to have contributed to the emancipation of the serf, still holds its own as a work of singular freshness and charm; Turgenev's mother said its prose reminded her of the scent of wild strawberries.

But the tale that exploits most effectively Turgenev's gifts of pathos and humor, insight and self-awareness—the strengths of his own passivity, so to speak—is "First Love." It is a masterpiece that shows the curious literalism of Turgenev's talent. He is best when eschewing all fancy stuff and describing exactly what happened, as he does in "First Love," in "A Sportsman's Sketches," in the miniature memoir "A Fire at Sea" and in his extraordinary eyewitness account of the death by guillotine of a French murderer, "The Execution of Tropmann." His famous style seems built for international consumption; he wrote in French as easily as in Russian, and he was fluent in German and competent in English, though the letters he wrote to English friends demonstrate a rather peculiar vocabulary. But appearances are misleading. Turgenev's Russian style, far from going easily into other languages, is exceedingly difficult to translate: the ordinary sort of faithful rendering, which will do nicely for Tolstoy or Dostoyevsky, quite fails to do him justice. The translator must understand, from inside, the wonderful supple intimacy of his Russian and evolve a comparable kind of ease in English idiom. This Isaiah Berlin has triumphantly managed, producing the best translation available of Turgenev's most effective tale.

Turgenev was more honest with himself than the other great Russian writers, and in his prose this transparent honesty combines with a profound sympathy for romantic delusion. In "First Love," the young Vladimir falls in love with Zinaida because he knows about love from reading Schiller and sentimental fiction. But the literary springs of his feeling do not in the least affect the passionate and spontaneous nature of the emotion. When she mockingly tells him to jump off his seat on a high wall if he really loves her, he finds himself falling as if pushed from behind. Going to bed, he lays his head down carefully, afraid of upsetting the precarious joy that fills his entire being.

Zinaida herself is by far the most realistic of Turgenev's heroines, and her passion for the boy's father has a kind of earthiness and substantiality that is wholly convincing. Turgenev knew how to render the erotic. The white blind that Vladimir sees suddenly and softly descend over the dark transparency of Zinaida's window is more suggestive than any account of doings in bed. Zinaida's mother, a slatternly old princess, and the hero's father, with his withdrawn and dangerous attractiveness, are memorable portraits from life. The events of the tale are certainly taken from the writer's own adolescence, his father having been a noted roué who married his mother for her money and died young.

The origins of "A Fire at Sea," another little masterpiece, are more curious. When he was nineteen, Turgenev obtained his mother's permission to visit Germany; he departed for Lubeck on a steamer that caught fire a few miles from its destination and was run ashore and burned out. Gossip began to find its way back to Russia that Turgenev had behaved in a comic and cowardly fashion, running distractedly up and down the deck and promising ten thousand rubles to any sailor who would save him, since he was his mother's only son and too young to die. Turgenev was never allowed to forget that story. Dostoyevsky mentions it with glee in his venomous caricature of Turgenev as Karmazinov in "The Possessed."

Turgenev's own attitude was a curious one; he seems to have defended himself, as he often did in contexts of political and literary controversy, by acting the buffoon, deliberately drawing attention to his own absurdity. (In this spirit, he once imitated a cancan dancer in the presence of the censorious Tolstoy, who noted curtly in his journal: "Turgenev—the cancan—sad.") That, at any rate, seems to have been Turgenev's intention when he gave some amateur theatricals on his big estate at Spasskoye and brought the house down by acting a scene in which a fire broke out and yelling at the top of his voice: "Save me! I am my mother's only son."

As Isaiah Berlin says, such behavior was characteristic of "his incurably ironic sense of his own person and conduct, which he often used as a defensive weapon to blunt the edge of the hostility and mockery he constantly excited in his native land." People in general, and especially Russian authors, don't forgive you for not taking yourself seriously enough. When he was dying of cancer of the spine—and, let it be said, dying heroically—Turgenev set down in French his own account of the fire at sea, showing that his talent for words had lost none of its magic. (He remembers the Danish sailors, with their "cold energetic faces.") In Mr. Berlin's words, "The memory of a moment of weakness that must have preyed on him for more than forty years was exorcised, turned into literature, rendered innocuous and delightful. His conduct becomes that of an innocent, confused, romantically inclined young man, neither hero nor coward, slightly cynical, slightly absurd, but above all amiable, sympathetic and human." Conrad's Lord Jim in reverse, as it were. But in a sense it is a judgment on Turgenev's art that it does transform everything into the innocuous and delightful.

That is one reason for the charm of his correspondence. David Lowe, author of the literary monograph "Turgenev's 'Fathers and Sons,'" has provided an admirable and scholarly two-volume edition of the letters, including more than two hundred translated for the first time. A. V. Knowles has edited a shorter selection, one that has the advantage of a more convenient apparatus, with a note on each correspondent prefacing the first letter to them, and notes at the foot of each page instead of in an appendix at the end. Anyone with a real interest in Russian literature will want to have one of these collections, and preferably both.

Though Turgenev's letters are not in the same class for literary interest as Flaubert's, some of the best and warmest are to the French novelist; that the pair got on so well together says much for Turgenev's charm. With his friend Pavel Vasilievich Annenkov he kept up a running commentary on the current literary scene in France, Germany, and Russia; and his few letters to Dostoyevsky have the peculiar fascination of two utterly opposed temperaments generously agreeing (in Turgenev's case, at least) to look beyond their own limitations. Both writers took part in the famous Pushkin Commemoration of 1880, in which Turgenev made a sensible and rational speech in praise of Russia's poet, doubting nonetheless that he was a "world poet," whereas Dostoyevsky inspired his audience to hysteria with his claim that Pushkin was Russia's ultimate gift to Europe, "re-creating Shakespeare, Goethe, and all the others." Turgenev's uninfectious common sense was coldly received, after that, by a Slavophile Moscow audience.

Some of the most touching and revealing letters are those to the illegitimate daughter, Paulinette—a name derived fondly but with singular tastelessness from Pauline Viardot, the love of Turgenev's life, whom he first helped into what proved a disastrous marriage and then supported in her cantankerous solitude. Mr. Facing-Both-Ways as he was, he possessed an unadvertised personal heroism. It comes out in a letter he wrote on his deathbed to Tolstoy, imploring that "great writer of the Russian land" not to forsake art but to write more novels and stories. From a writer to another who had always sneered at him, and from a writer who was dying by painful inches, that represented an uncovenanted nobility of spirit. But it was not at all untypical of Turgenev.

The New York Times, 1983

27

An Excellent Man

Anton Chekhov (1860–1904)

―――――――

Chekhov
by Henri Troyat, translated by Michael Henry Heim

CHEKHOV IS NOT a good subject for a biographer. He is too nice, too evasive, too lacking in the kind of temperament usually associated with writers and artists. He was in fact the kind of subdued heroic figure who in life is usually ignored by and depended on by everybody: an excellent man, in the sense of one of Barbara Pym's "excellent women." Transpose his sex, and he could well be the leading character in one of her novels, the kind of person whose virtue is taken for granted, and about whose emotional needs and private life no one is in the least interested. Ironically, he would never appear as a character in one of his own plays or stories. He was that rare thing, a literary genius who had no need or impulse to live what he wrote.

Nonetheless Henri Troyat has succeeded in doing an absorbing study of Chekhov, for whom he seems to feel more genuine affection than for the colorful characters of Russian literature—Pushkin, Gogol, Dostoevsky, Tolstoy—who are the subjects of his previous biographies. He finds the key to his hero's character in a remark made by Chekhov's deplorable friend Potapenko: "He resisted leading a private existence." With his usual subdued humor Chekhov himself was not far off the mark when he claimed that "if monasteries accepted the irreligious and permitted abstention from prayer, I'd become a monk." Potapenko, whose character is clearly visible in that of Trigorin in *The Seagull*, was in real life the playwright's rival for the favors of a lady called Lika Mizinova, who seems to have loved Chekhov but allowed herself to be seduced by his friend, the rake.

Did Chekhov love her himself? Possibly he did so in his own fashion, writing her tender letters, which left her, as Troyat says, "not knowing where she stood." When it came to the point he preferred to stand aside and leave her to Potapenko, seeing the pair of them, with his customary understanding and charity, as resembling the characters in his play. If Chekhov were a writer responding emotionally in the situation he would surely have pilloried Potapenko in *The Seagull*, had his revenge on him. As it is, he understands him, as he understands the girl whom he seduces. Not much reward for her perhaps, but in Chekhov that was the kind of lover she had to deal with — a baffling one for a warmhearted and impulsive Russian girl, the sort of girl who is the heroine of *The Darling*, the gently humorous tale about a woman who throws herself with passion into the lives and interests of her successive husbands or lovers, forgetting it all totally as each one dies or disappears. "That's what life is all about," Chekhov might have said; and an artist and consumptive cannot afford to get too involved with life in that sense.

D. H. Lawrence, fellow artist and consumptive, would have acrimoniously disagreed with him. Malice and revenge were a natural tonic and inspiration to Lawrence, although some of his best stories, particularly the early ones, have a remarkable affinity with Chekhov's. Tolstoy got Chekhov wrong, too, observing of *The Darling*, which he much admired, that the author had intended to satirize his enthusiastic heroine for her giddy commitment to each lover in turn, but, by writing about her with so much sympathy, had in fact exalted her. Chekhov must have deprecated that. Exaltation of the life principle, devotion to the channels in which life flows, as Lawrence's disciple F. R. Leavis put it, would have seemed to him cant, like all the other kinds of cant — political, social, and moral — that his friends and contemporaries were talking in Russia, as elsewhere. Life had no special charms for Chekhov. It was neither as good nor as bad as people made out, and it had to be got through somehow.

Psychiatrists today might call Chekhov a typical case of emotional disablement through parental tyranny. His father, the old patriarch of Taganrog, was despotic even by Russian standards, complacent, self-righteous, and cruel, a kind of quasi-Oriental Micawber, who in addition to being a drunkard and bankrupt, whose natural state was complete idleness, ruled his family with a rod of iron, drawing up detailed schedules for their hours of working, eating, and sleeping, and beating them ferociously for the smallest infraction of the rules. One of Chekhov's younger brothers, Troyat tells us, was mercilessly chastised for waking up a few minutes late, and another one, Ivan, howled so loudly under punishment that even in Moscow, where such manifestations of paternal zeal were tolerated and approved, there were strong complaints from all the neighbors.

A regime of this type might well have produced in those subjected to it an attitude similar to that summed up in Philip Larkin's poem: "Get out as early as you can / And don't have any kids yourself." But although he was a late starter, and possibly sterile through the effects of tuberculosis, Chekhov in middle age might well have become a devoted husband and father. When he at last took the plunge, late in his short life, he was deeply attached to his young wife, the actress Olga Knipper, but because of his health, which kept him in the south, and her work as a popular actress in Moscow, they were unable to live together for more than brief periods. Whatever the visible deficiencies of family life, which he had known from earliest childhood, Chekhov always remained a family man. He never seems to have resented the behavior of his father, who admittedly treated his eldest son better than the others, and quite early in life he took over as the counselor, comforter, and breadwinner for all the family.

Nothing is quite what it seems of course, and behavior is notoriously ambiguous where siblings and parents are concerned. Chekhov might well have been enacting his father's role, but enacting it in a spirit of proprietary benevolence. That an autocrat lurked somewhere in his nature is shown by his attitude toward the projected marriage of his beloved sister, Maria. After he achieved a measure of fame and financial success he bought a small estate near Moscow called Melikhovo. Himself the grandson of a serf, and a man who entertained no sentimental Tolstoyan nonsense about the sanctity and virtue of peasant life, Chekhov was immensely proud of becoming a landowner, even on such a modest scale. He rejoiced in his ability to entertain family and friends in the hospitable Russian manner, attracting a host of hangers-on who arrived for a few days, as in The Cherry Orchard, and were still there in the next year.

His sister was a pillar of this community and played a cardinal role in maintaining the equilibrium of his day-to-day existence. The time came when she received a proposal from one of his guests.

His name was Alexander Smagin. After a bit of innocuous courting Smagin suddenly made an impassioned declaration of love and asked for Maria's hand. At loose ends or, rather, panic-stricken, Maria needed someone to turn to. Her father? No, of course not. Her mother? No, not even her. Anton. Wasn't he the sage of the family? And so, mustering all her courage, she confronted him in his study with the statement, "You know, Anton, I've decided to marry." Since Chekhov knew who the prospective groom was, he did not ask, but his features seemed to harden. Maria was frightened by his silence. "When he failed to respond," she wrote in her *Memoirs*, "I sensed he found the news unpleasant. He held his tongue, though, and what could he say? I saw he couldn't admit that it would be hard for him if I went off to another home, a new family." She returned to her room in tears, having failed to coax a word out of her brother. Nor did he broach the subject with her in the next few days. "I gave it a great deal of thought. . . . I could consent to nothing that could cause him pain, upset his way of life, deprive him of the creative atmosphere I always tried to make for him. I informed Smagin of my decision, which caused him much suffering as well."

Chekhov heaved a sigh of relief. He had been very much alarmed. A not untypical Victorian situation. But it is surprising to find so gentle and humane a man as Chekhov acting in this way. In *The Unquiet Grave* Cyril Connolly wrote that when we see a man surrounded like a deep-rooted oak tree by friends and happy families, dispensing love and benevolence to all, "be sure that he is an ogre, and that human bones lie scattered round his roots." A sweeping generalization, but there is something in it. Even Chekhov was not entirely an exception.

The quotation above is a fair example of Troyat's style, which is relaxed, possibly rather too relaxed, and inherently difficult to translate, since it is suited to the biographical idiom of the French language rather than to that of the English, in which it sounds too loose and confiding, even arch. It is in fact the manner in which André Maurois used to write his popular biographies. But Michael Heim has done the best he could, and produced a very readable English version, which if it lacks the scope and detail of Troyat's big Tolstoy biography makes up for it in sympathy and insight. Although he does not attempt much in the way of a critical survey of Chekhov's writings, Troyat is good on the background of magazines and other such publications in which Chekhov's stories first appeared, and equally good on the situation and outlook of the Moscow theater companies by whom the plays were first produced.

Responsive as they were to the current *Zeitgeist*, with its emphasis on plangency, pathos, and nostalgic sentiment, the directors of the time saw in Chekhov's plays the perfect vehicle for this type of approach. Chekhov himself was much more old-fashioned, a devotee of traditional comedy, and he resisted to the end their attempts to sentimentalize his plays and make them broodingly symbolic. The farcical element in life was what appealed to his sense of theater, and he saw Madame Ranevsky in *The Cherry Orchard* as essentially a character from farce. He might have echoed Nietzsche's remark that the individual, closely looked at, is unavoidably comic, and his plays are always about individuals, never dramatic types. Deeply apolitical as he was, he could give neither his plays nor his stories a "moral" in the accepted sense, although his admirers never had any trouble in finding one. In this respect he is unique among Russian writers, and the older Russian critics were never able to accept or understand the admiring reverence with which, in the early twentieth century, his work came to be regarded in the West.

When he was writing *The Cherry Orchard* in a *dacha* near Moscow, his window blew open one night and scattered some pages of manuscript in the snow outside. When retrieved they were completely illegible. His friends said not to worry: he must remember more or less what he had written, but Chekhov protested that he could remember absolutely nothing at all. The story has a ring of truth in it. The secret of his work is its complete immediacy, its lack of anything deliberately considered or planned, even memorable in the utterance. The memorableness, like the meaning, had to be supplied by the actors, which is why reading one of his plays is an experience of remarkable vacancy, as well as of a kind of purity. That purity is most marked in his best stories, like "The Steppe," an early one, which relates in the simplest manner what happens to a young boy on a journey across the Don plain. The story ends with the boy's arrival at the place where he will go to school and his future life will begin. Since it was so successful, and earned him a lot of rubles per page, Chekhov toyed with the idea of writing a sequel to it, but he had only to begin the sequel to see it wouldn't do: the picture was artistically complete just because it was unfinished.

No one has ever been more levelheaded than Chekhov about those two giants of the previous literary age, Tolstoy and Dostoevsky. Tolstoy he admired immensely, but pointed out that much of his lesser work is marred by simple, willful ignorance. He will not look at the facts, whether they are about the way peasants live or women's attitude to sexual intercourse. Tolstoy was the supreme creator from his own experience, but his own experience, compared to Chekhov's, was remarkably limited; he did not know enough different sorts of people. Chekhov also greatly appreciated Dostoevsky, but unerringly drops in the *mot juste*. His works, in spite of their wonders, suffer from length and overemphasis. "Pretentious too." Yet it may have been *The House of the Dead* that gave Chekhov the idea of his journey, all the way across Siberia, to see and report firsthand on conditions in the penal colony island of Sakhalin.

This was a feat of astonishing bravery for a man in such poor health. Envious fellow writers said it was a publicity stunt, but nothing could have been further from the truth. Chekhov undertook it in the same spirit in which he had become a doctor and writer; he was moved by curiosity and compassion and the desire to see for himself. Sober and factual, his detailed report aroused no enthusiasm in revolutionaries and critics of the regime back home, who were less interested in convict conditions than in what could be made out of such matters politically. But the report was taken very seriously indeed by the government and civil service; and things in Sakhalin got better as a result.

It is hard to say how happy Chekhov's last time with Olga Knipper really was. Like everyone else, even his great friend and benefactor the self-made newspaper owner Suvorin, she seems to have regarded him rather absently, preoccupied as she was with other, more important things. He was never one to draw attention to himself. At the end, in a German spa, he could find nothing to say to a German specialist except to summon up what he could remember of the language and whisper the words, *"Ich sterbe"*—"I am dying." After his death the plaudits and the admiration really got going. Gorky, who led them, was deeply shocked that the corpse of the great Russian writer had inadvertently been shipped back to his native land in a railway wagon labeled "Fresh Oysters." Chekhov would have enjoyed the joke—in fact would barely have considered it to be one. It was not black humor: it was just the way life went.

The New York Review of Books, 1986

28

The Backward Look

Ivan Bunin (1870–1953)

The Life of Arseniev: Youth
by Ivan Bunin, Books 1–4 translated by Gleb Struve and Hamish
  Miles; Book 5 translated by Heidi Hillis, Susan McKean, and
  Sven A. Wolf; edited, annotated, and with an introduction by
  Andrew Baruch Wachtel

Ivan Bunin: Russian Requiem 1885–1920, A Portrait from Letters,
  Diaries, and Fiction
edited with an introduction and notes by
  Thomas Gaiton Marullo

Ivan Bunin: From the Other Shore 1920–1933, A Portrait from
  Letters, Diaries, and Fiction
edited with an introduction and notes by
  Thomas Gaiton Marullo

EXCEPT AMONG STUDENTS of Russian literature the name of Ivan
Bunin is hardly remembered in the West today. The title of one of
his most famous stories, "The Gentleman from San Francisco,"
may still strike a chord. The story survives well in translation, and once
read is not forgotten. D. H. Lawrence, who was not at all given to praising other writers, greatly admired it, and helped to produce the English
version; it could even be said to have influenced the technique of some
of his own later stories, though its most obvious resemblance is to Tol-

stoy's *nouvelle, The Death of Ivan Ilyich*. A rich elderly American comes to Capri, has a heart attack, and dies. That is the whole story, but the way it is done is masterly; and the stark and yet richly poetical overtones of its style are powerful and disturbing.

The story appeared in Russia in 1915 and was published in England and America in 1922, in a book of Bunin's stories that sold only very slowly. By that time however, Bunin, who had joined in the great diaspora of Russian émigrés and settled in Paris, was becoming a writer well known in European circles, partly through the sheer volume and variety of his output, which was brought out in journals and by the numerous and resourceful émigré publishing houses, as well as in the Soviet Union itself, at least up to the late Twenties. An old friend of Maxim Gorky, and before the war a fellow writer in his publishing concern *Znanie* (Knowledge), among a band of like-minded novelists whom the brilliant notoriety of the younger Gorky had attracted around him, Bunin possessed a genuinely Russian wealth of sympathy and versatility in his writing. He was both a lyric poet and a prose writer, often harmonizing the two media together in the same volume; but he was also the master of a detailed and pitiless realism, which he brought to bear on the backwardness and barbarity of provincial Russia.

Where the short story was concerned his master was Chekhov, and especially such a magical instance of Chekhov's art as one of his longer tales, "The Steppe," but in prose fiction Bunin's scope was far wider. His reputation in pre-revolutionary Russia was crowned in 1910 by his big *poema, The Village*. The Russian word signifies an epic of imaginative narration in either prose or verse. Both *The Village* and *Sukhodol (Dry Valley)*, which followed it, chronicle the destruction in the rapidly industrializing and socially changing Russia of the old patriarchal landowning ways and the class that presided over them. Both are "beautiful," in their writing and their sense of life, but uncompromisingly bleak and pessimistic in their view of the future. Bunin was not able or willing to summon up in his writing any of the utopian or merely hopeful prospects which were the stock in trade of the Social Revolutionary writers. Despite his versatility, and his understanding of the modern, Bunin really looks back to the classic age of Russian prose—Turgenev, Sergei Aksakov, and Goncharov—except that he was temperamentally disinclined to take even the cautiously liberal and progressive line that such writers thought proper to subscribe to, at least as a matter of decorum. He was raised in the Elets district of central Russia, in an ancient and impoverished family of country gentry, and real inspiration and nostalgia remained for him in the life he had before he was twenty—the world of experience lovingly recorded in the book he was to write in exile, *The Life of Arseniev*.

Always in love with the backward look, Bunin now found his true country in the past. Anna Akhmatova, in one of her poems written in a mood of stoical despair in St. Petersburg after the Revolution, knew that no new future awaits, "and that God has not saved us." In exile at the same time, Bunin set himself like Proust, the only modern French writer he admired, to rediscover the past. Since he was Russian the past was *Svyata Rus*, Holy Russia, the place where God had once been. And yet paradoxically Bunin was no sheltered introvert but a tough, combative, and ambitious writer: in the penurious and competitive world of exile one had to defend one's own corner as hard as one could—there was no chance of retiring into a corklined study.

Bunin exploited his fame among the émigrés as a famous prewar Russian writer and one of the gentry, one of themselves; and he continued to write as much as he could, and in the ways which had previously made him well known, including short stories and essays. It was this productivity in several literary fields, as well as his literary conservatism, that made him an obvious candidate, if the Nobel committee should feel it expedient for the first time to award the prize to a Russian—a non-Soviet Russian, naturally. Bunin and his friends in emigration lobbied as much as they could, and the distinguished award was duly conferred on him in 1933. By that time he and his devoted common-law wife, Vera Muromtseva-Bunina, had achieved a degree of prosperity that enabled them to live for much of the year in a villa near Grasse in the south of France.

This success and good luck did not please his fellow writers in exile. Even those who had worked hardest for him, like the influential critics Zinaida Gippius and her husband, Merezhkovsky, author of standard works on Tolstoy and Dostoevsky, now muttered that it was they, and not Bunin, who best deserved the final accolade of international recognition. The fiery poetess Marina Tsvetaeva was particularly infuriated.

I don't agree with it: Gorky is bigger, more human, more original, and more necessary than Bunin. Gorky is an epoch, but Bunin is the end of an epoch. But it's also a matter of politics, since the King of Sweden could not pin an order on Gorky the Communist. By the way, the third candidate for the prize was Merezhkovsky, who also undoubtedly deserved the award more than Bunin, for if Gorky is an epoch, and Bunin the end of an epoch, then Merezhkovsky is an epoch of the *end* of an epoch. His influence both in Russia and abroad is much greater than Bunin's, who never exerted *any* influence either here or there. And . . . to compare Bunin's style with that of Tolstoy . . . is simply shameful. . . .

I *don't love* Bunin. He's a cold, cruel, and arrogant *barin*.

For good measure Tsvetaeva adds that "everyone is afraid" of Merezhkovsky and Gippius, "for they are both mean, especially her." One can see that apart from the hardships of exile it was no joke being a Russian émigré writer surrounded with friends like these; and no doubt Bunin was wise to spend most of his time in the Alpes Maritimes. The mildest criticism he received was in an émigré journal, which dryly observed that no Russian writer had refuted as convincingly as Bunin "the old . . . half-truth that talents develop only on native soil." *Time* magazine approved the award, for Bunin was clearly "head and shoulders above all other White Russian authors," but remarked that Soviet Russia would be furious that Gorky had not been chosen, and that the award was "political." *Time* was right. Bunin's books were banished from the Soviet Union, and he only ceased being a non-writer there when the thaw came in the Fifties. His popularity in Europe had displeased the Soviet literary establishment, as did the fact that the Nobel committee had for the first time given their prize to what the American magazine called "a man without a country."

These comments are taken from Thomas Gaiton Marullo's two-volume portrait of the writer, based on Bunin's and his wife's diaries, later comments from the émigré press and from European critics, and occasional excerpts from Bunin's own novels and stories. The book is a highly skillful and scholarly compilation, giving an insight not just into Bunin's own work but into many other figures of Russian culture as it had spread out over Europe. And it is hardly Marullo's fault that neither Bunin nor his wife—a faithful and amiable but not particularly intelligent woman—is in the category of great or even interesting diarists. Although the Soviet authorities detested Bunin and his fellow émigrés, they profited indirectly from the widespread interest in Russian literature which these exiles had brought with them to Europe, producing the fashionable craze for Diaghilev's Russian opera and numerous productions of Chekhov's plays.

Bunin profited too. At the time of the prize he was continually interviewed, and was asked the usual imbecile questions about what he thought of modern civilization and the future of society. He replied that winning the Nobel Prize had made him "a great optimist" on all these matters. The same sardonic humor is evident in the "parody" stories that he now wrote in the style of Maxim Gorky, who had referred to him in his book about the Russian peasantry as a man well known in Russia for his hostility not only toward the new regime but even toward the spread of literacy among the citizens of the new Soviet Union. Not yet disillusioned with Lenin's and Stalin's regime, Gorky had set himself up as the archetypal opposite to his old friend and colleague in matters of class, literature, and ideals: he was the positive against Bunin's negative, and it is this "positive" aspect of Gorky's work that Bunin gently mocked in his story "The Made Artist."

If for Gorky Bunin was a nobleman who despised the new Soviet working class even more than the old peasantry—"a splendid artist, but that is all"—the envy and jealousy of some of his fellow emigrants began to make themselves felt even against his status as an artist. Didn't he belong *too* much to the past, even though as exiles they were bound to do so themselves? Mark Aldanov, who was acting as Bunin's chief lobbyist in the attempt to make his the best-thought-of Russian name for the Prize, wrote to congratulate him on bringing out, at the age of fifty-four, a new and wonderful love story. The poet Khodasevich, on the other hand, observed tersely to a friend that Mitya's love was "one percent *Kreutzer Sonata* and 100 percent distilled water." As poets, both Khodasevich and Marina Tsvetaeva seem to have been especially irritated by what they considered the spurious similarity between Bunin's work and Tolstoy's, whether it was Tolstoy's late and pessimistic tale of jealousy, *The Kreutzer*

Sonata, or his magical early trilogy, *Childhood, Boyhood*, and *Youth*, that is so much in the background of *The Life of Arseniev*.

And yet, for an English-speaking reader at least, this irritation seems unjustified. "Mitya's Love," which concerns the joys and sorrows of a boyish love affair, is lush and dreamy without being in the least sentimental: and while noting its place as "the culminating work of a specific tradition of Russian writing: the pseudo-autobiographical novel devoted to childhood," the editor of *The Life of Arseniev*, Andrew Wachtel, is surely right to claim it as "the crowning achievement of Bunin's illustrious career." Tolstoy himself in *Childhood* (1852), and Aksakov six years later in *The Childhood Years of Bagrov's Grandson*, had laid down the formula, as it were, aptly summed by Dr. Wachtel as "a happy, carefree time, spent in the countryside in the bosom of a loving family, that normally consisted of an essential, serious, loving mother, and a spendthrift, pleasantly disorganized father." A very Russian combination in the nineteenth century, when, as critics and historians have frequently pointed out, the women of the gentry class were usually stronger, more self-reliant, and more forward-looking than were its feckless and "superfluous" males. No wonder, though, that even the reactionary émigrés of the post-revolutionary period felt more than a little impatience with Bunin's wish to celebrate yet again the golden days gone by, days remembered only by a class that they themselves had mostly belonged to.

Nevertheless Bunin's late novel does indeed possess all the best characteristics of his earlier style and approach, developing a richness that is full and autumnal without being in the least decadent. Bunin's descriptive prose is alive in the same absolute sense as that of D. H. Lawrence, who had written of his own childhood twenty years earlier, a proletarian childhood, but dwelt upon in *Sons and Lovers* in the same warmly lyrical terms as those of the Russian gentry writers. Of course Bunin does not develop the same strongly probing themes, both modernist and "Freudian" as we should now consider them, which distinguish Lawrence's novel. The colors of a dreamy childhood are often visited by death—Bunin's most besetting theme—throughout his first four books: deaths of relatives, of a Grand Duke whose funeral train is seen returning from the Crimea to Moscow, and, in the fifth book, of Lika, the young woman with whom Bunin had been living for some years at the end of the period covered by the novel.

Death is equated in Bunin's work not only with the futility of material progress and prosperity, as represented by "the gentleman from San Francisco," but with the hateful vitality of revolution itself, the revolution that had forced Russia to "meet the fate she did, destroyed before our eyes with such miraculous rapidity." To that new Soviet death-in-life, Bunin, like Proust or Nabokov, opposes the truth of personal recall, of the moments subsumed in the Orthodox ritual and in the Church Slavonic funeral chant of "Eternal Memory." This desire and ability to record the past are the only immortality we possess. And as the nineteenth-century English parson Kilvert remarked in his diaries, which Bunin would have enjoyed if he could have read them, things from the past which are written down achieve a kind of holiness which was not given to them at the time, and which can never be felt in the passing moment. Bunin reflects:

> Do I remember many such days? Of course, very few; the morning which I imagine now is made up of patchy pictures, flitting through my memory from various times. Of noontides I seem to see only one picture: the hot sun, the stimulating smells from the kitchen, the keen anticipation of dinner awaiting everybody returning from the fields; my father; the sunburnt, red-bearded elder riding with a broad rocking amble on a sweating nag saddled with a high cossack saddle; the farmhands, who have been mowing with the mowers and now enter the courtyard on top of a cart full of grass and flowers mown together at the field boundaries, the gleaming scythes lying beside them; and the men who have brought the horses back from the pond, their coats shining like glass, their dark tails and manes dripping with water.
>
> At one such time I saw my brother Nicholas also sitting on top of a cart, on grass and flowers, returning from the fields with Sashka, a peasant girl from Novolselki. I had already heard something about them from the servants—something I could not understand but for some reason took to heart. And now, seeing them together on the top of the cart, I was suddenly aware, with a secret rapture, of their beauty, their youth, their happiness. Tall and slender, still no more than a girl,

with a delicate pretty face, she sat holding a pitcher, turning away from my brother, her bare legs swinging down from the cart, with downcast eyes; he, in a white peaked cap and a light cambric Russian shirt with unbuttoned collar—sunburnt, clean, youthful—was holding the reins; and he looked at her with shining eyes, telling her something, and smiling joyfully, lovingly.

The admirable translation, reproducing the creamy opulence of Bunin's style and avoiding unnecessary modernist touches, is equally at home in a winter landscape and at the hero's first ball.

> I recall impenetrable Asiatic blizzards, raging sometimes for whole weeks on end through which the town belfries barely loomed. I recall the Epiphany frosts that made one think of most ancient times of Russia, of the frosts that made "the earth crackle seven feet deep"; then, at night, over the snow-white town all drowned in snowdrifts, blazed menacingly in the raven-black sky the white constellations of Orion, and by day, crystalline and sinister, two dull suns shone; and in the taut and resonant immobility of the burning air the whole town was slowly and wildly besmirched with livid smoke from the chimneys and creaked and resounded all over with the footsteps of the pedestrians and the runners of sleighs. . . . During one such frost the mendicant idiot, Dunya, froze to death on the cathedral parvis; for half a century she had roamed the town, and the town, which had always mocked her with the utmost ruthlessness, suddenly gave her almost a royal funeral.
>
> Strange as it may seem, immediately after this comes to my mind a ball at the girls' school—the first ball I went. The weather was again very frosty. . . . On the way we met schoolgirls coming from their school, dressed in fur coats and shod in high galoshes, wearing pretty hats and hoods, with long frost-silvered eyelashes and radiant eyes, and some of them said in full, clear, affable tones as they passed, "Come to the ball!"—troubling one by that full, clear tone, rousing in me the first feelings of something which lay inside those fur coats, galoshes, and hoods, in those tender excited faces, in the long frosted eyelashes and quick ardent glances—feelings that were afterward to possess me with such force. . . .

Long after the ball I felt intoxicated by recollections of it and of myself—of that well-dressed, handsome, light, deft schoolboy in a new blue uniform and white gloves who, with such a joyously brave chill in his heart, mixed with the dense and elegant girlish throng, ran about the corridors and staircases, drank many almond syrups in the refreshment room, glided among the dancers on the floor sprinkled with some glistening powder, in the big white hall flooded with the pearly light of the chandeliers and echoing from the balconies with triumphantly resonant thunders of the military band, breathing in all that fragrant ardor with which balls drug the novice, and enchanted by every tiny shoe he came across, by every white cape, every black velvet ribbon on the neck, every silk bow in the braid, by every youthful breast heaving in blissful dizziness after a waltz.

The translators Gleb Struve and Hamish Miles have managed to convey much of what Bunin's Russian gives us, which Bunin himself dryly compares with the proverb "Russia's joy is in drinking," a joy which produces "that verbal sensuality for which Russian literature is so famous."

Throughout the novel there are intimations of the apocalypse to come—naturally enough, since Bunin is writing in the south of France a decade after his life had been torn apart by the revolution. His brother, a highly intelligent and well-qualified man, had been one of those gentleman subversives whose clandestine activities had been watched over by the Tsar's secret police, and whose services were both made use of and despised by Lenin and his professionals. Bunin is shrewd about their psychology and its real motivation, finding it in a sort of continuation of childhood by other means, "all that happy festive atmosphere amid which his youth had been flowing— . . . participation in all the secret circles, the holiday atmosphere of gatherings, of songs, of 'seditious' speeches, of dangerous plans and undertakings. . . . Ideas were all very well, but in these youthful revolutionaries how much was there also of the mere longing for gay idleness under the cloak of hectic activity . . ."

Nothing sharpens the memory so much as a divided life and that "lost childhood" of which Nabokov writes in *Speak, Memory*. Bunin was one of Nabokov's early admirers, remarking of *The Luzhin Defense*, Nabokov's *nouvelle* written in Russian in Berlin in the Twenties, that it already invented a new kind of Russian literary future and past, supersed-ing that of the writers of his own generation. Nabokov himself, as we learn from the end of Marullo's portrait of Bunin in his letters and diaries, perferred Bunin's "remarkable flowing poetry to the brocadelike prose for which he was famous."

> When I met him in emigration, Bunin had just received the Nobel Prize. He was terribly preoccupied by the passage of time, old age, and death; with pleasure he noted that he held himself more erectly than I, though he was thirty years my senior.
>
> I remember that he had invited me to an expensive restaurant for some heart-to-heart conversation. Unfortunately, I cannot stand restaurants, drinks, hors d'oeuvres, music—and heart-to-heart conver-sations. Bunin was taken aback by my indifference to pheasant; he was annoyed by my refusal to lay bare my soul. By the end of the din-ner, things had become intolerably boring for the both of us. "You will die in terrible torment and in complete loneliness," Bunin told me when we returned to the cloakroom . . .
>
> We used to meet often with other people; but for some reason we adopted a kind of depressingly bantering tone; in general, we never agreed on art.

One would hardly have expected them to have done so. One of Bunin's own themes, after all, is how the hungry generations tread down the memories of their predecessors and reject anxieties that lurk in their pos-sible influence. But Bunin's achievement is complete on its own, and as it stands. He most certainly remains one of the finest writers of the "Sil-ver Age," that period of creativity in the Russian arts which spanned two-thirds of his lifetime.

The New York Review of Books, 1995

29

Poems with a Heroine

Anna Akhmatova (1888–1966)

———————

Poems
by Anna Akhmatova, selected and translated by Lyn Coffin,
introduction by Joseph Brodsky

Akhmatova's Petersburg
by Sharon Leiter

ANNA AKHMATOVA had been in her youth one of the "Acmeist" poets, along with her husband Gumilev and Mandelstam. Acmeism was essentially a reaction against the symbolist movement in Russian poetry, a movement that tended, as such things do in Russia, to extremes, in this case extremes of uplift, mysticism, apocalypse. Acmeism by contrast was concerned with poetry as architecture, and poems as objects of weight and mass-produced as if in a workshop (the poets' guild or workshop was one of the group's other names for itself). The most important early influence on Akhmatova was her discovery of the poems of Innokenti Annensky, an expert translator and scholar of ancient Greek, who had written—they were published posthumously—a volume of verses called *The Cypress Box*. Her early poems are precise evocations of places, moments, loves, deceptive intensities of being, carved out with reticence and a kind of inner dignity.

It is significant that the Russian symbolist poets, notably Blok and Bryusov, hailed the revolution of 1917 in their whole consciousness. They were fascinated by the *idea* of such a thing. Their attitude was not unlike that of Yeats in "The Second Coming" and "Lapis Lazuli," joyfully greeting the end of order and the coming of the "rough beast" in a spirit of "gaiety transfiguring all that dread." Terror was merely an exciting and poetical idea to them, as the rough beast slouching toward Bethlehem was for Yeats. The Acmeists' reaction was very different: they recognized facts and truths when they saw them. Pasternak in *Dr. Zhivago* refers to Blok's line, "we children of Russia's terrible years," and he remarks dryly that those years really had been terrible for those who had been killed, bereaved, or imprisoned. The symbolic status of revolution was not the same thing as what actually occurred, and the Acmeists were only interested in what actually occurred.

Because of this common sense, as one has to call it, Akhmatova, like Mandelstam, can write about virtually anything. It is hard to think of any poetry in English, and certainly of none written in the last century, that has the range of hers, and the amazing power to rise to an occasion. Mandelstam said that great poetry was often a response to total disaster, and it is true that we may think of Milton, blind and at the mercy of his political enemies, setting out to write *Paradise Lost*. True in some heroic ages perhaps, but not much in our own, when poets in their sufferings have been more apt to lose themselves, like Pound muttering in his *Cantos*, or to say with Yeats: "I think it better that in times like these / A poet's mouth be silent." With her husband shot and her son imprisoned, Akhmatova wrote her poem *Requiem* between 1935 and 1940, telling of her experiences in the Yezhov terror. They were common experiences, as she emphasizes in the simple sentences of prose that preface the poem, describing how one day a woman in the great queue that stood permanently outside the prison recognized her and said in a whisper, " 'Can you describe this?' And I said: 'I can.' "

She could. Rare indeed for a poet to rise like that to such a challenge. But the whole poem has about it the dignity of utter simplicity, without false modesty or any attempt at the common touch. She describes her experiences as if they happened to her only, like words in a gospel, the equivalent in art of what she called the severe and shapely spirit of Russian orthodoxy. In this spirit she concludes by saying that if her countrymen ever want to make a monument to her she would consent if they put it outside the prison gates where she had stood, and where the news she longed for never came through the door.

> And may the melting snow drop like tears
> From my motionless bronze eyelids,
>
> And the prison pigeons coo above me
> And the ships sail slowly down the Neva.

That is D. M. Thomas's translation, from a rendering of *Requiem* and *Poem Without a Hero* published in 1976. In her version from a selection of Akhmatova's poems, Lyn Coffin attempts, and not without success, the flowing meter of the original.

> Let from the lids of bronze, unmoving eyes
> Snow melt and stream like the tears each human cries,
>
> And let in the distance the prison pigeons coo,
> While along the Neva, ships pass quietly through.

That has the movement but not the weight, or the calm simplicity. Thomas is better at giving an idea of that. As usual the problem is insoluble, but never mind: Coffin's is a good try that deserves as much credit as the cautious versions, or more. In her long poem sequences Akhmatova uses meters of great robustness and subtlety in the Russian which when transposed into English can often sound all too like Shelley or Poe at their most ebullient. The strong accents and stresses of Russian have a variety and flexibility that iron out a regular beat that would otherwise dominate the more docile English syllables. The meter of *Poem Without a Hero*, for example, has an extraordinarily commanding and stately rhythm, reminiscent of the *Dies Irae*, which could be Englished with its rhyme scheme as follows (the section refers to the ponderous march of the twentieth century, "the real not the calendar one," advancing on St. Petersburg like the stone effigy of the commander in *Don Juan*):

Thus up every street there came drumming,
So past every porch it was coming,
The shape finding its way in the gloom.
Gusts tore the placards off the palings,
Smoke spun a dance over the railings,
And the lilac flowers smelt of the tomb.

It was the metrical movement, percussive and minatory, that first started itself in Akhmatova's head, so she tells us, before any words came. In the Russian it sounds measured and relaxed, as calm as the stride of a great cat. The experts would say that the Akhmatovan line here consists of two anapests with an amphibrach, or two with an iamb, a combination so rare as to be virtually extinct, and certainly never found before on this scale. Annensky would no doubt have appreciated it, but it seems unlikely that Akhmatova herself would or could have worked it out theoretically.

The most complex and enigmatic of her works, *Poem Without a Hero* (*Poema bez geroia*), combines the personal and the historical somewhat in the manner of *The Waste Land*, but a great deal more dramatically. It is a poem of expiation, both for the personal sins she felt she and her contemporaries in St. Petersburg were guilty of, and for the national sorrows and horrors in part expunged by the great struggle for liberation against the Germans. It is certainly an arcane poem—Akhmatova called it "a Chinese box with a triple base," but its personal and literary allusions do not disturb its majestic liturgical flow. Even more than *The Waste Land* it is a poem that seems to call for explanations and yet does not really need them. It is essentially a voice poem, in the tradition that Pushkin stylized in the figure of the "Improvisatore" in "Egyptian Nights," who denies any idea of how complex verse can suddenly come into his head, rhymed and in regular feet, so that it can be instantly declaimed. Like many Russian masterpieces, especially by Pushkin, of whom Akhmatova was a profound student and critic, her *Poema* has the form of an open secret, at once spontaneous and enigmatic.

"I hear certain absurd interpretations of *Poem Without a Hero*," she writes in the foreword. "And I have been advised to make it clearer. This I decline to do. It contains no third, seventh, or twenty-ninth thoughts. I shall neither explain nor change anything. What is written is written."

And not in her voice alone, or that of her muse. She wrote the poem at intervals over twenty years, committing it entirely to memory because she feared to write it down, and it ends with a dedication to "its first audience," the fellow citizens who died in Leningrad during the siege. "Their voices I hear, and I remember them when I read my poem aloud, and for me this secret chorus has become a permanent justification of the work."

This combination of unashamed individuality with a public voice is characteristic of the best Russian poetry since Pushkin, who drew a sharp distinction between himself as an ordinary, idle, and fashionable man about town, gambling with friends and running after women, and himself as the vehicle for an unknown and inexplicable inspiration, a voice that might speak with the accents of private friendship or public authority. Akhmatova had something of the same dual persona: the dandy of St. Petersburg society, the arrogant beauty involved in bohemian intrigues at poets' cafés like the Stray Dog, and at the same time the grave poetic voice of conscience and religious awe, the voice of Russia's severe and disciplined spirit, silenced for a while by the anarchic envy and clamor of revolution, but speaking out in the fine series of poems dedicated to London at war (unprinted and unheard of, of course, while Soviet Russia was the ally of Nazi Germany), and in the sonorous poem "Courage," a summons not to the Soviets but to her fellow Russians, which appeared in *Pravda* a few months after the German invasion.

She was a Russian Orthodox believer and a Russian patriot. Her poetry flowed from both kinds of faith, and as the opening lines of *Requiem* pronounce, she was deeply proud, too, of having remained in Russia while so many others of her class and kind had fled into emigration. The four lines are very simple, but their tone sets a notorious problem for the translator:

> No foreign sky protected me,
> no stranger's wing shielded my face.
> I stand as witness to the common lot,
> survivor of that time, that place.

This attempt by Stanley Kunitz Americanizes the translation, and makes one realize how deep and subtle is the difference between "great simple verses" in the American tradition and in the Russian. The difference was even more marked when Robert Lowell reconstituted the lines in his own fashion.

> I wasn't under a new sky,
> its birds were the old familiar birds.
> They still spoke Russian. Misery
> spoke familiar Russian words.

Those are wholly American words, and an American tone. Lyn Coffin is the best at getting some equivalent of the original's weight and *gravitas*.

> No, it wasn't under a foreign heaven,
> It wasn't under the wing of a foreign power, —
> I was there among my countrymen,
> I was where my people, unfortunately, were.

"Unfortunately" could have been an unfortunate word, but its complex English connotations in fact just provide the right note, stopping just this side of the ironic. "Unhappily" would have verged on the portentous.

With the war over, the Soviet state returned to "normal." In 1946 Akhmatova was denounced by the cultural commissar Andrei Zhdanov and expelled from the Union of Soviet Writers.

> Akhmatova's subject matter is . . . miserably limited: it is the poetry of an overwrought upper-class lady who frantically races back and forth between boudoir and chapel. . . . A nun or a whore—or rather both a nun and a whore who combines harlotry with prayer. . . . Akhmatova's poetry is utterly remote from the people. . . . What can there be in common between this poetry and the interests of our people and state?

By using words like "overwrought" and "frantic" Zhdanov showed he had not the faintest conception of what her poetry—or any other, probably— was about. Remote from the people in a sense it certainly is, but the people did not seem aware of the fact. Her poems were immensely popular in *samizaat*, and the few official printings were instantly sold out. Perhaps the nun and the whore was the popular touch, as a symbolist like Yeats—oh so self-consciously—might have claimed. Yet the people who admired Akhmatova would not be likely to be interested in symbolist personas. Yeats or Blok might adopt the mask of libertine or sage, but Akhmatova, like Pushkin, was herself through and through, whether as woman or as poet.

Though she admired Blok, and perhaps briefly loved him, she regarded him as some sort of unstable demon, an actor in a seductive but dangerously wicked farce. She declared: "One does not ultimately behave like that," and she says the same thing in the same tone to state tyranny, to the horrors of the *Yezhovschina*, to all the destructive manifestations of inhuman conceit. She knows that offense comes, but woe unto them by whom it cometh, whether from the frivolity of the individual or the wickedness of the state. *Poem Without a Hero* (the ironic reference is of course to the new "Soviet-style" heroes of official Soviet poetry) irritated some of Akhmatova's own friends and well-wishers, as well as the Soviet officials, by resurrecting for guilt and expiation some of the old private St. Petersburg sins as if they were one with the new torments of Leningrad.

Lyn Coffin is probably wise not to attempt this poem, for her rhymed versions could not come near it, though they are frequently and rather unexpectedly effective when she renders in this way the shorter and earlier poems. Early Akhmatova often has a crisply matter-of-fact quality, which transposes well into an American idiom. Here is Coffin's version of one of Akhmatova's earliest poems, "While Reading Hamlet."

> A dust-covered patch to the right of the cemetery.
> Beyond that, a river of unfolding blue.
> "Get thee to a nunnery," you said,
>   "Or marry
> An idiot—It's up to you."
>
> That's the sort of thing princes always say,
> But I won't forget it as I grow older.
> May your words keep flowing as centuries wear away,
> Like an ermine mantle tossed over someone's shoulder.

"But I won't forget it as I grow older" hits just the right note, more so than Kunitz's more sober and impersonal "but these are words that one remembers." (Kunitz's version, though, had the Russian on the other side of the page—an excellent arrangement—and the added advantage of an essay by Max Hayward, by far the best and most concise introduction to Akhmatova yet written for readers in English.)

Lyn Coffin succeeds again in the short, tart poem in which Akhmatova glances at her unhappy relations with her husband, the poet Gumilev. She married him in 1910, after many proposals by him, one of them accompanied by a suicide attempt. Although an original poet, an explorer, and a gallant soldier (after the war he was shot by the Bolsheviks for alleged conspiracy), Gumilev was clearly not an easy man to live with, and Akhmatova herself seems to have been quite innocent of all the ordinary domestic virtues.

They had one son who because of his name was arrested in the purges, and for whom his mother spent the hours of anguish outside the Leningrad jail which are commemorated in *Requiem*. Released to fight in the war, he was re-arrested after it. Sadly, after his final release he became estranged from his mother. The son of the poet Tsvetaeva, who hanged herself in 1941, had done the same. Even in a situation of apocalypse the gap between life and art can often have the same dreadful old commonplaceness about it. Had it not been for revolution, tyranny, and violent death, Gumilev and Akhmatova would no doubt have quarreled, been jealous of each other's loves and poems, and finally separated like any other writers anywhere. As it is the little poem written only months after her marriage has a terse clarity about it which includes, even if it does not foretell, the future. There is humor in it, too, as well as sympathy and a kind of wry fellow-feeling.

> The three things he loved most in life
> Were white peacocks, music at mass,
> And tattered maps of America.
> He didn't like kids who cried and he
> Didn't like raspberry jam with tea
> Or womanish hysteria.
> . . . And I was, like it or not, his wife.

Kunitz's version has rival virtues, but ends, "And he was tied to me"—
which leaves the relationship ambiguous. Lyn Coffin cleverly gets her
rhyme on the first and last line even though she has to pad out the latter.
The Russian states merely: "And I was his wife."

There are some excellent versions, too, of the poems written during
the First World War and in the early days of the revolution, when Akhmatova was beginning, as it were, to rise to the occasion: "I hear the oriole's
voice," "The Tale of the Black Ring," "The Muse," and the magnificent
"Lot's Wife," which celebrates the woman who looked back at her old
home in "red-towered Sodom" and deliberately paid the price. "Dante,"
a poem on the same theme, was memorably rendered by Kunitz. The
poet sends Florence "a curse from hell / and in heaven could not forget
her": he refused to bow the knee to the town that was "perfidious, base,
and irremediably home." Lyn Coffin's version weakens this somewhat,
but her version of the almost equally memorable "Cleopatra" concludes well.

> Tomorrow they will chain her children. And yet
> She has something left in the world to do—one more jest.
> And the little black snake, as if a parting regret,
> With an equable hand, she puts on her swarthy breast.

In these poems Akhmatova invokes historical precedents for her fate without any scrap of pretension. The meter, unfortunately, is a mere jingle
compared to the Russian, but nothing can be done about that. What
comes faintly through is the quality that Joseph Brodsky isolates in his
preface to this translation—the true classic. "Nothing reveals a poet's
weaknesses like classic verse," he says, "and that's why it's so universally
dodged." As a poet in the same tradition, he is the best possible perceiver
of what gives Akhmatova's verse its inner strength.

Continually we hear echoes of the true classic in her verse, but they
are neither assumed nor something she is trying to conceal; they are
deliberate. As Brodsky says, "She came fully equipped, and she never
resembled anyone." She did not have to make herself like Yeats: she knew
what she was. She was Anna Akhmatova, not Anna Gorenko. Her father,
a naval architect of aristocratic birth, told her to write poetry by all means,

but not to "sully a good name" by publishing under it, so she adopted a name from the distant past of her mother's family, a name which, as Brodsky points out, has a distinctly Tatar flavor. It went with her appearance—"five feet eleven, dark-haired, fair-skinned, with pale grey-green eyes like those of snow leopards, slim and incredibly lithe, she was for half a century sketched, painted, cast, carved and photographed by a multitude of artists starting with Amadeo Modigliani." Bizarre, after this, that Brodsky compares her to Jane Austen (". . . her syntax resembles English. From the very threshold of her career to its very end she was always perfectly clear and coherent"), but the point is an exceptionally shrewd one. Neither cared in the least about originality, or even about being an "artist": they just were so. Akhmatova, according to Brodsky, disliked the very word "poet."

She was as much identified with St. Petersburg as her source of inspiration as Jane Austen with her "three or four families" in an English village. *Akhmatova's Petersburg* is a scholarly and imaginative study of her themes, her friends, and her poetry, in relation to the city that since its foundation by Peter the Great has exercised such a fascination over Russian poets and writers. Sharon Leiter quotes as one of her epigraphs a conversation with Akhmatova recorded by Lydia Chukovskaya in 1939, in which they agreed on the particular suitability of St. Petersburg as a setting for catastrophe. "This cold river, with heavy clouds always above it, these threatening sunsets, this operatic, frightful moon. . . . Black water with yellow gleams of light. . . . I can't imagine how catastrophes look in Moscow; there they haven't got all that." Blok and Bely would have agreed with her, while the stories of Gogol and Dostoevsky, and his *Crime and Punishment*, had already sounded the same theme.

And yet the town, like Dante's Florence, was "irremediably home." For her, as for her contemporary Mandelstam, it was the home of the "blessed word." There is a significant contrast here between the attitude of the two Acmeist poets to St. Petersburg (in my view Mandelstam's prose memoir *The Noise of Time* is the best evocation of it) and that of Blok. For Blok it was a symbolist hell, a *huis clos* whose only exit is bloody apocalypse. A famous two-stanza poem of his describes the immobile night scene, "a street, a street-lamp, a drugstore," with "no way out" in past or future. Akhmatova and Mandelstam let in all the light and air of story and legend (Acmeism for Mandelstam was "a nostalgia for world culture") and about the town they are, in their curious way, both more affectionate and more homely. In her "To Osip Mandelstam" she writes a poem of marvelous classic serenity, whose lilt—unheard before—nonetheless echoes both Pushkin's most famous lyrics and the nineteenth-century German lyrists who loved the Greeks.

> There, where Eurydices circle,
> Where the bull carries Europa over the waves;
> There, where our shades rush past,
> Above the Neva, above the Neva, above the Neva;
> There, where the Neva splashes against the step,—
> Is your pass to immortality.

The triumphant line—"*And Nevoi, and Nevoi, and Nevoi*"—with the accent on the last syllable of each phrase, conveys the dithyrambic movement, and Sharon Leiter's text is greatly enriched by making all quotations bilingual.

As she points out, the word "pass," *propusk*, is used by Mandelstam in his wonderful poem that begins, "We will meet again in Petersburg / As if we had buried the sun there."

> I don't need a night pass,
> I'm not afraid of sentries:
> For the blessed meaningless word
> We will pray in the Soviet night.

Though it was published in *Pravda*, as part of the official drive to mobilize the Soviet people's morale, Akhmatova's poem "Courage" also subtly undermined Soviet values by proclaiming that the struggle was to "keep you alive, great Russian word," the same word that Mandelstam invokes and prays for in the night of Leningrad. As Sinyavsky saw, the poet's word in Russia has an unambiguous authority that is the secular state's mysterious rival. The poet in Russia is the custodian of the word, and leaves the last word to God.

The New York Review of Books, 1984

30

A Poet's Tragedy

Marina Tsvetaeva (1892–1941)

————————

The Demesne of the Swans
by Marina Tsvetaeva, translated and edited by Robin Kemball

Tsvetaeva: A Pictorial Biography
edited by Ellendea Proffer, translated by J. Marin King

A Captive Spirit: Selected Prose
by Marina Tsvetaeva, translated and edited by J. Marin King

MARINA TSVETAEVA is the most Russian of poets in the same sense in which Hardy could be called the most English of poets, or Whitman the most American. Paradoxically Russia's greatest poet, Pushkin, is not, in the obvious sense, very Russian. Of course a Russian poetry lover would rightly say that this is a meaningless observation, but it does nonetheless remain true that Shakespeare and Pushkin are not placed by their nationality. Other poets are, and Tsvetaeva is one. It alters the case not at all—in fact it confirms it—that her family origins were also part Polish, part German: the most intensively English persons often come from Ireland, and American expatriates have been known to be more French than the French.

The Russianness of Tsvetaeva's poetry and prose—singularly direct and forceful as they are—consists in an obvious authenticity of the emotions. Everything is felt instantly and strongly; everything is *strashny* and *vesely*—terrible and joyful—and yet about this directness there is nothing histrionic, sloppy, or self-indulgent. It can however be contemptuous. Isaiah Berlin has remarked on the "emotional superiority" implicit in the Russian outlook.

> . . . a sense of the west as enviably self-restrained, clever, efficient, and successful, but also as being cramped, cold, mean, calculating, and fenced in, without capacity for large views or generous emotion, for feeling which must, at times, rise too high and overflow its banks . . . and consequently condemned never to know a rich flowering life.

The flowering of life is immensely strong, immensely spontaneous in Tsvetaeva's poetry, but that goes with an equally extraordinary precision and technical skill, an originality which was discerned by some of her poetic contemporaries, but both in émigré circles and the Soviet establishment not fully recognized until the Seventies.

But she has always been a poet's poet. Her first privately printed poetry, *Evening Album*, came out in 1910 when she was eighteen, and the young Pasternak was at once struck by the poems of her second collection, *Versty I*, written after Russia had been two years at war. He probably did not read them until the chaotic civil war years, when Tsvetaeva was producing her series of poems about the White Guard in southern Russia, *Lebednii Stan, The Demesne of the Swans*, which has appeared for the first time in an excellent bilingual edition with a scholarly apparatus and notes.

What impressed Pasternak, one supposes, was the absence of preciousness, of *littérature* in the sense in which it had obtained a stranglehold on symbolist and post-symbolist poetry. For Yeats, life existed to end up in a poem, and why not? But art must always try to crawl under the net of its own artifice. Probably it takes a poet, at the outset, to see how another poet has done it. Yeats made his style stark and brutal, saluting the arrival of the Savage God. Alexander Blok used meter and style in *The Twelve* to take the poem into the streets, among brutal, illiterate revolutionaries. But no one is deceived. Their poems remain as upstage as ever, which is not to say they are not marvelous and magical. "Gaiety transfiguring all that dread," writes Yeats, and a contemporary and friend of Blok observed that terrors and splendors for him were what could be made terrible and splendid *in poetry*.

Tsvetaeva's poems are not like that. Even her very great and elder contemporary Akhmatova can write of "joy and terror at the heart" without making the reader feel that these are anything but the emotions that the poet is working on. Brodsky compares her to Auden: a surprising judgment but one sees why. Both had very strong moral convictions—a rare thing among poets—which ultimately control their poetry, rather than the poetry creating by itself an image and likeness of the poet. Principle in both of them anticipates poetry. Tsvetaeva's passions, hatred of injustice, anarchy, and corruption, profound admiration for duty, honor, loyalty, and trust, are as it were the standard strong feelings, but they seem to belong to her as a person not as a poet, even when she is writing poetry. Nothing could be less modish than her feelings or her poems, which may explain why they have never quite fallen in with, or been discovered by, followers of poetic fashion, like the ones for confessions, suicides, the violence of nature, "The Savage God." Tsvetaeva's suicide cannot be seen as Sylvia Plath's could, as an aspect or requirement of her art.

It was simply the end of the road, a long and agonizing one. Like most Russian writers of the time, Tsvetaeva had a sheltered and happy childhood. Her father was professor of art history at the University of Moscow, and her mother, who came from both German and aristocratic Polish stock, was a lover of art and a talented pianist, a former pupil of Rubinstein. Tsvetaeva was educated at boarding schools in Switzerland and Germany as well as Moscow and later studied French poetry in Paris and attended lectures at the Sorbonne. Precocious, her verses had already attracted attention from Russian poets such as Gumilev (Akhmatova's husband), the symbolist Bryusov, and Max Voloshin, who ran a kind of permanent house party for young writers at his home in Koktebel on the Crimean coast. It was there at the age of eighteen that Tsvetaeva met Sergei Efron, who was a year younger than she and also hoping to become a writer. She made her decision in a typically firm and forthright manner. "I resolve that no matter what I will never part with him, and I [will] marry him."

Efron could be a character out of Conrad's *Under Western Eyes*: he would fascinate any great novelist. He was also the right choice for Tsvetaeva, at least insofar as she conformed to the description given by Nadezhda Mandelstam in *Hope Abandoned*.

She was absolutely natural and fantastically self-willed . . . cropped hair, loose-limbed gait—like a boy's—and speech remarkably like her verse. Her willfulness was not just a matter of temperament but a way of life. She could never have reined herself in, as Akhmatova did. Reading her verse and letters now I realize that what she always needed was to experience every emotion to the very utmost, seeking ecstasy not only in love, but also in abandonment, loneliness, and disaster.

Of course nobody, least of all a genius, quite conforms to that sort of stereotype. But the wish to shock, the bobbed hair, the cigarettes, the adolescent affairs—these are certainly the hallmarks of the period and were being tried out by strong-minded young women everywhere, by Katherine Mansfield in New Zealand and London, by the heroines of Lawrence's *The Rainbow* and *Women in Love*. Incorrigibly novelistic as we are, we could see Tsvetaeva as incubated in such emancipated fictional fashion worlds as those of Artsybashev's *Sanin*, or Bely's, or Remizov's, Lawrence's, too, if we transpose to an un-Russian key—but then entering and growing up into the real thing, into a work of Dostoevsky or Conrad.

The most touching photograph in the remarkable collection that appears in Ellendea Proffer's pictorial biography of Tsvetaeva shows her with Efron in the spring of 1911. With his childish good looks and party clothes, her soft hair and pince-nez and sturdily chubby features, they look like Hansel and Gretel, young lovers in a fairy tale. Four lustrous eyes gaze at the camera with stern concentration and melting candor. The features could be those of young revolutionaries from the Eighties of the previous century, but the look is wholly different, both gentler and more determinedly egotistical.

Their first child, christened Ariadna, was born a year later, and a second daughter in 1917. In the meantime Mandelstam had fallen in love with Tsvetaeva and pursued her from St. Petersburg to Alexandrov before giving up. Both commemorated the abortive affair in poetry, Tsvetaeva in the lyrical diary of *Versty I*. After the Bolshevik coup Efron got away to the south and joined the White army; she was caught in Moscow during the famine with the two children, and the younger died of malnutrition in the orphanage where Tsvetaeva had been compelled to leave her. From

1917 to 1922 she never saw her husband or knew if he still lived. She wrote in her diary: "If God performs a miracle and leaves you among the living, I shall serve you like a dog."

When she heard from him they agreed to emigrate together, and met in Prague, moving to Paris after a few years. Although Tsvetaeva had written a passionate and beautiful poem cycle celebrating the cause of the White army, she was not accepted or thought well of among the émigré sects. Though her sentiments were orthodox, even xenophobic, they sensed that her art was in its own way revolutionary. Good poetry has in any case its own ways of refusing to identify wholly with "us," as against "them," and perhaps nobody was ever so conscious of "us" and "them" as a Russian at that time. Number 36 of the Swan poem cycle gives us Tsvetaeva's own kind of poetic individualism, which her adored Pushkin would have appreciated. A "winged soul" is indifferent to class warfare, to the arrogance of the haves, and to the envy of the have-nots. "I have two foes in the world, twins inextricably interrelated—the hunger of the hungry and the glut of the glutted!" And though that sentiment would have got past the authorities in the Soviet Union, the technique, like Mayakovsky's, was too avant-garde for the growing conservatism of the new Red orthodoxy.

She herself put her dilemma pungently. "In the emigration they began (enthusiastically!) publishing me, then, on reflection, they withdrew me from circulation, sensing it was not in-our-line but from-over-there. The content seemed to be 'ours,' but the voice—*theirs*! . . . For those on the Right it is Left in form. For those on the Left it is Right in content." When Mayakovsky came to Paris she attended one of his readings at the Café Voltaire. When journalists asked her afterward what the recital made her think of the present Russia, she replied, "That strength is over there." She meant, which was true, that the best Russian poets were still in Russia, and it was their strength which was lacking among the poets of the emigration. But the comment was held to be pro-Soviet, and her work, on which her family depended for its small income, was boycotted from all the émigré magazines.

The same spirit of division obtained in the family itself. Efron, to whom she remained wholly loyal, had himself acquired Soviet views; their daughter and the son born to them in Czechoslovakia, now growing up, followed their father's example and wished like him to go back to Russia. They were desperately poor; at one time Tsvetaeva wrote that their only income was the four or five francs a day their daughter earned by making bonnets. This Dickensian touch was no doubt strictly accurate, though it is clear from the many photographs in the *Pictorial Biography* that things were not always so bad and that help of some kind was usually forthcoming. Nonetheless it seems that simple poverty was one factor in her family's wish to leave for the workers' paradise that Soviet propaganda depicted, despite the many disillusioned letters they had from friends who tried it.

There were other factors too. Efron, who was partly Jewish (his family were connected with the famous Efron-Brockhaus encyclopedia), had never been a convinced "Orthodox," and his experiences on the supply lines of the White army had not been such as to promote chivalric faith. It is touching that Tsvetaeva herself gloried in her husband's mixed ancestry and wrote a poem about his handsomeness, his face "narrow as a sword" and eyes "beautifully without purpose": "In his face tragically intermingle two ancient bloods."

> In him I am faithful to chivalry,
> To all of you who lived and died without fear!
> In times of fate such men
> Write verses—and go to the block!

Efron, one imagines, was not always disposed to follow this model, and the liberation of Russian Jews in the early idealist days of the revolution may itself have had an appeal for him. "If only you knew," his wife wrote to a friend, "how ardent, magnanimous, profound a young man he is." Though they were a loving couple, Efron's answer to this was to cultivate on the side his own style of individuality and dedication. One feels in him the odd presence of a wary, unspontaneous, perhaps bewildered man, weakened by illness and privation—he was a consumptive of long standing—and wanting to exhibit his own talents as a story writer. That may have something to do with his becoming involved in the most sinister of stories. Without telling his wife, he had joined in 1932 an organization known as "The Union for the Return to the Fatherland." He became a full-time official of what increasingly became a Soviet front organization—the name significantly changed to "Union of Friends of the Soviet Fatherland"—and was secretly recruited by the European department of the Soviet secret police.

In September 1937 the Swiss police discovered a bullet-riddled corpse in a country road near Lausanne. It proved to be that of a defected police agent who had been murdered by his former comrades on orders from above. Investigation clearly pointed to Efron as having helped to organize not only this killing but that in France of Trotsky's son Andrei Sedov. Efron had to disappear, and he did so via Republican Spain, ending up in the Soviet Union. Not long afterward he was arrested in the purges and summarily shot, presumably because he knew too much. His daughter Ariadna, who had earlier returned to Russia and become a devoted supporter of the regime, was sent into the Gulag and re-emerged in the Fifties—a crumpled photo in the *Pictorial Biography* shows a haggard woman with huge staring eyes. The eloquence of the photographs in this book is positively creepy. The last ones of Efron himself, in Paris and the Crimea, present a tragic yet strangely tranquil face, barely recognizable as that of the rather passive little dandy whom Tsvetaeva had carried off.

She refused to believe he was implicated in the murders, and when she heard he was in Russia prepared at once to join him there. It was her duty. Recalling the promise she made to herself at the time of their first separation, she wrote on the same page of her diary "*Voi i poidu—kak sobaka*"—"And here am I, about to go—like a dog (21 years later)." This recalls the archetypes of the strong loyal Russian woman and the weak indeterminate man she loves—Pushkin's Onegin, Turgenev's Rudin, Chekhov's Ivanov. But life is worse than fiction: the strength of that "fantastically self-willed" girl, whose loyalty was a kind of superb egotism, was nearly at an end. She was not persecuted in the Soviet Union. The authorities who had destroyed her husband and daughter, converts to the cause, seemed uninterested in one who had been always conspicuously against them. But to fellow writers she was bad news; they kept well away, and she and her son, now aged fifteen, were reduced again to extreme poverty and isolation.

She had been devoted to him as a little boy. Napoleon had always been one of her heroes, and physically her son resembled the great man to an extraordinary degree. "Mur lives torn between my humanism and the virtual fanaticism of his father. He is very serious. His mind is acute, but sober: *Roman*. He loves the magical too, but as a guest. All hope rests on that forehead. He loves me like his very own possession. And already—little by little—he is beginning to value me." But that relation seems to have vanished by the time they were back in Russia. Another writer recalled later her bewilderment and loneliness—"she and her son, in my observation, had no common language." Natural enough, at that age, but in the circumstances tormenting and heartbreaking. She felt that her position and reputation would ruin his life. When war came they were evacuated to Elabuga in the Tartar republic, and there, at the lowest ebb, she decided to carry out what she had long contemplated. "For about a year I have been looking around for a hook. . . . I think I am already posthumously afraid of myself. I do not want to die, I want *not to be*. Bitter wormwood."

When the house was empty she climbed on a chair by the front door, put a rope over a beam, and hanged herself. The note she left disappeared into Soviet police archives. Her son joined the army a year later and was killed, aged nineteen. In a strangely touching last postcard from the front he writes he is "absolutely confident that my star will bring me through this war unharmed and that success will certainly come to me." He has seen dead people for the first time in his life, for "up till now I have refused to look at the dead, even my mother."

Poets in Russia mourned Tsvetaeva, and felt guilty about her. Pasternak, who had visited her in France and been rather less than forthcoming in advice and assistance, wrote in his autobiography that "the common tragedy of her family exceeded my worst fears" and unhesitatingly answered "I am" when his friend Gladkov asked the rhetorical question, who was to blame? All of us, Pasternak added; but this is the natural display of guilt in a naturally warmhearted society where terror ruled, and where a fellow author would normally have been helped and cherished far more than in any comparable situation in the West. Pasternak described her as "more Russian than any of us . . . in the rhythms that inhabited her soul, in her tremendous, uniquely powerful language."

Those rhythms are indeed individual and highly effective, in prose as well as in poetry. Russian critics are perhaps apt to make too much of a mystery of the phonetic or acoustic side of Russian poetry, and the originality of new metrical or sound effects produced by Tsvetaeva or Mayakovsky. Russian poetry is deeply melodious and (as her translator Robin Kemball points out) even at its most modern retains much of the traditional harmony of meter, alliteration, and onomatopoeia. Kemball cites another expert, Simon Karlinsky, who remarks of Tsvetaeva's mature style that "words are not used to connote or to imply or to suggest: they are selected equally on the basis of their shape, sound, and meaning, each of these qualities being equally necessary for the total impression."

Well, yes; but the same could be said of almost any good poet in any language: the process is instinctive as well as individual, each poet producing his own kind of linguistic character by his own sense of words. The nature of Russian is apt to make the process more dramatic and emphatic, suited to a long tradition of recital. One feature of Tsvetaeva's style, on which Karlinsky writes very interestingly, is *bezglagolnost*—verblessness—a dislike of the verb compensated by a brilliant and characteristic use of inflection, especially dative and instrumental case endings, a tactic beyond the scope of any translator. As Kemball says, her syntax sets more problems than her prosody.

With this in mind he has favored metrical translations, unfashionable today, but in this case probably justified because they give some conception of the vigorous and vivid style of *The Demesne of the Swans*.

> Your temple, so stern and so stately,
> You quit for the scream of the square . . .
> —O, Liberty!—Beautiful Lady
> Marquis, Russian princes, found fair.
>
> So far we've some fearful choir practice—
> Communion has yet to take place!
> —O, Liberty!—harlot, seductress,
> In some giddy-brained soldier's embrace!

The trouble is that though the meter is the "same" as in the Russian you cannot really divorce meter from everything else in the poetry. In English it is bound to be non-poetry except for the meter and the rhyme, and thus the meter and the rhyme become non-poetry too: what jiggles in English does not appear to do so in its natural Russian.

> *Iz strogago, stroinago khrama*
> *Ty vyshla na vizg ploshchadei . . .*
> *—Svoboda!—Prekrasnaya Dama—*

The strength of the original, its discipline yet immediacy of response, expresses itself naturally in that forceful alliteration. Like much in this diary of poems, history is a kind of instant feeling: Philippe Egalité of the French Revolution and the aristocratic Decembrists of the Russian bid for liberty in 1825 are brought together with the drunken soldiers and their girls whom the poet had before her eyes in the squares of St. Petersburg, that town of severe harmonious lines which Pushkin in *The Bronze Horseman* had celebrated with the same alliterating adjectives.

> *Liubliu tebya, Petra tvorenie,*
> *Liubliu tvoi strogii, stroinii vid . . .*

> [I love you, Peter's creation,
> I love your severe harmonious look . . .]

When she made a fair copy of these poems before leaving for Russia in 1939, Tsvetaeva noted that her friend the poet Balmont, to whom she read the poem during the revolution, said, "I don't like the way you treat the harlot. Some harlots, well—" and he turned up his eyes. She replied, "What a *great pity* I can't say in answer to that 'Some soldiers—well.' " The rhythm of "To the cadets who fell in Nizhni" comes over very well, and is moving even in translation, a real tribute to Kemball's version.

> Swords held high—
> And the bugles sadly sighing—
> Bid good-bye
> To the dead.
> Cap with sprig of green-leaf lying
> At their head.

Another poem, glorifying and identifying with the White officers, was read by the author to thunderous applause at a recital in Red Moscow. Not really paradoxical: the poem does not mention the Whites specifically, and the idea of the officer, and officer qualities, was already just as popular—after the first giddy bout of egalitarianism—on the revolutionary side.

Ardis publishers are to be congratulated on the three excellent books under review, all lovingly produced and annotated. Marin King's edition of the prose and Kemball's of the Swan cycle are both supplied with a discerning and admirably complete *apparatus criticus*. This is the more desirable because Tsvetaeva, like many other Russian poets, is extremely allusive, and takes for granted the reader's familiarity with Russian history and poetry. Her prose does much the same thing, and is in its way as idiosyncratic as her poetry. Her description of Voloshin, in her portraits of contemporary writers, is memorable, and so is her account of her childhood in Germany in "The Tower of Ivy." (The title, as she tells us, came from her misreading of the name of Rilke's patroness, the Fürstin von Thurn und Taxis. *Thur* she connected with French *tour*, and she knew the botanical name *taxus*, yew, which she thought meant ivy.)

Her most interesting prose pieces, though, are her reflections on Pushkin, to which like Bryusov she gave the title "My Pushkin," and still more so her essay on Pushkin's two versions of the famous eighteenth-century Cossack rebel, Pugachev, one in his history of the rebellion and the other in his historical novel, *The Captain's Daughter*. The aesthetic implications of this are profound, and never more so than today, when art prides itself on getting things just as they were, and devoting its artifice to an appearance of factual realism.

Tsvetaeva, an idealist, will have none of this. For her the sober factual account of Pugachev in the history lacks the love with which Pushkin the poet created the portrait in his novel, a love which he made the hero feel for the villain, despite his villainy. For her, as for Pushkin—she quotes his poem "The Hero"—the idea of a hero is more important than any diminishing facts about him.

A truth, by the fact that it is low, is *not* truth anymore, and an elevating lie, by the fact that it elevates us—is *not* a lie anymore. There are no low truths and high lies, there are only low lies and high truths . . . there are happy cases, when destiny is perfected. What poet writing about Jeanne d'Arc does not adjust the record of the facts?

Hagiography has seen to it that she herself has become one of those "happy cases when destiny is perfected." In these three books we have both the legend of Tsvetaeva and her history. No doubt the legend has the greater appeal but the history is true too. And in its way as impressive.

The New York Review of Books, 1980

31

On the Horse Parsnip

Boris Pasternak (1890–1960)

Boris Pasternak: A Literary Biography, 1890–1928
by Christopher Barnes

Boris Pasternak: The Tragic Years, 1930–1960
by Evgeny Pasternak

Boris Pasternak
by Peter Levi

Poems, 1955–1959 and An Essay in Autobiography
by Boris Pasternak, translated by Michael Harari and Manya
    Harari

The Year 1905
by Boris Pasternak, translated by Richard Campbell

NOT UNMALICIOUS fellow poet once said of Pasternak that he resembled a horse: "the same big awkward profile and large eyes that seem to look intently without seeing anything." The horse-faced parsnip—*Pasternak* means parsnip in Russian. This is very endearing. What other great poet has the bigness and animal closeness of the equine, and words that plod like hooves with such delicate precision through twigs and grasses? The girls chanting the "candle" poem at his funeral must also have longed to have given him a lump of sugar? One of the best little scenes in *Dr. Zhivago* is the doctor riding home through the Urals forest, with his slow beast undulating under him, and "dry volleys of sound bursting from the horse's guts." As some of the photos in Evgeny Pasternak's splendid book reveal his father looks most at home wearing massive braces over his collarless shirt, like girths and a crupper.

Probably the best introduction one can have to Pasternak is to look at the poems in the *Penguin Book of Russian Verse*, selected by Dimitri Obolensky and provided with a plain and literal prose translation. There a reader without Russian can spell out the candle poem, "Winter Night," and suddenly see how and why it has such absolute authority and magic, like the prologue of Pushkin's *Ruslan and Ludmila* near the beginning of the anthology. *Svecha gorela na stole. Svecha gorela:* "The candle burned on the table. The candle burned." Where does the magic come from? It is one of the Zhivago poems, and is about two lovers exchanging "hands legs and fates" in the winter time in the Revolution. The candle burns when Zhivago writes his poems, the emblem and essence of what lives and matters. Lara is presumably in bed and asleep.

Put like that, it sounds a piece of bathos and this is the paradox of an art like Pasternak's, which is at once totally popular and totally narcissistic. Pushkin or Mozart effortlessly embody the same thing, but his period, place, and personality all made this effortlessness impossible for Pasternak. The paradox remains. His art is both brilliantly simple and personally portentous: the one cannot be separated from the other. He must have known it himself, but his vanity was as pure as his egotism, and he really did feel, in a sublime way, that he was the precious vessel of life which could burn up tyranny and ideology, save Russia and the world. Pushkin, too, was a kind of precedent, for though Pushkin would have laughed at the idea of his poetry saving Russia and the world, or anything else, Blok was not wrong in saying that Pushkin was the real inspiration of Russian life, that his "one bright name" was set against the whole gloomy roll call of tyrants and executioners.

Pasternak-Zhivago aspired to be the same, and of course there is something fishy about life worshipping life, extolling itself *as* itself against world and devil and Stalin's cockroach moustache. Schiller would have been puzzled by the notion of the naïve trying to appear reflective, the holy fool proclaiming life itself as a new "ism" under the pressure of the twentieth century's inhuman political ideals. Viewed in this way, the concept of life as its own kind of heroism might become as dated, in terms of art, as the titanic activities of those two terrible heroes of the century, as Carlyle would have seen them and as Heidegger has seen them, Hitler and Stalin.

Like every other Russian *intelligent* of his time, the young Pasternak saw Soviet man as the logical product of the life force—"the concept of Sovietness being the most elementary and evident of truths, residing in innocent and guilty alike." In a sense, he never changed his mind, although as a result of persecution he came to see himself as the only one in step, the only true heir of the revolution. At the end of his life, in "A New Year's Message" to his Western readers, he said that we must thank Russia and the Revolution for a new concept of life. "However great the difference between us, our revolution set the tone for you as well: it filled the present century with meaning and content . . . It's us you have to thank for this new man, who is present even in your ancient society, us you have to thank for the fact that he is more alive, more subtle and more gifted, than his pompous ancestors, for this child of the new age was delivered in the maternity hospital called Russia." There is a good deal of truth and justice in that, and Pasternak would certainly have recognized the truth in Thomas Mann's dry comment that "in our time the destiny of man presents its meaning in political terms."

Zhivay zhizn, Dostoevsky's "living life," duly becomes a political concept. But the ideology of life, as Pasternak necessarily and almost involuntarily developed it, is one fatally tainted with vulgarity. (He himself came to detest the title he had given his first collection of poems, *A Twin in the Clouds*, and the name of his third collection, *My Sister, Life*, a quotation from one of them, is if anything worse.) After this, it is a relief to learn from Peter Levi's lively and delightful biography that Dr. Zhivago (Dr. Alive) was a name Pasternak had seen on the cover of a Moscow manhole, rather as Dickens claimed to have spotted a Copperfield and a Chuzzlewit on the signs of poor London shops. Quite apart from its status in the war of ideologies, when the Soviet authorities refused to allow Pasternak to accept the Nobel Prize, critical opinion has always varied sharply about the actual merits of the book. A judge as sensitive as Stuart Hampshire finds its genius in the love relation between Lara and

Zhivago, while the poet Anna Akhmatova, although she admired Pasternak as a poet, could not take him seriously as a deep sage and public figure, or even as a lover, and professed maliciously to suppose that the Lara episodes had been written by Olga Ivinskaya, Pasternak's mistress, who had officially inspired them. Lara says that they loved one another "because all things around had wished it so, the land beneath them, the sky over their heads, the clouds and the trees"—which might have been written by Olga, by D. H. Lawrence on an off day, or by Pasternak himself. He could be equally rapt and romantic in his egotism about a hero who is often uncomfortably like "the most unforgettable character I have met," especially when his creator announces calmly that Zhivago's friends and helpers were only important because they had had the privilege of meeting him and living in his era.

The Russian novelist Slayavsky was probably closest to the mark when he called *Zhivago* "a weak novel of genius." The contrast, in a sense, is between the poetry in it—what other novel has for a hero a poet who could actually write the candle poem, "Winter Night"?—and the prose emotion, which is not up to a hierophantic and doctrinal task. But the horse plods on, and the vision of time and of failure is both compassionate and pitiless. Zhivago's genius crumbles into the maelstrom of Soviet life; Lara goes out on some household task and never comes back, vanishing into one of the innumerable camps. Olga Ivinskaya bore Pasternak's son stillborn in one of the camps, although she did come back. The book is so compromised with the horrors of a time and place of which, at least in the West, it has become a sort of symbol that it is impossible to distinguish the facts behind it from the imagination of life which it presents. Peter Levi is both just and generous in concluding that "in spite of its faults it seems to me better and more tragic every time I read it." Poetry must in its own way be perfect, but the novel, as Lawrence saw, is "incapable of the absolute," and gains in its own ways from its lapses and imperfections.

Peter Levi has a poet's eye for Pasternak's poetry, which he translates felicitously and comments on with gaiety and shrewdness. He does not take the subject too seriously either, which is a relief after the hagiographical approach of Guy de Mallac and others, worthy as their pioneering studies have been. But Christopher Barnes's "Literary Biography," of which this solid work is the first of two volumes, will certainly become the standard and indispensable guide for students not only of the poet but of his age and literary milieu. The popular Western image of Pasternak the holy Russian poet ignores the sheer density of relationship, the exigent business of literary life which he led, chaffering with a hundred writers and officials for space in periodicals, for rations and favored accommodation, intriguing against Grub Street intriguers, now armed and envenomed by the state and far more dangerous to life and reputation than anything Pope or Dryden had to contend with.

All this Barnes brings out with precision and omniscience. His approach is factual, his perception quite unsentimental: but his awareness of the youthful Pasternak's problems and evolution as a writer of verse, a student musician, a highly emotional and volatile being, is extraordinarily delicate and comprehensive. The clan, with its ramifying Jewish and Russian connection was cosmopolitan: Pasternak's father a prolific painter of great talent, while his mother had been an expert concert performer. The family were not orthodox, but the poet went further in a tacit, repudiation of his part Jewishness and a strong identification with Russian customs and ritual. He isolated himself in some degree from his family—in a way in which he could not isolate himself from the swarming importunities of Muscovite literary life and gossip, though the figure of Dr. Zhivago, who has no literary connections and whose training is technical and medical, shows that he might ideally have liked to do so.

All his life he had a passion for "ordinariness," all the more ironic in view of his present status as a sort of poetic icon. It helps to explain his feeling for Shakespeare and the strikingly subjective strength of his Shakespeare renderings, inaccurate and incomplete as they often are. Barnes quotes a significant passage from an essay claiming that "people of genius" are the most ordinary of all. "Only mediocrity is extraordinary, i.e. that category of people which from time immemorial has consisted of the so-called 'interesting person.' From ancient times he has shunned ordinary deeds and has been a parasite on genius . . . which he has always understood as some form of *flattering exclusivity* . . . Mediocrity has been especially fortunate in our day, when it has seized on romanticism, anarchism and Nietzcheanism."

These obsessions help to explain the oddity of Pasternak's work and its popularity—everyone likes the idea of genius as ordinary man—together with the often rather ludicrous contradictions involved. It is impossible to think of Mandelstam being made a fuss of, or making a fuss of himself, in this way: and yet Mandelstam is not only as great a poet as Pasternak but suffered a fate more exemplary and more terrible. The relations between the two were never good, Mandelstam taking what seems to have been a somewhat dry, professional attitude toward Pasternak's posturing, and the latter fulsomely praising his peer and colleague while—according to Akhmatova—never actually reading him. Waspish as poets are about other poets, and often unreliable, Akhmatova stressed that Pasternak, at least in his maturity, never did read verses other than his own, and that certainly goes with the Zhivago persona.

But it was Pasternak's other persona, that of the political survivor and professional man of letters, who was most crucially involved with Mandelstam at the time of the latter's arrest for writing a lampoon of Stalin. "You didn't tell me that and I didn't hear it," Pasternak is supposed to have said when Mandelstam met him in the street and told him the epigram: but when he heard what had happened he exerted himself in every possible way to save his colleague, getting in touch with powerful friends like Bukharin, who was himself shortly to go down in the purges. Probably as a result of this intercession, Stalin telephoned Pasternak, and there occurred the famous conversation the poet's account of which has been reported in a number of ways, and which he agonized over to the end of his life. The dictator seems to have been amused by the epigram, which Mandelstam in his quixotic fashion had told to a number of unreliable acquaintances, and he also seems to have been genuinely curious about the status of its author: was he a big, an important poet? As Levi comments, he was investigating the world of poets by stirring it with his boot, as a schoolboy disturbs an ants' nest. What appears to have happened is that Pasternak, naturally overwhelmed by the occasion, tried wildly to give his own opinions on poetry and Russian history until he was abruptly cut off. Stalin wanted a straight answer to a straight question, and Pasternak never forgave himself for failing to give it. A more adroit and in a sense a more unscrupulous man would have at once answered, "Yes, he is very important indeed," and left it at that: but in his Zhivago personality Pasternak was too separate—too "cloud-dwelling," as Stalin is supposed to have tolerantly called him—to have reacted expeditiously. In any case, as Nadezhda Mandelstam makes clear in *Hope Against Hope*, it would probably have made no difference, for Stalin's other and much more sinister interest was in finding out how far the epigram had gone, and in sealing off its source.

If Pasternak was obsessed with a sense of himself as the great but "ordinary" genius, Mandelstam, like Akhmatova and Tsvetaeva, had a much more confident sense of himself as unordinary poet. Like the two women, he saw the course the regime was taking as a crude threat to personality and to distinction, of which poetry was the natural expression. He knew it was a killer, whereas Pasternak, especially in his middle years, tried to identify himself with it as a great enhancement of life, and to make his works embody it as Shakespeare's embodied the being of his own age. The novel in verse *Spektorsky*, and his quasi-epical poems *Lieutenant Schmidt* and *1905* have much of the good qualities of his translations: that is, they achieve a wide but also meticulous impersonality of utterance, as if the poet, like his father the artist, were filling in canvases with professional skill and bravura, identifying himself with the big revolutionary themes and events, the urban perspective and the public emotion. These long poems are not well known in the West, and it is very useful to have Richard Chappell's version of *1905* in a paperback edition, with a translation in similar rhythms opposite the Russian. Equally valuable are Michael Harari's Russian plus English translation of the poems written between 1955 and 1959, published in the same paperback with Manya Harari's translation of Pasternak's *Essay in Autobiography*.

As Craig Raine points out in a witty and penetrating foreword, this *Essay* underwent a considerable gestation and metamorphosis, and was intended originally as an introduction, in 1956 or thereabouts, to a complete edition of Pasternak's poems. But in November 1957 *Il Dottore Zivago* was published by Feltrinelli in Italy, and from then on the essay acquired and became "a dangerous character." It also has "a cloudy twin," the memoir *Safe Conduct*, which the poet began late in the Twenties, and of which sections appeared in Soviet magazines. As Raine observes, there is a significant difference between the two, for in the *Essay* Pasternak not only displays lavishly his old youthful gift of acute poetic phrase

(Scriabin's repetitive goodbyes were "like a collar-stud that refused to slip into an exigous stud-hole) but has acquired an equally sharp sense of the author's absurdity, actual or potential. As a boy, the poet writes, he had fantasies of regaining a more pleasing, girlish, and fascinating earlier personality "by pulling in my belt so tight I almost fainted." Raine comments shrewdly on the difference between Pasternak in the early memoir being "rather too keen on savouring the flavour of his own uniqueness, his sensitivity, his passion," and the later version, which is much more aware of "human solidarity in silliness," for we all recognize that belt-tightening fantasy element from our own childhood. Rousseau's *Confessions* combine the same claim to uniqueness with an assertion of human solidarity in what Raine describes as the "endearingly discreditable." The older Pasternak indeed referred to *Safe Conduct* as being "spoiled by an affected manner, the besetting sin of those days," and a panic feeling of inferiority. The talent of Mayakovsky seems to have oppressed Pasternak even while he engaged in a love-hate relation with the young darling of the Soviet establishment, and he had to escape from him, as he may later have felt the need to cut himself off from Mandelstam.

But the poems are very much more remarkable than the prose. Apart from his magic Zhivago poems, which can sound like an improbable cross between an inspired Nineties symbolist and an Old Testament prophet, Pasternak's great strength is in his dynamically delicate fusion of words and objects, a feature noted years ago by the emigré scholar-connoisseur Prince Mirsky, who returned to Russia and ended as one of Stalin's victims. Nabokov's later prose tries for something similar, but neither prose nor English can do it naturally, although Craig Raine's own poems—particularly his superlative libretto on a Russian theme—sometimes achieve the same effect. full of "the dirty mauve" of February birches, or of "a Christmas tree half naked, preparing like the lady of the manor to puff out its bell-shaped skirts," Pasternak's Russian never sounds affected, as English inevitably does when pushed into ingenious contingencies of meaning and onomatopoeia. This is because it retains in every complexity the musical memorableness common to all great Russian poetry: its zany felicities linger in the mind as surely as Pushkin's incomparably simple ones.

His prophetic poems—Pushkin's poem "Prophet" reverberates

through Pasternak as through Blok—are easier to translate. But, as Raine notes, a sign of the intractability of his style is that it can sound better in imperfect and slightly eccentric English, as in the English versions produced by Pasternak's sister which Seamus Heaney feels to be more authentic than a professional job. Raine and his wife Ann Pasternak-Slater have themselves provided outstanding translations for Evgeny Pasternak's study *The Tragic Years*. The book has the special advantage of coming from right inside the family, and Evgeny Pasternak's portrait of his father is both affectionate and convincing. His grandfather, the painter Leonid Pasternak, would have been pleased too.

Michael Harari's attempts at some of the most difficult poems achieve their own kind of breakthrough. If poetry is what is lost in translation, we lose still more, as D. J. Enright pointed out, if it is not translated. But Raine is right that Pasternak's "brief lists" in sound and association have no way of surviving in English: in the marvelous poem "In Hospital," which describes one of his and Zhivago's heart attacks, the patient in the ambulance sees a confused blur of *militsia, ulitsa, litsa*—policemen, streets, faces—and later in hospital *palatam, polam, khalatam*—wards, floors, white overalls—all of which in English sound inert and rather obvious. Compare a real poem in English on the same theme, Larkin's "Ambulance," where the patient, "unreachable, inside a room / The traffic parts to let go by," is borne past "smells of different dinners," and where the quiet terror of the business is conveyed in the information that the vehicle has "arms on a plaque" and that "all streets in time are visited."

The poetic area of Pasternak is as distant as can be from what has to be called the Reader's Digest side of his story, the side somewhat exploited in Guy de Mallac's admittedly interesting investigation some years ago. Neither Peter Levi nor Christopher Barnes are guilty of such exploitation, and the memoir by the poet's son has its own special and authoritative interest. Yet it must be admitted that Pasternak's persona and career, compared, for example, with Mandelstam's, do lend themselves too readily to the kind of hagiographical publicity which is all too suited to a Goethe, but not at all to a Shakespeare. Pasternak translated both, and Shakespeare was his ideal: but Goethe was, so to speak, what he ended up with. The paradox would have amused but probably also saddened him, for he did not wish Dr. Zhivago to be at all like Wilhelm

Meister. Marina Tsvetaeva, with whom he once engaged in an ardently intense correspondence based on mutual Rilke worship, was down-to-earth enough to be a trifle amused by such lofty spiritual aspiration, unsuited, as she may have felt, to a poet whose gait and genius were essentially equine. In making that comparison, she added that Pasternak resembled the Arab, and also the Arab's steed. That is a real compliment, and one much more suited to him than are the all too spiritual portrait photos obligatory on the publishers' dust jackets. All steeds are horses, although not vice versa.

London Review of Books, 1990

32

The Hard Hitter

Isaac Babel (1894–?1940)

The Complete Works of Isaac Babel
edited by Nathalie Babel, translated by Peter Constantine, with
an introduction by Cynthia Ozick

LIKE SO MANY MEN who made their mark on the twentieth century,
Isaac Babel began as a Jewish revolutionary; like so many of them,
too, he died disillusioned and by violence. But in the process he
had become one of the century's most remarkable writers. He became
famous in Russia as a writer before his death at the hands of a secret
police firing squad; then he became a nonperson, until he was partially
rehabilitated in 1954. By that time, too, his name as a writer of brilliant
short stories had become known in the West. The collection *Konarmiya*,
"Horse Army" literally, and translated as *Red Cavalry*, which described in
graphic detail the abortive Soviet campaign against Poland in 1920,
showed that he had been an eyewitness and a sensational reporter of war
experiences, but his true stature and importance, for a long while
accepted and widely acclaimed in Russia, only became apparent in the
English-speaking world with the translation and publication of his complete works.

In the Twenties and Thirties, the years of his first success, Babel had
been one of the privileged children of the new revolutionary intelligentsia. Unlike his fellow citizens, he was allowed to travel; his wife settled in Paris in 1925, where his daughter was born in 1929 and where he
visited them, for the last time, in 1935. He felt a compulsion to return to

Moscow. In her preface to his *Complete Works*, his daughter, Nathalie Babel, writes that the demands and instructions of the state had completely disillusioned him. To write within the frame of the barracks mentality of Soviet ideology was intolerable for him, yet he didn't see how he could manage to live otherwise. Babel was fully aware of his predicament:

> I have a family: a wife and daughter. I love them and have to provide for them. Under no circumstances do I want them to return to Sovietland. . . . But what about myself? Should I stay here and become a taxi driver . . . ? . . . Should I return to our proletarian revolution? Revolution indeed! It's disappeared!

To his friend the critic Yuri Annenkov he uttered these dangerous sentiments in a confidential chat while they were in Paris together in 1932, and he concluded by saying: "Here a taxi driver has more freedom than the rector of a Soviet university."

Until the mid-Thirties Babel had a powerful political protector in the celebrated older author Maxim Gorky, who had encouraged him, and who published his early efforts in his own magazine, *Letopis*. With Gorky's death in 1936 Babel became particularly vulnerable, and the date coincided with the beginning of the great purges. As a Jew and an intellectual who had traveled abroad, Babel would in any case have been at risk; but what seems to have sealed his fate were his sometimes unflattering references in the *Red Cavalry* stories to three men—Semyon Konstantinovich Timoshenko, Semyon Budyonny, and Kliment Yefremovich Voroshilov—all of whom had become top men in the Red army, while the last two were old cronies of Stalin, who had a habit of sticking by his friends, particularly if they were slavishly faithful incompetents and offered no risk to his own power and position. They did not forget the truthfulness or the popularity of the *Red Cavalry* stories, and what Babel had said about them there.

In her introduction to *The Complete Works* Cynthia Ozick calls Kafka and Babel the "twentieth century's European coordinates" as writers, even though so different in language, style, and temperament:

> Each was an acutely conscious Jew. Each witnessed a pogrom while still very young, Kafka in enlightened Prague, Babel under a Czarist

regime that promoted harsh legal disabilities for Jews. Each invented a type of literary modernism, becoming a movement in himself . . . with no possibility of successors. To be influenced by Kafka is to end in parody.

This is a brilliant and a valid point, but though it must have been tempting for Ozick to make the same claim for Babel that she makes for Kafka—that he could not have followers or disciples who are even half original—the fact remains that Babel is a writer who submerged himself, as if deliberately, in the climate and idiom of his own age and culture, whereas Kafka was a solitary and a unique creature, a species of writer cut off by an act of his own will in his own self-determined world. Today we recognize that world instantly: we call it Kafkaesque, but it would make little or no sense to speak of a writer, or a kind of writing, as "Babelian."

Then there is the problem of translation. In any good translation Kafka still sounds inimitably like Kafka, and like no one else. He is a translator's dream, as Edwin Muir found when he discovered through his own version an almost perfect English equivalent. With Babel the problem is much more complicated. For one thing he is a chameleonic writer, quite happy in his early tales to resort to a vulgar and threatening bluster and to adopt the conventionally hectic revolutionary tone, and then abruptly change that tone for a detached and cool precision. Both he and his patron Gorky deeply admired the stories and the manner of Guy de Maupassant, sometimes adding their own kind of Russian warmth to Maupassant's Gallic objectivity. But in Babel's case at least, the spirit of Maupassant becomes unrecognizable to the reader, however much the Russian writer might hold it up for his own inspiration and guidance.

The irony of his own "story" "Guy de Maupassant," written in the time of Babel's greatest fame and success, probably about 1930, is that it is as unlike a Maupassant story as could be. Like many of Babel's stories of the time, it is really a sort of extended sketch, an inspired jotting on the verge of fantasy. The narrator, living from hand to mouth in 1916 in St. Petersburg (rechristened Petrograd during the war), meets a well-off Jewess, Raisa Bendersky, who tells him "Maupassant is the one passion of my life." She gives him her translation of "Miss Harriet," asking him to revise it for her, and put it into reasonably good Russian. Raisa herself writes "with laborious and inert correctness and lack of style," showing "no trace of Maupassant's free-flowing prose with its powerful breath of passion." But the narrator decides that the "work isn't as bad as it might seem." He then gives us Babel's own view of style:

> When a phrase is born, it is both good and bad at the same time. The secret of its success rests in a crux that is barely discernible. One's fingertips must grasp the key, gently warming it. And then the key must be turned once, not twice.
>
> . . . I spoke to her of style, of an army of words, an army in which every type of weapon is deployed. No iron spike can pierce a human heart as icily as a period in the right place.

In fact, for the non-Russian speaker, it is not at all easy to see how Babel writes, or even if he writes, in the usually accepted sense, well or badly. A foreign reader could well have the same trouble with, say, Kipling, whose style can be at once slapdash and refined, uncannily perceptive and vulgarly picturesque.

This makes matters almost impossibly hard for a translator; and Peter Constantine, although an expert and a veteran at his trade, is up against a problem as intractable, although in a wholly different way, as the problem of translating Pushkin. My own Russian is just about up to appreciating the subtle and limpid simplicities of Pushkin; but there is no way in which I can take in the richness of Babel's effects, which Russian speakers and readers rave about, no doubt justly. In English they often sound crude and overdone, or merely infelicitous.

When we meet Raisa's maid—"well built, nearsighted, haughty"—we hear that "debauchery had congealed in her gray, wide-open eyes." And that is exactly what the Russian says and means. A reader of the translation has no way of knowing whether "congealed" in Russian is just the right or the ironic word, the *mot juste*. He can only say that it sounds all wrong in English, strained and slightly grotesque.

But what can a good translator do? Peter Constantine's version does seem to me to have the disconcerting virtue of revealing the shortcomings, even the inherent vulgarity, of Babel as a stylist, although, as the story shows, a highly self-conscious one. But a Russian may receive quite the opposite impression, and Babel is indeed greatly admired for his style by sensitive and knowledgeable Russian readers. Kipling again seems a useful parallel, for what could be more effective, and in a sense Kiplingesque, than this description of the apartment in St. Petersburg where the Benderskys live?

> They lived at the corner of the Nevsky Prospekt by the Moika River, in a house built of Finnish granite trimmed with pink columns, embrasures, and stone coats of arms. Before the war, bankers without family or breeding—Jewish converts to Christianity who grew rich through trade—had built a large number of such spuriously majestic, vulgar castles in Petersburg.
>
> A red carpet ran up the stairs. Stuffed bears on their hind legs stood on the landings. Crystal lamps shone in their wide-open jaws.
>
> The Benderskys lived on the third floor.

The narrator is let in by the maid with the peculiar eyes, which in context seem expressive enough ("I thought how she must thrash about with savage agility when she made love . . ."):

> The brocade curtain that hung over the door swayed. A black-haired, pink-eyed woman, bearing her large breasts before her, came into the living room. It took me no more than a moment to see that Benderskaya was one of those ravishing breed of Jewesses from Kiev or Poltava, from the sated towns of the steppes that abounded with acacias and chestnut trees. These women transmute the money of their resourceful husbands into the lush pink fat on their bellies, napes, and round shoulders. Their sleepy smiles, delicate and sly, drive garrison officers out of their minds.

That is not only a vivid description in itself but an impression, both brilliantly exact and touchingly comic, of the way the boy from Odessa, which Babel had once been, would see Raisa's apartment at the corner of Nevsky Prospekt.

And yet this sketch entitled "Guy de Maupassant" still fails to accumulate into a story. Chekhov, one might feel, would have shaken his head, although the method is not so very different from the sketches he himself threw off so quickly when he was a very young man. But Babel was now in the full force of his matured talent, and taking his writing, as writing, very seriously indeed. Might the oddly disheveled quality that runs through all his work have been an effect that was sought after with care, rather than the spontaneous jotting process which it usually resembles? So strong is the magic of Babel's writing personality, however, that one comes to accept all this as it is, without any disparagement, and the more one reads such a story as "Guy de Maupassant" the more powerfully and seductively does Babel's medium of magic appear.

The last story in his 1925–1938 collection, "My First Fee," is also the best. The young narrator, the young Babel in effect, is living in Tiflis, working as a proofreader for the Caucasus Military District:

> A man who is caught in the noose of an idea and lulled by its serpentine gaze finds it difficult to bubble over with meaningless, burrowing words of love. Such a man is ashamed of shedding tears of sadness. He is not quick-witted enough to be able to laugh with happiness. I was a dreamer, and did not have the knack for the thoughtless art of happiness. Therefore I was going to have to give Vera ten rubles of my meager earnings. I made up my mind and went to stand watch outside the doors of the Simpatia tavern. Georgian princes in blue Circassian jackets and soft leather boots sauntered past in casual parade. They picked their teeth with silver toothpicks and eyed the carmine-painted Georgian women with large feet and slim hips. There was a shimmer of turquoise in the twilight. The blossoming acacias howled along the streets in their petal-shedding bass voices. Waves of officials in white coats rolled along the boulevard. Balsamic streams of air came flowing toward them from the Karzbek Mountains.

He meets Vera, a prostitute whom he passionately desires, and in order to try to interest her, starts to make up stories about his young life—how he ran away from home and lived with a man, then with an older, more repulsive one, a "church warden" (he has stolen the word from some novel). Vera looks derisive and, fearful that the spell of narrative isn't working properly, the young fellow hastens to embroider a still more absurd fantasy about the first man who had kept him, a generous and trusting man, ruined by his friends. "He gave them bronze promissory notes, and his friends went and cashed them right away." "Bronze promissory notes! I myself had no idea how I came up with that." But it turns out to have been a brilliant invention, like the sort of detail which used to be made up by the Magic Realists, or the genies and flying horses in the *Arabian Nights*. "Vera believed everything once she heard 'bronze promissory notes.' " (It is indeed a perfect example of what W. S. Gilbert's character in *The Mikado* calls "corroborative detail, designed to give verisimilitude to an otherwise bald and unconvincing narrative.")

But the real fantasy is in the actual prose Babel is writing, prose whose richness, at least in this story, never sounds artificial, but in the most grotesque or the ugliest and most realistic details always seems spontaneous and almost childlike. The young and aspiring writer is carried away by his own literary inventiveness and by the scraps out of books he has picked up. Self-pity "tore my heart to pieces" as he describes his life and the ways in which he has been ruined. "I quaked with sorrow and inspiration. Streams of icy sweat trickled down my face like snakes winding through grass warmed by the sun." (That sort of simile would sound affected and precious if used by other writers at that time—Hemingway for instance—but Babel gets away with it.)

"My story had come to an end." Vera, awakening from the spell of imagined narrative, makes her own unexpected but comprehensive comment. " 'The things men do,' Vera whispered, without turning around. 'My God, the things men do!' " As if he had passed some sort of initiation rite she now treats him as another and younger whore, her "little sister." She also initiates him in the arts of love. That is the effect his inventiveness has had, and she returns to him the two five-ruble coins—"my first fee"—with which he had paid her in advance. She in her turn has been the first person to pay for his services as a teller of tales.

In a short summary the story sounds as sentimental as one of O. Henry's, yet the tone and tempo are of course entirely different. Babel was experimenting with a kind of style and a use of words which would do their own work—sardonic and distant even in the midst of lushness. It is indeed a method unlike any other, and it is a considerable achievement by Peter Constantine to have brought it across in a translation as well as he has managed to do.

Babel's earlier stories, the famous *Red Cavalry* series, were, one imagines, a good deal easier for a translator to deal with. As is also the case with Kipling and with Hemingway, atrocities portrayed in a matter-of-fact and deadpan manner, which have their initial shock impact on the reader, don't have a lasting effect. Such subjects were less familiar in the writing of that time than they are today, although writers who had taken part in the First World War, from Erich Maria Remarque and Henri Barbusse to Siegfried Sassoon, were all good at describing horrors—in a sense there was nothing very difficult about it—but the art was to make it different from reportage or from a parade of feeling ("I was the man, I suffered, I was there").

It is here that Babel scores. He didn't just use his eyes. Like the young lad in "My First Fee," which is a far more accomplished tale than any of the *Red Cavalry* stories, he has already begun to mingle what he had seen with what he fantasizes and makes up, putting it across in a new and powerful species of linguistic idiom. Everyone who has ever read the stories remembers the Cossack commander, Savitsky, with his legs that resemble girls' legs encased in slim leather riding boots; but this is Babel's own flight of fancy, and has nothing to do with the Cossacks themselves and their own way of looking at things. Babel, a Jew and an intellectual, a complete misfit among these heroic beings, is in a sense bound to be making it all up, and being purely subjective while imitating total objectivity.

Here he is very different from Tolstoy, whose name he often mentions, half admiringly and half dismissively, but Tolstoy had at least attempted to see the Cossacks as they were, and to describe them in their own terms. For Babel they became the raw material for his personal experiment in style, idiom, and language, but it is impossible not to weary of the same Goya-like catalog of the disasters and horrors of war—looting, the raping of women, the shooting of prisoners. In some ways the diary Babel kept when he was actually on campaign is more bearable—less artful and so less repulsive—than the stories that were enlarged and devised out of the material. The terse and often horrifying jottings of the diary seem more authentic than the stories, in which the material was reshaped and carefully worked up. Admirably edited and translated, the diary is a master-piece in its own right and makes a good introduction to Babel's later work.*

"My First Goose," understated and Maupassant-like as it is, has all the hallmarks of an event reconstructed, perhaps even created, for effect. Savitsky of the famous boots, commander of the Sixth Division, who wants a clerk to do his military paperwork, sends for the newly enlisted Babel and asks, "Can you read and write?" With heavy humor the quarter-master who tells him where to find lodgings also tells his new comrades that there's to be "no funny business, . . . because this man has suffered on the fields of learning!" The new clerk's spectacles become a standing joke.

I went down on my hands and knees and gathered up the manuscripts and the old, tattered clothes that had fallen out of my suitcase. I took them and carried them to the other end of the yard. A large pot of boiling pork stood on some bricks in front of the hut. Smoke rose from it as distant smoke rises from the village hut of one's childhood, mixing hunger with intense loneliness inside me. I covered my broken little suitcase with hay, turning it into a pillow, and lay down on the ground to read Lenin's speech at the Second Congress of the Comintern, which *Pravda* had printed. The sun fell on me through the jagged hills, the Cossacks kept stepping over my legs, the young fellow incessantly made fun of me, the beloved sentences struggled toward me over thorny paths, but could not reach me. I put away the newspaper and went to the mistress of the house, who was spinning yarn on the porch.

"Mistress," I said, "I need some grub!"

The old woman raised the dripping whites of her half-blind eyes to me and lowered them again.

"Comrade," she said, after a short silence. "All of this makes me want to hang myself!"

"Goddammit!" I muttered in frustration, shoving her back with my hand. "I'm in no mood to start debating with you!"

---

*Isaac Babel, 1920 *Diary*, edited by Carol J. Arins, translated by H. T. Willetts.

And, turning around, I saw someone's saber lying nearby. A haughty goose was waddling through the yard, placidly grooming its feathers. I caught the goose and forced it to the ground, its head cracking beneath my boot, cracking and bleeding. Its white neck lay stretched out in the dung, and the wings folded down over the slaughtered bird.

"Goddammit!" I said, poking at the goose with the saber. "Roast it for me, mistress!"

The old woman, her blindness and her spectacles flashing, picked up the bird, wrapped it in her apron, and hauled it to the kitchen.

"Comrade," she said after a short silence. "This makes me want to hang myself." And she pulled the door shut behind her.

*   *   *

"So, what are they writing in the newspaper?" the young fellow with the flaxen hair asked me, and moved aside to make room for me.

"In the newspaper, Lenin writes," I said, picking up my *Pravda*, "Lenin writes that right now there is a shortage of everything."

And in a loud voice, like a triumphant deaf man, I read Lenin's speech to the Cossacks. The evening wrapped me in the soothing dampness of her twilight sheets, the evening placed her motherly palms on my burning brow.

I read, and rejoiced, waiting for the effect, rejoicing in the mysterious curve of Lenin's straight line.

"Truth tickles all and sundry in the nose," Surovkov said when I had finished. "It isn't all that easy to wheedle it out of the pile of rubbish, but Lenin picks it up right away, like a hen picks up a grain of corn."

That is what Surovkov, the squadron commander, said about Lenin, and then we went to sleep in the hayloft. Six of us slept there warming each other, our legs tangled, under the holes in the roof which let in the stars.

I dreamed and saw women in my dreams, and only my heart, crimson with murder, screeched and bled.

The goose is a symbolic bird no doubt, although certainly a memorable one; but the episode is not mentioned in Babel's diary and has the marks of being imagined rather than experienced. (Why, after all, was a fat goose still roaming around among these successive hordes of hungry soldiers? Surely in order that the narrator-hero might prove his mettle by slaughtering it, in the absence of a Polish prisoner to shoot or a fine lady to ruin.) So perverse is the way good art works, nonetheless, that the death of the goose is more memorable than the catalog of woes and horrors, the "disasters of war," that make up so much of the tales. The Jew among Cossacks who had "suffered on the fields of learning" is a brilliant touch, and so is the farmyard metaphor of Lenin picking out the truth as a hen picks up a grain of corn. As a passionate Communist and believer in Lenin, Babel ardently wished to proselytize his comrades, unpromising material as they might seem, and yet his art in the story has the last say, leaving us with the impression that the Cossacks were not interested in Lenin's exhortations, try as the narrator might to persuade them. It was the Jewish clerk himself they came eventually to accept as a comrade, rather than the distant leader of the revolution.

The narrator prays for what his experiences have made him feel is the simplest of all human abilities, that of killing one's fellow men. But the goose notwithstanding—and the function of the goose is of course ironical—he never achieves it. In "Dolgushov's Death," a comrade called Dolgushov, fatally wounded and afraid of falling into the hands of the Poles, begs the narrator to shoot him, but he can't do it. The narrator's "friend" Afonka rides up at that moment and does the job for him.

"Afonka," I said, riding up to him with a pitiful smile. "*I* couldn't have done that."

"Get lost, or I'll shoot you!" he said to me, his face turning white. "You spectacled idiots have as much pity for us as a cat has for a mouse!"

And he cocked his trigger.

I rode off slowly, without looking back, a feeling of cold and death in my spine.

"Hey! Hey!" Grishchuk shouted behind me, and grabbed Afonka's hand. "Cut the crap!"

"You damn lackey bastard!" Afonka yelled at Grishchuk. "Wait till I get my hands on him!"

Grishchuk caught up with me at the bend in the road. Afonka was not with him. He had ridden off in the opposite direction.

"Well, there you have it, Grishchuk," I said to him. "Today I lost Afonka, my first real friend."

Grishchuk took out a wrinkled apple from under the cart seat.

"Eat it," he told me, "please eat it."

Once again the effectiveness of the episode is obvious, more obvious than its truth, for this event also does not appear to figure in Babel's diary.

In the early stories, mostly about his early years in Odessa, although some of these are brief, Maupassant-style anecdotes which Babel must have picked up later in France, the method is already almost fully developed. There is nonetheless something still tentative and even innocent about it which is very engaging. The very first story, "Old Shloyme," is a case in point. The old man is devoured with anxieties, terrified he may lose his last warm corner in life. His story is soberly and convincingly recounted—old age imagined by the young Babel as vividly as the things he will make up and tell the prostitute ("bronze promissory notes") which win him his first fee. Shloyme, a poor old Jew in Odessa, whose family, he feels, may have to abandon him, gets up in the night, trembling with cold, and quietly, so as not to awaken his daughter-in-law, goes outside and contrives to hang himself, managing with his dimming eyes to gaze at the town "he had not left . . . once in sixty years":

There was a strong wind, and soon old Shloyme's frail body began swaying before the door of his house in which he had left his warm stove and the greasy Torah of his forefathers.

TURGENEV IS SAID to have remarked that all Russian prose narrative had really come out from under Gogol's story "The Overcoat"; and in the same way all the best qualities of Babel's best writing could be said to come out from under his own first brief tale. Nonetheless, in a comparatively short writing career Babel tried out and tested his talents in a variety of different forms—stories, propaganda essays, plays that could not have been at all easy to cast and to produce, film scripts, and projects for new kinds of film. They seem not to have had much success. In his tales and even at times it seems in his diaries he mixes the true and the imagined, reportage and Soviet uplift and ideology, so that it is sometimes hard to tell one from another. Sergeant-Major Trunov, good-hearted, of peasant stock, a prototype of the military Stakhanovite, is held up as an example to all in an article in the magazine *Red Cavalryman*, "What We Need Is More Men Like Trunov!" Out on the steppe Trunov defended his company to the last against attacks by White airplanes dropping bombs and led, rather improbably one might think, by an American pilot called Major Fauntleroy. (Remarkably enough a Major Fauntleroy did actually exist, and was one of the mercenary adventurers flying Spads and Camels for the White general Wrangel and his army.)

On some occasions Babel's taut prose, at once excited and blasé, can become almost elegiac—the tone of Wordsworth's "Old unhappy far-off things / And battles long ago." At other moments in the *Red Cavalry* stories his voice is carried away by the sheer excitement of what he is doing, and by a remarkable mixture of feverish uplift and weary disgust with all the pointless and aimless brutality which so much revolutionary fervor has brought about.

The "Reports from Petersburg, 1918," which precede the *Red Cavalry* tales in date of composition, although they come after them in this *Complete Works*, may remind us of another Wordsworthian comparison, the ecstatic moment in *The Prelude* when the young man is traveling in France just after the Revolution has broken out and exclaims retrospectively,

> Bliss was it in that dawn to be alive,
> But to be young was very heaven!

Babel of course had never given himself entirely over to the heady unrealities of revolutionary idealism. As a writer he could cast a cold eye even when most carried away by the fervor of the moment. Nor did he ever lose his Jewish sense of humor, that irrepressible amusement at the woodenness and deviousness of Soviet conformists which was to cost him his life many years later, from the long memories of malign thugs like Budyonny and Voroshilov.

Amusement and enthusiasm intermingled animate Babel's reports from St. Petersburg, most strikingly in the piece "The Palace of Motherhood," an example of Babel's pro-revolutionary style at its most exuberant and uninhibited, and yet still with a slight undercurrent of skeptical comedy:

Eight women in bedroom slippers shuffle with the heavy tread of the pregnant through the Rastrellian halls, their large bellies sticking out. There are only eight. But the palace belongs to them. And this is why it is called the Palace of Motherhood.

Eight women of Petrograd with gray faces and legs swollen from too much walking. Their past: months of standing in lines outside provision stores, factory whistles calling their husbands to the defense of the Revolution, the hard anxiety of war and the upheaval of the Revolution scattering people all over the place.

The recklessness of our destruction is already dispassionately handing us its invoice of unemployment and hunger. There are no jobs for the men returning from the front, their wives have no money to give birth, factories raise their frozen chimneys to the skies. A paper fog— paper money and paper of every other kind—flashes eerily past our stunned eyes and vanishes. And the earth keeps turning. People die, people are born.

I enjoy talking about the flickering flame of creation kindled in our empty little rooms. It is good that the buildings of the institute have not been snatched up by requisition and confiscation committees. It is good that oily cabbage soup is not poured from these white tables, and that no discussions of arrests, so common now, are to be heard.

This building will be called the Building of Motherhood. The decree says: "It will assist women in their great and strenuous duty."

This palace breaks with the old jail-like traditions of the Foundling Home, where children died or, at best, were sent on to "foster parents." Children must live. They must be born for "the building of a better life."

That is the idea. But it has to be carried through to the end. We have to make a revolution at some point.

It could be argued that shouldering rifles and firing at each other might occasionally have its good points. But that is hardly a complete revolution. Who knows, it might not even be a revolution at all.

The tone of the piece is unique to Babel, though it may owe a little to his admired preceptor Gorky; but one can only wonder that when writing like that, the young Babel managed not only to stay alive but to prosper. One may feel nonetheless that like many really talented Soviet writers — Zamyatin and Bulgakov for instance — he had come to the end of the road as a writer before the worst of the purges began. There can of course be no certainty about this; had the times become more favorable, so many good writers who were compelled to cultivate what Babel called the "art of silence" might have come back to life; while in any case the sheer toughness and in a sense the self-sufficiency of poets like Pasternak and Akhmatova was to see them and their genius through the worst days to come.

Without a chance to see them performed it is almost impossible to assess the potential of Babel's two plays, *Sunset* and *Maria*. But it scarcely seems as if he had much gift for the theater. He was at the same time too much of a loner and too ebullient in the pursuit of what was ultimately a very solitary vision to subdue his hand, as Shakespeare did, to the needs of the stage. The screenplays seem much more promising, and one can imagine Babel working effectively with Sergei Eisenstein and the teams who made *Battleship Potemkin* and *Ivan the Terrible*. And yet as Babel's daughter, Nathalie, the editor of the *Complete Works*, more than once points out, and rightly, these screenplays read more like works of literature than scenarios. The editing in general is first class, although for some reason "Bezhin Lug" — a Soviet propaganda rewriting of the story of the same name by Turgenev which was Henry James's favorite — seems to have been missed among the screen scripts.

Nathalie Babel's afterword is of particular interest. She and her mother were living at Niort in the west of France at the time of Hitler's invasion of Russia, when all the Russians in German-occupied France were automatically arrested and sent to camps, to be followed by many of the Jews. Nathalie's mother remained under arrest, the Gestapo completing in the family circle what the KGB had begun, and her daughter

valiantly importuned the German authorities until the town comman-
dant consented to see her and to release her mother on condition that she
report to him every day. Neither Nathalie nor her mother ever wore the
Yellow Star that Jews in occupied Europe were condemned to wear, nor
did they even declare their Jewishness. They were all too familiar with the
ways of every new revolutionary totalitarianism, as in his own bitter way
Nathalie's father had himself become. As she wisely says, "My father was
. . . filled with many contradictions, which are apparent in his stories and
books. Perhaps his future biographer will explore further the many incon-
sistencies that marked his brief life." On this matter Babel would have
been in wry agreement with his daughter, as "The Palace of Motherhood" shows. At an early date Babel was very much aware not only that
revolutions cease to be revolutionary but that they take to devouring their
own children.

Nathalie's mother, ill with cancer, told her daughter, who had not
been much of a success at a French *lyceé*, of the domestic complications previously unknown to her, which her father had got himself into
in Moscow. "You have a half-brother," her mother said. "I left Russia
mostly because of an affair your father was having with an actress, a very
beautiful woman. . . . She wanted him and his fame, and had a son by
him. Perhaps one day you might meet this man, and you should know
he is your half-brother and not someone you could fall in love with." In
fact Nathalie never did meet him, although while she was working as a
guide in Moscow at the time of a visit by a French workers' delegation
she met the members of still another of Babel's families in Russia, blurt-
ing out her own name when she met Antonina Nikolayevna Pirozhkova
and her daughter, Lydia, Nathalie's half-sister, who emigrated to America in 1996.

The ambiguous figure of Ilya Ehrenburg, a natural survivor if ever
there was one, enters the story when he seems to have been sent on
Moscow's orders to mislead and confuse Nathalie's mother with reports
that Babel might still be alive, might indeed have survived the war under
house arrest or in exile prior to his rehabilitation. From reliable sources
Babel's wife knew this to be untrue; but Ehrenburg's superiors presumably hoped that the word might get about among French Communists
and intellectuals, many of whom were still enthusiastic Stalinists, that

Babel was alive, or at least that Stalin's secret police had never executed him. Babel's wife came to detest Ehrenburg as a man who, having won all too many Lenin and Stalin prizes, and been on the inside of the Soviet establishment, might at least have done something to help her husband.

But even in the days of his first excitement and hope over the revolution Babel had never been a licker of the grander Communist boots, and it is doubtful if anything could have saved him. He had made too many enemies in high places who bided their time and did not forget. Budyonny launched his first attack on the *Red Cavalry* stories in 1924, but it was not until fifteen years later, when the new Communist, or rather Stalinist, anti-Semitism had become widespread in the higher circles of power, that he and his old cronies were able to take action.

However carefully he wrote, and however carefully he studied and worked at his effects, Babel remained deliberately a raw writer, concealing his skills under cover of an almost knockabout casualness; he was out to grate on his reader's nerves, to shock, to disturb, and to horrify. Peter Constantine as a translator seems to me to understand this very well. Russian seldom or perhaps never sounds ugly, but he is careful to convey Babel's new-style colloquial Russian at its most harsh and unaccommodating, rather than to smooth it down into a feebler and gentler English. The great nineteenth-century masters of Russian prose—Turgenev with his deliciously "creamy" style, as it has been called, Tolstoy's long, agile sentences, even Dostoevsky's rapid and clumsy euphony in such a key work as *The Underground Man*—Babel in one sense rejected them all, no doubt intentionally, as he gradually found how to say things in his own way, a revolutionary way.

Even so Babel remains a chameleon. One cannot pin down Shakespeare's style, or (if one were a translator) settle into an idiom which would convey Shakespeare's "style" in another language. The same must be true of Babel, and Peter Constantine makes the point very explicitly. He has found it fascinating, he says, to see how Babel's style changes from work to work. "We are familiar with terms such as Proustian, Chekhovian, and Nabokovian, but, as I soon realized, the term 'Babelian' is harder to define."

Babel's first published piece, "Old Shloyme," has very little in common with the style, or even with the linguistic feel, or rhythm of his second story. When writing about Odessa gangsters Babel uses an "elegant and surprising prose," and the diction of the *Red Cavalry* stories are just as surprising, just as varied. Even the two plays, Constantine tells us, sound different from each other, and one would hardly believe that the man who wrote the powerful and appalling story "The Road," about the murder and sexual mutilation of a Jewish intellectual on a train—a story which has haunted me since I first read it—could have produced the wholly different tone and style of "My First Fee." Babel's "ugly" effects should, as Peter Constantine obviously feels, be rendered into a similar style of English; he is surely right to avoid what might seem an elegiac ending to "My First Goose"—"My heart, stained with bloodshed, grated and brimmed over"—rendering it instead literally and with all the histrionic violence Babel sometimes adopts: "My heart, crimson with murder, screeched and bled." That hits hard in either language, but then Babel was a hard hitter by nature, intent on making a new literature to go with the new world he saw coming; a world that was first to disillusion and finally to destroy him.

The New York Review of Books, 2002

33

A Prig of Genius

Aleksandr Solzhenitsyn (1918–)

───────────

The Oak and the Calf: Sketches of Literary Life in the Soviet Union
by Aleksandr I. Solzhenitsyn, translated by Harry Willetts

"I AM A *littérateur*," wrote Belinsky. "I say this with a painful and yet proud and happy feeling. Russian literature is in my life and blood." Many other Russian writers could say the same, and Aleksandr Solzhenitsyn above all. He belongs wholly to the committed tradition of Russian literature, which Belinsky inspired, and which regarded writing as the lifeblood of ideas, progress, social truth. Belinsky detested art with a conscious social purpose, just because it *was* conscious: for him good art was the natural, the inevitable, the only weapon in the struggle for truth and justice, and he revered Pushkin and Turgenev as great artists who could not help but light up the human condition and banish the repulsive gloom of tyranny, hypocrisy, and superstition.

This precious essence, far more precious than can be imagined by Americans who live under the humane and far-seeing dispensation of the Founding Fathers, is contained in such a writer as Solzhenitsyn as if in some holy vessel. As a religious man Solzhenitsyn is no doubt humble; as a writer he is sublimely conceited. Conceit rather than pride seems to be the word, for pride goes with humility, and Solzhenitsyn is still, and no doubt always will be, the fearless, intelligent, self-centered prig whom he portrayed with such endearing accuracy in "Prussian Nights," that long rambling poem about himself on campaign in Germany just before his arrest in 1944, which he composed and committed to memory in one of the Gulag camps.

A fearless prig, and a prig with genius. But it is not the genius itself that produces the effect but what the possession of genius means in the context of Russian history and the Soviet state. "For a country to have a great writer is like having another government." Imagine that comment being made with reference to America, or England, or even France. But Solzhenitsyn, though he does not say so, was only echoing another radical, Vladimir Korolenko, who at the beginning of this century said: "My country is not Russia, my country is Russian literature." Solzhenitsyn might say, "My country is not the Soviet Union: I *am* Russian literature." *The Oak and the Calf* reminds us again and again of the conviction the author holds that no Communist, no citizen even who collaborates with the Soviet state, has the right to call himself a Russian. "Russia," he once wrote, "is to the Soviet Union as a man is to the disease afflicting him. We do not confuse a man with his illness: we do not refer to him by the name of that illness or curse him for it."

And so the Russian calf butts the Soviet oak. *Bodalsya telenok s Dubom*—the calf butted the oak—comes out of that great stock of Russian proverbs which have always had a strong attraction for Solzhenitsyn. Here he gives us a few more, such as "If trouble comes, make use of *it*, too," and we might remember that the last line of one of Pasternak's most moving poems is the peasant saying: "It is harder to live your life than to cross a field." Like all his predecessors in the nineteenth century, Solzhenitsyn has a deep feeling for the virtues and the sanity of the Russian peasant, and two men of that peasant stock were saviors to him as a writer. Khrushchev cared nothing for *One Day in the Life of Ivan Denisovich*, or for its author, but he saw how it could be made use of in the cautious attempt to demythologize Stalin. Moreover its hero was a peasant, and that he did approve of, being one himself. It is curious how Russian accounts of convict life—Dostoevsky's *House of the Dead*, Shalamov's *Kolyma Tales*, and the story that rocketed Solzhenitsyn to fame—all specifically decline the documentary approach and opt for the distancing process of art, the art conferred by a narrator who is a stranger to the author, a different sort of man.

Solzhenitsyn's real savior and the most important figure in this book was Aleksandr Tvardovsky, the editor of *Novy Mir*. This magazine, heir of the old "thick" magazines of the nineteenth century, had become the nearest thing in the Soviet Union to an organ of the intelligentsia, that vanishing class of open-minded, intellectually voracious persons which had been built up so painstakingly in the nineteenth century and virtually destroyed by the Red reaction of the 1920s. Everything in *Novy Mir* had to be passed by the censorship of course, and its editorial board was well supplied with Agitprop stooges, but its editor was a man who understood and worshipped good literature and, as Solzhenitsyn tells us, prospected for real writers with the unremitting zeal of a prospector hunting gold. What makes *The Oak and the Calf* fascinating reading, even for those who have little interest in the arcane gossip and the endless infighting that characterize the literary power struggle in the Soviet Union, is the spellbinding narrative power with which the author tells the story of his relations with Tvardovsky and the magazine.

Tvardovsky owed everything to the regime. As he said plaintively to the author in the many Dostoevsky-style dialogues between them—"Where should I have been without it?" He loved not the power it had brought him—he was no good at power and felt sick on the tightrope every such apparatchik has to walk—but the trappings of Soviet success: the car, the dacha, the dark suit, even the pleasures of bullying those below him and placating those above. He drank a very great deal even by Russian standards—he was referred to once as "a distillery in trousers"—but drink did not spoil his nose for good literature or his ability to fight for its survival, to intrigue on its behalf. Solzhenitsyn was as energetic an intriguer on his own behalf: he had to be, his genius on its own would not have got him anywhere. And with the luck essential to a good conspirator and commander (he talks of moving his proliferating manuscripts westward "like divisions or army corps") he succeeded in landing the "lightened" version of *One Day in the Life of Ivan Denisovich* on the desk of Anna Berzer, a devoted workhorse of the magazine.

She contrived as it were to toss it over the heads of the intervening "drones and deadheads of Agitprop" so that it landed on the editor's desk. "This is about the experiences of a peasant in the camps." That decided Tvardovsky to read it. Wild excitement. Ever since he had learned verses of Nekrasov as a barefoot boy, writes Solzhenitsyn, "Russian literature alone had sustained him," and here was a real morsel, and a morsel that promised an endless feast. He came to love Solzhenitsyn as he loved his own paper; glory for the one would mean glory for the other, even though he, a man without true friends, could never really relax with his new author, alternately patronized and pleaded with him, ordered him to wear the proper uniform of a successful Soviet author instead of going around with his shirt hanging out. Khrushchev's support sent Tvardovsky into ecstasies ("What a warm-hearted and clever man he is!—how lucky we are to have such a man over us!") and he recounted eagerly the enthusiasm of the people "up there," even coming to believe (though Solzhenitsyn does not) that Khrushchev and he had discussed together the complete removal of the censorship from serious works of art and literature.

But the usual farce and tragedy attend progress toward socialism's yawning heights. *Ivan Denisovich* finally appeared at the time of the Cuba crisis. Khrushchev's days were numbered. The Stalinists were getting seriously alarmed. And some odd tricks were used to discredit the giddy success of *Novy Mir*'s new baby. The editor of *Izvestia*, Khrushchev's son-in-law Adzhubei, trying to seize the initiative from Tvardovsky, harangued his editorial staff on their incompetence in not "opening up" this important theme. Someone helpfully recalled that a story about the camps *had* come in a while back and of course had been instantly suppressed. The wastepaper baskets were feverishly searched: no go; but the author's name had been filed (for reasons that might at another time have boded ill for him) and so G. Shelest found himself bemusedly dictating his tale long distance from some far provincial backwater to an eager *Izvestia* subeditor. It was shoved in the holiday issue without any comment, "as though stories about camp life had been appearing in newspapers for forty years and were boringly familiar to everyone." There is something in this of all newspaper life, anywhere.

"In our country abuse and praise alike are always carried to extremes." Solzhenitsyn was determined not to be seduced by praise into appearing to give any kind of aid and comfort to the regime, and this could easily have happened. Instead, as he now thinks, he made the opposite mistake, "completely failing to understand my new position and my new possibilities." He refused every interview, thus missing, as he afterward felt, the chance of saying what he liked. He turned down the most tempting offers from other publishing houses—Soviet editors compete with each other much more fiercely than their Western counterparts—and thus threw away the chance of getting his great accumulation of other material into print when the atmosphere was still cautiously liberal and he was riding the crest.

Besides, he owed his loyalty to Tvardovsky, who was passionately anxious to retain him in his bosom. And Solzhenitsyn never attempts to disguise the naïve streak in himself, the conviction that the walls of Jericho will fall flat if he blows his trumpet loud enough, that the oak tree will be pushed over by the calf. Years later, when he was re-arrested and about to be deported from the country, he was convinced that he was going to be able to confront the Soviet leadership and harangue them on their misdemeanors. As he paced his cell in Lefortovo prison,

> I was mentally in conversation with the Politburo. Something told me that given two or three hours, I could budge them, shake their certainty. There would have been no getting through to the fanatics in Lenin's Politburo, or the sheep in Stalin's. But these people I (foolishly?) thought could be reached. Why, even Khrush had shown some signs of understanding.

It is magnificent but it is not politics. Yet that word "foolishly," and its question mark, too, are not inserted for nothing. There are two Solzhenitsyns, one the believer, the sublime prig, the only man in step; the other, the novelist who watches himself as acutely as he does other people, who looks into himself and them with the penetrating eye of a Tolstoy, but also with the same worldly understanding, the same charity. Certainly, without drawing any other comparisons, one can see repeated in Solzhenitsyn the same Tolstoyan dualism between novelist and prophetic sage. And Tolstoy as a novelist saw himself as clearly as he saw other people.

Solzhenitsyn's political shrewdness comes out in his superb portrait of Lenin in the short novel *Lenin in Zurich*, to my mind one of the best things he has done. This really is Lenin, the conspirator, the cynic, the man of genial intelligence and inflexible willpower. And as a portrait in a novel it convinces where Solzhenitsyn's own dogmatic assertions about the nature of the Soviet state do not. Solzhenitsyn has deeply irritated some of the best among his own countrymen, and liberals in the West as well, by deriding the notion that communism can ever conceivably develop, modify itself, acquire a human face. It is, he says, utterly unredeemable. And that is a theological concept, meaningless to politicians and liberals alike. But novels know nothing of theology, and the portrait of Lenin before he came to power shows why this view of the matter could be, and probably is, empirically true.

History does not offer many examples of the kind of organization which Lenin perfected, and which was thus able to survive him. But if Robespierre had not fallen, no one believes that terror would have ceased to be the instrument of government, that things under such a man would have tended to "get better." No one assumes the Mafia improves with time, civilizes itself, and liberalizes itself as it acquires more experience. Communism may not be damned theologically, as Solzhenitsyn would have us suppose, but it may well be irreversibly condemned by the logic of its own political techniques.

All this is implicit in the long and extremely detailed account of the author's relations with Tvardovsky. The editor was a committed man, who had put all his spiritual and creative capital into the system. Fundamentally it was antipathetic to him, but it had given him riches and a job he loved, had praised his poetry and sold it in huge editions. Solzhenitsyn praises the poetry, too, rightly observing that the narrative poem about a Soviet soldier, *Vasily Tyorkin*, is the only work of its kind about the war which does not tell lies, which stops short of the *poshlost* and the mechanical patriotism that are the hallmarks of the vast Soviet war-book industry. It appeared when the war was still in progress, and the gunners of Solzhenitsyn's own battery enjoyed having it read to them, together with *War and Peace*. That is praise indeed. But for all his real creative achievement as a poet, and the sterling work he had done at *Novy Mir*, Tvardovsky was a wretchedly unhappy man. It is a tribute to Solzhenitsyn's skill as a novelist that we believe this, not because he says so but because it seems to emerge as the truth of the portrait, just as truth emerges in the portrait of Lenin.

Indeed the division of a soul appears, ironically, in two different forms. Tvardovsky could not reconcile the demands of God and mammon, his poetic soul and love of literature, and the demands of his robot masters. Solzhenitsyn, on the other hand, appears to have no difficulty at all in reconciling the Pyotr Verkhovensky side of himself—the charming, ruthless extremist, sacrificing everything, wife and children, too, if need be, to his books and their survival, pouring out with joyful ebullience the details of his successes, his immense and legendary reputation in the underworld of *samizdat*—with the novelist who, wryly and humanely, observes, judges, and understands. But there is no justice about such things, as he himself would probably be the first to admit. Tvardovsky died of his contradictions, virtually died of a broken heart when he was eased out of the editorship in 1970 after the final defeat of the liberalizing policy of *Novy Mir*. Solzhenitsyn goes on from strength to strength, and "when trouble comes, makes use of *it*, too."

Perhaps that toughness is something he acquired as a *zek*, in years of prison camps. One of the most touching scenes in the book is the account of Tvardovsky's stay with the Solzhenitsyns at their humble flat in Ryazan, so that he could read *The First Circle* well away from the office. He was genuinely delighted to be asked and even enjoyed being an ordinary citizen, buying tickets and food like everyone else instead of in the special shops and agencies, keeping off the bottle for a couple of days while he devoured the manuscript and then letting go on the vodka and cognac while he asked his host endless questions about *prison*, what it was like, what they did to you, and finally lamenting that he had never experienced it, but perhaps he would one day. It is not only in the West that some people feel they lead, as it were, sheltered lives.

Of course Tvardovsky emerges as by far the more sympathetic character. We can all side with weakness, with Ismene rather than Antigone, even when weakness and accommodation is on the side of the big battalions. Solzhenitsyn chides his friend and guardian angel for not doing more, but such a man, in such a situation, most certainly did all he could. It was not his fault that the Lenin prize he strove to get for Solzhenitsyn was awarded to some party nonentity, or even that the entire staff of *Novy Mir* was compelled to vote "unanimously" in favor of the invasion of Czechoslovakia. Such things were simply the facts of life in the place he had to live it: courage comes in various kinds and Tvardovsky had as much of it in his own way as his friend and critic.

Moreover, it is by no means clear that his policies and aims have been totally defeated. As Geoffrey Hosking points out in *Soviet Fiction Since Ivan Denisovich*, there are writers published today, and not in *samizdat*, who are good in any case, writers such as Maximov, Voinovich, and Trifonov. Unless you think that the art of the possible is always a vile and degrading compromise, the policies of *Novy Mir* must be seen to have achieved some kind of success. On the literary front at least, Soviet "normality" has been marginally modified.

More ironically, the decline and death of Tvardovsky make Solzhenitsyn's memoir, which has been hovering unapologetically on the verge of tedium, now become positively boring. The points are made obsessively, the feats of Jack the Giant-killer mount up to more and more legendary proportions; and of course the stifled yawn the Western reader cannot help indulging would be taken as one more proof of how unfeeling, corrupt, and incapable of salvation he has become. But the *novelist* is always alive, never taking himself quite seriously, and the detailed account of his final expulsion is a masterpiece of humor. This, too, is its only retrospective element: the rest was written at top speed more or less at the time it was taking place, while Solzhenitsyn was violently reacting to an article in *Stern* which asserted that *August 1914* was an allegorical and not a historical novel—a decidedly stupid criticism—and while *The Oak and the Calf* itself was being circulated around Moscow and multiplying in *samizdat*. So the somewhat gimcrack air, as of things and persons and thoughts disturbed and *couchés provisoirement*, is itself a proper part of the effect this memoir creates. Solzhenitsyn's regular novels and *povesti*, whatever the difficulties of their conception and birth, are more solidly fixed in art and time.

The memoir prompts us to ask: what really is Solzhenitsyn's position, and how should we reasonably respond to him? I would reject at once the charges that he is as intolerant as his opponents, a reactionary fanatic, a dotty Ayatollah who takes more relish in lambasting the corrupt West than in denouncing the Eastern Antichrist. That is all beside the point, and some of the liberals who resent his reproaches—no one is more offended by contempt from such a source than a right-minded Western liberal—seem to do so because they are sensitive above everything to having the right position, not only to be washing their clean linen in public but to be seen to be doing it. As Irving Howe put it in an "Open Letter to Solzhenitsyn" in *The New Republic*: "We were opponents of every dictatorship, Hitler's and Stalin's, as later of Pinochet's and Castro's." Yes they were, and all honor to them, but that does not alter the fact that their decision to be against them was a matter of intellectual and emotional propriety; it could not involve the whole man, and for a Russian like Solzhenitsyn the whole man must be involved.

It's unfair, but there is a gap, and an unbridgeable one, between the *bien pensant* and the soldier at the front, the believer who has witnessed in the arena. Maybe Solzhenitsyn has been too eager for martyrdom, and to tell us all about it, but that does not make him any less of a great man, a man entitled to utter what Howe calls "coarse jeremiads" against the Western world whenever he feels like it.

Understandable, too, though definitely misleading, is his insistence that Russia is a blameless victim, a captive maiden kidnapped by the Soviet Union. To imagine her free and mistress of her destiny he would have to go a long way back, to a time before the rulers of Moscow learned to behave like the Mongols of whom they were the vassals. This is historical commonplace. But there is *some* sense, even so, in which he is right even here, for the attachment to an idea of Russia, her faith and literature, overrides historical consideration. "If England was what England seems," as Kipling put it.

There is a moving moment in *The Oak and the Calf* when a friend who has also been in trouble says to the author that "life would be impossible anywhere but in Russia." Solzhenitsyn feels this, too, however much Russia may have become the Soviet Union, which is why he carries his idea of her about with him. Pushkin and Tolstoy did the same. "Of course I despise my country from head to foot," wrote Pushkin in a letter, "but it makes me furious when a foreigner shares my feeling." Tolstoy was even more shamelessly and magnificently illogical, remarking that he could feel really free in Russia because he hadn't made the laws, much freer than the English and Americans felt in their own countries, where because they had made them they had to support them.

More important, the uneasiness which Solzhenitsyn stirs up in the liberal bosom is a very fundamental one indeed, and it is central to the whole function and nature of religion. The open society takes it for granted that religion is a voluntary affair, that one can take it or leave it, as one can anything else in the society, from education to cosmetics. To Solzhenitsyn this view of the matter is profoundly shocking, as shocking as a comparable nineteenth-century attitude was to Kierkegaard. Events today merely underline the lesson that real religion, and real morality, too, as opposed to the negative virtues which even a free society cannot do without, are intimate not with freedom but with authority and power. Perhaps Solzhenitsyn is hoping one day to return in triumph to Moscow as Khomeini returned to Iran. The idea is not wholly chimerical. "Why," inquired Herzen with grave irony, in his memoirs *From the Other Shore*, "is belief in God and the Kingdom of Heaven silly, whereas belief in earthly Utopias is not silly?" Communist theology has not yet found an answer to that question.

The New York Review of Books, 1980

PART IV

American Poetry

34

Songs of a Furtive Self

Walt Whitman (1819–1892)

---

*The Trial of the Poet: An Interpretation of the First Edition of
    Leaves of Grass*
by Ivan Marki

THE ENGLISH WRITER Edward Carpenter, who inspired both
E. M. Forster and D. H. Lawrence in his time, had a number of
conversations with the aging Walt Whitman, and was startled to
hear him remark of himself, in the third person: "There is something in
his nature *furtive*, like an old hen." It is a most endearing remark, and
shows the kind of lordly shrewdness and self-awareness that must be in the
bedrock of Whitman's genius. Carpenter, and many of his disciples, had
more than a bit of the old hen in them too, but one cannot imagine them
coming out with it like that. Their image of social and sexual emancipation, on behalf of which they fought a courageous but necessarily devious
campaign, did not include that particular sort of avian behavior pattern;
but Whitman, who in the preface to *Leaves of Grass* inserted what Ivan
Marki in *The Trial of the Poet* well calls "a veritable ornithological
litany"—

The wild pigeon and highhold and orchard-oriole and coot and surf-
duck and redshouldered hawk and fish-hawk and white-ibis and
indian-hen and cat-owl and waterpheasant etc., etc.,

—found room for a hen in it, and would no doubt have celebrated hen-like behavior in his barbaric yawp, as he celebrated most other kinds.

Nonetheless, furtiveness is a vital ingredient in the extraordinarily rich and autonomous world of Whitman's poetic language, all the more so because—as Marki implies in the course of his analysis—it mostly masquerades as an extreme and challenging openness. The "curious triplicate process" of *Song of Myself* may in some ways remind us of Henry James's dream of pursuit by a shapeless terror in a nightmare in the Galerie des Glaces at Versailles, and how he nerved himself at length to round on it and chase it all the way back down the hall. It is of significance that James understood Whitman, accepted and admired him to the point of hardly troubling to comment, or to isolate him safely on the pedestal contemporaries had hastened to provide. He knew what it was all about; and it would not be fanciful to see an alembicated cousin to Whitman's in the style James evolved, a medium as equal to startlement as it was at home in depths of equivocation, adapted to agility as to repose—just as an old hen is in fact.

"The expression of the American poet is to be transcendent and new. It is to be indirect and not direct or descriptive or epic." Whitman's words in the preface are certainly true although, as Marki implies, the indirectness has often been overlooked, even by such sympathetic and perceptive scholars as Allen, Rubin, and Catel. The fact is that Whitman was not really doing anything American at all in *Song of Myself*, whatever the appearances; he was creating a new language and style for self-expression—the physical sense of self—as Keats had done thirty years or so before. Keats's sensuality of language can often be slightly shamefaced, but it is not furtive: furtiveness implies a carefully worked out undercover program, such as the genius of Whitman could organize.

The effects of Keats's language, though, are remarkably similar to Whitman's—"The Eve of St. Agnes" and *Sleep and Poetry* are in terms of their verbal world the nearest kind of poetry to *Song of Myself*. Even Keats's neologisms have an exact parallel in Whitman's exuberances and demotic oddities. Marki observes disapprovingly:

Whitman's silly habit of flaunting the five or six [foreign] words that he knew has been, from the first, a matter of so much gratuitous mirth on the part of his readers and therefore has become so tediously familiar that beyond a short note of 'acknowledgment' it can be safely ignored.

This is surely on a par with the critics who wince at Keats's verbal ardors and gentilities; Whitman's gallicisms are an essential part of his style, its total and original 'campness,' and like Keats's intuitions in language of the nature and feel of the body, Whitman's sense of it seems also to need that posture of touching and unwitting absurdity and vulnerability which belongs to human nakedness. This his fervency of language, like Keats's provides.

> The young men float on their backs, their bellies bulge
> to the sun, they do not ask who seizes fast to them,
> They do not know who puffs and declines with pendant and
> bending arch,
> They do not think whom they souse with spray.

Like Keats's, Whitman's language has what might be termed erectile tendencies ("Those movements, those improvements of our bodies," as Byron blandly remarks) and its exuberance and oddities seem wholly natural for this reason. There is nothing pretentious or metaphysical about the neologisms of either poet; they seem to expand into a world not of ingenuity but of vivid physical simplicity, a verbal equivalent of what Whitman calls "the curious sympathy one feels when feeling with the hand the naked meat of the body," and its "thin red jellies."

Discovering the body in poetry was not quite the same thing as discovering America. More fortunate than Keats in this as in other ways, Whitman did not feel that he had to pass himself for the higher life in order to discover America. Furtiveness came naturally to him, but it had the simple health of inner shamelessness: he was not in thrall to romantic ideas of the European tradition, the spirit and its lofty destiny, as Keats was. The age and the expectations that ordained for Keats the romantic hero's role, in opposition to his own poetic genius, left Whitman wholly free to loaf about on fish-shaped Paumanok, clam-digging and declaiming Shakespeare to the waves.

The impressive thing about his poetic self, and the language in it, is the freedom it achieves—from the self as an abstract identity—by remaining as it were bewitched by the body. In what James called "the spacious vacancy" of America, the way to be alive was to touch oneself, a strangely original activity for the poetic. And it is no sense narcissism. Berryman, who achieves in *Dream Songs* something of the marvelous insouciance of Whitman's style, is nonetheless a self watching itself pen in hand in the rocking chair, and making poetry out of finding this "I" to be a case. The new American *sum* soon became as absorbed with itself as the European *cogito*. Hemingway addressing himself as "you," drinking the whisky, putting the bait on the hook, feeling good, is a kind of ghastly parody of Whitman, even down to the use of foreign words—before the hero of *A Farewell to Arms* is blown up by a shell, and finds himself leaving his body, he has just been consuming a mass of cold "pasta asciutta" with some Italian privates: mere macaroni would not have been worthy of his style of self-intentness.

Tocqueville observed that Americans do not converse but address, and that they will instinctively address a single interlocutor as "Gentlemen." Whitman virtually addresses his body as "Gentlemen" in *Song of Myself*, and the effect is seraphically funny. It is the nuances of this process in which Professor Marki is interested, and he has many admirable and penetrating things to say. He uses a more or less formalistic technique to analyze the undercover workings by which Whitman arranges either to address us, or to be overheard addressing himself; and this can lead to whole paragraphs in which we seem to be nowhere near the poetry at all. But, most endearingly, the critic has caught from his great original some of the inability to be afflated and rhapsodic for long, so that he drops down again into a simple exclamation of pleasure or the expression of a personal preference.

In *Walt Whitman Reconsidered* Richard Chase analyzed some time ago what he called "the paradox of identity" in the poet, and traced the "comic drama of the self," unfolding in the great poem through the self's "escaping a series of identities which threaten to destroy its lively and various spontaneity." "A comic drama" might not appear to consort with "I lean and loafe at my ease . . . observing a spear of summer grass," but it is just Whitman's trick (again one might think of Keats and "I stood tip-toe upon a little hill . . .") to present physical indolence and self-absorption in terms of a dynamic process of courting and evading the kinds of experience and identity which consciousness plays with and is threatened by the consciousness that

> Looks down, is erect, bends an arm on an impalpable certain rest,
> Looks with its sidecurved head curious what will come next.

Marki handsomely acknowledges Chase's book, as also E. H. Miller's *Walt Whitman's Poetry: A Psychological Journey*; but he has his own individual method of feeling the way into the world of the poetry and exploring the nature of its originality. He lays particular stress on the preface to *Leaves of Grass*, which in its way demoralizes the reader by its very lack of commitment and clarity, preparing him for the real clarity and unexpectedness of the poem. I think Marki is too ingenious when he claims that "the sketchy, improvisational quality of each single image or phrase is the most convincing proof of the validity of the total effort," which is as much as to say that *because* the preface is so muddled and evasive it is doing its work properly and saying what it has to say; but this is undoubtedly a notion along the right lines, for like some preliminary recitative of poor quality, the nullity of the preface ("America does not repel the past"—what *does* it do then?) makes the sudden bursting forth of the aria all the more impressive. Even the "nationalistic turgidity," as Marki calls it, is not very positive, giving as it does muffled hints of the poem's joyful peculiarity—the rivers and "beautiful masculine Hudson" being there to "embouchure where they spend themselves," and also to "embouchure" into America's bard.

The permament scaffolding of Freudian interpretation has always been wasted on Whitman as his more enlightened critics have realized—"Did you fear some scrofula out of the unflagging pregnancy?" the poet enquires—and the same is probably true of other theories and interpretations of the self, Hegelian or otherwise. Lawrence, who much admired Whitman but could not resist trying to cut him down to size, as he did with all manifestos but his own, replied to his expansive query, "What is impossible or baseless or vague? . . . all things enter with electric swiftness softly and duly without confusion or jostling or jam" with "if that is so, one must be a pipe open at both ends, so everything runs through." This metaphor of aliment and excretion—"a pipe open at both ends"—is indeed perfect for Whitman, and higher praise than Lawrence presumably realized. It expresses the physical relief and freshness ("The bowels sweet and clean") he gets into poetry, and suggests, too, the lapses into vacancy when we are not concentrating on it. It leaves little or no mark on the memory or mental consciousness, and is then renewed when we go back to it again and plunge in.

Hence he is a poet of release rather than accretion—we do not add to our knowledge of him and our participation in him, as time goes on, in the way that we do with every other great poet. The slate is wiped clean each time: coming back to him we immerse ourselves afresh. Hence, it must be admitted, the comparative pointlessness of academic criticism, even though the stylistic analyses of Professor Marki and his predecessors do give us a clearer view of Whitman, as "the equable man" in his poetry, than do the more straightforward earlier debates about his attitudes and message. In fact probably the best as well as the briefest thing about him is Louis Simpson's poem, "Walt Whitman at Bear Mountain," with its epigraph from Ortega y Gasset, "life which does not give the preference to any other life . . . which therefore prefers its own existence." In this admirable poem Simpson speaks of "the realtors, pickpockets, salesmen and actors performing official scenarios" who turned a deaf ear to him, having "contracted American dreams." But:

> the housewife who knows she's dumb,
> And the earth, are relieved.
> All that grave weight of America
> Cancelled!

Naturally enough the grave weight of Soviet Russia does not see it like this. Whitman must there be seen to be (and he is immensely popular) an American poet in the sense in which a Soviet poet is a Soviet poet. Maurice Mendelson is an experienced and erudite scholar, in the admirable tradition of Russian critical scholarship on poetry which has produced so many good Pushkinists, but given the Soviet line on Whitman he has no chance to say anything of interest, although the biographical side of his book, *Life and Work of Walt Whitman,* is well done. The "puzzles" of Whitman, however, are of a different kind to those which receive the attention of Professor Marki. Leslie Fiedler is indignantly castigated for his view of Whitman the impostor, and the correct dialectic is set forth:

> Was Walt Whitman a skilful demagogue playing at democracy, or a poet whose world view was that of the democratic masses . . . was the poet bound hand and foot by bourgeois individualism, or did his strength lie in an emotional and intellectual leaning towards collectivism?

Gorky saw Whitman as "Calling on man to merge with mankind," and Commissar Lunacharsky "shrewdly remarked" that the "real foundation of his poetry was not individualism but just the opposite." This is all perfectly rational in terms of Newspeak, but one suspects that the Soviet masses in fact simply read their Whitman with the same kind of relief that the rest of us do.

On the Civil War and slavery Mendelson's attitudes have a better cause, for Whitman was more deeply involved in the war between the states than any other great poet has been in a national or civil war, not even excluding poets who have fought in one. The Soviet imagination has always been caught by the Civil War—on the side of the North of course: a recent Soviet novel by Alexander Borshchagovsky tells the true story of a Tsarist officer, Turchin, who emigrated to America and became a colonel in the Illinois regiment. Soviet society would feel much more at home with Whitman's letters from the military dressing station where he worked, and the articles he wrote about it, than with his poetry, and indeed these are deeply moving in what they express about the war and Whitman's feelings about it, feelings common to all good men. There is of course not a whisper in Mendelson's book about Whitman as homosexual, "Extoller of armies and those that sleep in each others' arms"— only a commendation in the preface for Emory Holloway's book *Free and Lonesome Heart,* which condemns speculation about his "alleged homosexuality." Specific queries here are certainly beside the point, but it is surely impossible not to feel that the war for Whitman was a profoundly, indeed sublimely homosexual experience, of which his great work among the wounded was very much a part, and to which the most moving poems in *Drum-Taps*—"The Wound Dresser" or "As Toilsome I wander'd Virginia's Woods"—bear witness in a manner as uncompromising as it is dignified.

The Times Literary Supplement, 1977

35

Mothermonsters and Fatherfigures

E. E. Cummings (1894–1962)

Complete Poems, 1910–1962
by E. E. Cummings

Dreams in the Mirror: A Biography of E. E. Cummings
by Richard S. Kennedy

AMERICAN POETRY has two traditions: open and closed. The first may well be the mutated offspring of the styles of poetry shipped over wholesale, at one time or another, from England; the second represents the more or less systematic repudiation of those ready-made poetics by the developing American consciousness. "Closed" poetry is in fact usually much more original in technique and tone than "open" poetry, and it reveals its ancestry only in its degree of encapsulation. Its idiom is self-defining: it does not merge with or enter other poetic areas; it cannot breed, and can hardly even metamorphose.

The immense and various achievements of American poetry owe much to the difference between these two traditions, and to their possible modes of combination. Robert Frost might be said to write a closed sort of poetry that looks as if it were open: the style of the first deviously and beautifully works to give the impression of the second. Something altogether more complex but not wholly dissimilar seems to be taking place in the poetry of Wallace Stevens and John Berryman. But the boldness of American poetry is toward the previously undefined and unexpressed, although poets of the open tradition—Robinson Jeffers, Robert Lowell (who at moments can sound so strangely like him), William Carlos Williams, A. R. Ammons, John Ashbery—are not only obvious heirs of Whitman but are all, as it were, on the best of terms with the laborious traditions and hermetic practices of closed poetry; they are as familiar with Emily Dickinson as they are with Ezra Pound, and with Edwin Arlington Robinson, John Crowe Ransom, Marianne Moore, and E. E. Cummings as well.

What do not pass from one tradition to the other are the sense and the uses of time. "Closed" poets may have long careers—some of the longest, steadiest, and most prolific—but time seems to stand still for them (and so for their readers). They do not, like the two spectral poets in the waning dusk of *Little Gidding*, "urge the mind to aftersight and foresight." Again, the cause may be essentially historical. In 1867 Henry Timrod composed an "Ode for the Commemoration of the Fallen":

> Stoop, angels, hither from the skies!
> There is no holier spot of ground
> Than where defeated valor lies,
> By mourning beauty crowned!

The homely "spot" does not prevent the poetry from slipping effortlessly, and very movingly, into the English idiom of more than a hundred years earlier, the commemorative idiom of Collins. But there is nothing derivative or old-fashioned about the sound of it: it ignores times, standing in its own enclosure outside it. The Timrod syndrome, as we might call it, is surprisingly endemic in closed American poetry; an idiom, once fixed (and no matter where it comes from), has its own special place. English and European poetry, by contrast, is a great deal more corporate and collective, moving all together when it moves at all. And Cummings offers a striking example of the Timrod syndrome in a very different guise; he too can tranquilly ignore what is going on outside his own self-occupied enclosure, impervious to fate and history, of which contemporaries like his friend Allen Tate, and the younger generation of Robert Lowell, were so wonderfully aware. No poetry could be less closed than the "Ode to the Confederate Dead":

Turn your eyes to the immoderate past,
Turn to the inscrutable infantry rising
Demons out of the earth—they will not last.

It is the implicit claim of American open poetry not "to last," but to be in
just that state of instability and turmoil which, as it does also in Lowell's
"For the Union Dead," joins the personal to the public chimera, the
predicament of now to that of the past.

Such poetry is its own continuing drama, and also an index of changing awareness. Inside their own closed idiom, a John Crowe Ransom or
an E. E. Cummings can do almost anything, provided they do not reveal
themselves to be sensitive to outside possibilities. The poems they make
must not show signs of wanting to be "understood." Ransom perceived
this very well: "little helpless," as Cummings's first wife called him, did
not. The wife, Elaine Thayer, also made the memorable comment: "I
don't like people who want to be understood." A perpetual child, Cummings did like to be understood, and his charm made his friends eager to
help and protect him. But in his best poems he is absorbed, like a good
child in its toys, and isn't in the least concerned with understanding. The
analogy is exact, for the reader must get down with the poet among the
building blocks on the floor; it is no good meeting him when he is charming the grown-ups—especially the more sentimental ones—with his cute
ways. Auden once wrote that "to grow up does not mean to outgrow either
childhood or adolescence but to make use of them in an adult way." By
this criterion Cummings's poetic techniques are designed to perpetuate
adolescence, both in the poetry and the poet.

Most good poets suffer for their gift and use it to make such suffering
visible—to write out the nature of it is to enhance its reality. Cummings
uses the gift to retain and maximize the insulation of a happy childhood.
Poetry is his toy, but not "his toy, his dream, his rest," as it was for Berryman and Lowell, the plotted and cultivated scenario of an otherwise distracted existence. It is a paradox that although Cummings's typographical
dodges seem to be drawing attention to themselves they in fact come off
best when they are at their least self-conscious. The poems that are
admirable in *Tulips and Chimneys* (published in 1922, a memorable year
in literary annals) are the series of "Actualities" and "Post Impressions."

Sexual experience with ladies like Marj and Lil provided Cummings with the perfect subject for his format: detachment in comic physical involvement; the agilely precarious recording of experience and appearances, even as the poet lies passive in the sleazy, clumsy, but not hostile machine which he is laboriously manipulating. Experience, particularly sexual experience, is like a new American mechanism to be spryly mastered (as in that splendid poem "she being Brand"), and the poet in the happiest way is both operator and passive recorder.

All his life Cummings was able to write such poems, but they alternate with the winsome and folksy type which became more common as time went on. Here his best technique goes bad on him; artful verbalization emphasizes rather than remakes cliché, as it often does in the poetry of Dylan Thomas, with which Cummings's has many affinities. But what suits the rhymed sentences of Patience Strong sounds worse than banal in the arrangement of such virtuosos:

> the trick of finding what you didn't lose
> (existing's tricky: but to live's a gift)
> the teachable imposture of always
> arriving at the place you never left

A poem from Cummings's juvenilia borrows Keats's thrush:

> Music is sweet from the thrush's thoat!
> Oh little thrush
> With the holy note,
> Like a footstep of God in a sick-room's hush
> my soul you crush.

That is engaging, but the note is still being struck fifty years later.

> o purple finch
> please tell me why
> this summer world (and you and I
> who love so much to live)
> must die

Finches, unlike thrushes, do not in fact sing; but this special bird, "eagerly sweet caroling," informs the poet that it would not be able to do so if it had anything to tell him. The early thrush poem seems an honest effort, but the purple finch has acquired a style quite incongruous with what it is required to say.

The young Cummings was clearly very bright and quick to learn, but unlike his master Pound he has no real intellectual curiosity, and little wish to understand other sorts of art than the ones he could make use of. Unlike most good poets he was inarticulate in a critical context. His attempt in the 1920s to write about T. S. Eliot's poetry for the *Dial* had to be rejected after he had produced a few comments on the level of "this is one of the few huge fragilities before which comment is disgusting." His prefaces to his collections make embarrassing reading, and are not unlike Dylan Thomas's comments on his own verse. In the 1950s Cummings too became a great draw on the poetry-reading circuit, his Peter Pan charm making a special appeal to female students. But he was happiest whittling away in the Wendy house at Patchin Place, Greenwich Village, or at Joy Farm, the New Hampshire holiday home of his parents.

In a political sense he was equally naïve. He had met and admired Aragon in Europe, and in 1931 translated his laborious (and unpunctuated) long poem *Front Rouge*: it is hard to say whether the translation or the original is the more *ennuyant* today. Cummings's own visit to the Soviet Union where he had no one to look after him, was such a chapter of minor accidents and misfortunes that he does not seem to have had time for any of the larger statements of retrospective admiration or disillusion customary among writers at the time: he was too busy recording the minutiae of what happened to him. Late in life, in 1956, he produced a little poem about the martyrdom of Hungary which must have brought a blush for poetry to the cheek of W. H. Auden, if he ever read it (it is instructive to compare Auden's own succinct poetic comment on the event: "The ogre does what ogres can . . ."). On the other hand the poem beginning:

> 16 heures
> L'Etoile
> the communists have fine eyes

is highly memorable because it uniquely and effectively registers a chaotic, child's-eye impression of the genuine Cummings sort. It is the difference between the private and public face, the public and private comment. Poets march against the Bomb and make their own protests, but Cummings's public announcement that he could "never forgive" President Truman for dropping the bombs was merely absurd. It sounds like a small boy who says he will never forgive you for sneaking off with his pencil sharpener. After which he would soon recover what Cummings artlessly referred to as his "natural buoyancy of spirits."

Not unnaturally, father figures were important to Cummings. His own father was a remarkable man, a self-made Baptist minister who became influential in cultural circles in Cambridge and Boston and well known throughout the United States for his writings and the causes he sponsored. He also made a fair amount of money. He was obsessively devoted to his son, to whose interests as an artist, writer, and erratic husband he devoted himself tirelessly; but he was also anxious to keep Cummings permanently captive in the family on a regular allowance. Cummings had to escape from this overpowering solicitude, but he never escaped very far, and he always hero-worshipped his father ("He is a famous man whereas I am a small eye poet") and ran for help to him in crises. He was also very close to a warm and sympathetic mother, the closer after his father, motoring up to New Hampshire, was killed by a train on a level crossing in a snowstorm: his mother survived with a fractured skull.

The oedipal experience finally liberated Cummings, and significantly stabilized his own private life. Of his three beautiful wives, the only one who responded to and got on with his mother was the third, Marion Morehouse, an ex-model and failed actress, and she and Cummings remained happily married until his death in 1962. Elaine Thayer, his first wife, was also socially the grandest, a demurely dazzling little rich girl, married to the young millionaire dilettante Scofield Thayer, who admired Cummings's verses at Harvard, became his first patron, and sent a check for a thousand dollars for the epithalamion Cummings wrote for his wedding. (Cummings senior was greatly displeased.) Thayer took an emancipated view of marriage, lived in a bachelor penthouse, and neglected his wife, who inveigled Cummings into a kind of Peter Pan and

Wendy affair, as a result of which a daughter was born. After divorce and remarriage to Cummings, Elaine reverted to type and became disenchantedly toughminded, soon going off with an Irish banker. For many years Cummings was denied access to his daughter, who grew up not knowing he was her father. Cummings went from frying pan to fire: his second wife was a demonic lady who when in liquor, as she usually was, complained loudly and publicly about the small size of his penis.

These facts about Cummings's life are not unusual, given the time and the milieu he moved in, but they have no relation to the poet and his poetry. We cannot feel, as we do with most imaginative writers, that the life helps us to see more deeply into the art, to understand it better. This might be a sign that the art itself is inferior, but in Cummings's case we can hardly say that. Most bad art is an involuntary pastiche of what was going at the time: his is certainly not. He was a genuine original, like John Crowe Ransom, who has also been the subject of a big biography, Thomas Daniel Young's *Gentleman in a Dustcoat*. The charm of both books is that they could in a sense have been written about anybody, and their accumulation of careful, often pedestrian detail is interesting in itself rather than for the light it throws upon the subjects. They are "pure" biographies, like an old-time Bradshaw. Ransom was of course different, a Southern gentleman, a scholar, golfer, and quietly devoted family man. A hood seems to cover his personality; nothing can be flushed out from the darkness under it, and—as in the case of Cummings's more conventionally rackety life—there was probably nothing much there. The main interest of Ransom's biography is in the group of critics and poets with whom he was associated.

With both, the talent for composing a "closed" kind of poetry seems independent of the nature of the poet, even seems to act as a substitute for it. Both live in the ponderous past, encased in solid Victorian three-decker jobs which might have been composed about the time George Eliot died and bespoken by the family of an influential bishop. As we move on from winter engagements to summer vacations ("there was some talk of their going again to Bangor that year but in the event they did not"), we marvel at the meticulousness of the research (Cummings's Aunt Jane left him seventeen thousand, four hundred, and twenty-three dollars and sixty-four cents) and come to love it for its own sake. The tone, a little owlish in its reverence for the past, seems as appropriate to the vanished 1930s as art deco. It is with this sort of decorum that Richard S. Kennedy discovers for us that the Cummingses sometimes stayed in the summer with Max Eastman and his wife at Martha's Vineyard, and that the Eastmans "had a private beach that allowed nude bathing. Marion especially enjoyed it, for, proud of the beauty of her body, she liked to share it with intimate friends." A grainy photograph shows nice faces, teeth, and smiles, but discreetly cuts out anything below them.

Even Cummings's experience in France in the First World War—experiences that led to the writing of *The Enormous Room*—become part of the family archive. His duties were limited to washing down ambulances behind the lines, and even there he behaved so irresponsibly that he and a fellow delinquent were sent to a detention center for dubious foreigners and minor offenders. This was like a mad school, which suited Cummings exactly. He loved the misfits there—"delectable mountains" as he calls them—and his lively account of the place is still highly readable. Despite the occasional tedium of the macaronic style, its vision of excremental innocence still survives while *Three Soldiers*, the more painstaking war novel by Cummings's friend Dos Passos, has become hardly more than a curiosity.

At its best, *The Enormous Room* has the clear ebullient vividness which Cummings got from his hero Joyce: in 1918 bits of *Ulysses* were appearing in *The Little Review*, where he found them shortly after he had also discovered Pound. The poem that came as a revelation to him was *The Return* ("Slow on the leash, pallid the leash-men!"), and he wrote soon afterward a poem which, however much it owes to the classical aura of Pound, HD, and imagism, is unmistakably his own.

> Tumbling-hair
>   picker of buttercups
>   violets
> dandelions
> And the big bullying daisies
>   through the field wonderful
> with eyes a little sorry
> Another comes
>   also picking flowers.

The iconography of the Dis and Persephone story ("herself a fairer flower") is compressed into a new and successful form. From his Harvard days Cummings had a grounding in the classics—a considerably better one than Pound—and a good teacher had encouraged him to attempt translations, both free and exact. His technical breakthrough, which still owed much to Pound and was probably not consciously arrived at, was the discovery that the same idiom would fit any situation. Joyce's grand style adapted itself deliberately to the meanest context, and Cummings's miniatures learned to do the same. A simple example is one of the "Portraits" in *Tulips and Chimneys*, "i walked the boulevard":

> i saw a dirty child
> skating on noisy wheels of joy
>
> pathetic dress fluttering
>
> behind her a mothermonster
> with red grumbling face
>
> cluttered in pursuit
>
> pleasantly elephantine
>
> while nearby the father
>
> a thick cheerful man
>
> with majestic bulbous lips
> and forlorn piggish hands
>
> joked to a girlish whore
>
> with busy rhythmic mouth
> and silly purple eyelids
>
> of how she was with child.

There is here the same dependence on a neat "point" which marks all Cummings's successful poetic contraptions, though the point may build up in the poem's shape and not be sprung in the last line. There are contexts, like the "war" poems and the semi-political squibs where such a point will not work, and where Cummings's cute cursory innocence does not answer. But point can come in the form of an excellent descriptive conceit, like the sky in "Impressions II," first resolved "by the correct fingers of April" into "a clutter of trite jewels,"

> now like a moth with stumbling
>
> wings flutters and flops along the
> grass collides with trees and
> houses and finally
> butts into the river.

Himself a painter and draftsman, though of no great originality or power, Cummings at his verbal best often suggests the painterly techniques of the impressionists and post-impressionists and their admiration for Japanese art. His verse in fact is at its best when it draws attention not to its own words but to the picture they are bringing into existence. That is the kind of observation that would mean nothing in connection with most poetry, but with Cummings there can be a real sense of space between the words on the page and the mental images evoked. In the best poems, and the ones that best stand rereading, we seem to slip straight into the mental images. The zestful verbal capers, anthology pieces such as "anyone lived in a pretty how town," have a short reading life: their verbal substance is not of the kind that survives prolonged acquaintance. The poetry is at its worst when the verbal and sentimental are made to play engaging games together, as in "my father moved through dooms of love" or "sons of unless and children of almost."

This indicates a matter of great importance in relation to Joyce's verbal art. *Finnegans Wake* not only remains wholly and eerily alive but it can move us deeply in the simplest way. Joyce has in a sense found the modern way of doing what Dickens did in relation to crossing-sweepers and the deaths of children and Barkis going out with the tide and David

Copperfield's vision of his mother holding up her baby in her arms. Cummings often seems to be looking for the modern way of doing such things, and not finding it. It is of course invidious to compare a great writer with a minor verbal artist, but the point is nonetheless a valid one. Cummings almost never moves us: he is his own child, too self-absorbed.

Almost never, but he approaches tenderness sometimes, as in the "etcetera" poem, in which the word falls through successive slots of meaning—a way of dismissing sentiment, of pushing detail impatiently aside, evading parental exhortation, shrugging off oneself and one's dreams— until it falls into its final and tenderly intimate meaning, all the more tender and intimate for being a euphemism and earning a capital letter.

> (dreaming,
> et
> cetera, of
> Your smile
> eyes knees and of your Etcetera).

In general, though, Cummings has none of the artist's sensitivity to the outside world and to the reality of other people and their responses. Nothing shows this more clearly than a small poem which must upset friends and fellow artists, the non-Jews, as is the way with such things, more than the Jews themselves.

> a kike is the most dangerous
> machine as yet invented
> by even yankee ingenu
> ity (out of a jew, a few
> dead dollars and some twisted laws)
> it comes both prigged and canted

—"pricked and cunted" in the original version, which had to be bowdlerized when submitted to the *Quarterly Review of Literature*. It appeared in 1950 in the collection *Xaipe*, published by Oxford University Press after Cummings's American publishers had declined to continue making losses on his work.

Despite remonstrances Cummings insisted on including it, whipping out his smallboy reaction and protesting that a kike was not a Jew but an American hybrid, which was the point of the poem, and citing his recent experiences in Hollywood ("a wailing wall for Christians") where he had endeared himself to no one and failed to obtain employment. Many Cummings poems, especially in the *Xaipe* volume, are wishfully satirical, but to be effectively bitter a satirist must be involved. Memorable open poetry is subversive in its very nature, but a closed poetry cannot go out to subvert. Shock words like "kike" and "nigger" do not quite seem quaint, however, even in our unshockable era; liberal America minded them very much, and perhaps would still do so. The real trouble is that they point to something mean—in both the American and the English sense—in the poet's satiric impulse. As his biographer shrewdly observes, Cummings could only see the world as directed at him and "emblematic" of his situation. So does everyone at times, poets particularly, but while poets like Yeats and Lowell return by this very process to the universal, Cummings remains in his own area of smallness.

Out of it come his own special effects, which are certainly like no one else's. He is a poet for do-it-yourself readers, and the best criticism of his poetry, like Norman Friedman's *E. E. Cummings: The Art of His Poetry*, takes a technical and structural line and gets down to close analysis of the typography. This collected edition is austerely and beautifully produced, without notes or introduction, but these are not missed. There are felicities every few pages and once in a while a whole poem that succeeds. Cummings's own way of treating the mythological flourished and persisted: one of the best poems that he wrote toward the end of his career, harking back to the Persephone piece, recounts the tale of Venus, Vulcan, and Mars, and the laughter of the gods when the lovers are taken in the artificer husband's web:

> my tragic tale concludes herewith:
> soldier, beware of mrs smith.

The Times Literary Supplement, 1982

36

Lowellship

Robert Lowell (1917–1977)

Robert Lowell: Essays on the Poetry
edited by Stephen Axelrod and Helen Deese

Collected Prose
by Robert Lowell, edited and introduced by Robert Giroux

IF ROBERT LOWELL had not been a Lowell would he ever have had
the confidence to write the poems he did? It is impossible to imagine
the scion of a distinguished English family using that family now as a
basis for poetic composition. But all Lowell's poems are about being a
Lowell, or rather, more specifically, about being this Lowell. Only in the
home of democracy, probably, could the personality of the poet as aristocrat be asserted today in this fashion.

It is an irony which strikes deeper with each rereading, and the realization of it comes each time to seem more important to the status and
success of the poems. It is the regal touch. *Life Studies* are Lowell studies, in the same way that a prince of the blood might become absorbed,
without either self-consciousness or false modesty, in compiling an intimate dynastic chronicle. The word "Lowell" occurs and recurs in the
same spaciously necessary way. The Poet's father wears his "oval Lowell
smile" as naturally as a Hapsburg his lip; and there is a casual, humorous
assumption of *lèse-majesté*, as between poet and reader, in the news that
the poet's mother's coffin had the misspelled name "Lovel" on it when it
was sent home from Italy. Doubtless that was put right before the coffin

took it place in the family vaults. In terms of solid pomp Schonbrunn or the Escorial have nothing on the funerary monuments of an American Cemetery.

The irony multiplies when the Lowell entourage is considered. Every difficult poet has his devoted following, but even so Lowell's case is remarkable. Those who were in attendance upon him found it natural to look on egocentric follies or irresponsibilities as acts of heroic virtue, a testament to the wonderful fact that America had produced what was once seen in Europe as civilization's diadem: a great poet who was also a patrician. Whereas a noble lord who wrote verse could scarcely be conceived as being more than a figure of fun in contemporary English circles, the rhapsodies which greeted Lowell's early poems in the American press surely indicated a deep if obscure feeling that the United States had, in the cultural sense, finally arrived. More than one contributor to the collection of essays on his poetry refers dryly to the headlines in the American press ("MOST PROMISING POET IN 100 YEARS") which greeted the publication of *Lord Weary's Castle* in 1946, and remarks on the total indifference of the popular publicity machine in America to the achievements of other new American poets.

Lowell himself deepens the ironies. What an extraordinary analogy to take with his poetry, that of Vermeer, and Vermeer's paintings and interiors! One of the editors, Helen Deese, writes a highly perceptive essay on the relation of Lowell's poetry to the visual arts, but she seems to take it for granted that the Vermeer analogy invoked, for example, in Lowell's "Epilogue" is a natural and normal one. It seems to me nonsensical, one of the most blatant indications of Lowell's kingly habit of assuming he owned the country.

> Pray for the grace of accuracy
> Vermeer gave to the sun's illumination
> Stealing like a tide across a map
> To his girl solid with yearning

Those lines seem to me not only bad but remarkably vulgar as well, with the sort of involuntary vulgarity which upper class assumptions of universal ownership entail. "Solid with yearning" is an almost perfect description of something in Lowell himself, but merely makes a graffiti scribble across the simple mystery of *Woman in Blue Reading a Letter*. Vermeer is the reverse of a king; his art the very opposite of Lowell's credo that "the artist's existence becomes his art." Vermeer's pictures are endlessly mysterious and commonplace precisely because the artist is not in them, has been able so completely to exclude himself. And this is the mystery which is wholly lacking in *Life Studies*. There is a final logic in the fact that Lowell's success in those wonderful poems is its own nemesis, a perfect verbal score—"twenty-twenty," like his father's vision. "Nothing is real until set down in words," and what is set down is the "living name." The grace of accuracy is not that of a Vermeer but of a superb photograph, the split-second reality which sums it all up. Lowell's eye in art is

> Fifty years of snapshots,
> The ladder of ripening likeness.

In his introductory essay Steven Gould Axelrod writes that "Lowell felt so personally contingent that he dedicated himself to a task of self-creation in an unfinishable discourse, spent his life pushing across the borders of his previous texts, lived only in the ever-shifting frontier of an immanence he variously termed his 'style,' his 'voice,' his 'texts,' his 'poems,' his 'living name.'" Could a poet with any other name have done the same? Byron wrote "Byron" on the temple metope, and Byron is the name invoked by everything he wrote, and in the breast of every admirer. Invoking Milton's Satan, or Napoleon, or George III (in a long and elaborate poem), Lowell does not so much identify with those persons as cause them to appear in a new light as Robert Lowell. Who else could they be? What else could the poets and poems taken over in *Imitations* be? It is significant that Byron distinguished between himself as Byron and as a writer who, like Pushkin, another aristocrat, wrote for money and reputation. This separation of the social and the scribbling self ("I hate a fellow that's all author") is important to the persona of the European writer as aristocrat. Lowell is the first of the genre to need his status as an aristocrat while identifying wholly with it as a poet.

In his introduction to the *Faber Book of Modern American Verse* W. H. Auden pointed out that "every American poet feels that the whole responsibility . . . has fallen upon his shoulders, that he is a literary aristocracy of one, whereas a British poet can take writing more for granted, and so write with a lack of strain and over earnestness." From an aesthetic point of view this second attitude can be an asset to the reader, as it is to the viewer of Vermeer's pictures: he can feel that the poet or artist has a life of his own outside his art. It makes both for interest and for repose. Neither, in a way, is possible or relevant to Lowell's "living name," or to the seriousness with which it must be established. John Berryman as a poet was not so different, but it is extremely relevant that Berryman, like other self-creating poets, had to invent a persona—that of "Anne Bradstreet," or "Henry Pussycat"—in order to become his real self set down in words. Lowell had no need for that: his self and his persona were both absolute Lowell.

Yet he did share with his peers the general characteristics stated by Auden to be typical of American poets—an unremitting professionalism like that of crack golfers, tennis players, race-car drivers. It is this which makes their essays and criticism, their letters and public pronouncements, so strangely depressing. The reader eventually becomes fed up with "poetry," with the techniques and reputations of those who practise it, in the way he would if he were listening to the perpetual shop of experts who think and talk of nothing but their ruling passion, and their colleagues, in its practice. The thing to them is literally a matter of life and death; but it is also, paradoxically, totally a matter of the trade and the business. The great tycoons who shaped American material prosperity, and built their American fortunes, understood very well how it must be—and can only be—both. Axelrod quotes as high praise, and as something to which Lowell's censorious biographers pay too little attention, the words of his second wife, Elizabeth Hardwick. She said that "texts had been his life." A tycoon's widow might equally say, and in the same spirit, that "money had been his life." The sharpest point that Marjorie Perloff makes is to quote from Ian Hamilton's biography of Lowell, recalling his treatment of one of his mistresses, the Lithuanian dancer Vija Vetra, for whom he declared "undying love," and whom he set up in a Manhattan flat, rented in the name of Mr. and Mrs. Robert Lowell. A few weeks later she was summoned by Lowell's solicitor and told to quit the premises in two days. "Heartless, absolutely heartless" was Miss Vetra's not unjustified comment: "But that's the American way, Very ugly." Marjorie Perloff cannot resist remarking that the dancer "did not know who the Lowells of Boston were, and did not fully appreciate that her lover was a Great Poet." More to the point, perhaps, Lowell's behavior was not only that of a poet-king in disguise but that of a tycoon acting in the normal way.

Axelrod spends much of his introductory essay denouncing Ian Hamilton's biography of Lowell, while admitting its authority and its sense of what the Lowell legend is all about. I feel a good deal of sympathy for Axelrod's contention that the biography largely ignores the fact of genius, and its fruits, while cataloguing the bad behavior of the poet with an air of clinical detachment, and even a slight suggestion of English superiority. There does seem to be a kind of animus in Hamilton's account, and a tendency to imply that Lowell's manic periods, when an unbalanced cerebral chemistry drove him certifiably insane, were somehow his fault. George III was not, after all, responsible for his kingly porphyria. Yet madness had nothing to do with some of Lowell's more repellent traits: his casual bullying, that of the spoiled prince setting about the courtiers, or the bred-in-the-bone snobbishness which seems to have dictated at least one of his sudden matrimonial swoops. Against that, Lowell was surely more aware than most poets (more than Shelley, for instance) of his own failings, and his power of working through them is equally bred in the bone of his best poetry. If there was something rotten in him, his art confronts it, possibly even exploits it, but never merely exhibits it involuntarily.

Marjorie Perloff's essay, the most combative in the book, would not agree with that. She sees both Lowell and Berryman as unfree, in a way that American poetry should not be: cribbed and confined not so much by willful violence or compulsive neurosis, as by a fundamentally "un-American" social background "Both Lowell and Berryman were, in a curious way, perfect preppies. They had been to the right schools (St. Mark's for Lowell, South Kent for Berryman); they assiduously avoided Bohemia . . . and Lowell's brief 'rebellion' against Harvard, which brought him first to Vanderbilt and then to Kenyon, should not obscure the simple truth that he was, like Berryman, the ultimate Ivy Leaguer, the educated genteel intellectual who would spend a good portion of his life on campuses like Harvard or Princeton. Yet the other side of the preppie portrait is that of the Wild Man . . . the aggressively promiscuous macho poet." The social detail accumulated here is itself revealing, as if Perloff was giving all the evidence she could to place and pin them down in a way that could not be done with real American poets—Carlos Williams, Wallace Stevens, John Ashbery. She even places Lowell inside a critical trope. "The New Critical doctrine that every poem is a little drama built around a central paradox is . . . in the very fabric of their lives . . . especially Lowell, whose life is the emblem of New Critical tensions." He is the New England Puritan aristocrat who is also a relentless womanizer, the "Mayflower screwball" (a satisfying oxymoron out of Hamilton), the conscientious objector hectoring on about Hitler's "brilliance."

Now this is a very shrewd way to depreciate Lowell's achievement. Perloff is surely quite right to see that Lowell's life studies are also critical exercises; that he uses his complex social and personal status, as Hamlet might have done, to create living and lively metaphysical paradoxes. Newer critics than those of the New Criticism might say that he had no choice; that this is what literature is in any case all about; that Lowell willed his life into making the sort of poetry he had been taught to admire as a student—clever, metaphysical, and British. The heart of Perloff's attack is that Lowell lacks the Continental, Jewish-type cosmopolitanism proper to an American intellectual. He and Berryman were not continually excited by experiment, as American intellectuals ought to be. They show not "the slightest indication of interest in the dominant art movement of their time, Abstract Expressionism, or in its successors, Pop Art, Minimalism and Conceptual Art."

Bully for them, one might all irreverently feel. Those things represent American seriousness of another kind, and one which Lowell and Berryman, obsessed with the techniques of their own sport, had neither time nor inclination to study. In the same way Lowell's "politics" are really only cosmetic, a question of good manners. Perloff's reservations here are sound and need to be attended to. There is a strong feeling of the best school traditions in the behavior of the pair—win or lose, play the game to the limit—with Awful Behavior, and concentration on the poetic ball, as substitutes for the school code. "To have no outlet but the literary life on the campus or in the quarterlies is not as unconnected as it might seem to the endless cycle of broken marriages and mental breakdowns, alcoholism and suicide, that characterised the lives of what we might call the tragic generation of genteel posts." "Genteel" because never really involved, and (though Perloff specifically denies this) in much the same situation as earlier *poètes maudits* like Baudelaire, who had to manufacture their own hells, because life, war, politics had put them, as true participants, to one side. "We asked to be obsessed with writing," said Lowell, "and we were." And to Berryman he wrote about their troubles that "these knocks are almost a proof of intelligence and valour in us." How unimaginable that Wilfred Owen should have written such a thing from the trenches, but then he was pushed into being a poet by circumstances. Like Baudelaire, Berryman and Lowell had to make their circumstances: otherwise they would have decayed like their parents and their parents' friends into class-ridden depression.

Perloff concludes that the "Age of Lowell" has already vanished, because it marked "the end of an era rather than ushering in a new one," and this view is echoed by some other remarks quoted in the book. Young poets at poetry readings say that almost every other poet is "their contemporary," but not Lowell. Like Colonel Shaw of *For the Union Dead* he is "out of bounds" now, left behind like a museum exhibit, a period photograph, while abstract expressionism, or whatever its equivalent in ongoing American poetry may be, continues its fissiparous course. Is Lowell the victim of what he himself called "the bravado of perpetual revolution, breakthrough as the stereotype, with nothing preserved"? That, in a sense, would be a fit end for a king, remaining embalmed in the history books, in anecdotes, stories, and tableaux.

But it is not the impression one receives from the essays of the other contributors to this volume. One and all, they seize with old-fashioned avidity upon the facts in the poetry—the skunks and the cars and the localized despairs. George McFadden is particularly good on the diminished intimacies of the last *Day by Day* collection, and Alex Calder writes about the "process poems" of *History* and *Notebook*. All this criticism of the poetry has to center on its human and biographical aspect. There is a certain comedy in the way in which academics trained in modern methods have to come to terms with this, and do so with a sometimes grudging admission of continued admiration. "To enter any one of the poems," writes Sandra Gilbert, "was like entering a darkened, heavily curtained room where someone has been living a very long time with too many family relics. Dusty, sadly factual, sardonically circumstantial, they were like endless anecdotes told by an ancient mariner. Why did one continue to sit in the darkened parlour?" And she goes on: "That I then did not understand quite why I went on reading and rereading *Life Studies* even while I continued to pore (and that seems an appropriate word) over the grimiest details of the poems shows just how valuable an exercise continual rereading is. Because I think I know consciously now what I unconsciously intuited then: that Lowell's poems really were the aesthetic paradigms of the 'tranquillised Fifties,' poems of—yes—the mid-century, and this was one source of their almost perverse appeal." The critic is severely aware of what she not unjustifiably calls Lowell's "misogyny" in "Skunk Hour," though it takes a "secret, subtextual" form, but she nonetheless finds the poem "not just fearsome but, to be honest, rather wonderful." Shying away from the need for such an engaging conclusion, Albert Gelpi suggests, in what from the point of view of the higher criticism is a superb essay, that the best Lowell is the early Lowell of *Lord Weary's Castle*. There we have a genuine Emersonian metaphysical wrestle instead of the self-indulgence of *Life Studies*. The critic puts up an admirable case, yet it seems to be one that can only be designed for fellow scholars or advanced students; just as a poem like "Skunk Hour" can seem almost as if designed to be analyzed, in such circles, by the techniques of the highly advanced critic Riffaterre.

It is Sandra Gilbert, surely, who comes closest to what still has to be called the common reader's response to Lowell. That reader does indeed "pore" over the details, not with the "close reading" of the expert, but with the hooked absorption of, say, the Dickens or the Sherlock Holmes fan. Lowell appears himself to have been an ardent Dickensian, and the best things in what is otherwise a rather stagey unfinished essay he wrote on "Art and Evil" is an inspired commentary on Mrs. Gamp as a detailed "life study." There is certainly a Miss Havisham in the background of many of his poems. There is further irony in the fact that by now the common reader probably knows and cares little about the status of the Lowell family, and yet Lowell, with none of the inventive genius of Dickens, could not have become himself in the poems without it. As with Dickens (David Copperfield, Pip, "George Silverman's Explanation"), the detail in the writing has a strong diagnostic slant. Dickens's heroes, like Lowell, are seeking to explain their present selves: but with the important difference that such explanation for Dickens is itself connected with the romance of fiction and the fictionalized life. There is no such romance in Lowell's self-discovery. The knowledge of the self hoarded in the poems' compulsive details in "frizzled, stale, and small" ("Home After Three Months Away"). It is part of the power and originality of Lowell's self-presentation that, unlike almost all such presentations in writing, it contains no element of literary excitement. "Alas, I can only tell my own story" ("Unwanted") has a tone of parody, the parody of something obsessionally, in a sense boringly, true. Familiarity with Lowell is like the slightly sickening familiarity most people can remember having with someone at school, someone whose dottiness, tiresomeness, overbearingness, were accepted with fatalistic incuriosity. Although, as Sandra Gilbert says, the reader or rereader of middle and late Lowell does indeed continue to "pore" over the information the poems offer, it is not in the spirit of wonder or speculative inquiry.

Lowell has seen to that. The strange element of self-discovery, itself seemingly unfamiliar and unexpected by the poet, which reveals itself in the most characteristic poems of Edward Thomas, is wholly absent from the world of his poetry. So is the sense of easing himself, in the expression of grief or pleasure, which is natural to Hardy. No word could be less suitable for these Lowell effects than "confessional," which suggests outpourings and confidences. The poems are far too structured for that, and far too cunningly set up. Their closest analogue, in fact, seems to me with poems of Philip Larkin like "I remember, I remember" and "Dockery and Son." However different the Larkin atmosphere, there is a similarity in terms of bravado, shared relish, the turned-around humor of the trench. This is why, in the case of both poets, "serious" attention to their social and personal attitudes is beside the point.

In the cases of Edward Thomas and Thomas Hardy there is often an embryonic trace of the short story, something much more developed in some of Larkin's poems. The point of such a story is the degree of uncertainty about it, the poet's art being to leave in doubt just what some episode in his life meant and how it affected him. ("Well, it just shows how much, how little . . ." the poet in "Dockery and Son" reflects in a railway carriage before dozing off.) The story technique, with its build-up and dissolution into unresolved possibilities of meaning, is quite alien to Lowell's snapshots, which represent an advanced poetic technique for turning subject into object. The special interest here is the relationship of this technique nonetheless to the wry Larkin persona, and its distance from the "warm," simple, recollective writing—on mothers and fathers, uncles and aunts—of Seamus Heaney and some of the other Irish poets. Affection and recollection are too facile in them, making a too easy basis for a poem that may be beautifully crafted and expressed.

Lowell's later poems have by contrast the ghastly matter-of-factness of a psychiatric report. Possibility is swallowed up in unavoidable knowledge. And there is no difference between what that knowledge means and what the poem says. Lowell as unwanted child, and the mother who told him that when she carried him she wished she were dead, have ceased to be the kind of discovery that poems can make. But even this is an achievement which links with the rather different Lowell who used poetic rhetoric in an earlier poem as Byron, or as Larkin, might have done.

> Always inside me is the child who died,
> Always inside me is his will to die.

That makes a slight mockery of self-absorption, as so many of Larkin's poems more obviously do, bringing to mind the way Byron's lines at their most moving proclaim that grief is itself a form of rhetoric, like self-reproach or self-advertisement.

The final virtue of Lowell, like that of other poets who write about and reveal themselves, is that the reader's bosom returns an echo to what is "human, all too human." In spite of distaste for some of his ways of being himself in poetry, and boredom with his frenzies, the final effect—like that of Baudelaire's "Spleen," or the boredom of Larkin's nonexistent childhood holidays—is vivid and exact and compelling, alive as only good art can make things alive. His poetry can love, and learns to love, his parents, his relations, everything in his life. And these essays on him celebrate that fact. The big technical question still sticks out, however. The situation of Lowell's mother and father, and its effect on their son, are so boringly overfamiliar that if one were to meet it in Hampstead or

Hackney or the New York slums, treated in whatever genre by a writer from those backgrounds, it would almost certainly be even more boring. Can it be that Robert Traill Spence Lowell intuited that in his royal dynasty nothing was boring, and founded his poetic art on that equivocal fact? Can it be that he was right, and that art still endorses Aristotle's dictum that tragedy can only occur in a few good families? The marriage of a Lowell and a Winslow, like that of Agamemnon and Clytemnestra, may still be the right matrix for a rare kind of art?

The earliest piece printed in the *Collected Prose* is an essay on the *Iliad*, written when Lowell was eighteen and a senior at St. Mark's school. It is remarkable for its conciseness, good sense, and grasp of the issues: but even more for the effortlessness with which Lowell identifies with the hero, Achilles, and for the way in which he emphasizes the healing role of Thetis, the mother of Achilles. He concludes that after she has restored Hector's body "the strongest and most violent character in literature is once more at harmony with the world." Twenty years later, in the unfinished lecture on "Art and Evil," he is identifying in the same way with Rimbaud, with Grandcourt, the villain of George Eliot's *Daniel Deronda*, and with Milton's Satan. Grandcourt, the bored aristocrat, has "an inner life like a dentist's drill hitting a nerve twenty-four hours a day." More subtly, Lowell perceives that C. S. Lewis's new "brilliant scolding little book" on *Paradise Lost*, with its emphasis on a Satan who "really is diabolic . . . a creature sleeplessly thinking about himself, and one whose speeches are interminable autobiography," is actually an even more sympathetic hero to the modern reader than the old, defiant hero of Blake and Shelley.

These intuitions are based on identity, and are the critical cousins of Lowell's autobiographical pieces, "91 Revere Street" and "Near the Unbalanced Aquarium." These are superb: the first cherishes Lowell's parents as a literate Achilles might have cherished Patroclus and Thetis. His own comments on "Skunk Hour" are less satisfactory, a bit of a show-off, a relaxed tale the king tells his ministers, although the boasting way of revealing a debt to a verse of Hölderlin, or of Annette von Droste-Hulshoff, is a revealing kind of kidding on the level. No doubt such moments in arcane foreign poems, or random unused images like the famous "blue china door-knob," are where "real poetry came from," rather than from "fierce confessions." Like other great poets, Lowell can absorb literature invisibly and make it look like more than life. What he steals invisibly in this way is infinitely more precious than what he took over openly in *Imitations*. In terms of literary reference "Skunk Hour," that fabulous poem, is the "Xanadu" of our day. Yet the Lowell family itself was a more potent inspiration than any literature.

This in itself disables Lowell as a critic. He treats other writers with wary courtesy; he pretends to be someone else, much more judicious; he forfeits the manic precision with which he pursued family anecdotes and humiliations. In a sense, he becomes almost like Byron despising a fellow that's all author. And yet not so, for no one could have flung himself more determinedly into the milieu, and identified more with that almost gay, charmed, doomed circle—John Berryman, Randall Jarrell, Delmore Schwartz, Peter Taylor. They are written about not as authors but as friends, or, like T. S. Eliot and John Crowe Ransom, avuncular elders to be lovingly gossiped about. Eliot, on their second meeting, asked him if he didn't hate being compared with his relatives? "I do." There followed a reference to a review in which Edgar Allan Poe had "wiped the floor" with two Eliot forebears. "I was delighted."

When he gets outside the circle Lowell can be very shrewd. The best criticism, also one of the earliest, is a short piece on Wallace Stevens written in 1948. A master with very different method, and Lowell diagnoses it instantly, in relation to the way he feels he must come to write himself. He saw that the emperor of ice cream often had no clothes, and that delight in the way his poetry after *Harmonium* "juggles its terminology with such lightness and subtlety" does not conceal its appearance on rereading as "muddled, thin and repetitious." Few poets of Stevens's stature "have tossed off so many half-finished improvisations . . . there seems to be something in the poet that protects itself by asserting that it is not making too much of an effort."

Lowell's poetry always seeks to make that effort, to score absolutely, to be solid, old-fashioned stuff that would, so to speak, have rebounded from Dr. Johnson's toe had he kicked it. The fashion in American poetry that Stevens represents, that Marjorie Perloff praises by implication, evades the personal as it evades the fact. "Cloudy, cloudy are the stuff of stones," wrote Richard Wilbur about Johnson's kick. If Lowell's factuality, like his status, is un-American, then the American poets of today are those who, like John Ashbery, are without this kind of substance, living syntactically among shadows, anonymous and generalized feelings and beings, subway sensations. Such a poetry is as original as Lowell's and expresses the common lot as effectively as his can, though from a different premise and by a different method. Lowell, like Larkin, is unique, and his very uniqueness makes him unfashionable today: it means that his lines have to be studied not like seminar poetry but like a royal family tree.

London Review of Books, 1987

37

"One Life, One Writing"

James Merrill (1926–1995)

A *Different Person: A Memoir*
by James Merrill

Selected Poems: 1946–1985
by James Merrill

A LITERARY CATEGORY much more common in Europe than in
America depends on its unliterary charm: the author seems to
take being a writer as a purely social phenomenon, without either
the trouble of a sought-for vocation or the wish to make money by writing books. He writes as he might eat good food, wear good clothes, visit
the right people and the right places. Sometimes a writer like Byron or
Pushkin, who half despises the medium his genius compels him to work
in, makes a nostalgic gesture toward the other sort of gentlemanly life he
would half prefer to be living. "I hate a fellow who's all author," said
Byron, with feeling, longing in patrician disdain to stand apart from the
inky tribe.

The opposite attitude toward the literary vocation—or was it really
quite the opposite?—was taken by Robert Lowell when he spoke of himself in a poem as "one life, one writing." One suspects that what Lowell
really meant was that his life was so absorbing to him—its ancestry, its
relationships, its social detail—that he knew as if by instinct that it must
be more important to others than anything else. The sheer confidence of
Life Studies is more than regal. And it comes, in the last resort, from

assumptions that royalty or aristocracy make about themselves. Or used to make. Today there is bound to be a faint air of the *ancien régime* about any writing of the sort one finds in *Life Studies*.

The same air of confidence hangs rather bewitchingly about the memoir by James Merrill, who was himself of course, with his well-to-do family, not far from the world of Robert Lowell. Lowell might himself have recognized, I suspect, the sheer ease with which Merrill's memoir begins, the endearing lightness and self-confidence which has absolutely no need for defense or aggression, no need to explain or to apologize for itself.

> Meaning to stay as long as possible, I sailed for Europe. It was March 1950. New York and most of the people I knew had begun to close in. Or to put it differently, I felt that I alone in this or that circle of friends could see no way into the next phase. Indeed, few of my friends would have noticed if the next phase had never begun: they would have gone on meeting for gossipy lunches or drinking together at the San Remo on MacDougal Street, protected from encounters they perhaps desired with other customers by the glittering moat, inches deep, of their allusive chatter. I loved this unliterary company; it allowed me to feel more serious than I was. Other friends, by getting jobs or entering graduate schools, left me feeling distinctly less so. On the bright side, I had taught for a year at Bard College, two hours by car from MacDougal Street. My first book of poems had been accepted by the first publisher I sent it to. And I had recently met the love of my life (or so I thought), who promised to join me in Europe in the early summer.

A different phase, a dedicated, literary, unsocial phase, is about to begin, but the reader already knows that it won't go as planned. And the writer knows that the reader knows. The Jamesian charm of this opening depends on the immediacy of this relationship, so swiftly and unerringly established, as much as on what seems the wholly natural felicity of the writing. (The fact that the "glittering moat" should only be "inches deep," where the metaphor seems to call for something much more hyperbolical, is just one instance of this unobtrusive felicity.)

And so begins Europe, and psychoanalysis, and a long affair with Claude, unagonizing and affectionate, with all the implications of that "or so I thought"; and the round of rich Americans in Rome. It is like eating a dish which has taken someone time and trouble to prepare, but whose deliciousness depends on its simplicity and lack of pretension. And the "phase" is always the same phase: "one life, one writing," again though in a very different style from Lowell's. The "unliterary company" too is a blessing: such a relief from the contemporary climate of literature which is solely concerned with its own possibilities in being literature.

Merrill's memoir is in one sense as simple as a diary in which events appear to lead their own lives, as it were, and to be greeted in passing by the author's unfailing sense of good manners. Even an acute attack of dysentery in the Greek islands is treated by the author with his usual exquisite politeness; and the treatment given in Athens by white nuns and French-speaking doctors is described as meticulously and courteously as the beautiful little needle case given him quite casually one day by a friend who has had it since she was a child. He is never intense, never anxious: if he has any anxiety at all it seems to be the fear of boring the reader, and right from the first page we know that is not likely to happen. For one thing he is easily bored with himself, by himself; and that goes with his sunny lightness of touch, and his sense of humor.

So he starts dreaming about "poor plain pious Mademoiselle," who had been his governess in his childhood, and had boarded out her own daughter in East Hampton the better to care for him. "At nine and ten, when my mother's troubles gave her scant time for me, I transferred, day by day, more and more love to this good soul." One day he made the mistake of telling her he loved her more than his mother, and after that nothing was quite the same again. When his parents separated, "it was felt that I could do with masculine supervision." A young Irishman was hired— "handsome as Flash Gordon"—but this was a failure. The youthful Merrill behaved so badly that the young man gave up ("and how badly in that Depression year he must have needed the job"). Through slitted eyes the author used to watch him undress, as he had with Mademoiselle, and he had often ached to lie in the arms of both of them.

The past is certainly a foreign country, as the English novelist L. P.

Hartley observed, where they do things differently. Merrill's formidable mother, who came intensely to resent her son's homosexuality, seems to have made every mistake in the book. Or don't the upper classes ever make mistakes, by definition? Merrill is hilarious about his psychiatrists, though not exactly unkind, and they are only wheeled on for a few deft moments. The Irishman supplanted Mademoiselle, but Dr. Detre urges his patient to remember that she had originally been hired "to supplant your mother, so that *she* would have more time to attend to your father's needs." But what about his father? By seeking custody after his parents' divorce, "hadn't he aimed at taking my mother's place himself?" (" 'We're getting warm!' Dr. Simeons would have exclaimed; Dr. Detre let me find my own footholds.") But wait—hadn't he become a supplanter himself—"according to an appendix in *Webster's Collegiate Dictionary*, my very name, James, meant 'the supplanter' "—and what about Mademoiselle's little daughter, boarded out in East Hampton? What, come to that, about the nice young Italian police cadet, Luigi, whose fiancée he's attempting to supplant? Such people flicker in and out of the pages with extraordinary vividness but they don't appear for long. As for this supplanting caper, after his visits to the psychiatrist, "Reaction set in on the bus home. How deeply, how unspeakably, such perceptions bored me."

Dr. Simeons and Dr. Detre continue to appear occasionally, like the comic couple in a film, and they are always welcome. Once the author told Dr. Simeons the following true story. After their marriage in 1925, his parents lived in a brownstone on West Eleventh Street in New York. "By autumn my mother was, as they used to say, 'expecting'—her close friends already knew the thrilling news." The expectation was of course of young Merrill. One day an ex-beau named Frank Huckins, who was shortly getting married himself, came to tea. As the butler showed him in, Mrs. Merrill got up with deliberate awkwardness (she was only three months pregnant) and taking his hand pressed it against her stomach. The young man was aghast as "his palm sank into a deep, unnatural softness." Smiling mischievously she removed the down pillow she'd stuffed into her dress. When Dr. Simeons heard about this "his face was a study, his laugh reluctant." Not surprisingly perhaps: but the psychiatrists must at least have discovered that the young man had inherited his mother's sense of humor. I've always wanted to write a pillow book, he told Dr. Simeons.

Dr. Detre (he lived in Rome) was especially exercised when Robert turned up. He and Merrill had become lovers ("Over meals we talked inventively, self-delightingly—no tense misunderstandings, no restful silences"). But when Robert left for home (his grandfather had died: his mother needed him), the doctor was inclined to fear that his patient had been "creating a duplicate self out of Robert." A different person again. But was that so bad? Wouldn't he be learning to love himself?

> "No doubt. But there is only so much to gain from paying court to
> the mirror."
> "None of it gained by the mirror . . ."
> "Regrettably so. It is a onesided transaction."

When Robert left, Merrill got down to his translations of two poems by Eugenio Montale. He allows us here a quick glimpse of the hard professional within. It didn't matter that he had to look up most of the words in an Italian dictionary; the "essential failure" lay, he felt, in the realization that he was not yet a complete master of his own language. Montale, Rainer Maria Rilke, or Pablo Neruda do a lot of accidental harm to the budding poet, he ruefully concludes, by encouraging a sort of "baby talk" in them, based on the accessibility of a user-friendly version of these great poets.

W. H. Auden, that more openly tough egg, would certainly have agreed. At one point in the memoir there is an inspired recollection of his talk, and the kind of things he said. Auden is introduced characteristically, on a visit to Athens. "Catching sight of me, he smiles. Although we aren't yet the intimates we shall become after his death, he approves of my work and fancies that I exemplify moderation to Chester." (If so, to no avail alas, for Chester Kallman continued in his undefiant good-natured way an indefatigable pursuit of *evzones*, the Greek kilted soldiers.) Auden meets Merrill's friend Maria Mitsotaki—"the closest I'll ever get to having a Muse"—and is soon expounding to her his views on the shortcomings of Latins. "They can't be bothered to learn our language, they've no conception of culture, ours or theirs. I mentioned guilt in a talk I once gave in Rome, and it was translated over the earphones as gold leaf. South of the Alps guilt has only its legal or criminal sense. The rest is all *bella figura.*"

Arguably, and on the evidence of the *Selected Poems*, Auden was a better companion poet for Merrill than Robert Lowell. One cannot say more inspiring, because from his earliest volume Merrill's verse was in its own way much too sure of itself to need such an inspiration. But he did indeed become intimate with Auden "after his death," and the result can be seen in such a masterly poem as "The Blue Grotto," from the 1985 collection, *Late Settings*. With its elegance and its dry but wholly forgiving humor the piece is pure Merrill. Everyone knows about the grotto. "That often sung impasse. / Each visitor foreknew." So how to confront the real spectacle?

> But here we faced the fact.
> As misty expectations
> Dispersed, and wavelets thwacked
> In something like impatience,
> The point was to react.

The boatload react in their different ways. Don "tested the acoustics / With a paragraph from Pater." "Jon shut his eyes—these mystics," and thought about his mantra.

> Jack
> Came out with a one-liner,
> While claustrophobiac
> Janet fought off a minor
> Anxiety attack.
>
> Then from our gnarled (his name?)
> Boatman (Gennaro!) burst
> Some local, vocal gem
> Ten times a day rehearsed.
> It put us all to shame:

The astute sob, the kiss
Blown in sheer routine
Unselfconsciousness
Before one left the scene . . .
Years passed, and I wrote this.

The weight on the word "unselfconsciousness", the deft and comprehensive modesty of the conclusion, and the frown of memory in the first line of the last verse which produces Gennaro's name triumphantly in the second—these are the sorts of felicities not lightly achieved by any poet. In aggregate they produce the comprehensive grace of a long poem like *The Changing Light at Sandover*, or the shorter "Bronze," which has its origin in the 1972 discovery, by a skin diver off the Calabrian coast, of an arm thrust upward from the sandy bottom. It proved to be a Greek original, a god in bronze, but so encrusted with lime and silica that it took nine years to restore in Florence.

With characteristic acuteness the distinguished poetry critic Helen Vendler has observed that the "puns, ambiguities and the stanzaic shapes of English" have been used by Merrill as Matisse used the flat motifs of Muslim decorated art. The analogy sounds apposite but rather too heavyweight: Merrill's lines are in fact as engagingly devoid of the repetitive as they are of compression or concentration. They "save themselves," as the French say, by a lightness of touch that Auden must have envied, and that is indeed one of his own special trademarks. (Incidentally Auden would have absolutely agreed with Dr. Simeons, author of *Man's Presumptuous Brain*, still to be found in "holistic bookstores," that every physical symptom—those of piles for example—is in fact psychological.)

Perhaps Merrill's least successful verses are those which recall Lowell's *Life Studies*, for Lowell etched every apparently throwaway line of those as deeply as an engraving. For Merrill, on the other hand, the significant gift of his teens was a Ouija board. It "put me in touch with a whole further realm of language." Messages were arresting from the start.

. . . born in Cologne
Dead in his 22nd year
Of cholera in Cairo, he had KNOWN

NO HAPPINESS. He once met Goethe, though.
Goethe had told him PERSEVERE.

"These lines, for all their parlor-game tone, turn out to be as crucial to my poetry as Aeschylus's bringing on-stage an 'answerer' . . . was to the development of Greek drama. Two voices—my narrative one in lower case, the young German ghost's in upper—together compound the cozy lyric capsule. A promising start . . ." Certainly, and by a clear paradox a "cozy" one, but Dr. Detre did not wholly approve. Another "different person" had become involved.

The most vivid glimpse of all in this undeniably enchanting memoir is of the author's father, "silver-haired, his round face lightly tanned, a small, compact figure in smart clothes." Both clearly felt deep affection for each other, enhanced when traveling together in Italy by the absence of other company, beyond that of nurse and valet. Father "dreaded the company of his third wife, for love of whom he'd left my mother, and her absence from the scene added measurably to the charm of Naples and its bay. That was merely a smoking volcano in the distance, not Kinta with her whims and irascible vapors." Kinta was to be compensated back in Southampton (" 'Don't count on it,' sighed my father") by twenty identical models of her favorite shoes, made by a cobbler on Capri.

The complications of family life among the very rich are all around us, but the reader never feels excluded. The secret of this book was brilliantly summed up by the critic and novelist Edmund White, who commented that Merrill has contrived in it "to trade in the family drama for the human comedy." In a sense he could only do that by becoming a different person, while remaining in fact always very much himself. Nor is A Different Person in any sense a shallow book. Its "glittering moat" can safely be reckoned in fathoms, not in inches.

The New York Review of Books, 1993

38

Richly Flows Contingency

John Ashbery (1927–)

Flow Chart
by John Ashbery

B ROWSING THROUGH the *Complete Poems* of that onetime whiz
kid of Soviet poetry, Yevgeny Yevtushenko, I found myself thinking that this is now the sound of poetry for the Soviet public at
large. When declaimed, it sounds right and natural, the proper noise that
a poet should make, just as Tennyson sounded in his own time, or Yeats
and Auden in theirs. Without having to use the obvious cliché that this is
what it means to be "a major poet," one could and should say that this is
what real achievement in a contemporary poet consists of: he has laid
down guidelines and made his mark on the language of the tribe.

John Ashbery is doing the same in America and in the English-
speaking world. His early poems and collections—*The Tennis Court
Oath, Rivers and Mountains*—still had the exoticism of new device and
a new speech, but his voice today is certainly that of "poetry" as she is now
spoken. It is an unemphatic though far from monotonous sound, combining courteously indeterminate distinction with a seeming unawareness of the old idea that poetry should be—as Auden once called
it—"memorable speech." Ashbery in his own way often *sounds* memorable, yet I should doubt if any of his readers actually carry any sequence
of his lines in their memories, or could recall more than a passing phrase.
At the same time his lines and sentences have the unusual ability to
weave themselves into the reader's mind, to take over his own silent

speech cogitations as a virus takes over and uses the cells of the body. Inside his own head the reader may begin to think and to talk like Ashbery, in the way that a reader fifty or sixty years ago might have been reciting bits of Auden in his head, and taking up for a moment, like Walter Mitty, their appropriate mental stance.

To have sounded, in poetry, the standard tones of the age, is no small feat. Philip Larkin talks in a poem of jazz being, when he was young, "the natural noise of good." Anything new by Ashbery has become for poetry the natural noise of now. A number of talented poets, Steven Vita in America and Mark Ford in England, for example, have begun to sound rather like him, achieving something of the same kind of gripping but unidentifiable monologue. Authoritative and subtly influential as it has become, Ashbery's natural voice leads us into shopping malls and to visiting the "mottled houseplants" sold to homemakers; to dreaming of a hyena or a great speckled hen and a number of other things that will not last out today, except, perhaps, in the words of this poet, or of others who have come to be like him.

> But the sum will get lost anyway
> in the crowd, unless drastic measures are taken. And who is to take
>   them?
> Because you, walking around comparison-shopping, are its
>   infrastructure
> and the only one who will bring it to the edge of a cross-section of the
>   people's imaginings.
> See, there might be already a little canopy over the pier
> but more likely not; it's still early in the season; the river's rank winter
>   smell
> still pierces the air's musky crevices; the grass isn't right and
> *there's too much pre-freshness. The real thing won't be around for days,*
>   *even weeks.*

The real thing will probably never be around, but that is not the point. Because we live in contingency, a poetry can be wholly contingent and yet make out of that very circumstance its own power to focus and to fascinate the reader's mind. Because we live in contingency, neither the spring nor anything else—as art—comes in the form in which we expect it. Previous dwellers in art, it may be, saw no need to recognize this, but continued to strive for what seemed essential and locate their consciousness in it. Today things seem different. In making its thing of this, Ashbery's poetry makes use of the way things seem in a manner seemingly close to styles of modern painting and music. Prose, as the matter of ordinary communication, cannot present itself wholly as a medium in the way that poetry and painting and music now can.

This evident, indeed obvious, quality of what he writes explains why Ashbery is baffled and (to judge from interviews) sometimes annoyed at the idea that there is any difficulty in his poetry. To be difficult a poem has to be about something; and the efforts of critics who are themselves baffled to produce a suitable subject matter—love, death, loneliness, angst—are all okay to a poet who says that any interpretation will do, and that he doesn't care what meaning his readers find there. Yet this seems a little disingenuous, for it is the special character of the poetry—compared, say, with that of Wallace Stevens—not to proffer but to block off the directions taken by meaning.

Is this a special trick? In a sense, yes. Ashbery's bland, undisturbing clarity has learned how to flow toward, between, and over meaning without rupturing the surface. The continuum diary, as he has called *Flow Chart*, free associates with the weather and thoughts about the past "and comes up with all kinds of extra material that doesn't belong—but does." The poetry is placid, even facile: even making a virtue of this facility, as it does of the contingent. No "intolerable wrestle with words and meanings," as for T. S. Eliot at his desk—Ashbery never seems to "work" apparently— but a sure, rapid, and effortless natural growth.

Flow Chart, a poem of more than two hundred pages, came into existence in about six weeks. Thought, letter, diary—and yet with communication left out, except in one vital respect. This natural noise of the present hypnotizes the reader and takes him over, or is taken over by him. How the stuff at its best can so grip and absorb—and *Flow Chart* is Ashbery's best poem in his own genre to date—is Ashbery's own trade secret.

If this facility is the key, it negates modernist insistence on the "mystery," the specialist or hermeneutic knowledge necessary to "read" new music or painting. And Ashbery must needs be less than popular in circles where this expertise is current. (An unusually pungent aside in *Flow Chart* says, "I will show you fear in a handful of specialists.") Nor does any kind of Zen intuitiveness seem apposite to the case. It is natural enough to claim, as Christopher Benfey has done in a review in *The New Republic*, that this poetry "makes enormous demands on the reader to assimilate it," and that "it's hard to say precisely what the poem is about" and "what flow it's meant to chart." Critics are rightly employed to get to the bottom of these things, but in the case of Ashbery does it matter? His equable flow certainly reminds us how challenging, how up-to-date with an assertiveness asking for the critical process, were Ezra Pound and William Carlos Williams and Wallace Stevens and all modernists in search of an exegete. The postmodernist in Ashbery seems to look for nothing but anonymous and invisible readers; and the transaction should not appear arduous, either to his readers or himself.

But the fact is that the technique associated with postmodernism can be seen to direct us, although probably with no consciousness of doing so, in contradictory ways. On the one hand the medium is the message: words, notes, paint their own separate thing. Asked if an object on the canvas was a man's back or front, Delacroix said it was neither—"*C'est la peinture*"—and that was long ago. Even before that Wordsworth needed to say that new things must create the taste by which they are to be judged. The see-saw between the demands of a new expertise and the proclamation of a new liberty is in motion all the time. Judgment suits Ashbery no better than interpretation, and yet of course something irrevocably and personally fastidious does emerge from the industrial process which digests his love of art deco and old B movies, and—to quote *Webster's* dictionary on the term—shows "the progress of materials through various stages by means of a manufacturing process." That "schematic diagram," claims the jacket copy, is "nothing less than the entire poem itself."

Industry is now old hat in poetry, but perhaps not quite in this sense. Ashbery's total and seemingly effortless absorption in the dense technology of modern living is a million years away from the days of the Thirties, when poets self-consciously made pylons stride across the uplands like nude giant girls. And yet Ashbery begins with "an emptiness / so sudden it leaves the girders whanging in the absence of wind." His "newness" has a long history behind it, a history of poetic properties broken down for recycling but suddenly reconstituted in unexpected and effective ways, to lie around like the stranded monster rotting in the reeds of Rimbaud's *Bateau Ivre*.

> Sad grows the river god
>   as he oars past us
> downstream without our knowing him: for if, he reasons,
> he can be overlooked, then to know him would be to eat him,
> ingest the name he carries through time to set down
> finally, on a strand of rotted hulks. And those who sense something
> squeamish in his arrival know enough not to look up
> from the page they are reading, the
> plaited lines that extend
> like a bronze chain into eternity. It seems I was reading
> something . . .

As with early Wallace Stevens there is a suggestion of romantic pastiche; which is natural enough, because from Poe to Mallarmé the romantic impulse in poetry was to avoid meaning (*Flow Chart* warns that "the force of meaning never extrudes") in its concentration on the aesthetically beautiful. Of course we, and Ashbery, know that meaning cannot be avoided; but the impulse remains interesting, for Ashbery is clearly in revolt against modern academic and deconstructive practices where poetry is concerned: against the whole apparatus of university English departments. Whether deliberately or not, those departments have downgraded the idea of responding to the "beauty" of poetry, presumably because it might be construed as an elitist approach, the suggestion of a gift possessed by WASPs with hereditary taste buds. No English department I know of now dares to assume that some students have no gift or taste for poetry.

Instead modern critical methods are designed to blur the possibility of such distinctions. Suitably trained, anybody can master the business of reading poetry. Enjoying it may be another matter. The instinct in Ashbery's poetry—the instinct of one who is essentially a born-again romantic and Victorian—is to rebuff the academic approach while at the same time steeping his poetry in the flow of "ordinary" experience, the banality of throwaway perception and being—lowering the tea bag into a mug, or standing around in a seersucker suit. Treated in this way it ceases to be banal. The drowned Lycidas, or Phlebas the Phoenician sailor, appear in pictures or used-car lots and are also ingested in the poem's grainy but exotic texture. If we have it, we have a taste for these things, and a taste for his poetry, as for all poetry, is something Ashbery rather magnificently takes for granted. It can seem like something halfway between reflective introspection and watching television.

> Voices of autumn in full, heavy summer;
> algae spangling a pool. A lot remains to be done, doesn't it?
> I haven't even begun to turn myself inside-out yet, and that
> has to precede even an informal beginning. Try making up those
>   childish itineraries we were once
> so apt at, and you'll see. Even my diary has become an omen to me,
> and I know how I'll have to go on writing it; it would be disappointed
> otherwise. And those days we have to get through! Afternoons at the
>   store,
> and when bluish evening, the color of television
> in a window high above the street, comes on, who has the strength to
> judge it all . . .

Sex makes charmingly evasive swirls and eddies in the movement, almost as a part of its humor, or of Auden's "secret clearings where the shy humiliations / Gambol on sunny afternoons." The poem can be very funny about the days (strangely enough its own days, for "we all live in the past now") when it seemed important to understand, to get things right, and (to quote Auden again) "make action urgent and its purpose clear."

> . . . maybe
>   these were the things
> they were saying then in the theater or writing about in novels so that
> people would understand and thereby save themselves a lot of trouble
> and floundering. In the unprincipled mire we walk about in today,
>   nobody bothers even

to warn you about the perils of white slavery (to cite an extreme example), but then again
nobody is forcing you to save yourself either.

Sex should be a way of not specifying; and that is what it becomes in the
poem, where it takes its proper place in the provinces of daydream. At the
same time the humor of *Flow Chart* ("stockings are of secondary importance") consists in the poem's full awareness that it is part of a *literary*
consciousness in which when "we are surprised yet not too surprised / By
every new, dimpled vista," we automatically feel—involuntarily dialing
Wordsworth—"I knew then that nature was my friend." Sex is a part, no
doubt the most important part, of a literary consciousness; and there is
charm in the fact that the word "dimpled" could refer to a momentary
impression of either sex as well as to the fact that even "nature" itself can
seem kind at times, when our thoughts are all moving agreeably and in
the right direction, as they do in *Flow Chart*. The poem is happy because
it charts the harmonious processing of daydream, as if "nature" had
become (as no doubt it has) a process in which mind and matter cooperate in a kind of complex industrial miracle.

There is indeed a mellowness in *Flow Chart*, as in Keats's "Ode to
Autumn," which has replaced the often disturbing unease and transparency of *Shadow Train* and *April Galleons*, in which poems like "Forgotten Sex" ("They tore down the old movie palaces . . .") enact the
fragility and fright of "transparent bricks / in particular dreams," and the
moment when consciousness yields to the present—"As it comes time to
stand up like a sheet of metal / in the blast of sunrise." *Flow Chart* locates
itself safely in the past, the haunt of consciousness, where it seems more
normal to wonder about white slavery than about AIDS.

The game, or trick, in *Flow Chart* connects with its curious air of
patrician safety and pleasantness, as if the author were absolutely sure of
himself, and displaying the villanelles and triple sestinas which are part
of his ornamentation in a spirit of pure courtesy, like Browning's duke
showing off his wondrous possessions. After the calculated angst and self-
conscious uncertainty thought proper in most contemporary poetry, Ashbery's frank and calm display comes as a great relief, as well as justifying
itself as a sign of mastery. As his art criticism, *Reported Sightings*, shows,

as well as his most famous poem, "Self-Portrait in a Convex Mirror," Ashbery has, as it were, looked into the existential question and the identity problem—as these affect art—and has disposed of them in a manner that befits this ringmaster of the romantic effect. Those once-fashionable ideas from Marx or Heidegger are used to build a new style of Victoriana, in which tableaux—like a girl's mind as she is being proposed to in the back of a car ("It was so *good*—and underneath I was saying, all men are rogues, but I guess I like them") climb up for a few well-put-together sentences and are dismantled. This is Ashbery's highly effective version of a romantic paradox which only the best poets of the genre can pull off. When A. E. Housman ends a poem "In all the endless road you tread / There's nothing but the night," or Auden promises that "In headaches and in worry / Slowly life leaks away," the reader feels positively bucked up, is given a new shot of *joie de vivre*; and the same thing happens to the punctilio with which Ashbery's lines celebrate the baroque reign of insufficiency and contingency.

It seems that Ashbery was an old-fashioned child, brought up on a farm and befriended, as if in an early Henry James story, by an elderly grandfather and a rich neighbor. He went to Deerfield Academy and thence to Harvard, where he was the contemporary of poets and writers like Robert Creeley and Robert Bly, Donald Hall and John Hawkes. For the New York school with whom he then became identified, poetry could be a close relative of painting and music, although the affinity of Ashbery's poetry with these other arts may now seem more notional and cosmetic than deeply integrated. But the Ivory Tower is one aspect of romanticism that means nothing to him. John Cage taught him that "whatever interruption happens is part of the piece of music." Answering the phone and talking to students are as much at home in the consciousness of his poetry as doing the chores in the office when he worked on *ArtNews*. He now teaches part-time at Bard College and lives much of the time near the Hudson in a house furnished to resemble his grandfather's.

Reviewing Ashbery's *Selected Poems* in *The New York Times*, the English poet James Fenton said, "There were times . . . when I actually thought I was going to burst into tears of boredom," and wrote of "this excursus into the meaning of meaningless." Significant perhaps, all the same, that Fenton made such boredom sound emotional and dynamic. It is part of the Ashbery paradox that boredom is as compelling as day-dream, the routine coming and going of consciousness as masterful as the deeds of an old-time extrovert film hero. The Bloomsbury critic Desmond MacCarthy, whose talk was the most fabled of his time, was once captured unbeknown to him by an early recording machine as he sat at the dinner table. Results were null: nothing seemed to make sense at all. And yet the talk *had* been fabulous. Ashbery's speech seems deliberately to play with and to court such an outcome: and to gain authority from making the challenge, by becoming the natural noise of the contingent present. Transformed this way we feel we too can speak it by a new style of romantic alchemy.

The New York Review of Books, 1991

PART V

Out of
Eastern Europe

39

The Power of Delight

Bruno Schulz (1892–1942)

Letters and Drawings of Bruno Schulz with Selected Prose
edited by Jerzy Ficowski, translated by Walter Arndt with
    Victoria Nelson

O NE ODD FEATURE of twentieth-century literature is a metamorphosis to childishness. Childhood had been a subject for great
literary artists—Wordsworth, Dickens, Tolstoy, Aksakov, Alain-
Fournier—for almost a hundred years, but they had always created it retrospectively, revealed it from the standpoint of maturity. The war, and
Freud, possibly Dada and surrealism too, seemed to change all that.
Childishness began to extrude itself into literature on its own terms, as it
were; it crawled out raw and unmodified from the subconscious.

After the First World War the new state of Poland seemed a suitable
experimental region—"God's playground" as it had been called, where
the ruling classes had never taken power and politics seriously, and with
to them fatal results. The grown-ups of Russia, Germany, and Austria had
closed the place down. But the Polish intelligentsia had never lost its
identity, or, in a sense, its wonderful irresponsibility.

The period between the wars was Poland's heyday. Warsaw intellectuals and lively periodicals like *Skamander* inaugurated new kinds of writing that drew inspiration from other European authors—Proust, Joyce,
Kafka, Thomas Mann—but possessed a very definitely Polish personality
and Polish characteristics. Witold Gombrowicz, who achieved international fame in 1938 with his novel *Ferdydurke*, had for some years before

been publishing in Warsaw his stories and studies of adolescence. Ignacy Witkiewicz, usually known as Witkacy from the way he signed his paintings, was perhaps the most versatile Polish artist and writer of the time, pioneering and encouraging new cliques and movements. He committed suicide during the German and Russian invasion of 1939, and Gombrowicz had emigrated to Argentina the year before, never returning to Poland.

The two made a trio with a small, shy Jewish writer from the provincial Galician town of Drohobycz (now in the Ukraine), whom Witkacy championed in 1934 as the most significant contemporary phenomenon in Polish literature. This was Bruno Schulz, whose fantasy *The Street of Crocodiles*, sometimes translated under the title *Cinnamon Shops*, had just appeared. Unremarked before Witkacy hailed it as a masterpiece, the gestation of Schulz's book was itself sufficiently extraordinary. The son of a dry-goods merchant, and himself the drawing master at a local high school, Schulz depended on letters to friends for intellectual support and nourishment. In 1929 a fortunate chance introduced him to Debora Vogel, a girl from Lvov who was a poet and had a doctorate's degree in philosophy; she had scored a critical success with a book of imaginative prose called *The Acacias Are in Bloom*. They began writing letters to each other, and Schulz's letters developed postscripts, of greater and greater length and originality of fantasy, with a mythology of his childhood, his family, and the town where he lived.

In 1938, when he was well known in writers' circles, Schulz wrote to the editor of a literary periodical, modestly disclaiming that he had been an influence on Gombrowicz, whose *Memoir from Adolescence* had, he pointed out, appeared in 1933, *The Street of Crocodiles* a year later. "What led to the association of our names and respective works were certain fortuitous similarities," he wrote. When *Ferdydurke* appeared in 1938 Schulz wrote an enthusiastic review of it in *Skamander*, reprinted in *Letters and Drawings of Bruno Schulz*. He observes that "until now a man looked at himself . . . from the official side of things," and that what happened inside him led "an orphaned life outside . . . reality," "a doleful life of unaccepted and unrecorded meaning." It was this inner childishness that he and Gombrowicz sought, in their separate ways, to mythologize. "Gombrowicz," Schulz wrote,

showed that the mature and clear forms of our spiritual existence . . .
live in us more as eternally strained intention than as reality. As reality we live permanently below this plateau in a completely honorless
and inglorious domain that is so flimsy that we also hesitate to grant
it even the semblance of existence.

("Flimsy" is a key word here.) *Ferdydurke*, in which the middle-aged narrator hero has been transformed into a schoolboy, "breaks through the
barrier of seriousness with unheard-of audacity."

Schulz himself did not use such comparatively direct methods. His
child's-eye vision is utterly natural, perpetuating into middle age the
humble, celestial rubbish that filled our consciousness in infancy, and
helped to pass its time. There is no sense of looking back; "not a touch of
whimsy in it," as V. S. Pritchett, a devotee of Schulz, has commented.
Since Schulz's time childishness has been both stereotyped and made
use of—we can all fondly play catcher in the rye—and Gombrowicz, who
struggled heroically to free himself from the coils of theory and literary
fashion, eventually succumbed to being typecast as one of the early
"mad" writers.

It is impossible to typecast Schulz because, to quote Pritchett again,
"his sense of life is a conspiracy of improvised myths." Again, the word
"improvised" is crucial. As his postscripts grew and flew off to his correspondent, Schulz's imagination dissolved, reformed, liquidated itself. His
wonderful language—a kind of sparkling liquid Polishness, as an admirer
has said—is almost impossible to translate into a less vivacious and ebullient medium. Even Goncharov's fantasies of the Russian village of Oblo-
movka, or Proust's magical first sentences in *A la recherche du temps
perdu*, seem set in monumental majesty—very unchildish—compared to
the eddies and spiraling paragraphs of "Cinnamon Shops" and "Crocodile Street," two of the chapters, sections, or stories in Schulz's book,
which was followed a year later by a similar compilation called *Sanitorium Under the Sign of the Hourglass*.

In these stories, the father figure, then hero, almost becomes a bird or
a cockroach, as he acts out internal fascinations not normally on adult display. Adela, the housemaid, has only to wag her finger at him—the sign
of tickling—for him "to rush through all the rooms in a wild panic, bang-

ing the doors after him, to fall at last flat on the bed in the farthest room and wriggle in convulsions of laughter." Perched on the pelmet he becomes an enormous bird, a sad stuffed condor; once, as an enormous cockroach, he is almost served up in crayfish sauce at a family dinner. He breeds strange birds in the attic, which fly away and return a few chapters later in outlandishly spiky forms, flying on their backs, or blind, or with misshapen beaks like padlocks, or "covered with curiously colored lumps." Debora Vogel, the recipient of these amazing reveries (which do not in the least seem like fantasy) has herself a surname that in German means "bird." Perhaps his postscripts were Schulz's strange way of making love to her—strange and, at the same time, delicate, unimportunate, unpretentious.

In one of his letters Schulz refers to a door, the good solid old door in the kitchen of his childhood. "On one side lies life and its restricted freedom, on the other—art. That door leads from the captivity of Bruno, a timid teacher of arts and crafts, to the freedom of Joseph, the hero of *The Street of Crocodiles*." In an introduction to the book, the Polish poet Jerzy Ficowski, who has helped to do for Schulz what Max Brod did for Kafka, comments that "behind the mythological faith of the writer there peers, again and again, the mocking grin of reality, revealing the ephemeral nature of the fictions that seek to contend with it." That seems to me misleading. There is no Peter Pan element in Schulz's imagination; rather does he show, with a tender excitement far removed from the calculated shamelessness of Gombrowicz's *Ferdydurke*, that we really and always do live in two worlds, and that the ability to live in and with both is a sign of sanity. Not many of us can turn the compulsive contingencies of the inner life into art, but when it has been done—and in so magical a form as this—we recognize its truth from our own inner experience.

No whimsy there, and nothing coy either. Schulz as a writer was a grown man, whose sexuality is immanent in the marvelous agitations of his world: in Adela's silken legs, the motion of her finger as she threatens to tickle the father, and in an idiot girl's frenzied rubbing of herself on an elder tree by the town rubbish dump. In his drawings, particularly the ones from a collection called "Idolatry," two-dimensional sex takes over, its fixed poses replacing the dynamic three-dimensional fantasy of "Crocodile Street" and "Cinnamon Shops." In a sense we are now in the nightlife of Weimar Berlin—and indeed a Gestapo officer is said to have admired Schulz's drawings—but even so there is a fluidity, a childishness, an innocence in these beautiful fetishistic little sketches that wholly removes them from the pornographic fixity in the pictorial world of— say—Balthus. There is rather a touch of Fragonard, more than a touch of Picasso, in the slender nudes with their big heads and bobbed hair, who stretch out an alluring toe toward their groveling male devotees, whose nakedness has the pathos of desire but also its dignity. There is a singular naturalness and unself-consciousness in Schulz's graphic world, in which he often features himself, surrounded at times by the higgledy-piggledy intimacy of a big patriarchal Jewish household. For his engraving he used the laborious cliché-verre technique, drawing on gelatin-coated glass and developing the print like a photographic negative. It produced for him lines and shadings of great delicacy, effects entirely his own.

Schulz admired and translated *The Trial*, but his world does not in the least resemble Kafka's. There is no quest, no terrible unknown compulsions, no anguish before the law. Schulz's family, with whom he was in his own peculiar way on good terms, had no Yiddish or Hebrew but spoke German and Polish. In Polish he was as at home as Paul Celan, another exile and victim, was to be in German, or as Italo Svevo, otherwise Ettore Schmitz, was in Italian. And like Osip Mandelstam, Schulz acknowledged no particular Jewish identity; he was just different from everybody. Gombrowicz, who came from a Polish gentry family in Samogitia, the heart of old Lithuania, was much more aware of his background than Schulz was, and always felt divided between his own "schoolboy" personality and his semiaristocratic provenance. In an open letter to Schulz commissioned by the editor of *Studio*, beginning "My Good Bruno," Gombrowicz cannot help patronizing his friend, even while praising him, and rudely dwelling on the fact that he has not actually *read The Street of Crocodiles*, even though he is sure he admires it. (In his diary he comments more candidly that Schulz's stories "bored him stiff.") Schulz's letter for *Studio* in reply is a model of rational self-explanation, ignoring the innuendo of class and race that Gombrowicz—perhaps deliberately, perhaps not—had let emerge in his own letter, and that seems to reflect the jealousy of the conscious and determined intellectual for the natural and involuntary fantasist who had crawled out as if from the woodwork.

"Dance with an ordinary woman" was one of Gombrowicz's more bracing prescriptions. Schulz indeed had done so, and become engaged to her: a Catholic girl named Józefina Szelinska for whom he felt a naïve warmth and affection, which was evidently returned. But somehow it all petered out, and his many letters to his one-time fiancée have disappeared, whereas Kafka's to his Milena have survived. Even in the matter of marriage, though, the pair of writers were probably very different. Schulz was timid, poor, and constitutionally reluctant to leave the place he worked and dreamed in, the burrow of Drohobycz, no matter how much he might have seemed to want to.

In his letters to Romana Halpern, a handsome, clever, and sympathetic woman who worked as a journalist and was to be killed by the Germans in Warsaw just before its liberation, he confided his plans for change, wider recognition, a job in Warsaw. She helped him; in 1938 he even spent three weeks in Paris. But the war found him still back home, and in 1942, after a temporary respite during which Galicia became part of the U.S.S.R., the Germans reoccupied the area and started to carry out their Final Solution. Cornered on the street one day during a "drive," Schulz was shot in the head by a Gestapo man named Günther, who no doubt felt—if he felt anything—that he was casually stamping on a cockroach. Friends had already prepared non-Jewish papers for Schulz, and had plans to help him disappear into the Polish countryside, but he had been characteristically reluctant to take the step.

Illustrating his own books, Schulz felt himself to be akin to a medieval priest or craftsman. And like a good child he dreamed and scribbled and drew, secretly and spontaneously. From his letters to Romana Halpern it is clear that his sudden literary fame depressed and disturbed him. He consulted her anxiously about his plans for marriage, which she hinted might be bad for his writing and make him "middle-class." He refutes this, defending his fiancée warmly; but Romana, herself a divorcée, probably had a clearer idea than Schulz himself did of what might go wrong. By the late Thirties he is very low, unable to write, planning masterpieces commensurate with his new reputation; but obscurely longing, one senses, to return to that womblike existence in which his real books had gestated, and in which he had drawn his haunting little pictures of bearded rabbis at their sabbath meal, or slim-legged blondes gazing impassively at their prostrate suitors.

Gombrowicz understood Schulz's plight. "He approached art like a lake, with the intention of drowning in it." His masochism made it impossible for him to impose himself on a project, or to plan a work ahead. *Cinnamon Shops* and its successor, *Sanitorium Under the Sign of the Hourglass,* remained his only achievements, although he meditated on blending them in some way into a long work to be called *Messiah,* perhaps inspired by his deep admiration for Thomas Mann's encyclopedic novel *Joseph and His Brothers.* Nothing of this survives, if it ever existed. Yet on the strength of his two little books Schulz is undoubtedly one of the masters of our century's imaginative fiction. He himself probably wrote the anonymous blurb for *Sanatorium,* in which he spoke of fiction's "dream of a renewal of life through the power of delight." That is an accurate description of the way his books work on us.

The New York Review of Books, 1989

40

Something Childish

Witold Gombrowicz (1904–1969)

Diary, Volume I
by Witold Gombrowicz, edited by Jan Kott, translated by
Lillian Vallee

EVERY SO OFTEN one runs across a sort of fugitive from the literary
world, a volume that seems to be forever on the run, flitting across
frontiers, denied a residence permit, only one jump ahead of the
immigration authorities and the secret police. There is often an element
of playing hard to get about such books, which makes them still more of
a legend and increases the potential reader's curiosity.

Ferdydurke is a prime example. In an interview in the *New Left Review*
Sartre once observed that the "naive" novel "is now quite impossible,"
and went on to say that the analytic novel of the future had been invented
by Witold Gombrowicz, whose books were also designed "to self-
destruct." Yes, but who is this Gombrowicz? Intellectuals would know,
perhaps; the common reader, although by now quite familiar with Sartre
or Beckett, might still be baffled. Now that *Ferdydurke* is a Penguin paperback, beautifully introduced by the poet and Nobel Prize winner Czeslaw Milosz, all becomes clear.

Gombrowicz was a Polish gentleman, child of an old landowning
family. (The word "child" is highly important in his context, as we shall
soon find out.) He did not fit into such a heritage. Joining the Warsaw
intelligentsia he began to write: unprinted essays, stories, and a play,
Princess Ivona, written in 1934 and performed in England, where it

seemed familiar to audiences accustomed to Beckett and Ionesco. He attracted no special attention until 1937, when *Ferdydurke* was published. Gombrowicz was then thirty-three. His book created a sensation in Polish intellectual circles, where an international future was predicted for this scandalous work. Then in 1939 came the German invasion. Polish discussion disappeared. It is worth remembering that throughout the war Sartre, whose novel *La Nausée* appeared just before it, continued to write and to talk in Paris. Gombrowicz was in exile in Argentina, where *Ferdydurke* was published in Spanish in 1947. Its author noted in his diary that "*Ferdydurke* had been drowned in the sleep-walking immobility of South America."

Gombrowicz had in fact reached Buenos Aires before the Polish apocalypse, whether out of prescience or for some random reason is not now apparent. In his introduction to Volume One of the diary, Wojciech Karpinski tells the story, admittedly legendary, of Gombrowicz taking passage for home on a Polish vessel just before war broke out, and an instant before the final whistle blew running back down the gangway with his two suitcases. What had called to him from South America? Something to do with emptiness, with the lack of meaning, with youth, or rather the idea of youth; perpetually unfulfilled in maturity? There is a suggestion that he never intended to stay in Buenos Aires, but had merely taken the opportunity offered by his acquaintance Stempowski, director of the Gdynia-America line, to make the inaugural voyage in his role as a Polish intellectual, landowner, minor celebrity. In that case his decision to "jump," to maroon himself on another continent, seems comparable to that involuntary step taken by Lord Jim, the great creation of an earlier Polish writer.

Joseph Conrad settled in England: Gombrowicz abandoned himself to isolation like another of Conrad's characters, Martin Decoud in *Nostromo*. Decoud, the arch-intellectual, involving himself in a hazardous political adventure, cannot stand for more than a few hours the loneliness of an uninhabited island. Grasping that he has no existence outside the pages of a book, conversations, theories, the endless chatter of the bookish cafés, he shoots himself, or rather allows himself to be shot by himself. Gombrowicz was clearly very different, although in the contrast itself there is a kind of relationship. He once remarked, "I am not Gombrowicz the writer. I am just Gombrowicz, and not even that." He did not depend upon intellectuals and yet he was obsessed with them, obsessed with escaping from them and becoming a sort of intellectuality of one. He is the anti-intellectuals' intellectual.

Sartre, in writing *La Nausée*, was setting out his ideas, finding an embodiment for his concept of the existential. Gombrowicz, as he tells us in an afterword to the novel, began *Ferdydurke* as a satire against the whole august European tradition of thought systems.

> How could I, a Pole, believe in theories? That would be grotesque. Against the Polish sky, against the sky of a paling, waning Europe, one can see why so much paper coming from the West falls to the ground, into the mud, onto the sand, so that little boys grazing their cows can make the usual use of it. But these theories, which drift across the sky, become ridiculous, blind, ignoble, bloody, vain. Gentle ideas are pregnant with mountains of corpses. What can one do? Everyone sees the world from where he stands. It is not for nothing that I come from the plains which separate Europe from the rest of the world.

Or that separate Argentina from Europe. Perhaps Gombrowicz found his own Poland in South America? Observing (a point on which Conrad was silently very sensitive) that "it is not right that a Pole should have to sacrifice all his humanity to Poland," Gombrowicz goes on to say that large countries do not lay such burdens on the writer. But in minor countries, like Poland, Argentina, Norway, and others, "it is really a matter of life and death to break away, to keep one's distance." It is a familiar argument, but Argentina may have offered Gombrowicz the chance to embrace his Polish plains by other means. For this child of squires there were more ways than one of remaining with the landed gentry. And in *Ferdydurke* (a meaningless nonsense word, by the way, unsuited to any known language) the whole question of who makes you, and how you make yourself, becomes a wild, prolonged, and lonely joke.

Conrad's Martin Decoud, in his few hours on the barren island, would certainly have recognized the truth of this note from Gombrowicz's diary, a truth promulgated in its entries over a quarter of a century or so, the truth about how the diarist spent a Sunday in Buenos Aires.

Tragedy.

I walked in the rain, hat perched over my forehead, collar raised, hands in my pockets.

After which I returned home.

Then I went out again to get something to eat.

Then I ate it.

The most "authentic" thing about Gombrowicz, in existentialist jargon, is that he seems to be a natural, a "naive" writer, who discovered existentialism by mistake. His fellow countryman and intense admirer, Bruno Schulz, said in a lecture on Gombrowicz that "he did not follow the smooth path of intellectual speculation, but the path of pathology, of his own pathology." Schulz, himself a brilliant imaginative writer, one of a constellation in Polish literature before the war, understood the wholly unabstract nature of Gombrowicz's talent. *The Street of Crocodiles*, Schulz's own enchanting fantasy on petit-bourgeois Jewish life in provincial Poland, is quite a different matter, intensely stylish in the way that Kafka is stylish, and in some degree inspired by Kafka's own fantasies. Schulz, who was gunned down in his native city by the German SS during the occupation, has the kind of style that comes over in translation, and—again like Kafka's—adapts admirably to style in a different tongue. Alas, one has the impression that the reverse is true with Gombrowicz. His translators have done their best, but in English he sounds awkward, colorless. The reader has a baffling sense that he must sound wonderful, sure, and strongly flavored in his native Polish, but that does not come over. Much else, fortunately, does.

This is only the first volume of Gombrowicz diaries, but it reads more like a selection than extracts from a more comprehensive diary, which he kept over the years in Argentina. Gombrowicz spends some time reconsidering his past writings in the light of later trends and contemporary fashions.

In 1956 Gombrowicz noted with his usual openness in his diary that existentialism and Marxism were two "bankruptcies" in which he had found himself unwittingly involved:

I wrote *Ferdydurke* in the years 1936–37, when no one knew anything about this philosophy. In spite of this, *Ferdydurke* is existential to the marrow. . . . In this book, practically all the basic themes of existentialism play fortissimo: becoming, creating oneself, freedom, fear, absurdity, nothingness . . . with the single difference that in addition to the typical existential "spheres" of human life, like Heidegger's banal and authentic life, Kierkegaard's aesthetic, ethical, and religious life, or Jaspers's "spheres," there is yet another sphere, namely, the "sphere of immaturity." This sphere or "category" is the contribution of my private existence to existentialism. . . . For Kierkegaard, Heidegger, and Sartre, the more profound the awareness, the more authentic the existence. They measure honesty and the essence of experience by the degree of awareness. But is our humanity really built on awareness? Doesn't awareness—that forced, extreme awareness—arise among us, not from us, as something created by effort, the mutual perfecting of ourselves in it, the confirming of something that one philosopher forces onto another? Isn't man, therefore, in his private reality, something childish and always beneath his own awareness? And doesn't he feel awareness to be, at the same time, something alien, imposed and unimportant? If this is how it is, this furtive childhood, this concealed degradation are ready to explode your systems sooner or later.

Well, as can be seen from such entries, Gombrowicz is determined to show that he is in the forefront of the conceptual battle, slugging it out with the most revered names in the philosophical fashion business. This is how we keep abreast of things in the wilds of South America. There is something engaging in his tone, too, in these diaries, a lightness, a lack of solemnity that suits the inherent shrewdness of the point Gombrowicz is making. Furtive childhood is, as it were, always lying in wait for the pompous Heideggerian. That is what animates and determines the method of *Ferdydurke* itself. "It is as though we were simultaneously at the table and under the table."

For his first novel Gombrowicz borrowed, no doubt without knowing it, a theme around in literature long before the Victorians, although it made a specially nightmare appeal to the Victorian imagination. It was the theme used in Mark Twain's *The Prince and the Pauper* and in F. Anstey's once immensely popular Victorian classic, *Vice Versa*, about the

heavy Victorian father who finds he has changed places with his schoolboy son. Toad, the real hero of Kenneth Grahame's *The Wind in the Willows*, also has his persona of comfortable, overbearing, conceited squire
magicked or disguised into a reverse and humiliating role. In *Ferdydurke*
the middle-aged hero finds himself led off back to school by a ludicrous
professor.

Such transformations could be, as Kafka saw, the terror lurking in the
modern fairy story; and both Bruno Schulz and Gombrowicz may have
had Kafka's example directly in mind. In *The Street of Crocodiles* the
tyrannical Jewish father becomes an exceedingly lifelike cockroach, or
rather a type of domestic lobster, who even temporarily survives being
cooked and eaten for the family dinner. This coruscatingly pathetic and
funny sequence was much admired by the Polish literary intelligentsia in
the prewar years. But Gombrowicz, as he often tells us, will have nothing
to do with Freudian images or significances. He takes the idea literally
and simply: his hero finds himself back at school and that is all there is to
it. Where nightmares or degradations are concerned there is no need to
go further.

Ferdydurke divides more or less into three parts. The school sequence
is followed by grotesque French farce, the encounter with a family consisting of Mr. and Mrs. "Youthful" and their daughter Zutka; and this
transforms itself into the hero—still dogged by a schoolboy "friend"—
meeting up with his landowning relations at their country place. The two
latter episodes are highly satirical, in the Gombrowiczian manner: the
"Youthfuls" representing enlightened modernity, the new bourgeois ethos
(there is a charming moment when Mrs. Youthful retires into the water
closet and emerges looking even more progressive and civic-minded than
when she went in), and the squires in the country standing for the wholly
conditioned and most classbound race imaginable.

But Gombrowicz is not a satirist; his pictures of how people live and
have their being are all the more vivid for their utter lack of the "grown-
up" reforming instinct. *Ferdydurke* also takes an authentically child's-eye
view of sex, a grotesque but compulsive activity that causes people to act
in odd ways, and is somehow associated with backsides or bottoms, which
figure largely in the general atmosphere of startled and outraged immaturity. Gombrowicz's greatest strength is the absolute consistency with

which he sticks to "the path of pathology," never letting on that he, as author, is anything other than he appears to be in the terms of the fable. This is a rare thing, and it brings him closer to Swift or Defoe than to any "absurdist" modern writer, in all of whom one can detect the authorial manipulation from a concealed vantage point different from the one the book is offering. "Immaturity," for example, is hard to create or dissemble. Holden Caulfield, in *The Catcher in the Rye*, can now be seen to be a made-up figure, like Peter Pan, embodying the author's wistfulness for what he was, or thought he might have been. In his diary and novels alike Gombrowicz is all of a piece, operating, as he puts it, at the "level of our own inadequacy"; but though we feel familiar with him we never know quite where we are. He is indeed more like a piece of daily existence than like a writer whose method and tactic can be worked out.

Gombrowicz obligingly offers in his diary a suggestion for how to read him.

> To persons who are interested in my writing technique I offer the following recipe:
> Enter the realm of dreams.
> After which begin writing the first story that comes to mind and write about twenty pages. Then read it.
> On these twenty pages, there may be one scene, a few sentences, a metaphor, which will seem exciting to you. Then write everything all over again, attempting this time to make the exciting elements the scaffolding and write, not taking reality into consideration, and striving only to satisfy the needs of your imagination.

Sounds easy? The recipe is certainly typical of Gombrowicz's literalness and lack of pretension. "After which you read in the press," he goes on, "in *Ferdydurke* Gombrowicz wants to say . . . ' " But "who has decreed that one should write only when one has something to write? . . . Art consists in writing not what one has to say, but something altogether unexpected." He was happy to meet an Argentine writer who taught philosophy part-time, and who said his method was *hay que golpear*—"one must strike." "One must tear them away from the reality to which they have become accustomed," so Gombrowicz suggests in his diary. "Knowledge, whatever it is worth, from the most precise mathematics to the darkest suggestions of art, is not to calm the soul but to create a state of vibration and tension in it."

True, and because he does not write "what he wants to say" Gombrowicz has always evaded predictability. And yet his point about the shock effect of the unexpected is only half true, as he knows very well. Milosz has speculated about his relation to Dostoevsky and the Underground Man—the hero from under the floorboards—and Dostoevsky has indeed the same capacity to immerse the reader in the atmosphere his hero inhabits. But just by "living there" we come to take aesthetic comfort and calm in that situation; for the reader too is adaptable, and will find reassurance and familiarity in the most unlikely places. Gombrowicz is by no means as familiar as Dostoevsky, but he could become so if he were not in other ways so elusive, simultaneously close to us and far away.

Yet in some ways his life proceeded like that of any other modern intellectual. In the Argentine he continued to write novels—*Cosmos, Pornografia, Transatlantic.* All follow the general pattern of *Ferdydurke*; and *Pornografia*, especially, uses Gombrowicz's preoccupation with immaturity—in this case the fascination it can have for the elderly, who are not so much mature as set in their ways. The scene is Poland during the war, and the novel takes place in a country house, where two elderly gentlemen hatch a plot to persuade two fresh young teenagers to go to bed with each other. The love scene never comes off, but murder does—just because the teenagers are so innocent. The atmosphere is murky, and the story does not appear very persuasive, but Jan Kott has pointed out how well Gombrowicz understood the wartime atmosphere, which also haunts his play *The Marriage.*

Like Sartre's *Huis clos, The Marriage* starts from the notion of a small group who cannot escape each other's company. The actual and humdrum situation of being shut up together for twelve hours or more arose from the imposition of the curfew in occupied Warsaw and Paris. Anyone who gave a "party" had his guests on his hands till next morning; there was no way they could leave or he could get rid of them. Hell is other people, but the "I" is also somebody else. As Gombrowicz puts it in his preface, "Being united, people impose upon one another this or that manner of being, . . . each person deforms other persons, while being at the same time deformed by them."

Kott recalls that in the winter of 1943, at one of these all-night Warsaw parties, he saw two young men engaging in a grimacing match, in the manner made popular by the duel of faces in *Ferdydurke*, which the narrator watches among schoolboys after he has been metamorphosed into one of them. The two dueling young men of the wartime night in Warsaw later became famous writers—Czeslaw Milosz and Jerzy Andrzejewski, author of *Ashes and Diamonds*.

Jan Kott writes in a preface to *The Marriage* that in *Ferdydurke* "we have the whole Gombrowicz," and that out of the duel of grimaces in *Ferdydurke* "developed the Gombrowiczian theory of social behavior and particularly of aggression and mutual debasement." Maybe so. But it may be, too, that Gombrowicz stayed in South America to escape the kind of typecasting that intellectuals impose upon one another. *Ferdydurke* is certainly a spontaneous work, but the *Diary* is even more so, and to the extent that it is, even more rewarding. One pays it a high compliment by saying that one would hardly guess it was written by a well-known intellectual; and this in spite of the fact that every page contains speculation and query about the human condition, brilliant perceptions and criticisms of Rimbaud or Sienkiewicz, Nietzsche or Camus. Nonetheless the spirit of openness, of innocence, of a certain dishevelment, is always present, as is a singularly personal awareness of and response to the Argentine scene, the emptiness of the pampas and islanded estuaries, the farms and *estancias* with their dark rooms and long avenues of eucalyptus. Gombrowicz may have been lonely in his new country, sometimes bored, often poor, working as a clerk or in some other humble occupation. His solitude indeed seems that of a truant schoolboy, but his individuality is always present, as in this late entry when he tells us about his day:

> I get up around eleven, but I put off shaving until later because it is very tiresome. Then comes breakfast, consisting of tea, baked goods, butter, and two soft eggs on the even days of the week and two hard ones on the odd. After breakfast, I get down to work, and I write until the desire to stop working overcomes my reluctance to shave. When this breakthrough occurs, I shave with pleasure.

He puffs on his Dunhill pipe, smoking Hermes tobacco, writes for the local paper in the afternoon to earn some money, goes to supper at the

Café Sorrento, spends most of the night reading books, "which, unfortunately, are not always the kind I really desire to.read." He records with satisfaction the purchase of six summer shirts "on sale for a very good price." He certainly avoided being forced into the mold of a philosophical writer, although in his later books he found it harder and harder to avoid the proleptic attentions of critics like grimacing schoolboys saying "what Gombrowicz intends to say is this." Eventually he gave in and returned to Europe, to France, spiritual home of all intellectuals, where he died in 1969. The existential establishment, with their all-too-predictable fashions and slogans, embraced him in the end, and he saw that it must be so. Yet he still felt like Rabelais, who had no idea or intention of producing "pure art," or "articulating his epoch," but who "wrote the way a child pees under a bush, in order to relieve himself."

The New York Review of Books, 1988

41

Poet of Holy Dread

Paul Celan (1920–1970)

Paul Celan: Poet, Survivor, Jew
by John Felstiner

IT MAKES LITTLE SENSE to ask who is the finest poet of the postwar era—Robert Lowell, John Berryman, Elizabeth Bishop, Philip Larkin might all seem to qualify if we are considering Anglo-Americans—but there seems little doubt who has the strongest claims to being unique. Paul Celan's subject was something about which no true poetry came from any other poet—the Holocaust. Many poems have been written that speak about it, in the appropriate style of emotion, but they do not become it: they cannot realize it in the unique voice of poetry. Celan alone made its world his own, as a poet.

The German-Jewish philosopher Theodor Adorno, with whose writings Celan was familiar, suggested after the war not only that it couldn't be done but that it shouldn't be done. To compose lyric poetry after the world experience of Auschwitz could only be, he felt, a "barbaric" act. Something impossibly insensitive and philistine, a stupidity or unawareness from which a real poet could only withdraw; be present in absence; be silent. Celan showed Adorno that he was wrong. He was, perhaps, the only poet who could have done so.

He was born Paul Antschel, sometimes written Ancel, in a Jewish community settled in Bukovina in northern Romania. Celan was an anagram which he used as a poet from 1947, and which became in effect his real name. That in itself is typical of a poet who called one of his collections *Die Niemandsrose—The No One's Rose*—a beautiful untranslatable German word which holds a haunting image of a poet who gives the impression of knowing that he has no existence, except in the words he creates. His father was a builder, a keen Zionist, with whom his talented son (one remembers Kafka) was never much in sympathy. His mother he loved deeply; and it was she who used to read with him the German classics and poetry. One of his most moving couplets makes on this a lilting comment that is itself no comment.

> *Und duldest du, Mutter, wie einst, ach, daheim,*
> *den leisen, den deutschen, den schmerzlichen Reim.*

> (And do you suffer, mother, as you did, ah, once at home,
> The gentle, the German, the painbringing rhyme.)

Celan never got over his mother's death. In 1942, a year after the German invasion, his parents were sent to a concentration camp in the Ukraine, where his father died of typhus and his mother was killed, probably shot in the back of the neck by the Germans after she fell ill and was unable to work. In a different work camp back in Romania their son survived, managing to emigrate to Vienna from Bucharest two years after the end of the war and, later, to Paris in 1948; but in a sense he had left himself behind, in the Ukraine, where his mother had vanished. He recorded her death in the unbearably simple words of another early poem, "Espenbaum" ("The Aspen Tree").

> Aspen tree, your leaves glance white into the dark.
> My mother's hair never turned white. . . .

> Round star, you coil the golden loop.
> My mother's heart was cut with lead.

> Oaken door, who forced you from the hinges?
> My gentle mother cannot come.

For Celan the only language in which such a loss could truly be expressed was the German language, the language spoken by the people who had brought it about. Although she of course also spoke Romanian and Yiddish, Celan's mother clearly felt that German was her native tongue; and as her son was to say, "Only in the mother tongue can one speak one's own truth. In a foreign tongue the poet lies."

His mother, who, as he once wryly remarked, sometimes had her doubts about him and his future, however close their early relationship had been, never saw his German verses. The convoy with which his parents voluntarily decided to leave started from Czernowitz on a day when Celan himself seems to have been accidentally absent. But something far deeper than survivor's guilt made it impossible ever after for him to "pluck from the memory a rooted sorrow." Shakespeare's words in *Macbeth* express a common phenomenon, and one all too terribly common at the time; but Celan spoke its own truth for himself in the tongue both of his mother and of her German executioners.

In fact, as John Felstiner shows in his admirably detailed and understanding study, Celan had very little idea at the end of the war whether he could be a poet at all, and if so in what language he could write. He was at home in Romanian and attracted to its own special qualities, suited to the surrealist verse which many Romanian poets of the time were writing. He was almost equally at home in French and Russian—he had visited Paris before the war with plans to become a medical student—and even during the war he was translating his favorite Russian poets like Sergei Esenin and Osip Mandelstam. All his life he made translations from every sort of poet—Andrew Marvell, A. E. Housman, and Emily Dickinson among many others—but his own truth could only be uttered in what had been literally his mother's tongue.

There have been innumerable studies in many languages of Celan, many of them elaborately theoretical and recondite to the verge of portentousness. For another unspoken irony is that the extraordinary simplicity and directness of what he writes has sent commentators scurrying about in search of every kind of hidden meaning and allusion. Celan himself always vehemently rejected this sort of approach, protesting that his poetry was "absolutely not and in no way 'hermetic.' " And it is the great merit of Felstiner's study not only to put Celan's life and achievement in a detailed but homely perspective which should help to make them much better known among English speakers, but to have presented the poetry in a sensible and straightforward way, with an unpretentious comparative commentary. Celan, even in English, is not difficult to understand and to be deeply moved by, as is shown by the two examples I have already quoted; but the weighty tradition of Germanic exegesis has fastened itself upon him with what one might naturally suppose to be almost guilty obsession. Felstiner's book helps in the best possible way to dispel all this.

Like his adored Mandelstam, for whom poetry was simply "world culture," Celan gives the impression of taking in everything in poetry that Europe and America can offer, while remaining at the same time wholly and often agonizingly his own self, inside his own predicament. The paradox is equally evident in Kafka, some of whose stories he translated into Romanian toward the end of the war. As Kafka startles many of his foreign devotees by turning out to have been a strong and patriotic believer in the old Hapsburg Empire, so Celan regarded Vienna, one of the most anti-Semitic cities in Europe, as the natural mecca of any cultured Central European. As Felstiner says, "people living in those outposts of the Austro-Hungarian Empire saw Vienna as their spiritual home."

Celan made his way there with great hardship and difficulty in 1947, and presented himself and his poems at the offices of a magazine. A Viennese acquaintance wrote later that he came literally out of nowhere, a condescending view which upset Celan's compatriots back in Bucharest, and which was echoed by a Swiss editor who published some of his poems in 1948. ("The Aspen Tree" was published three times that year.) The Swiss naïvely praised Celan for the difficult feat of mastering the German language to the point of being able to write verses in it. How could a young Romanian Jew from some rural backwater have done it? And this was being written of a poet who had read Goethe and Schiller with his mother as a young boy and lived in his teens in the poetic world of Freidrich Hölderlin and Rainer Maria Rilke! No wonder Celan signed himself in a letter to a Bucharest friend "sad poet of the Teutonic tongue." And yet he was immensely gratified by the praise his poems received in Vienna—"God knows I was happy when they told me I was the greatest poet in Austria, and—so far as they know—in Germany as well."

The main reason for instant fame, and one which Celan came

afterward bitterly to regret and even to dissociate himself from, was the quickly spreading notoriety of the amazing poem he had written soon after the war—"Todesfuge" ("Deathfugue"), about which Felstiner has a chapter titled "A Fugue after Auschwitz (1944–1945)." In fact it first appeared in a Romanian magazine and in a Romanian version translated by a friend of Celan's, who could himself have written the poem in the same language, of course, but did not. The translation is called "Tangoul Mort'ii" ("Death Tango"), and it seems at first suitable that the Latin civilization which produced the tango should mordantly contrast with the German musical culture from which came the fugue. In fact, however, not only did Celan himself first call the poem "Todestango," but that name was actually dreamed up by an SS lieutenant who ordered a Jewish orchestra in one of the camps to improvise one and to play it. A recording of their composition exists; it is based on the Argentine Eduardo Bianco's prewar hit. This same tango was being played in Paris when Celan was there early in 1939, and the same band from Paris later entertained Hitler and Goebbels, who greatly preferred the tango to what they considered the decadence of New York jazz.

Whether tango or fugue, Celan's extraordinary poem is wholly unlike anything else, even—as must be the case with a genuine work of art— quite unlike the awful things which it describes, and which generated it. It is not that the poem transcends in any sense those terrible happenings, but that it creates its own absolute vision of them, as Grünewald created his dead Christ, or Titian his sublime late painting of the hideous flaying of Marsyas by Apollo. The greatest poetry inevitably brings to birth a world of its own. We are right to be suspicious of the paradox; and there is something decidedly suspicious about the immense popularity of "Todesfuge" in Germany after the war, particularly with the young, among whom it became a cult. As Auden said, "No poet can prevent his poetry being used as magic." "Todesfuge" gave the Germans a kind of enormous and magical relief, the equivalent in great art of the black joke current at the time: "The Germans will never be able to forgive the Jews for Auschwitz." But the poem itself—though not its author—is sublimely indifferent to all these crooked reactions and responses of the human heart.

Celan was acutely aware of German reactions. In his later talks about his poetry in Germany he combined civilities with a sharp reminder that the "euphony" of traditional German poetry had during the war years been able "more or less untroubled to trip tunefully alongside the most frightful things." The "euphony" of his own poem was not like that. It *was* trouble; and yet by a supreme irony it could also lay trouble to rest in the hearts and minds of many Germans, who could feel their guilt wonderfully, and painlessly, through its medium. No wonder Celan later refused permission for it to be used in readings or reprinted in popular anthologies; and no wonder that he himself came to feel increasingly miserable and uneasy when he visited Germany, where he was fêted and received praise and rewards. He felt himself to be a tame Jew, whose famous poem made Germans feel better: worse, that his poem was being debased into a kind of pop music by whose means the younger generation could bait and glibly condemn their elders.

None of this affects the potency and the hypnotic, inscrutable force of "Todesfuge." Felstiner translates it brilliantly, and comments on it in telling detail, from its celebrated opening section —

> Black milk of daybreak we drink it at evening
> we drink it at midday and morning we drink it at night
> we drink and we drink
> we shovel a grave in the air there you won't lie too cramped
> A man lives in the house he plays with his vipers he writes
> he writes when it grows dark to Deutschland your golden hair
> > Margareta
> he writes it and steps out of doors and the stars are all sparkling he
> > whistles his hounds to stay close
> he whistles his Jews into rows has them shovel a grave in the ground
> he commands us play up for the dance
>
> Black milk of daybreak we drink you at night
> we drink you at morning and midday we drink you at evening
> we drink and we drink
> A man lives in the house he plays with his vipers he writes

he writes when it grows dark to Deutschland your golden hair
    Margareta
Your ashen hair Shulamith we shovel a grave in the air
    where you won't lie too cramped. . . .

—to the electrifying close, which has already appeared in the poem in different keys of the fugal repetition. For this Felstiner supplies no translation and none is needed. He has already given a gloss of the words— "Death is a Master from Germany / Your golden hair Margareta / Your ashen hair Shulamith"—so that, as they recur, the lines gradually take on the cadenced beat of the original, and, at the end, the German words appear like returning ghosts in Felstiner's translation, now as terrifyingly comprehensible to the foreign reader as they are in the true language of the poem.

> . . . der Tod ist ein Meister aus Deutschland
> dein goldenes Haar Margarete
> dein aschenes Haar Sulamith.

Celan's poetry is never "meaningful," in the sense in which a conductor gives a meaningful glance or gesture to his orchestra or to some part of it. ("A Celan poem is wholly without intention," wrote one reviewer, with unconscious irony.) There is no underlined contrast between the Faustian Margareta's golden hair and the ashen hair of Jewish Shulamith. The words do nothing but realize themselves totally within the holy dread of the poem. Bach wrote *The Art of the Fugue*, and is, as Felstiner says, "our paragon *Meister aus Deutschland*," but Bach is not mocked by the words. In the "Todesfuge" German art is met in a new and terrible celebration and recognition of a new voice, one that inherits all of that art's powers.

A dozen or so years after "Todesfuge" Celan wrote a poem on the same theme, "Engführung," the term for a form of counterpoint in a fugue. *Eng*—narrow or cramped—is again a key word, but in this deathly quiet, almost breathless poem, words compress themselves, as if into a tunnel in which there can be no turning back, and in which they have breath only to whisper. Introducing "Engführung," Felstiner writes,

In everyday idiom, a whole population and anyone entering this poem is "Taken off to the terrain with the unerring track" to find

> Grass, written asunder. The stones, white,
> with shadows of the blades.

Had Celan written no more than these two marvelous poems he would be one of the greatest poets of the century. He wrote of course much more, always making his poetry, as he put it, "expose" rather than "impose" itself. With Celan's poems an elaborate commentary seems out of place, but John Felstiner's observations, and his excellent rendering of the verse into an at least related kind of English, are of immense help to the reader who is trying to get to know the poet. (This is also true of Michael Hamburger's bilingual selection, published in 1988 by Persea Books.)

Some of Celan's poems have a reputation for extreme difficulty, but they and their language always have the same heroically absolute quality of being themselves, and not another thing. For this reason it is for the reader not so much a question of "understanding" them as of perceiving, in the fullest sense, their mode of existence. In the matter of language Celan was greatly interested in Heidegger, philosopher of existence as the poetic, the "secret king of thought," as Hannah Arendt called him. A strange and moving poem of Celan has the title "Todtnauberg," the name of Heidegger's mountain retreat; and the poet encountered there the philosopher who had remained always as silent about the fate of the Jews as about his own political past. It has been said that Heidegger made himself absent, or never received Celan, but in fact there is a good deal of evidence that their relations, whether by letter or meeting, were in fact both cordial and helpful to the poet.

Let us hope so; for the loneliness and depression of Celan's late years were in fact considerable, and crushing. When awarded the Bremen Prize for his poetry in 1958 he was genuinely and humbly grateful, but his speech of thanks let his listeners know that *Denken* and *Danken*—to think and to thank, which are "from one and the same source"—remind us of "others" who also spoke "our language"—*unsere Sprache*—a finely courteous shaft of sarcasm from a Jew in postwar Germany. Despite his many friends, loneliness must also have extended into every corner of his own postwar life as a "no one's person." Living in Paris he worked and translated at the Sorbonne, and in 1952 he married Gisèle de Lestrange, a young graphic artist whose parents came from a noble French family. (Another strange transformation for the dispossessed stranger from Central Europe.) Although they lost their first child soon after birth, the marriage seems to have been a happy one, given the touchingly odd position of the poet, outside all nationality and yet inside all language, and his increasingly despondent feelings about Europe, the Jewish question, and his own poetry.

He was hounded, too, by accusations of plagiarism, rumors—certainly baseless except for the coincidences arising from the friendship of two poets—which were set off by the vindictive wife of his old friend, the Franco-German poet Yvan Goll. Part of the misunderstanding may have arisen from Celan's own multifarious translations, the genius—akin to that which wrote his own poetry—for understanding the unique nature of another poet in his own words; he seems to have offered in friendship to translate some of Goll's French songs into German. The stigma of malicious gossip among his own circle of poets hurt him deeply, no less deeply than the signs of latent or reviving anti-Semitism, and the resentment of a Jewish writer who wrote in German, which he thought he detected on his visits to the Federal Republic, however much it might officially honor him.

Paradox, often tragic paradox, continued to haunt his sense of language. A poet who could only be himself, and "speak his own truth," in the language of his people's oppressors, could also travel from tongue to tongue as if with fire at Pentecost. But not as a poet; for that the German tongue was his sole being. All real poets know the truth of T. S. Eliot's comment that "the bad poet imitates, the good poet steals." Even the wonderful word *Niemandsrose* is in a sense not wholly Celan's—why should such a word belong to any one poet?—since one of Rilke's *Sonnets to Orpheus*, a series much loved by Celan, speaks of "Rose, oh pure contradiction, desire / To be no one's sleep under so many / Lids." There is also a marvelously touching side to Celan's devouring fascination with the "poetryness" of all other poetry. It led to his making versions of Shakespeare's sonnets, of Rupert Brooke, of Lewis Carroll's "Jabberwocky," and even, as Felstiner tells us, a perfectly singable version of Yeats's "Down by the Salley Gardens." (But how very different is "Todesfuge" from Yeats's beautiful but somehow bogus and merely poetic refrain "A terrible beauty is born," although Celan's poem—all his poems—could make the same claim in their own very different way.) Incidentally, the thirteen-year-old who wrote to his aunt "Speake-you English?" later wrote, when visiting a friend in London, a little poem called "Mapesbury Road," which could almost be a distillation of the poetic spirit of John Betjeman, and of the North London school of painters.

But Celan's last years were sad, and, above all, lonely. Remaining married, he craved solitude nonetheless and went to live by himself in a small flat on the Left Bank in Paris, in a quarter in which he knew every house where a writer or artist had once lived. But he had always suffered from what the Jewish writer Emmanuel Levinas once called "insomnia in the bed of being." One dark night in 1970 he went down to a bridge over the Seine. No one saw him go into the water. He and his wife and child used to have their holidays on the Breton coast, and he was a strong swimmer. But he let himself drown, and his body was not discovered for some time, far down the river. On his desk back at his flat was a biography of Hölderlin, in which Celan had underlined a sentence by the poet Clemens Brentano: "Sometimes this genius goes dark and sinks down into the bitter well of his heart."

"*Paul Celan est mort*" said the front-page headline of a leading Paris literary weekly, but the story added that in France he was unknown. A final paradox, spelled out in the country where he had chosen to live; for although he had often been invited to emigrate to Israel, which he had visited, he could never bring himself to do so. But his last poem, written shortly before his death, was called "To the Sabbath."

The New York Review of Books, 1996

42

The Art of Austerity

Zbigniew Herbert (1924–1998)

Selected Poems
by Zbigniew Herbert, translated by Czeslaw Milosz and Peter
   Dale Scott

Report from the Besieged City and Other Poems
by Zbigniew Herbert, translated by John Carpenter and
   Bogdana Carpenter

In *The Unbearable Lightness of Being,* Milan Kundera imagines his fiction in terms of a metaphysics of history. Since nothing repeats itself, nothing really happens—if by "happening" we mean an event of permanent human significance, an event which causes us to weep or rejoice, to feel indignation and anger, as we do in response to the things that touch us nearly in our daily lives. A fiction can be imagined in terms of the German saying, *einmal ist keinmal*; what takes place in it has no reality, since what happens once has not happened at all. Hitler or Genghis Khan can kill as many people as they want: it is merely one more for the book, and a novelist can re-create in his own devices its lack of significance.

What about a poet? Poetry cannot sound like history. By its very nature it cannot *say einmal ist keinmal*: if it comes anywhere near doing this it ceases to be itself. T. S. Eliot comes dangerously near it in *The Waste Land* by his use of the word "unreal," arranged in a pattern of typographic isolation. It was modernism's gesture to the non-event of recent events, but fortunately the rest of the poem redeems this by its impenetrable singularity. W. H. Auden came close to it in "Spain," which is precariously saved by the authenticity of its parts and details, though the poem's facile proclamation of faith would otherwise be a particularly blatant acceptance of historical meaninglessness—meaninglessness in the form of Marxist "meaning." "Today the struggle," like *"La lutte finale,"* is an especially insidious version of *einmal ist keinmal.*

In *The Unbearable Lightness of Being,* Kundera contrasts the state of total inner political cynicism in which people live in Eastern Europe, and which supplies the idea behind his title, with the weighty permanence of personal lives, the state of chance relations and events which has brought about commitment and finality. His doomed couple— doomed by the meaningless fact of the fiction, but also, and savingly, by the inevitabilities of any individual life—live for each other and for their dog, who dies agonizingly of cancer. Dogs embody the heaviness of being, and its inescapability, like the pebbles in a poem of Zbigniew Herbert's. Dogs are also powerless, with that powerlessness which is the true fate of the single individual. So are poems, which, as Auden said, make nothing happen. Elias Canetti, in his aphorisms, says that as long as there is one totally powerless person left in the world "I cannot lose all hope." That is both portentous and tiresome, but it links up with Tolstoy's curious observation that freedom consists "in my not having made the laws." The English fancy they are free, said Tolstoy, with that majestic cynicism which often characterized the old man, because they have made their own laws. "But I, in Russia, am truly free, because the laws have nothing whatever to do with me."

The relevance of all this for a poet like Zbigniew Herbert is that it stands on its head the Marxian commandment that freedom is the recognition of necessity. Politics can never recognize necessity; only powerlessness can do so. The paradox today is that this most politically aware poet is also the poet whose works most absolutely reject the unbearable lightness of the political. A. Alvarez, in his introduction to the Carcanet paperback reissue of Herbert's *Selected Poems,* stresses that this poetry is "unremittingly political," but he does not seem to have asked himself why this should be so, and on what contemporary central European paradox this unremittingness is founded. Alvarez makes a ritual contrast between the poets of the West, with their "cosy, domesticated, senselessly sensible way of life in a mass democracy," creating "worlds which are autonomous, internalized, complete inside their own heads," with the stark poetry of the East which is "continually exposed to the impersonal external pressures of politics and history." But such a contrast is all but meaningless except in so far as it reflects the pleasurable sense of guilt and self-accusation which some critics and commentators always express when implying that artists who have really been up against it must be politically *dans le vrai.* All poets and their poetry are subject to the "impersonal external pressures of politics and history." The real contrast today is between those poets who have not made the laws and those who have helped to do so, or are at least conditioned to feel that they have helped, and are helping, to do so.

For the latter kind, poetry can make things happen, in a modest way, like any other form of social action. The Ulster poets write poems about the Irish situation which not only give it a cultural status but arguably help to form attitudes, at least among the small minority, perhaps mostly students, who read them. Such poetry is itself a form of social and political discussion, in tone sardonic and reasonable, and all the more effective in its moderate office for not claiming too much. It may be on the side of what Alvarez calls a "cosy, domesticated, senselessly sensible way of life," but it is certainly not "autonomous" and complete inside the poet's head: if it were it might, as poetry, have a greater impact. The autonomous and wholly personal idiom of Auden's early poems has, in retrospect, very much the air of belonging to a poet who has not made the laws, and who has the freedom that comes from being outside them. Yet Auden's idiom seemed precisely that of its age's political anxieties; and so today does Herbert's. Arguably the most "unremittingly" political poetry gets written by poets who are most detached, even—in the special way poets can be—indifferent. Only the powerless really reveal the nature of power; only the nonpolitical understand the nature of politics. This is shown by one of the most "unremitting" political poems ever written—Pushkin's *The Bronze Horseman*—and also by such poems of Herbert's as "Five Men" and "Preliminary Investigation of an Angel."

"Five Men" records the execution of the men, presumably Poles, by a platoon of soldiers, presumably Germans. It refuses to be moved, or moving, and its weight falls on its own question and reply.

> what did the five talk of
> the night before the execution
>
> of prophetic dreams
> of an escapade in a brothel
> of automobile parts
> of a sea voyage
> of how when he had spades
> he ought not to have opened
> of how vodka is best
> after wine you get a headache
> of girls
> of fruit
> of life

After this the poet does not have to answer his own question.

> I did not learn this today
> I knew it before yesterday
> so why have I been writing
> unimportant poems on flowers

The question answers itself. The word "unimportant" disclaims any irony, just as the absence of punctuation—none of Herbert's poems is punctuated—turns all query into statement.

As the tone of "Five Men" resembles exactly the ending of *The Bronze Horseman*, so that of "Preliminary Investigation of an Angel" resembles the tone of Kafka. The angel sheds his angelic being as the investigation proceeds until from his hair "drops of wax run down / and shape on the floor / a simple prophecy." Angel and candle, points of lights, are inter-metamorphosed, not by Kafka's nightmare but by the spoken and unspoken nature of Herbert's poetic language. Herbert's detachment is of the kind that takes a lot for granted: there is no point in going on about the nature of things. The last poem in the *Selected Poems*, "Why the Classics," tacitly but significantly takes Thucydides for the poet's hero, and in a sense for his model too. In the fourth book of his account of the Peloponnesian War, Thucydides refers briefly to his own minor unsuccessful military assignment to relieve the Athenian colony of Amphipolis before the Spartan general Brasidas got there. He made a quick winter passage with his seven ships but nonetheless arrived too late—an everyday sort of setback for a commander in a war which was fought with dogged persistence rather than strategic brilliance. Herbert is interested in the perfunctoriness with which Thucydides refers to the incident, and contrasts it with the memoirs of "generals of more recent wars" who belittle their colleagues and display everything to their own advantage. The lesson is for art.

> if art for its subject
> will have a broken jar
> a small broken soul
> with a great self-pity
>
> what will remain after us
> will be like lovers' weeping
> in a small dirty hotel
> when wall-paper dawns

"Classical" is the word most often used to describe Herbert's poetry, both in Poland and among readers who know his work in the West. The word is necessarily ambiguous. T. S. Eliot often appealed to the traditions of classicism, and implied, as did Ezra Pound in his way, that his own poetry endorsed them. But the interior of Eliot's poetry is deeply personal, full of romantic secrets and intimacies. These are notably lacking in Herbert. Not that Herbert is impersonal: he presents a Horatian simplicity and openness, a temperament like that of a traveler or classical scholar. His collection of essays on European cultural sites, *Barbarian in the Garden*, contains some of the best travel writing of our time, but is almost disappointing in the way it reveals nothing about the inner life or history of the man himself. One cannot imagine him writing a love poem, or investigating his emotion with the zestful precision of a Robert Graves. His poetry reveals sharply and by contrast how much modern poetry has come to depend on versions of self-pity, and on the way it feeds and builds up the individual interior of a poet's work.

This is not all gain where Herbert is concerned. His poetry can seem flat, formulaic, and predictable. Even in the crisp and impeccable translations of Czeslaw Milosz and Peter Dale Scott there is a certain sameness about the parallels along which each poem develops that may not show up in the variety and intimacy of its native tongue, where nuances of idiom and cadence would give it a specialness not available in English correspondence. As the translators point out, Herbert is not classical in the sense of using traditional meters or rhymes; his poetry is more like a spare form of conversation, obviously depending a good deal on word order and on the subtle use of cliché. Well-known poems like "Apollo and Marsyas" and "Elegy of Fortinbras" are no doubt much funnier in the original. In English they depend rather too much on the points they make. In "Apollo and Marsyas" the god of restraint, proportion, and clarity, having flayed the faun and cleaned his instrument, departs along "a gravel path hedged with box," leaving his skinless victim uttering one immense howl on a single note, perhaps a new kind of "concrete" poetry. The joke, at the expense both of classicism and of pop art, has a tenderness, but in English the message arrives without the full depth of its implication. No doubt the cruelty of art—even Herbert's own art—arises from the fact that in the very act of creation it necessarily separates itself from human suffering, which cries out from the force and nature of its whole body and blood, and is thus abhorrent to the "god with nerves of artificial fibre."

The impasse left on the English page has no doubt all sorts of sly entrances and exits on the Polish one. The same is probably true of "Elegy of Fortinbras." Fortinbras explains the needs of the world to the dead Hamlet, and tells him that "the rest is not silence but belongs to me."

> I must also elaborate a better system of prisons
> since as you justly said Denmark is a prison
> I go to my affairs This night is born
> a star named Hamlet We shall never meet
> what I shall leave will not be worth a tragedy

On the face of it the poem has too much point to have a proper inside territory; but the contrast between the two characters may well have a greater significance in the original. Hamlet has understood the nature of action: he has in fact "understood," just as a poem does, but what Fortinbras says of Hamlet—"you knew no human thing you did not know even how to breathe"—is also true of a poem.

A brief preliminary note by the translators is oddly defensive, and yet makes a firm and just point:

> Control, conciseness, honesty and soberness are not always to be condemned, least of all when these are qualities of a poet who received a proper European initiation into horror and chaos. In these times sanity may become as much of a corrective to normalcy as the absurd was in an earlier era.

It is indeed a striking thing that so many European poets, who when young went through the full terror of the Second World War, have written in consequence a poetry of extreme simplicity and precision, avoiding any overt expression of emotion, and setting the highest value on the old artifices of logic and reason. Vasko Popa in Serbia was one such, and Czeslaw Milosz is himself another. Man in extremity does not imitate the abyss and its moppings and mowings, but strives rather to detach himself from its absurdity. And it is a paradox that the sort of sounds made by Marsyas proceed, in our day and climate, not from anguish and loss of freedom and fatherland, but from the kinds of boredom and meaninglessness inherent in the affluent society. As Milosz implies, being a Pole connects one, in an intimacy which is almost comfortable, to the unchanging horrors of history. The idea that we live in a very special time that calls for a very special art would cause a Pole to smile. For him it is always the mixture as before, so that the attitudes and practices of classicism represent no arbitrary whim on the part of the poet, but rather the most natural response in art to the imperatives of survival. Herbert's poetry lives in the flow of history, and among the artifacts of European culture, as naturally as a pebble in the bed of a stream.

Herbert's great-grandfather was English, and the bizarre coincidence of his name with that of two English poets sharpens the fact of his wholly

European rather than Polish status. The family split into two branches, one Catholic and one Protestant, and Herbert's branch settled in Lvov, in the eastern marches, where Polish, Ukrainian, and Jewish cultures made a richly cosmopolitan mix. The east has always been a fertile ground for Polish poetry. Adam Mickiewicz came from Vilna, on the borders of Lithuania, as did Milosz. Herbert's mother was Armenian; his father, a professor of economics, a practising Catholic; his grandmother Orthodox. "And, all around, evidences of Hasidic culture . . . hence my syncretic religion." Herbert's cousin, son of an Austrian general on the other side of the family, was one of the thousands of Polish officers murdered by the Russians at Katyn in 1940.

Paradoxically, this almost too nutritious background has probably been instrumental in producing the austerities of Herbert's verse. Instead of submerging itself in the past and in its milieu, with all the helplessness of which some modern poetry makes a virtue, Herbert's poetry detaches itself into a thinner air, almost that dimension of logic and mathematics in which recent Polish scholarship has specialized. Many of the poems in *Report from the Besieged City* employ a persona called Mr. Cogito, a not altogether serious figure (sometimes he becomes "the suckling Cogito") who devotes himself nonetheless to some highly serious and abstract questions—on eschatology, autocracy, or death—varied by encounters with a monster who cannot be seen ("the proof of the existence of the monster / is its victims") or with Maria Rasputin, the historical daughter of that Siberian shaman who exercised his influence in imperial St. Petersburg.

Mr. Cogito "would like to remain faithful to uncertain clarity," and rejects "the artificial fires of poetry."

> the piano at the top of the alps
> played false concerts for him
> he didn't appreciate labyrinths
> the sphinx filled him with loathing . . .

> he adored tautologies
> explanations
> idem per idem

> that a bird is a bird
> slavery means slavery
> a knife is a knife
> death remains death

Of course, poetry is always rejecting its own devices, and acquiring new ones in the process. But Herbert is not just saying "My mistress' eyes are nothing like the sun"; his equivalents are precise and cryptographic. The poem "September 17" refers to the precise date in 1939 when the Russians invaded eastern Poland, ten days after the German army had struck in the west. But the date is only allowed its precision in and for itself: the poem is saying the opposite of *einmal ist keinmal,* for in Poland invasion is invasion, a simple and continuous fact and, as Pushkin put it tersely, more than a hundred years earlier and from the eastern side: "The history of Poland is and ought to be a disaster."

> knights sleeping in the mountains continue to sleep
> so you will enter easily uninvited guest

Herbert is not in the least afraid of the kind of platitude which goes with his simple and perpetual equivalents in history and logic.

> My defenceless country will admit you invader
> and give you a plot of land under a willow and peace
> so those who come after us will learn again
> the most difficult art the forgiveness of sins

At the end of the book the title poem, "Report from the Besieged City," explores the same ground and reaches the same conclusion, a conclusion that has none of the brilliance of Milan Kundera's formulation but a great deal more good sense. Since the poet is too old to bear arms

> they graciously gave me the inferior role of chronicler
> I record I don't know for whom the history of the siege . . .
> all of this is monotonous I know it can't move anyone

Nothing can be less exciting than the history of the siege, and once again the conclusion is what anyone might have expected.

> cemeteries grow larger the number of defenders is smaller
> yet the defence continues it will continue to the end
> and if the city falls yet a single man escapes
> he will carry the City within himself on the roads of exile
> he will be the City

Both in relation to Poland and to humanity at large the meaning is as obvious as a syllogism, but it carries its obviousness with the weight and delicacy which makes Herbert so peculiar and so individual a poet.

The Times Literary Supplement, 1986

43

Return of the Native

Czeslaw Milosz (1911–2004)

The Issa Valley
by Czeslaw Milosz, translated by Louis Iribarne

Native Realm: A Search for Self-Definition
by Czeslaw Milosz, translated by Catherine S. Leach

Emperor of the Earth: Modes of Eccentric Vision
by Czeslaw Milosz

Bells in Winter
by Czeslaw Milosz, translated by Lillian Vallee

The Captive Mind
by Czeslaw Milosz, translated by Jane Zielonko, with a foreword
    by the author

"*B*IN GAR KEINE RUSSIN, *stamm' aus Litauen, echt deutsch.*" (I am not Russian at all; I come from Lithuania, a true German.) The twelfth line of *The Waste Land*, a fragment from the poet's reading in a German memoir, raises more echoes than even T. S. Eliot was likely to be aware of, and certainly more than are grasped by most of his readers. The connection with the poem is minimal, but as in so many of its other lines randomness has achieved an air of inevitability, in its suggestion of unhappy and not-so-far-off things, unknown lives, and fates, the product of complex histories, the inspissated rivalries and relations of Lithuanians, Balts and Letts, Jews, Germans, and Russians.

With them no one could have a more natural familiarity than the poet and winner of the 1980 Nobel Prize for literature, Czeslaw Milosz. He too stemmed from Lithuania. But not with any conviction of purity; and during a century when the now small but once enormous country has been successively Russian, German, Polish, Lithuanian, Russian, German, and Soviet Russian again. Like most of the native sons of the town known in Polish as Wilno (German and Russian *Wilna*, Lithuanian *Vilnius*), Milosz is a Polish speaker, and it was in Polish that he began to write his poems. With a hint of irony he remarks that natives of his province are more inward, with the deeper intimacies of the Polish language, than are their metropolitan cousins at the center in Warsaw. The "Polish Pushkin," Adam Mickiewicz, foremost of native poets, began to write under the inspiration of the land of Polish Lithuania.

But whereas a poet from Dublin or Edinburgh would advance in all seriousness the proposition that the English language at its liveliest and most sensitive was to be found in those towns (and a bookish native of New York, Chicago, or Los Angeles might do the same), Milosz is unquestionably amused by the complacency of his own claim that languages are richest at their cultural edges. Nationality is not a thing he can take seriously: it would be hard to imagine a greater writer more emancipated from even its most subtle pretensions.

Nevertheless his genius flourishes and finds its subject in the many degrees of consciousness nationality implies; and to feast on such things and yet remain free of them is in itself a gift of genius. Language and nationality are haunts of the irrational. They are also the root of the well-grown ego, the base of that *samodovolnost*—self-satisfaction—which Tolstoy (whose forebears, before rising in the Tsar's service, had themselves stemmed from Lithuania) perceived as the beginning of all lively and healthy human activity. Our natures grow and flourish by denaturing those who are not planted in the same bed. The snobberies of race and language are even more needful in us, more deeply intertwined in the unconscious, than the associated snobberies of class. And, so far from diminishing, this tribal mentality is now everywhere more virulent, more local, than ever before.

Native Realm: A Search for Self-Definition is thus an autobiography with a real title, and not just a fashionable quest for roots. The genius of Milosz is far too confident for him to wish to "rediscover" himself: it is a question of seeking to embody in consciousness and in poetry the individual's complex and precious sense of itself. Looking back in 1968, when the book was first published in both Polish and English, he saw the forests and swamps of Lithuania as a rich manure heap out of which grows the butterfly of a detached and poetical awareness. With his secret fastidious humor, his natural delicacy, Milosz is fascinated by the vagaries of class in such a situation, no less than by those of race and language. Abruptly, when Milosz was a child, Lithuania became a sovereign state again, a minor result of the cataclysm of the First World War, which had severed one Tsarist province from another, as if New Jersey abruptly found itself an independent neighbor of New York, a contiguity that brought out every old sort of enmity and rivalry and fostered a whole lot of new ones.

Lithuanians now reserved their animus particularly for Poles, whom they assumed, not without justification, to be gentry, landlords, and oppressors, disaffected from the new state, as in the case of Ireland or Finland, but with a special degree of complication that could only be found in the marches of Eastern Europe. With the incomprehensible logic of time, the Lithuanians, tardy converts to Catholicism, had slipped into the position of perpetual peasants, uncouth younger sons, their new religious devotion confirming their ineradicably junior status. In the days of their pagan ascendancy, worshippers of Peruna, the god of thunder, of the oak tree, and of Ragutis, the leering corpulent satyr hewn from it, had conquered all Eastern Europe to Kiev under their grand dukes Gudimin and Olgerd, and in the spirit of such a conquest had entered into partnership with the Poles. With the help of religion the Poles soon reduced them to the state of country cousins.

Northward, superiorities were of a Teutonic kind, bourgeois and Lutheran. It is significant that in Milosz's wonderful autobiographical novel, *The Issa Valley*, a Lithuanian peasant speaks admiringly of life in Sweden—the Swedes too, like everyone else in that quarter, have been through Lithuania in their time—and of the prosperous northern neighbor as a model state for rural egalitarianism. And though the gentry spoke

Polish, Lithuania still had its language, one of the oddest and most ancient of Indo-Germanic survivals, akin to Sanskrit, the object of studious enquiry by philologists in Munich and Berlin. To have such a language was itself a form of superiority.

In *The Issa Valley*, Milosz portrays himself as Thomas, grandson of a minor landowner whose gentility is based on Poland and Polish, though his name and some of his forebears are Lithuanian. The novel is an idyll of immense charm and poetic depth, a story without much conventional plot about a boy growing up in the Lithuanian countryside and raised largely by grandparents proud of their Polish background. The sensitive translation by Louis Iribarne gives at least a good idea of what must be the quality of the original, first published by an emigré press in Paris in 1955. Its quality lies in its solidity—it is as solid as the oak-hewn figure of Ragutis himself.

The portraits in this novel will remind readers of those classic figures drawn from Tolstoy in *Childhood* and *Boyhood*, and by Aksakov in his family memoirs. But Milosz is more humane than Tolstoy and less "creamy" (in literary historian Prince Minsky's word) than Aksakov. The child of *The Issa Valley* accepts his elders with unconscious and uncomprehending love, but the pattern of their days and their being is created with a great poet's unobtrusively vivid power. As the book progresses we understand more and more of the nature and outlook of the hero's grandfather, who is at first a painting in words, like Ghirlandaio's *Old Man*. The hero's grandmothers are similarly memorable. One despises regular meals and nibbles tidbits of sweet and sour, lifting her skirts to warm herself at the porcelain stove. The other, raised in cities, lives a more anxious life like a squirrel in its hole. Her death near the book's conclusion is a sign to the young hero—his first—of his true identification with the ground she goes to rest in.

Meantime he's growing up, hunting and dreaming, taking in portents both from nature and from the age-old accessibility of the human consciousness around him. He communes, too, with lives that form subplots to the novel: the mistress of the priest who killed herself with rat poison when he sent her away; the forester haunted by the Russian soldier he has stalked and killed in the forest; a Polish small landowner who teaches the hero to shoot, and whose Lithuanian housekeeper—primitive, contemptuous, and bewitching—leads her own mysterious life in a corner of the narrative.

It is an ancient world over which Milosz has mastery here, but there is nothing self-conscious in its ancientness. I have stressed the Lithuanian provenance of Milosz because it seems to me the clue to something in his work that is unique: the reality of the *thing*, the return of the *thing*. It is no accident that structuralism and deconstruction, as critical and reading techniques, have banished physical realities from literature, replacing them with the abstract play of language, "the game of the signifiers." They were on their way out anyway; they were leaving literature; and the critical process, as usual, found ways of explaining and rationalizing their departure, even of suggesting they had never been there.

Why "things," in this profound sense, should have faded out of literature, leaving not even the grin of a Cheshire cat, is a question of great complexity, but one reason is certainly what has to be termed the Americanization of the field of literature itself. Things, in the sense in which the nineteenth-century novel—Dickens and Hardy and Tolstoy—both assumed and created them have not been central to the American literary consciousness. In their place have been legends and ideas and consciousness itself. The Deep South and Wild West with its Indians and cowboys which captivated the European imagination (Milosz often refers to them as part of his own boyhood awareness) did so because they had never existed. Like so many other American stories, these were an effort of consciousness to create experience, to give itself something to live by.

In Europe things preceded consciousness; in America they had to be created and commemorated by it. Most literary creation in America is factitious, in the sense that it has to be an advertisement for itself; and this leads naturally to the world of actual advertising—of news, of lifestyles, of literary fields—which dominates the modern consciousness. New styles of reading and of analyzing texts represent a recognition and an intellectualization of this process, which has come to be the norm in every contemporary culture.

It takes a masterpiece to reveal the sheer unreality of our modern creative modes and poses, and Milosz's novel is such a masterpiece. Its account of childhood in a valley inhabited by an "unusually large number of devils" has no obvious originality, nor is it in any sense a strikingly

distinctive work; but, strangely enough, even the fact that it is a translation only appears to accentuate its closeness to real things, for it seems to
be about those things and not about the author's invention of them, odd
or novel. It makes us realize the extent to which an American masterpiece tends to be about itself only, and has to be. *Winesburg, Ohio;
Appointment in Samarra; The Great Gatsby; The Heart Is a Lonely
Hunter*—they all have to clutch their discoveries to themselves, creating
a new consciousness that does duty as a new world. Such comparisons are
not wholly invidious: it is a fact that a writer like Milosz is effortlessly master of a primeval world, of which the art of the West no longer has any
conception, and can only reconstitute in solipsistic magic, the supermar-
ket gothicism of Edna O'Brien or Joyce Carol Oates. Even Faulkner's
world is as willed as theirs, crafted straight from vacancy into myth and
symbol.

The significance of this was touched on accidentally by Milosz himself in his essay "On Pasternak Soberly," printed in the collection entitled
Emperor of the Earth, published in 1977. *Dr. Zhivago*, he writes, has been
misunderstood in the West because we have forgotten how to read and to
recognize a primitive work. All those events and objects and people, the
products of that hymn "Eternal Memory" which is being chanted in the first
sentence—these are real, with the reality conferred by primary art; they
are not the "web of symbols" ingeniously discovered by Edmund Wilson,
just as they are not the soap opera, with the "Lara theme" and the sword-
waving Cossacks dashing over the snow, into which the publicity agents
of the West converted them. But *Dr. Zhivago* is a primitive tale about a
society in an ageless state of barbarism now grown dynamic, full of the
chances, the coincidences, the collisions that actually occur in such a
society and thus in a story about it. Milosz points out, for example, that
Yuri Zhivago's half-Asiatic natural brother Yevgraf, who appears mysteriously from time to time to sort out his problems, and who has been taken
as some kind of symbolic figure, is in fact just the kind of person you find
both in Soviet and in primitive heroic societies—the archetypal Great
One who offers some protection against perpetual threats and hazards.

Of course there is a strong element of pastiche in *Dr. Zhivago*, an element of fin-de-siècle fantasy, and *The Issa Valley* is not free from pastiche
either. It could hardly be otherwise with a book written today about a boy

growing up in the small valley, the countryside of the author's childhood. But both Pasternak and Milosz are poets, poets of the first class though of very different kinds, and this difference is shown in the texture of their prose. In the case of Milosz, experience emerges as a quality that over-rides the impossibilities of translation. A poet so good that he can be translated is a supreme paradox, one which many poets today, and read-ers of poetry, would refuse to recognize, so strong is the tendency now for poetry only to congeal and inhere in the carefully exploited accuracies and idiosyncrasies of a language.

But if nobody thought Dante and Shakespeare untranslatable it was because of what they said; how they said it was of course another matter. The fact that what Milosz says comes across with such primary force and impact is itself an indication that, as a poet in the largest sense, he is an ideal kind of recipient of the Nobel Prize. It is possible that there are real differences here, though of a wholly indefinable kind, in the nature of languages themselves: some are more amenable than others to moving sideways, to acquiring a kind of international potential. Not for nothing, perhaps, was Esperanto invented in Poland.

In *Native Realm* Milosz writes with admirable humor and dispassion about the lightness of his native tongue, its adaptability, its centuries-old cultivated Westernness, as contrasted with the poise and weight, the inevitability, as it were, of Russian syllables and syntax. Observing that his countrymen are fascinated by Russian because it "liberates their Slavic half," because in its menace and seduction it "is all there is to know about Russia," Milosz tells how he and his friends used to perform a certain exer-cise which gave them "a good deal to think about." First they uttered in a bass voice the Russian words for "A deep hole dug with a spade," and then chattered quickly in a tenor the verbally very similar Polish equivalent.

> The arrangement of accents and vowels in the first phrase connotes gloom, darkness, and power; in the second, lightness, clarity, and weakness. In other words, it was both an exercise in self-ridicule and a warning.

Be that as it may, it is certainly true that such Russian syllables, if they become poetry, are untranslatable in consequence. Milosz discovered

Pushkin on his own, which is the right way to do it, and was captivated. "My native tongue was incapable of such power of expression, of such masterful iambs, and I had to admit it." But as an embryonic poet he soon began to distrust the lyricism "which seemed to unfold from itself as if born of the very sounds themselves." Pushkin doesn't happen to talk about a deep hole dug with a spade, though if he did it would become poetry, as it does when he writes of "the sea where ships were running," or "a forest on the banks of the Dnieper." Such poetry is untranslatable because it says nothing, but exists merely and absolutely in its own tongue, and so in another language is flat and banal.

The poetry of Milosz, as of Mickiewicz, is not like that; it has a timbre, a clarity of desire, an urgency of sense which forces itself out of its own language into others. The Spanish of Pablo Neruda, the Italian of Eugenio Montale, can today still do the same, availing themselves of the Latin camaraderie which is so immanent also in Polish religion and culture, if not in the language itself. In the lines of Mickiewicz's "Forefather's Eve," which Milosz quotes, there is an acoustic forcefulness which proclaims itself as poetry in whatever language. The poet's hatred for Russian tyranny contrasts with his sympathy for its victims, whom he sees not from the inside, as Pushkin and Gogol did, but with the brutally lucid incredulity of an outsider. He contrasts the faces of Europeans, an articulate record of intelligible emotion and feeling, with the Russian face.

> Here, people's eyes, like the cities of this country
> Are large and clear; never does the soul's tumult
> Move the pupil with an extraordinary glance,
> Never does desolation cloud them over long.
> Seen from a distance they are splendid, marvelous;
> Once inside, they are empty and deserted.
> The body of this people is like a fat cocoon,
> Inside which sleeps a caterpillar-soul . . .
> But when the sun of freedom shall rise,
> What kind of insect will fly out from that shroud?

A poem written by the young Milosz, before the war, will serve as an example of his special quality, as well as of his extraordinary translatability. Written in 1936 and collected in *Bells in Winter* (1978), it is called "Encounter."

> We were riding through frozen fields in a wagon at dawn
> A red wing rose in the darkness.
>
> And suddenly a hare ran across the road.
> One of us pointed to it with his hand.
>
> That was long ago. Today neither of them is alive,
> Not the hare, nor the man who made the gesture.
>
> O my love, where are they, where are they going
> The flash of a hand, streak of movement, rustle of pebbles.
> I ask not out of sorrow, but in wonder.

Even more striking than the fact that this poetry remains poetry in another language—with the advantage, it is true, of having been translated in collaboration with the poet himself—is the sense of a shared experience that Milosz manages to give, a limpid repose upon the way things are that is no less than our sense of wonder at them. What prompted the writing of *The Issa Valley* in 1955 was the same kind of emotion that found expression in this poem, and Milosz was then an exile in America, collecting and perpetuating the wonderings of his adolescence.

There is in a way nothing personal about them. Milosz's world is collective—a place for everything and everything in its place. He is one of the few poets who does not give the impression of seeing something in his own special way. The self in his poetry is not impersonal but effortlessly manifold, like the emotions and sensations in its records. As he puts it in his poem "Ars Poetica?" which appears in *Bells in Winter*:

> The purpose of poetry is to remind us
> how difficult it is to remain just one person,
> for our house is open, there are no keys in the doors,
> and invisible guests come in and out at will.

We become our relations, our moments, each other, even our graves; at least we do so if we live in the kind of dense and populous relation with the world which Milosz records and celebrates. The relation to the past moment in his poem is the same as that to his grandmother's grave in *The Issa Valley*. In *The Issa Valley* too we see the beginnings of the poem "Diary of a Naturalist," however much later on that poem was written, in an experience of the young boy.

> One winter Thomas spotted an ermine on the bank of the river Issa. Frost and sunlight made the twigs of the bushes on the steep shore of the opposite bank stand out like bouquets of gold, lightly tinged with gray and bluish purple. It was then that a ballet dancer of remarkable grace and ability would appear on the ice, a white sickle that would arch and straighten again. With a gaping mouth Thomas stared at it in bewilderment and ached with desire. To have. If he had had a rifle with him he would have shot it, because one could not simply stand still when one's wonder demanded that the thing arousing it be preserved for ever.

The overwhelming impulse that wished to have the creature—shoot it if need be—later became the impulse of the poet. Milosz does not sentimentalize the adolescent's worship of nature, as predatory as the beasts it moves among. *The Issa Valley* is full of hunting and hunting expeditions, as memorable as those in *Pan Tadeusz*, or Aksakov and Turgenev. Of particular note is the stalking of the capercailzie (the translation, in most respects excellent, calls it a grouse—quite a different bird) when that fabulous fowl of the spruce woods, as wary as a cat throughout most of the year, is temporarily deafened by the noise of its own ritual mating call.

The characters in *The Issa Valley*—grandfather, grandmothers, neighbors, the local forester, are all members of a household, even though the Lithuanian peasant shows at moments an atavistic hostility to the Polish *pan*, or local gentry. As in Tolstoy, the more closely integrated the members of a family, the more peculiarly individual they appear. In this pre-American melting pot the racial and social mix produces not uniformity but a matured exactness of distinction, of the kind found in nature itself and worshipped by Milosz when he writes as a botanist and ornithologist.

That habit of exactness explains the twin paradox of Milosz's distinction as a poet: his sense of things as they are, and yet his power—almost a conscious power it sometimes seems—of projecting what he writes out of the absolute linguistic form which poetry usually demands. His own poetic temperament and upbringing again offer a clue. He has a sense of a poet as "not just one person," an instinct akin to Keats's perception of the poet as a man in whom personality has been exorcised in the intensities of negative capability. But Keats's poetry, in all its richness, its vulnerability as language, is held down to the very words in which it was first uttered. Milosz's seems to aspire to some ideal language, almost to Wordsworth's "ghostly language of the ancient earth," and not the earth only—the sky too, the steady rationale of a sentient universe.

It is the same with the novel. Despite its immensely local subject and setting there is nothing in the least provincial about it. A friend of Milosz, the poet Tomás Venclova, a native of Vilnius/Wilno, notes the same characteristic about it from the viewpoint of a native professional, a connoisseur, as it were, of the interplay of linguistic factors, and of their transcendence.

> It always seems to me that this novel belongs to a certain conceivable, ideal Lithuanian literature. In that literature [as in the work of Donelaitis] we have these types and motifs, there are these landscapes and seasons, but, alas, we have no novel in which everything could be united into such an integral and beautiful entity. The novel belongs to Polish literature. However, from a certain point of view, this is ultimately unimportant.

Unimportant because a true transcendence of nationalism is produced not by simplification and standardization but precisely by that linguistic interplay, rivalry, and synthesis of which the background of Milosz's writing affords such a remarkable example.

There is another factor involved. The whole movement of American and English poetic writing, of such writing in the West in general, has tended toward the linguistic justification of the individual, of the poet as self-explorer and self-proclaimer. In proclaiming himself, Walt Whitman

gave a voice to America, but the modern poet has for the most part settled to invent only his own language and his own self. By belonging to
themselves—and to the poet—so completely, his poems elude any
authenticity other than their own personal one; they not only avoid any
other and wider version of themselves but disown it. Their art is devoted
to remaining just one person, one poem, one life-study. This is as true of
Robert Lowell and John Berryman as it is of Philip Larkin and Seamus
Heaney. The Irish poet writes fondly and with devout precision of the
nature of bogs, of their soft dark provenance in his soul; but this is bog as
he owns it, as he has found it—as Yeats found and made his own Ireland.
That bog so dependent on its personal verbal artifact ("The squelch and
slap / Of soggy peat, the curt cuts of an edge") is a far cry from the forest
swamps of Lithuania, which, through Milosz's mediation and advocacy,
are an open place alive with invisible guests and no longer centered in
his own self.

This is not to attempt a qualitative judgment. Milosz is not better than
the best poets of the West, but he is certainly different, and the difference
declares itself as a question of open poetry and an open mind, an openness manifesting itself out of a society closed by the Iron Curtain. The formidable talent of an American artist in our time seeks in one sense relief
from freedom: it needs the prison of its own self-creation, one suggested
in that grimly revealing little exchange between the painter Edward Hop-
per and an admirer—"What are you after?" "I'm after me." Perhaps one
can pay too high a price for one democratic tongue and one democratic
kind of solitude.

Milosz is not after himself but after that old European goal of cultiva-
tion and understanding, enlightenment and *humanitas*. Often, no doubt,
his open poetic pronouncements upon that goal may look like cliché, to
poets and their readers conditioned to come at it—if at all—through the
honing and perfecting of the ego. And there is a certain irony in the fact
that while a poet and critic like Donald Davie may have learned from
Milosz and deeply understood his old-fashioned creative intellectualism,
Milosz is also admired in America by an open tradition of poetry which
is the reverse of intellectual. As Milosz himself has recognized by quoting
it in his own poetry, Allen Ginsburg's *Howl* is paradoxically closer to his

own poetic outlook than is that of the sophisticated and egocentric poetic styles of today.

Openness in Milosz as an artist is also rare in terms of his openness of genre. By writing in every form, he writes virtually in one: and he instructs in all. *Native Realm* and his earlier essay *The Captive Mind*, which first appeared in English in 1953, are among the most illuminating books to come out of recent history and its debate on ideology. It is so much an index of how good Milosz is as a critic, historian, and philosophical commentator that if one knew his work only in those reflective forms one would not guess that he is also a novelist and poet. Only very good poets and novelists have these comprehensive and Goethean abilities, though Milosz's creative outlook has none of Goethe's deliberative importance. He excels at the rapid focus, the quick glimpse that finds the inner dimension of a subject.

In one of his essays, "Brognart: A Story Told Over a Drink," collected in *Emperor of the Earth*, he relates almost as Joseph Conrad might have done the story of a young Frenchman of peasant origins, who visited a friend in Poland in 1939 and was caught by the war. Because he remained bent, in his logical French fashion, on finding a consul and repatriating himself, because, in effect, he persisted in behaving as if he were not in a world where civilization had ceased to have meaning, he was eventually picked up by the Russians and shipped off to a camp near Archangelsk, where he lasted until 1951, still making efforts to get in touch with a French consul.

As a Pole, eternally caught between two incompatible power centers, Milosz profoundly understands the total incomprehension that exists between states and individuals of quite different provenance. No other phenomenon is historically more important, and its importance today continues to increase. It made any mutual understanding impossible between Neville Chamberlain and Hitler in 1939, and equally impossible between poor Brognart and his persecutors. Incidentally, this terrible little true story has something in common with Conrad's meticulous tale, "Amy Foster," in which a shipwrecked immigrant pathetically attempts to adapt himself to life in an English village.

Milosz's essay on Apollo Korzeniowski, in *Emperor of the Earth*, the doomed, tormented, and idealistic father of Conrad the English novelist, is more illuminating in a few pages than most of the critical books on Conrad's novels. So, in a different way, is his passing reference to the fact that the Poles who would not let Jews join their first partisan detachments during the war would have been genuinely amazed if their behavior had been criticized as racial discrimination—not that this was any comfort to the Jews. Such things to them were facts of nature; and as such were intimately connected with the fact that prewar Poland had nothing resembling the fanatical and hysterical anti-Jewish policy carried out in Germany. The "gentrification" of that great Polish-Lithuanian *respublica* which stretched from the Baltic to the Black Sea may have been politically disastrous, as was shown in its easy liquidation by the servile empires of the Teutons and Slavs, but it also means that an idea of civilized behavior, of moral *comme il faut*, penetrated from above into the humblest reaches of Polish society.

And yet Milosz's uncle, Oscar Milosz, himself half Jewish and a distinguished French poet, used to admonish his young nephew on his rare visits to the East to remember that "in Europe there is nothing more stupid or more brutal in its petty hatreds than the Polish gentry." And that was true too. The remarkable father of this cosmopolitan poet, who became the first Lithuanian delegate to the League of Nations, had been a Polish landowner who saw a portrait of his future bride—she happened to be a beautiful Jewess—in a Warsaw shop. The fact that he determined on the spot to marry her was itself a manifestation of the proud independence befitting a Polish gentleman, but it also meant that his caste ostracized him and his family. For all his French domicile and reputation the son expressed as plangently as Chateaubriand a homesickness for what he regarded as his native Lithuania—"*une vaste étendue de lacs obscurs, verdâtres et pourissants, envahis par une folie des tristes nymphéas jaunes, . . . O Maison, Maison! Pourquoi m'avez-vous laissé partir?*"

Milosz regained his home through writing about it in *The Issa Valley*. He was conscious always of the precarious and provisional nature of the country in which he grew up, and how complete would be its extinction when the moment came. France, he points out, survived a German invasion and conquest without undue discomfort, and would have done so even if the Germans had remained the winning side. For Poland—the new nation—defeat would mean calamity and extinction. The young

Milosz got the nickname of "catastrophist" from the tone of the poems he wrote in the years before the war, but, though history was to prove him altogether too accurate a prophet, his own survival during the time of apocalypse chastened him. He was too honest not to see that survival is its own form of humiliation, one that subdues not only pride of the ideological visionary—and Milosz was then a believing Marxist and revolutionary—but the impulse to denunciation of such ideology, a counter-attitude.

Life itself, and the reverence for it, becomes then the precious thing to be explored and celebrated. It is this lucid humility which sets Milosz apart from Solzhenitsyn, a self-martyred soul who inhabits a country where conviction is more important than reflection, where the vowels are deeper, the shapes of speech more minatory. Solzhenitsyn's power as a writer demands that life should be intensified, directed, and organized in the Russian style; Milosz's provenance makes him conservative and freedom-loving in a wholly different sense. In his novels and poetry, life and time are caught in an unending study of awareness: the gesture of a man pointing to a hare that runs across the road.

The New York Review of Books, 1981

PART VI

Aspects of Novels

44

The Point of Novels

"WHAT IS THE *POINT* OF IT?" The novel remains vulnerable, as no other art does, to this traditional philistine query. For unlike that of a vase, a picture, a poem, or a play, the form of the novel does not contain in its own self the reason why it "is what it is and not another thing." And the more new novels I read, the more I feel it not only natural but discriminating to ask myself if they have a point, and if so, what?

Conversely, it is a sign of success if the query seems truly irrelevant. The novel has achieved a self, has coincided with a notion of its form. This has occurred to me lately only twice: in *We Think the World of You,* by J. R. Ackerley, and in Brigid Brophy's novel *Flesh.* Yet neither seemed to me about anything in particular: they explored no new world of technique or feeling; they flung down no challenge for Our Time; they exhibited no profound understanding; they were not compassionate, indignant, or even especially meaningful. Both clearly drew upon personal experience but remained impersonal in tone; and both were completely absorbing, not by virtue of subject and treatment, but through their discreet self-confidence as works of art.

This is not to say I have enjoyed no other new novels—I have had pleasure from several. But with most of them I felt, like those readers of poetry whom A. E. Housman deplored, that I was enjoying not so much the novel as something *in* the novel. A tiresome and dangerous distinction? Yet it is far truer of the novel than of poetry. The daily life, say, of a girl just down from the university and grappling with her job, her apartment, her young men—this interested me because it extended my awareness of what is actually happening to such a person at the moment, and fed the social curiosity which in life is usually nipped off or left unsatisfied. What interested me was the continuation of social awareness by literary means. That, for me, was this novel's point. I was also interested, say, by a fiction about what it is like to be a steward on a Cunarder or a chemist in Nairobi, or about every moment on a journey in a continental express. And here my curiosity was being fed by vicarious experience of an unfamiliar kind.

The point of such novels does not lie in fiction but in fact. All great novels have of course dealt in plain fact in one sense—look at Balzac on printing or Tolstoy on battles—but it is fact that has been surrounded by the novelist's imagination. Have we another criterion here? If we feel the novel had better have been a memoir, an account, a true story, something has gone wrong. We may feel this about quite famous works: I do about A *Farewell to Arms* and *Seven Pillars of Wisdom*. In these cases the author's personality has not transmuted fact, but has interposed itself between fact and ourselves.

There are two troubles here. One is the mere *consciousness* of the writer—eyeing us, cajoling us, taking cover from us, exhibiting or concealing the indulgence of fantasy. The other is his pretension that he is at last bringing us the truth, lifting it above the serried ranks of his predecessors for us to see. "Life is not like that, it is like this"—how many times the cry has gone up. But the novelist who begins with "life" begins with a theory. Most novel readers are less interested in life itself than in its happenings, money-making, love-making, committee-sitting, being young, growing old. What actually happened to Arnold Bennett's old wives will probably survive Virginia Woolf's "luminous envelope" or Robbe-Grillet's obsessed lens.

Not that I am suggesting anonymity, the author *absconditus*, as a criterion for the good novel. We would not wish to forgo the personality of Hardy or Evelyn Waugh or Norman Mailer. But it becomes increasingly rare to find pleasure in the personality of a novelist as it appears in the novel, and the reasons for this, though extremely complex, are perhaps worth investigation. As I have implied, the novelist strikes one as being more and more on his own, interpreting and manipulating his material.

An easy and *self-confident* relation to his tale (as in the two novels I mentioned earlier) becomes increasingly rare. An unself-confident novelist is a lowering phenomenon, and the increasing sophistication and self-imposed importance of his office make it an always more common one. Particularly so, possibly, in America, where the novelist's lack of self-confidence may reflect that of a whole culture. Even in so accomplished a writer as J. D. Salinger, a lack of self-confidence may be at the root of indefinable failings which the reader feels impelled to censure with the use of that handy shotgun word of distrust, *bogus*. It is used more frequently of novels than of any other art form, and usually seems to mean that the reader has detected in the novelist a lost feeling, a suspicion that compassion, cleverness, and *me* are not enough, and a corresponding determination to make out of them a formula that will be.

It is here that the non-novelist scores, for as he relates his war experiences, or takes us on his travels through the jungle, he can be himself without bothering about what sort of self it is, or what sort of point he is making. Paradoxically, his relation to his material is closer to the fictional dawn of Fielding and Dickens. We see this very clearly in the contrast between accounts of "extreme situations"—wars, concentration camps, Houses of the Dead—and in novels about them. The novelist casts about for the true significance or *donnée* of this theme, and quite rightly, for unless he finds it he has not written a true novel; and yet if he does not find it he had better not have manipulated the stark fact of his material by attempting to do so. His path is a hard one, and its difficulty is shown by the apparent absence of any masterpiece about the last war and its accompanying and succeeding horrors. Novels, as opposed to accounts, of these things lack an imaginative justification for being what they are. And yet at any moment a genius may stumble upon their point.

Novel readers are not a demanding race; they can like almost everything but it is always worth their while to ask themselves why they are liking it, and what for.

The Times (London), 1962

45

Gossip in Fiction

Gossip
by Patricia Meyer Spacks

I N *Northanger Abbey* we learn that nothing very awful in the way of immurement or assassination of wives, or any such Gothic goings on, can occur in an English village, because of its "neighbourhood of voluntary spies." In this chilling phrase Jane Austen indicates the social benefits of gossip, and also implies with secret amusement that the moral benefits of novel-reading follow from the fact that the novel is a licensed vehicle for gossip. In the course of an intelligent and informal analysis of the concept, chiefly in its relation to literature, Patricia Spacks remarks on the absence of adolescent pregnancy in China, and connects it with the compulsory retirement, under the Communist regime, of men at fifty-five and women at fifty. There is thus a vast reserve of voluntary spies whose socially acceptable—indeed more or less compulsory—occupation is to keep an eye on young love and nip it in the bud.

Jane Austen, and Georgian and Victorian society, would hardly have been surprised at this. For comprehensively ideological motives, a Communist society applies exactly the same sort of social pressures to its members as did an old-fashioned "free" society. Both have ways of making you conform. In such an environment gossip is an instrument with real teeth: your job and your home may depend upon it. Is gossip still a killer in the Western world? Liberalism has gone to a lot of trouble to draw its teeth, and to make sure that whatever you do you won't have to suffer for it physically at society's hands. In her novel *The Groves of Academe*, Mary McCarthy has a no-good college teacher who can't be got rid of, in the earnestly liberal atmosphere of a campus, once he has cunningly spread the rumor—quite untrue—that he had been a member of the Communist Party. This bestows tenure, a job for life; a modern version of the secret sexual license acquired by Horner in William Wycherly's play *The Country Wife* when he has gossip give out that he has been made impotent by venereal disease.

The author of two good books about poetry, and of two studies on fashionable contemporary themes, *The Female Imagination* and *The Adolescent Idea*, Professor Spacks is also listed on the cover of her new book as chairperson of the English Faculty at Yale, once an academic center for the more arcane sorts of abstract literary theory. Perhaps this means that the teaching of literature is reverting to its old comfortable function of gossip about the people in books. Is Satan good or bad? Why exactly did Iago hatch his plot, or Isobel Archer decide to marry Gilbert Osmond? Such speculations need the exercise of just as much intelligence as does the higher jargon, and for most people they are more fun to make. Dr. Spacks ends her preface with the comment that although the ambiguities and perplexities associated with gossip appear endless, "to explore them has been great fun." A heart-warming point, and we can have it both ways because, as she implies, there is just as much material for class or seminar in this way of doing things as there is in the verbal meccano-work of literary theory.

In conclave with her admiring if skeptical husband in Henry James's novel *The Golden Bowl*, Fanny Assingham remarks of her efforts on behalf of the Prince and Charlotte—efforts which involve, at the highest level, resources of query, speculation, understanding—that whatever happens it will all have been "great fun." To which her husband retorts: "And you call *me* immoral?" The notion of "fun" is indeed compromised in the context of gossip, but Dr. Spacks is surely right to bring it sturdily back into the world of academic thinking and reading, as of conversing and living. In both fields, she suggests, the effect can only be therapeutic. She does not mention Mary McCarthy or Fanny Assingham, both of whom seem to claim that the gossip market can be played—judiciously—for higher stakes than that. Nor does she make much of the gossip industry as it is harnessed and manipulated by government and publicity media, usually for shabby purposes, although it is possible now to imagine a crisis in which we should have to be encouraged to report on AIDS-risk rumors, as the older Chinese are said to be enlisted to keep an eye on youthful sex. Even among us today gossip can still ruin a politician or make a lot of inside money.

But, like white magic, it can be a good thing, and never more so than between the pages of a book. Or in a bookish context. Side-stepping the traumatic link between gossip and power, Dr. Spacks suggests that throughout history it has been chiefly both the weapon and the consolation of the powerless, a special bond of female solidarity. She begins the book on a personal note. Over a number of years she and a woman colleague, equally "beleaguered by trying to sustain families and careers," used to meet every morning for half an hour of coffee and chat.

> Sometimes a male colleague would come in, his expression conveying, or so we fancied, contempt at our verbal trivialities as our talk moved from details of our own lives to speculation about others, or from discussion of novels to contemplation of friends' love affairs. Our husbands couldn't understand why, considering our frequently proclaimed, desperate need for more time, we counted these morning minutes sacred: only dire emergency interfered with them. Both married to unusually sensitive, understanding men, we felt shocked to discover their incomprehension of this essential part of our lives. But we couldn't explain to them; nor did we ever fully explain to ourselves.

This sensibly asserts what women were once conditioned to deprecate, or even masochistically hold up for masculine ridicule, as in the case of Clare Booth Luce's play, *The Women*. The extraordinary success of Barbara Pym's novels in America shows they seem to minister to the same assertiveness, and the same desire for separation. A perennial Pym scene, drawn from life once or twice in her Diaries, is of the women's part of the office, and the calm insolence with which they treat male incursions, continuing to discuss their own affairs. It seems that the strains of sexual equality require a stylized separation into two camps, in which the "sensitive and understanding" man and the emancipated woman can nonetheless assert their ritual difference from one another: the point being that such a difference is no longer involuntary and fundamental but deliberately chosen.

This seems to be what drew Dr. Spacks to gossip as a theme for exploration. It is the handiest medium for deciding what sex you want to be. In practice, one suspects that men's gossip is no different from that of women, although it may take pleasure in a masculine setting and flavor, as theirs in a feminine one. Significant that Henry James's two greatest gossipers are a married couple, as if he felt—rather touchingly—that the principal pleasures of marriage must be sharing impressions of other people's lives. As with Jane Austen's "neighbourhood of voluntary spies," there is something a bit chilling in the lifestyle implied in Dr. Spack's personal account: only the women gossiping together, with the men doing their thing in lordly incomprehension. On the other hand, it must be admitted that something historically feminine in the nature of gossip has contributed one of the most important elements—perhaps *the* most important—to the deep structure of the novel form.

This is the element of equivocation, or at least indirection. As Dr. Spacks points out, Fanny Burney's *Evelina*, one of the liveliest novels of the late eighteenth century but fully embodying its moral norms, is built on a hidden paradox. Evelina can only achieve her womanly goals, a good marriage, an intelligently loving husband, by pretending, at least till she gets them, to be what she isn't. Lord Orville rewards Evelina for her good behavior by marrying her, and good behavior means that she is gentle, silent, discreet, not a gossip—the gossip's role being insensitive, malicious, and dangerous, ultimately alarming to the male persona. Yet the novel in itself articulates those tendencies, and the will to use, exploit, and embody them. As teller of her story, Evelina is the opposite of herself as character in it: and this will become something deeply true of the autobiographical aspect of the novel in general. In being Madame Bovary, Flaubert necessarily forsakes the persona and the intelligence which contemplates her.

The juxtaposition in Evelina is cruder, of course. The young woman reporting—judgmental, necessarily malicious, confident, observant, highly verbal—is the opposite of the young woman set up for judicious appraisal: kind, timid, quiet, vulnerable, always frightened of causing offense. The paradox is notable in Jane Austen, in a much more subtle and humorous way, and is one which used to produce, and perhaps still does, a common masculine reaction to her. How to reconcile the virtuous heroines of her humane comedy with the harpy who wrote the letters, and of whose tongue, as Mary Mitford said, "everyone was afraid." The answer is that it is the contrast and Jane Austen's ways of dissembling it that make the novels the works of art they are. The true moral discovery comes out of the dissembling. Jane Austen was more like Isabella Thorpe than Catherine Morland, and her "Evelina" characters—Fanny Price, Anne Elliott—have a relation to their creator which is ingeniously compounded in Emma, the heroine whom "no one but myself will like," who said things that Jane Austen would probably herself have wished to say.

The novel never admits that gossip is its life, moral matters only its underpinning. As Dr. Spacks remarks, "fiction exercised subversive pressure on the standards it apparently upheld . . . fiction by women explicitly preached doctrines long enforced in female lives." But its plot and technique suggested a "problematising" of moral doctrine. Without this unconscious advantage George Eliot turns the risk, it seems to me, of being a sibyl with too simple and explicit a message—a risk evaded by Jane Austen or the Brontës because of the way women's fiction worked in their day. The mainspring of fiction may be the equivocations and uncertainties of the gossip world, or the Olympian and scientific urge to get things defined, sorted out, pinned down. A combination of the two is not uncommon, but can have its drawbacks, exemplified in *The Great Gatsby*. Gatsby is the ideal person to be talked about, and Nick Carraway, Scott Fitzgerald's narrator, come to New York from the Middle West, can both identify with Gatsby as a figure of mystery and charm, and also consider him objectively as a focus for speculation. Gossip and speculation go together. Anthony Powell's narrator, Nick Jenkins, has the engaging habit of pondering, on our behalf, the possible implications of others' behavior. Surmise and romance go together, putting fascination in the place of knowledge. In Edith Wharton's novel *The House of Mirth* Lawrence Selden sees Lily Bart at Grand Central Station, and wonders "what she was doing in town at that season." He entertains various possibilities because "he could never see her without a faint movement of interest: it was characteristic of her that she always aroused speculation."

So does Gatsby, but in order to make his story come out Fitzgerald has to explain Gatsby, refer him to his origins, terminate our own and the narrator's speculation. This in itself is effective, but it has the drawback that Gatsby's romance can no longer be situated in the realm of gossip, but has to be generalized at the rather lush level of the narrator's sententiousness about boats against the current and the dust that floats in the wake of dreams. Ideally Gatsby should have remained a man of mystery, in the unknowable world in which Henry James is careful to keep Millie Theale, his fabulously rich young lady in *The Wings of the Dove*. The rich, as Fitzgerald knew, are different from us, and hence ideal inhabitants of the gossip world.

The ideal gossiper is an outsider with no hope of penetrating the secrets that absorb him. Dr. Spacks says that she and her friend "moved from details of our own lives to speculation about others, or from discussion of novels to contemplation of friends' love affairs." A natural transition, seemingly, and yet there is a big difference. One's own love affairs are as vulnerable as those of the friends who may be even now discussing them; and however engrossing, such a mutuality is both dangerous and self-limiting. True gossip should not only offer a state of perfect relaxation but of perfect ignorance as well, with only imagination to do the work.

London Review of Books, 1987

46

Little Green Crabs

Marcel Proust (1871–1922)

The Book of Proust
by Philippe Michel-Thiriet, translations by Jan Dalley

Marcel Proust: A Biography
by George D. Painter

Marcel Proust: Selected Letters; Volume 2, 1904–1909
edited by Philip Kolb, translations by Terence Kilmartin

ONE OF MARCEL PROUST'S FRIENDS is supposed to have said of him that "beauty did not really interest him: it had too little to do with desire." A remark which is not entirely lacking insight. It might be said that the relation of the two fascinated Proust as they had fascinated no writer before him, and he perceived that the kinds of pleasure involved in the two concepts were indivisible. He was the brilliant analyst of sensations and experiences which the Victorians tasted and created without critical examination, and not the analyst only but the chemist who broke down this matter into its component parts, which have subsequently remained separate. A *felix culpa* in some ways, no doubt, but the disastrous results also, for the wholly unself-conscious energy which fused the pair in, say, the best poetry of Tennyson and Browning now becomes so well aware of what it is up to. Had he come across it, Proust would have been enchanted by Browning's "Meeting at Night," with its astonishing report of the concentration of desire:

the startled little waves that leap
In fiery ringlets from their sleep
As I gain the cove with pushing prow
And quench its speed i' the slushy sand.

Proust's predecessor Baudelaire would have been enchanted, too, but also incredulous—did the poet really not know what he was talking about? Baudelaire has his own kind of innocence, as has even Proust, but the latter merges into a whole perspective of nostalgia and desire such erotic tableaux as the steeples of Martinville, or the spectacle of Mlle de Vinteuil and her friend pursuing each other round the table with the absorption and the awkwardness of large birds, or the moment before the hotel at Balbec when the narrator is accused by Charlus of the solecism of having anchors embroidered on his bathing dress. The significance of all these things is clear, and Proust's consciousness explores what that clarity might mean for a complete understanding of our erotic and aesthetic life, an understanding only immanent and never fully realized in the English novels Proust most admired—Hardy's *A Pair of Blue Eyes* and *The Well Beloved*. Did he ever read, one wonders, the sword display of Sergeant Troy to Bathsheba in *Far from the Madding Crowd*?

Part of the secret of his art is how it manages to convey that though the apple had been eaten, innocence has been retained. Like all snobs, Proust understood everything about the objects of his snobbery except their own simple view of themselves. His ultimate naïvety was his failure to perceive theirs. Jacques Porel remarked that Proust knew everything, "but his viewpoint had not been deformed by erudition. He was simple, like an innocent boy, or pretended to be." Pretended to be? There is a great deal of pretense involved, but the reader, too, is not deceived by it, accepting it in the spirit of its own art. Proust compelled his erotic life, which was also his social life, to identify itself with an aesthetic, and it was this, perhaps, which aroused the envy and wonder of Virginia Woolf, who found herself unable to work the artistic miracle the other way round, to move from the aesthetic and the social into the world of desire which unites and animates the two.

In a sense, the most blatant of Proust's pretenses is the whole form, pretension, and "secret" of his work, the idea of Time Regained. Once again the genuine element is an erotic one, the intense pleasure, comparable to a solitary orgasm of quite special felicitousness, when consciousness slots into alignment with the feel of uneven stone under the foot, or the taste of a special flavor on the tongue. Imbued with the whole theater of the French metaphysical tradition, Proust must have seen at once that this idea could not only be worked up into an impressive intellectual and imaginative thesis, but that it could also appear to be the key to an artistic unity, and a completed human drama. This Racinian drama was the inner life of the narrator-author, and the way it resolved itself in an act of sublime renunciation that was also one of ultimate discovery. Every reader is fascinated by the simultaneous image of the author completing his work and the narrator discovering his vocation, and renouncing the world in order to fulfill it. The two coincide and change places while retaining the dramatic span of separation.

Like most funny writers, Proust started out as a highly accomplished parodist, but all this big stuff, not unlike the Ulyssean framework of Joyce's epic, had the effect not only of ensuring the profound respect of the cultured French audience but of convincing them that something much more important was going on than a voluminously chatty novel—a *roman à clef*—about high society. A rejoinder that the young Proust once made to Anatole France, the old master on whom Bergotte was chiefly modeled, is revealing in this context. The famous writer who admired him, and who in 1896 had written a preface for the young Proust's first book, *Les Plaisirs et les Jours*, began a conversation admiringly with "You, Marcel, who so much love the things of the intelligence"—only to be interrupted by Proust saying that he did not love the things of the intelligence at all: "I only love life and movement." Kidding on one level, and yet true in the same sense that he preferred, as his friend observed, desire to beauty and that his real obsession, like that of his contemporary Robert Musil, was uniting the two by the same aesthetic. How he must have responded to Ruskin's comment, in *The Stones of Venice*, that it was just as exciting to study the little green crabs in the weed on the mooring stage as it was to disembark and enjoy the Titians in the Venetian palazzo. The crabs in Proust's case were the denizens of Sodome et Gomorrhe, as well as of the Faubourg St-Germain.

The critics are still not quite allowed to say that we value *A la*

Recherche for its life (the extremely hostile literary mandarin Paul Souday admitted that if one can bring oneself to plunge in "one does not let go" because its "prolixity . . . always conveys the feeling of life") and for its humor, its marvelous and endlessly discriminatory sense of the ridiculous. But because it is so close to poetry, humor is the first thing that fails to surface even in the best translation. *A la Recherche* can be funny in Scott Moncrieff's Bloomsbury accents, funnier still in the admirable version of Terence Kilmartin, and yet Proust's own peculiar feeling for human comedy cannot in the end be divorced from language. Charlus's mixture of preciousness and pomposity emerges in one word when he is offered a glass of orangeade at the Verdurin salon and expresses a preference for *sa voisine*, the raspberry cordial. Reading Proust in English, I had frequently gone straight over a scene between Swann and Dr. Cottard until I happened to open it at that page in the French. Cottard is offering Swann a free ticket to a dentistry exhibition, but warns him that no dogs are allowed in the building, adding in his benevolent way that he thought he'd better mention it because several of his own dog owning friends had been turned away disappointed.

Although wholly idiosyncratic and personal, Anthony Powell's humor shares with Proust's the same irresistibly comic feeling for human differentiation, and the immovable misunderstanding which results from it. If there is any summing-up to *A Dance to the Music of Time*, it is in the narrator's observation that whatever happens to people comes in time to seem appropriate; and this is not only a logical consequence of our differentiation and misunderstanding but completely harmonious with André Gide's words on *A la Recherche*: "If I try to find the quality I most admire in this work, it is its gratuitousness. I don't know of a more useless work, nor one less anxious to prove something." Probably it was natural that the apostle of the *acte gratuit* should find what so much absorbed him in Proust, but Gide's observation reminds us that it is pointless to get so worked up—as Edmund Wilson did—about Proust's dogmas on love, jealousy, or sex. These are indeed not intended to prove anything. We come to accept them, surely, as bees in the bonnet of an old friend, for it is one of the last secrets of Proust's art (and, in consequence, to some extent Powell's too) that the narrator-author is one of his own characters, whose foibles are as much their justification as their intelligence and esemplastic powers. If they want to bore us, or to impress us with their grasp of unmanipulated form and secret harmonies, let them: they have earned the right, and it is all part of the fun.

"My poor friend, our little Albertine is no more. Forgive me for breaking this terrible news to you who were so found of her. She was thrown by her horse against a tree while she was out riding beside the Vivonne." Albertine is probably the most intensely conceived and rendered object of love to be found in any fiction. Her sex is not important, although her feminine charm is all the more absolute for being so strangely equivocated. Nor does it matter that both Marcel and his creator can be tiresome, pretentious, and boring. Proust may well have been conscious that he had gone on too long about Albertine, because in the new version which has come to light, deftly introduced and translated by Terence Kilmartin, he compresses the whole episode, giving it what for him is an almost brutal concision. It is much more powerful like this; it is also in a sense less Proustian; and though he might well have gone on to enrich and ornament it with his usual mass of afterthought and interpolation, there seems no doubt that it was intended as the final and definitive rewriting.

"The world is not created once and for all for each of us individually. There are added to it in the course of our lives things of which we have never had any suspicion." The telegram from Mme Bontemps arouses in the narrator a final agony of futile jealousy, because it was near the Vivonne that Mlle was living, and the telegram inadvertently confirms the narrator's worst fears about Albertine's secret lesbian life. (Never mind if this was really Proust's chauffeur Agostinelli's private heterosexual life.) After this what was the point, Proust may well have felt, of a further hundred and forty-odd pages of musing and meditation? The final twist of the knife are the two posthumous letters the narrator receives the next day: the first promising that Albertine will try and persuade her friend Andrée to come and live with him; the second—written within a few minutes of the first—begging to come back herself. No matter that this is a soap opera situation, almost a travesty of the romantic convention that you don't want the girl until she is absent, and then you want her very much indeed. Proust's final version moves by its air of restraint, and seems without effort to resolve and summate all the pathos of social being and all the contingent secrecies of private life. Proust usually reaches feeling by the road of affectedness, but Agostinelli's death in an aviation accident, and a posthumous letter from him so like Albertine's, show a reliance, in this extremity, on what life rather than art can do.

In its loving detail and its quiet humor George Painter's today quite undated biography matches and complements Proust's own method, and his own dedication. He is especially good at bringing out the ways in which real life could *not* be used by Proust, supreme as were his digestive powers where the metamorphosis into art was concerned. Hence we see a Proust who does not appear in or dominate his novel, and this is always engaging, often revealing. The same applies to the other characters who had to be transformed before they could be used, like Monsieur Arman with a wart on his nose, the original of Monsieur Verdurin but a quite different and more formidable personality, unamenable to Proust's alchemy. He contributed a yachting column to the *Figaro*, the journal that Proust and most of his friends read and wrote for, under the *nom de plume* of "Jip Topsail," and mercilessly teased Anatole France because the *maître* had once attempted to enrich his column with some purple patches about blue skies and white sails which the editor had carefully cut out. Like most of the great ladies who ran a salon, Madame Arman may have been an intellectual snob but was certainly not a social one: she was proud of owning Anatole France but was not in the least gratified when Count Robert de Montesquiou, one of the originals of Charlus and a devastating snob himself, made up to her. All such matters had to be modified until they could become part of Proust's world; and Painter shows how the complication and contingency of real lives were never simplified or sacrificed in the process.

Rather touchingly, Proust, when a young man, had a passionate wish to join the army and do his military service, not so much out of patriotism, although that motive cannot be discounted, but from the thought of living at close quartets with all those young fellows. Madame Arman's own son Gaston was doing his service with the Artillery, and although Proust had not yet met this high-spirited young man, who was to be one of the models for St. Loup, he very much desired to emulate him, and listened wistfully to the news of his glories and sufferings, the jokes in barracks, and the horseplay on route-marches. The influence of his famous father, one of the best-known doctors in France, could have excused Proust on health grounds, and exemptions were in any case granted to those taking a university course: however, if he served in the ranks for a year as a volunteer it would definitively release him from the longer period which new regulations were about to bring in. As things turned out, he loved it, though indulgent superiors probably let him down lightly, and Orléans/Doncières became for him a town of romance and nostalgia. He even begged to be allowed to stay on in the army a few months longer, but that, alas, could not be arranged, possibly because when he had been given clerical work "the chief of Staff, not without reason, was exasperated by my handwriting, and threw me out."

Proust had also wanted to emulate his younger brother Robert, a tough young heterosexual who followed his father by becoming a brilliant and successful doctor. Although Marcel as mother's boy had been extremely jealous, they became very fond of each other as adults, and Proust adored his little niece Suzy and once offered to buy her anything she fancied. She asked for a flamingo, and her uncle would have got her one somehow, if her mother had not intervened. Painter suggest that Proust as a young man was genuinely bisexual; and that his affairs with young girls—though not with his admired Jeanne Pouquet, who married Gaston Arman and was one of the models for Albertine—were at least up to a point physical love affairs. But Philippe Michel-Theriet, who compiled the invaluable *Book of Proust*, now very well edited and translated, is confident that Proust was exclusively homosexual even as a young man, however much he may have been attracted by the spectacle of *jeunes filles en fleur*, and even considered, as a kind of aesthetic scenario, the possibility of marriage with one of them, or with Anatole France's daughter Suzanne. Admirably organized, *The Book of Proust* contains all possible information about provenance, period, and lifestyle, down to such details as who owned the freehold of the Prousts' vast apartment at 45 Rue de Courcelles (the Phénix company), the history and fortunes of the Ritz Hotel, and which sentence in the works is the longest. Of special interest is the material on the parents. Mother a Weil, a rich Jewish family, originally German-speaking: father descended from solid village stock at Illiers in the Beauce near Chartres—Jehan and Gilles Proust in the sixteenth century finally made it to the ranks of the rustic bourgeoisie. It would be difficult to find a more promising genetic background.

His letters, surely, are not his strong point, however much they reveal about him, and Kilmartin's introduction and selection reveals a great deal. Proust could be *bête*, unexpectedly so, in his letters to friends, showing them too clearly, one would have thought, what he expected from them, and his own self-absorption. Marie Nordlinger, a serious and scholarly girl who had given him a lot of help with Ruskin, is treated with a patronizing gallantry which must have upset her. "I am all on fire for *Sesame*—and for you" is not quite the right phrasing for what Marie construed as an amorous advance; and it can't have helped that, when she let her feelings show, he professes to detect "a vague allusion to some sadness which you don't express," Deprecating her health and vigor, he accuses her of offering "a moral blood transfusion" and finally observes that he is the last person who could dispel her melancholy, advising her to accept a job in America.

The other young woman, the actress Louisa de Mornand, is quite different, and Proust is much more at home with her. She was the mistress of his friend Albufera, and fond enough of Proust to give him a delicious blue enamel repeater watch. He thanks her for it in an ecstatic letter in which he tells her that he feels as if he were pressing other enchanting "buttons" about her own person. Painter opined on these grounds that she must have granted him physical favors, but Kilmartin more plausibly assumes that he was flirting at second hand with her lover Albufera, to whom, incidentally, she was notoriously unfaithful. For a man as devious as Proust, it was easy to seem daring with such a girl, each understanding the other. So did Proust and Count Robert de Montesquiou, whose exchanges, printed together, are perhaps more predictable than entertaining: though it is significant that the Count (invariably addressed as "sir") sees through his "dear Marcel" and has the measure of him in a way that Proust the author would never have allowed Charlus. The most moving thing—it must surely have moved even the Count—is the letter Proust wrote him after his mother's death. "My life has lost its only purpose, its only sweetness, its only love, its only consolation." Among all the maneuvering and the subtle malice of the flowery compliments this stands out, like Proust's anguish after the death of Albertine-Agostinelli, as no more nor less than the truth. Art was to be the only surrogate con-solation. The letters carry us back into a vanished world, in which one can hardly believe that people had the leisure, the space, the social resources to live as they did. By contrast, the world of Proust's novel is as much alive as if it were all still going on.

London Review of Books, 1989

47

The Order of Battle at Trafalgar

———

S OME YEARS AGO, Lionel Trilling was writing in *Partisan Review*
about the "unargued assumption" of our time that the one true
object of the intellectual's imaginative life was the modern world
and its preoccupations. He expressed a certain nostalgia—even though
rather diffidently—for "a quiet place" in which today's intellectual "can
be silent, in which he can *know* something—in what year the Parthenon
was begun, the order of battle at Trafalgar, how Linear B was deciphered:
almost anything that has nothing to do with the talkative and attitudinis-
ing present." Things have changed a bit since then of course. I do not
know whether the intellectual at the time was at all heedful of Trilling's
point, but I suspect that for his successor in the next generation—the
present—the status of facts as facts has been still further diminished.
Knowing something, in the sense Lionel Trilling had in mind, may seem
to him more naïve than ever.

The climate of structuralism has something to do with this, particularly where the study of literature is concerned. Rejecting "the meta-
physic of presence" we study "self-consuming artifacts"; codes and
strategies have replaced facts and objects. The past, in literature, no
longer consists of events and things. There may be at least one elementary and grim reason for this shift of attitude toward the past, the negating
of any cherished sense of it, and this is that so much in the immediate
past will hardly bear thinking about. The Germans for many years res-
olutely refused to think about it at all. The railway timetables that dispatched trains to Auschwitz do not bear contemplating with the same

sense of knowledge—the same "fond participation" in Henry James's phrase—as does, say, the order of battle at Trafalgar.

In his Charles Eliot Norton Lectures, published as *The Witness of Poetry*, the Nobel Prize winner Czeslaw Milosz talked about the implications of this, and how Polish poets like Zbigniew Herbert, Alexander Wat, and Anna Swirszcynska, had reacted to it. A poem of Herbert's implicitly rejects the nightmare of memory in favor of contemplating a pebble.

> I feel a heavy remorse
> when I hold it in my hand
>
> and its noble body
> is permeated by false warmth

and he foretells of such stones that

> to the end they will look at us
> with a calm and very clear eye

"The Pebble" does without the past in an honorable sense, not the sense in which the past has been rejected by today's critics on the ground that there can be nothing outside the area they control. Reductive as it may be, the poem does not seek to escape from human events or to deny that they ever take place. "The fact," for Roland Barthes, "can only exist linguistically, as a term of discourse," so that the statement "Napoleon died at St. Helena on May 5, 1821" merely shows that there is an item called "historical truth" in our culture codes. The fact that Poland was occupied by the Germans from 1939 to 1945, and that millions of Poles and Jews died as a result, strikes poets who were close to and intimate with these events in a rather different light.

Herbert and the other poets had come up against the fact—for that is what it seems to be—that certain other facts are not susceptible to being dealt with either by our culture codes or by our capacity for human feelings. They remain outside us, like the pebble in the hand, "permeated by false warmth." Much has been written, often histrionically, about the inability of language to confront Auschwitz, but it is not language which is at fault—language as description will do all that is asked of it—but our awareness of facts which remain outside the possibility of feeling. Milosz remarks that many poets tried to bring these events, and their proper feelings about them, into poetry and as poetry. Such attempts were honorable but a complete failure. Herbert's pebble, looking at us with a calm and very clear eye, shows us why this is the case. Poetry, in such cases, must respect what has happened by acknowledging that it cannot feel it. Paradoxically it will then be in accord with that other sense of the past which Lionel Trilling was thinking of. In both cases the mind reaches out to facts outside itself: in the one case, facts in which the mind can participate just because they are outside; in the other, those in which it cannot participate for the same reason. It is the externality of the past, as of the pebble, which makes art possible in some cases and impossible in others.

The question we have to ask when Barthes tells us that "the fact can only exist linguistically, as a term of discourse," is "why does he want to say that?" The answer may be that history and the past, where so-called facts are, have come to repel him, and that he wishes to seal off the language of art and our response to it. That would be in effect a kind of higher escapism, an intellectual elaboration of the theory of art for art's sake. But the more probable explanation has to do with the necessary division between the past and ourselves, between works of art and literature and ourselves. We abolish this division by refusing to admit that the past exists or that the facts of literature are anywhere but in our own codes of discourse. The technique is to insist that what is self-evidently true is therefore comprehensively so. Barthes might have said: "I can only exist biologically, as a function of cellular activity," and thus taken for granted that he cannot think, suffer, or recognize the external world for what it is and has been.

Herbert's pebble is irreducible for his consciousness, bringing its own kind of comfort, giving its own kind of feeling. It is "the feel of not to feel it," as in Keats's poem "In a Drear-Nighted December," which concerns the difference between natural objects which have no memory, and therefore feel no pain, and human subjects which do. Comfort? Certainly; any honest poem is comforting, because it tells the truth about our feelings, or lack of them, our powers, or lack of them, in the face of externality. The sort of poem which Milosz mentions, one in willed pursuit of "proper" responses to the Holocaust, to the scale and terror of the death camps, has to construct its message in codes which are familiar without being really felt. Faced with Herbert's pebble, on the other hand, we catch a glimmering of what the horror is really all about. The poet did not know he was doing this, did not understand what he was doing. In the phrase of Valéry, he only knew what he had said when he had said it. The sense of the past revealed itself to him in an unexpected way.

Barthes and the structural analysts would scarcely find a way of understanding this, because their methods do not recognize the absolute existence of the past or of the fact outside ourselves. Wittgenstein's reasons for saying "the limits of my language are the limits of my world" were strictly and intently philosophical: his statement has had an unfortunate effect, nonetheless, on the software of literary theory. Dr. Johnson broke the Berkleian hypothesis, to his own satisfaction, by kicking a stone, and common sense is always trying to disenmesh itself from literary theory in the same way. Richard Wilbur, like Wittgenstein, may have been expressing a certain kind of truth when he protested:

> Kick on, Sam Johnson, till you break your bones,
> But cloudy, cloudy, is the stuff of stones

but in using stones as a "term of discourse" he was not saying that was the end of the fact of them. For the structural analyst, however, literature and the past have no existence outside his own analysis of them. One result of this is that he cannot understand why a poem cannot be written "about" a concentration camp.

Such a poem would revolt us by its attempt to merge and be with its subject, by its inability to realize that any feeling it concocts is wholly alien to the fact it describes. This is an extreme case of what structural analysis does to literature itself, and to the past and the events on which literature depends. The common critic, like the common reader, has always been conscious that whatever he thought about the works he read, whatever the degree of his fond participation in them, they remained outside himself, their existence was different from his own and would remain unchanged by it. I am now myself trying to say something about the relation of literature and the past, their relation and their externality; trying, like all critics, to make a point. Whatever its validity, however, I know that what I think about it has no significance whatever in contrast with literature itself, and the past in which it lives. The ingenuities of structural analysis—and they can be very ingenious indeed—rest on the premise that the facts in literature are themselves as transparent as the critic's words, into which they merge and are reconstituted.

Again it is necessary to ask the simple question: why do the new analysts want to look at things in this light? The answer, too, seems simple. They are dissatisfied with the traditional position of critics and teachers as on the sidelines of the real, watching the actual ball game, so to speak, and commenting on it as spectators. They wish to seem, by their processes, to be manufacturing the stuff itself, to manipulate and metamorphose it into endless new shapes, so that it becomes a cloudy constituent of the climate of the modern world. The process needs no facts and truths—the death of Napoleon or the battle of Trafalgar: these have only a relative existence, if any, in the new discourse.

The neoclassic critics and the old rhetoricians were, to be sure, almost equally and confidently dogmatic, and their exercises were often judged not by how much truth they revealed but by how much ingenuity they displayed. Day could be darker than night if the virtuoso produced enough ingenious tropes to prove it so. But the paradox of such ingenuity was that its liveliness depended on a deep belief in the truths and facts available to common sense. It would have been pointless otherwise. Novels today are often written under the influence of the modern critical climate, but it is noticeable that the liveliest ones often resemble old rhetorical practice in that they involuntarily underline the significance of fact even while modishly engaged in calling it in question. Thus in Julian Barnes's novel, *Flaubert's Parrot*, the narrator becomes obsessed with finding the stuffed parrot which Flaubert had on his desk while he wrote *Un Coeur Simple*, a story about a woman who is, among other things, devoted to her parrot. He finds what purports to be the real stuffed parrot in a museum, but then finds a rival parrot in another shrine devoted to Flaubert relics. Flaubert's writings, and what the narrator makes of them, mingle with a sense of unreality presided over by the ambiguous legend of Flaubert, the disappearance of things under close scrutiny, the impossibility of the past itself.

These are the modish notions canvassed by the novel, but the impression it makes on the reader is rather different. The past, the parrot, and Flaubert himself all come most vividly to life, as if to confirm that there *was* a parrot, however now unverifiable, just as there was a real moment (among many others) when Flaubert sat down one afternoon to write *Madame Bovary*, the novel which neither he then, nor its readers now, have ever been quite sure about. The conscious implication of *Flaubert's Parrot* is that since we cannot know everything about the past we cannot know anything; but its actual effect—and its success—is to suggest something different: that the relative confirms the idea of truth instead of dissipating it, that the difficulty of finding out how things were does not disprove those things but authenticates them. It may be that few things happened as they are supposed to, and many things did not happen at all, but why should this be a reason for abandoning traditional conceptions of history, of art, of human character? All three depend upon our sense of the past, and are confirmed by the unknowability of the past. Is it the influence of science, a horror of the past, or a passing fashion of defeatism, which makes us reluctant today to speculate in Lionel Trilling's "quiet place," to assemble the materials of creation and participation?

Our conception of character depends on our conception of history, and can either be seen to be dissolved in the dissolution of history, or actually confirmed by the impossibility of knowing what things and people were like. In the case of Hamlet the uncertainty produced by the brilliance, or perhaps the inadvertency, of Shakespeare's art makes the Prince more of a character, not less of one. He has all the magnificence and the despair, the familiarity and the hauteur, which history suggests about the character of the Renaissance ruler. The contradictions make the man. It is significant that historical novels which try to recreate the past, particularly the distant past, seem unable to make use of the uncertainty which marks the idea of a character at any point in history. Novels about ancient Greece, say, construct a Theseus or an Alcibiades who is held together by the fatal assumption, on the novelist's part, that he must be coherent, recognizable, just like one of us. The element of mystery which determines the possibility of a true character is sacrificed to the attempt to produce a convincing and consistent historical picture—"what it must have been like." This is even more marked in science fiction and fantasy, where the

Lord of the Rings, or whoever, is a flat figure without any of the queries and incongruities which history supplies. Such fictions are the abdication of that consciousness of the past which was once second nature to all novelists, who instinctively set their period thirty or forty years before the time they wrote, in order that it might become part of the memory and retrospection of the reader, who was unconsciously creating himself and his own past through the medium of the novel.

That instinct of the novel comes to its full and conscious fruition in Proust, who reconstitutes himself from the past and becomes his own novel in the process. Hamlet is a figure of mystery because he lives in the unknowable past, but this does not stop us from having, like Coleridge, a lot of Hamlet in us. What we do not have in us is a character fixed in a historical role decreed by the writer—Tito Melema, say, in George Eliot's *Romola*. The author spent laborious years getting the background of the novel right, and putting Tito—the man who is a complete self, living only in and for the self—into it. The result is that Tito is neither alive in history nor in the present, nor can we be alive in him. He resembles one of those sad statues on the Albert Memorial in London, in a stony limbo of art which has neither the truth of a photograph album, nor the mystery that continues life and joins past with present.

Trilling's "quiet place" is not quiet in the sense of being fixed and definitive. It is, on the contrary, a place of perpetual speculation, contemplation calmed by an awareness of fact, the fact that lies behind history, art, and human character, and makes them one and indivisible. The line of battle at Trafalgar is well known, amply documented. We know the moment of the day and the look of the calm sea when the *Victory's* bowsprit surged into the gap between the *Redoubtable* and the *Bucentaure*. All else beyond the fact is mysterious, given over to the possibilities of historical personality. Did Nelson say "Kiss me, Hardy" as he lay dying that evening in the flagship's cockpit? How much it reveals about him if he did, as about his flag-captain, the big, bluff, invulnerable Captain Hardy, who was not to die until a generation later, full of years and honors. By the end of the century expectations of behavior had radically altered, and his admirers had elected to forget what seems to have been Nelson's feminine, histrionic, emotional nature. What might a man with a stiff upper lip say as he lay dying, something that sounded like "Kiss me,

Hardy"? Perhaps, "Kismet, Hardy"? Nelson had been in the Middle East, after all, and had dealings with the followers of Islam. For the contemporaries of Sherlock Holmes it seemed the kind of thing that a naval or military man might utter, with a slight smile, a notional shrug of the shoulders.

The example is comic, certainly, but at the heart of the comedy is the stuff of true fiction, as it is the stuff of the past. It is because fiction cannot deal in fact that it absorbs us in the nature and reward of fact. In disqualifying the category of fact from text and discourse the modern critic often shows a curious naïveté about its historical relation to fiction. In an essay on how we should read novels today David Lodge notices the moment in Arnold Bennett's *The Old Wives' Tale* when Sophia, foreseeing difficulties in the future, decides to relieve her drunken new husband of his money and secrete it about her own person. His wallet she hides at the back of the cupboard in their hotel bedroom, "where for all I know," writes the author, "it is there to this day." It would be a very naïve reader, comments Lodge, who might wonder if the wallet really was still there, in that hotel in the French provincial town. This comment seems to me to miss the point in a potentially disastrous manner. The reader does not need to be reminded that he is reading fiction: but the author has just shown him how clear, how close, how unmistakable is fiction's relation to fact. How peculiar as well. "There to this day . . ." Sophia and her experience are abruptly brought out of the past where, in an obvious sense, all fiction resides, and into the present. The interchange shows art's simultaneous dependence on its relations with the concepts of past and present, the invented and the real.

Those relations form a crisscross pattern. Hamlet the character is a literary invention, but he carries his own personal reality both into our sense of history and into our contemporary experience of life. Was he in love with Ophelia? The play gives us no answer: the idea that he might have been increases nonetheless his potential as a fictional character because it is precisely the same kind of possibility which attends our experience of other people in life. Fiction and life are, so to speak, continually changing places, each under the scrutiny that produces art. In theory we can know everything in a fiction, and about a character in fiction, and very little in life, or about the people we meet in life. In practice fiction

avails itself of the disablements of life, and under the guidance of a master hand is enriched by them. In *The Princess Casamassima* Henry James
gave up the completely rounded fictional form which defined the character of Christina Light in *Roderick Hudson*. As the Princess Casamassima Christina has become, as it were, an "unsatisfactory" character, the
sort of person often met with in real experience who calls forth our
curiosity without in any way satisfying it. Christina simply continues
through her "life." In his later preface to *Roderick Hudson* James was to
write that "relations stop nowhere," and that the artist's problem was "to
draw, by a geometry of his own, the circle within which they shall happily
appear to do so." He may have been reflecting, at least in part, on the way
in which the circle drawn in the earlier novel was ruptured by the reappearance of Christina in *The Princess Casamassima*. She disappears as
the completed concept of a character and comes back in a secondary
role, seen differently because she is now free to carry on living in an ordinary untidy way. James has washed his hands of her; she is no longer
determined by the resolution of the plot and by a completed role in fictional history. The "fond participation" he was to write of in the New York
preface to *The Princess Casamassima* hardly includes her, and this
reminds us that characters, although they have to be regarded from the
standpoint of art, whether we are reading about them or experiencing
them in life, have also their own unshaped existence which we cannot
enter, and about this speculation is wasted.

A singular instance of the writer removing a character from the flux of
events in order to perpetuate him for the "inward eye" occurs in the original version of the *Lyrical Ballads*. In 1797 Wordsworth saw an old man
traveling, and composed a sketch on the subject, subtitled "Animal Tranquillity and Decay." What struck Wordsworth, and makes the crux of his
description, is the fact that the old man does not seem conscious of the
impression he most makes on others—that of patience and "settled
quiet." He doesn't seem to "need" the tranquillity his outward form
exhibits, and "the young behold / With envy, what the old man hardly
feels." Wordsworth observes appearances with the keenest possible eye,
and from them draws conclusions familiar to himself, and with their own
sort of comfort for himself and his readers. In the poet's eye the old man
does indeed, in some sense, "exist linguistically, as a term of discourse."

We are impressed by our own conception of him rather than by the man himself, as is evident from Wordsworth's peroration.

> He is by nature led
> To peace so perfect, that the young behold
> With envy, what the old man hardly feels.

But this view of the matter is completely blown away by the last few lines of the original poem, which Wordsworth dropped in the 1800 edition of the *Lyrical Ballads* and never afterward restored.

> —I asked him whither he was bound, and what
> The object of his journey; he replied
> "Sir! I am going many miles to take
> "A last leave of my son, a mariner,
> "Who from a sea-fight has been brought to Falmouth,
> And there is dying in an hospital."

Even the original punctuation, with the speech commas at the beginning of the lines, indicates the totality of the contrast with what has gone before. The old man shows that he is neither led by nature to peace so perfect, nor that he is indifferent to the calm about him which is the envy of the bystander. So far from being subdued to settled quiet, he is concerned with one overriding purpose, to see his wounded son before he dies, the son who has been present in a battle at sea.

This collision of fact with appearance was first presented by Wordsworth with complete fidelity, as if he were unconscious—as perhaps he was—of the contrast between his view of the old man and the old man's real preoccupations and place in things. The poem has stubbed its toe on a fact which has brought it to an end; but because it is a poem, and a very successful poem, a remarkably fitting end. There is no incongruity between the old man's speech and the impression that he made on the poet, but Wordsworth later became sensitive about such things, and by removing the end of the poem spoilt the wonderful interplay in it between character, fact, and history, the interplay which was not "subdued" to poetic discourse but left in what can only be described as its natural state, the state where our sense of these things is most receptive.

Wordsworth's original poem is both close to Herbert's poem on the pebble, and opposite to it. It is close in the involuntary way it opens itself to history and the fact, to what is going on. Both poems contain a great weight of implication of things the poet knows about but lets only look over his shoulder. Herbert's pebble knows nothing of what has been happening, of all miseries since the world began, and it lets its "noble body" be permeated by the "false warmth" of the poet's and reader's vision of it, and the comfort it brings. Poetry cannot take over the pebble, and this is an obscure earnest of the dire truth that poetry also cannot approach or explain the recent past and its horrors, the massacres and concentration camps.

"Old Man Travelling" takes over its subject, the old man, but is then forced to relinquish him when he opens his mouth and speaks, stating things which the poem cannot handle and take over, which can only be dealt with by their removal and suppression in all subsequent editions. His poetry can deal with "old unhappy far-off things," as Wordsworth did in his poem "The Highland Reaper," where subject and vision remained wholly in his mind. But these instances all emphasize the way in which the recalcitrance of the past, its separation from us, confronts art as firmly as does the individual character, and in the same way. Art must both use and respect them; the reader himself feel their presence as separate entities, and speculate on their several realities, as he does in that quiet place where he can learn in what year the Parthenon was begun, and what ships formed the battle line at Trafalgar.

Salmagundi, 1986

48

In Which We Serve

Patrick O'Brian (1914–2000)

———————

The Aubrey/Maturin series
by Patrick O'Brian

Master and Commander
Post Captain
H.M.S. Surprise
The Mauritius Command
Desolation Island
The Fortune of War
The Surgeon's Mate
The Ionian Mission
Treason's Harbour
The Far Side of the World
The Reverse of the Medal
The Letter of Marque
The Thirteen-Gun Salute
The Nutmeg of Consolation

IN ALDOUS HUXLEY'S first novel, *Crome Yellow*, a man of action recounts an escapade of his youth, and comments that such things are only really agreeable to look back on after the event. Nothing is exciting as it happens. Warriors in heroic times only knew what they had been through when they heard about it from the bard in the mead hall. Armchair warriors who have never performed such feats can nonetheless become connoisseurs of them at second hand. In the same way, it is possible to become an expert on the apparatus of the old-time naval world—backstays and top-gallants, twenty-four pounders and hardtack—without having the faintest idea how to fire a gun, reef a sail, or fother a ship's bottom. Naval novels today are unique among the genre in this engaging respect: author and reader are alike innocent of the experience graphically conveyed by the one and eagerly appreciated by the other.

This may seem a good reason for not taking such books very seriously. The Frederick Marryat who wrote *Mr. Midshipman Easy* and the Herman Melville who wrote *Moby-Dick* had themselves been to sea, as frigate officer and as a whaling hand: they knew what they were talking about. So, too, with Joseph Conrad. But that is scarcely relevant to the genre of nautical fiction today, which can seem more like the genre of science fiction or fantasy, even of "magic realism." The fashionable thing in the theory of the novel at the present time is to do it, so to speak, without hands; to recognize the totality of fiction, its arbitrariness, its success not in relation to "life" but in purely literary terms. On the other side, the new historicism has created a genuinely authoritative style of fiction—Gore Vidal and Simon Schama are formidable exponents of it—which researches the legend of the past while demonstrating the seductive unknowability of the real thing. Gore Vidal's *Lincoln* is a special and incontrovertible masterpiece of such a kind.

Like his compatriots J. G. Farrell and John Banville, Patrick O'Brian does not really fit into any of these more up-to-date categories. In their own different ways they are at once too traditional and too idiosyncratic. Loosely linked by the theme of an empire in its decline, the novels of Farrell's trilogy—*Troubles, The Siege of Krishnapur, The Singapore Grip*—were a great success from the fashion in which they combined fantasy and erudition with an original imagination of how a particular culture saw itself, spoke, and showed off to itself. They made something new, fresh, and hilarious, out of being bookish. In his own subtle and leisurely style Patrick O'Brian does something of the same sort, making extensive use of the pleasure that fiction addicts find in feeling at home, recognizing old faces, old jokes, the same social occasions and regimes, the same sort of exciting situation. His most time-honored ploy is the two-man partnership, the accidental coming together of a dissimilar pair—Don

Quixote and Sancho Panza, Holmes and Watson, Hergé's Tintin and Captain Haddock—who from then on are indissolubly wedded in terms of the reader's expectations and the novels' success.

O'Brian's couple are Jack Aubrey and Stephen Maturin, who meet at Port Mahon in Minorca in the year 1802, when Jack is a lieutenant in the British Navy hoping for promotion to commander, and Stephen is a bit of a mystery man, a half-Irish half-Catalan scholar in medicine and botany, down on his luck. After a mild quarrel at a concert—passionate music lovers both, Jack will play the violin and Stephen his cello throughout many a subsequent saga—they take to each other, and Jack offers Stephen a berth as surgeon in his first command, the fourteen-gun sloop *Sophie. Master and Commander* inaugurates a relationship that will continue through the vicissitudes of the service in every ocean and latitude, through marriages and bankruptcies, promotions, dismissals, windfalls, and losses of prize money, until with *The Nutmeg of Consolation* (the name is that of a jewel of a little corvette built in Borneo to replace the shipwrecked HMS *Surprise*) we end up on the shores of Botany Bay, among the convicts of the new colony of Australia.

In strict terms of time and sequence, the war against Napoleon should by now be over, and the Treaty of Ghent signed that ended the war of 1812 between England and the United States. But O'Brian has cunningly allowed history to expand, as it were, so that his own episodes can continue while the larger process marks time. In one introduction he confesses to this method, for he is too sound a chronicler to play fast and loose with what actually occurred. In the middling novels of the series there are memorable accounts of historic actions, like those of the French and English frigates and East Indiamen at Mauritius, and the unequal but epic fight in the Indian Ocean between HMS *Java* and the USS *Constitution. The Fortune of War* actually ended with the battle outside Boston harbor of the *Shannon* and *Chesapeake*, while *The Surgeon's Mate* opens with the burial at Halifax of Captain Lawrence, the *Chesapeake*'s gallant commander.

But by the time we reach *The Nutmeg of Consolation* such main events have tactfully withdrawn into the background and the chief action—a very thrilling one to be sure—is an attack by Dyaks and their pirate queen on the shipwrecked crew of the *Surprise*. (This frigate was Jack's favorite command and gave her name to the third novel in the series.) The flora and fauna of the far Orient, and of Australia itself, are of the deepest interest to Stephen and his chaplain assistant, and *The Nutmeg* ends with a marvelous account of the duckbill platypus and the hazardous consequences of being bitten by one.

The above may give the idea that adventure is paramount in the series, and that the novels are further examples of the naval-romantic genre inaugurated by C. S. Forester with the exploits of Captain Hornblower, and copied since by several inferior cutlass-and-carronade performers. Nothing could be further from the truth. Many of the Hornblower books were superb examples of their craft, and Forester remains unequaled for dynamism of narrative and precision of encounter: his single ship actions are surely the best ever described. O'Brian's technique and achievement are of quite a different kind. For a start, although he is dutiful about giving us marine warfare, meticulously reconstructed and fleshed out from the dry pages of naval historians like Robert Beatson and William James, his real interest is in the ships and the crews, in naval custom, habit, and routine, the daily ritual of shipboard life, and the interplay of personality in the confinement of a wooden world. His ships are as intimate to us as are Laurence Sterne's Shandy Hall or Jane Austen's village of Highbury in *Emma*. Like Jane Austen, O'Brian is really happiest working on two or three inches of ivory and turning into art the daily lives of three or four families in a locality—except that his village happens to be a wooden ship of war at the apogee of a great navy's world sea power in the days of sail, and famous for the skill and discipline of its officers and men. Jane Austen, two of whose brothers ended up as admirals, would have understood all this very well, and would no doubt warmly have approved O'Brian's spacious but modest undertaking.

Stephen is being shown over the *Sophie* by young Mowett, a midshipman with a taste for writing verse, by no means a rare accomplishment at a time when learning to play the German flute was a popular relaxation in the gun room, and captains might stitch petit point in the lofty seclusion of the great cabin.

"You are studying trigonometry, sir?" said Stephen, whose eyes, accustomed to the darkness, could now distinguish an inky triangle.

"Yes, sir, if you please," said Babbington. "And I believe I have nearly found out the answer." (And should have, if that great ox had not come barging in, he added, privately.)

"In canvassed berth, profoundly deep in thought,

His busy mind with sines and tangents fraught,

A lid reclines! In calculation lost.

His efforts still by some intruder crost," said Mowett. "Upon my word and honour, sir, I am rather proud of that."

"And well you may be," said Stephen, his eyes dwelling on the little ships drawn all round the triangle. "And pray, what in sea-language is meant by a ship?"

"She must have three square-rigged masts, sir," they told him kindly, "and a bowsprit; and the masts must be in three—lower, top and topgallant—for we never call a polacre a ship."

"Don't you, though?" said Stephen.

In one sense the technique—clueless landsman much respected nonetheless as a doctor—is as time-honored as it is in Smollett, but O'Brian contrives to give it back a sort of innocence, which goes with his extraordinarily adroit individualization of minor figures. Two novels later in the series Jack is giving a dinner party on board his new command (he has just become a post captain) and is as relieved as a suburban hostess would be that the burgundy and the plum duff ("Tiggy-dowdy" to the service) are doing their job in loosening tongues and promoting social ease. Stephen is in conversation with the marine lieutenant, a Highlander called Macdonald, and they are growing a little warm over the Ossian question, Stephen pointing out the absence of manuscript sources:

"Do you expect a Highland gentleman to produce his manuscripts upon compulsion?" said Macdonald to Stephen, and to Jack, "Dr. Johnson, sir, was capable of very inaccurate statements. He affected to see no trees in his tour of the kingdom: now I have travelled the very same road many times, and I know several trees within a hundred yards of it—ten, or even more. I do not regard him as any authority on any subject. I appeal to your candour, sir—what do you say to a man who defines the mainsheet as the largest sail in a ship, or to belay as to splice, or a bight as the circumference of a rope? And that in a buke that professes to be a dictionary of the English language? Hoot, toot."

"Did he indeed say that?" cried Jack. "I shall never think the same of him again. I have no doubt your Ossian was a very honest fellow."

"He did, sir, upon my honour," cried Macdonald, laying his right hand flat upon the table. "And falsum in uno, falsum in omnibus, I say."

"Why, yes," said Jack, who was as well acquainted with old omnibus as any man there present.

Not only do the natural passions—indeed obsessions—present in any small community receive at the author's hands the most skillful and sympathetic testimony, but he makes graphic if unobtrusive display of the diversity of types, interests, and nationalities always present in a naval context. The hazards, too. A day or two later Stephen has to amputate Macdonald's arm after a cutting-out expedition, and they take up their conversation again in the hospital.

O'Brian is equally and fascinatingly meticulous on questions of geography and natural history. *The Nutmeg of Consolation* is embroidered with the flora and fauna of the East Indies; and an extraordinarily gripping sequence in the previous novel, *The Thirteen Gun Salute*, recounts the danger to a sailing vessel of approaching too near in a calm to the nine-hundred-foot cliffs of Inaccessible Island, which rise sheer out of the depths of the South Atlantic not far from Tristan da Cunha. Whalers had been drawn by the mountainous swell into the giant kelp at the cliff's foot and perished with all hands. The crew of the *Surprise* are enjoying a routine Sunday morning when this danger threatens, and are plucked from divine service by the urgent need to get out the boats and row the becalmed frigate clear into safety. It is then revealed by a white-faced carpenter that the long boat had a couple of rotten strakes which he has cut out and not yet had time to replace. Like the young captain in Conrad's *The Shadow Line*, who fails to check that what is inside the bottle in the ship's medicine store is indeed quinine, Jack Aubrey is faced—and not for the first time—with the implacable crises of life at sea, to survive which every last detail must be kept in mind and under eye. There is nothing in the least approximate or merely picturesque about O'Brian's handling of any marine situation, or even the most conventionally spectacular kind of naval action. In *Master and Commander* he took us, together with the unskilled Sophies, through every detail of the drill required to fire a single gun of the broadside.

Of course he has his failures—what novelist embarked on so amply comprehensive an undertaking could not have them? The women are a problem; although it seems unfair they should turn out to be, for Jack's amiable fiancée and then wife, his far from amiable mother-in-law, and Stephen's own heartbreaker, Diana Villiers, with whom he is on and off through several books, are as vigorously and subtly portrayed as the men, and come alive as much as they do. No more than Conrad is O'Brian what used to be called a man's man, and he has as many women as men among his fans. Nonetheless it is with a feeling of relief that we leave Jack's Sophia in the little house near Portsmouth, or Diana in Mayfair, and embark upon our next commission. The reason is plain. It is not that O'Brian's women are less interesting than his men, but that a single domestic background is essential to the richness and vivacity of the work. Not being a bird, as the Irishman said, O'Brian cannot be in two places at once, and he cannot successfully locate the women in one background and his seagoing population in another. Were he able to take his ladies to sea (he does have some memorable gunners' wives and East India misses) it would be another matter, but here history is against him—naval wives often took passage but could not be closely involved in the life of the ship—and O'Brian has total respect for the niceties of contemporary usage and custom.

Another important narrative theme is more suitably ambiguous. Almost unknown to Jack, at least in the earlier books of the sequence, Stephen is an undercover agent of naval intelligence. Nothing improbable in that, and it does lead to some interesting situations, although the reader may feel that such goings-on are there more for the benefit of plot and adventure than real assets to the felt life of the fiction. The two traitors inside the Admiralty who are a feature of the later novels bear a not altogether comfortable resemblance to more recent traitors like the all too real spies Burgess and Maclean. There are moments, too, when Stephen's erudition and expertise in all matters except love become a little oppressive, as does Jack's superb seamanship and childlike lack of business sense. But these are the kinds of irritation we feel at times with those who have become old friends. Stephen and Jack have their occasional quarrels, too, and their moments of mutual dissatisfaction.

For indeed the most striking thing about the series is the high degree of fictional reality, of Henry James's "felt life," that it has managed to generate. This may be partly because we grow accustomed and familiar, as in the homelier case of the comic strip; and yet the more surprising and impressive virtue in the novels is their wide range of feeling and of literary sensibility. At least two tragic characters—Lieutenant James Dillon in the opening novel, and the erratic Lord Clonfert who makes a mess of things in *The Mauritius Command*—have their psychology subtly and sympathetically explored; and there are some scenes in the series of almost supernatural fear and strangeness: two pathetic lovers seeking sanctuary on a Pacific island, or the weird and grisly chapter, like something out of *Moby-Dick*, when a Dutch seventy-four pursues Jack's smaller vessel implacably through the icebergs and mountainous waves of the great southern ocean. And no other writer, not even Melville, has described the whale or the wandering albatross with O'Brian's studious and yet lyrical accuracy.

The vicissitudes in Jack's naval career—the many fiascoes and disasters as well as the occasional triumphs—come from naval careers of the period, like that of Lord Cochrane, who was dismissed from the service for alleged financial irregularities. Such resourceful heroes often made a second career for themselves—Cochrane became a Chilean admiral in the South American war of liberation—and there seems every hope that Jack and Stephen may turn up in those parts when their author can no longer put off the conclusion of hostilities in Europe. Most historical novels suffer from the fatal twin defects of emphasizing the pastness of the past too much while at the same time seeking to be overfamiliar with it ("Have some more of this Chian," drawled Alcibiades). O'Brian does neither. Indeed "history" as such does not seem greatly to interest him: his originality consists in the unpretentious use he makes of it to invent a new style of fiction.

That unpretentiousness has become a rare asset among novelists. The reader today has become conditioned, partly by academic critics, to look in Melville and Conrad for the larger issues and deeper significances, rather than enjoying the play of life, the humor and detail of the performance. Yet surface is what matters in good fiction, and Melville on the whale and on the *Pequod*'s crew is more absorbing to his readers in the long run than is the parabolic significance of Captain Ahab. Patrick O'Brian has contrived to invent a new world that is almost entirely in this sense a world of enchanting fictional surfaces, and all the better for it. As narrator he never obtrudes his own personality, is himself never present in the role of author at all; but we know well what most pleases, intrigues, and fascinates him; and there is a kind of sweetness in his books, an enthusiasm and love for the setting of the fiction, which will remind older readers of Sir Walter Scott. It is worth remembering that Melville too worshiped Scott, and that the young Conrad pored over the Waverley novels in Poland long before he went to sea.

The New York Review of Books, 1991

49

Seer of the Ego

Stendhal (1783–1842)

Stendhal
by Joanna Richardson

IN THE LAST full-length biography of Stendhal in English—now
thirty years old—F. C. Green observed that the impression Stendhal
makes "derives from a quality rarely found in imaginative literature—
the unswerving respect for the truth." The point would be to define, as
Green did not, what is the use made of the word "truth" in this context,
and by Stendhal himself. Dante or Shakespeare or Milton did not exactly
tell lies: the splendor of their art lies in the way it takes for granted not
only natural appearance and human activity but the great metaphysical
cosmologies which grew up with these and gave them the coherence of
a second nature. In this sense even Homer, the great truthteller, is simply
endorsing an accepted view of things. And this acquiescence is always as
true as the opposing challenge—that the emperor has no clothes. But
there are times when this kind of truth is truer than the other, more vital
to perception and reflection alike; and Stendhal's was emphatically one
of them.

So, no doubt, is our own; which is why Joanna Richardson remarks
modestly that the immense accretion of Stendhal studies in the last thirty
years justifies a further biography, and a reappraisal of what Stendhal
means to us today. Stendhal said in the 1830s that he would really be read
"round about 1900," and his forecast was so far accurate that it would be
true to say he has meant much the same thing, to the same sort of peo-

ple, for the last hundred years. He is not the first of the *authentiques*, but he is certainly the most authoritative. He made a particular kind of dynamic solipsism seem the only honest way of looking at life. His version of the Cartesian *cogito* is: "what I experience must be the case," and most novelists who have come after him have said the same, though seldom with so much instinctive conviction.

Nothing illustrates this better than Stendhal's celebrated discovery about the true nature of a battle. Such a thing never takes place where I am; hence, can it really be said to take place at all? In his capacity as supply officer to the Napoleonic armies Stendhal took part in the retreat from Moscow as well as in the Marengo campaign, and he experienced his share of military hardships and discomfort. But he was only present at one major battle, Bautzen, fought during the retreat across Germany in 1814.

> From noon to three we saw perfectly well all one can see of a battle, in other words nothing. The pleasure consists in the fact that one is a little moved by the certainty that something is happening there which one knows is terrible.

It was in this fashion that Fabrice, in *La Chartreuse de Parme*, will be present but not present at the battle of Waterloo. Stendhal would have been the first to admit that his perception of this truth proceeded from the way in which such things had happened to him personally, hanging around— as he did—on the skirts of Napoleonic glory, passionately romantic about "this young General Bonaparte who will perhaps make himself king"; and yet always finding himself cast for some comparatively humble and workaday role, ordering linen covers to preserve the imperial furniture at Fontainebleau from the damp, or taking inventories of flour kegs at Milan. It was this mixture of the heroic dream with the factual reality which Stendhal perceived as characteristic of the modern spirit, and of the way things must appear to it.

It is of course an alienated vision in the classic Hegelian sense. And from a literary point of view Stendhal also owes much to Voltaire's technique of irony: the deliberate alienation of language itself from its customary associations. It is significant that Tolstoy, who learned so much from Stendhal, employs both the Stendhalian and the Voltairian technique, describing the events of a battle in such a way as to "make it strange," as the Russian formalists say, to abolish the *idée reçue* and what Stendhal himself called "the done thing." Thus young Rostov at Austerlitz has for some of the time the same sense of total unmeaning as young Fabrice at Waterloo.

But it is also significant that Tolstoy does not stop there. Stendhal never, as it were, puts himself outside the alienated vision, but Tolstoy widens the panorama to include every possible kind of perception, from the conventional and Homeric—action taking an orderly and for that reason an idyllic course—to the intrusion of total absurdity, the nightmare of naked and unaccommodated awareness. The strength of Tolstoy is that he thus avoids the menace to literature of the predictable, for Stendhal's vision of things, once made into a formula—and what writer since the mid-nineteenth century has been able to perceive the reality of war in a fashion different from his?—has become just as much "the done thing" as any other ancient stereotype, any other version of what Stendhal dismissed as "the noble and emphatic."

The young Henri Beyle (Stendhal was the romantic-sounding pseudonym he adopted when he began writing) spent his early years detesting his father, a bourgeois of Grenoble, and worshipping the memory of his mother who had died when he was seven. "It seems that my memory is only the memory of my sensibility," he was to record in his journal, and all his life he was strangely indifferent to fact and physicality, living largely on the recollection of and nostalgia for his various loves, and seeking for others in order to add further chapters to his memory. In his stylized autobiography, the *Vie de Henri Brulard*, he shows a remarkable perception—which like so many of the discoveries of the romantics anticipates Freud—not only of the sources and prognosis of the Oedipus complex, but the ways in which the political and ideological convictions and alignment of the adult are determined by childhood emotion. The Beyles were legitimist and devoted to the Bourbons, and Henri's father awaited with anguish the news from Paris of the outcome of the trial of Louis XVI.

When the news of the condemnation arrived my family were in absolute despair. "But they'll never dare to carry out that infamous sentence," they said. "Why not?" I thought—"if he was a traitor?"

I was in my father's study in the rue des Vieux-Jesuites, at about seven o'clock in the evening. It was quite dark. I was reading by the light of my lamp and separated from my father by a very large table. The house was shaken by the mail coach arriving from Lyon and Paris.

"I must go and see what those monsters have done," said my father, rising to his feet.

"I hope that the traitor has been executed," I thought. Then I reflected on the extreme difference between my feelings and those of my father. . . . I was judging the case between my family and myself when my father came back.

"It's all over," he said, heaving a deep sigh. "They have murdered him."

I was overcome by one of the most intense feelings of delight which I have ever known.

That is Stendhal's style at its best, at once pregnant and uninsistent ("*Comme il insiste peu!*" said André Gide), detached and yet intimately commonplace. There is something to be said for the view that *Henri Brulard* is his best work, for Stendhal talking about himself is more suited to his own manner, as it were, and to his own personality, than when he is cooking up the romantic self-projections of Julien Sorel and Fabrice del Dongo. Both in a sense are case histories (Julien Sorel is based on a newspaper account of a young man called Berthet who murdered his mistress), and the history and fate of both are totally determined by their early experiences. Both appear to be infinitely free, plunging into a Stendhalian *chasse au bonheur*, and endowed with all the potentialities for the career that Napoleonism had opened to their talents; but they end up where they began, their worldly skills condemned to the service of an imprisoning memory and sensibility. It is the same with Octave in *La Armance*, whose impotence—never openly stated by Stendhal, but most subtly and pervasively suggested—has its unrevealed sources far back in some childhood situation.

It is likely that the reason why Stendhal never finished *Lucien Leuwen*, a shapeless and contradictory though in many ways a fascinating novel, is that he could not see how to chain up its aimless young hero satisfactorily in the past. Lucien gets involved in politics, the details of which have considerable interest and show Stendhal in his most disenchanted and also his most Balzacian vein, but the main interest is his infatuation with Madame de Chasteller, an entirely suitable and admirable girl, whom Stendhal cannot convincingly relate to any childhood need or disability in his hero; hence he has to concoct a ludicrously contrived separation, in which Lucien is led to believe that she has just had a child by another man though he has seen her—quite evidently unpregnant—a few days before.

To these shifts was Stendhal reduced when he had to invent a novel instead of drawing on his own powers of self-analysis. And the clumsiness points to a more serious weakness: Stendhal's romantic inability to understand or bother about the feelings of anyone but himself and his hero; or rather perhaps—though it comes to the same thing—his lack of interest in the actuality even of the persons who stirred his sensibility. His famous phrase about the novelist being "the mirror in the roadway" is scarcely true of himself. The mirror reflected only his own reactions to what was passing, but its picture of these had total fidelity.

So analytical a talent must also be abstract; and the reason why the treatise on love, *De l'Amour,* is such a tedious work is its mania for categorization—it makes a ghost of the whole flesh and blood business. Not that categories need necessarily be bloodless—the *Kama Sutra* and Theophrastus show that, as well as Tolstoy's post-Stendhalian tales—but like many apparent sensualists and *roués,* Stendhal was genuinely uninterested in physical phenomena. If asked about the physical details of lovemaking with a particular woman he would have honestly replied, like the artist womanizer in Anthony Powell's novels, that he "hadn't noticed." What appealed to him was the accumulation of nostalgia, and the triumph of impulse over hesitation. How many young men have been encouraged and inspired by Julien Sorel's silent resolution to embrace Madame de Renal before the clock shall have struck nine? In *Les Grands Timides* Dugas announces that the center of Henri Beyle's life was the struggle against his own timidity; and one of his most perceptive French critics, Louis Brombert, has suggested that the false accouchement of Madame de Chasteller, which deceives

Lucien, is a parody of Stendhal's own permanent need to be the dupe of love.

And though the dupe of love may understand it from his own point of view, he can hardly be sensitive to the needs of others. Tolstoy's art is as transparently and stimulatingly solipsistic as Stendhal's, but because he was a "seer of the flesh" Tolstoy understood the language of the flesh in others—hence the marvelous intimacy of our rapport with Anna Karenina, Natasha, or the Little Princess. Stendhal's heroines may appeal to those who are somewhat obliquely constituted—the arrested, the masochistic, even the cryptohomosexual—but to the more conventional majority they can never be anything but stuffed dummies.

Madame de Renal and Madame de Chasteller are mere pillow dreams of their creator, and as for that devastating bore, the Duchesse de Sanseverina in *La Chartreuse de Parme*, no one could bear to go near her except the Stendhalian fanatic, the adept of the interior will, determined to erect the image of a "brilliant woman" and to become her creature. They may in fact not really be women at all, but figments of a will and imagination essentially bisexual. Stendhal records in his journal how he suddenly "fell in love" with a handsome young Russian officer of the occupying army at the Paris opera in 1814, but this was one emotional challenge he did not pursue.

Joanna Richardson is much too shrewd and perceptive a biographer not to find all this something of a handicap when she comes to give—as she rightly desires to do—a three-dimensional picture of the many women in Stendhal's life. They all remain very shadowy, wraiths whose intelligence, vivacity, and charm we have to take for granted. Their interior being, even the ordinary details of their personal lives, is something that cannot quite get itself into the framework of the picture. It is significant that the most solid of them—in every sense—is Madame Daru, wife of the secretary of the ministry of war, whose robustly easygoing features gaze at us with such unromantic geniality from the portrait by David.

Pierre Daru was from Beyle's background, an able bourgeois on the make, to whom the revolution and the Empire gave his chance to rise to great heights. He launched Stendhal on his career in the commissariat, and his wife—who died at the birth of her seventh child—was briefly Stendhal's mistress, but it is clear that he only made use of her while sighing after more spiritual even though no less attainable mistresses. The career of the Darus also shows us something of great significance about the Stendhalian personality: though he prided himself on being in the swim and on the make, a Napoleonic man, party to all the dynamics of the new state, he was in reality neither competent nor single-minded enough to be a success in that tough and glittering world. One could not serve both Napoleon and the interior sensibility, even though—as Stendhal was later to boast to Byron—he actually accompanied the emperor for part of the Moscow retreat, noted his behavior, and heard his conversation.

It was no doubt for this reason, rather than because of Napoleon's downfall, that Stendhal failed to make the success of his life that his bourgeois origins and convictions made him ambitious for. He knew it himself—rueful and humorous honesty is one of his most attractive characteristics—and he constantly lamented his failure to make the income he thought due to *l'homme stendhalien*, just as he lamented his failure to settle down with a rich and amiable heiress. It was his destiny and his ultimate wish to remain on the outside looking in, confident that the complexity and truth of his message would one day be fully recognized.

Le Rouge et le noir had indeed a great *succès d'estime*, but Stendhal wryly noted that *De l'Amour* sold only a few copies, a fact that seems to show his contemporaries found the book no more diverting or convincing than we do. There is a sense, of course, in which Stendhal is scarcely for Anglo-Saxons anyway—at least where his concept of Woman is concerned—although his romantic and accurate dramatization of intrigue and the will has probably appealed more to our modern culture—and especially to its novelists—than it has to his more habituated fellow countrymen. To us he offered—still offers—the appeal of a stimulating and challenging lifestyle, but to the French he is perhaps chiefly unique and remarkable as a literary stylist, whose matter-of-fact absence of fine writing did much to emancipate French prose from the rules of classicism and good taste.

In his later years Stendhal languished as consul at Civitavecchia, a poky and provincial seaport near Rome, submitting to a succession of raspberries from higher up on account of his negligence, his tendency to sneak away from his duties to Rome (whose society was in any case uncongenial to him), and even for his extravagance in matters of postage. As he had never found his ideal woman, so he was never able to settle in the town of his dreams—Milan—where he had first undergone that heady experience, part worldly, part visionary, which started him on the *chasse au bonheur*; and which caused him to ask for the words *Arrigo Beyle, Milanese*, to be cut on his tombstone. Intensely French in many ways, he despised his fellow countrymen and adored an Italian ideal, as he adored a feminine one. In this he was true to himself, revealing not only how compatible is the romantic spirit with the most down-to-earth and searching personal analysis, but how close together, in the *homme stendhalien*, were the impulses of tough calculation and worldly snobbery with delicate ideals and timid and vulnerable yearnings of the soul.

The New York Review of Books, 1974

50

What Will You Do to Keep the Ship from Foundering?

Joseph Conrad (1857–1924)

Joseph Conrad: A Biography
by Jeffrey Meyers

Joseph Conrad and the Modern Temper
by Daphna Erdinast-Vulcan

IN ONE OF George Eliot's *Scenes from Clerical Life* a lady addicted to reading tracts skims rapidly over references to Zion or the River of Life, but has her attention immediately caught by any mention of "pony" or "boots and shoes." A reader of modern biographies can see why. The best things in them are usually the facts, the objects, the unexplained and inexplicable things that cluttered up the lives of the august and famous, as they do everybody else's, and now find a place in the story. The greasy trilby hat Ford Madox Ford put to dry in Jessie Conrad's oven, provoking the only outburst of wrath even seen on the part of that placid lady; the "good sandwiches" which the soon to be cast-off Hadley Hemingway promised to make for her husband's outing to the races at Longchamps, "black-eyed Susan," the New Mexican cow beloved by D. H. Lawrence: these are the things that stay in the mind when diagnoses and depreciations are forgotten.

Jeffrey Meyers, who has done solid biographies of Lawrence and Hemingway and has now done one for Conrad, is particularly good on — as it were — the boots and the shoes. It makes his biographies not only readable but in their own way memorable, for their subjects appear in a

satisfyingly crude state, touchingly touchy and vulnerable, enmeshed in
contingency. This is in some ways preferable to elegant analyses or magisterial summings-up. Meyers's robust but sympathetic treatment worked
well with Lawrence and is equally effective for Conrad: the reader can
supply the fine tuning and the critical speculation for himself; perhaps on
the basis of such alarming questions as Conrad had to answer when he
was examined for his certificates as chief mate and as master. "You are
totally dismasted and consequently quite unmanageable: what will you
do to keep the ship from foundering by the sea striking her astern or
amidships?"

That was one of the easier ones. When Captain Thompson—
"motionless, remote and enigmatical"—piled on the agony with fog, a
lee-shore, and a lost anchor cable, Conrad explained that he would "back
the bow anchor and tail the heaviest hawser on board on the end of the
chain before letting go, and if she parted from that, which is quite likely,
I would just do nothing. She should have to go." This reply struck a chord
with Captain Thompson, and Conrad got through the ordeal in record
time. Fatalism had not only paid off but had impressed the practical no-
nonsense seaman, and Conrad left the interview with the same ineffable
sense of achievement felt by the youthful mate Powell in *Chance*. As
Meyers points out, Conrad's real knowledge—as opposed to the sort of
thing that Kipling picked up and made use of—comes out at moments
like the abandonment of the *Patna* in *Lord Jim*, when the officers in the
boat see her lights vanish in the squall, and conclude she must be safely
sunk. In fact, she is so far down by the head that she swings head to wind
"as sharply as if she had been at anchor," and the change of position cuts
off the sight of her lights from the dinghy to leeward.

Meyers rather spoils his point, however, by observing that one of the
questions—"How is the lacing rove on the lower part of the luff of a
spanker?"—might have been associated by the examinee "with sex rather
than with seamanship." Well, hardly. Conrad's nautical English was—
had to be—perfect to the point of instinctiveness; his mastery of the language was clearly much more complete than he himself sometimes liked
to pretend. He used his foreignness as a cover in several ways: to explain
the agonizing slowness with which he composed his first novels, and to
preserve the aura of the outlandish and the exotic which both intrigued

the inquisitive and kept them at bay. As he became more famous, he cultivated his mode of speech for the same reason: friends commented that his accent grew worse, not better. But he was always proud to have been accepted so completely in his chosen métier, even if he had been known as "Polish Joe" before the mast, and sometimes later on as "the Russian count" by fellow officers behind his back. Apprentices remembered him with great affection. As he himself put it, he "had proved to the English that a gentleman from the Ukraine could be as good a sailor as they."

It was this kind of thorough expertise that lay behind the famous wish "to make you see"; and there is even more than that to Conrad's compelling accuracy of thing and detail. It does the deep work for him, making supererogatory many of his more explicitly intellectual *démarches*. Or should one rather say he would not have such authority as a writer if he had not been a first-class seaman, of a quite unique sort? Writers about "the human condition" who were deeply influenced by him—André Gide, André Malraux, Albert Camus, Graham Greene—are notably lacking in this sort of homely and instinctive expertise: they are "writers" pure and simple. Conrad was certainly a born writer in one sense, and yet he might easily never have become one had he not invested his skill and training in the dying craft of sailing ships. Long after he had taken his certificate and been acting captain of the *Otago*—an experience he wrote of later in *The Shadow Line*—he was still trying for humbler and already dwindling jobs of junior mate in sail, and taking them when he could.

For a psychologist, the striking thing is the magnificently determined way he spent twenty years of his life mastering a craft that then turned out to be obsolete, while at the same time remaining in many ways helplessly dependent, irresponsibly juvenile. An orphan from early years, he might easily not have survived at all without the paternal affection and anxiety of his uncle Tadeusz, who, as he confessed in later life, "cared for me as if I were a little child." Conrad not only borrowed without shame but when he was in particularly low water, took refuge on the distant estate of his relative, where he was clucked over and cosseted. Uncle Tadeusz, who took enormous pride in his nephew's achievement in the English merchant marine, died before Conrad made his name as a writer. Another relative by marriage, Marguerite Poradowska, a Frenchwoman married in Brussels to a Polish refugee, had had two tasteful but insipid romances published in the *Revise des Deux Mondes*. Conrad wrote to her archly as his "dear teacher," and proposed they should collaborate on a translation of *Almayer's Folly*, still unaccepted by any English publisher, for the same magazine. Marguerite was nine years older but still a beauty—"the most beautiful woman I ever saw," Jessie Conrad was later to observe wistfully. The mayor of Brussels was a suitor in her widow-hood, and Conrad himself may have proposed and been turned down, although they continued to be on very affectionate terms, and Conrad seems to have expected his wife to wait on Marguerite when she came to visit them in later life. He always had an eye for a *grande dame*, but Jessie was the permanent nurse and mother figure he needed and depended upon; and though he ungallantly told his friends that his "intended" was extremely plain, from her pre-wedding photo she looks in her quiet dark way decidedly attractive—rather as one imagines Winnie Verloc. By an odd coincidence Marguerite was the niece of Dr. Paul Gachet, who had looked after Van Gogh in the months before his suicide. Himself a highly disturbed personality, Gachet had a flat full of paintings which Conrad—so admirer of modern art—compared to the lunatic asylum at Charenton.

It is arguable that Conrad's peerless sense of fact is the most vital ingredient in his genius, as it was the most original. All his most success-ful fictions—yarns one could be quite properly inclined to call them—radiate from some central object, and Conrad's intense perception of it: the fire in the hold in *Youth*; the quinine in *The Shadow Line*, horribly changed from a healing substance "light as feathers" to a heavy sludge, the incarnate malignancy of the dead captain who has substituted it. In *Lord Jim* some nameless obstacle, lurking beneath the calm surface of the sea, rips out the *Patna's* keel, and with it Jim's image of himself. Often Conrad's perception of the object takes the form of confrontation, some-times speechless or in slow motion. In the bravura passage at the end of *Youth* the men of the East confront the sleeping castaways, Razumov meets his fate in his own room in the figure of the sleeping terrorist Haldin; and again, in the office of the bureaucrat Mikulin, when he asks "to go right away" and receives in reply a gentle "Where to?" The climac-tic moment in *Heart of Darkness* is not the melodramatic business of finding and bringing out Kurtz, but the "extraordinarily profound and familiar look" directed at Marlowe by the mortally wounded black steersman, and his blood in the wheelhouse filling Marlowe's shoes and socks. The desire to change these becomes his single fixation, but at the same time the African's blood and the look in his eyes has fixed the pair forever in a terrible intimacy.

Sometimes this slow-motion narrative has a mesmeric drollness, as in the perfect comedy of "The Secret Sharer." Conrad, who used on occasion to vie with his friend and agent Edward Garnett in yarn-spinning, told him that his tale "between you and me, is *it* . . . every word fits and there's not a single uncertain note. Luck my boy. Pure luck." The sense of fitness was what most impressed D. H. Lawrence, who observed of one of the last novels, *The Rover*, that it still showed that unique "momentum": "Magnificent. He could write in his sleep." *The Rover* has indeed something of that verbal satisfaction which attended Henry James's style, and grew on it and with it to the point where idea and intention became superfluous. "I'm never sure what it is I'm affirming," Conrad said despondently at this late time to a young French writer, but "affirmation," in the sense that French writers and intellectuals understood it, had never been his thing. If he had opted for the French language, as could have happened if he had married Marguerite Poradowska and settled on the Continent, he might have gained a different sort of fame and reputation: more likely he would never have been heard of, or only in some Gallic charmed circle.

The primacy of things is still strong in *The Rover*, ruling over the old smuggler Peyrol's elaborate plan to immolate himself in order to deceive and disinform the British captain. It rules in the great flake of rust which springs off the straining bulkhead, and convinces Jim that the *Patna* is about to sink, in the revolver which secures Falk's cannibalistic preeminence over his shipmates, and in the carving knife which Winnie Verloc snatches from beside the cold mutton to impale her trusting spouse; even in the cupboard and bed at "The Inn of the Two Witches," a far more haunting version—slight as it may be—of the prototype tales in Edgar Allan Poe and Wilkie Collins. On the other hand, too ponderous a reliance on the procession of the factual can be a nemesis for Conrad's method, as it is in the leaden apotheosis of *Nostromo*, the fatalistic adventure epic of Patusan in *Lord Jim*, and the excessively slow-motion charade of *Victory*. The reader gets a nose, too, for the moments when Conrad is deliberately vague over the facts, or lines them up too economically to point in a desired direction. There is a famous moment in *Heart of Darkness* when Marlowe, on his way out to the Congo, sees a French cruiser apparently shelling the empty bush: a symbol of the evil fatuity of colonial penetration. In fact, as Conrad knew quite well, the ship was taking its important allotted role in the conquest of the powerful local fortress town of Dahomey, key to the French empire of West Africa. However wicked, the aggression was far from futile. But symbols do have a tendency to stray too far from their base, and Conrad is always at his best when they do not, as if were, become separated and fully formed. Nothing like that occurs in *The Nigger of the "Narcissus,"* whose center point is the scarlet thread running from the mouth of James Waite, the dead Negro seaman. Conrad had seen the man dying of consumption on board the real *Narcissus* and "known" the whole thing by immediate instinct.

This is very different from what his admirers soon began to take for granted as a fine performance on the Conrad. Indeed so much for granted that nobody noticed for years and years the misprint at the end of the first paragraph of *Heart of Darkness*, the full oddity of which was pointed out by Frank Kermode. "Gleams of vanished spirits"—no doubt the souls of all the sailormen haunting the Thames since the savage early days of Roman conquest—seemed acceptable Conradian language, in keeping with the tale's general atmosphere, except that what Conrad actually wrote was "gleams of varnished sprits" a reference to the big oblique spar supporting the red mainsail of Thames barges. (Some later editions print an even more bizarre "varnished spirits.") Clearly the word was strange to the printer, who substituted a more familiar one, and the adjective to go with it. The assumption behind the readings makes a neat little summation of what E. M. Forster called the "misty" side of Conrad and the writer who was a practical seaman. Of course the combination made his genius what it was, but nonetheless there remains a distinct gap between the two Conrads: the writer and the "intellectual."

It is naturally enough the latter in whom academic these are chiefly interested; and *Joseph Conrad and the Modern Temper* is in its own way a brilliant study of the ways in which Conrad has been perceived as exemplifying the post-Nietzschean world outlook. Both its author and Meyers quote the relevant letters to Cunninghame Graham in which he expatiates on the "no God, no morality, no truth" theme: probably laying it on for the benefit of his melodramatic but not wildly intelligent correspondent. "Nothing. Neither thought, nor sound, nor soul. Nothing." And having got that out of the way we can go back to the business of living, and writing. Art can only deal in "comfortable untruths," including the Nietzschean one: but all the more reason for devoting oneself to it.

That at least is the suggestion which *Joseph Conrad and the Modern Temper* follows through. Daphna Erdinast-Vulcan makes good use of Hans Vaihinger's *The Philosophy of As If*, a post-Nietzschean follow-up in the first years of the twentieth century to which thinkers and philosophers have not since paid much attention, but whose implications for the state of the art in fiction can now be seen to be of some importance. The climate of assumption it helped to produce in Conrad's milieu—he was certainly familiar with it—is as evident as it is later on in the work of Kipling, Hemingway, or Joyce: all take for granted in their different styles a total absence, filled with "good work," with the burden of what must be done, with the heroic pattern fulfilling itself like fiction in the lives of those for whom, whether they know it or not, "truth is no more immortal than any other delusion." It seems to be highly significant that all four writers clung to fact, making almost a fetish of it in Bloom's breakfast kidney, Kipling's immaculate screws and engines, and Hemingway's food and drink and weapons, as well as in those significant objects which dominate Conrad's best fiction. It is also important that, though fiction immortalizes fact, its powers of doing so appear to be on the wane. The words that despise it and have replaced it in modern fiction reduce it to conscious literariness and care for it no more than they do for other kinds of truth. Facts used to be the determinants of a work of fiction, ensuring that its plot became its destiny. But perhaps Conrad did not really believe in plot, or in character? For the modern temper his special interest is that he was one of the first novelists not so much to recognize as to exhibit that artifice creates "reality," which can only exist in fictional versions.

For me there seems to be a hiatus in his work, for this reason, between fact—the rock that nearly sinks the *Patna*—and fiction: Jim's fiction about himself, the French lieutenant's myth of honor, and the tale that Conrad afterward makes up about Jim's exploits and death in Patusan.

The hiatus illustrates both art and the failure of art, and is deeply and characteristically Conradian. Following to some extent Gerald Graff and the other modern critics, Dr. Erdinast-Vulcan sees things rather differently: but her clear and thorough analysis of Conrad in relation to contemporary critical thought makes her study the most stimulating yet on this subject, particularly as it is independent of critical jargon. She sees Conrad's later characters as becoming "uncomfortably conscious of their own fictionality," and this is surely true. With the man who wrote to the *New York Times* in 1901 that "truth was no more immortal than any other delusion" was trying twenty years later to persuade both his characters and his public that the books they read or had a part in were visionary and profound, the public responded by finding them as comfortable as any other popular romance. They bought them by the thousands and made their author a rich man. Romancers, then, had to believe in their romance. The modern novelist turns this "fictionality" of his characters to good account, making it both conscious and comfortable: but for Conrad the game was up.

London Review of Books, 1991

51

Look Here, Mr. Goodwood

Is Heathcliff a Murderer? Puzzles in Nineteenth-Century Fiction
by John Sutherland

A LEARNED, INDEED AN ERUDITE little book; but also one that is so absorbing, so readable, so quietly and deftly humorous, that it shows up all the dull pretentiousness of nine-tenths of the stuff that gets written nowadays about English literature. A fascinating and major paradox is involved; but what would be the point of the author displaying it when a fabulous gathering of fictional puzzles will do it for him? The best critic, like the best novelist, leaves the reader to decide. The paradox remains, however. On the one hand, the novelist must tell the truth, and want to tell nothing else: on the other, he has the irresponsibility of a creator whose fondness for his creatures is no guarantee that he will not kill them or save them at a whim, show them up or let them down. You want a happy ending? Dickens, Hardy, and above all Thackeray will oblige, however much with tongue in cheek. Dickens and Hardy will do it, while taking the opportunity, in letters or prefaces or afterthoughts, of making clear that it goes against their artistic consciences Thackeray will exhibit the absurdity of novel-writing with a shrug and a smile of apparent shamelessness.

> You, the reader, may settle your fable-land in your own fashion. Anything you like happens in fable-land. Wicked folks die . . . annoying folks are got out of the way . . . the hero and heroine happy ever after

. . . Ah, happy harmless fable-land, where these things are! Friendly
reader, may you and the author meet there on some future day! He
hopes so; as he yet keeps a lingering hold of your hand, and bids you
well with a kind heart.

Overdoing things in that fashion, as Thackeray does at the end of his massive saga-novel *The Newcomes,* has a certain subtlety of purpose behind
it. The reader is made to feel a bit embarrassed and ashamed, as if he
were being wheedled in oily tones by the proprietor of a pornography
shop, who at the same time impresses on him the fact that, while completely in sympathy with his client's requirements, he himself, the
novelist-pornographer, is above such matters. It's far more effective, as
well as more evidently sincere, than the defense Thackeray made to some
intellectual friends of George Eliot, who got at him in his own coin by
teasing him about the happy end they would wish for two of his characters.
He could only reply: "the characters once created *lead me,* and I follow
where they direct." Oh yeah?

As Sutherland intriguingly shows, many Victorian endings cause puzzles. Was Becky Sharp a murderer at the end of *Vanity Fair?*—did she kill
Jos Sedley? Thackeray here is being even more smilingly serpentine in
the way he deals with his reader. He hints, nudges, and winks, encouraging the reader to feel how clever he is not to miss the hints, such as the
fact that Becky's solicitors have the names of well-known murderers. In
seeming to blunder by making Becky at the end entirely out of character,
as a murderess, Thackeray manages to show that there are some things
the little adventuress will not do; but since she has no reputation left,
everyone, including many of his readers, will be happy to think she might.
As Sutherland puts it: "Does Becky kill Jos? Of course she doesn't—but
maliciously wagging respectable tongues will never believe otherwise."
The reader who wants her to be as bad as her reputation is wrong-footed.
Respectability is always at a shady premium in *Vanity Fair,* and by not
having any, Becky remains her own kind of heroine.

Then what about the puzzle that concludes *Villette?* Did Paul
Emanuel survive the storm and return to marry Lucy Snowe? Or was he
drowned? Charlotte Brontë produces a subtle variation on the gross
Thackerayan formula. The "kind heart" and "sunny imagination" is

allowed to conceive "the delight of joy born again fresh out of great terror. Let them picture union and happy succeeding life." But Lucy Snowe is being her own Thackeray. The end has something of the complex irony which attends that of *Wuthering Heights*, where the foolishly good-natured narrator Lockwood cannot himself picture unquiet slumbers for the sleepers in that quiet earth. Loneliness and loss have made Lucy Snowe as narrator calm in another sense. Her farewell is uttered years after the event. She knows: does it matter what her reader thinks? It is probably the first instance of the device of a genuine double ending, implicit in the psychological and dramatic circumstance of the narrative itself. Mrs. Gaskell was fairly hamfisted about it: "the idea of M. Paul Emanuel's death at sea was stamped on her imagination, till it assumed the distinct force of reality; and she could no more alter her fictitious ending than if they had been facts which she was relating." Hamfisted it may be in its assessment of Charlotte's state of mind as an artist, but it goes to the heart of the reader nonetheless. The artfulness of the ending lies in its contrasting the sadness of a fact with the consolation of a fiction. What the fiction insists on is that neither Lucy nor her creator can alter the facts. Art gives the double ending a kind of truth which a single one could not have had.

This is worth pondering in relation to the bogus double endings and "do what you wills" of postmodernist fiction, and of an elaborate affair like *The French Lieutenant's Woman*. By the time such fictions have set themselves up, we couldn't care less about the fate of their characters, or indeed the outcome of the story itself. "Fiction" has devoured itself. True, what Sutherland calls the "epidemic" of Victorian double endings, all briskly defended by their authors, were in response to the pressures of a new reading public, which could make its wants felt. It wanted respectability, and it wanted happy endings. As Sutherland says, novelists like George Moore and Thomas Hardy "were enraged by the constraints that Mrs. Grundy (alias Mr. Mudie, the nursemaid of literature) were imposing on their art and their claims to the privileges of realism." And yet there is a sense in which writers who were rightly Mr. Mudie's enemies brought in time a kind of nemesis on themselves. Say what you like about the constraints which watched over the Victorian novel, they did at least have the rather mysterious effect of making readers believe what the novel was telling them. They were a paradoxical index of seriousness: the absorption in the story of the novel's reader, and the diplomatic but nonetheless wholehearted dedication of its writer. The more emancipated the novelist, and the freer he is of social and sexual constraints, the less seriously the form comes to be taken by its equally emancipated readers.

The involuntary connection of seriousness with strict convention where the novel form is concerned is shown by novels as different as *Tess of the D'Urbervilles* and *The Portrait of a Lady*. The "puzzle" in the former concerns, for Sutherland, the question of whether Alec D'Urberville is to be regarded technically as a rapist. Was Tess raped, or was she seduced? Sutherland, taking this as an important legal question, inclines to the view that Tess must herself in the end be considered more guilty of murder than Alec is of rape. Writing in *Blackwood's Magazine* in 1892, in a review more or less contemporary with the novel, Mrs. Oliphant took the same view. But in 1968 Tony Tanner took both social injustice and Sophoclean irony for granted, observing that "she who is raped lives to be hanged." Sutherland makes the permissible retort that she who was seduced in 1892 has become she who is raped in the permissive Sixties. It could be argued, however, that it is part of Hardy's unconscious technique in presenting Tess to shy away from the both the idea of rape and the idea of seduction. In the latter case her purity would be impugned: in the former the dream image he has of her would be compromised by brutal rather than pathetic association. For Tess leads her multiple existence entirely in Hardy's imagination, and the remarkable achievement of the book, which infuriated a neorealist like George Moore, was Hardy's power to install her in his readers' sensibilities, too—effectively, neither raped nor seduced.

The query raised by the ending of *The Portrait of a Lady* is, as Sutherland rightly contends, not a query at all. Was Isabel Archer's loyal suitor, Caspar Goodwood, left by the last words of the novel with any hope that she might turn to him in time, and abandon her husband, the repellent Osmond? No, he was not. And the ending congests, both lightly and weightily, all the seriousness of the novel, all its moral point. But that seriousness would run the risk, like all too much straight seriousness in novels (George Eliot's, for example), of being merely tiresome, if the ending of James's story had been other than it is. Its fascination was recognized, and absurdly misunderstood, by the well-known and influential critic R. H. Hutton in his review in the *Spectator* of November 1881. He praised the novel highly, but abominated what he regarded as James's open hint that his "ideal lady" saw, at the end, "a straight path" to a liaison with her rejected lover. Henrietta Stackpole has demonstrated all the banality of common sense by taking his arm and saying, "Look here, Mr. Goodwood, just you wait!"—which are almost the last words of the original novel. The reader may feel that the brash female journalist is privy to some secret intention on Isabel's part: but James's own artistic purpose—a sufficiently clear if subtle one—is to underline the vulgarly simple point she is making. There is of course no other possibility for James's own "ideal lady" than to know her fate and see it through to the end. As for her admirer, he is young, and time will do its trick. He will not pine after Isabel forever, and if he does it will make no difference to the decision she has made.

Hutton had done worse work than most critics of a novel can boast of, however, and Sutherland's chapter is well called "R.H. Hutton's Spoiling Hand." The living seriousness of the nineteenth-century novel was underlined by the consequence, for, in some distress of mind, James brooded on the matter and finally, in 1908, he added a final paragraph which loses the moving subtlety of the early version and adds nothing but the needless certainty that Caspar Goodwood has, where Isabel is concerned, nothing to wait for. It is a fetching example of James's late style: Henrietta "stood shining at him with that cheap comfort"—having told him he is still young—"and it added on the spot, thirty years to his life." Caspar Goodwood, we feel, will join—has already joined—the ranks of those doomed Jamesian bachelors whose destiny is to live out a dignified and somehow aesthetically noble life of selfless earning, toiling, and non-living.

The titular question—"Is Heathcliff a murderer?"—turns out something of an anticlimax. Heathcliff certainly brings about Hindley's death by encouraging—almost forcing—a man already an alcoholic to drink himself into a coma. Perhaps he also stands by while Hindley chokes on his own vomit? Perhaps he stifles him? The interest here lies not so much in what happened as in how the author saw Heathcliff, and how the novel expects that the reader should see him. And here we are very much in the dark: not for nothing has Ian Jack, its meticulous editor, noted that "*Wuthering Heights* is one of the most enigmatic of English novels." Much depends on how Emily Brontë imagined her hero, as well as very skillfully creating him, and covering her authorial tracks. I would say that as a young woman she had daydreams about herself as a male vessel of roughness and violence, no doubt in contrast to what was expected of women at the place and time. Daydreams are in the head, and so is Heathcliff, which is the novel's chief weakness; for the more often one reads it the less one believes either in Heathcliff's "real" wickedness or in the deathless "passion" of the lovers, which has promoted so many sentimental films. What one admires more and more, on the other hand, is Emily's skill at disciplining her daydreams into a superb plot, and thumbing her nose invisibly at the domesticated "little me" outpourings of her sister Charlotte. Being in the head, daydreams of passion can be purely abstract; but there is no doubt of Emily's daydream feelings being those of Heathcliff himself, murderous and destructive as they seem to be. In a sense, of course, Heathcliff himself is no more than the old Byronic hero with his "one virtue and a thousand crimes," the one virtue being his "undying" passion for Cathy, his alter ego.

There would be grounds for saying that *Wuthering Heights* is not only the most enigmatic but also the most misunderstood of Victorian novels. Its Gothic features have been so intelligently domesticated, so ironized through the media of innocent Mr. Lockwood and the shrewd servant Nelly, that the reader is apt to be distracted from the wanton, irresponsible violence—and revelry in violence—in which Heathcliff and his author have colluded. Heathcliff expresses a seething cauldron of black humor at someone's expense—and whose if not the constricting world in which Emily lived, and from which her brother broke out? The spiritualizing of Heathcliff's "love," no more in itself than a necessary mechanism of the brilliant Gothic adaptation, took in all Emily's fans, especially the male ones, and was tartly put in its place by—of all people—Ivy Compton-Burnett, for whom the novel had "received a great deal more than its fair share" of adulation and reverence. It is impossible to imagine Emily writing prefaces as Charlotte did, but had she done so she might have made the same claim—and with a lot more secret point and pungency—that her novel was as "unromantic as a Monday morning."

Puzzles like these go to the heart of a novel and its author—to its viscera, too, perhaps, in the case of Mary Shelley and her monster, which may have produced misunderstandings akin to those of *Wuthering Heights*. Frankenstein's monster, as Sutherland brilliantly implies, was at once and blandly taken over by the male science fantasy establishment, with Mary Shelley's connivance in a sense, for her doctor scientist is of course a male. And yet the creation of the monster is essentially one of the horrors of birth, as young Mary, whose mother had died giving birth to her, and who was pregnant with a third child as she wrote *Frankenstein*, may have come to conceive it. As the Brontë critic Ellen Moers suggested, birth might well have seemed sometimes to Mary the process of "filthy creation" that it became for Frankenstein: something disgusting in itself and the cause of endless trouble. The more purely masculine business of electricity and engineering, on which all the many *Frankenstein* films have been based, came later.

Sutherland must, one suspects, be the first critic to notice in print what poor Hetty, in *Adam Bede*, is waiting for, although the point may have been unconsciously taken by many if not all of George Eliot's female readers. Pregnant by Donnithorne while betrothed to the virtuous Adam, Hetty in her great dread "had waited and waited in the blind vague hope that something would happen to set her free from her terror." The vocabulary is that of the Gothic damsel in distress, but the meaning is indeed as domestic and as unromantic as Monday morning. Hardy is similarly explicit/inexplicit in *Jude the Obscure*. At a memorable moment of the novel the earthy Arabella flings at the hero a "piece of flesh, the characteristic part of a barrow-pig." Periphrasis here merely heightens the reader's knowledge of what has taken place, and exaggerates its significance, already considerable for Jude, who grasps "that it had been no vestal who chose that missile for opening her attack on him." But the sleuth critic Sutherland admirably persists in asking what exactly it is that Arabella *does* throw, and thus reveals the full rural complications of Hardy's hidden irony. Kate Millett in *Sexual Politics* says it's a scrotum, implying a pig's full sexual apparatus. But a castrated barrow-pig has no scrotum, only a sexually dysfunctional penis, "useless for any other purpose" than to grease a countryman's boots. In country matters poor Jude might be considered just as useless and dysfunctional. But Hardy is much too good an artist to give the reader nothing but such a brutally ironic realism. What we should add to the down-to-earth picture, surely, is the wonderful symbol which he sets against it: that of the sudden dawning for Jude of "fresh wild pleasure"—the pleasure of a sexual awakening—coming after the fall of a candle that has blotted out the lifeless inscription on a tomb. Jude is perfectly capable of his moment of sexual realization and joy, however ill-starred it may turn out to be.

So the puzzle-illuminations continue in this absorbing little critical study, the author always leaving the reader, in the last instance, to make up his own mind. Almost the last of them is the gripping question of why H. G. Wells's Invisible Man doesn't take the trouble to make himself a suit of invisible clothes. This must have occurred to every reader of Wells's brief and powerful fantasy; and the answer of course has got to be that if he had clothes he would be much more boringly successful than he is, and all the *Gulliver's Travels*–type grotesque episodes—the London mud that reveals his ankles, the curious dog, the cold weather that drives him shivering into a lair behind the carpets in a huge department store— would not have held us spellbound. But there is a metaphysical reason, too, which makes Wells's tale much more than a science fiction. The invisible man is naked and alone in a heartless society. Nobody marks him or cares about him; and all he has left at the end is his own personal delusion of difference and solitary power.

London Review of Books, 1996

52

In Praise of the Amateur Approach

———•———

A VISIT TO THE EXHIBITS at the Tate Gallery short-listed for this year's Turner Prize shows how professionalism today runs not only artistic theory but art itself. There was nothing to take in except the theory of it. Animated discussion, even cries of pleasure and pain, were to be heard from the neighboring exhibition of the strange and superb work of Gerhard Richter. But from the viewer of "the best that is being done by younger British artists today" no ordinary expression of opinion seemed worthwhile, or indeed possible. Amateur appraisal had become pointless. I was reminded of a pamphlet called "Speaking for the Humanities," issued by the American Council of Learned Societies, which stated that since the humanities are under threat they must be run by those who take them seriously—"by professionals rather than by amateurs"—and by specialists who do not make the mistake of assuming an audience "both universal and homogeneous."

The pamphlet was quoted by John Gross in an afterword to a revised edition of his book *The Rise and Fall of the Man of Letters*. Gross assumed a combative stance, calling his piece "the man of letters in a closed shop," and speaking of the "cold horror" that filled him when he contemplated the professionalization of criticism today and the spread of literary theory. But he also recognized that there was something forlorn about such aggressiveness which only made the professional men more cocky. Their chief weapon is to present their opponents as unconscious and thus benighted theorists, "unselfconsciously sustaining traditional social and cultural exclusions." The old-fashioned humanities man who thinks he has an open mind is "simply in the grip of an older theory."

That truism is apt to have a boomerang effect, for new humanities men often seem equally unconscious that their political and ideological role is a surrogate one. The stuff of art is less important to them then correct attitudes and procedures. The professionalized response is good at taking over when there is nothing much to respond to, as in the case of the Turner Prize exhibits. On questions of art or literature the man of letters did at least say straight out what he thought, however much he may have been conditioned to think it. He did not compel a work of art to understand, indeed to create, itself: he gave his own response to it, his own awareness of approval, curiosity, or dislike, which he could justify only in part or not at all, since they came out of him as the work of art from its source, albeit on an appropriately lower level. Amateurs and professionals of the humanities should nonetheless be able to live with each other quite happily, but politics—a surrogate politics that claims to be present in all their responses—requires them to wage factitious war as a matter of display. The cuckoo may be determined to take over the nest, as Gross fears, but that, too, is seen from both sides as more show, gambit, and stratagem than reality: an aspect of the technique of presenting the literary past and present in ritualistically political terms.

Professionalism can genuinely threaten the amateur, however, by making his approach seem inconclusive—again like a work of art itself. Technicians are expected to exercise control. Art's public today is naturally agoraphobic, and instant high-tech is above all reassuring, just as it must have been reassuring to hear from Roland Barthes that "literature is what gets taught"—that is, literature is what I am teaching you. A representative high-tech man tells us that literary criticism "has come a long way" since the days of the man of letters, which is reassuring in the sense that we know a word-processor is now easy to use just because it is complex—with a little tuition anyone can operate it. The theory processor is not concerned with natural talent, any more than with the vagaries of opinion, but men of letters are, or were, in the paradoxically more tricky position of having to write both for those who can and those who can't— for readers with a gift for understanding and appreciating literature as well as for those with little or none. Like artists, they must illuminate, intrigue, and divert at the same time, which is why a master of the genre like V. S. Pritchett is himself both critic and creator.

As man of letters and critic, Pritchett covered all the ground. His collected criticism, a rich and massive volume, examines as many authors as all twelve volumes of *Scrutiny*, and indeed it now appears that Pritchett's powers of detecting and instructing are not so different from those of the F. R. Leavis collective, though never needing its authoritarian pose. Good critics—Leavis and Randall Jarrell, John Updike, A. S. Byatt, Pritchett himself—are more alike than not. In contrast to high-tech men, they share with the authors and novelists who are their subjects a readiness to enter into the diversity and viscosity of the written word, the blatant assault of the personal. The act of liking or disliking a novelist can still seem a sudden intimacy: whether or not you get on is your own affair, and as used to be said, there is no accounting for tastes. The best critics are not necessarily teachers, but theorists almost invariably are, and they have come to dread the direct untreated response by their students, pronouncing E. M. Forster soppy, or Virginia Woolf a bit of a bitch. High-tech negates such responses, rescuing itself from social and worldly critical converse—the medium in which the novel naturally swims. To discuss in the old fashion the characters of *War and Peace* or *Anna Karenina* is to let loose a bedlam of chat in which callow innocence and worldly wisdom are equally happy to take part, leaving the technician gibbering on the sidelines. The man of letters does not mind this—it constitutes a challenge to his skill, but no wonder the high-tech men dread it, and they hasten to restore order by treating the writer as if he were somehow privy to the new linguistic structure they set up within him, which thankfully will put an end to discussion of his books as experience.

It is true that the reception theorists and Stanley Fish have discovered a more ingenious and less obvious tactic: confusion and viscosity can themselves be turned to account, when the text becomes an aporia awaiting a battery of interpretative machines. But how much more illuminating as well as entertaining to manage it in one of the ways Pritchett can do.

I have been reading Dostoevsky again: *The Possessed*. You know the sensation. You are sitting by the fire reflecting that one of the things that reconciles you to life, even at its most tragic, is the low clear daily monotone of its voice. Suddenly comes a knock at the door, there are cries. A man has been murdered at a house down the street. You put on your thickest coat and go out . . . people go rushing by. Who is it this time? Shatov, you hear, the ex-student, the ex-radical, the believer in the Russian Christ. Good Heavens! There was no one more serious, more honest, more likeable than Shatov, rather difficult in argument because he had never got over a sort of angry awkwardness about his class. He was tongue-tied and shy one moment, violently angry the next. His anger soon passed, however, and then he smiled repentantly. There was absolutely no malice in Shatov.

Unlike most belletrists, Pritchett never repeats a gambit, but his way here of carrying the reader into Dostoevsky country is remarkably effective — effective for this particular case. What he goes on to say is, in fact, very similar to Bakhtin's magisterial analysis, which was only available in English long after this essay was written; but in saying it he makes the novel and its characters "alive," as used to be remarked and alive on their own terms. Shatov, whose name means the "unstable one," joins the throng of what Bakhtin was to call "polyphonic" voices and apparitions. Yet the student of today who reveres Bakhtin would not begin to know how to extract the same message from Pritchett. The student is not on the same wavelength. The appeal to experience would bother and embarrass him; he feels far safer with a critic whose method and vocabulary are as distant as possible from those of his subject, and whose message is correspondingly detached, wrapped and processed for separate consumption. Bakhtin has the line on Dostoevsky: Pritchett merely plunges into him.

But if the intellectual classes no longer know how to read a man of letters, and sad as this may be it is probably true, there would be no better way of rediscovering the art than through Pritchett's essays. Their variety is huge and their range encyclopedic. Nor do they offer the slightest evidence anywhere of those "traditional social and cultural exclusions" of which the new humanities men are so keen to discover unconscious traces in their predecessors. A self-made man of letters, Pritchett had none of the subsidies and privileges that post-war intellectuals came to expect the state and the university to shower on them. He found the Russian, French, and Spanish masters for himself, and as a novelist and story writer worked his own way into them, as into every other conceivable literary corner. William Hazlitt—somewhat ironically, the darling of radicals who would dismiss the essay genre in general—was an ignoramus compared to Pritchett, and with a far less open mind. Pritchett approaches politics, like everything else, through the books he discusses and the findings of the people in them; the kinds of common sense which result are not afraid to sum up, for example, what Dostoevsky conveyed to the world in his novels as the varied, vivid, muddled thinking "typical of a confused Russian middle-class intelligentsia, with equal leanings towards populist mysticism and populist progress." Much the same could be said of *Mein Kampf*. And yet novelists, as Pritchett's exposition goes on to demonstrate, can penetrate through silliness into profound imaginative command, and this is specially true of Dostoevsky.

Behind Pritchett's exact and brilliant seizure of the thisness of any given work are the outlines of wider ideas, as rational as they are unpretentious, never grounded in academic self-satisfactions. In a piece on Mrs. Gaskell, "The South goes North," he indicates unobtrusively the dependence of the Victorian novel—a conditioned reflex in almost every work except *Wuthering Heights*—on the inculcation of responsibility, the ethic of self-improvement. How easily and naturally the novel worked, what a proper inevitability its form possessed—like that of classic tragedy—when it strove instinctively upward, toward the better thing and the higher conclusion! Our own novels, on the contrary, "seek to impress us with ideas of self-sufficiency and guilt." Written decades ago, that remains true today, revealing not only that the ludic preoccupations of the modern novel are not based solely on a changed view of language, but that a craving for those Victorian directions is still in the bones of the modern novel reader, and in novelists as different as Iris Murdoch and Margaret Drabble. Such readers and writers are in no sense Victorian throwbacks, yet they know in their bones that the true English novel is destined to a Victorian purpose and persona, in whatever modified circumstances. Pritchett understands this. He observes in passing as he writes about George Eliot that now "we do not wish to be better than we are but more fully what we are." Most of us, perhaps, but not all, and certainly not all readers of novels.

His droll precisions—as when he writes of W. W. Jacobs "living in an ivory foc'sle"—are a particular joy. Yet his pleasure in Jacobs is such that he makes us want to rush off at once and discover or rediscover the world of Ginger Dick and Peter Russet. He draws the most subtle of distinctions between Jacobs's unerring sense of the human will to be one up and how it gets its way in his elemental contexts, and the bogus literary tradition in which Jacobs had to write to sell his work. A couple of quotes from August Strindberg's "Getting Married" make the point, with hardly anything else needing to be said, that there is a kind of offhand piercing gaiety of intelligence in the man, and in the way he writes, that makes this so-called misogynist a bosom pal of D. H. Lawrence, with equally abrupt insights into the ways in which sex makes people behave.

The most striking thing about the man of letters, exemplified at his best in this collection, is the absence of tunnel vision. It is improbably comic to think of Pritchett taking part in one of those Sunday books of the year surveys, and adding his quota to their self-important predictability. Traveling widely, he owns no field, has no place to take over and develop as an authority. He loves without possessiveness. Nor does he suffer from the conscientious urge to be with it, which today can afflict both the writer of reviews and the novelist and story writer determined to show that all modern living can be fitted into their art, from the clitoris to Cambodia. Symptoms of this engaging but also rather depleting condition can be detected in the collected review essays of John Updike, *Odd Jobs*, a volume as massive and as rich as Pritchett's. Perhaps because the status of the man of letters was never recognized in America he cannot be said to have either risen or fallen there. *The Shores of Light*, Edmund Wilson's best collection, and Lionel Trilling's on the liberal imagination, are from masters of the art who would nonetheless have recognized a fellow master in Pritchett. It is true that they—Trilling especially—could be anxious where Pritchett is cheerful, and portentous where he is brisk and insouciant. Trilling's anguish over the fate of writers—Conrad, Kafka, Dostoevsky—whose ferocity is not only lost upon the young but tamed into domesticity by English departments, would not have worried Pritchett, whose direct access to books has never been mediated through theory or seminar. Let us hope he will not be the last of the breed: at present he is certainly its most distinguished son.

53

Death and the Dichter

Robert Musil (1880–1942)

———

Posthumous Papers of a Living Author
by Robert Musil, translated by Peter Wortsman

Five Women
by Robert Musil, translated by Eithne Wilkins and Ernst Kaiser

Robert Musil
by Lowell A. Bangerter

T HE GERMAN TERM *Dichter* is not at all readily translatable. It has a wider sense than "poet," and a more transcendental one than "writer." Goethe, the archetypal *Dichter*, created masterpieces in every genre, but was also the model of thinking and being, in the science and ethic of a civilized state. Never much like its English, French, or Russian counterpart, the German novel, coming from the pen of a *Dichter*, has always more resembled an enterprise of the philosophical imagination.

Frank Kermode gave this interpretation of *Dichtung* when he spoke of its "elaborate attempts to use fiction for its true purposes, the discovery and registration of the human world." That might mean much or little. A modest masterpiece, like a novel of Jane Austen's, could be said to achieve such a goal as effectively as a work of vast and deliberate metaphysical scope, if not more so. It's a question for the reader, and for the way his mind works. In the relative world of the novel revelation may come to him from an unexpected quarter. Or the discerning reader may go only for a novelist-*Dichter* with whom revelation is an open promise. Milan Kundera, a lively, but it must be said exceedingly naïve, commentator on these matters, assures us that the novelist is an "explorer of existence, . . . man's being, which the novel alone can discover."

In a sense Kundera and Kermode are on sure ground, but there is a snag. By hailing the novelist as a *Dichter* (the word has unfortunate if fortuitous connotations with *Diktat*) they bestow on the novel a conscious and transcendent function, one that goes with the German and Goethean tradition.

A *Dichter* can remain a *Dichter* only by asserting his own absolute preeminence and authority; and, as D. H. Lawrence very sensibly put it, the strength of the novel is that it is "so incapable of the absolute." Nothing is more absolute than an idea, and the naïveté of a lively and creative intellectual like Kundera emerges in his persistent belief that the more striking its ideas, the more effective the novel. All his disclaimers, all his insistence that the novelist is not playing with ideas but exploring human individuality, serve only to emphasize his real allegiance. For him the three great novelists of the twentieth century, the ones who really matter, are all men—all, one might say, specifically *masculine*—and all Central Europeans: Hermann Broch, Franz Kafka, and Robert Musil. And of these the real intellectual's novelist, the one most committed to ideas, is Musil. He is the apotheosis of the modern *Dichter*, one who has passed beyond life into a world of abstract inquiry about it. In the foreword to his essay collection, *Posthumous Papers of a Living Author,* as in its title, he made a joke of this. "Can a *Dichter* still speak of being alive?"

Well perhaps not. The author of *Axel's Castle* observed that the artist's valet would do his living for him: Musil in the next century allots the same role to thought. He was frank about this. In his diary in 1910 he wrote: "Where I cannot elaborate some special idea, the work immediately becomes too boring for me." In one of the essays and dialogues assembled in his book *The Art of the Novel,* Kundera observes that Fielding *tells* a story, Flaubert *describes* a story, and Musil *thinks* a story. The odd and indeed slightly comic paradox in all this is Kundera's insistence, where Musil and the modern novel are concerned, on the Heideggerian existence—*in der Welt sein*—of Musil's apparently "unliving" characters.

"Making a character 'alive,' " says Kundera, "means getting to the bottom of his existential problem . . . nothing more."

But people don't walk around with an existential problem. They walk around worrying about a visit to the dentist, buying a pound of sausages, wondering if their husbands are being unfaithful. The novel has always known this and has invented itself accordingly. As Kundera elsewhere implies, and rightly, the novel has always known what the existential thinkers in our time have been preaching as a new gospel: and yet he is himself most impressed and influenced by those novelists who have made the most elaborate attempts to use fiction for the discovery and analysis of "existence." It is a question of which comes first: the novel, or thoughts and ideas about the novel, the metaphysical uses that the form can supply after the event. Walter Benjamin—no mean judge—saw this clearly, and said that Musil was a thinker but not a novelist: a thinker who made use of the novel.

Musil himself might well have agreed. He was not dogmatic on such issues. As *Dichter* he saw himself primarily as an explorer of "the other condition," which is both the goal and the process of thinking about one-self, experiencing oneself. And by experiencing oneself one may reveal one's experience to others. This is the delicate point in our relations with Musil—are we sharing an experience, or being asked to admire a highly complex and specialized one of his own? Is he, like Tolstoy, a solipsist who speaks for us all, or one who is only interested in a unique self?

It is the same kind of contradiction as that between man as an existentialist and as someone who is preoccupied about his pound of sausages; and to do Musil justice he is neither disturbed by it nor even made self-conscious. Of the triad of novelists exalted by Kundera he is closer to Broch than to Kafka, or to other intellectual European novelists like Elias Canetti and Thomas Mann. But he remains very much a writer on his own. It is obvious that when we read Kafka, a very different sort of writer, we are no more meeting fully recognizable individuals than we are in the pages of Musil. Kafka's figures are so compelling because we are at once engrossed in their experience, becoming a beetle with Gregor Samsa in "The Metamorphosis," or the victim of a mysterious trial with Josef K. What happens to them is so absorbing that we are not interested in what they are like. But with Jane Austen's *Emma,* say, interest is divided between

Emma as a personage, presented for our acquaintance and amusement, and Emma as a set of experiences that the author invites us to share. With Musil we have something quite different, none of these more familiar introductions to the world of other people, but simply to the mind of a man who once said that he made fictions because they were the only vehicle for the unphilosophical view that everything in thought and experience can be simultaneously true and false.

Hence the unpositive nature of Musil's world, its lack of "characteristics." Most novels depend on emphasizing, even exaggerating, the characteristics of things and people, so that we soon recognize everything and begin to feel at home in the world the novelist invents for us. Musil's long, unfinished novel, *The Man Without Qualities*, which should really be given in English the clumsier title of "The Man Without Characteristics," pretends to use some of the usual business of the novel. There is the "Collateral Campaign," a society project for rehabilitating the Austrian Empire; there is much satire on bureaucracy; there are investigations of a sex murderer, Moosbrugger, and of the incestuous love between Ulrich, the man without qualities, and his sister Agathe. There is the suggestion of a world on the brink of the disaster of the First World War. There are also portraits *à clef* of powerful women of Musil's acquaintance, such as Lou Andreas-Salomé.

But all this is of little importance beside the play of thought—and it must be said, style—which is the real Musil experience. Musil's triumph ultimately is to do what all other great novelists do: that is to say, compel us to share the authenticity of his world; but it is a world in which fact, event, and consideration are, as it were, ineradicably interchangeable. That is why it would be vulgarly misleading to speak of Musil's world as existing on the brink of the abyss of war and anarchy, because the abyss may cease to exist or turn out to be something quite different. For the same reason the novel could not end, but would merely go on, until its author, impoverished and ill, died in Switzerland in 1942, just after completing a sentence. Like fiction's version of Penelope's web it secretly and mysteriously unraveled itself even while it was being so delicately and carefully woven.

In some metaphysical way that might be considered the highest destiny of the novel form, its ultimate essence; and it is certainly true that highly intelligent people who do not read ordinary novels will read Musil with deep admiration. He is a philosopher's pet, like Wittgenstein, perhaps because philosophers, who try to establish what can be known, are seduced by a world of such palpable intelligence in which knowledge and experience remain absolutely free and uncommitted.

Intelligence, for Musil, is embodied in the erotic, in its sensations and discoveries, and the most graphic passages in all his books deal with sexual musings and intimations as a part of the "other condition," the state that medieval mystics, in whom Musil was much interested, frequently likened to certain kinds of erotic experience. A tiny essay in *Posthumous Papers* called "Maidens and Heroes" muses about the thoughts, or nonthoughts, of servant girls exercising dogs. Is their world one of Zen-like calm, or of "thinking that the movie's about to begin"? Another, in a style even more mesmeric and haunting, describes the narrator going to bed in a hotel room with a slight fever, and listening to the woman with him making her own preparations "in the realm of reality":

Incomprehensible, all the walking up and down: in this corner of the room, in that. You come over to lay something on your bed; I don't look up but what could it be? In the meantime you open the closet, put something in or take something out; I hear it close again. You lay hard, heavy objects on the table; others on the marble top of the commode. You are forever in motion. Then I recognize the familiar sounds of hair being undone and brushed. Then swirls of water in the sink. Even before that clothes being shed; now again: it's just incomprehensible to me how many clothes you take off. Finally, you've slipped out of your shoes. But now your stockings slide as constantly over the soft carpet as your shoes did before. You pour water into glasses, three or four times without stopping. I can't even guess why. In my imagination I have long since given up anything imaginable, while you evidently keep finding new things to do in the realm of reality. I hear you slip into your nightgown. But you aren't finished yet and won't be for a while. Again there are a hundred little actions. I know that you're rushing for my sake, so all this must be absolutely necessary, part of your most intimate I, and like the mute motions of animals from morning till evening, you reach out with countless gestures, of which you're unaware, into a region where you've never heard my step!

In such explorations of the erotic consciousness, as a form of prolonged meditation, Musil the *Dichter* does indeed seem to forgo the authority of that high poetic intelligence, and take on some of the novel's diffidence, its relative and nonabsolute qualities.

Musil was, like Wordsworth, "a traveller, whose tale is only of myself." And yet like many if not most mystics he was an eminently practical man in daily affairs, by turns a mathematician, engineering student, successful soldier in the First World War; and then a prolific reviewer and essayist, and editor of a periodical. He wrote one play that was a failure and another that had a considerable success. It is true that all this brought him little profit. His touchy independence and reluctance to commit himself to offers meant that he and his wife lived on the edge of poverty. Friends even set up a *"Musilgesellschaft,"* into which subscriptions were paid for their support. As *Dichter* on the one hand and day-to-day man of letters on the other he led a double life, one not uncommon in an artistic setting but carried by Musil to extreme lengths. *The Man Without Qualities* was incessantly restarted and revised, and the publisher, Ernst Rowohlt, grew reluctant to pay further advances. He continued to do so nonetheless, remarking later that though many authors threatened to shoot themselves if support were withdrawn, Musil was the only one he thought might really do it.

In all these vicissitudes Musil's wife, Martha Marcovaldi, was both pillar of strength and alter ego. Seven years older than her husband, she had been married twice before, first to a young man who died and then to an Italian merchant by whom she had two children. He made trouble about a divorce, which eventually had to be obtained in Hungary. In all his difficulties Musil came to see her as "another side of himself." He wrote in his diary that she "was someone he had become and who had become him." Fortunately Martha was tough enough to stand up to this most invasive of solipsists. In his helpful study Lowell Bangerter records that Musil's first German biographer, Karl Dinklage, announced in an address that "Martha was for Robert Musil the intellectual, spiritual, physical complement that was necessary for him to become what he is today for us and the world."

In a sense all Musil's fictional situations take for granted such an interchangeability. His characters are all himself, or, as he would probably have put it, he has the power of endowing with himself anyone he creates. The same might, after all, be said of Tolstoy, or any other great novelist. Yet it remains true of Musil in a special sense, the sense in which he can be said to *think* his characters and their "story." His first and most popular novel, *Young Törless*, which came out in 1906, already demonstrates this tendency. Outwardly a more or less conventional *Bildungsroman* concerning the events in a military academy, it represents more convincingly the play of mind in a single person: the brutal cadets Reiting and Beineberg and their victim, the cowardly theif Basini, are acting out the "larval" impulses of young Törless in his search for his true selfhood in the "other condition." But the book owed its success to being received by its readers, in the bourgeois era, as a steamy revelation of what actually went on in such a school.

Musil himself saw the "special idea" of his novel as a kind of microcosm of contemporary society, the idea adumbrated — but also, as was typical with Musil, eluded and contradicted — on a much larger scale in *The Man Without Qualities*. Much later, in a diary entry during the Thirties, he referred to his brutal pair of cadets as "today's dictators *in nucleo*," but that seems like the hindsight of a writer who was always, and deliberately, pretentious. Musil, as much as Joyce, is an intensely personal and domestic bard, although all great writers can, of course, be seen, or can see themselves, as prophets of political doom, civilization's collapse. "We cannot halt the deluge," Musil exclaimed in the Thirties. But the way he thinks a story echoes the title he gave his essays: it does not depend on the daily vicissitudes of life and history. The mystically erotic transcends such things, as it transcends conventional sex barriers. Törless's homosexual experiences are no more specifically homosexual than the relations of Ulrich and his sister Agathe in *The Man Without Qualities* are specifically incestuous, or Moosbrugger is a real sex murderer.

All these things are in the mind, or, as we should have to say in the case of a cruder writer, in the sexual fantasy. Moosbrugger believes that the world's existence depends on his crimes, an exaggeration of Ulrich's search in incest for his other self, a total relation such as Musil saw in himself and Martha. Musil in fact exemplifies perfectly, on the highest of planes, the way men cannot help imagining women. His female characters, like Joyce's Molly Bloom and Gretta Conroy, are themselves male fantasies. There is a certain irony in the fact that the untrammeled exercise of the intelligence on the novel, by so supreme an intelligence as Musil's, results in a rarefied form of something with which men are all too familiar—dreams of fair women. Shakespeare does not in this sense imagine Lady Macbeth speaking of the tenderness of suckling a child; and Tolstoy does not fantasize about Natasha Rostov's translation from coltish girl into slatternly earth mother. These are matters of universal knowledge and experience, as a down-to-earth genius presents them. But Musil's touchingly and indeed hauntingly objective presentation of Tonka, one of the "Three Women" in a short collection with that title published in 1924, is not quite what it seems.

The real Tonka was a simple working-class girl called Herma Dietz, with whom Musil lived for a time while working as a young man in technical and scientific institutes. The story explores, thinks as it were, her simplicity; and how it dissolves the distinction between deceit and innocence, so that Tonka can be, in some sense, faithful to the narrator, even when it is obvious that she has made love with another man and contracted venereal disease. The story is not really interested in her as a social being, but in the metaphysical status the narrator confers on her. What fascinates him is that she has no power of speech, and thus embodies something his own intelligence has with infinite subtlety concluded: that an idea or a person—anything in the world—can be simultaneously true and false, existent and nonexistent.

Three Women is combined in a paperback volume with two earlier *nouvelles* published in 1911 with the title *Unions*. All are concerned with women of the imagination, Tonka being the most notable, and the most elaborate a meditation entitled "The Perfecting of a Love." A woman travels to see her daughter at school, her husband absorbed in his work remaining at home. As in a modern film she encounters the shadowy figure of a man who stands outside her hotel door at night, and with whom she eventually makes love, feeling the moment to be the perfection of her union with her husband, "a state that was like giving herself to everyone and yet belonging only to the one beloved." "Grigia" reverses the pattern, a husband parting from his wife to work on a project in the South Tyrol, where he makes love with a peasant woman, whose husband lures them down a mine shaft and blocks the entrance. The girl escapes, but the narrator appears to have been seeking the perfect venue for a mystical *Liebestod* with his own wife, which then takes place, at least in the narrator's and the reader's imagination. Musil certainly puts queer ideas into other people's heads.

Published in Zurich in 1936, the ironically named *Posthumous Papers* contains a number of short sketches and stories written for magazines over the previous years, often terse reminiscences in miniature of the longer *nouvelles*. Some are dry and witty comments in newspaper style. Ably rendered as they are by Peter Wortsman, they cannot convey a great deal, in English, of the elliptical symmetry and richness of Musil's German. As a prose poet he is at his best over short distances, moments of what the critic Frederick Peters, in his 1978 study entitled *Robert Musil: Master of the Hovering Life*, defined as "ultimate narcissism." Nothing of course is "ultimate" in Musil, but "hovering life" conveys very well that flashpoint of the solipsistic and the external worlds which he conveys so marvelously, sometimes in images like that of the gathering of people in *The Man Without Qualities*, who seem to take wing in a myriad of mental impressions before alighting "like waders on a sandbank."

An ironic little essay in *Posthumous Papers* called "Black Magic" conveys as well as anything in his work its simultaneous feel of density, mathematical logic, and seductive unpredictability. Like Kundera, and indeed like most representatives of the culture in which the expressive word originated, Musil is fascinated by the relation of kitsch to life and to art. Kundera claimed, from extensive experience of the political systems of Eastern Europe, that ideals like "the Brotherhood of Man" were only possible on the basis of kitsch. Musil's more subtle view has the same implication. For him "art is a tool which we employ to peel the kitsch off life." Kitsch may be life's answer to "the horrible gaping contingency of all one does," but art—and especially the art that really explores sex—can do the job much better. Art strips life layer by layer. "That in life which cannot be employed for art's sake is kitsch."

It is the center of Musil's philosophy as *Dichter*. Or is it? Abruptly he switches away into a pattern of seriocomic syllogisms:

> Art peels kitsch off of life.
>> Kitsch peels life off of language.
>> And: The more abstract art becomes, the more it becomes art.
>> Also: The more abstract kitsch becomes, the more it becomes kitsch.
>> These are two splendid syllogisms.
>> If only we could resolve them!

He proceeds to do so in a few sentences worthy of Alice in Wonderland, or Wittgenstein's *Tractatus* run mad. "Art equals life minus kitsch equals life minus language plus life equals two lives minus language."

Then the essay, one of a collection entitled "Ill-tempered Observations," switches as it concludes into quite another key again:

> A black hussar has it so good. The black hussars swore an oath of victory or death and meanwhile stroll around in this uniform to the delight of all the ladies. That is not art! That's life!

Where do these black hussars come from and what do they mean for Musil? Are they a *Dichter*'s companions, the bodyguard as it were, who protect his genius, or the escort who have him under arrest? The artist swears an oath, but the man who lives continues to stroll around day by day, in his artist's uniform, to the delight of the ladies? Art is like death: it swallows up its devotee, who continues to lead a posthumous life.

The New York Review of Books, 1988

54

Fighting for the Crown

Angela Carter (1940–1992)

Wise Children
Love
The Bloody Chamber and Other Stories
Heroes and Villains
The Infernal Desire Machines of Dr. Hoffman
Come Unto These Yellow Sands
The Old Wives' Fairy Tale Book (ed.)
The Sadeian Woman: An Exercise in Cultural History

POSTMODERNISM IN THE ARTS notoriously starts from the premise that "anything goes," but this is no great help if we are trying to find out what sort of fiction today is actually thought and spoken of as postmodernist. The expression has often been used about the books of Angela Carter, and so has the rather more easily definable term "magic realism." Indeed when she first started to publish in the Sixties her novels were hailed in England as an enterprising native version of the kind of thing that was being done in North America by Thomas Pynchon and in South America by Gabriel García Márquez.

The link between magic realism and the more evasive concept of postmodernism in the novel probably was that everything goes: that the hitherto separable conventions of fantasy and realism, satire and social comment, could be fused together in a single permissive whole. The process was a very self-conscious one; the novelist knew exactly how new and up-to-date he or she was being, while at the same time being careful in an egalitarian way to avoid the more exclusive and old-fashioned label of "experimental": the rigors of formalism were definitely out. But if this was postmodernism it could still be said to have been around for a long time, for critics were beginning to detect just the same brew of ingredients, even if less deliberately mingled, way back in the history of the novel. Looked at under modern eyes even *The Mayor of Casterbridge*, say, Thomas Hardy's sturdy down-to-earth survey of the rise and fall in a country town of a man of character, begins to assume a fantastic aspect, with the author's dreams and fears of failure and success clothing a fairy tale in the sober hues of business and property.

Fantasy, in short, can be seen as the basis of every novel: what matters today is the individual and original use made of it. Angela Carter scored high marks at that, from her first, *Shadow Dance* (1965), to her last, *Wise Children*. Although she is an enterprising and versatile writer, always exploring fresh themes, there is about all her novels a strong element of continuity, even communality, which may remind the reader of the claim often made for postmodernist art as "a single ongoing subcultural event" that does not distinguish between intimacy and togetherness, any more than between high art and pop art. Like other very capable modern authors Angela Carter is good at having it both ways, dressing up pop art in academic gear and presenting crude aspects of modern living in a satirically elegant style. In *Love*, her most effective and memorable novel of the Sixties, she cunningly drew a pair of youthful student hippies as a version of many traditional fraternal prototypes, including Ivan and Alyosha Karamazov. The brief novel is Dostoevskian in other ways, dramatizing a triangle of unbalanced passion and possessiveness and placing it in a squalid urban setting among students of the post–Lucky Jim type. Lee and Buzz are brothers, with an incestuous closeness between them, and Lee is pressured by her parents into marrying Annabel, who is trying to paint, and who already has episodes of madness.

The subsequent explosions leading to Annabel's suicide as she lies in bed watched over by Buzz, who has fulfilled one of her desires by shrinkingly raping her, are done with a vigor and understanding that remain impressive today, even after such Gothic goings-on in the novel have become commonplace. Carter controls the Gothic element, as well as her other literary devices, with characteristic brio, driving it firmly to a polemical end, and not indulging it for its own sake. Among other things, *Love* is a vaudeville version of the Sixties, and of the young people seduced by the heady climate of the revolution seemingly so near at hand, and licensing in a communal setting whatever private violence was haunting them. A thoroughly professional artist, Carter obviously took what the fashions and emphases of an epoch sent her way. In her after-word to the revised edition of *Love* she imagines with rapid and sardonic precision the later lives of her youthful cast, who were

> not quite the children of Marx and Coca-Cola, more the children of Nescafé and the Welfare State . . . the pure perfect products of those days of social mobility and sexual license.

In the epilogue we learn that Buzz has now come out of the closet and plays in New York punk bands, meanwhile dabbling in real estate "with some success." Lee stays in dull old England, where he has found a bossy woman to patch him up after the trauma of his wife's suicide; he teaches school and becomes responsible and respectable on sound socialist lines. He is devoted to his children and severe with them, his wife having little time for them, engrossed as she is with feminist concerns:

> They row fiercely. The adolescent daughters in their attic room turn up the volume of the record player to drown the noise. Upstairs, the baby cries. The telephone rings. Rosie springs off to answer. It is the Women's Refuge. She begins an animated conversation about wife-beating, raising two fingers to her husband in an obscene gesture. . . .
>
> Suddenly the whimpering baby yawns hugely, quiets and sleeps, looking all at once like a blessed infant.
>
> The father kisses her moist meagre hair and lays her down upon her side. The older girls, trained in deference to her tyrannic sleeps, snap off their loud music but, cold-eyed strangers that they have become, continue to discuss in muted whispers their parents' defi-ciencies as human beings.
>
> Oh, the pain of it, thought Lee, thinking about his children, oh! the exquisite pain of unrequited love.

Note that the children of the flower children are all girls, preparing in their unillusioned and disenchanted way to lead their own styles of life. In its vigorous way the novel celebrates the Sixties but also moves on from them, questing for new directions. It is also very funny at moments about sex, briskly aware that many happy solutions in this sphere have led to so many yet darker complications. Poor near-psychotic Buzz is excluded from what seem to the young its newly liberated joys.

> "Open your legs," he said. "Let me look."
>
> . . . Buzz crouched between her feet, and scrutinised as much as he could see of her perilous interior to find out if all was in order and there were no concealed fangs or guillotines inside her to ruin him. Although he found no visual evidence, he remained too suspicious of her body to wish to meet her eyes.

The notion of the "perilous interior," with its medieval and literary antecedents in perilous chapels and seas, affords Carter and her readers some subliminal amusement; but although she is sorry for Buzz she sticks even here to the party line: instructing us that female bodies must not be treated as objects. Still less of course as mechanical traps. Indeed if there is a common factor in the elusive category of the postmodern novel it is political correctness: whatever spirited arabesques and feats of descriptive imagination Carter may perform she always comes to rest in the right ideological position.

This was the case with her other dazzling performances in the Sixties' milieu: *The Magic Toyshop*, which was made into a film, *The Passion of New Eve*, and *Heroes and Villains*. She shows great brilliance in updating literary and social stereotypes, and upending them as well. She herself invoked Benjamin Constant's *Adolphe* as the model for the doomed relationship described in *Love*. (*Adolphe*, as it happens, was also made very conscious use of in one of Anita Brookner's quietly perceptive fictions. Constant would recognize his hero and heroine in her fictional milieu but hardly in that of Carter.) And another bygone French author, Charles Perrault, would be surprised at the use Carter has made of the fairy tales he collected and popularized in his own elegant tongue. The stereotypes of Red Riding Hood and Bluebeard's wife have had their roles very much reversed in Carter's lively storybook *The Bloody Chamber* (1979). Perrault's tales, like their venerable originals, reveal the cheerful but often chilling matter-of-factness of the implicit horror, the time-honored suspense and relief: "Sister Anne, sister Anne, do you see any-one coming?" and "All the better to eat you with!"

Carter not only switches her narrative into the wholly explicit but turns the passive predicament of the heroine into one in which the con-vention of female role-playing seems to have no part, only brisk and deri-sive common sense, the best feminine tactic in a tight corner. Her Red Riding Hood is a slyly confident adolescent, removing her clothes with a sneer to enter the wolf's bed. When he speaks the hallowed formula, "All the better to eat you with!" "the girl burst out laughing: she knew she was nobody's meat." The wolf is not discomfited, but being a politically cor-rect animal at heart he enfolds her in an egalitarian embrace, and they go blissfully to sleep in the eaten-up granny's bed.

Bluebeard's latest wife is equally cool-headed in her sexual collusion with the demon lover who is both father and husband. Interestingly, Carter's new-style heroines have one point in common with many of their prototypes in fairy tales: they could come from any country and belong to any class. Carter's brand of magic realism is also a democratic magic. In her introduction and arrangement of the stories collected in her anthol-ogy, *The Old Wives' Fairy Tale Book*, she distinguished between the dif-ferent traditional feminine categories: natural witches; bad, because resourceful, girls; "good girls and where it gets them." The same enlight-ening categorization is to be found in her essays and theoretical writings, *Nothing Sacred* and *The Sadeian Woman: An Exercise in Cultural His-tory*. The latter is a sardonic study of the two types who have supplied the mainstay of pornographic literature: the virtuous and therefore helpless girl, and the wicked lady. They are the Justine and Juliette of de Sade's fiction; and Carter's arguments emphasize that de Sade performed an important service in drawing attention by pornographic means to the tyranny that such man-made stereotypes imposed on women of the time, and for centuries before and since. As Voltaire satirized in *Candide* the fate of innocence and optimism in a wicked world, so de Sade revealed the fate of all women, who in a man's world had no choice but to be what men required. Justine was the stereotype of the abused wife, and Juliette the seductively wicked prostitute mistress.

Carter's essays are as vigorous as her fiction, but necessarily dated now that such insights have become received wisdom and thus commonplace. However "correct" Carter's novels may be, they all demonstrate the brio and originality of true personal talent, as she showed by excursions into her own style of science fiction—*Heroes and Villains* and *The Infernal Desire Machines of Dr. Hoffman*. Although written with all her ebullience, these books seem to me less memorable than earlier novels like *Love* and to be more purely "performance" novels, designed to appeal to a diverse audience.

Another of postmodernism's purely negative qualifications is that it is not "elitist": that is to say, does not possess the kinds of private and individual distinction which recommend themselves to a small audience. *Heroes and Villains* is a romp allegory appealing to everyone suspicious of such minority tastes, for the heroine is a professor's daughter who has to live down that stigma by being captured by a beautiful barbarian and carried away to a paradise of primitivism, sex, and greenery. Carter uses a scenario similar to those of Swift or Orwell but without any apparent irony (irony is necessarily elitist because some may not see the point) although—to be fair—irony comes into her work of science fiction, *The Infernal Desire Machines of Dr. Hoffman*, in which a war is fought against the diabolic doctor who wants to destroy the "reality principle." A grotesque embodiment of the male principle, Dr. Hoffman is a mad scientific deconstructionist, part Mary Shelley's Frankenstein, part Dostoevsky's Grand Inquisitor.

In 1985 Carter's first experiment in radio drama produced *Come Unto These Yellow Sands*, based on the unnervingly beautiful fairy paintings of Richard Dadd, the Victorian artist who went mad and killed his father. She even spoke of "re-inventing" the paintings of Jackson Pollock with the same kind of drama performance, remarking in her cheerful way, "*That* would be a challenge." Meanwhile she exploited her talent for colorful and rollicking vaudeville plots in *Nights at the Circus* and in her latest—and, alas, last—novel, *Wise Children*. Carter's imagination has always been inspired by a stage ambiance, and the kinds of living that go with it, but *Wise Children* also associates itself with a new sort of fashion in fiction, one very effectively exemplified by two short and modest English novels: David Lodge's *Paradise News* and Penelope Fitzgerald's *The Gate of Angels*. It is well known that in the novel a good man is hard to find: one of the most convincing appeared a long time back in Saul Bellow's *Mr. Sammler's Planet*. With the two other English novels, *Wise Children* sets out on the same journey, to explore the quality and desirability of virtue, the nature of the *honnête homme* or the *honnête femme*.

Carter's honest narrator in *Wise Children* is one of a pair of twins who have spent their lives in show business: the London music halls when young, and Hollywood in their later years. Inspired no doubt by the Dolly Sisters, a charming photo of whom decorates the cover, these heroines were conceived and born in unprepossessing circumstances, their mother being a waif of the stage door known as Pretty Kitty. Throughout an eventful lifetime the pair have remained innocents at heart, and virtuous as well, although not, of course, in what used to be the technical sense. Carter sets herself to demonstrate that the jungle law of the casting couch and the tawdry world of stage and screen can nonetheless be pure at heart, peopled not by tigers but by does and fauns, creatures who may be grotesque but are also endearing. It says much for Carter's literary charm and drive that she makes this seem perfectly possible. Her own brand of magic seems to infect her cast, and to make them believe in the magical reality of the tinsel and trappings in their hard-worked lives.

Literary models lurk as usual in the background. Dickens would at once have seen the point of *Wise Children*, and might have suggested calling the pub where its characters meet, "The Twelve Jolly Thespians," after his own Thames-side pub in *Our Mutual Friend*. Carter has also skillfully taken a leaf out of J. B. Priestley's best-seller of the Twenties, *The Good Companions*, stripping its romance of sentimentality and giving its hearty fellowship the proper party line. She is also well aware that bewitching foundlings are a sure hit with any audience. Dora and Nora Chance—it is the first named who writes the record—have been on the boards from their tenderest years up to the moment when Nora begins to throw her heart away "as if it were a used bus ticket."

> She had it off first with the pantomime goose, when we were Mother Goose's goslings that year in Newcastle upon Tyne. The goose was old

enough to be her father and Grandma would have plucked him, stuck an apple up his bum and roasted him if she had found out, and so would the goose's wife, who happened to be principal boy. . . .

The goose had Nora up against the wall in the alley outside the stage door one foggy night, couldn't see your hand in front of your face, happily for them. You don't get fogs like that, these days. . . .

Don't be sad for her. Don't run away with the idea that it was a squalid, furtive, miserable thing, to make love for the first time on a cold night in a back alley with a married man with strong drink on his breath. He was the one she wanted, warts and all, she *would* have him . . . while I stood shivering on the edge like the poor cat in the adage.

But we never found out she was pregnant until she lost it in Nottingham, the Royalty, when she haemorrhaged during a *fouetté*, we were a pair of spinning tops. Nothing like real blood in the middle of the song-and-dance act. It was long past pantomime, the goose gone off to Glasgow to do a *Chu Chin Chow*, he never wrote. Nora cried her eyes out but not because she'd lost the goose. . . . No. She wept the loss of the baby.

Oh, my poor Nora! She was a martyr to fertility.

"Nothing like real blood in the middle of the song-and-dance-act." Carter has always been keen on blood as a symbol of sexual emancipation. The wolf-girl from her updated fairy stories in *The Bloody Chamber* is inducted via menstruation into a correct and liberated social and sexual awareness. The title *Wise Children* is reminiscent of that controversial Seventies study of the subject called *The Wise Wound*, which equated the feminine cycle with all the female virtues opposing male violence and aggressiveness. But it is only fair to say that in *Wise Children* the men are as warmhearted and as essentially humane as the women. Nora and Dora Chance turn out to be the illegitimate children of—who else?—Sir Melchior Hazard, the greatest Shakespearean actor of the day, whose hundredth birthday celebrations lead to the novel's inevitably hilarious climax. The reader more or less immune to stage charms may have experienced a certain amount of tedium by then, but it has been a gallant show, the cast supported by a producer nicknamed Genghiz Khan, and an elfin Irish alcoholic and scriptwriter who becomes Dora's boyfriend, possibly even the love of her life.

As she grows older Dora's mellowing mimetic arts let slip the occasional Wildean epigram such as "Every woman's tragedy is that after a certain age she looks like a female impersonator." One of Carter's chief talents has been to help create a new kind of persona for real women to copy. The Carter girl of the Eighties, with her sound principles, earthy humor, and warm heart, has become a recognizable type: in a sense all too recognizable, for if you are not like that by nature you have to work hard at maintaining the pose. In Carter's latest writing the show is the thing, and as every pantomime-goer knows, putting on a prodigious warmth of heart for the benefit of the kiddies can look like and even be the real thing. Dora's solid eighteen-carat whimsy rejoices in "laughter, forgiveness, generosity, reconciliation," and also in the well-timed wink with which she tells us such things will be "hard to swallow, huh?" Not necessarily. *Wise Children* is very readable, though it may not appeal to admirers of Carter who prefer her in a more wild and provocative mood.

The stage is the beginning of sincerity, as Oscar Wilde might have said. Carter's questing intelligence and the theatrical virtuosity of her language have greatly assisted her championing of new ideas and causes. But would her fictions invite a second reading, or does the vitality die in the performance? Would she continue to move us? *Love* may have the edge there, for its forlorn trio lingers in the mind with the pathos of those abandoned in a former lifestyle, although she sought in her afterword to bring them up to date. The impact of her plots and her prose can nonetheless seem to coincide too exactly with what enthusiasts and publicists say about them. No one who reads the glittering superlatives on a novel's jacket expects to find them precisely mirrored by the writing inside, and it is a trifle disconcerting to find in a Carter novel just those "stylish, erotic, nightmarish jewels of prose," and "a colourful embroidery of religion and magic," which reviews and blurb had promised. A process of inflation seems unavoidable.

In one of her *Common Reader* essays Virginia Woolf remarked of Jane Austen's juvenilia that they contained phrases and sentences clearly intended to outlast the Christmas festivities for which they had been written. However effective and well done they may be, few novels today seem aware of the old canonical notion of "good writing": they can even seem programmed for auto-destruction and replacement by more of the same. In postmodernist terms that is not necessarily a bad thing. It indicates that the job has been done, the point made. Archetypal narrative is founded on what is written but unspoken; modern narrative on what is said and claimed, and therefore can be superseded. Even when transmitted through the warm-hearted wisdom of Dora Chance, Carter's own message is unmistakable; the same could be said of her rewritten fantasies and fairy stories. Told by Grimm or Perrault, or even by Andrew Lang in his "Fairy Books," blue, green, and red, those old tales remain free and enigmatic. Retold by Angela Carter, with all her supple and intoxicating bravura, they become committed to the preoccupations and to the fashions of our moment. When Beauty is in the power of the Beast, in his baroque sinister palace, she cannot help letting out "a raucous guffaw: no young lady laughs like that! my old nurse used to remonstrate." In Carter's pages all young ladies do.

A room of one's own, or a bloody chamber? The new role model for women may seem to deny them the literary gift of privacy. But it is sad that so gifted a writer as Angela Carter, who died of cancer at the early age of fifty-one, will not be continuing to explore and define her new worlds in fiction. Her great talents would certainly have come up with new surprises. They say that wise children know their own fathers, and she certainly knew hers, while rejecting any concept of patriarchy. Jane Austen and the Virginia Woolf of *Orlando* and *The Waves* would have recognized her as one of themselves and been greatly interested by her books, although they might have missed in them the privacy and individuality, the more secret style of independence, which they valued as much as good writing, and which is the supreme gift to us of their novels. Carter's achievement shows how a certain style of good writing has politicized itself today, constituting itself as the literary wing of militant orthodoxy.

This was of course not true of an earlier generation of "magical" writers like Vladimir Nabokov, Jorge Luis Borges, or Italo Calvino, who assumed that male experience was central. Margaret Atwood, author of *The Handmaid's Tale*, has written movingly of Carter as the fairy godmother who herself so wonderfully looked the part, seeming to offer a talisman which would guide her friends and readers through enchanted forests and charmed doors. For Atwood, Carter was the supreme subversive; but the magic talisman of female subversion, though it could turn even de Sade's victims into early feminists, was also an ambiguous gift, making imagination itself the obedient handmaid of ideology. That would not worry many in the latest generation of critics, who read literature past and present by the light of political correctness. But Carter's new woman combines correctness with being a sort of jolly feminine Tom Jones, what the publisher Carmen Callil in a loving obituary has called "the vulgarian as heroine." "*Wise Children,*" she continued, "is a novel of Thatcher's Britain, a Britain split in two." This of course may not be of great interest to Europe or America, but Mrs. Thatcher as the national anti-heroine certainly looms in the background of Carter's work. She and Angela Carter could be seen as making a new heraldic opposition on the royal crest: the lion and the unicorn still fighting for the crown.

The New York Review of Books, 1992

PART VII

Correspondences

55

Sons and Brothers

Henry James (1843–1916) and William James (1842–1910)

The Correspondence of William James
Volume 1: William & Henry 1861–1884, Volume 2: William &
    Henry 1885–1896
edited by Ignas K. Skrupskelis and Elizabeth M. Berkeley

The Correspondence of Henry James and the House of MacMillan,
    1877–1914
edited by Rayburn S. Moore

Collected Travel Writings
Volume 1: Great Britain and America (English Hours, The
    American Scene, Other Travels), Volume 2: The Continent
    (A Little Tour in France, Italian Hours, Other Travels)
by Henry James

Lettere a Miss Allen (Letters to Miss Allen), 1899–1915
by Henry James, edited by Rosellina Archinto (in English and
    Italian)

The sky is white as clay, with no sun
Work has to be done.
Postmen like doctors go from house to house.

The end of Philip Larkin's great and gloomy poem "Aubade" is anachronistic, but in the happiest sense. Without looking back, or appearing to do so, it re-creates what for the poet had never come to an end: a world in which letters were greedily received and faithfully dispatched; in which the telephone was an expensive and barbarous mode of communication for business use (in Larkin's dawn poem "telephones crouch, getting ready to ring / In locked-up offices"); and letters, here the household remedy relied on to combat the ills of daily existence. For poets or artists letters could be an extension of their art by other means; a way of exploring their own individuality and bringing it home to others.

The epoch of romanticism exploited correspondence for this purpose, and has continued to do so until our own day, when technology has all but killed off the form. Heroines and heroes of their time, like Richardson's Clarissa and Goethe's young Werther, came alive in their letters: Byron, Keats, and Charles Lamb used them spontaneously for the same purpose. But in the grand epistolary epoch it was a question of outpourings of wit or passion, not of humble therapy in comradeship, as wryly envisaged in Larkin's poem. To "long for certain letters," as Auden remarks in another poem, is to be fully human, and to admit a common humanity. Devoted sisters Jane and Cassandra Austen took that for granted. As devoted brothers, William and Henry James did so, too, with the addition that words were to both of them not only communicative intimacy but the stuff of reflection itself, the medium of thinking and being, the matrix not only of art but of all religious and spiritual experience.

Through the medium of their correspondence Henry can turn his frantic and highly practical queries about the obstinate constipation that plagues him amid the splendors of Florence and Rome into a whole rhetorical saga, a dramatic narrative of daily hopes and disappointments that is quite as eloquent as the diplomatic gambits of *The Ambassadors*, or those of the resourceful narrator in *The Aspern Papers*. And William, the medically trained elder brother, had verbal resources equal to the case, probably a great deal more effective than the actual practical remedies he prescribed, some of which now seem as outlandish as Dr. Frankenstein's galvanic experiments.

He also seems to have taken in good part his younger brother's despairing quip, "It's no more than just that the family should in some form repay themselves for your medical education." Money was discussed between them as frankly as the bowels, and with the same deft mutual intelligibility. "What is a doctor meant for," asks Henry, "but to listen to old women's *doléances?*"—and he adjures his brother not to "lose sight of that good news about my back" (he was sure that "obscure hurt" was benefiting from the beginning of an improvement in his internal condition) while touchingly recalling the brotherly duty of reciprocity. "To shew you haven't taken this too ill, for heaven's sake make me a letter about your own health—poor modest flower!" ("Make me" gives a subtle indication of the brothers' attitude in composing their letters. The art of the maker was always as present to them as the mere desire to communicate.)

William duly obliged. His own health obsessed him as much or more, though its manifestations were less down to earth, chiefly concerning the nervous system and the eyes. He could read only for short periods; and it is natural to wonder whether his symptoms didn't include some reluctance, born of his father's example, to engage in the hurly-burly of earning a living, and of studying for that purpose. And yet he and Henry were in no doubt that it must be done, for financial reasons as well as on the grounds of their own *amour propre*. They wanted independence from their father and family; and at the same time to remain uncompromisingly within its bosom; and this as much because of their father's verbal and spiritual ambiance—that mystic web of words he had himself woven about them—as from motives of piety, domesticity, and cupboard love. The web was also a social one, of course. The brothers were even more at home in the old American aristocracy of New England than Henry was one day to be in the *haute monde* of the Old World.

The point is well made in Gerald E. Myers's introduction to the superb first volume of William and Henry's correspondence, running from 1861, when William was nineteen and Henry a year younger, to 1894, when William had been for some years a married man and teacher at Harvard, and Henry had made himself an international reputation as a writer. Father and mother were dead, but both writers remained closely bound to the old family home, with its rituals and responses, and to the *manes* of their all-embracing parent. Henry was not using words idly— he never did—when he read his absent brother's "letter of farewell" at the father's graveside—"which I am sure he heard somewhere out of the depths of the still, bright winter air." As Myers observes, "the sons had been reared on their father's linguistic inventiveness." If you could *say* it—in the fullest sense—you believed it. "What language can do for nuancing ideas was not lost on these sons of a father who could complain . . . about a traditional concept of God: 'Against this lurid power—half pedagogue, half-policeman, but wholly imbecile in both aspects—I . . . raise my gleeful fist, I lift my scornful foot.'" Gleefulness in expression— spirituality as a kind of freedom, and as the power to verbalize belief— was indeed a common factor for all three of these remarkable Jameses.

At the same time they were all very much in the air, as it were: a constant prey to the vertigo of non-being, non-sensation. The father's famous "vastation" is well known: that dreadful occasion near Windsor Park in England, when after a tranquil supper on a summer evening the sense of nothingness suddenly overcame him with such force that he could not get over it for months, and suffered a periodic recurrence of the horror for the rest of his life. His two eldest boys were especially well acquainted with similar sensations—it was probably in some form or other a genetic inheritance for the whole family—and quite apart from their detailed epistolary exchange of what we should now call psychosomatic symptoms, their letters suggest a constant need for the healing balm of each other's company in the written word.

When they were physically together things went less happily, although their closeness of affection was undoubted and even took on occasion a quasi-physical form. What photograph of the pair could be a happier choice than the one the editors of this admirable volume have chosen for the jacket? It shows them somewhere near Rye on the Sussex coast, when Henry was living at Lamb House in that little town, and William was visiting. Like a couple of good schoolboys from some superior academy both are attired in dark coats and waistcoats, gray woolen trousers, white shirts, and ties. Each carries a hat. William's arm is protectively around Henry's shoulder, and Henry's large bald head and ample, now shaven features incline at a startling angle toward the reassuring neighborhood of his brother's whiskers and sharp kindly eyes. The light across the Sussex pasture is of a calm sunset. Who took the picture? William's wife, Alice, or his son, the youngest Henry? At any rate it is now in the Houghton Library at Harvard, with whose permission it is reproduced.

There is something intensely vulnerable and childlike in the portrait *à deux*, a speaking glimpse not only of interdependence but of a kind of mutual loneliness. And yet both were well equipped to fight life's battle on their own, in foreign hotels and at London dinner tables not less than in the arduous hours of study and composition and in the even more exacting business of seeking contacts and driving bargains. Both needed solitude—William acquired the habit of leaving his sensible wife for weeks at a time, particularly after she had just given birth—and yet each needed to feel his own constant presence in his brother's life and in their communion of letters. One of the most spellbinding elements in this interchange—when we do not yet know, as it were, how the plot will turn out—is to watch Henry briefing his brother on how to visit Europe and where to stay. We cannot be quite certain—perhaps he was not certain himself—whether Henry really wanted William beside him in his cherished European haunts; or, indeed, whether William himself, despite the nature and detail of his queries, really wanted to undertake an expedition so indebted to fraternal assistance. The letters conceal as much as they reveal or more; or rather, as with Henry's own fiction, their concealments are their own kind of revelation.

So it is bewitchingly hard quite to judge the tone in which Henry for example, after judiciously opining that his brother "might subsist very comfortably *in Rome* on the footing you set forth," since "the place . . . is peculiarly adapted to help one get through time," concludes that "of course my society would fill up a great many crevices." For a writer so jealously conscious of time's winged chariot that was an assurance both handsome and no doubt sincere. Henry needed society and knew that William did so, too, so he recommended Rome both for things to see, and for people (by which of course he meant American and English expatriates) to converse with. Florence had plenty of such society but a harsher climate and fewer "resorts and lounging places": Naples "a *belle nature* but very little society."

William in fact did not avail himself of any of these suggestions—it was the summer of 1873—but betook himself to the Isles of Shoals, off the Maine coast, from which he wrote his brother letters about the idyllic surroundings—"absolutely barren rocks with a great & first class hotel on two of them"—as rich and vivid as any of the accounts he was receiving from Europe.

> I just lay around drinking the air and the light & the sounds. I succeeded in reading no word for three days and then took Goethe's Gedichte out on my walks, and with them in my memory the smell of the laurels & pines in my nose, and the rythmic pounding of the surf upon my ear I was free and happy again. How people can pass years without a week of that *Normal* life I can't imagine.

Henry hastened to reciprocate about the joys of *dolce far niente*. "Every word you say about Nature & the 'normal life' has an echo in my soul. I enjoy them more the older I grow and acquire a fatal facility in sitting under trees letting the hours expire without *particular* fruits." Was each brother secretly relieved to be enjoying the "normal life" on his own, with the pleasure augmented by telling the other all about it? Henry had certainly done his best; and so had the postmen: but it is astonishing to remember that there was no speedier mode of detailed communication at that date than by letter. Like Stanley and Livingstone in Africa the brothers hoped to run up against each other in London or in Paris, or perhaps in Rome, in the course of what must necessarily be uninstructed wanderings. William urges Henry to write back as soon as he can, or he will not be able to get himself a good berth on the Cunarder, on which he will venture toward some meeting-place outside the reach of letters. Perhaps after all he was wise to remain in New England.

As the critic Geoffrey Myers points out, "in William's psychology and Henry's fiction the 'evanescent' in experience is all-important." From an early date William was uncompromising on the role of the "aesthetic," not only in philosophical matters (that point made in the last chapter of *The Principles of Psychology* appeared years earlier in an 1878 essay) but in the physical sciences. The kind of "impressions" garnered in letters to his brother were themselves in a sense the essence and foundation of pragmatism. It is striking to notice, as we read on, how much more "advanced," in a technical literary sense, than that of his brother was William's instinctive mode of retailing those impressions. It is he, not Henry, who anticipates what later became called the "stream of consciousness" technique; and yet one feels that it was Henry's example and peculiar talents that inspired his brother to a kind of emulation. William was not going to let the younger, and as he was once memorably to call him, the more "frivolous" brother eclipse the elder as wordsmith and man of letters.

That is apparent in the collection's first missive: William's impression after leaving the family at Newport of his new lodgings — "drear and chill abode" — in Cambridge, where he was to enter Harvard's Scientific School. The war was on, but neither brother noticed the fact much in correspondence: their bad backs and delicate health, as well as the virtual paternal veto, made it seem natural to leave the fighting to their tougher and fitter young brothers, Wilky and Bob. The interest of William's early letter is in the conscious sense of *contrast* — in this case between the happy ambiance of Newport and the bleak one of his Cambridge lodgings — and its affinity to the kinds of contrast Henry will specialize in as a novelist, from the great Europe versus America theme to the detailed contrasts and comparisons of English, French, and Italian landscape, custom, and appearance. Nothing came more naturally to them as correspondents than to play off one place, as it were, against another:

> As I write now even, writing itself being a cosy cheerful looking amusement, and an argand gas burner with a neat green shade over it merrily singing beside me, I still feel unsettled. I write on a round table in the middle of the room with a red and black cloth upon it. In front of me I see another such-covered table of oblong shape against the wall capped by a cheap looking glass & flanked by 2 windows, curtainless and bleak, whose shades of linen flout the air as the sportive wind impels them.

William's observations convey the impression of a frugal lodgment in the same way that Henry's later fiction evokes an interior in Venice or London. There is a kind of displaced possessiveness too, of a brotherly sort, in

the way in which he seeks to impress his own image, in its own surroundings, on his more peripatetic sibling, as if bringing Henry to heel.

> At 10.30 arrived your letter of Jany. 26th . . . At 12.30 after reading for
> an hour in Flints physiology, I went to town paid a bill of Randidge's,
> looked in to the Atheneum reading room, got 1 doz. raw oysters at Hig-
> gins's saloon in Court Street, came out again, thermometer having
> risen to near thawing point, dozed 1/2 an hour before the fire, and am
> now writing this to you.

Meanwhile Alice—the sister, not the wife—is seized in the midst of her
toilet by an acute colic, caused by sewer gas in the pantry where she was
washing up "in the lack of a 'parlor girl' "; and William, leaving her
behind, is off to a party in Boston with Mr. and Mrs. Child—"Child curs-
ing and swearing all the way in." Undeterred, William much enjoys sitting next to "the beauteous and adorably naive miss Mary M," while Mr.
Morse is "squinting & showing his dazzling teeth in a lady like manner
at the head of the table." On return he was glad to find Alice had been
"relieved 'copieusement' (proving cause of trouble) and was all right."

William indeed is on a par with Joyce in his capacity to immortalize
the "evanescent," while in the same letter he gives his brother a brisk critique of George Eliot's *Middlemarch* ("Ladislaw-Dorothea suggest too
much and solve too little.") The one left out in the cold is poor sister
Alice, having her own psychosomatic troubles over the washing up, and
thus unable to attend the Morse dinner party "wh. was a pity, as the party
was given in her name." Whatever her own feelings for William, about
which much has been speculated, he appears oblivious. At least he gives
no sign of them in his communion with Henry, but that is just another
item in the plot dimension of this exchange, in which impressions are
many but relationships few.

Henry's marvelous vignettes of Oxford, and of the fair-haired young
giants in their blue and white flannels punting and rowing on the river,
are about as far as he goes in his own particular emotional direction, and
with his own talent for suggesting much and resolving little. And yet the
way he revels in art—Tintoretto and Veronese, but Titian his true
favorite—is both perspicacious and joyously infectious.

A second volume of William and Henry's letters, which runs from 1885 to 1896, makes equally compulsive reading, although we miss the bubblingly youthful and sanguine note of the brothers in their younger years. While never ceasing to cling to and confide in each other they became more formal: more harassed, too, by unremitting activity, and the wear and tear of their remorselessly busy careers. These were the years both of achievement and of an increasing melancholia and disillusionment. Often they met and read the same new authors. Both were enthusiastic about Robert Louis Stevenson, and Kipling, too, when what William called the "dear little genius" hove upon the literary scene, visiting William in America and Henry in London, and later in Rye.

The letters the pair exchanged about the death in England of their sister Alice are copious and moving. Henry wrote to William from her deathbed, "She is perfectly clear & humorous & would talk if doing so wouldn't bring on spasms of coughing. But she does speak in a whisper— & gave me, in my ear, very distinctly, three words to cable to you." The cable read, "Tenderest love to all farewell Am going soon." On the day after her death, William replied, "Poor little Alice! What a life! I can't believe that that imperious will and piercing judgment are snuffed out with the breath. Now that her outwardly so frustrated life is over, one sees that in the deepest sense it was a triumph." William reports about his own health and that of his children, and Henry makes surprisingly frequent references to regret at his continuing bachelorhood. It is clear that the brothers were franker with each other than with any other mortal: in William's case, even with his own wife, Alice. The volume ends with William comforting Henry for his disappointment of his dramatic debut with *Guy Danville*; and with what the editors justly call the "interminable elongation" of his own work on *The Principles of Psychology*.

Henry's own relation with publishers was on the whole cordial but nothing if not demandingly inquisitive. He took a great liking to the young Frederick Macmillan, which was quickly returned, to their mutual benefit, although Henry lamented long and loud that his growing reputation was not matched by anything Macmillan's could do in the way of sales. Macmillan uncle as well as nephew did their best—Henry confided to his brother that "old Macmillan physically *hugs* me"—but although the famous publishing house was "caressing" and "everything that's friendly," "the delicious ring of the sovereign is conspicuous in our intercourse by its absence."

The Macmillans were the first to regret the fact. As correspondents they could be as voluble, and as acute as Henry himself, and the latter frequently found in Frederick a correspondent worthy of his steel. Very few publishers today would write a letter as forthcoming as this one, mildly deprecating the fact that James had decided to try placing one of his children with Chatto and Windus.

> I confess I did feel hurt about "Confidence." Of course we don't pretend to any claim over your work, but as we have been your publishers hitherto I am sorry you should have gone elsewhere merely because you wanted some ready money. If you had written to my Uncle proposing that we should advance you £100 on account of future profits, you would undoubtedly have received a cheque by return of post. Certainly the money result last year was not very encouraging, but you must remember it was the result of your first year before the British public as a writer of fiction. No doubt the flavour of your work is too delicate to be at once appreciated by the palates accustomed to coarser food, but I believe that the cordial recognition your books have received from the critical papers & reviews will in time have its effect on the sales, indeed I think this is already evident as each book seems to do better than the last.

Bracing words, which Henry must have recalled with a mournful irony as the sales of his later fiction went down instead of up. But the firm certainly did their best for him; and young Mrs. Macmillan, who had a soft spot for Henry, brought back jars of maple syrup for him when she visited the United States with her husband. Professor Moore has shown here, as in "A Literary Friendship," his selection of the correspondence between Henry and that ubiquitous Edwardian, Edmund Gosse, that the native James genius for letter writing could also be an inspiration to their friends.*

*Rayburn S. Moore, ed., *Selected Letters of Henry James to Edmund Gosse, 1882–1915.*

The same sort of rapprochement recurred, in a rather different context, when Henry was much older, during the productive but also sad decade which saw the publication of *The Ambassadors, The Wings of the Dove, The Golden Bowl*, but also the death of his beloved brother, and his own increasing vulnerability to periods of illness, loneliness, depression. In 1899, at the Palazzo Barbaro in Venice, Henry was a fellow-guest of Jessie Allen, an English maiden lady with aristocratic connections, who spent her days traveling and staying at houses on the continent. She was a very different sort of person from poor "Fenimore"—Constance Fenimore Woolson—the American writer whose attachment to James ten years earlier had become something of a source of embarrassment to him, until she killed herself while in a depressed state in Venice. He and Miss Allen were of much the same age (she died in 1918, two years after Henry) and took a shine to each other immediately. Miss Allen soon became his "Goody Two-Shoes," to whom he confided his numerous woes, lending her counsel and comfort in return.

Compared to the correspondence with his brother, the letters—heretofore unpublished and now issued by an enterprising Italian publisher—are those not only of an older but a more distracted and increasingly helpless man, clinging for sympathy to this kind and lovingly undemanding woman, and pouring out his recital of the ailments that increasingly plagued him—gout, shingles, irritable bowel syndrome. His letters are not only less on top of things than they once were, but are also more chaotic, more mannered, more inclined to exaggerative whimsy, even while they are as capable as ever of expressing the warmest affection and the most humorous sense of the human comedy. By no means indifferent to Miss Allen's connections in high society, though she herself like many quasi-aristocrats, seems to have been both self-assured and unassuming, Henry found her a good audience for his lamentations about a very different female admirer—Edith Wharton—with whom bondage, gilded, could also be oppressive.

An hour ago there arrived Mrs. Wharton from Paris, by motorcar—from Folkestone—it is now 7 P.M. and she left it this A.M.; and she stays till Tuesday; and she then proposes to sweep me away, in her car, on a tour (of these islands) against which all my necessities and conveniences frantically protest. I snatch this scrap of communion but by her lying down before dinner; and even while I trace these rude characters for your slight benefit I strive to brace myself for that discussion of the immediate future which is sure to break upon me this evening. I shall not get off without *some* surrender; when a lady has motored straight across the Channel to ask one to oblige, one must go some little part of the way to meet her—even at the cost of precious hours and blighted labours and dislocated (say rather quite smashed) thrift and order.

By 1912 the motor-car had already become something of a tyrant, at least when at the command of as dominating a lady as Mrs. Wharton; but of course James was far from reluctant to be borne away, like some faintly protesting and far from youthful Ganymede, by this masterful female Jove. He only compensated—not revenged—the inconvenience by writing, when his captor was resting upstairs at Lamb House, to that other, more understanding and more comfortingly congenial, friend, his "dearest Goody," whom he sees in a characteristic metaphor as being always available as a restorative snack—"a slice of cold or cooling Goody—with a sense of her being quite the ornament of my sideboard." What would the other lady upstairs have thought of this employment?— but then, one of the great pleasures of a correspondence (Philip Larkin's letters certainly bear this out) is to say just what one likes about some of one's friends to other friends, to whom one will shortly be writing in the same vein.

The New York Review of Books, 1994

56

Milan Kundera and Jane Austen

IN *The Art of the Novel* Milan Kundera speaks of his "disgust" with those who reduce a work of fiction to its ideas. Yes, but who watches the watchers, who preserves the critic from this primal fault, when the critic is also a novelist? It might seem that there is no answer to this question. Kundera is a writer very different from his admired Kafka, who has no "ideas," who made a world of his own, a private world in which privacy had no existence; and who thus anticipated—as Kundera says—the society of totalitarianism and the concentration camp. Kafka knew nothing of such a society, and had no idea of prophesying it: his own world was both personal and obsessive, and yet it has become one that is public and accepted, universally recognized.

It is difficult to imagine such a process occurring with Kundera. Many if not most good novelists could indeed be described in the words that Mallarmé used about Poe. Time has changed them into their real selves. Posterity has revealed what they could not have known about their own creation. But could this apply to Kundera, remarkable novelist as he certainly is, or to the other contemporary novelists he admires—Hermann Broch, Witold Gombrowicz, Vladimir Nabokov, Italo Calvino—novelists all concerned in their different ways with that twin activity Kundera himself has described: the "appeal of thought," and "the appeal of play." It is tacitly accepted in critical circles today that the ludic function of the novel produces a created equilibrium with its ideas, its thought content; that the two together somehow vouch for each other, canceling the charge of either frivolity or academicism. But if so, what is the reality about them that their authors do not know, and which future readers and critics will discover?

The question is whether Kundera has, so to speak, any *future being* as a novelist *apart* from what now declares itself with such vitality and lucidity in his novels, and in what he has himself written about them. What secret world might be left to declare itself to a coming generation? On the face of it, none, and yet the question is not so simple as that. Oddly enough the work that occurred to me in comparison with Kundera's here is one apparently as unlike his as possible. It seems likely that he has never read Jane Austen's *Northanger Abbey*: possibly nothing by Jane Austen at all. One can imagine him saying, like Conrad, if her novels were brought to his attention, that he could not see the point of them; and it is certainly the case that in his essays and interview discussions in *The Art of the Novel* he mentions no women novelists. There seems to me to be no male chauvinism in this: only an honest unawareness that women write novels, and write them, usually, in a different way from the male novel, which for Kundera is always, if it comes off, a "conquest of being." That is of course a significant phrase. Kundera sees the novelist as successively annexing new areas of experience *(Ulysses* "undertakes" the immense theme of vulgarity), and the parallel with science, war, exploration, is obvious enough. As so often, Kundera is paradoxical here. His disgust with ideas is also a disgust with male conquest by metaphysics. He quotes Heidegger: "Since reality consists in the uniformity of calculable reckoning, man too must enter monotonous uniformity in order to keep up with what is real. A man without a uniform today already gives the impression of being something unreal which no longer belongs." In spite of Kundera's disgust, male novelists must be, for him, men in uniform.

Nonetheless, Kundera as a novelist does overcome his own intellectual paradox. The example of Jane Austen's first, most youthful novel helps to show how. She began *Northanger Abbey* as a skit on the Gothic novel. Not on Mrs. Radcliffe, whom she greatly admired, but on that great novelist's imitators, who were springing up on all sides. Her simple recipe was to involve her young heroine in a commonplace social situation, which she, the heroine, would contrive to see as a "Gothic" one: with the consequence of social follies and misunderstandings. Intent on the development of her idea, Jane Austen did not see that her novel would in time reveal something quite other from what she had planned: would reveal, indeed, an extraordinarily original image of the self, in relation to the fashions and distractions which she portrayed as creating it. Catherine Morland, her heroine, possesses a good nature and a capacity to love that overcomes all the social "Gothicism" that her author contrives to put in her way. Jane Austen's deliberate and secondary satire goes to show that respected social figures, like General Tilney, are in reality just as much ogres and monsters as the stereotype Catherine—her head stuffed with romances—conceives them to be. Jane Austen was deliberately showing that Gothic novels were far more realistic, in the society in which they were so successful, than their besotted and daydreaming readers could possibly have supposed.

But beyond that she had done something she knew nothing of, which has secured a deserved immortality for that first slight novel, an immortality which would have come to pass even if she had written no later and more mature masterpieces. She has made a real person out of wholly artificial conventions and contrivances. Her heroine manages somehow to elude the successive tones of satire, amusement, delicate burlesque in which the novelist has presented her. The novel has escaped from ideas and purposes, from what we might now consider—following Kundera— to be the pattern of "thought" and "play."

And it seems to me that something very similar is happening in Kundera's own best novels, particularly in *The Unbearable Lightness of Being*. The novel's true and distant meaning—its meaning, if not for "eternity," then at least for the following generations—lies in some other dimension than the schema propounded by its author, however much his own deliberate "conquest" of new reality may contribute to it. *The Unbearable Lightness of Being* not only subsumes the rich underside of Kundera's writing but may reveal an unexpected meaning beyond its schematic one. As *Northanger Abbey* takes the Gothic as its inspiration and starting point—what Kundera would call "the already known," from which the novelist must seek his or her new departure—so *The Unbearable Lightness of Being* begins with the idea of kitsch.

The word is an old piece of Austrian slang which, as Kundera is at pains to explain in an analysis of it, signifies a peculiarly Central European concept of the vulgar-romantic, the facile, the sentimental, the false. Like the Russian *poshlost*, kitsch signifies a dimension of life which developed as a kind of popularization of the romantic experience of the early nineteenth century; and in exploring and analyzing it Kundera gives it an extra political dimension. The Brotherhood of Man, that politically romantic ideal, can only be achieved, he tells us, "on the basis of kitsch"; and kitsch is the chosen instrument of the Communist Party in their manipulation of social consciousness. All pictures of smiling sunburnt farmers, little girls in flowery meadows, contented old grannies—in a word, all *advertisement*, whether capitalist or communist, which takes an implacably rosy view of human possibility, is the groundwork or raw material of kitsch and its various social and artistic ramifications.

Kundera sees human consciousness, particularly under a communist regime, as besieged by kitsch: and the chief function of art today as having the duty to disown, denounce, and replace it. This can be done by the novel in its ludic role and as the natural vessel not of negation but of skepticism—"consubstantial irony." Irony is the natural enemy of kitsch, its antidote and opposite. But how should the novelist use irony? Kundera is as cunning about this as one would expect. Irony in the novel must be an invisible presence, not an aggressive weapon, as it is used by the satirist. Just by being a novel, in the true sense, the form can dissolve the kitsch universe.

But kitsch possesses a reassuring solidity and weight. That is why the lightness of being seems so intolerable when compelled to a confrontation with it. In Kundera's novel Sabina is the chief anti-kitsch partisan, and it is part of the book's invisible irony that this role destroys her. The "honesty" of communism—the drabness, the shortages, the food queues—she can tolerate, even approve; what she detests are its hypocritical pretenses, its façade of a glittering socialist palace. She develops as an artist an unnerving technique for destroying her enemy through subtle kinds of distortion. Having been trained in a socialist art school she applies its precepts to her painting; but in every canvas representing a sheet-metal workers' factory meeting, or happy schoolchildren at play, she contrives to insert some disturbing touch—a few blood-red dots, or a scrawny bird outline etched in black—which arrests and reverses the reassuringly kitschy expectations the audience has from the picture.

Sabina's tactic earns her fame abroad, when her pictures are smuggled out of the country and become known in the capitalist West. She herself emigrates and becomes successful and prosperous. But she is soon disgusted with the way in which her paintings are, as it were, turned back into kitsch for the benefit of a society which in its own way is just as hungry for it as the Soviets desire their own subjects to be. Her exhibitions are advertised by crafty photos of machine-gun watchtowers seen from below, or tasteful patterns of barbed wire surrounding the text of the announcement. She realizes that her enemy now possesses her, is inside her, and her gaiety and promiscuity cover a deep foundation of despair.

Sabina's predicament is, in a sense, that of the novelist himself. In his attack on the *idea* of kitsch Kundera has put himself in a decidedly tricky situation. For the idea of the separation between the two worlds—that of kitsch and non-kitsch—is as artificial and as constricting as any other "idea" to which Kundera hates the novel to be reduced. By attacking kitsch has he, like Sabina, fatally involved himself in it? Whereas Jane Austen could expand her whole universe of irony, and also of daily commonsense, by means of her play with the Gothic, Kundera has apparently boxed himself in by making too purely partisan an approach to that anti-world which confronts the novel—the world of kitsch.

This, however, is where the true future of his novel beckons. Jane Austen got her own truth out of the Gothic by naturalizing it in everyday life: Kundera gets his unexpected and "non-partisan" value from kitsch by an invisible accommodation with it, in terms of the art of his novel. This is done in terms of the "hero and heroine" (itself a pretty kitschy notion) of the novel—Tomas and Tereza.

Tomas is like the hero in a soap opera. But the reader does not think of this; nor, apparently, does the author. And Tereza is, of course, the right foil for a soap opera hero. Theirs is the real thing, true love, which will last as long as they live. He is redeemed from promiscuity and aimlessness by the love of a good woman. He sacrifices his career for her. They withdraw from the world to love in a cottage. But so brilliantly has Kundera deployed his ideology and set the scene that these things, in a sense so evident, even so obvious, seem wholly new and fresh, as if "true love" were being discovered in the novel for the first time. In fact, true love has indeed been realized and attained in the creation of the novel, but by the agency of its consciousness of kitsch, in the same way that an absolutely real young woman is established in *Northanger Abbey* through the medium of the Gothic novel and Jane Austen's use of it. Neither author, it seems to me, is fully, if at all, conscious of the operation, and there is a particular interest in the fact that *Northanger Abbey* (first titled *Susan* and then *Catherine*) was published only after Jane Austen's death, nearly twenty years after she had written it, and at a time when the inspiration she had received from the Gothic novel, and the use she had made of it, would have been much more apparent than when she first composed the work at the end of the eighteenth century.

To what extent is Kundera aware of the peculiar use he has made of kitsch in his novel? I doubt if he is, for the paradox involved depends on what he himself has called the novel's "radical autonomy." Although Jane Austen was much better disposed towards the Gothic novel—particularly the novels of Ann Radcliffe—than Kundera can be assumed to feel about contemporary artistic and political kitsch, it is nonetheless kitsch in a metamorphosed form which triumphs in his novel, just as the Gothic reversed does in Jane Austen's. *The Unbearable Lightness of Being* could well have started out by being called *Tereza*, for it is Tereza who is both the counterpart to kitsch and its apotheosis.

As it happens, one of Kundera's own admired group of Central European novelists may have accidentally suggested to him a key aspect of Tereza. Kundera himself mentions the episode in Gombrowicz's *Ferdydurke* when the modern young Polish matron goes nonchalantly into the lavatory, drawing attention to the fact, because she regards such frankness as the modern and emancipated line to take. It is an exceedingly funny moment, but also a conscious and satiric one. If Kundera recalled it when writing *The Unbearable Lightness of Being* he certainly changed its significance. Tereza sitting on the toilet is of course an epitome of the helplessness of physical being—that heavy helplessness which draws Tomas inexorably towards her—but she is also, and by a piece of much more involuntary mystery, a figure of beatified kitsch. Out of Kundera's hatred for this concept, and for its domination of all political and aesthetic life in the Soviet bloc, there has unexpectedly emerged a particularly strange and satisfying case of the novel's radical autonomy: the emergence of something new in place of the "already known." The invisible and consubstantial irony in the novel unites Tereza and Tomas, as it were, on the toilet seat, in all the saving helplessness of physical dependence. Kitsch has triumphed at the last, but in a transcendent, almost unrecognizable guise. Kundera has endorsed, and perhaps without meaning it, an epigrammatic saying of the Austrian novelist Robert Musil, that the novel exists to overcome kitsch. We could turn that around and say that the novel cannot exist without kitsch, whose function is to be transformed by the novel.

Like Catherine Morland, Tereza emerges as a character entirely clear and authentic from a background of literary artifice and guileful intention. As I have emphasized, it seems likely that neither author planned the character who emerged: Catherine and Tereza are not like James Joyce's Molly Bloom or Henry James's Isabel Archer. They are not portraits of ladies. And although Tereza "stands" for weight, the saving and inevitable burden of life, she is saved from any theoretical status as a character by the bizarre shadow of the kitsch that makes her both "ordinary" and admirable, while redeeming her from intellectual personification. Terezas are in a sense what every advertiser aims at, and every *Reader's Digest*–style priest ("the most unforgettable character I have met") exhorts his flock to resemble. She is faithful, patient, long-suffering, and kind, and uses (or would use if she had the opportunity and the resources) all the right consumer durables. Like Catherine Morland she is everybody's nice girl; and yet both in their contexts escape the label, become apparently unique individuals.

It is revealing to compare Tereza not only with her Polish counterpart in *Ferdydurke*, whose toilet-going activities are simply a way of satirizing what was then the modern cultural attitude, but with the haunting heroine of Robert Musil's novella *Tonka*. Tonka is a simple girl of the people who becomes the narrator's mistress, and in her speechless and undefining way is apparently loyal and faithful to him; but she contracts venereal disease while living with the narrator, and this can only mean that she has had relations during that time with some other man. The hero intuits— indeed *knows*—that what she says is both true and false, and from this experience in the realm of the erotic he deduces that everything in the world, and in human experience, can be both false and true at the same time. The narrator, and his author Musil, are in fact using Tonka as an example of thinking-about-the-world metaphysically, and especially in terms of erotic metaphysics. The mysterious Tonka, although she makes a deep appeal to the narrator-author, and—because the novella is unquestionably successful—to the reader as well, remains nonetheless a character perceived and manipulated by pure intelligence, not the unconscious work of creation that seems to have gone into Catherine, or into Tereza.

Kundera himself remarks that while most novelists invent or describe a character, Musil *thinks* a character. This is certainly true, and it remains the reason why Tonka is an aspect of erotic investigation, and hence, for Musil, of discovery about the nature of the world. But Tereza, no more than Anna Karenina, is not there for the purpose of adding a new dimension to our sense of human beings. She is simply *there*—an achievement more common among classic novelists of the nineteenth century than it is among novelists today. The type of the achievement remains alien to the modern writer. And the novelist of the former time could hardly have said himself how he brought it about. Henry James said of one of Balzac's female characters that it was not by knowing her that he loved her: he knew her by loving her. That gives an important clue to the process.

Tonka dies at the end of her story, seemingly of the complications of pregnancy attended by venereal disease. The significant thing is that she dies, just as the old-time heroine who had "gone wrong" used to die in the novels of the past. A Tonka who simply disappeared into urban limbo would not, oddly enough, have been so effective a vehicle for Musil to think with and through, in terms of his discovery that something may be simultaneously true and false. He needs the old-fashioned solution of death to round off, as it were, the modern problem. For Kundera the problem, too, comes first: comes, that is to say, before the character, and it seems likely that Kundera follows Musil not only in *thinking* the character, but in using an old convention to close down the situation which has explored the thought.

"To begin perfect happiness at the respective ages of twenty-six and eighteen, is to do pretty well." So Jane Austen takes leave of her hero and heroine at the end of *Northanger Abbey*. She too is using the convention, but using it in such a way that it operates in the opposite sense to the one it states. From this the reader knows—if he cares, and the success of the story will have been to make him do so—that a pair of perfectly ordinary lives, with the usual ups and downs, joys and sorrows, are in prospect. As Musil wrote, the novel at its best kills kitsch, but does it by removing the distinction between kitsch and "reality." Kundera completes his novel by means of a convention similar to Jane Austen's, though more radical: he tells us what happened after the novel is over, and in place of perfect "felicity" this is random death in a road accident. Just as Jane Austen's tone does not in fact mock, but rather enhances, the realities that have appeared in her story, so Kundera's ending serves to emphasize the contentment of Tomas and Tereza in their "togetherness." Kitsch wins by losing; or, alternately, the novel wins by understanding the truth of kitsch. As an intellectual novelist Kundera is especially aware of two things: the novel's need to escape ideas on the one hand, and kitsch on the other. One of the major pleasures of reading him is to see how he does both. At the same time he shows us how the modern novelist's fear of ideas is intimately connected with his fear of kitsch. The novel needs both, but should also lose both in the telling, as the young Jane Austen lost both the Gothic novel and a satire on it in finding her own person, her own place.

The Review of Contemporary Fiction, 1989

57

Balzac Possessed

Honoré de Balzac (1799–1850) and Roland Barthes (1915–1980)

Balzac
by V. S. Pritchett

S/Z
by Roland Barthes

T HE GREATEST *PROPRIÉTAIRE* in literature has always made a contradictory appeal to those who travel light. And to a remarkable extent he has become an author's author. Proust and Gide adored him; Yeats was an addict of the *Comédie Humaine*; it was certainly the greatest single influence on the *oeuvre* of Henry James. What fascinates other writers about Balzac is probably the way in which he identified creation with greed, art with acquisitiveness; he made no distinction between inspiration and appetite, seizing everything that lay about him with infantile abandon. For him art was no problem, and this in itself makes him the artists' hero. Though the contemporary Hegelian consciousness, the spirit developing in alienation and solitude, is in a sense his own, it is surrounded today with every kind of formal block and impediment, often self-created, every barrier which the ironies of extreme self-consciousness can put in its way. Balzac's is the ego uninhibited by alienation: possession was all, and to possess he had only to put pen to paper.

Balzac had a typically Napoleonic upbringing; the *carrière ouverte aux talents* exemplified in him its most characteristic paradox: that the talented ones become rapacious beyond anything dreamed of by the old regime. His subject is the madness of those who are liberated by revolution into the possibilities of an infinite takeover—"mad in pursuit and in possession so." His father, born into a large peasant family in the Tarn district in the south of France, came to Paris just before the revolution to seek his fortune. Oddly enough he was a royalist by conviction (his son of course was an instinctive absolutist, like all fundamentally apolitical people) and was in some danger under the Terror. But he soon managed to make himself necessary in the new world of buying and selling, married a draper's daughter with a small fortune, and got a steady job in Tours as a military supplier. His son always liked to think of himself as a Tourangeau, from the most fecund and Rabelaisian district of France.

Young Balzac was sent away to school with the Oratoriens, a priestly seminary run on Spartan lines, where for five years he was totally miserable. But the fathers had an excellent library, bought up cheap from the revolutionary mobs who had looted the great châteaux of the area, just the kind of transaction that Balzac was to take such pleasure in detailing in his own novels. He spent the time in a dream, soaking himself in literature and particularly in the English novel, from Defoe and Fielding to the trashiest Gothic romances. By the time the family moved to Paris he was well equipped to find employment in a pulp fiction workshop, reeling out melodrama and near pornography anonymously and by the yard.

V. S. Pritchett points out that Balzac had three mothers. They all adored him, and he returned their affection while exploiting them shamelessly and without scruple. The Balzacs—they were by this time calling themselves the *de* Balzacs whenever feasible—made friends in their quiet village outside Paris with a former aristocrat, Madame de Berny. Balzac was sexually timid with and indifferent to young girls, but he was bold enough with women twenty-five years or so older than himself. Madame de Berny became his mistress, and for the rest of her life looked after him and lent him money in collaboration with his real mother; she died both poor and neglected, for Balzac's continued fondness for her stood no chance in the face of his innumerable other obsessions and commitments. She was deeply jealous of his third mother, the Duchesse d'Abrantès, a slatternly beak-nosed lady of literary pretensions, who had been married to General Junot, and who in return for Balzac's help with her memoirs was able to supply him with invaluable material about high life and intrigue under Napoleon.

For yesterday in France, as Balzac realized, was already history in the grand Scott style. In his first serious novel, *Les Chouans*, he treated the Breton insurrection of 1800 in Scott's manner, but one remembers that *Waverley*, Scott's first novel, is subtitled " 'Tis sixty years since" and offers Bonnie Prince Charlie as a bygone romance. History for Balzac was what was still in progress, and although years were to pass before he found the title for his great work, the conception of it was already in his head. He was no longer "Lord R'Hoone," the grotesque would-be English pen name he had concocted out of an anagram of his own. Gigantic projects were hatching in his head, in business no less than in literature. He bought a printing works on credit, which under his management promptly went bankrupt, and he had to be bailed out by his mother and Madame de Berny.

From then on the pattern was set: an immense and increasing load of debt arising from extravagance and speculation—Balzac only had to touch a stock for the bottom to drop out of the market—against which were mortgaged the plans and profits of novel after novel. He turned his hopes and disasters into fiction as he lived through them, becoming, in turn, César Birotteau, Père Goriot, Vautrin, Grandet, Gobseck, and Nucingen. Edmund Wilson's premise, that the novelist creates his characters merely out of different aspects and impulses of his own nature, is in fact generically true of Balzac, and his most obvious point of contact with early nineteenth-century romanticism.

Such creation is far from being the Shakespearean one of "negative capability," and indeed nothing could be further from the imaginative process of most novelists, including Dickens, with whom Balzac is so often compared. But Dickens was both worldly and adroit: where Balzac's Paris paper lost money spectacularly, Dickens's *Household Words* prospered: Dickens's fantastics are extrapolated from a deep level of his unconscious, whereas Balzac's are an aspect of his day-to-day life; one cannot imagine Dickens confusing reality with invention as Balzac is reported to have done, calling out in his last illness for Bianchon, the doctor he had created in the *Comédie Humaine*.

Yeats, as I have said, adored Balzac, but nothing could be less Balzacian than his edict that "the intellect of man is forced to choose perfection of the life or of the work." Like a madman writing about madmen, a man on the run dreaming up tales of men on the run, Balzac compelled life to behave to him in the style in which he imagined his own creations.

The great and final love of his life, Madame Hanska, was a case in point. Rich, passionate, and vivacious, with an ailing husband and an estate in the Ukraine as large as a French department, she seemed the answer even to megalomania on his scale. But the scope of the allure turned out to be—as his fiction required it should—a tragic mirage. She encouraged and rebuffed him; summoning him to Russia and to the life of a prince and potentate, and dispatching him back to France still deeper in debt and unable even to find the ready money for coach hire. Her husband dead, she only gave in and married him when she saw that he himself was a dying man. On their last homecoming to Paris they found Balzac's house a shambles—his butler had gone mad and refused to admit them—and when, a few weeks later, Balzac was on his deathbed, Madame Hanska withdrew from the scene: only his own mother, reduced to poverty by his endless demands on her, was with him at the end.

V. S. Pritchett is another novelist and storyteller who has come under Balzac's spell, and he writes about him in a manner suited to the subject—Balzac would have enjoyed his book. The derogatory epithet "coffee-table book" is often applied to illustrated biographical studies of this type, but I cannot see why a great number of prints and portraits, admirably chosen and reproduced, should be assumed to diminish the value of a serious work, or why it should be taken for granted that people who put books on coffee tables look at nothing but the pictures. In any case, Balzac loved display, and nothing could be less literary than his hold over his original clientele; his appeal was to their sentiment and curiosity, their snobbery, greed, and sensationalism—all the things be wrote about himself.

On the face of it there could hardly be a greater contrast than between V. S. Pritchett's straightforward and pragmatic relish in his subject and the approach of Roland Barthes in *S/Z*, a structuralist critique of Balzac's story *Sarrasine*, which appeared in the Paris critical series *Tel quel*. But the two are really not so dissimilar: both are trying to reanimate Balzac's image for the modern reader, Pritchett by British empirical methods, Barthes by the latest style of Gallic formalistic analysis.

Why should Balzac need this treatment? Largely because of the defects of his own virtues. Where Dickens will reveal considerable depths, both of conscious sophistication and unconscious meaning, in the context of a normal critical discussion, Balzac's great effects are always on the surface. His very energy and flamboyance make him the most obvious of writers; he has no buried riches for the critic to harvest and for the modern student to rediscover. That, again, is why other novelists have loved him: they can deepen and equivocate his graphic situations of power and the will. Henry James did it in *The Aspern Papers*, that most Balzacian of tales, metamorphosing his hero from the adventurer who fails—if fail he does—in the external power struggle, into the no less unscrupulous and determined would-be possessor who is undone by a growing inner awareness of what his conduct implies, an awareness which James converts into dramatic narrative.

Pritchett's task, well accomplished, is to remind us that Balzac is an extraordinary man, worth reading for the sake of himself and his characters (Pritchett is very good on the device of the recurring figure in the *Comédie Humaine*). Barthes uses Balzac as a *"texte ancien, très ancien,"* for explication on a linguistic basis. He segments and categorizes the Balzacian cliché to show what stock response was expected, and, by liberating us from any collusion with the historical unself-consciousness of the author, ends up with what he calls a *"théorie libératrice du Signifiant."*

This process of transforming our consciousness of the past in order to surprise us into a consciousness of the present is very much in the French critical tradition, and at its best Barthes's manipulation justifies itself by giving us an image of *Sarrasine* both as a historical phenomenon, a story composed at a certain epoch by Balzac, and as a timeless artifact of language, whose internal logic and effect can be deduced by an equally enclosed and quasi-mathematical analysis.

The results are certainly illuminating, but they will afford most profit and pleasure to that numerous class of persons who have no instinctive enjoyment of literature and yet feel they ought to get something out of it. This is certainly a way of getting something, and I suppose that support should not be withheld from any techniques today which encourage the precise examination of verbal structure and a discriminating sense of words and meaning. Unfortunately Barthes's style is portentous and his build-up of jargon formidable beyond necessity. In this context as in others, linguistic and critical discrimination calls for the use of Occam's razor, not for the deployment of a new para-language.

The New York Review of Books, 1973

58

A Complex Relationship

Alexander Pushkin (1799–1837) and Lord Byron (1788–1824)

BYRON WOULD HAVE greatly enjoyed a touch which Pushkin eventually omitted from his great poem—one of his last—*The Bronze Horseman*. The poem tells the story of a young clerk in St. Petersburg, whose ancient and distinguished family has come down in the world (Pushkin here was probably thinking of his own family), and who is in love with a young woman who lives with her mother in a modest cottage on the other side of the river Neva. In one of the great October floods which occurred periodically in the capital which Peter the Great had erected on a Finnish swamp—a highly unsuitable site—the cottage is swept away and the women are drowned. Poor Evgeny, the clerk, goes mad, and one night threatens with his puny fist the bronze statue of the emperor, rearing his horse on its great red granite plinth beside the Neva. It seemed to Evgeny that the terrible emperor's head turned slowly toward him, and he flees distractedly about the town all night, pursued, he imagines, by the hollow hoofbeats of the bronze steed. Later his body is found on a small island where the remains of a poor cottage have been washed up.

A sad tale, as Pushkin says, and one which he tells with typical concision and restraint. Nonetheless it has all the elements of a romantic tale, the sort which Byron had exploited with such extraordinary verve and success in *The Giaour* and *The Corsair* and *Parisina* and the others— poems which Pushkin had read with rapture, like almost every other educated young European, and which had inspired him in "eastern" poems ("Vostochnaya Poema"), *The Captive of the Caucasus* and *The Fountain of Bakchisarai*. It is often said, by Russian critics, that Pushkin "outgrew" Byron, and that even in these early Eastern poems he shows a sense of discipline and dramatic economy alien to the romantic genre and to Byron's use of it. There is something in this, but it is far from being the whole truth. Both Byron and Pushkin developed as poets in their own ways, but the development of each could be said in odd and interesting ways to remain in sympathy with that of the other. The Byron of *Don Juan* would have fully appreciated Pushkin's novel in verse, *Evgeny Onegin*; and he would also have seen the point of Pushkin's later poem, and later hero, the poor clerk who is also called Evgeny.

The touch he would have especially relished is a typical piece of deadpan Pushkinian comedy. When the flood is at its height a senator looks out of the window of his mansion, and is amazed to see a general going past in a rowing boat. He thinks he must be "seeing things," because his cushioned lifestyle in his great house has enabled him to ignore such things as floods, and indeed to be unaware of their existence. Only after he has called his servant, and confirmed that he, too, has seen the strange spectacle outside, is he able to relax once more, order a cup of tea, and dismiss the matter from his mind.

Byron's sense of humor would certainly have responded to this: indeed it is the kind of story he might have recounted with great brio in one of his own letters. He would have seen it not only as funny in itself but as significant in terms of poetic "message." Not only are the great ones of this harsh and unjust world made comic by its events, over which they have no control, but their attitude shows their lack of realization and compassion. Why then did Pushkin, whose sense of the ridiculous was very like Byron's own, finally omit this scene from his poem? The answer seems to be that whereas Byron was always ready—and particularly in his Don Juan period—to break off to make a pointed and witty aside, to denounce tyranny and injustice, or to express his own feelings about some current event, Pushkin always possessed an inexorable sense of what the form of a poem required, and what such a form itself could do to determine the work's own peculiar being and discourse. Byron's requirement is different. "I want a form that's large enough to swim in, and talk on any subject that I choose." It suited him; and when Pushkin came to write his novel in verse, *Evgeny Onegin*, he, too, followed this prescription in his own way. Yet *Evgeny Onegin* remains a very different sort of poem—naturally enough even though it is full of Byronic asides, witticisms, personal observations. Pushkin himself "knows" Evgeny, his hero, and recalls how they used often to stroll together on fine summer evenings along the embankment of the Neva. Such a comment to the reader stylizes the whole relationship, reveals the total artifice of the poem by exaggerating its apparent frankness and informality. Although Byron claims to have "known" Juan in the same way, his hero was a real extension of himself, and the whole poem an aspect of his being.

In fact that word "deadpan" does in some degree sum the matter up. The law of Pushkin's artistic being was to let effects speak for themselves, never to draw attention to them by his own commentary. An agreeable instance of this occurs in *Evgeny Onegin* after Tatiana has rashly declared her love in a letter to the hero, and he has met her in the garden and lectured her on the folly of her actions. The scene is touching and dramatic, high-minded and romantic: the girl near to tears, the young man approaching almost like a spectre, it seems to her, as she stands trembling; the talk about love, the pitiful renunciation of it on her part, the somber refusal on his. "He offered her his arm. Sadly (as the phrase is, "mechanically") Tatiana leaned on it in silence, bending her poor little head. Home they went round the kitchen garden."

A Russian critic has pointed out how characteristic of Pushkin's novel in verse is that casual reference to the vegetable garden, at the moment when Tatiana's heart is breaking. Pushkin does not rub home the point, as Byron might have done, by saying how typical this is of the way life goes. By his silence he makes clear that it is his hero Evgeny himself who is unconscious of life's little incongruities, because he is absorbed by his own role as the world-weary man of experience, whose duty (and pleasure) it is to reveal her folly to the poor girl, and how he might have taken advantage of it. Crushed Tatiana and complacent Evgeny are wholly integrated in the poem, as are its meaning and its message. However informal its tone may seem, as opposed to its meter, nothing is allowed to stand out and call attention to itself.

This is even truer of *The Bronze Horseman*. The interesting thing is that Pushkin's late *poema* still has a lot in common with Byron's early poetic and romantic narratives, which Pushkin had so much admired.

"Read *Parisina*" he exhorts a friend, who had applied to him for a good poetic model. It was sound advice, which Pushkin himself had followed out in ways that might have surprised Byron. For there seems to me no doubt, however surprising it may appear, that Pushkin learnt the clue of how to be deadpan from Byron himself, even though the English poet never systematized the technique, and indeed forsook the kind of poems which revealed its possibilities to Pushkin. Byron went on to make his own special mode of the wonderfully unbuttoned and talkative Juan: Pushkin developed his own later version of the romantic and dramatic narrative, and stayed with it, as *The Bronze Horseman* shows.

It is for this reason that Pushkin so carefully pruned any relaxed or impersonal elements from this masterpiece of a poem. Not only the general in the boat had to go (he draws the reader's attention too much away from the central drama, as well as making too clear a satirical social point), but Pushkin even omitted eventually one of his most delightful passages, which put before us the inner thoughts and feelings of his humble hero, Evgeny. On the night before the storm and the flood he lies awake in bed, dreaming about Parasha and their hopeful future, dreaming, as Pushkin says, "*kak poet*"—"like a poet"—a quietly ironic touch, because Evgeny's personality and his simple ambitions are deliberately made as unlike those of a poet as possible. Pushkin is doing the same thing that Byron so frequently does in *Don Juan*—depreciating the inky tribe and "a fellow that's all author"—but instead of suggesting, like Byron, that noblemen are not like common authors because they can think of something else than writing, Pushkin puts his hero as far from literature as possible by making him a young man with the simplest and least aristocratic ideas, although he comes (like Pushkin himself) from a once distinguished family.

> Get married? Me? Well, why not? It would be tough going of course but then I'm young and healthy and ready to work day and night. Somehow or other I'll fix up a simple modest little place for Parasha to settle down in. A bed, two chairs, a bowl of soup—I'd be my own master and what more would we need? We wouldn't have big ideas. On Sundays we'd go out together for a stroll in the country. And after maybe a year or two I'd get myself well dug in with my job, and leave

the management and the kids' upbringing to Parasha . . . and so we'll
live, and so we'll go down hand in hand to the grave, and our grandchildren will bury us.

Evgeny's simple hopes are all doomed of course, and perhaps Pushkin
was right not to underline so much the contrast in the poem between the
simple aspirations of a nobody, and the imperial dreams of the great Tsar
Peter, when he stood on the deserted shore of the Gulf of Finland and
meditated the creation of his capital. Pushkin wanted his poem to be
swift, dramatic, and objective, in keeping with the terse comment in his
prologue—*Pechalen budet moi rasskaz*—"Mine will be a sad tale"—a
line which he first used and discarded in an early tale, *The Fountain of
Bakchisarai*.

Nikolay Chernyshevsky, the influential critic later in the century who
wanted literature to be the handmaid of social and political reform,
agreed that too many homely and personal details would have detracted
from the stark contours of the poem, but nonetheless regretted that
Pushkin had not retained his Evgeny's meditation, as a pointed illustration of what the "little man" wanted out of life and from his rulers.
Chernyshevsky's wish shows exactly what Pushkin's instinct was to avoid:
an obvious message. For Valery Bryusov, the symbolist poet of the 1890s
who wrote an excellent study of Pushkin, the latter was quite right to
depersonalize his poem as much as possible. Bryusov pointed out that
Pushkin had even removed, at an early stage of his draft, the name of
Peter himself from the prologue of the poem, substituting the bare mono-
syllable "He"—("On a shore washed by the desolate waves *he* stood, full
of high thoughts, and gazed into the distance"). There is a briskly discreet
parallel, not dwelt upon, between the figure of the Tsar and the equally
depersonalized figure of Evgeny. Part of Pushkin's intention was no doubt
not to upset the censorship, but even so only the prologue of the poem
was published in his lifetime.

There is a contrast, too, between the statue of Peter on its massive
plinth, surrounded by iron railings, and the "unpainted fence" beside the
river which encloses the willow tree and the shabby little house in which
live Parasha and her mother, the little house which is the goal of Evgeny's
dream. Later writers like Gogol and Dostoevsky were to make much of

the "poor folk" theme, which is implicit in *The Bronze Horseman* but never systematically deployed. Pushkin carries a terse impersonality in his completed poem to the extent of leaving in a state of uncertainty, even mystery, what exactly happened to poor Evgeny. Nor do we ever meet Parasha and her mother, presumed victims of the great flood. All we know is that the remains of a cottage, "like a black bush," are washed ashore on a small island in the gulf, and that the body of the deranged clerk is found there, on the threshold. Here again Pushkin is taking a leaf out of Byron's book, and his early poems. In his favorite, *Parisina*, the unfortunate heroine, presumed victim of a jealous husband, simply vanishes from the scene. "Parisina's fate lies hid / Like dust beneath the coffin lid." It was certainly part of Byron's technique, in his early romantic narratives, to end the poem in an obscurity which was part of its romantic aura, and Pushkin gives an unexceptionable tautness and economy to the same device. We see it at its most effective and moving in *The Bronze Horseman*.

Much earlier on, in *The Fountain of Bakchisarai*, Pushkin borrowed the figure of Seyd from Byron's *The Corsair*, and turns him into Girey, the Tartar Khan of the Crimea who captures and falls in love with Mariya, the Polish princess. In his harem Mariya is the innocent and unintentional rival of the passionate Zarema, a situation that echoes to greater effect that of Byron's Medora and Gulnare. "It was enough—she died— what reck'd it how?" says Byron at the end of his drama, and Pushkin turns this into a more dramatic and enigmatic climax. The young Pushkin himself thought this end, as he writes to a friend, "dramatically effective." It is amusing, too, that Pushkin, following Byron's offhand expertise with oriental titles and properties, perpetuates the howler that the latter made in *The Corsair*. In both poems the guard of the harem is referred to as the Kislar, which in fact is a Turkish word meaning "girl." Pushkin borrowed the term and the mistake from Pichot's French translation of Byron, as his English at that stage was not up to reading the original poem.

After his romantic and Eastern poems, and his starkly dramatic poem *The Gipsies*, which does not fit into either category, Pushkin produced in *Poltava* a poem combining both the heroic and the romantic modes. It tells the story of the conspiracy in the Ukraine against Peter the Great, in which the Hetman, Mazepa, allied himself treacherously with Charles of Sweden. He contrived to turn Peter against Kochubey, Peter's loyal supporter in the Ukraine, and had him executed. Kochubey's daughter, the beautiful Mariya, had earlier conceived an extraordinary passion for the aged but still handsome Hetman, and had run away to him. All this is historical but dressed up in romantic form, although done with Pushkin's usual beautiful economy and terseness. But in its second part the poem switches to the heroic mode. The great battle of Poltava, at which Charles's army was annihilated by Peter, is described in detail, and the poem ends by placing its own events in a legendary perspective. The story of Mariya has become one of those "old unhappy far-off things," to be comfortably remembered in song and story.

> Only the blind Ukrainian bard, at times when he recites the Hetman's songs before the villagers, recalls in passing to the young Cossacks who listen the name of that abandoned girl.

Byron, like Pushkin, had a keen interest in history, and a serious feeling for how the artist should make use of it. He was also just as aware as Pushkin of the difficulty of reconciling bald fact with pleasing fiction, "romantic" requirement with historical truth. An amusing instance of this difficulty occurs in Pushkin's first narrative poem, *The Captive of the Caucasus*. The captive manages to escape with the help of a beautiful Circassian maiden, who has fallen in love with him. It is a hopeless love, however, because she realizes that the captive officer is only availing himself of her services, and that his one idea is to escape and get home. She guides him to the Russian outposts, and as he leaves her, she plunges to her death in a mountain stream. Her lover hears the splash, but does not turn back to try to rescue her. Pushkin's friends, and the young ladies who read the poem, were indignant at this unchivalrous behavior, so inappropriate in a romantic hero of the time, and Pushkin defended himself as Byron might have done, by pointing out the facts of the case. "Try jumping yourself—I have swum in the rivers of the Caucasus—and my captive is an intelligent and sensible fellow."

Byron's *Mazeppa*, which recounts in its words a story from the hero's youth, makes use, like the *The Prisoner of Chillon*, of first person narrative to close the gap between historic event and subjective romance. Far from being a sinister, obscure old power broker, seen only through the consequences of his acts, as Pushkin's Mazepa appears to us, Byron's is a garrulous and courtly old party whose function it is to entertain Charles of Sweden with a tale, while he and the monarch are on their arduous journey together, after the rout of Poltava, to the safety of the Turkish border. Byron catches admirably the tone of reminiscence:

> I think 'twas in my twentieth spring—
> Ay, 'twas—when Casimir was king—
> John Casimir—I was his page . . .

and in so doing implies a decided contrast between the old fellow who faithfully attends on the fallen Charles and the dashing Ukrainian blade who once cuckolded a nobleman and was bound in revenge on the back of a wild horse. Byron's technique is to bring his character close up and personalize him in the romantic way with a love exploit which—like those in the other narrative poems—makes failure and even death worthwhile. Pushkin's is to distance everything, so that motive and personality remain enigmatic in the perspective of history. Mazepa and Mariya are not the hero and heroine of Poltava, but two shadowy figures in its rich narrative and historic background. We do not even know, because history does not tell us, whether the crafty old Mazepa "loved" the rash girl who became infatuated with him, or whether he just made use of her, as an item in his intrigue against her father Kochubey. Pushkin makes one concession to romance of the stock kind, when the young Cossack, who has hopelessly loved Mariya from afar, makes a gallant single-handed attack on Mazepa on the battlefield, and is shot down by his entourage.

But Pushkin's chief method is to distance by swift deadpan touches, which are naturally dramatic. On the eve of her father's execution by Mazepa, Mariya's mother manages to make her way to her errant daughter, and begs her to plead with the Hetman for her husband's life. So lost in her own infatuation is the girl that she cannot understand what is being asked of her, and replies in stupefied tones, "What father?" Pushkin makes a marvelously dramatic *tour de force*, too, of the execution scene itself, describing the animation of the crowd and the appearance of the headsman ("In his white hands he grasps and plays with the heavy axe, jesting with the excited mob") with Shakespearean speed and vividness. Maurice Baring, a great admirer of Pushkinian effects, remarked on the economy of that touch about the *white* hands, invisibly contrasting, as it does, with the blood that will soon flow. Both Pushkin and his friend Ryleev, who also wrote a *poema* on the subject, borrowed the business about the headsman from Byron's *Parisina*.

> The headsman with his bare arm ready,
> That the blow may be both swift and steady,
> Feels if the axe be sharp and true
> Since he set its edge anew:
> While the crowd in a speechless circle gather . . .

Pushkin reverses Byron's emphasis on the hush of the moment. He was unaware, of course, of the difficulty of double rhymes in English, and their inherent tendency to sound a bit absurd. Pushkin in fact was borrowing—and improving—at two removes, because Ryleev's poem was written before his own. Writing to another friend he says that Ryleev "has in his poem a hangman, with his arms bare, for whom I would give a great deal." It was typical of Pushkin's generosity and sense of friendship to admit where he got things from.

Typical of him, too, to pick up and perfect touches from any kind of source, as he would do later with Barry Cornwall's "Dramatic Scenes," turning them into the elegant form of his own "Little Tragedies." Although he admired Byron's plays, and appreciated the scrupulous sense of the historical which Byron put into them, particularly the Venetian ones, he criticized the way in which the new romantic tragedy tended to rely on doing things "characteristically," a convention it had inherited from neoclassic drama, where a soldier always behaved in a soldierly fashion, and a villain in a villainous one. As Pushkin put it in a long letter to his friend Raevsky,

> When a character of this sort is conceived, all he is made to say, even
> the most random things, bear his essential stamp. . . . A conspirator

says "Give me a drink" conspiratorially, and that's ridiculous. Look at
Byron's Hater (Pushkin is referring to Loredano, in *The Two Foscari*),
this monotony, this affectation of the laconic, this continual rage. . . .
Is this nature? Look at Shakespeare—read Shakespeare—he is never
afraid of compromising his character.

Pushkin was struck by the fact that Shakespeare never "compromised" his
characters, in the sense that they were always free to do or to say irrelevant or uncharacteristic things. Hamlet the revenger reveals a keen interest in amateur dramatics; Iago the villain is a witty man and something of
a complacent philosopher; Shylock the miser is a man of passionate
resentments and family pride. So struck was Pushkin by this Shakespearean "freedom" that he returns to the idea again and again, and made
his own version of it in his *poema Andzhelo*, based on *Measure for
Measure*, and in his "Little Tragedies," where Don Juan, for example,
becomes a man who not only loves his conquests for their own sake but
takes a great personal interest in them, rather as Pushkin did with his own
girlfriends.

Like other English writers in the native tradition, Byron was inhibited
by Shakespeare, in spite of the vigor of his own genius. Pushkin, like
Friedrich von Schiller and Heinrich von Kleist in German, was more
detached, and thus more able to use the great dramatic inspiration from
another country. Indeed it is a striking thing, to which comparative critics have still not paid enough attention, that Pushkin shares with Kleist,
although the latter belonged to the previous generation, the distinction of
grasping the inner significance of Shakespeare's characterization. Other
playwrights like Victor Hugo in France, and there were very many of
them, did their best to exploit the Shakespearean scene in terms of history
and humor, local color, the picturesque. Kleist, in both his plays and his
stories, developed something much more complex: the unpredictability
from minute to minute of the Shakespearean character (Hamlet is the
obvious example) and the fact that he cannot be understood from an
external viewpoint. Human nature is not only infinitely various but infinitely variable. Pushkin perceived something very similar, and pursued it

in his short enigmatic plays and sketches, like "Rusalka," and in his ideas for novels. Byron himself had come to something not so different in his Don Juan, and both poets—had they lived—might have produced work still more closely related in feeling and sympathy.

The Byron Journal, 1988

59

Doubles

Fyodor Dostoevsky (1821–1881) and
J. M. Coetzee (1940–)

———————

The Master of Petersburg
by J. M. Coetzee

Doubling the Point: Essays and Interviews
by J. M. Coetzee, edited by David Attwell

Demons
by Fyodor Dostoevsky, translated by Richard Pevear and
  Larissa Volokhonsky

A YEAR OR SO AGO, talking to the leading contenders for a prestigious new fiction prize awarded in Moscow, I was struck by the wry defeatism displayed by writers who had been the most successful. One of them remarked: "We Russian novelists cannot do without the tyranny of history any more than Fyodor Dostoevsky could do without God. And we haven't learnt the Western trick of being interested in individuals for their own sake." I said I thought Western novelists were no longer much interested in individuals for their own sake, and added that Tolstoy had surely been the grand master of this particular literary field. He agreed, but said that Tolstoy was of no possible use now to a Russian writer, as the weakness of Solzhenitsyn's recent work had so clearly demonstrated; and, moreover, that both he and Tolstoy had relied on Russian history to the point of identifying the novel with it. Without the total domination of the first the second could not exist.

I recalled this conversation while reading J. M. Coetzee's novel, *The Master of Petersburg*. The master is Dostoevsky, and Coetzee's intention seems to have been to analyze the great writer's psyche in fictional terms, rather as literary critics once used to analyze "character" in their surveys of the nineteenth-century novel or of Shakespeare's plays. Coetzee, a brilliantly analytical writer, seems to have decided, at least for the moment, to abandon history in the Russian, or indeed the South African, sense—history, that is, as an essentially dynamic and ever-present process—in favor of history as the past, and thus as the sphere in which "character" as a literary concept is situated.

So Dostoevsky becomes a character from the past in Coetzee's novel, as if he were a character in one of his own novels; for that seems to be the effect that the author is aiming at. And in one way he is remarkably successful, combining a deeply pondered imaginative sympathy with the professional and academic sharpness one would expect of a novelist who is also a professor of general and comparative literature. The effect is not so unlike that achieved by Jay Parini—also an academic—in his excellent short novel *The Last Station: A Novel of Tolstoy's Last Year*. And yet of course Dostoevsky's life, and his inner psychology and motivations, are far more complex and more mysterious than Tolstoy's, and fundamentally more unknowable, as well as indefinable. Coetzee duly pays tribute to their unknowable nature, but he manages to suggest the certain and yet disconcerting truth that even a very great novelist like Dostoevsky was not only timid and diffident about his writing, and how to write, but that he was quite simply abashed—when it came to the point—by men of action and politics who were ruthless and determined, and who knew how to get what they wanted. For no matter how powerful and influential his voice may be, any great writer in the end is himself powerless, betrayed from within by his own uncertainties and connivances.

With whom does he connive? With the very people, of course, whose influence he most fears and rejects, and against whom he is writing. In this case the terrible figure is that of Nechaev, the real-life model for the demonic young Pyotr Verkhovensky, villain of the novel which the Dostoevsky of Coetzee's book will soon be writing, and whose title, *Besy*, has been variously translated as *The Possessed*, or *The Devils*, or most recently and accurately, *Demons*. The real Nechaev was a terrorist intellectual who, either directly or through his malign influence over his fellow con-spirators, committed several murders in the tsarist Russia of the late 1860s and 1870s, most notably that of a student who was suspected of taking a Christian attitude, backsliding from the revolutionary cause, and who appears in *Demons* under the name of Shatov, from a Russian verb mean-ing wavering, uncertain, or, by extension, unconvinced.

In Coetzee's novel Dostoevsky returns in 1869 from Dresden at the news of the sudden and untimely death of his stepson Pavel. Pavel has fallen from a tower on one of the St. Petersburg quays—was it an acci-dent? Was he pushed by the Tsar's secret police, as the terrorist fraternity have claimed? Or were the terrorists responsible, among them Nachaev himself, with whom Pavel may or may not have had a secret connection? All is suitably ambiguous and uncertain; and the author of the novel reveals his hand, perhaps prematurely, in stressing from the outset the doubleness, or tripleness, in the soul of the tormented author who has returned to Russia. Doubles are Dostoevsky's thing: he has written a novel with that very title.

He has also, of course, written a novel called *Crime and Punishment*, in which the hero Raskolnikov seeks redemption in suffering in a Siber-ian prison for his murder of an old money-lender, and is redeemed by the Christ-like love of the heroine, Sonya. When Dostoevsky the writer meets Nechaev, the terrorist ironically reminds him of this, indeed flings it in his face, wickedly implying that all novelists only invent things like suf-fering and redemption for artistic purposes, and to edify their readers. The confrontation between Dostoevsky and Nechaev, the subversive whom he will subsequently triumph over and, as it were, emasculate on paper in his novel *Demons*, is one of the most powerful scenes in Coet-zee's novel. Nechaev baits the writer by suggesting he make a statement, in the manner of literary men, any statement he pleases, and the conspir-ators will print it word for word on their little "Albion-of-Birmingham" printing press.

> "My statement?" he [the Dostoevsky character] says.
> "Yes, your statement. Whatever statement you choose to make. You can write it here and now, it will save time."
> "And what if I choose to tell the truth?"

"Whatever you write we will distribute, I promise."

"The truth may be more than a hand-press can cope with."

"Leave him alone." The voice comes from the other man, still poring over the text in front of him. "He's a writer, he doesn't work like that."

"How does he work then?"

"Writers have their own rules. They can't work with people looking over their shoulders."

"Then they should learn new rules. Privacy is a luxury we can do without. People don't need privacy."

Now that he has an audience, Nechaev has gone back to his old manner. As for him [Dostoevsky], he is sick and tired of these callow provocations. "I must go," he says again.

Almost as if he were in collusion with Nechaev, everything has been calculated by Coetzee to reduce Dostoevsky as a man—not a "master," but a real man living in the real world of St. Petersburg—to total discomfiture. He is put to shame by the suffering of the wretched woman who is landlady of the foul cellar where Nechaev lives; by the questioning of the doltish girl who adores Nechaev and has supplied another girl, a fellow conspirator who is under arrest, with poison on Nechaev's orders. These are, so to speak, living and breathing inhabitants of St. Petersburg, and not the "suffering" characters whom Dostoevsky will invent and put into his novels.

But he is shamed most of all by Nechaev's easy victory in argument, and in the duel of wits that takes place between them.

As if sensing his weakness, Nechaev pounces, worrying him like a dog. "Eighteen centuries have passed since God's age, nearly nineteen! We are on the brink of a new age where we are free to think any thought. There is nothing we can't think! Surely you know that. You must know it—it's what Raskolnikov said in your own book before he fell ill!"

"You are mad, you don't know how to read," he [Dostoevsky] mutters. But he has lost, and he knows it. He has lost because, in this debate, he does not believe himself. And he does not believe himself because he has lost. Everything is collapsing: logic, reason. He stares at Nechaev and sees only a crystal winking in the light of the desert, self-enclosed, impregnable.

"Be careful," says Nechaev, wagging a finger meaningfully. "Be careful what words you use about me. I am of Russia: when you say I am mad, you say Russia is mad."

Nechaev has got him, because whatever truth the writer utters can be twisted by the terrorists to their own purposes and the author will necessarily collude with the terrorists just by writing for them and about them. The irony in the fact that "writers have their own rules," and can only tell men like Nechaev that they "don't know how to read," graphically expresses the helplessness of Dostoevsky the actual man, who now longs above all to escape from this all too real world from which he will take refuge, it is implied, by reinventing it in his next novel, *Demons*. In the meanwhile he longs above all to get away from "the maelstrom of St. Petersburg."

> Dresden beckons like an atoll of peace — Dresden, his wife, his books
> and papers, and the hundred small comforts that make up home, not
> least among them the pleasure of fresh underwear.

At the end of the book we see Dostoevsky sitting down to write *Demons*.

It is of course not without significance that Coetzee has written perspicaciously and with authority on the latest academic theories about how novels are read and written; or that, as a teacher of literature, he may well be thinking of the remark Joseph Conrad made off the cuff about his own African novel, *Heart of Darkness*. He had written it, said Conrad, in order to get rid of having experienced it. By implication he had been shamed not only by the horror of what he had seen but by the ignoble part he felt he had played in it, and by his covert desire to conquer and put it behind him by writing the novel.

Writing of this sort might be seen as itself a form of confession, and yet Coetzee seems not at all sure about that. In an interview reprinted in *Doubling the Point*, his book of essays and interviews headed "Autobiography and Confession," he discusses the kind of interest he had in Dostoevsky and in the question of the novelist's ambiguous attitude to his subject matter.

> Against the endlessness of skepticism Dostoevsky poses the closure not of confession but of absolution and therefore of the intervention of grace in the world. In that sense Dostoevsky is not a psychological novelist at all: he is finally not interested in the psyche, which he sees as an arena of game-playing. . . . To the extent that I am taken as a political novelist, it may be because I take it as given that people must be treated as fully responsible beings: psychology is no excuse. Politics, in its wise stupidity, is at one with religion here: one man, one soul: no half-measures.

These are wise words. And yet it remains true that in this novel, as opposed to his essays and theoretical writings, and indeed to his earlier novels with a South African background, Coetzee is very much interested, as if by necessity, in individual psychology, and in the psychology of the double or triple man like Dostoevsky, whose attitude to everything he deals with artistically remains profoundly ambiguous. In order to overcome Nechaev on paper, and turn him into his own invented character Pyotr Verkhovensky, he must endow him with the same qualities that he himself possesses. The author's own secret shamelessness must become open in the character he is creating. Dostoevsky cannot afford to let Nechaev/Verkhovensky appear as a simple and principled, if ruthless and dedicated, fanatic. He must behave (and in *Demons* does behave) as Saint Augustine tells us, in Book II of his *Confessions*, that he did when he and his young friends stole some pears "for the pleasure of committing a forbidden act . . . having no inducement to the evil but the evil itself."

Augustine is quoted in an essay of 1985 from *Doubling the Point* called "Confession and Double Thoughts: Tolstoy, Rousseau, Dostoevsky." Coetzee points out that confession on the orthodox Christian pattern should be followed by penitence and absolution; but he suggests that for such a writer as Dostoevsky the act of writing is *itself* the bestowal of absolution, however equivocally, by the writer himself. At the end of *The Master of Petersburg* Nechaev, soon to be arrested, is moving around the city in disguise, and Dostoevsky, unable to establish what killed Pavel, has escaped back into writing, even though the process "tastes like gall," and makes him feel that "he has betrayed everyone." The child of Pavel's exlandlady, with whom Dostoevsky has developed a fixated quasi-sexual relation, puts the matter naïvely by wondering that authors get paid "lots of money for writing books," and even before he begins to write the new novel, Coetzee's Dostoevsky begins to feel "that he had to give up his soul in return." But to quote again from the 1985 essay, "until the source from which the shameful act sprang is confronted, the self can have no rest."

The irony of which Coetzee seems to be aware, but Dostoevsky may not have been, is that the real Nechaev was certainly himself a double agent, subsidized in secret by the Tsar's police. Dostoevsky may well have intuited this. But the crudity of that simple form of duplicity would have had no appeal to the artist who wrote *Demons*. Equally alien to such an artist would be Coetzee's use of another, rather obvious, irony, which makes the tormented novelist pine for the order and comfort of Germany: petit bourgeois order and comfort being just the things that the "Russian" Dostoevsky felt that he most despised. But this is as much as to say that Coetzee the novelist has bravely put himself in the impossible position of writing about a novelist who himself wrote his novels in quite a different dimension. Instead of the Dostoevskian polydrama Coetzee gives us a sharp, meticulously brooded-on analysis—an analysis of the genesis of a novel—that has to make its points, and then adhere to them. He has to follow Freud in positing that the repressed irrational, the fundamental dishonesty of the human soul, is yet "accessible to the language of rationality."

The phrase comes from another essay in *Doubling the Point*, an essay on the Austrian novelist Robert Musil. It gives the key, in a certain sense, to the methods on which all of Coetzee's fiction is based, and it shows the kind of intelligence he has brought to the problems he faces in them. A fellow countryman of Freud, Musil is famous for his lengthy unfinished novel *The Man Without Qualities*, in which he draws a continuous distinction between what is rational and predictable in human behavior, and what he calls "the other condition," in which anything goes. Musil, says Coetzee, draws a line between the province of *Wissenschaft*, or science, and the province of *Dichtung*, which is poetry; and it is as a *Dichter* that he sets out to explore the submerged "other condition."

No doubt Coetzee's profound sympathy with Musil, as with Dostoevsky, would have made him wish to follow their example in his own writing of fiction, but the academic precision of his own creative intelligence seems to preclude this. Thus *The Master of Petersburg* remains an admirably imaginative critical commentary by one political novelist about another, rather than a novel in its own right. It is a fascinating book for all that, not least for the light that it sheds upon the problems of the novelist who writes about South Africa, and the tyranny of its history. About such a question Coetzee is too clear-sighted not to be ambivalent. For is it not the case that, as with Conrad and Dostoevsky, the novelist who writes about a terrible political situation is involuntarily freeing himself in the process from the darkness and the impossible complexity which it presents?

In a dialogue with Coetzee on "Autobiography and Confession" his editor, David Attwell, certainly suggests something of the kind. He gives as an example the writer's last novel about South Africa, *Age of Iron*. Its heroine, who is dying, finds herself regarding death as both escape and absolution from the seemingly hopeless politics brought about by the States of Emergency in South Africa. South Africa, like Russia, was in the grip of a historical tyranny which had forced this heroine to speak out, as it had compelled novelists like Coetzee and Nadine Gordimer to write the kinds of novels they have written.

But Coetzee's heroine feels that the imminence of death will not only release her from the compulsions of the historical situation in which she finds herself, but permit her for a time to enter again the world of the purely individual. It is toward that world which Coetzee himself seems to be turning in composing this study of the past. The character and individuality of Dostoevsky's novels are, in their own way, a gift of absolution from the past. Thus the novel need not just seek to interpret history, but in its own terms can overcome history's legacy, showing how Musil's "other condition" is within the novel and its reader, as it is within the novel's own creative power. A masterwork so thoughtfully if abstractly conceived as *The Master of Petersburg* deserves to be read along with the admirable translation of Dostoevsky's *Demons* by Richard Pevear and Larissa Volokhonsky. The two throw light on each other, and the newer novel has much to suggest to us about the way in which the older master-piece might have been written.

The New York Review of Books, 1994

60

The War Between the Diaries

Leo Tolstoy (1828–1910) and
Sofia Tolstoy (1844–1919)

Tolstoy's Diaries
edited and translated by R. F. Christian

The Diaries of Sofia Tolstoy
translated by Cathy Porter

L EO TOLSTOY was much preoccupied with questions of identity. His brutally penetrating intelligence, as well as the instinctive self-confidence of an aristocrat, were always running incredulously up against the fact of existence, and the certainty of nonexistence. What and who was he at different moments of the day? One of his earliest attempts at writing is a history of twenty-four hours, a record of his various selves during that period. His early diaries have the same feel to them. This is not like the stream of consciousness, but something far more urgent, emotional, and volatile. "My God! Where am I? Where am I going? And what am I now?" That is almost exactly like Natasha's exclamation at the death of Prince Andrew, which the translators weaken by paraphrase, finding its literalness too disconcerting. It should be: "Where is he and who is he now?"

Who is he now? Tolstoy's sense of identity was so strong that it would obviously survive death. But because so strong it was also so fearful and so tormented—joyous, too, but never taking itself for granted for a moment. Solipsism is an index of immortality. Tolstoy's intellectual real-ization that he was going to die, dramatized in A *Confession* but vividly present in the pages of his earliest diary, engaged all his life in the most literal of struggles with the conviction that nothing of the sort could possibly happen. It is the first of the paradoxes of his life and writing, and the one that underlies all the rest. The Jewish philosopher Lev Shestov, his most perceptive critic, dryly remarked that Tolstoy struggled against solipsism all his life, because he didn't know what to do with "this impertinent thing," but that eventually he gave in to it, as one does give in to the thing in one's life that really matters. At the age of twenty-nine he was already writing: "Thoughts of approaching death torment me. I look at myself in the mirror for days on end." The last entry in the diary, not long before pneumonia caused him to lose consciousness, runs: "Here is my plan. *Fais ce que dois, advienne que pourra.* And all is for the good of others and above all for me."

Above all for me. The magnificent obsession conjures into positive and nightmare being—as if it were the witch Babi-Yaga rushing through the forests in her hut on fowls' legs—what is for most people the normal neutral background of life. Tolstoy's sense of himself was so strong that it must be the most important thing in the world, to which he incessantly called everyone's attention. So strong, too, that it communicates itself to the rest of us. That "who is he now?" underlies every word he wrote and every character he created. Stiva and Vronsky, and the mare Frou-Frou, and the horse Kholstomer in the short story, are possessed of the same inner life, that presence of interior being which Tolstoy can suggest like no other writer. So "who is he now?" seems the one question worth asking when somebody dies. He must still have being, for nothing makes sense otherwise.

Tolstoy, aged twenty-eight, was traveling in Switzerland when he jotted in his habitual telegraphic manner the query about where he was and what he was. It is perhaps significant that he had just had an encounter, later described in his story "Lucerne," with an itinerant singer whom he had invited into his hotel for a drink. The waiters sneered at the man and put the couple in a room by themselves, away from the hotel guests. Earlier, Tolstoy had been incensed by the fact that the public had listened to the singing, but then turned away without giving the performer any money. The singer himself proved to be "a commonplace, pathetic person." But the incident shows how Tolstoy's sense of himself, almost mystical later on that evening as he looked out of his hotel-room window on "darkness, broken clouds, and light," was particularly responsive to encounters of this sort. Toward the end of *Anna Karenina* Levin has a similar encounter with a peasant, which suddenly reveals all that matters to him. Solipsism, unexpectedly, is both intensified by other people and intensely responsive to them. Tolstoy's social instincts were always generous and immediate, but what mattered to the artist and writer was the encounter itself, and its effect on the ego. There are highly memorable ones in *War and Peace*: Prince Andrew on the retreat to Moscow, for example, meeting the two little girls in the garden who are stealing plums, and Pierre's encounter with the party of Russian soldiers after the battle of Borodino.

His diaries have been well used by every biographer, but a proper English version has not appeared before, and Professor Christian has done an excellent job on this selection of them, as he did a few years ago on Tolstoy's letters. The second volume, from 1895 to 1910, when the man has become an adjunct of the legend, is mostly rather boring except to Tolstoy addicts. The most striking thing, to the reader who is familiar with his life and works, but who now reads the diaries consecutively for the first time, is the way in which his ambition to be a great writer had always come first. Though biography gives the impression of him blundering around, and trying first this and then that, the diaries unobtrusively emphasize the overpowering will to be a great writer, a "general of literature," and the efforts to write in all situations. They only really begin when Tolstoy goes as a cadet to the Caucasus in 1851. This was a sudden impulse—his elder brother Nikolai, who was already an officer in the army, was returning there. All his life Tolstoy enjoyed making sudden decisions, like the one at the end of his life when he left home and died at Astapovo railway station, but the idea of going to the Caucasus was one that any other ambitious young Russian writer might have had. Since Pushkin and Lermontov it had been the prime place to seek romantic experience and copy.

The second impression the early diaries give one, apart from Tolstoy's firm ambition to become famous through authorship, is how easy it was for him to lead the kind of life that made this possible. Dostoevsky, not the most unenvious genius in the world, used to complain that he would be able to write a real masterpiece if only he had the time and the resources that Tolstoy and Turgenev had. In fact, of course, Dostoevsky wrote best under great pressure—debt or prison or the firing squad were challenges that brought his most characteristically brilliant responses— but he himself probably did not see matters in that light. Like him, and like Pushkin, the young Tolstoy gambled heavily and got into debt, actually having to sell the big house on his estate at Yasnaya Polyana after one crushing loss at cards in the Caucasus. But however often this occurred ("16 *April. Staro gladkovskaya* . . . Lost 100 silver roubles effortlessly to Sulimovsky"), it was not really a serious matter. Tolstoy got up in the morning full of remorse and doggedly proceeded with trying to write *Childhood*, or *The Cossacks*, or one of his brilliant stories of army life in the Caucasus.

In fact, his army routine was the most leisurely affair possible, consisting almost entirely in talking and trying to compose stories, shooting hares and pheasants, having affairs with Cossack girls, and getting treated for gonorrhea at the local spa. Neither then nor later in the Crimea, at Sevastopol, did military duty interfere in any way with such things. Though he does not seem to have exploited his name and aristocratic rank, there is no doubt that a privileged position was tacitly allowed him by senior commanders. Everything conspired to help him become a writer. There is a parallel here with the military experiences of his admirer and self-proclaimed rival, Ernest Hemingway, who spent less than a week at the Italian front as a Red Cross welfare officer, distributing oranges and chocolates. Having had the luck to be wounded by a shell at the end of that time. Hemingway subsequently invented for himself and in his writings, a whole saga and mystique of heroic military service, the real facts only becoming known after his death.

Tolstoy's service was not like that, for though the diarist often accuses himself of being a coward, he behaved bravely enough on the few occasions when he was in actual danger. Like Hemingway, though, he was both obsessed with the need for a macho image and at the same time privately disgusted with the need and the idea. *War and Peace* is far more frank and open about all this than Hemingway could ever be. Nonetheless, the resemblance goes further than the marked self-division in both writers, and the popularity of Hemingway—seen as a sort of disciple of

Tolstoy—in Russia. Both men were quite unable to get on in the marriage relation, because—as Sofia Tolstoy was to write in her diary—"he doesn't want me to have any life of my own." Hemingway's wives made the same point, and no doubt it is and was a frequent complaint against husbands who have no claim to be great writers. Yet in all cases, even the most commonplace, it arises from the husband's obsessive fear that his wife has seen through his childlike macho image, and is secretly mocking it. Hence the abuse and distrust of wives, and the desire that they should have no private or secret life of their own.

In her diary for 1898 Sofia Tolstoy recorded an evening in which her husband and his sister were reminiscing about their childhood:

> It was such fun. Mashenka told us about the trip they had all made to Pirogovo when Lyovochka Tolstoy, then a boy of about fifteen, decided to run behind the carriage for the first five versts to *impress* everyone. The horses were trotting along but Lyovochka didn't fall behind, and when they stopped the carriage he was gasping so heavily that Mashenka burst into tears.
>
> Another time he wanted to *impress* some young ladies (they were staying in Kazan at the time, in the village of Panovo, their uncle Yushkov's estate) and he threw himself fully clothed into the pond. But he couldn't swim back to the bank, so he tried to touch the bottom, found he was out of his depth, and would have drowned if it hadn't been for some peasant women haymaking in the fields nearby, who saved him with their rakes.
>
> Yes, he always wants to *impress* and *impress*—he has been like that all his life. Well, he certainly has impressed the world, as no one else!

Rambling, full of vague detail and the teasing malice of its emphases, Sofia's journal is very different in tone from that of her husband. For one thing, her voice can be heard, and its mixture of tones is quite subtle. She wants to take Leo down a peg, of course, and to show to herself and posterity what it is like living with this childish great man. She is possessive about him: but she is also full of the vitality which Tolstoy once so much admired in her and her sister Tanya, and portrayed in the character of Natasha in *War and Peace*. At such moments there is visible in her diary, though not in his, the cheerfulness that must have kept breaking in all the time. "It was such fun . . ." Like many powerful men who need to "impress," Tolstoy also needed to be laughed with, even—by a loving wife—to be laughed at. With his wife and sister, and in the bosom of his family, he probably entered with amusement even into stories of how he had been saved from drowning by the rakes of the women haymakers.

Being taken down a peg, openly or secretly, was probably the least of his matrimonial troubles. Sofia must have possessed from an early age all the latent intolerableness which is apt to go with great physical vitality. As her husband was to remark of certain sorts of powerful and sensational novels, you see the point and then you become bored. Sofia must rapidly have developed into the most formidable of all bores: not the monotonous sort who merely send you to sleep, but the kind who demand from their vis-à-vis an equal display of gratuitous energy. Like Natasha in *War and Peace* she had flashing self-regard without any corresponding powers of self-analysis; immense subjective drive without any objective talent. Indeed, perhaps the most cunning achievement of Tolstoy's essentially cunning talent is to portray in *War and Peace* a wonderful heroine who seems to exemplify and gather to herself so much of the open space, power, and joyous movement of the book, but who is really a monster.

Her monstrousness is just ripening into maturity as the book ends. Pierre her husband will receive the full force of it in that speculative future which stretches out at the end of many great novels, and *War and Peace* most of all. An additional irony is that Tolstoy toyed with the idea of making Pierre a Decembrist, who after the abortive liberals' plot against the Tsar in St. Petersburg would be sent into exile in Siberia. Many of the Decembrists' wives voluntarily accompanied their husbands to Siberia, and heroically endured great hardships. Natasha would have been tailor-made for this role. Disaster and challenge would have brought out the very best in her. And the same sort of destiny would have done the same for Sofia Tolstoy. As it was, she had nothing to do but endure her husband, incessantly bear his children, copy his manuscripts until three in the morning, put up with his Christian principles and with the fact that in spite of them he always expected and got the best of everything for himself. Siberia would have been a more acceptable alternative.

The Christianity must have been the hardest to bear.

What sort of *Christian* life is this, I should like to know? He hasn't a drop of love for his children, for me, or for anyone but himself. I may be a heathen, but I love the children, and unfortunately I still love him too, cold Christian that he is, and now my heart is torn in two with doubts: should I go to Moscow or not? How can I possibly please everyone? Because as God is my witness I am happy only when I am making others happy.

That is touching, and one believes every word of it. But it also has the involuntary humor sometimes displayed by those who have absolutely no sense of humor at all. Being made happy by Sofia can have been no easy task, and no wonder her children, as well as her husband, came to flinch from it. In the meantime "Lyovochka is being quiet and friendly at the moment—and extremely *amorous*." She notes that he has begun reading English novels, which is a sure sign that he will soon be starting to write a novel of his own. In 1891, at the age of forty-seven, she is expressing what is in many ways a conventional Victorian view of herself and her sexual destiny. She longs for all *that* to be over and done with. "All my life I have dreamed sentimental dreams, aspired to a perfect union, a *spiritual* communion, not *that*. And now my life is over and most of the good in me is dead, at any rate my ideals are dead."

Yet on the same morning she had felt differently.

Horribly dissatisfied with myself. Lyovochka woke me this morning with passionate kisses . . . afterwards I picked up a French novel, Bourget's *Un Coeur de Femme*, and read in bed till 11.30, something I normally never do. I have succumbed to the most unforgivable debauchery—and at my age too! I am so sad and ashamed of myself! I feel sinful and wretched, and can do nothing about it although I do try.

All *that* evidently still has its attractions. She was in a muddle, and the muddle, together with all her loves and fears, prejudices and passions, goes instantly into the diary.

Tolstoy was a good father when the children were young, but as they grew older only the daughters had any appeal for him. "My sons, of whom I seem to have about a hundred," were "impossibly obtuse," filled "for all time with impregnable self-satisfaction." The diaries are continually noting self-satisfaction in others, with censoriousness but also sometimes with a kind of envy, as if the tormented genius who sought always to find out the Hedgehog's secret, "the one big thing," secretly knew that what he saw and rejected in others was indeed the proper and human way to get through life. His art knows it. *War and Peace* celebrates the rightness, indeed the necessity, of human self-satisfaction, as if Tolstoy knew that his own brand of dissatisfied egoism—a very different thing—was not likely to produce the harmonious outlines of a Russian idyll.

He identified the "stupidity" of his children with that of the mother, which was natural enough, a ploy used by many parents in the marital struggle, though usually more good-naturedly. Tolstoy wanted to rub it in. One of his sons has "the same castrated mind that his mother has. If you too should ever read this, forgive me: it hurts me terribly." Probably the son Seryozha read it in time, but his mother was reading such things in her husband's diary almost every day. At the same time there may have been some comfort and reassurance for her in the comically universal, James Thurber–like nature of Tolstoy's complaints and self-pity. Naturally his family "don't see and don't know my sufferings." What wife hasn't heard that her spouse is "depressed . . . a worthless, pathetic, unnecessary creature"? What wife or husband doesn't know that "I'm the only person who isn't mad in a house full of mad people, run by mad people"?

Self-knowledge, difficult enough for anyone at any time, and especially for Tolstoy's Lear-like genius, was made possible for both of them by the war between the diaries. While Tolstoy was presenting himself as a suffering martyr, his wife noted how everything in the house was done for his benefit, how he, who had run a school at Yasnaya Polyana in order to "impress" people, would not take the slightest interest in his own children's education. It is significant, too, that Tolstoy's novels, multitudinously true and perceptive as they are about the nature of family life, contain no real hint of what was going on; just as his early stories of the *Childhood* sequence never contained the sort of facts about himself which his sister remembered and shared with his wife. Honesty with each other, parodied by the ritual of reading each other's diaries, and by Tolstoy's insistence that his young fiancée should know all about his early sexual adventures, made it all the more impossible for them to be honest with themselves, was a kind of substitute for such self-knowledge.

So indeed was the kind of honesty which Tolstoy could always deploy in his writing. As with D. H. Lawrence, everything that went in was true but a good deal was left out. Both can only appear to their own advantage in their autobiographical novels, however much a Pierre or a Levin is presented as comical, a Paul Morel or Rupert Birkin as priggish. Both were deeply inspired and supported by their wives, yet if he had lived long enough Lawrence might well have left Frieda, as Tolstoy left his Sofia. The last ingratitude is the need to leave the person who has helped you become what you are. Lawrence at least had the good fortune and the intelligence to be genuinely classless: he never had to struggle, as Tolstoy did, with the clutches of a way of life which would not give him up, and which he could only defy in himself and his family by the absurdest of gestures, like cobbling his own boots, which he did very badly. Lawrence, for all his frailty, was physically a far more efficient person, for whom it was natural to do all the chores.

> Mowed. Stitched boots. Can't remember what I did. The girls love me. Masha clings to me. Letter from Chertkov and an officer.

Like so much in both diaries that sort of entry is touchingly commonplace. Everyone "forgets what I did," and wants wives and daughters to love them. Happiness in families is all the same, as stated in the opening sentence of *Anna Karenina*, but the unhappiness of the Tolstoys certainly had some rather special features. There was Chertkov for one thing, an insinuating aristocrat and former guards officer who had seen the light and become one of Tolstoy's most dedicated disciples. Sofia couldn't stand him and in this her instinct was surely right; he was a home-breaker of the most disagreeably high-minded kind. Sofia even goes so far as to suggest in her diary that there is between him and her husband a homosexual attachment. Here she was clearly wrong, but pardonably so when one considers that she was dealing with a man who was trying to get all the family assets, copyrights, and literary properties into his own hands. He haunts the pages of her diary before her husband left home to die.

In the early entries, when he was stationed in the Caucasus, Tolstoy is predictably frank about his sexual feelings, about both men and women. Lust he regarded as an illness, attendant on seeing a desirable woman, and to be got rid of as soon as possible by having her. Disgust of course afterwards. "I have never been in love with women," he remarks at that stage. He finds it embarrassing to look at men he is—or has been—in love with, as with a company commander whom he regards as a good solid homely type, backbone of the Russian army. But in general he believes he has fallen in love with men for some sort of excitement or delicious fear, "the fear of offending or not pleasing the object of one's love."

> I fell in love with men before I had any idea of the possibility of *pederasty*, but even when I knew about it the idea of the possibility of coitus never occurred to me. A strange case of inexplicable sympathy was Gautier. Although I had absolutely no relations with him except for buying books, I used to be thrown into a fever when he entered the room. My love for Islavin spoilt the whole eight months of my life in Petersburg for me. Although not consciously, I never bothered about anything else except how to please him . . . I always loved the sort of people who were cool towards me, and only took me for what I was worth . . . There is the case of Dyakov . . . I shall never forget the night when we were travelling from Pirogovo, and wrapped up under a travelling rug, I wanted to kiss him and cry. There was sensuality in that feeling, but why it took that course it's impossible to decide, because, as I said, my imagination never painted any lubricious pictures; on the contrary, I have a terrible aversion to all that.

This is straightforward enough. Shakespeare and Stendhal probably had the same sort of feelings, and Tolstoy had them on the same scale as he had everything else. But it is easy to see why his wife hated Chertkov so much. Nothing could be more infuriating than a man like that whom your husband was always trying to please, though he never made an effort to please you. No doubt with Chertkov, a guardsman and aristocrat with whose upbringing he felt in deep if unconscious accord, Tolstoy may have experienced in some way "the fear of offending or not pleasing the object of one's love." Even though Chertkov was his disciple, Tolstoy saw in him an idealized version of himself, free from his own humiliating family entanglements.

It is an odd paradox that Tolstoy's novels seem so "English" — as he wanted them to be — but his family life and temperament were as "Russian" as could be: mad, grotesque, touching, funny as anything in Dostoevsky. Boring too. You see the point and it begins to bore you. Unlike her husband, Sofia was a bore in herself, but her diaries are more vivacious than his, more zestful and surprising. Part of the pleasure is to see her getting her own back while at the same time cosseting her husband, who was that not unfamiliar type, a red-blooded hypochondriac. Both were also masochists on a truly Dostoevskian scale, and Sofia seems to have enjoyed nothing more than copying out her husband's diaries. "There is no such thing as love, *only the physical need for intercourse and the practical need for a life companion. I* only wish I had read that remark 29 years ago, then I would never have married him." (Tolstoy, one notes, rejected romantic "love" as emphatically as D. H. Lawrence was to do, as something fit only for women.)

> Self-admiration runs through all his diaries. It is strikingly obvious that people exist for him only if they directly concern him . . . He would like to destroy his old diaries, as he wants to appear before his children and the public as a patriarchal figure. Still the same old vanity!

Copying the diaries was no doubt a way of preserving her spouse's feet of clay for posterity. It grieved her terribly when he shouted at her, as he did most days, that he must leave this "hell": and yet few days passed without a reconciliation, tears, kisses, and hugs of love. Like many marital opponents, they needed each other in spite of everything, and it is likely that the final departure would only have been temporary if Tolstoy had survived.

London Review of Books, 1985

PART VIII

*How It Strikes a
Contemporary*

61

Conducting the Music

———

Books Do Furnish a Room
by Anthony Powell (1905–2000)

REVIEW IN THE *Stuttgarter Nachrichten* of the German translation of *A Dance to the Music of Time* finds that "of all big post-
war novels" it comes nearest to the ancient epic. This may startle
English devotees who welcome each installment as one welcomes a fresh
bout of gossip about the latest dirt on old so-and-so and who made what
scene at the party, but it is indeed true that in tone and form Anthony
Powell is closer to Homer than to Proust. Epic blends the natural and the
naïve with a sophisticated narrative art, presenting stylized encounters
and relations in a pattern of time-and-place cross-reference so true to our
factual experience that every bosom must return an echo. Not for nothing did Matthew Arnold select as one of his touchstones of great poetry
the moment when Helen recalls her brothers, unaware that they have
long since been in their graves back home in Lacedaemon. Not so differently did Pamela Flitton, in *The Military Philosophers*, obscurely refer to
an earlier relation with her uncle, Charles Stringham.

Pamela is a formidable figure, a wartime member of the women's
army corps with a twisted provenance and a sullen rage against life
(revealed in a penchant for vomiting with impassive malignancy into
fonts and Chinese vases) which in conjunction with her blank beauty,
makes her sexually irresistible to a great number of men, agile stoats of
the battlefield like Odo Stevens as well as the chairborne warrior and

power specialist Widmerpool. *The Military Philosophers* ended with Pamela married to Widmerpool and threatening as fateful an influence on his prospects as Hallgerd in *Njalsaga* had upon the lives of her successive husbands. *Books Do Furnish a Room* opens with Widmerpool a Labour MP and Pamela casting about for fresh experiences.

The secret of Pamela, as of all Anthony Powell's most memorable characters, is inaccessibility. Widmerpool, for example, is identified only by anecdote on an appropriate formulaic pattern. The author never succumbs to the lure of close analysis—even through the medium of a sedulous narrator—or of taking possession of him for moral and intellectual ends. The high intensity of intelligence which produces—in Henry James's phrase—characters "deeply studied and elaborately justified" is wisely eschewed by pseudo-epic craft. And paradoxically, its formalism produces characters not only more lifelike than those who are studied for a purpose, but far more durable over a prolonged period of acquaintance. Our curiosity about Pamela, Jeavons, and Widmerpool, as about Stringham and Templer (who have now died, respectively, in Singapore and Yugoslavia), is never satisfied, as it could not be in life. We welcome each meeting all the more because the genre in which they have their being is by definition not equipped to satisfy our curiosity, only to keep it alive.

Not that Nick Jenkins, the narrator, is sparing of comment and opinion, but his generalizations about life and literature, sex and society, do not impinge directly on the characters: they rather act as a kind of choric background. The author (again unlike Proust) has provided a contemporary Burton or Aubrey, with whom we are wholly at home but who has a better opinion of himself and his insight than we need to have. Apparently more coexistent with his creator than are Lockwood and Nelly Dean with Emily Brontë, or Marlowe with Conrad—for he also writes novels and works on seventeenth-century authors—he has much of their function: and this is ironically confirmed when he observes—inadvertently, as it were—on the last page of the novel, that "a novel is what its writer is," and that "this definition only opens up a lot more questions." Even so, this opinion is not his own but that of the writer X. Trapnel, another character who comes into the baleful orbit of Pamela Flitton.

Despite this kind of virtuosity the narrator is in fact helping to keep the work on a genial, naturalistic plane: though tone is of vital importance, it is not the unwavering tone of a Compton-Burnett or *nouveau roman*. Narrative naturalizes, as do those of the early Russians whom Anthony Powell admires—Mikhail Lermontov in particular. Even the evasions and insubstantialities enhance the overall choreography— humor can appear laborious when the actors require it, or seem a sudden deadpan flicker from further back. Social attitudes are pre-Victorian, with the unself-conscious crudeness of the fully assured, and so unaware of the contemporary need to show yourself—one way or another—on the side of decency, social justice, human values, etc., that it comes as something of a surprise to find—as the whole light project voluminously unfolds— that what survives is the significance of the last sentence of Chateaubriand's *René: Il n'est de bonheur que dans les voies communes.*

The method works best for families and for the numerous class of persons who have nothing to offer but themselves, but whose every word and gesture is designed to emphasize and advance that self. With intellectuals it is less happy. It brings out their absurdities, but cannot suggest the conjunction of these with real talent and sensibility—inaccessibility is a handicap here rather than an asset. The composer Moreland, who makes a brief appearance in *Books Do Furnish a Room*, seems to me a failure because endowed with an almost supernatural flow of learning, wit, and epigram. Yet, as Jenkins says, "it is not what happens to people but what they think happens": in a sense the novel shows not what Moreland says but what he thinks he is saying.

The Military Philosophers fell somewhat below the level of Anthony Powell's form: here he is right back on it. But the reasons for the lapse are not uninstructive. Jenkins became too important; he was too much in the limelight. Allied with this was a swerve to the documentary, too overt an attempt to enfold the atmosphere and personnel of the period, even down to recognizable sketches of top brass. Now Jenkins is back in focus. Unlike Proust's Marcel he should pervade his world without dominating it, for his experience of time is not the conquest of the *madeleine* but a passive recognition of the vagaries of chance. The metaphysical notion of time regained becomes for Anthony Powell the technical one of time as coincidence, bringing all home to the same party, pub, or country house. In many who thus arrive or return we can take no interest, just as we could not with their counterparts in life, but all alike convey precisely the right glint of familiarity without the vulgar possibility of a *roman à clef* identification. Evelyn Waugh—a good witness, one would have thought—pronounced himself unable to place any of them. (His own narrative methods, one might assert, are notably lacking in a comparable aesthetic harmony—personal romanticisms and obsessions worked off via the heroes of his novels have no place in his more equable and ultimately perhaps more congenial memoirs and travelogues narrated in the first person.)

It remains to ask whether the dramatis personae of *The Music of Time* are not too clannish and class-oriented to appeal to the audience of today and tomorrow. Must we know the language, recognize the form and the nuance, to be at home? I think myself that the answer is no, and that those who deprecate Powell as the chronicler of a localized culture group are on the wrong track. It is true that his range is less wide than it looks: the earls at one end and bohemians at the other have a lot in common, not least a kind of masonic preoccupation with their fellow members. But this itself helps to create a structure and density of felt life rarely attained by the novelist who attempts to confront the contemporary social scene without such a convention. The form requires Jenkins to be an assiduous cultivator of his acquaintance not on his own behalf but on ours. Indeed I suspect it is not the kind of circles he moves in who best relish reading about his social Odyssey, but those anti-Jenkinses who do their best not to recognize a chance-met acquaintance and hope that he in turn will do the same by them.

The Listener, 1971

62

Proud Prisoner

The Gulag Archipelago
by Aleksandr Solzhenitsyn (1918–)

SHELLEY REFERRED TO POETS as "the unacknowledged legislators of the world": Auden observed that the secret police would be stronger candidates for that title. Such a body personifies the state in its worst aspect, the aspect in no way related with *us*, but purely and wholly *them*. Yet, historically, the secret police has been associated with a high degree of civilization: with the Chinese and Persian hegemonies, the Roman Empire and the Byzantine, the Florentine and Venetian republics, as well as with the dynastic practices personified by Tudor monarchs, and by Louis XIV, Peter the Great, and Napoleon. Nor should one forget the special contribution of the Roman Church, whose aims and methods as the heir of Imperium have at times anticipated those of contemporary police-supervised ideologies. Dostoevsky gave a powerfully imaginative portrayal of them in the fable of the Grand Inquisitor in *The Brothers Karamazov*.

Although in *The Gulag Archipelago* Aleksandr Solzhenitsyn is concerned, above all, with handing on the truth and setting the record straight—"that is not how history is written," he remarks in parenthesis about some Soviet version of events—and although he is well aware of the long perspective of tyrants' techniques, he is emphatic in asserting that nothing in history is in any way comparable with the Soviet system, except that of Hitler. In one sense this is misleading. For overwhelmingly cogent geographical and historical reasons, Russia has always been a police state, and her intellectuals have always been aware of that fact and its seeming immortality: they have even taken, as Pushkin did at times, a sort of fierce and rueful pride in it, both hilarious and xenophobic. Someone in *Dr. Zhivago* refers to the Cheka as "these new *oprichniki*"—the *oprichniki* were the special security and terror troops of Ivan IV—and Colonel Pestel, the most formidable of the Decembrist conspirators against Tsarist absolutism in 1820, took it for granted that the new regime of enlightenment would employ the methods of the old. For the Bolshevik intellectuals, what was wanted was a simple transfer of the existing power structure, the dictatorship of the proletariat; and their assumption that methods did not matter, provided that the new philosophy of the state was "correct," entailed on Soviet Russia the same continuity of oppression, well before Stalin was able to take advantage of the fact.

Solzhenitsyn would certainly agree that the only hope for the individual lies in complex disunity and equilibrium inside the state: the laborious, wasteful, time-honored, and time-consuming chess game between divided centers of influence and authority (it is odd that the word "divisive" should be bandied about among us today as a political insult). The remarkable thing is that he has dared to contrive to set himself up in Russia as such an independent influence and center of power, frail and precarious, but authentic in the vital sense that the authorities at the moment find it more expedient to play chess with him—however brutally one-sided the game—than to abolish him. Such a stand, against such odds, exhibits all the drama of heroism and ideals which is notably lacking in our mundane, if freedom-enhancing, system of confrontations, dialogues, and *impasses*. Youthful radicals might note that he combines the charismatic appeal of a freedom fighter with the humanity and common sense of some unromantic ideologue of the Open Society.

The sense in which Solzhenitsyn is right in claiming that the Soviet system can only be compared to the Hitlerian lies in the widespread consent of the governed under those two tyrannies, in their profound and sinister popularity. Historical tyranny does not greatly concern itself with anything beyond the acquiescence of the masses: in exacting obedience, it is indifferent to the freedom implicit in our remaining *us*. Not so the modern version. Solzhenitsyn's most heartbreaking and uphill struggle is the effort to divide and segment a popular monolith, to restore, if he can do nothing else, the categories of *we* and *they*. Yevgeny Zamyatin in the Thirties set himself the same task in his satirical novel, *We*: to proclaim the tyranny of unanimity. By an obvious paradox, the islands of the "Gulag Archipelago," the myriad prison compounds scattered across the great sea of the Soviet Union, are also spots of freedom, places where *we* are on our own, because *they* have paid us the ultimate compliment of expulsion from the overwhelming category of their own first person plural.

Solzhenitsyn's novels, *Ivan Denisovich* and *The First Circle*, have made the point with all the space and impact of art. The account of arrest and arrival at the Lubianka in the latter novel is the most sustained imaginative sequence in his work: it describes initiation, indeed ordination, because a detainee, a *zek*, becomes in a few traumatic seconds a spiritually free man. It is this paradox which underlies the ambiguity of Solzhenitsyn's approach to political imprisonment in Russia, and his own imprisonment in particular. Although the point in *Gulag* is scorn and indignation for the repulsive facts, there is the same emphasis on the intellectual freedom of the camps, which makes a striking contrast with the nightmare of claustrophobia in Dostoevsky's *House of the Dead*, the nightmare of being cooped up month after month with the same terrible people.

But everywhere in the old Russian consciousness there is a mystique about jail, *ostrog*—that "good old Russian word" as Solzhenitsyn calls it. He has a streak in him of the mystical conservatism of Dostoevsky and Volashin. He sees the trauma, the division in his own life and consciousness, as a necessary liberation. There is no need to invoke Freud in recognizing Solzhenitsyn's unconscious and compulsive urge to become a martyr, to put himself outside the system by embracing *tyurzak*, the title of one of his chapters and, like *Gulag*, one of the many Soviet-type portmanteau words for the prison organization. He was thus the exact opposite of those earlier victims of the Soviet system, Kamenev, Bukharin, and the other Bolshevik intellectuals, who, after a lifetime's dedication to building the machine, were mentally and spiritually unable to resist or redefine themselves when arrested, and often could only cooperate with the machinery destroying them.

Underlying all Solzhenitsyn's work is a deep disillusion with, and distrust of, populist conformity, a system that can count on an overwhelming show of hands. He does not speak to the masses—to whom in the nineteenth century a Nekrasov or a Tolstoy saw themselves as appealing, and tailored their propaganda works accordingly—but to the historian and the nonconformist. The history he passionately records may be only for the few, but that is all the more reason for recording it. Of course, like Pushkin's Prophet, he would wish to set fire to the hearts of all his fellow countrymen, but that is not the way things are. From Radischev onward, the history of Russia is full of martyr intellectuals who hand on the torch, not to the many, but to others like themselves. For the trouble with political prisoners is that they cannot but constitute a classless elite, a *separate* body, with different standards and different ideas, and the masses are never much concerned with the fate of an elite—why should they be? Inevitably, in Russia, they were far more concerned with economic than with political freedom.

Few historians are impartial, however priceless the facts they hoard and transmit, and it is natural that Solzhenitsyn should play some things up and others down. This seems to be the case in his account of Vlasov's army, a large force commanded by one of the most able Soviet generals, who was cut off and surrendered in 1942 after the High Command had compelled him to continue a hopeless offensive, not unlike that of the German 6th Army at Stalingrad. Disgusted by stupidity and callousness at the top, Vlasov went over to the Germans, followed by the bulk of his command. What sort of a regime is it, demands Solzhenitsyn, from which so many good men could be so completely disaffected, even to the point of fighting against their mother country? But—at least to an outsider—the striking thing about the war years is not how many Soviet citizens turned against the regime, but how few did: and this cannot have been altogether because of police terror, or even "Mother Russia" and German brutality, but because of a genuinely heartfelt if propaganda-fed support for Stalin and for the truth and justice of the communist system.

This, of course, is the kind of support that Marxists dream of and call true democracy, in contrast to which bourgeois democracy of the ballot box invites a gesture not of solidarity but of separatism. (One would like to hear Solzhenitsyn's comment on a recent *New Statesman* correspondent's claim that "communists are *ipso facto* democrats who do not believe that democracy consists in voting for a new government every five years or so.") Solzhenitsyn sees Soviet democracy as the force that made possible the continued existence of the Gulag Archipelago. For, like Komsomols or the Co-op, the KGB are, in a sense, a genuine consensus phenomenon. Not everyone works for them, but a surprising number of ordinary citizens are affiliated on a part-time basis, as it were for mail order or advertising. They do not, no doubt, want to hear or to know what may be the end product of their activities—to that extent the secret police remain secret—and a Russian might retort that capitalism produces its own lugubrious crop of vested interest—

> Half-ignorant, they turned an easy wheel,
> That set sharp racks at work, to pinch and peel—

but it is certain that the ingrown nature of the system makes Solzhenitsyn's appeal all the more likely to fall on wary ears, even if it could be published in Russia. Western capitalism, as Watergate witnesses, is as eager at the popular level to expose and exacerbate its sores as Russia—by long conditioning—is to conceal and deny her own.

In the Paris YMCA-Press edition of *Gulag* is a photograph of Artillery Captain Solzhenitsyn in February 1944, the three stars on his shoulder straps proudly in evidence. It bears the ironic title *nezadolgo pered*—not long to go. After his abrupt arrest at the front, for criticizing Stalin in letters to a friend also on active service, his first friend and fellow-captive was an Estonian, who fascinated him with accounts of the political arrangements of that small bourgeois democracy. What seems to have struck him as wonderful, indeed incredible, was a social system that calmly accepted the discrepancy, even incompatibility, of individual aims and goals; and his growing sense of the freedom to be found in incarceration began to arrange itself around such centers of independence.

In his novels, as much as in the explosive immediacy of these notes and records for a future generation, Solzhenitsyn seizes on moments that begin to unravel the density and weight of the great political lie. Just after his arrest he met two tank officers in the same case, relieving themselves outside the communal cell. One of them quietly replies to the KGB man's order to hurry up: "We do these things slowly." "Where?" "In the

Red Army." These are the sentiments—true at any time, anywhere—of the fighting soldier about the staff-wallah, but they also reveal the point where *we* and *they* can at last be openly invoked. Although his badges had been cut off, Solzhenitsyn at first found comfort and pride in the thought that he was an officer; his moment of truth came when he started to feel pride only in being a prisoner.

Moments of revelation, of sudden and often oppressive and demoralizing freedom, are not uncommon in the great Russian novels. In the same East Prussia in which Solzhenitsyn was arrested, Nikolai Rostov, in *War and Peace*, undergoes a similar experience when his Colonel gets into trouble with the authorities, and all sorts of frightening and dangerous thoughts about power and injustice, about the adored Emperor and the peace he has just made with Napoleon, begin to crowd into Rostov's mind. They do not remain there of course: he can burrow back into the enormous friendly bosom of the Russian family, the home and haven of the novel, though in its final chapter such ideas are beginning to raise their heads again. But the comparison serves to underline Solzhenitsyn's point: tyranny, even Russian tyranny, was as nothing in the past, compared to the present; its present monumental scale and scope dwarf the majestic proportions of Tolstoy's novel to a kind of childlike innocence. If Solzhenitsyn still thinks of Russia as a family, it is clearly as one in which, to adapt Orwell's phrase, the wrong members are in charge.

Solzhenitsyn wrote *Gulag* in the Sixties, taking ten years about it, and the Russian-language version which has now appeared in the West contains only the first two of seven parts. He intended to keep its existence a secret indefinitely, but the KGB got wind of its existence, and Solzhenitsyn authorized publication of a copy which had long before been smuggled to the West. Unfortunately, the material with which it is packed full and tight would be far more disconcerting and compulsive reading to the Russians than it is to us, and there is very little likelihood that they will ever see it. We ourselves have already supped full of these horrors, and can only hope we do not bring too much of an element of the consumer's morbid self-indulgence to this further banquet.

The book is certainly written with immense nervous force and feeling, idiomatic, allusive, and filled with exclamation and parenthesis which in Russian give an impression of total unself-consciousness, but which would be exceedingly difficult to translate in such a way that their almost Voltairian tone came across. There is a great contrast with the calm and craftsmanship of the novels; and much of the edgy, explosive reminiscence exhibits that curious lack of verisimilitude which shows the author to be a novelist who needs to distance and regroup his material before it takes on the three-dimensional truth of fiction. A slight instance: the tank officer's reply to the KGB man is no doubt based on fact, but as recounted here it seems *voulu*, almost in the category of retorts we doubt ever got retorted. Strong feeling, however justified, does not always have its will with an intimate buttonholing technique, and the more impersonal sections, particularly those on the history of capital punishment in Russia, or on the way that camps were run as a business are in some ways even more absorbing than the immediate experience of the man who suffered and was there.

The Listener, 1974

63

Too Good for This World

High Windows
by Philip Larkin (1922–1985)

A LTHOUGH THERE ARE not so many of them, Philip Larkin's poems enclose on first impression a large and rather featureless area of our inner and outer geography, an area where vocabulary is usually limited, since it has only to convey a sense that we are not so young as we were; that life has made us and not we ourselves; that we seem to have missed our chances, if any; and that much more in life is to be endured than enjoyed. Pleasures here approximate to the moments when we leave off banging our heads against the wall, or having them banged for us.

The poems that explore this familiar place with such inimitable skill have the air of being very meticulously mounted and developed, as if they had spent months in the darkroom or years at the workbench in the garden shed. "In every sense empirically true"—like the young lady in the photograph album—they are coaxed on to the careless celluloid as if to give the poetic equivalent of its dim candor, and as if, too, they would accept with bleak, sardonic relish the fate of its image:

> Unvariably lovely there,
> Smaller and clearer as the years go by.

They are also epiphanic intermissions: equivalents in art to the moments when we leave off banging our heads against the wall.

If that does not sound much, it would also be true to say that they are the most refined and accurate expression possible of a national as well as a universal area of awareness: they are very English in fact. They are not sentimentally so, as John Betjeman's deliberately are—it is not in the least a pejorative word to use in appreciating *him*—and they reject with equal deliberation any kind of eager or enthusiastic response from the reader. Enthusiasm is not this artist's state of mind. The great virtues of the culture he celebrates—for celebrate it he does—are negative ones. Dim, decent, dignified, and nowadays decidedly old-fashioned—those virtues were never conditioned to feel that we have the right to get, and should get, much out of life. The comfort lies in the conviction that there is very little to be got, and in the gratification of this awareness.

There *is* life before death, but not much. It is the philosophy of the urban Victorian world that Mayhew examined, and it is significant that a fine poem in Larkin's first major collection, *The Less Deceived*, is concerned to set up and imagine the situation of one of his child prostitutes. Others, of course, have got the same apprehensions into poetry. They are the natural base from which Hardy went on to build his more intellectual and metaphysical theories of disconsolation. Kipling took his customary and slightly sinister pleasure in the dignities of deprivation (a nurse in one of his stories observes: "I don't want anything, thank you, and if I did I shouldn't get it"). Eliot pervaded *The Waste Land* with the sense of such things: overdoing it, indeed, in the first and longer version of the poem.

Larkin certainly does not overdo this, or anything else. But *High Windows* differs a little from its two predecessors in sometimes taking a more swingingly satiric, even ribald, view of its own *Weltanschauung*:

> Sexual intercourse began
> In nineteen sixty-three
> (Which was rather late for me)—
> Between the end of the *Chatterley* ban
> And the Beatles' first LP.

"Annus Mirabilis" is typical of Larkin's kidding on the level; the envy of the young that it mimes with such wryly glum delicacy is both heartfelt and judiciously contemptuous. The same is true of the title poem "High Windows," which develops a typically lucid Larkinian rumination:

> When I see a couple of kids
> And guess he's fucking her and she's
> Taking pills or wearing a diaphragm,
> I know this is paradise

The vocabulary shows that Larkin has moved with the times since the *Chatterley* ban while retaining as a piquant foil some old box-camera phrases. (Surely "wearing a diaphragm" lingers on an unsettling archaism with the same deliberation as T. S. Eliot's "stockings and slippers, camisoles and stays"?—femininity is invented in words by men, and to make it old-fashioned is a well-known self-seducer.) Only the young seem free, and the poet imagines himself looked at in turn when young:

> *He*
> *And his lot will go down the long slide*
> *Like free bloody birds.* And immediately
> Rather than words comes the thought of high windows:
>
> The sun-comprehending glass,
> And beyond it, the deep blue air, that shows
> Nothing, and is nowhere, and is endless.

"Sun-comprehending glass" is as triumphant as Yeats's "rook-delighting heaven" in the way it sweeps an ancient majesty of language right up to the moment. The arresting image, with all its bravery on and tackle trim, is typical of Larkin's way of verbalizing oblivion—"the solving emptiness / That lies just under all we do"—as he did in "Next, Please":

> Only one ship is seeking us, a black-
> Sailed unfamiliar, towing at her back
> A huge and birdless silence. In her wake
> No waters breed or break.

But as always with Larkin the cogitatory life of the poem is more absorbing and ambiguous than its rhetoric. Perhaps the young really *are* getting it, now? The poem knows the irony: that deprivation and desire for oblivion can be held in an image, but not the unreflected and unreflecting existence envied in the poem's opening. The image is needed by the poet to exorcize the thought of free animal being, and also to justify his own exclusion from it and distract us from the mastery that licenses exclusion. These deep images of living are strictly and bleakly behavioral —

> . . . though our element is time,
> We are not suited to the long perspectives
> Open at each instant of our lives.
> They link us to our losses . . .

In Yeats's "The Road at My Door" the sight of soldiers sent him off into an image of what he could be or might have been:

> I count those feathered balls of soot
> The moor-hen guides upon the stream
> To silence the envy in my thought;
> And turn towards my chamber, caught
> In the cold snows of a dream.

In the introduction to his first collection, *The North Ship*. Larkin wrote that he spent three years "trying to write like Yeats, not because I liked his personality or understood his ideas but out of infatuation with his music." Music — a quite different music — wonderfully continues, but there may have been one or two other things that stuck too.

Poetic egotism certainly did not, for personality is dissolved in these poems into all our behaviors: while their verbal fastidiousness never seems to patronize the vaguely dolorous nature of humdrum self-awareness, but to be its natural secretion. In the *Dream Songs* Berryman, in the persona of "Henry," has something of this power of pulling us instantly into the quick world of the poem, while not seeming to be poetic at us:

> Life, friends, is boring. We must not say so.
> . . . and moreover my mother told me as a boy
> (repeatedly) "Ever to confess you're bored
> means you have no
>
> Inner Resources." I conclude now I have no
> inner resources, because I am heavy bored.
> Peoples bore me,
> literature bores me, especially great literature,
> Henry bores me . . .

That is certainly not boring! But what Berryman discovers to us as sedi-tious is to Larkin self-evident. And under the kidding there is something portentous (in no bad sense) in the American's tone with us that is quite alien to Larkin, who is far too English to claim a peculiar wound, and whose intimacy is that of the lounge bar, never the psychiatric couch. That, too, distinguishes his from Auden's more coterie-type intimacy, though the magic life of *things* in his poems has a marked resemblance to many of Auden's.

Image of thing and place has a particular importance in Larkin's poetry. As a superb poem like "The Importance of Elsewhere" shows, he can make a difficult concept pellucidly clear by sheer accuracy of phrase and nuance, but this metaphysical skill is overshadowed by verbal imagi-nation of another kind. It shows the big difference, which revealed itself in the wake of the first romantic poets, between what might be called a poetry of artificial arrest, like his, and the poetry of natural progression. Larkin is careful never to let us know what happens between our odd meetings in that lounge bar: he vanishes; and this sort of vanishing com-pels us all the more because it does not come into the common cate-gories of life or apply to its normal relations. It is exotic, and aesthetic, as if indeed we were meeting someone who fascinated us into making things up about him, in default of finding out the reality. This seems fanciful no doubt: but think of the poetry of progression in the same social terms. Wordsworth, or William Carlos Williams, or Robert Lowell, we have with us always, as one of the family; and very boring their company can be.

The peculiar intensities of the poetry of arrest are all internal—total reality focused by the intent gaze of imagination. It cannot be "on the side of life" as a continuous and contingent process, because its subject is contingency itself, distilled—Larkin's supreme speciality—into verbal essence. For such a poetry any continuity is impossible, would entail boredom and disenchantment. Yeats flirted with a doctrine of arrest: Keats and Tennyson are its great involuntary exponents. "He will not come," says Mariana, for the poem would not exist if he did. Perhaps he came later? Perhaps: but that is not what either a Tennyson or a Larkin poem can afford to be about. Larkin's "nutritious images" are those of the photograph album, the master-image of arrest.

This seems worth emphasizing, because of the assumption which gives Larkin his credentials among students—and not among them only—that he is a poet of today's "lifestyles," celebrating our common surroundings, customs, and mode of being. "Here" appears in university entrance papers in expectation of such a response. (Betjeman has called Larkin "the John Clare of the building estates." Though one can see how the misunderstanding arises this is surely misleading: one might equally, on the strength of "The Eve of St. Agnes," call Keats the poet of social life in castles.) In fact Larkin's imagination of his material is in the most absolute sense aesthetic and ironic. A lot of his poems take such a moment as that in which Keats's lovers of St. Agnes' Eve "fled away into the storm." They are starting their honeymoon, looking at an old songbook, being looked at in the snapshot of—

> a past that no one now can share
> No matter whose your future

—but there can be no progress into what Wordsworth called "the world which is the world of all of us—the place where in the end we find our happiness, or not at all." It is by seeing that world in the mirror that the poet gives us such dazzling glimpses of it.

There is thus a droll sense in which his poems, like the poster-girl of "Sunny Prestatyn"—"She was too good for this life"—really are too good for it. They cannot, as the poetry of progression can, unbend into verbosity or miscalculation, enlarge into extended explanations or into prose. The comparison often made with *Life Studies* is again only true up to a point, for Lowell's poems lead into the kind of life that cannot be arrested or preserved: the poetry like the life recognizes the inevitability of its own alteration—perhaps into more and worse words but different ones—a poetry that is hurried on by change, and subject both to the indignity and the dignity of its laws. Lowell is not a greater poet than Larkin, nor was Wordsworth than Keats; but the poetry of Lowell and Wordsworth has a more extended and more native residence in the world that is the world, undergoing the infirmities of its span.

Even Larkin's two novels are not prose in the same sense in which the poetry of natural progression can be. *A Girl in Winter* is an astonishing tour de force, one of the finest and best sustained prose poems in the language. Beside it everything comparable—by Virginia Woolf or Stevie Smith, say—seems uncertain or shrill or self-absorbed. Technically it is profoundly original, but it not only seems tranquilly unconcerned with technique and experiment, it can also be devoured like a real novel, with total engrossment in what is going to happen. And yet it is a still life, longer but no less perfect than the sonnet in *High Windows* called "The Card Players." *Jill* is perhaps less successful partly because it is set in Oxford and absorbs a more stylized and general apprehension of that place, and partly because Jill herself is a parody of the Larkin genre girl, proffered too sardonically at second hand.

We never discover what country Katherine, the foreign heroine of *A Girl in Winter*, comes from, and the few clues about her background appear in the form of glimpses through a window. In a most ingenious sense the book takes on the vision of a double voyeur: we and the author see Katherine as if in the context of a vivid, inexplicable and seductive life, the vividness depending on the voyeur's awareness that for him it has no past or future; while simultaneously she (and we) see her English experiences in the same way, as a funny and fascinating pattern that is not her "real" life. This sounds tiresomely intellectual and theoretical, and in a *nouveau roman* it would certainly be so; but in Larkinian fashion it is done with such blandness and ease, and so much deadpan social comedy, that it seems as if nothing at all unusual were occurring. So much so that the book appears to have fallen into a kind of quiet slot, well away from fashion and sex and all other forms of literary preoccupation or engagement. Neither of Larkin's novels seems to be easily available today, and oddly enough neither appears on the list of his publications opposite the title page of *High Windows*. One would almost believe a conspiracy to keep quiet about them, as if the secret reader who is looking in at the window does not want to find himself part of a large audience.

The poem "The Importance of Elsewhere" reveals the secret of the Larkinian aesthetic. In his world we (and he) are in a foreign country, ticket of leave men, licensed to see without taking part. The insistent and utter familiarity of what we are shown ("This is a real girl in a real place / In every sense empirically true") becomes for us the fascination of a strangeness, of the once glimpsed and never forgotten. In the poetry of progression we are in our daily lives, where "no elsewhere underwrites my existence." In the Larkinian suspension we are abroad, knowing our proper place to be dully if reassuringly back home. The sense of exclusion is turned into the reward of art, but the poet recognizes wryly that when he is at home his existence cannot be underwritten by this art: he must find "customs and establishments" invisible to it, unpartaking of it. The paradox is that by pretending to the absolute commonplace the poetry shows just how far away that commonplace really is.

But it is not a cold or cruel paradox: there are none of the attitudes here of art for art's sake. To put it in an Irishism, in Larkin the poetry of arrest has moved a stage further. For with him it is the characteristics of arrest itself that both make the joke and move the poem: Larkin's humanity is in the humor, as Owen said his poetry was in the pity. One would not insult this poetry with clichés about "compassion," any more than one would emphasize "the pity" in Owen's finest poems, like "The Send-Off":

> So secretly, like wrongs hushed up, they went.
> They were not ours:
> We never heard to which front these were sent.

Feeling is best registered in both poets by a kind of withdrawnness, appropriate to the craftsman of arrest, which creates an effect both searching and impassive. And the moralist in Larkin is of course peculiarly deadpan, his assertions being themselves a form of humor, as in the concluding stanzas of the first poem in *High Windows*, "To the Sea":

> If the worst
> Of flawless weather is our falling short,
> It may be that through habit these do best,
> Coming to water clumsily undressed
> Yearly; teaching their children by a sort
> Of clowning; helping the old, too, as they ought.

One of the glimpses through the window of *A Girl in Winter* is of a woman deprived of all other human choice by having to look after a bedridden mother, while an extended genre piece, the most comical and moving in the book, describes taking a sufferer to the dentist. In all such matters Larkin is close to Hardy, his great love, from whose miniature masterpieces like "The Self Unseeing" or "The Parasol," he has drawn so much profit. But Hardy does not limn in the mirror, or does not seem to; his verse is more casually attached to the world than Larkin's can afford to be, and its banality is never quite so meticulous, never so advertently adroit. It has the dilution and the garrulity of unself-consciousness, that goes with the poetry of progression. Keats, too (*pace* Christopher Ricks), seems quite unconscious of what it means to be a voyeur: he just devoutly is one, while Larkin quietly and sardonically gloats over that status, and the refinements he brings to it.

The importance of Larkin's consciously turning a virtue out of arrest and exclusion cannot be overstressed, because it makes him wholly original and independent of the conservative conventions and influences he otherwise depends on. Take the opening of the second stanza of "The Whitsun Weddings":

> All afternoon, through the tall heat that slept
>   For miles inland,
> A slow and stopping curve southwards we kept.

Beautiful, but the lilt and the word order are purely Hardy's; while those of stanza seven's beginning are entirely Larkin:

> Just long enough to settle hats and say
>> *I nearly died,*
> A dozen marriages got under way.

The reason is the discreet hilarity of Larkin's own position, looking on. To find himself onboard a trainful of brides would certainly have inspired Hardy, but to something nearer the grim Fun of Folklore. Larkin's response is the more subtle for being more separated, as things are today. "Got under way" is a parody of what the Larkinian moment cannot do, and the point is emphasized in the marvelous close—

> . . . it was nearly done, this frail
> Travelling coincidence; and what it held
> stood ready to be loosed with all the power
> That being changed can give. We slowed again,
> And as the tightened brakes look hold, there swelled
> A sense of falling, like an arrow-shower
> Sent out of sight, somewhere becoming rain.

"All the power that being changed can give": the power of the poet—and he knows it—is in the function of not being changed. The tension between their standing ready to be loosed, and his not being, is poignant and extremely funny: what Keats called the "swelling into reality" goes on out of sight, where the rain it raineth every day, and this poetry would be dissolved if it followed. For the strange romantic beauty of those last images also have a dense Shakespearian suggestiveness about them, an inwardness printed in every detail.

Is this to say that it is the poet and not the weddings that the poetry is looking in at? Almost, if not quite: the two complement, forming a magic dual interior. Hardy's confrontation with an unborn pauper child, or journeying boy at midnight on the Great Western, is absolute: Larkin's with the raped girl of "Deceptions" is characteristically elliptic:

> Slums, years, have buried you. I would not dare
> Console you if I could. What can be said,
> Except that suffering is exact, but where
> Desire takes charge, readings will grow erratic?
> For you would hardly care
> That you were less deceived, out on that bed,
> Than he was, stumbling up the breathless stair
> To burst into fulfilment's desolate attic.

The metaphysical point is bound to usurp the actuality, as the poet knows and needs: it is this poetry's way of making "all disagreeables evaporate": "Self's the Man," as another title tells us, and self is there, implying all fulfillment in this hideous form, the breathless stair leading here to the desolate attic, but everywhere in life to the "cold hill side." Yet that is less than just, for Larkin can move most by suspending the secret humor of his own self-perception and imposing a real gravity ("For you would hardly care") in the necessary gap between poet and victim.

Not the straight face but the face unconscious of itself is needed here; and yet the pervasive drollery of the poetry—and how many modern poets can make one suddenly guffaw as Larkin does?—is usually brought about by keeping a straight face in the mirror, as in "I remember, I remember," where it is precisely the substances of the past that feed the poetry which are revealed as not being really there:

> . . . I'll show you, come to that,
> The bracken where I never trembling sat

The mirror—"that padlocked cube of light"—turns out in his own case to be empty; the snapshots to be greedily devoured are never of one's own past: of that, all that can be said is that "nothing, like something, happens anywhere."

"Vers de Société," one of the best and funniest poems in *High Windows*, is a superb piece of Larkinian introspection along the same lines, as enlightening as it is relaxed:

My Wife and I have asked a crowd of craps
To come and waste their time and ours: perhaps
You'd care to join us? In a pig's arse, friend.
Day comes to an end.
The gas fire breathes, the trees are darkly swayed.
And so *Dear Warlock-Williams: I'm afraid—*

Funny how hard it is to be alone.

The poem uses in its own unique way the Yeatsian rhetorical mode—query, demurring, and restatement. Considering the point of parties, it suggests that an underlying need hiding under a mask of reluctance and boredom are all that is left now of religious observance. Adapting Von Hügel, we meet people not because we like them but in order that we may like them, a compulsion leading to typical Larkinian crucifixion—

Holding a glass of washing sherry, canted
Over to catch the drivel of some bitch
Who's read nothing but *Which*

—but such a view of social life conceals in its turn a simpler sort of desperation:

Are, then, these routines

Playing at goodness, like going to church?
Something that bores us, something we don't do well
(Asking that ass about his fool research)
But try to feel, because, however crudely,
It shows us what should be?
Too subtle, that. Too decent, too. Oh hell,

Only the young can be alone freely.
The time is shorter now for company,
And sitting by a lamp more often brings

Not peace, but other things.
Beyond the light stand failure and remorse
Whispering *Dear Warlock-Williams: Why of course—*

The down-to-earth elegance reminds us that Larkin's originality was incubating at the same time as Kingsley Amis's; and "The Old Fools" is on a very Amis-like topic:

This is why they give

An air of baffled absence, trying to be there
Yet being there. . . . and them crouching below
Extinction's alp, the old fools, never perceiving
How near it is. This must be what keeps them quiet:
The peak that stays in view wherever we go
For them is rising ground. Can they never tell
What is dragging them back, and how it will end? Not at night?
Not when the strangers come? Never, throughout
The whole hideous inverted childhood? Well,
        We shall find out.

Admirable as they are, these big and more impersonal poems—"Show Saturday" (a country fête was also a set piece of *A Girl in Winter*), "The Old Fools," and "The Building" (about hospital)—they do lack the secret drama to which one becomes so addicted in Larkin, the peculiar drama of intimacy. It shows his range, among other things, that he is as good at the big quiet subjects as on those swift mirror-like confrontations; but one learns more, in every sense, from this latter sort, which in turning away from life ("Beneath it all, desire of oblivion runs") show us so much about how life is actually got through. It would not be invidious to say that Amis's world lacks among other things the inner dimension of refinement, which proceeds from a total absence of go-getting in this art, and from its motions of withdrawal which are also motions of perpetuation—no poetry seems less to score while sending every ball to the boundary.

Larkin's only danger is the kind of success that removes him from us into a less refined area of feeling—it happens in the beautifully crafted bespoke poems in this volume—"The Explosion" and "Going, Going"—and makes them resemble those now-all-too-famous masterpieces, "Church Going" and "An Arundel Tomb." (This latter, in particular, shows the dangers of bringing a nimbleness rather too morally fluent to a theme deserving Hardy's tough antiquarian piety.) These poems are arrested in the only pejorative sense which the word could carry in a Larkin context, in that we begin to have the sense in them of rereading as replay—a fine performance on the Larkin.

One mentions such an impression only because it is so rare, and because the slow-grown perfection of each piece might lead one to think it more common: in fact it is one of the typical surprises of Larkin that a poem with the almost Mozartian lightness and grace of "Cut Grass" (or the earlier "At Grass") should also reveal such a considered specific gravity.

Such pieces combine miraculous performance with the strange expectancy and reticence of being that shines in the depth of a Vermeer interior—still life unending in what it can both query and prolong. The reticence is more a feeling than a fact—we learn, as I have suggested, much about the poet—but the relief of not having to, of entering a relation in which old-fashioned manners play so large a part, is as great as the fascination of gazing into lighted interior or indeterminately civic mood. Larkin is as little on the side of togetherness as he is on the side of life, which shows by contrast just how vulgarly *intrusive* and unprivate is the premise of most art today, in the theatre and novel above all, but in poetry too.

It goes without saying that the techniques are also traditional—it is pleasurable to observe the adaptation of Praed's social stanza in the trilogy poem "Livings," or to compare Larkin's use of sonnet rhymes or of the ode stanza, interpolating a short line among pentameters, with that of Spenser, Keats, and Matthew Arnold. But more important is his updating of the fundamental aesthetic which they all in different ways took for granted: that the business of poetry is to delight and console, to calm and to satisfy, above all to entrance into completeness the inadequacy and the "disagreeables" of living. It is to the interest of many writers now to assume the opposite: that what is boring and squalid—or, worse, merely grossly familiar—should be faithfully enlarged and underlined in any art that is honestly and fearlessly "with it." They do so because they are incapable of achieving that paradox of transmutation which this poetry displays, on a scale as spacious and felicitous as that of its many English predecessors.

The Times Literary Supplement, 1974

64

From the Ridiculous to the Ridiculous

Napoleon Symphony
by Anthony Burgess (1917–1993)

IN THE FERTILITY of his enterprise, his louche congenial knockabout confidence, Mr. Burgess may remind us of one of those Elizabethan professionals, like Thomas Nashe or Thomas Deloney, who tried their hands at practically every species of literary composition, always coming up with something readable and rewarding, but curiously unsettling, too, as if their freewheeling methods cast a kind of doubt on the more accepted kinds of literary achievement. There is a sense in which *The Unfortunate Traveller*, for instance, deflates the artificial pretension of *The Shepheardes Calender* or *Venus and Adonis* so that we feel—not so much "Ah, here is life at last," as "Why do Spenser and Shakespeare have to go to those lengths to get it into literature?" The effect is deceptive. Burgess, no less than Nashe, is an artificer in his own line, but he does not seem to take us so far from presentness and actuality as do in their various ways James Joyce or Scott Fitzgerald or Saul Bellow or Anthony Powell.

This is only partly a compliment. Such "real authors" (if one may rather uncivilly beg the question) as those I mention work the magic in two ways: by making contingency itself into form—thus removing us from its actual daily pressures—and by removing all traces of the workshop from our immediate gaze. Mr. Burgess, whenever we remeet him in a literary setting, seems to be standing knee-deep in the shavings of new methods, grimed with the metallic filings of bright ideas. A *Clockwork Orange*, for example, was a book which no one could take seriously for what was supposed to happen in it—its plot and "meaning" were the merest pretenses—but which contained a number of lively notions, as when his delinquents use Russian slang and become murderous on Mozart and Beethoven. In a work by Burgess nothing is connected necessarily or organically with anything else but is strung together with wires and pulleys as we go.

Thus we can discount at once the claim, hopefully supplied by the blurb, that what we have here is "a grand and loving tragicomic symphony to Napoleon Bonaparte." The symphonic stuff—a novel in four movements and so on—is no more than bits of string, and it is one of the many endearing things about this author that he does not really bother us (and possibly irritate us) by pretending it is anything else. He is as enterprising as Nabokov, but his flair does not need pretension to keep it going: he is not an aesthete but a man of letters. Why should he have wanted to write about Napoleon? Probably because of the interesting technical challenge involved—an almost impossible challenge, but writers like Burgess and his predecessors are not worried about finicky matters of possibility provided they can keep a workshop going and amuse themselves and their public.

Burgess is immensely well informed; he has read everything on the period, and relished it. His fondness for Napoleon in some sense echoes the strange obsessive reverence paid by Kafka and Henry James, whose diaries are full of meditations on the great man's doings—James, indeed, in his last days, had Marbot's memoirs constantly beside his bed. All writers are apt to admire men of power and decision who alter the face of Europe with a few battles and a few strokes of the pen, but Burgess's interest in Napoleon, like that of his in some sense predecessors Tolstoy and Hardy, is less with the facts and the fascination of power than with the psychology and motive of the period that let him get away with it, wooed him, applauded him, and finally had enough.

For Tolstoy, Bonaparte was the supreme egotist (and egotism was a subject Tolstoy knew all about) who opposed himself to the processes of life—life being represented by the Russian family. Mr. Burgess takes a simpler and more down-to-earth view of the matter: his Napoleon is reminiscent, it must be admitted, of his portrait of Shakespeare in an earlier historical fantasy, and both have a good deal in common with the durable figure of Enderby, the protofigure of many of Burgess's fictions. They are, that is to say, observant, civilized, distracted, victimized, and endowed with a rich stream of consciousness. Burgess's Napoleon is always being got at by someone in the imperial entourage; generals have a go under their breath on the subject of his many failings; Josephine despises and cuckolds him; Marie-Louise patronizes him; but he is really much *nicer* than any of them. In the background is Leopold Bloom, image of what we all are or would like to be, no doubt, in and to ourselves, and archetype of what I am afraid would have to be described—in view of later developments—as the new permissiveness in characterization.

Mr. Burgess's very wide knowledge of and sensibility to literature (inside this kind of writer an autodidact don is always struggling to get out) makes him an admirable popularizer of works by—to risk the phrase again—"real authors," and he has adapted the Joycean stream of consciousness to a popular level for almost any use. *Napoleon Symphony* is in a good and modest sense a popular novel, using highbrow techniques in a not too demanding way, and throwing in plenty of eating (chicken marengo after the battle and Napoleon's favorite Chambertin), sex, and jokes, with all the agreeably ghoulish details of battlefields and frozen corpses. Seriousness of vision there is none, nor can there be any attempt at subtlety of insight. Facility—and Bloomian good nature—are all. Here, to illustrate the point, is Napoleon on the Queen of Prussia:

"There was a moment, Talleyrand—" He mused, amused, bemused.

(One must interpolate at this point that one of Mr. Burgess's more self-indulgent practices is a kind of verbal doodling, less Joycean than laxly Euphuistic and Elizabethan, which sometimes cannot be restrained from breaking out into sections of verse, not seriously intended, one assumes, to underwrite the symphonic image, or to be admired in their own right, but to jolly along the pleasantly undemanding associations of Hardy's Dynasts or Tchaikovsky's Overture.)

"She was sitting in her carriage, waiting, while the King was having
a final word with young Alexander. Eyes full of tears, smiling bravely,
so beautiful and so much *alone*—because that long-faced bastard

she's married to is no good to man, beast, woman, Prussia, or anything else. There was a moment, I say, when I nearly jumped in
there and gave her what she so obviously needed—passionate kisses
on mouth and neck and bosom, a pair of strong arms around her.
And then, of course, she would have gone on about dear suffering
Prussia, and then I would have said, Oh, have it all back, poor angel,
what is a kingdom compared to a woman's tears? The world well lost,
there's a play about that, I think. But I was strong, Talleyrand, I did
not yield."

This is boneless stuff, no skeleton of point beneath it. Is it irony? he was
not strong. Or pity? the great cannot yield to their impulses and be
human. Or a demonstration of the commonplace? history is a bundle of
trivial and misshapen needs and muffled impulses. All that really emerges
is that Napoleon is nicer than Talleyrand—the Blazes Boylan of the
book—and must be so, because it is his consciousness that author and
reader inhabit. Mr. Burgess's problem, which he cannot be said to have
solved, is that his more informed readers cannot really need this kind of
thing to imagine themselves into the Napoleonic era, while all the sound
knowledge—of corps commanders, horse batteries, Continental System—which he strews so prodigally but inconspicuously around cannot
do much to edify his more popular readership.

On the other hand the book is genuinely funny at times, and it is then
that history virtually becomes bunk for Mr. Burgess. A picaresque Every-
man takes over, finding himself (as picaresque heroes and Marx brothers
do) in situations that are none of his making and certainly not to be
understood by him. And here Mr. Burgess does catch the tail of a certain
imaginative truth, seen in historical perspective. Napoleon did not know
he would win Marengo and lose Waterloo; Alexander had no intuition
that he would find himself a hero after the retreat from Moscow. The
reader knows the score of the symphony but the players do not, and the
fun of this to some extent saves the day, for in works whose pretensions
cannot be taken very seriously by anyone, the author least of all, it is
humor that must—and often can—step in with the meaning. Here are
Napoleon and Alexander dividing their global interests on the famous raft
on the river Niemen.

"One of our philosophers has said that the deeper purpose of war is nothing more terrifying than a need to communicate."

"Really? Interesting." N looked warily at Alexander, something of an intellectual then, a bit of a nuisance, might come up with other intellectual gobbets like *Who controls Poland controls the world.*

There is a suggestion of Nixonian grotesque, and for good measure Napoleon feels physically attracted to Alexander, touches his "bony knee, a boy's"; gives him sound advice about the leadership of men, and finds that even he is slightly abashed by so much hero worship.

"How do you do it?" Alexander asked. "Can it be taught? Could I, for instance, learn it? Your really *incredible* record of military achieve-ment—"

"Well," N said modestly, "you have to have a certain talent for it."

Alexander's tone ("Could I, for instance, learn it?") is just right, and the spirited brio of the scene suggests that Mr. Burgess had Shakespeare's scene on Pompey's galley in mind—not a bad model if you feel up to tak-ing a crack at it. The sentiment of the troops who struggle back across the Berezina is rendered in a more straightforwardly Joycean idiom, which gets the authentic army note of pith mixed with wind.

Apprise the men of the inevitable difficulties of the constructive task that lies ahead, laying particular emphasis on the need for the utmost in improvisatory skill and stressing the importance of speed, General Eblé said. . . . Sergeant Rebour said: Right lads, as you know, we lost the fucking pontoon train. . . . The primary need, General Eblé said, is to obtain the requisite structural materials and this will certainly entail the demolition of civilian housing in the adjacent township . . . the only way to get it is to pull down all those fucking houses.

All good fun, even if it isn't quite war, as one of the next Napoleon's gen-erals more or less remarked in the course of the next contest. After the retreat from Moscow, Napoleon said that from the sublime to the ridicu-lous is but a step: he did not, however, add that they are both the same thing. Mr. Burgess is far too intelligent and thoughtful a writer not to have reflected on the curious fact that we can no longer render the past in terms of its pomp and circumstance, the sublime as well as the ridiculous. We can only do it—perhaps we can only do ourselves too?—as creatures of fantasy and farce.

The New York Review of Books, 1974

65

Moral Magic

Darkness Visible
by William Golding (1911–1993)

JORGE LUIS BORGES has written (and it is certainly true of Borges)
that the writer is like a member of a primitive tribe who suddenly
starts making unfamiliar noises and waving his arms about in strange
new rituals. The others gather round to look. Often they soon get bored
and wander off, but sometimes they become hypnotized, remain spellbound until the rite comes to an end, adopt it as a part of tribal behavior.

A simple analogy, but it does fit some novelists and tale-tellers, preoccupied in the midst of us with their homespun magic. They are not modish, not part of any literary establishment. Nor is there anything of the
showman about them: Dickens was magician in another sense, the sense
that goes with the melodrama and music hall, and tribal magicians are
not creators as Dickens and Hardy were. They do not invent a whole natural world of their own in which the client can lead a solitary life; their
appeal has something communal, as the Borges image suggests, and the
shareability of a cult. A largely Anglo-Saxon phenomenon, with a suggestion of Beowulf about it (another of the Borges admirations), and *The
Lord of the Rings* as one of its longer more popular texts. America lacks
this type of magician—the shamans there are grander, more worldly,
more pretentious—and the German-style version of Hermann Hesse or
Günter Grass is too instinctively metaphysical, not homespun enough.

Richard Hughes was one of our most effective local magicians; John Fowles has become one; William Golding has had the status a long time.

Darkness Visible confirms Golding as a master craftsman in his particular sort of magic. It is beautifully constructed, it grips the reader—so much so that its effectiveness gives it the air, a little disturbingly, of being closer to one of those rather different pieces of master-craft by Graham Greene or John le Carré than to its own progenitors. But this resemblance is no bad sign. It indicates change and maturity, a greater toughness and naturalness. In fact, this seems to me Golding's best book yet, compounding and refining the virtues of *The Lord of the Flies*, *Pincher Martin*, and *Free Fall*, and avoiding the weaknesses of *The Spire*—that all too Shavian exercise in the medieval picturesque—and the rather nervelessly genteel social reminiscence of *The Pyramid*, Golding's last novel.

The weakness of *The Pyramid* has been turned in some measure into the strength of *Darkness Visible*. Its meticulous, uneasy kinds of social questioning, seeming there consciously muted and damped down, have now found a new kind of certainty and force. *The Pyramid* was a depressing book: *Darkness Visible* is in a sense a hopeless one but far from depressing.

> . . . yet from those flames
> No light, but rather darkness visible
> Served only to discover sights of woe,
> Regions of sorrow, doleful shades, where peace
> And rest can never dwell.

Milton's lines were presumably very much in Mr Golding's mind. His narrative begins in the Blitz, when the firemen manning a pump see a burnt child approaching them down a burning street. The creature is eventually reconstituted after long spells in hospital, sent to school, found a sort of job in a moribund hardware emporium. No one knows where he comes from; he fits in nowhere; he seems barely to belong to the human race. His scarred appearance is so repulsive that he is disliked all the more by those who show him charity, because their principles compel them not to turn their heads away. At school, a master who loves boys is accidentally exposed by him, which results in dismissal and imprisonment, while the boy the master loves is found dead after falling off the roof.

Matty, the name given the misfit, is deeply but confusedly troubled by these events. He discovers the Bible: he goes to Australia. After various jobs and difficulties he comes back, still trying to find out who he is, and what he is *for*. He keeps a diary, and becomes convinced that angels of a kind are giving him commands and leading him toward some event. He gets a menial job at a posh private school where the well-brought-up little boys take a polite but wholly natural interest in his disfigurements. This makes him love them. He still mourns for the fate of Mr. Pedigree, who couldn't bear him. He sees two angelically beautiful small girls looking into a bookseller's window, and he prays for them also.

At this point Part I ends. Part II takes up the life of the little girls, twins: Toni, the odd dreamy one, and Sophy, with whose consciousness we are in touch. Their divorced father is vaguely distinguished and well-off, a chess and music critic; they live with grans, mistresses, au pairs. Golding's brilliance at conveying the consciousness of the young has never been more exact, but to what purpose? We apprehend through a growing and repulsive sense of tedium, tedium conveyed (as it might be in Gogol, who ends a story with the words: "Things are tedious in this world, gentlemen") through a narrative grip and persuasiveness which is the very reverse of tedious. Neither hell nor heaven lies about the infancy of these two, but something worse. What is it for? The reader's first reaction is to feel that here is magic turned inside out; that, although wonderfully under control, the novel has joined the ranks of those numerous other more or less modern novels whose pride and purpose seems to consist in establishing the dullness of experience, its inherent squishiness, its *nausée*.

Not so, however. There is a reason why growth in this case is the growth of absence, non-feeling. At seventeen or so Toni leaves home and becomes, by easy stages—overland to Afghanistan, conferences in Cuba—a presumptive terrorist. Piqued into competition, Sophy joins the criminal classes via a series of hitchhiking experiences, deliberately incurred. The twins, "everything to each other," have felt too little for hatred or love. They come together again as the novel gathers itself carefully together and pours itself over the edge of an effective climax: the school, hostages, fire, and Matty, seeking to save, vanishing into it as he had emerged from it at the beginning. The end, which succeeds the climax and brings Mr. Pedigree back, is extremely moving.

Reaction afterward, though, may be disappointment at what seems the patness of the fable: terrorists, hostages, the emptiness of evil, all things running down into aimlessness. It is an odd thing, certainly, that any novel today which tries to make use of what seems the all-important topicality risks the slightly forlorn air of yesterday's newspaper what seems all important has inevitably moved just a shade further on. But this is not a real disability, and Golding is right to stare it down. Novels have always had a time lag between their sense of a subject and the present—Dostoevsky's Devils were some way back, as was Dickens's Circumlocution Office and Hardy's "new woman," Sue—and it is not the fault of the contemporary novel that the lag may look obvious if it is no more than a weekend.

A truer weakness could be the schematic contrasting of the characters: Golding has always been a little uncertain on the natural reality of the figures whom he manipulates for thoughtful, magical ends. How misfits grow up cannot easily be demonstrated convincingly by a novelist who has planned what is to happen (Elizabeth Bowen failed at the same technique in *The Heat of the Day*), but at the same time the childhood of those two is given a wonderfully creepy quality, which would not be retrospectively diminished had they settled down as blameless housewives in Gerrard's Cross. Unfeelingness, like goodness, can take any way. But the real triumph of the book is Matty himself. Golding makes no attempt to suggest that someone like this would come out of that kind of early experience. Matty is just good, in his own laborious hopeless way, and to make that clear—and the place of his desperate, do-it-yourself religion in it—is a remarkable achievement.

For Golding, the magical and the moral are very closely allied, may even be the same thing. The source of his success, and his stature as a novelist, lies in the way in which he can persuade us that the novelist's manipulation of his material—his magic power—is essentially a moral activity (which is not the case with those conventionalized moral formulae through which a Graham Greene or le Carré operate). To succeed, such a novelist must work outside his convictions—if indeed he has any—and must allow the hypnotic concentration of his originality to do the job for him. Often Golding has failed in this: Piggy in *The Lord of the Flies* was too evidently preselected as the decent human norm. But Matty is a different matter. There is nothing normative about him at all, but virtue shines forth and the fire displays it, making other things than darkness visible. As well as hope, the novel casts out nostalgia, but Matty's Bible is there, and the impulses that lead him to others; his nature is determined as much as that of Mr. Pedigree, the lover of little boys. But what of the undetermined nature, the sort that like Dostoevsky's Svidrigailov is "nothing in particular"? It is into that gulf that the novel runs down, carrying our interest every inch of the way.

London Review of Books, 1979

66

Professional Strategies

The World, the Text, and the Critic
by Edward W. Said (1935–2003)

PROFESSOR STANLEY FISH of Johns Hopkins tells us that this book by Edward Said, the critic and professor of literature at Columbia University, "speaks with a particular and moving urgency to the issues facing criticism today." A word, as so often, gives the game away. Urgency? Is science about to destroy the world, or the superpowers each other? Is capitalism or communism about to collapse? Quite possibly. And the scientist, economist or political theorist who takes up a pen to face these matters might reasonably claim, or have it claimed on his behalf, that the task was an urgent one. But in this context the word is factitious.

Not to Professors Fish and Said, however, for whom literary criticism is not only as serious a matter as science and politics but one equally to be conducted by professionals. Literature departments in universities exist to prove it. In a recent number of *The* (London) *Times Literary Supplement*, Mr. Fish pointed out, incontrovertibly, that as long as there are literary studies there will be professionalism, and that we cannot, "by the waving of a magic moral wand," return to some happy and simple amateur attitude toward books and texts. With a rare and refreshing honesty Mr. Fish said straight out that academics seek ideas and cultivate theories about literature because these are "the goals, purposes, and authorized strategies of the profession." Because the don is a don he ought to behave like one and not pretend that he is enjoying and thinking about literature for its own sake.

That is a salutary reminder. Everyone knows that the worlds of science and economics, their structure and terminology, are invented by brilliant men dedicated to advancement in their profession. Freud did not make discoveries: he was determined to invent things in order to impose his will on his colleagues and gain a reputation. In literary criticism, structuralists and deconstructionists do the same thing. But where invention is concerned, the literary worker lacks a basic self-confidence: he is always looking over his shoulder, not only at other critics but at literature itself— that massive, varied, indifferent presence that will still be in the libraries when his ideas about it have vanished, even though his constant effort today is to persuade us that literature only exists by virtue of the critic, just as science exists by virtue of the scientist.

The whole tendency of Mr. Said's book is to discount the kind of claims that latent feelings of anxiety and inferiority lead some critical practitioners to make. As a scholar and a man of great erudition in many fields and languages, Mr. Said obviously knows deep down that the "enterprise" of critical theory has reached full circle and that the academic critic now best makes his mark by announcing his total independence from it—even if he has to erect in the process a gigantic monument to all other critics and their systems.

In one sense, therefore, Mr. Said's book is an attack on the critical industry, proclaiming the now unfashionable view that human truths and the human world are as important as the sacred "text" of the structuralists and actually dwell inside it. Of course this does not mean becoming once more a simplistic amateur of letters, boring students with one's own enthusiasm for stories and poems about real life and real people, even while rigorous and exciting new modes of making them unreal are being cooked up by the professionals elsewhere. And yet Mr. Said's prospectus does often sound like a return to amateurism by professional means, as it were: a return to the world by renouncing the critical devil in the text.

What else does it mean when the critic thinks that he should "maintain a distance" from the "dogmas and orthodoxies" of the systems, and when he advocates responsiveness to "political, social, and human values" and to "the heterogeneity of human experience"? No doubt he is against sin and the man-eating shark. What amateur of letters ever thought otherwise? Common sense and the common reader may not be "daring," but they have known this all along. Yet for "contemporary literary theory" it does indeed represent "a new departure."

"My position," Mr. Said writes, "is that texts are worldly, to some degree they are events, and, even when they appear to deny it, they are nevertheless a part of the social world, human life, and of course the historical moment in which they are located and interpreted. Literary theory, whether of the Left or of the Right, has turned its back on these things. This can be considered, I think, the triumph of the ethic of professionalism."

He goes on to connect this ethic, interestingly if unprovably, with "the ascendancy of Reaganism" and the jargon of the new cold war. However that may be, let us raise a cheer for the new amateur professional, falling back at last on what Henry James called "the critic's only weapon, the exercise of his intelligence"—in every department of literature and life. What has bedeviled literature departments for so long is the search for shortcuts and blinkered minds, and for systems and strategies to aid and comfort the baffled student who cannot otherwise make out what great books are all about. The inculcation of a critical system is no substitute for the free play of Jamesian intelligence which, like taste itself, cannot be taught. For professionals, everything in a literature course can and must be taught.

In a sense there is a real book inside Mr. Said's official one, and the real book is relaxed and discursive, original, immensely learned, fluently written. It is essentially a book of essays, Victorian essays (perhaps we may soon revive that admirable Victorian critic, E. S. Dallas, who spoke of criticism, God help him, as "the gay science") that slip easily and illuminatingly from one thing to another—from Swift and his politics to Conrad and Filiation, to the comparative examination of religions and romance by way of reflections on Freud and on the American left, or on the critic Raymond Schwab and the difference between culture and system. On all these matters Mr. Said has something of great interest to say and the fruits of encyclopedic reading to share with us. His chapter on Conrad is superb: old-fashioned criticism of the best kind is combined with modern scholarship; nothing better has been written on this novelist.

Mr. Said is particularly illuminating on the contribution of Islam, at all stages of its history, to the development of literary and political theory. Possibly Islam's conservatism and its capacity for a natural synthesis between life and literature, religion and society, have influenced not only the intellectual curiosity that lies behind his learning but its tendency to return to time-honored platitudes, to what he calls, quoting Kipling, "the Gods of the Copy-Book Headings." It is a singular reflection on our academic culture that, to establish what is or should be simple and obvious, Mr. Said's book has to masquerade as yet another daring display of critical theory.

The New York Times, 1983

67

Writeabout

The Songlines
by Bruce Chatwin (1940–1989)

THE WELL-KNOWN SPEECH in Dryden's play *Aurungzebe* beginning, "When I consider life, 'tis all a cheat," has the emperor
gloomily observing that we still expect from the last dregs of life
"what the first sprightly running could not give." The empress, however,
takes a different line: keeping going is what matters.

> Each day's a mistress, unenjoyed before;
> Like travellers, we're pleased with seeing more.

The metaphors are instructive, contrasting as they do the disillusion of
the sedentary, who wait in one place for what life may bring them, and the
instinct of the migrant to get somewhere, anywhere, on his own feet.

Bruce Chatwin's latest book is about the idea of being a nomad. From
his experiences in Australia he builds a case for fairly aimless wandering
about, over large distances, as the way of existing most suited to human
consciousness. Traveling of this sort, once a necessity for food-gathering,
can now only be done very artificially, when it constitutes a way of life
summed up at the end of Philip Larkin's sardonic poem as "reprehensibly perfect." The natural thing today is to travel as if sitting in a room, an
airplane, or a car. Instant arrival leaves us sitting in another room, waiting for more drops, sprightly or otherwise, from the state's life-expectation

machine. That may be a cheat, but at least it seems to most of us the natural cheat. It takes care of our restlessness no more but no less effectively than migration on foot would do.

Although as an artist he is a black pessimist about the nature of existence, Bruce Chatwin would probably not agree. Like the Empress Nourmahal, he has always been in favor of pressing onward, even though it gives him little pleasure. Larkin himself would have approved his passively meticulous sense of place, and indeed Larkin was a passionate admirer of his three earlier books, particularly *In Patagonia*. It is a travel book like no other, by far the most interesting recent example of the genre. Its writing reverses our expectations, setting us down at the end of an outlandish continent in a place which seems stalely familiar, but that is no doubt the proper reward of travel, and to the true traveler—still more to his reader—it can be made a satisfying one. Just as compulsively memorable, or more so, this book takes us to the Australian Outback, the central and northern territories. They are, of course, awful—like a lay-by on Western Avenue frequented by gypsies and tinkers.

But Chatwin's notion was to get to know the lore of the "songlines" or "dreamingtracks" which run invisibly all over Australia, and which the Aborigines used and use in their endless wanderings-about. These rather sloppy-sounding phrases are presumably renderings from an Aboriginal language, which saw the recognition tracks as bound up with tribal and personal identity, a repetitiveness of the sacred, a way of feeling in past and present, of being both dead and alive. They also involved a complex system of land tenure, based, not on blocks of tribal or personal property, but on an interlocking network of "ways through." What the white men saw as the meaningless habit of "Walkabout" was a kind of bush-telegraph stock-exchange, spreading news of commodities and availability among peoples who never saw each other, and might even be unaware of each other's existence. Since goods were potentially malign, they would work against their possessors unless they were kept in perpetual motion. Nor did they have to be edible, or useful: people liked to circulate useless things, like their own dried umbilical cords, or a shell that might have traveled from hand to hand from the Timor Sea to the Bight.

Chatwin is uncannily good at conveying the sense in which the transmission of such matters into English, for the benefit of anthropologists and the kind of nuts who get enthusiastic about them, takes away their meaning by making them sound interesting and mysterious. But poetry is what gets left out in translation. His informants seem to have been rather like the lizards who leave their tail in the captor's hand and wriggle off to grow a new one. Chatwin was told about the ceremonial centers where men of different tribes would gather. "'For what you call corroborees? 'You call them corroborees,' he said. 'We don't.'" By describing one's life and beliefs, one not only falsifies them but creates a picture of unreality, which may seem all the more seductively comprehensible to others. Margaret Mead was taken for a ride by the New Guineans because she wanted them to be the only way they could describe themselves. No one could be less like Raymond Chandler's schoolmarm at the snake dances than Chatwin. He makes no comparison or comment, and draws no conclusions: but his reader has the impression that anthropologists can't do other than mislead, just as the early explorers and artists did, though in a different and perhaps a more deadening way. Chatwin seems aware of doing it himself, and that gives a kind of wry and secret satire to his most hypnotically vivid conversations and encounters. These are the real point of his book, as they were of *In Patagonia*. So overwhelmingly actual is the writing, in its power of putting places and moments before us, that questions relating to theory and "Society" seem left awkwardly behind. They are there, nonetheless, making their point all the more effectively for being pushed aside by what, quite simply, goes on, as it does anywhere. The author meets a young Australian working in the Land Rights movement called Arkady, whose father was a Ukrainian Cossack displaced between Germans and Russians in the last war. Miraculously saved from both, he ended up in Australia, but always pined for his homeland, which he once contrived to revisit. His sons are wholly Australian. In a pub up north, Arkady and the author meet a policeman who has thought of a marvelous title for a best-seller, to rival *Killer's Pay-Off*, *Shark City*, or *The Day of the Dog*. Convinced he can sell it for fifty thousand U.S. dollars, he is reluctant to impart it to the author except on a basis of literary partnership, but eventually does so, closing his eyes in ecstasy. It is *Body Bag*. Sleeping Aboriginals are not infrequently pulverized, it seems, by the trucks of the huge road-trains from Alice to Darwin. I should have thought it an excellent title, though Chatwin did not. Meanwhile Aboriginals in the bar are listening to a big white man who has fought in France and married a girl from Leicester.

He had heard we were surveying sacred sites.

"Know the best thing to do with a sacred site?" he drawled.

"What?"

"Dynamite!"

He grinned and raised his glass to the Aboriginals. The birthmark oscillated as he drank.

One of the Aboriginals, a very thin hill-billy type with a frenzy of matted hair, leaned both elbows on the counter, and listened.

"Sacred sites!" the big man leered. "If all what them says was sacred sites there'd be three hundred bloody billion sacred sites in Australia."

"Not far wrong, mate!" called the thin Aboriginal.

Arkady and the policeman are meanwhile discussing the drinking laws, and the policeman is saying how much he likes Aboriginals, who are nonetheless standing in the way of progress. "You're helping them destroy white Australia." Arkady says he thinks the surest way of judging a man's intelligence is his ability to handle words.

Many Aboriginals, he said, by our standards would rank as linguistic geniuses. The difference was one of outlook. The whites were forever changing the world to fit their doubtful vision of the future. The Aboriginals put all their mental energies into keeping the world the way it was. In what way was that inferior?

The policeman's mouth shot downwards.

"You're not Australian," he said to Arkady.

"I bloody am Australian."

"No, you're not. I can tell you're not Australian."

"I was born in Australia."

"That doesn't make you Australian," he taunted. "My people have lived in Australia for five generations. So where was your father born?"

Arkady paused, and with quiet dignity answered, "My father was born in Russia."

"Hey!" the policeman tightened his forelip and turned to the big man. "What did I tell you, Bert? A Pom and a Com!"

That well-known artistic Pom, William Blake, did an engraving of "A Family of New South Wales" which is reproduced on the cover of Chatwin's book. In a touchingly direct way it expresses the old ecstatic unrealities which anthropologists have since been adding to with all the devices of scientific "objectivity." Blake must have been told something about Aboriginal style and equipment, perhaps by the authors of *An Historical Journal of the Transactions at Port Jackson*, in which his picture appeared. But the faces of his naked family—father, mother, two children—have the ideal look, not so much of the Noble Savage who was a cliché in cultivated circles at the time, as of a contemporary Social Democratic Party family, or the grouped models in color-supplement advertising. It is a striking picture, all the same, full of the "wiry bounding line" which the artist sought for. But it is a product of the need to imagine something different from ourselves: ourselves as we might be if we could only live differently. Blake's near-contemporary Dr. Johnson, whom he so much abominated, was inclined to take a deterministic view of human lifestyles. When we can get something "better," we do—not because it makes us happier but because it represents current possibility. An Aboriginal wants an old car, to drive if possible but if not to live under, as a kind of "humpy." Those who persist in following the old ways now find themselves living the artificial life, becoming "reprehensibly perfect," like Blake's imagined New South Wales family. As birds and animals have no objection to squalid surroundings, the modern Aboriginal lives in a mess of plastic bags, rusty cars, candy-bar wrappings, which presumably become part of his Songlines. His wish to keep or to revive the old ways seems to be mainly a way of getting at the Government, inhibiting land development, and upping the welfare check.

The poetry of Chatwin's remarkable pages flitters quietly about among these matters, steering a course, as it were, between William Blake and Dr. Johnson. He is particularly skillful with his own version of that time-honored literary ploy, the most unforgettable character. We meet briefly—and the wiry prose makes them unforgettable—a discontented septuagenarian acting out an Australian image in the solitude of the bush; an Irish priest living in a tent on a sand dune by the Timor Sea, and getting so fond of his hermitage that he has decided to leave and look after derelicts in Sydney; an Aboriginal "hunter" who skillfully chases kangaroos through the spinifex in an old jalopy, and knocks them down. This last treats the author as his slave, forcing him to make pits with a digging stick to change a wheel, and to hold his cigarette as he fumbles with the carburetor. These people are an aspect of journeying, as in immortal books like Evelyn Waugh's *Ninety-Two Days*, or Peter Fleming's *News from Tartary*.

Bruce Chatwin's narrative is divided by pauses for quotation and reflection. He has more than a touch of Rimbaud in him, and indeed he quotes from *Une Saison en Enfer*: "For a long time I prided myself I would possess every possible country." He reminisces here about the nomads he once met in the Sahel, and about the customs of Mauritania. A waiter in a Timbuktu hotel gave him the menu and said: "We eat at eight." This turned out to mean that the staff ate at eight, the guests at seven or at ten; and, dropping his voice, the waiter intimated that seven was the better time, "because we eat up all the food." We hear of a meeting with Konrad Lorenz in Austria, and Chatwin must have thought of him when he suggested to some elderly Aboriginals that their songs were territorial, like those of birds, and they gravely agreed. Every quick glimpse, everything related here, is in a sense an anti-traveler's tale, a brilliant focus from the reverse end of that hoary old convention. As in Julian Barnes's *Flaubert's Parrot*, one discovery contradicts another, each aperçu wipes out the one before. We read that "by spending his whole life walking and singing his ancestor's songline a man becomes the track, the ancestor and the song," and this at least seems satisfyingly familiar. We recall the bowler and the bat, the leaf, the blossom, and the bole. But with a shrug the author leaves the idea, like the lizard its tail, and quotes from the *Chinese Book of Odes*: "Useless to ask a wandering man advice on the construction of a house." He says that "after reading this text I realized the absurdity of trying to write a book on nomads."

Whatever it is about, the book is a masterpiece. Very briefly the author meets a young Australian teacher from Adelaide who could in one sense be an alter ego. Graham has gone native, like many young Australians who work in Aboriginal settlements. He found the boys of the Pintupi tribe were born musicians, and so founded his own rock band, making songs with names like "The Ballad of Barrow Creek" and "Grandfather's Country," which became the song of the Out-Station Movement and number two in the Sydney charts. The band were about to take off for a Sydney visit at a time when they were supposed to undergo their tribal initiation ceremonies, and the elders were very angry. Nothing was sorted out, of course, a depressing impasse remaining which was not helped by young Graham wanting to be initiated, too, and telling the senior woman teacher that he refused to teach in a school run by "racists." "The education programme," he told her, "was systematically trying to destroy Aboriginal culture, and to rope them into the market system. What Aboriginals needed was land, land and more land—where no unauthorised European would ever set foot." She very sensibly pointed out that the South Africans had a name for the line he was taking: they called it Apartheid.

The author leaves Graham in limbo on the road as he leaves everything else. But the process is neither callous nor reluctant: we sense in some way that the author's troubles, about which no word is uttered, are metamorphosed into those of the people he meets. Arkady has, in fact, bought him a paperback of Ovid's *Metamorphoses* at the Desert Bookshop in Alice. That legendary process, metamorphosis, is, as Ovid's stories show, as unsatisfactory as every other in living, but it takes care of the next stage of the journey. *Solvitur ambulando*, as the ancients used to say. A baby will cease to cry if it is walked about.

London Review of Books, 1987

68

Country Life

———

The Enigma of Arrival
by V. S. Naipaul (1932–)

IN HIS LONG, still much undervalued poem *The Age of Anxiety*, W. H.
Auden's heroine in New York likes to imagine "one of those lovely
innocent countrysides" that are "familiar to all readers of English
detective stories."

> There was Lord Lugar at Lighthazels,
> Violent-tempered; he voted against
> The Banking Bill. At Brothers Intake
> Sir William Wand; his Water Treaty
> Enriched Arabia. At Rotherhope
> General Locke, a genial man who
> Kept cormorants. At Craven Ladies
> Old Tillingham-Trench; he had two passions,
> Women and walking-sticks. . . .
> . . . At Lantern Byepew
> Susan O'Rourke, a sensitive who
> Prayed for the plants. They have perished now; their
> Level lawns and logical vistas
> Are obliterated; their big stone
> Houses are shut.

Rosetta's fantasy is probably shared by a good many nostalgic middle-class English persons, for whom the idea of country life and country houses in the shires is one that continues to make an appeal. Some time ago—how long exactly remains uncertain in his account of it—V. S. Naipaul went for a season to live in the heart of just such an English rural scene; and as one might expect from so curious and sensitive a writer his vision of it has a profound, tender, and disquieting originality, as if Eden was being seen for the first time by someone with much sharper eyes than Adam and Eve.

To a personal, self-protective fantasy, like that of Auden's Rosetta, he would be very sympathetic. As a stranger and pilgrim like her, coming from an island far away from England, he would be aware of the desire to romanticize the old, new-found country whose language he has always spoken; to allow himself to luxuriate in its strangeness and exoticism, as E. M. Forster and J. R. Ackerley did in *The Hill of Devi* and *Hindoo Holiday*, books that recorded their stay in the domain of an Indian prince. Their India was his England, the country he had read so much about during his boyhood, in poems and novels. And the unique quality of his discourse, in *The Enigma of Arrival*, is in the way it combines the sense of innocence and wonder with an eye and an understanding that are quietly and totally penetrating. It is a combination unlike any other, and no other writer today could produce anything like it.

The new England revealed is, spoken of as a residence, situated in one of the country's richest as well as one of its most picturesque areas, the one that Hardy would have called North Wessex, lying at the confluence of the chalk streams of Wiltshire which flow toward Salisbury. It is, coincidentally, not only Hardy country—although Hardy located there no major novel, only stories—but the setting of E. M. Forster's own favorite among his novels, *The Longest Journey*. South from Salisbury the Roman road runs straight to Blandford Forum—whose ancient name itself sounds as if straight out of Auden or Betjeman—and on to Dorchester, Hardy's Casterbridge. A few miles south of Salisbury, too, lies Southampton, the port at which V. S. Naipaul first arrived from Trinidad by way of New York, and whose name then struck him as "especially beautiful." Perhaps that arrival also suggested to Naipaul the Chirico picture from which he took his title. North from the village, or rather manor, he came to live in, forming the background of his book, are the chalk downs whose summit could be reached in an afternoon's stroll, and from which Stonehenge is visible.

Property values are higher in this part of England than in any other, not because the farming land is especially profitable but because so many retired or semiretired people with a lot of money—judges, generals, financiers, former colonial administrators—come to live there. But the country is not suburban: it clings, with a perhaps rather too great and increasing self-consciousness, to a traditional rural image. Naipaul is well aware of this. The manor he came to live in—he does not tell us just how—was one of the older "big stone houses" of the neighborhood, owned by the descendant of a great family who had acquired land and a fortune in the early days of the Empire. This figure has become a recluse, still living most of the time in the big house, and referred to rather enigmatically by the writer as "my landlord." We hardly meet him, but his presence is a potent factor in the strange, rather disturbing charm the place comes to possess for the writer; and it is also the invisible focus for extended sketches of the people we do meet—the "locals"—gardeners, caretakers, drivers, not so much retainers of the manor as hangers-on.

"My landlord" was evidently in his youth a well-known figure. One day the taxi driver abruptly takes from the dashboard shelf a thin volume and puts it in the writer's hand. It is a little *jeu d'esprit* of the landlord's late teens, an Evelyn Waugh type fantasy about a society girl, privately printed, long since gathered into the vale of lost things. How has the driver obtained a copy? Why does he now wish to lend it to the writer? Such episodes generate a slightly eerie atmosphere, as if in the world of Proust, or of Alain-Fournier's romance *Le Grand Meaulnes*, but they are also significant in simple commonplace ways. The driver, a typically rootless, undeferential, uncentered contemporary English person, nonetheless clings to this evidence that the man at the manor is somebody, or was once somebody, a reassuring figure from a now nonexisting hierarchy. Naipaul understands this well, for it corresponds to something in his own psychological makeup, which the book explores as softly and delicately as it explores the place and the people with whom he comes in contact.

To such a writer as Naipaul, for the purpose of understanding himself and others, and for the purposes of fiction, it is clearly necessary to have a deep and imaginative sense of the dual nature of individuals, their existence in two worlds, both in different ways precarious. Naipaul thoroughly understands the romance of himself—what the novelist John Cowper Powys called his *life illusion*—the inner saga of himself and his destiny which each person secretly carries alongside the physical circumstances of his existence. His own sense of himself comes out in this book with a gentle, meticulous candor, wholly absorbing and illuminating. He wonders at the strangeness of the contiguity: the invisible partnership between "my landlord," living alone across the garden in the decaying great house, and himself in his rented cottage by the old farm buildings. The atmosphere of the place mingles with that of his own distracted and distant provenance:

> To see the possibility, the certainty, of ruin, even at the moment of creation: it was my temperament. Those nerves had been given me as a child in Trinidad partly by our family circumstances: the half-ruined or broken-down houses we lived in, our many moves, our general uncertainty. Possibly, too, this mode of feeling went deeper and was an ancestral inheritance, something that came with the history that had made me: not only India, with its ideas of a world outside men's control, but also the colonial plantations or estates of Trinidad, to which my impoverished Indian ancestors had been transported in the last century—estates of which this Wiltshire estate, where I now lived, had been the apotheosis.

He is sensitive to all the physical manifestations of change, the rawness of the old–new country and the mechanism that exploits it—the concrete silages and driveways, the milking parlors and mounds of black plastic weighed down by motor tires. At the same time he is exactly fitted to be the recorder of what rural England now actually looks like, the old and the new continuing together in some bemused and placidly doomed relationship. The British Empire, as a parting gift to her talented son (and no mean one considering the old lady was on her last legs), had given him a language and an education, a jackpotful of scholarships and grants which had brought him to England, to Oxford, and to this beadsman's existence— peaceful and fruitful—in the autumnal peace of a Wiltshire cottage.

The history I carried with me, together with the self-awareness that had come with my education and ambition, had sent me into the world with a sense of glory dead; and in England had given me the rawest stranger's nerves. Now ironically—or aptly—living in the grounds of this shrunken estate, going out for my walks, those nerves were soothed, and in the wild garden and orchard beside the water meadows I found a physical beauty perfectly suited to my temperament and answering, besides, every good idea I could have had, as a child in Trinidad, of the physical aspect of England.

Nonetheless, the god Siva, the destroyer and creator, was at work in Wessex, as in Trinidad or in India.

Meeting distress halfway, I cultivated old, possibly ancestral ways of feeling, the ways of glory dead, and held on to the idea of a world in flux: the drum of creation in the god's right hand, the flame of destruction in his left.

Let loose in the peaceful heart of England, this atavistic Oriental understanding—itself ancient, embracing, comprehensive—forms a strange and beautiful artistic amalgam, produces a unique novel. Its center, its *clou* as Henry James would say, is the shadowy relation between landlord and novelist: the former barely seen by the latter, but admired, sympathized with, even identified with. Naipaul does not luxuriate in the poetry of decline, but he admires the spirit that recognizes and accepts it:

I felt a great sympathy for my landlord. I felt I could understand his malaise; I saw it as the other side of my own. I did not think of my landlord as a failure. Words like failure and success didn't apply. Only a grand man or a man with a grand idea of his human worth could ignore the high money value of his estate and be content to live in its semi-ruin. My meditations in the manor were not of imperial decline. Rather, I wondered at the historical chain that had brought us together—he in his house, I in his cottage, the wild garden his taste (as I was told) and also mine.

Round this relationship are grouped, almost symmetrically, more down-to-earth and humdrum ones—with "Jack," another quasi-retainer whose cottage and garden were close at hand, with the regular gardener, the manager, agricultural workers and their wives. As we gradually get to know these people and enter their lives, the sense of a country as it really is, at this moment, is extraordinarily strong, as if the quiet magic of Naipaul's prose were catching these people in a temporary lull, a shared backwater on their way to dissolution. The writer knows that his time in this place cannot last; but his fleeting companions seem to know it, too, of their own lives: so far from being rural and static they are constantly borne onward in the shoddy mechanisms of modern change, failing in subtle ways to be themselves, or discovering unexpected ways of beginning afresh—another job, religion, a new car or wife. In the course of the book all these relations come to an end or peter out, but while they last they are wry and genuine, types and symbols of the way we know one another in the alienated world of today, and explored by Naipaul with an equal sympathy and a lack of any stereotyped sentiment.

These relationships, and the regular rhythms of his day, are the heart of the book. Stonehenge, so near at hand across the downs, and the river beside him ("Avon," he discovers, is a generic name for river: there are many Avons in the English south) still exercise the power that Richard Jeffries, in his country studies a century ago, would recognize as insensibly calming and shaping the country person's sense of himself. It is striking that when the personal narrative of the book carries the author briefly to other parts of the world—Trinidad, Africa, New York—the reader cannot wait to get back again to the peace and meditation of the Wiltshire valley. To Naipaul it was so clearly "home"—whatever that means today. The valley and the mysterious landlord had to "take him in," in a way that nowhere else could do, not London, not the New World, or any other, more exotic, part of the old.

It is significant, and rather touching, that this rural peace is also, for the author and participator, a sexless world. He records the "Gala Dance" on the boat over from America, and how a "dainty" girl (the adjective is typical of Naipaul's gently romantic accuracy) with whom he had happily conversed about books during the voyage, had suddenly ceased to recognize him and become "moist-eyed" in the company of some tediously uneducated fellow, "as though worked upon by forces outside her control." Those forces are notably absent from the Wiltshire valley, and from the experiences that determine there its value for the author. For both himself and his reader a rest from sex seems especially agreeable, in the context of life or of letters; for, as the novel implies, sex in our modern age has come to seem not something that puts down deep, established, accustomed roots, but an urge as involuntary as it is desolating and nomadic—the urge that produces Rosetta's lost cry in *The Age of Anxiety*:

> Wafna. Wafna. Who's to wind me now
> In this lost land?

There are still unexpected ways, as Naipaul's book so beautifully demonstrates, of rediscovering and repossessing such a land, in the experience of art, and of art as a part of living, even while recognizing and knowing it to be lost.

The New York Review of Books, 1987

69

Class Act

Palimpsest
by Gore Vidal (1925–)

ONE OF THE MANY fascinating photographs in *Palimpsest*, perhaps indeed the most fascinating of the lot, is of the author's grandfather, Senator Thomas Pryor Gore, having his portrait painted in old age. Reticently distinguished, the subject sits in his chair, ignoring the canvas, a remarkable likeness of him on a properly heroic scale, and presided over by the artist, Azadia Newman, whom we learn was soon to be married to the film director Rouben Mamoulian. The expression on her beautiful face, with its plucked eyebrows, is quite deadpan. Like a portraitist of the Renaissance she is doing her job, and has no special feelings about it or the sitter. But the photograph seems a revelation not only of the society in which Gore Vidal grew up—a very uncommon one in what Roosevelt was even then calling the Age of the Common Man—but of Gore Vidal's ability to put his reader inside that society, to give us a happy and an unfamiliar sense of familiarity with it.

The reader—the English reader in particular—is here somewhat in the position of one of the characters in Anthony Powell's long sequence of memoirized fiction, *A Dance to the Music of Time*. Marrying accidentally into the *haut monde*, this chap sets himself to find out all about its peculiar ways, while not for a moment aspiring to be part of it himself. Vidal's skill as a memoirist puts his reader in the same privileged and enviable position. And he is very funny about it. Ever a stickler for elegance of language, he is careful not to use the word "palimpsest" in any merely approximate sense.

> "Paper, parchment, etc., prepared for writing on and wiping out again, like a slate" and "a parchment, etc., that has been written upon twice; the original writing having been rubbed out." This is pretty much what my kind of writer does anyway. Starts with life; makes a text; then a *re*-vision—literally, a second seeing, an afterthought . . . , writing something new over the first layer of text. . . . I once observed to Dwight Macdonald, who had found me disappointingly conventional on some point, "I have nothing to say, only to add."

It might well have amused Proust, a great palimpsester, to have made a rather similar claim. And for the memoirist-novelist, as Proust and Powell would have agreed, the most essential thing is humor. True snobbery is always solemn. After the wedding of Vidal's half-sister, Nina Gore Auchincloss (her marriage was a failure, "as family tradition required"), Vidal finds himself driving to the reception with the young Jack Kennedy.

> In the back of the limousine, Jack and I waved to non-existent multitudes, using the British royal salute, in which the fingers of one hand unscrew, as it were, an invisible upside-down jar of marmalade. Jack thought that Nini had made a mistake in not marrying his brother Teddy. I had no view on the matter. Absently, he tapped his large white front teeth with the nail of his forefinger, click, click, click—a nervous tic.

The reader feels right there, with it and in it; and so effective is the superimposed ripple of Vidal's style and personality (the palimpsest at work?) that a kind of innocence of absurdity—as with the marmalade jar—easily mingles with an effortless and knowing sophistication. Brought so fascinatingly close to us, the Vidal world seems both exotic and domestic, glitzy and homely, and is presented with a deft economy that is itself highly droll.

> That winter Paul and Joanne and Howard and I took a house together in the Malibu Beach colony. Each had a small car. Paul left for Warn-

ers at dawn, as that studio was in the far, faraway San Fernando Valley. I left second, to drive to MGM in Culver City. Finally, Joanne made her leisurely way to Twentieth Century-Fox in nearby Beverly Hills. . . . Weekends, the house was full of people that, often, none of us knew. Christopher Isherwood and Don Bachardy were often there, as were Romain Gary and his wife, Leslie Blanche, and . . .

I am at the point I have been dreading: lists of names of once-famous people who mean nothing, by and large, to people now and will require endless footnotes for future historians. One might just pull it off if one had something truly intriguing to say about each name or if I had, like so many contemporary autobiographers, tempestuous love affairs, bitter marriages, autistic children, breakdowns, drugs, therapy, a standard literary life. But I was to have no love affairs or marriages, while casual sex is, by its very nature, not memorable. I have never "broken down" as opposed to slowly crumbling, and I've steered clear of psychoanalysts, nutritionists, and contract-bridge players. Joanne Woodward and I were nearly married, but that was at her insistence and based entirely on her passion not for me but for Paul Newman. Paul was taking his time about divorcing his first wife, and Joanne calculated, shrewdly as it proved, that the possibility of our marriage would give him the needed push. It did.

In 1958 they were married at last and we all lived happily ever after.

Not only does Vidal have original things to say on many subjects, but the reader feels himself becoming one with the characters in the book: a sure sign of a literary master at work. He has, for example, a good point about class. He is amused by the British class system, and by romantic English writers—W. H. Auden was one—who loved the idea of America as the classless society while firmly asserting their own status back home (upper-middle in his own case, Auden insisted—he was the son of a doctor). Of course America has its own class system, says Vidal, just like Britain. The difference is that most Americans don't even know it. The few that do are well aware of the exclusion zones and neatly roped-off areas which it takes either privilege of birth or dazzling social and intellectual skills (Vidal had both) to enter and enjoy. Whereas the Englishman knows his place, and is prepared either to put down his inferiors or to be put down—ever so unobtrusively—by his betters, the American really can change his class, if his talents or chutzpah are up to it. All this is very politically incorrect, but it probably happens to be true; and Vidal, as a natural classicist and an admirer of Montaigne and Cicero, thinks it is likely to go on being true.

Incidentally, the "Howard" referred to in the passage quoted above has been Vidal's almost lifelong companion. " 'How,' we are often asked, 'have you stayed together for forty-four years?' The answer is, 'No sex.' This satisfies no one, of course, but there, as Henry James would say, it is." Howard Auster was born in the Bronx, worked in a drugstore to put himself through New York University, and tried to get a job in advertising. At that time Jewish persons were discouraged in that profession, so Vidal recommended that he change the *r* at the end of his name to an *n*. He did so, and was at once taken on by an agency. Class is less visible than racism, but no doubt the two always have and always will be intertwined. (Austen, by the way, or its variant Austin, is a respectable though not a grand name in England, not like Talbot, say, or Villiers. Jane Austen knew her class—roughly upper-middle, like Auden's—and kept a beady eye above and below it, for like many such families she had some connections grander than herself, and others less grand.)

His needle-sharp curiosity and humor make Vidal a natural enjoyer of all such matters. He revels, as already noted, in a sort of sophisticated innocence. P. G. Wodehouse would have been delighted by the idea of Paul Newman and Joanne Woodward and the author each setting off for their respective studios at different moments in the early morning: yawning, no doubt, as they brushed the crumbs away. A super sophisticate in the public estimation, he has a ruefully witty tale or two to show with what unjust firmness that persona has clung. An actress once told him that *everyone* knew Noel Coward had one really rather disgusting sexual habit. "I was horrified. I knew Coward well. He was as fastidious about sex as about everything else." When Vidal saw the actress later she said she'd never forgotten what *he* had told her about Coward's sex kink. "Thus I have been transformed into the source of a truly sick invention that will be grist to the Satanic mills of Capotes as yet unborn."

The two most important people in *Palimpsest*, and the ones most movingly brought to life, are his Gore grandfather, the senator, and Jimmie Trimble, the fair-haired boy he met in Washington, killed in 1945 with the marines on Iwo Jima. Vidal loved both, and it is love that brings them so much alive in his memoir. Thomas Pryor Gore becomes for us as memorable a figure as the old patriarch grandfather in Aksakov's well-known memoir *A Russian Childhood*, but there is nothing patriarchal about him. Rather he is a distant, detached, and slightly sardonic figure, which itself may give a clue to the difference between the naturally big man in a Russian nineteenth-century family and in a twentieth-century American family. Power in an up-and-coming American family was a more subtle affair than it had been in the Russian context, and it had to be more skillfully exercised. Freedom in America was always there for the rest of the family to walk away into if they wanted.

T. P. Gore, in any case, was not inclined to control his family by means of money, or through the prospects of inheritance. He was blind from ten years old: as his grandson says, an extraordinary trick of fate. "The odds are very much against losing an eye in an accident, but to lose two eyes in two separate accidents is positively Lloydsian." And fate had more freakish adventures in store for him. He was a friend of Clarence Darrow, and at a time when he was visiting one of Darrow's court cases he was himself about to be tried for rape. He had backed the Indians against the oil interests in Oklahoma, where he was senator, and after ignoring threats to soften up he had the "badger game" played on him. A woman constituent rang him with some request, and after leading him to her hotel room, in the absence of his male secretary, tore her clothes off and started screaming. Two handy detectives rushed in and said, "We've got you!"

A jury took ten minutes to exonerate the Senator, who, as it happened, had already once found himself in a "shotgun" situation over a young woman. And she too had been blind. Her family accused him of raping her—the youthful pair were living in the same boarding house in Corsicana, Texas—and demanded marriage. A real shotgun was produced, but the future senator walked away saying, "Shoot, but I'm not marrying her." The facts of what happened remain obscure, as family facts perhaps always do and should do; but making his own inquiries in later years the grandson found some evidence to suggest that the Senator had indeed been guilty in this instance. Surmounting all the odds he was already on his way to becoming a quietly charismatic personality and a brilliant and dryly Ciceronian speaker; but even he might have been overhandicapped by becoming a partner in a blind marriage. He met his wife—they became known to the family as Dot and Dah—at a political meeting in Texas. After hearing her beautiful low voice he said at once, "I'm going to marry you."

There is more than filial feeling, strong though that is, in the vivid way Vidal recreates a grandfather who may have meant far more to him than his own father, Gene Vidal, the athlete and airline president. From the Senator, doubtless, came not only the literary gift but the abiding fascination with the personalities of power—power in any era. Reading for hours a day to a grandfather whose affection never took, then or later, the form of gratitude, the seven- and eight-year-old Gore must have unconsciously begun to learn how things go in those power circles. It was to be a lesson put to good and apparently effortless use in the brilliant studies of Caesar and Julian the Apostate, as well as in those of Lincoln and Burr. The young Vidal also saw senatorial ruthlessness in action. If he ever gave up on the reading aloud—always history, poetry, or economics: novels were despised—his grandfather would blithely remind him that both Milton's daughters themselves went blind, reading to their old tyrant of a blind father.

Language was clearly the Senator's being. After he had made a fine political oration in Texas, a group of Baptist ministers were so impressed that they offered him a fat salary and fine house to become their minister. When he courteously declined, on the grounds that he did not believe in God, they told him, "Come now, Mr. Gore, that's not the proposition we made you." The Senator's own brand of eloquence was what mattered. "Dah," says his grandson, "had a curious position in the country, not unlike that of Helen Keller, a woman born deaf, mute, and blind. The response of each to calamity was a subject of great interest to the general public, and we children and grandchildren were treated not so much as descendants of just another politician but as the privileged heirs to an Inspirational Personage."

Jimmie Trimble, appearing, Vidal tells us, in many photos with no smile on his handsome face, and with his eyes looking away, is the image of Delphic Charioteer, or Shropshire Lad, who would have been recognized at once by the poet A. E. Housman. Housman knew that real love was once and for all, and that the knowledge went, rather more ambiguously, with an unconscious lust for the loved one's early death. It did not happen in his case. His fate was to love a young undergraduate who in fact lived a long and useful life, but at least in the poet's memory he became one with "the lads who will die in their glory and never be old."

Jimmie was nineteen when he was shot and bayoneted, asleep in his foxhole, by a Japanese raiding party at midnight on Iwo Jima. Vidal is of course fully aware of the irony that now veils the myth of the young dead soldier; but he has the kind of style that can admit all that irony and yet achieve a moving and classic simplicity as well. Jimmie's single reappearance is both plangent and matter-of-fact, like the visit that Odysseus, after he has drunk the black blood, is permitted to make to the world of the dead. The blood-drinking ritual for Vidal was smoking ganja in Katmandu, "not an easy thing for a nonsmoker to do."

> But as I gasped my way into a sort of trance Jimmie materialized beside me on the bed. He wore blue pajamas. He was asleep. He was completely present, as he had been in the bedroom at Merrywood. I tickled his foot. The callused sole was like sandpaper. It was a shock to touch him again. The simulacrum opened its blue eyes and smiled and yawned and put his hand alongside my neck; he was, for an instant, real in a hotel room in Katmandu. But only for an instant. Then he rejoined Achilles and all the other shadowy dead in war.

Jimmie had been an excellent athlete and a reluctant soldier, who did his best both not to be where he was and not to die where he did. Like Vidal, who was serving as a mate on an army landing craft in the dangerous waters of the Aleutians, he strongly resented the fate that had brought him into war. Had he survived he might never have mattered very much to the author, who dedicated a novel, *The City and the Pillar*, to him, and who recalls telling an inquisitive journalist that JT " 'was the unfinished business of my life.' A response as cryptic as it was accurate." Certainly the living have not the powers of the dead, and power is of course Vidal's most writerly theme. Finding out about the dead man, chiefly from his mother, after his own brief idyll with the living one, was clearly as important to Vidal's subsequent and protean development as the relation with his grandfather had been. *The City and the Pillar* still reads as a most impressive novel, far more powerful and also closer to life than the homo-erotic novels of its own or of a previous time. Like the Greeks and Romans, the young Vidal could always find sex at the same time bleak, lyrical, and funny, whatever form it took.

His powers as novelist and writer, not only thoroughbred ones but gifts that are truly his own, are at their strongest in this search for the past which gives us his own family, his Gore grandfather in particular, and his love for Jimmie Trimble. Jealousy, although in this case a retrospective jealousy, is the side of love most familiar to Proust. For Vidal, perhaps, love could only become fully aware of itself when the sources of jealousy were revealed, for others beside the young Vidal had been smitten by Jim-mie. Vidal himself was then well able to plunge into a dazzling career of sex, entertainment, and hard work—turning out novels, plays, and film-scripts, even while his unconscious mind was carrying on its "unfinished business."

The more gossipy and predictable side of *Palimpsest* is beautifully done, economically funny and elegant, but by necessity a conducted tour rather than what can seem—especially in the first section of the book—a true conversation of discovery with the reader. And yet, as *Myra Breck-enridge* long ago showed, Vidal can be more classically funny than most writers in this vein since Petronius Arbiter wrote of Trimalchio's Feast. Every page of *Palimpsest* has some pleasurable absurdity, usually a good-natured one, that stays in the memory, and often with an aroma of poetry about it, as on the pages which return us at intervals to the author's villa at Ravello, where the memoir is being written. Swimming under the cypresses in the navy-blue pool and rescuing a small drowning lizard, he recalls the exceedingly grubby swimming pool at the Windsor Castle Royal Lodge, where he and Princess Margaret saved a number of bees from drowning, she exhorting them "in a powerful Hanoverian voice" to "go forth and make honey."

The snapshot of E. M. Forster, patron saint of the English gay com-munity, is not only dreadfully funny but revealing. Forster, as Vidal per-ceived, held perpetual court in both senses, and his judgments had an "unremitting censoriousness" quite alien to the free and easy living of

American gays. Forster twinkled at adoring acolytes like Christopher Isherwood, even while ignoring the book Isherwood had recently sent him. He invited Vidal and Tennessee Williams to lunch at Kings College, Cambridge, for he was shrewd enough to wish to patronize a rising celebrity, even an American one. Williams wisely declined, but Vidal was prepared to undergo a droll experience.

> We had a bad boiled lunch. "You must have the steamed lemon curd roll," Forster said. But as there was only one portion left, which he so clearly wanted, I opted for rhubarb. "Now," he said, contentedly tucking in, "you will never know what steamed lemon curd is."

Forster was also highly secretive. Lionel Trilling had just published a study of his novels but had no idea that their author was queer, and was astounded to be told so by Truman Capote. For once, as Vidal dryly remarks, Capote had no need to be inventive.

At this time, in the late Forties, after *The City and the Pillar* had become a best-seller on the *New York Times* list, Vidal "wanted to meet every writer that I admired. I met several; as a result, I never again wanted to meet, much less know, a writer whose work I admired." But the great exception was Tennessee Williams, "the Glorious Bird." The essential homeliness, even shyness, of this exotic figure is what comes across in *Palimpsest*, whether in Rome or New York, or on the Left Bank, as if such descriptions of him might be of Julius Caesar, in a domestic light with his wife Calpurnia. Vidal possesses the gift for seeing life, as it were, on its snug, unbuttoned side, perhaps because, as the Bird once remarked, "Gore gets on even less well with people than I do." It takes the born outsider, which most good writers are, to show the way of the world unbeglamoured, and as it really strikes them.

Vidal shared rooms on the Left Bank with the Bird in the early Fifties, at a time when both were on the edge of success. An American female academic, who was doing a biography of Tennessee Williams, asked Vidal whether they were lovers at the time. Vidal replied that "in my experience of real life it was unusual for colleagues to go to bed with each other. Of course, I added tolerantly, to show that nothing human was alien to me, I did understand that it was known for tenured lady professors to go to bed with each other. . . ." It was a neat way of turning the tables, and one would like to know what the professor came up with in reply. *Palimpsest* is much too urbanely written to bother with reticence, but it contains not a hint of either the vulgar betrayal of friends, or a pseudo-radical confession about the self. As the Bird pointed out, intellectuals usually prefer to talk to each other rather than to go to bed together. At least it was so in his case. " 'It is most disturbing to think that the head beside you on the pillow might be thinking, too,' said the Bird, who had a gift for selecting fine bodies attached to heads usually filled with the bright confetti of lunacy."

As if he were living in an Elizabethan age, the worlds of fashion and frivolity were as natural for Vidal, given his background, as was the world of politics and power. In Camelot the two were the same, and the Kennedys were typically anxious to meet and to mingle. A photo shows Jack Kennedy with Vidal and the Bird, who have driven up from Miami to greet him. "Far too attractive for the American people" was the Bird's verdict. That was in 1958, when Kennedy was already running for president. Two years later Vidal himself would be running for Congress in upstate New York on the Democratic ticket. Truman came to help out in Poughkeepsie, remarking "I hope I haven't done you any harm" as he left. But Vidal's interest in politics was more that of a writer than that of a dedicated player of the game: his interest in Kennedy, as friend, near-relative, and political phenomenon, was, so to speak, Shakespearean rather than professional. The true goal of Vidal's politics was surely his own books, particularly *Julian*, *Lincoln*, and *Burr*, which came out of both his own experiences and the feel for things he had acquired at the knee of his senator grandfather.

It is far from easy to say how balanced or how deeply felt is his own political philosophy. The image of Lincoln-Macbeth, the reluctant tyrant agonized by the consequences of his own tyranny, is a striking one, but it may belong more to the study and the theater than to any real political world. On the other hand, Senator Gore used to say, and with some justification, that Lincoln's sober rhetoric was as inherently meaningless as the flowery sort. "Was there ever a fraud greater than this government of, by, and for, the people? *What* people, *which* people?" No wonder that his grandson has considered the greatest presidents to be simply the most

Machiavellian, manipulating an attack on Fort Sumter, or on Pearl Harbor, in order to do what they, and not the people, wanted.

If Vidal's political views are in keeping with his family background there is no doubt about the part their basic assumptions have played in his own career. He once attended a literary conference in Sofia, Bulgaria, at which he encountered that great memoirist, Anthony Powell, together with the English novelist C. P. Snow, who liked to think he frequented in his own fashion the corridors of power. Snow was no match for his Yankee counterpart, who ruthlessly dismissed any genteel plea that the conference might be about "culture." Authors, like other men of the world, care for nothing but fame and fortune. The *enfant terrible* who discomfited the English delegates has never been backward about opening his mouth in settings where the conventions of hypocrisy are respected. Goaded in this manner, an exasperated pedagogue at the memoirist's prep school once told his colleagues that he wanted to be a bull. "So that I could gore Vidal."

The New York Review of Books, 1997

Credits

The following pieces originally appeared in *The New York Review of Books*:

"The Genius of Shandy Hall"; "Double Life"; "Best and Worst"; "Living with Trollope"; "Eminent Victorian"; "The Two Hardys"; "The King's Trumpeter"; "Life in the Head"; "The Last Puritan"; "God's Greene"; "Family Man"; "The All-Star Victorian"; "An Art of Self-Discovery"; "Fun While It Lasted"; "Gallant Pastiche"; "Under the Overcoat"; "An Excellent Man"; "The Backward Look"; "Poems with a Heroine"; "A Poet's Tragedy"; "The Hard Hitter"; "A Prig of Genius" (originally titled, "The Two Solzhenitsyns"); " 'One Life, One Writing' "; "Richly Flows Contingency"; "The Power of Delight"; "Something Childish"; "Poet of Holy Dread"; "Return of the Native"; "In Which We Serve"; "Seer of the Ego"; "Death and the *Dichter*"; "Fighting for the Crown"; "Sons and Brothers"; "Balzac Possessed"; "Doubles"; "From the Ridiculous to the Ridiculous"; "Country Life"; "Class Act."

The following pieces originally appeared in the *London Review of Books*:

"Nothing Nasty in the Woodshed"; Like Ink and Milk"; "Baby Face"; "Mr. Toad"; "Unmisigiving" (originally titled "Sexist")"; "The Best of Betjeman"; "The Last Romantic"; "Cutting it Short"; "On the Horse Parsnip"; "Lowellship"; "Gossip in Fiction"; "Little Green Crabs"; "What Will You Do to Keep the Ship from Foundering?"; "Look Here, Mr.

Goodwood"; "In Praise of the Amateur Approach"; "The War Between the Diaries"; "Moral Magic" (originally untitled); "Writeabout."

The following pieces originally appeared in the *Times Literary Supplement*:

"The Flight of the Disenchanter"; "Songs of a Furtive Self"; "Mothermonsters and Fatherfigures"; "The Art of Austerity"; "Too Good For This World."

The following pieces originally appeared in *The New York Times*: "The Strengths of His Passivity"; "Professional Strategies."

The following articles originally appeared in *The Listener*: "Conducting the Music"; "Proud Prisoner" (originally untitled).

"The Point of Novels" originally appeared in *The Times* (London); "The Order of Battle at Trafalgar" appeared in *Salmagundi*; "Milan Kundera and Jane Austen" appeared in *The Review of Contemporary Fiction*; and "A Complex Relationship" appeared in *The Byron Journal*.

Index

About the Author

Born in India in 1925, John Bayley was educated at Eton and Oxford, and he served during World War II in the Grenadier Guards. He became a fellow of New College in 1955, where he taught English. In 1956, he married the novelist Iris Murdoch, who was then teaching philosophy at St. Anne's College. In 1973, he was appointed Warton Professor of St. Catherine's College.

Bayley has written numerous works of criticism—notably, *The Characters of Love, Tolstoy and the Novel, Pushkin: A Comparative Commentary,* and *Shakespeare and Tragedy.* He has also published several studies about Thomas Hardy, Jane Austen, and Henry James, as well as a history of the short story. His most recent book, *The Widower's House,* was published in 2001.

Nothing in recent literary memory, however, compares to the response given the publication of *Elegy for Iris,* a *New York Times* bestseller, which has spoken to readers the world over about suffering, sacrifice, and love. Together with its sequel, *Iris and Her Friends,* Bayley wrote these beautiful tributes to Murdoch during her struggle with Alzheimer's disease, to which she ultimately succumbed in 1999. In 2001, Jim Broadbent won an Academy Award for his portrayal of John Bayley in the film adaptation of *Elegy for Iris.*

Bayley remarried in 2000, and he lives and writes in Oxford, England.